CAPTURING LIGHT

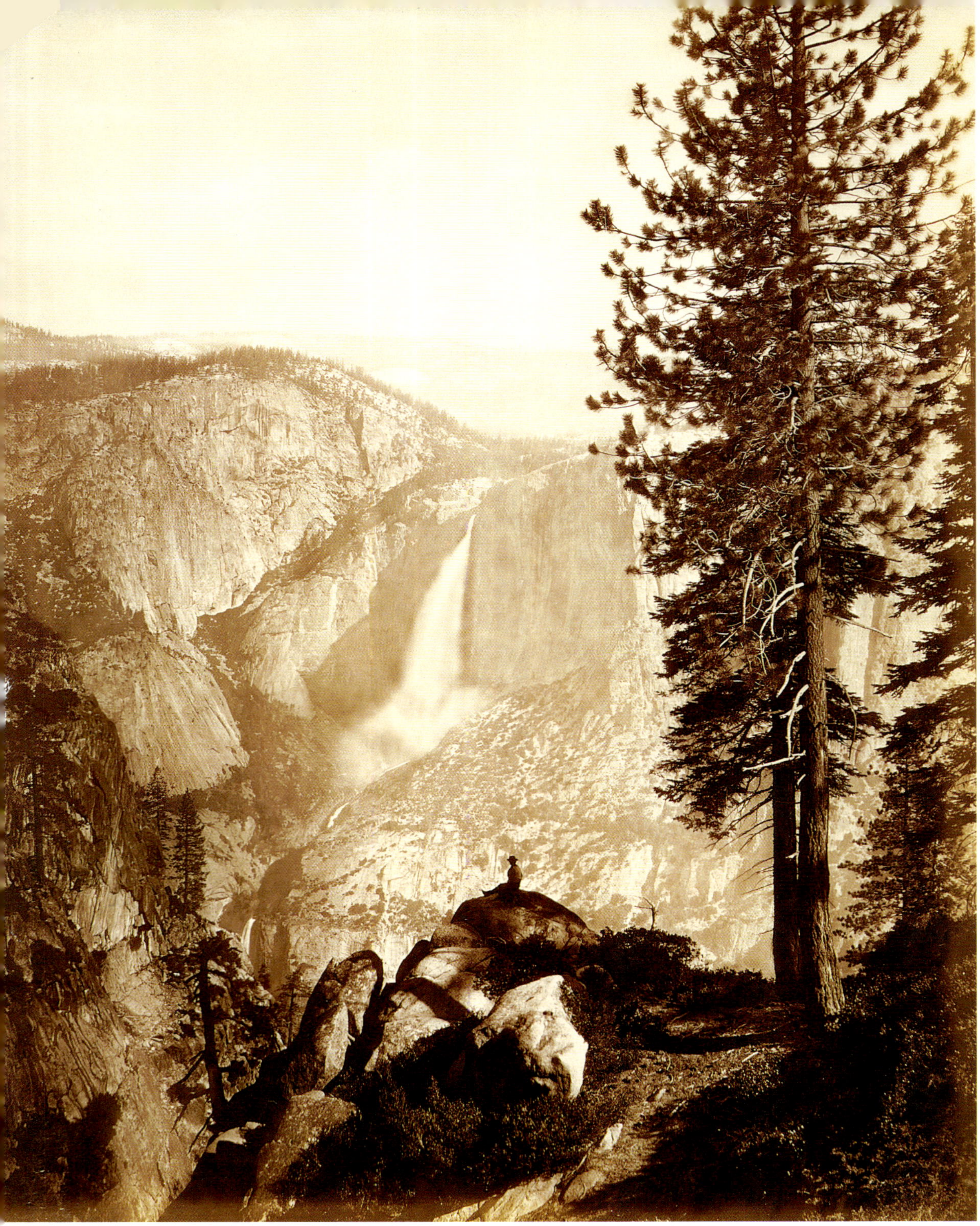

Capturing Light

Masterpieces of California Photography 1850 to the Present

EDITED BY
Drew Heath Johnson

FOREWORD BY
Therese Thau Heyman

ESSAYS BY
Peter E. Palmquist
Naomi Rosenblum
Sally Stein
Andy Grundberg

PHOTOGRAPHS FROM THE COLLECTION OF THE OAKLAND MUSEUM OF CALIFORNIA

OAKLAND MUSEUM *of* CALIFORNIA
OAKLAND

in association with

W. W. NORTON & COMPANY
NEW YORK LONDON

This book is published on the occasion of a major exhibition, *Capturing Light: Masterpieces of California Photography, 1850–2000,* organized by the Oakland Museum of California with the generous support of the Oakland Museum Women's Board and the National Endowment for the Arts, a federal agency.

FRONTISPIECE:
Eadweard Muybridge, *Falls of the Yosemite, from Glacier Rock,* 1872.
Mammoth plate albumen print, 21½ x 16¾ in. Gift of Robert B. Honeyman, Jr.

Printed in Hong Kong
First Edition

ISBN 0-393-04993-0

LIBRARY OF CONGRESS CATALOGING-IN-PUBLICATION DATA

Capturing Light: Masterpieces of California Photography, 1850 to the Present / edited by Drew Heath Johnson.
p. cm
Includes bibliographical references.
1. Photography—California—History. 2. California—Pictorial Works. 3. Oakland Museum of California—Photograph collections. I. Johnson, Drew Heath.
TR24.C2 C37 2001
770'.9794—dc21 00-055419

Oakland Museum of California, Art Department, 1000 Oak Street, Oakland, California 94607
www.museumca.org

W. W. Norton & Company, Inc., 500 Fifth Avenue, New York, N.Y. 10110
www.wwnorton.com

W. W. Norton & Company Ltd., 10 Coptic Street, London WC1A 1PU
1 2 3 4 5 6 7 8 9 0

The text of this book is composed in Bembo
With the display set in Frutiger Light
Manufacturing by South China Printing (1988) Ltd.
Composition and Book Design by Gordon Chun Design, Berkeley, California
Copy Photography by M. Lee Fatherree, Oakland (color plates) and Camera Corner, Oakland (essay illustrations)

CONTENTS

vii FOREWORD *Therese Thau Heyman*

ix INTRODUCTION & ACKNOWLEDGMENTS *Drew Heath Johnson*

PORTFOLIO I: The Pioneers 1850–1900

3 The Pioneers: Landscape and Studio *Peter E. Palmquist*

21 PLATES

PORTFOLIO II: Mood and Symbolism 1900–1935

61 California Pictorialism *Naomi Rosenblum*

75 PLATES

PORTFOLIO III: Seeing Straight 1925–1945

121 Starting from Pictorialism: Notable Continuities in the Modernization of California Photography *Sally Stein*

145 PLATES

PORTFOLIO IV: California Dreaming 1945–1980

193 A New and Different Kind of Art *Andy Grundberg*

211 PLATES

PORTFOLIO V: Toward the Millennium 1980–2000

259 EPILOGUE

261 PLATES

295 NOTES TO THE PLATES

315 BIOGRAPHIES

363 INDEX

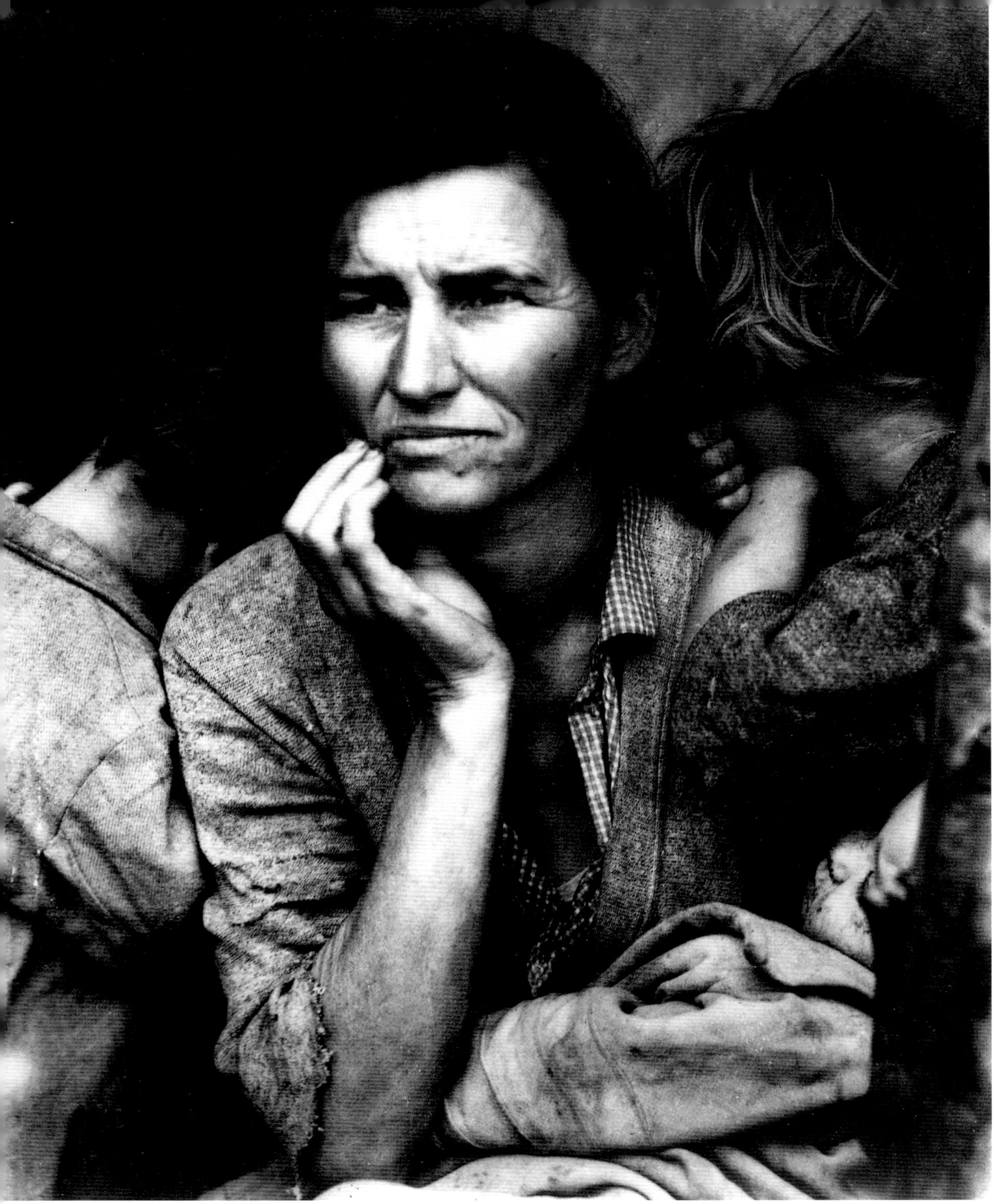

DOROTHEA LANGE
Migrant Mother, Nipomo, California, 1936
COLLECTION OF THE OAKLAND MUSEUM OF CALIFORNIA, GIFT OF PAUL S. TAYLOR

FOREWORD

GOOD FORTUNE AND PHOTOGRAPHY have been joined in California from the beginning. As news of the gold discovery of 1848 spread, as "the world rushed in," the hunger for information and news became insatiable. Headlines screamed and letters from the mines confirmed that riches could be had for the picking. The excitement generated by the remarkable discovery at Captain Sutter's sawmill instantly inspired images—drawings, maps, cartoons—which were distributed to the eager and ignorant around the world. In 1849 thousands of voyagers set out for California's gold fields.

Fortunately, this massive migration was witnessed and recorded by the newest visual invention. The daguerreotype had amazed the French when it was announced in 1839, and the process was quickly taken up by Samuel F. B. Morse and others in America. When gold was discovered, photographers were ready to drop everything for the chance to document history in the making, shipping cameras and copper plates "around the Horn" to California even as aspiring miners carried their shovels and pans on the arduous journey to El Dorado.

Photographers prospered as the ranks of forty-niners increased, yet the fragile copper and glass plates, once very numerous, are now maddeningly rare. For thirty years the Oakland Museum of California has collected, displayed and published its collection of fine, cased images depicting the lives of miners and the instant metropolis of San Francisco, the most photographed city of its day. Within a decade of the gold discovery, photographers were trooping to the Sierras, replacing pioneering images of human activity with majestic scenes of vast western mountains. Carleton Watkins, well represented in the Museum's collection, made portfolios of Yosemite and other Western wonders for rich patrons and the general public alike.

This new western landscape demanded large-format photographs. The steady invention of new photographic methods and equipment made it possible for artists such as Watkins to capture the "best general view." Human enterprise continued to be celebrated as well. The push to build a cross-country railroad provided opportunities and challenges for Andrew J. Russell and Alfred A. Hart. Russell's large collection of glass-plate negatives documenting construction of the Union Pacific Railroad form the best-known holding of the Oakland Museum of California History Department.

As brilliantly as these early photographs pictured the terrain, its mineral deposits and landscapes, they also raised questions. The place of photography, its very nature, was always in dispute. Was the camera merely a machine that recorded light? Or could the light that was captured also reveal elements of art? This set of choices motivated a few museums, including the Oakland Art Museum, precursor of the Oakland Museum of California, to take up photography shows in the early 1930s. In the twentieth century the Pictorialists, and later the influential Group f.64, consciously declared in favor of photography as an art by creating carefully made prints designed for exhibition. Whether characterized by color pigments and inky use of light, as in the first group, or by clear, sharply seen objects, as in the second, these photographers left no doubt as to their identity as artists. Many of the best California images from these groups remain in the collection at Oakland.

When I began adding to the small number of photographs in the Museum's Art Department in the 1960s, the strength of the holdings was contained in a few important gifts made by dedicated donors. I quickly found the family of Anne Brigman, a Pictorialist and member of Alfred Stieglitz's Photo-Secession, who made all of her significant images available, along with a set of fascinating personal letters and notes. Ansel Adams endorsed the idea of the collection's California focus with key gifts of early images from the 1930s. Willard Van Dyke, another influential member of Group f.64, sold us prized pictures from the group, as well as his own exhibition prints. Simply by searching phone books, I found that many of the originators of West Coast photographic styles still lived in the San Francisco Bay Area. It was our good fortune that they, too, encouraged our emphasis on photography as a major collection area. Oscar Maurer, Francis Bruguière (through his estate), Peter Stackpole and the rebellious Imogen Cunningham, all one-time Pictorialists, and Sonya Noskowiak among many others, made it possible to represent them with important work, from early vintage prints to family snapshots.

Most significant, Dorothea Lange and her husband Paul Taylor's remarkable gift of Lange's archive, containing negatives, signed prints, letters, books and tapes, gave great distinction to the Museum. Even the family of Florence Thompson, Lange's Migrant Mother, added their insights in the form of reminiscences describing their role in photographic history.

As the Oakland Museum prepared to open in its new building in 1969, donors Shirley Burden, Stanley Truman and Dr. and Mrs. Dudley P. Bell made it possible for me to make very significant purchases for the collection. I often found important work at auctions: out-of-fashion California landscapes, portraits by Arnold Genthe and Margrethe Mather, timed motion studies by Eadweard Muybridge, portfolios by Edward Curtis and George Fiske. Although it is hard to imagine today, photography was the bargain of the art world. Five hundred dollars could win Man Ray's California Images. Early vintage prints by Edward Weston, Mather and Cunningham, often platinum prints, were sold for no more than what a single lunch might cost today. Younger photographers such as Robert Dawson, Anthony Hernandez and Richard Misrach, just beginning to receive recognition, also aided our search for the best in California photography, donating work or making it available at a fraction of its present-day value.

Today Drew Johnson, who has headed the Art Department's photography section since 1995, successfully continues acquiring what is significant in the new market for photography, no longer the low-cost medium it was when I was fortunate to have been building the basic collection.

Therese Thau Heyman
Curator Emeritus and Research Curator
OAKLAND MUSEUM *of* CALIFORNIA

INTRODUCTION & ACKNOWLEDGMENTS

Everything worth photographing is in California.

– Edward Weston

Photography came to California in the midst of an international mass hysteria, known today as the Gold Rush of 1849. In an unlikely historical coincidence, news of vast amounts of gold in Sierran foothills reached the East Coast of America just as the infant art of photography was approaching maturity.[1] Loosed on the world in 1839, the daguerreotype initially was little more than a primitive, if startling, curiosity. Daguerre himself had declared photographic portraiture a practicle impossibility, thanks to exposure times of twenty minutes or more. Just a decade later, on the eve of the Gold Rush, photographs were a commonplace feature of American life, with hundreds of professional photographers producing untold numbers of inexpensive and technically accomplished images. Like the countless multitude of bakers and schoolteachers seduced by tales of gold, these daguerreotypists were ready to drop everything for the romance and fortune contained in the word *California*.

It now seems appropriate, given the way we think of California, that photography should arrive in the region at a time of such national lunacy. Gold Rush California was a notoriously peculiar place, free from traditional social restraints, a multicultural jumble where ordinary moral, religious and sexual standards were more or less ignored. "You cannot know the perfect freedom and independence that characterizes all our relationships," wrote a San Franciscan in 1852. "Society if it exists at all is freed from the multitude of prejudices and embarrassments and exactions that control the Eastern cities."[2] There is more than a little resemblance between this statement and the words of Edward Weston who, a century later, found California "unhampered by tradition, less bound by convention, more open, free, youthful,—physically and psychically, [affording] untilled soil from which will appear a new feeling for, and manifestation of, life."[3]

What makes California photography Californian? Aside from the obvious quality of having been made within the state's borders, can there possibly be common threads which unite the photography of, say, Eadweard Muybridge and Judy Dater? There is the landscape, certainly, a feature so remarkable to nineteenth-century eyes that photography was initially required just to verify the outlandishness of the descriptions. The phrase "California photography" immediately calls up visions of Yosemite and Point Lobos, and it does not require too great an insight to see a link between the work of Carleton Watkins in the nineteenth century and Richard Misrach in the late twentieth.

Then there is the unique social milieu which so intrigued Weston, the freedom to ignore or revise artistic canons from without. This quality has been reinforced by a series of events (each in turn described as "second Gold Rushes") which brought new people and new cultural influences to the state: The rise of the film industry and Hollywood culture, the economic boom brought about by World War II, waves of immigration from Asia, Latin America and the South, the youth revolution of the sixties, the rise of Silicon Valley. Each has changed the state permanently, yet each seemed somehow wholly consistent with what had gone before.

These two threads, the inspiration provided by California's landscape and a quest for personal freedom, are perfectly embodied in the person of Anne Brigman (plates 51 and 52). "My pictures tell of my freedom of soul," she declared, "of my emancipation from fear." Camping in the high Sierras in the first decade of the twentieth century, Brigman experienced an epiphany: "One day during the gathering of a thunder storm when the air was hot and still and a strange yellow light was over everything, something happened almost too deep for me to be able to relate . . . I turned full force to the medium at hand and the beloved Thing [camera] gave to me a power and abandon that I could not have had otherwise."[4] The only West Coast photographer anointed a fellow of Alfred Stieglitz's prestigious Photo Secession, Brigman went on to serve as role model and mother figure to a younger generation of California camera artists.

Much of what we think of as Great American Photography can be claimed as Californian. Names such as Weston, Watkins, Ansel Adams or Dorothea Lange are among the first that occur to us when we consider the history of the medium worldwide. In spite of this prominence, however, California photographers have historically felt isolated, removed from the mainstream and overlooked by East Coast arbiters such as Stieglitz. Those who break through this isolation cease to be regarded as California photographers. This may have as much to do with geography as the prejudice of Eastern critics. As more than one essayist here points out, the state was not often at the forefront of aesthetic trends, in photography or the other arts. But California artists unquestionably have shown unusual flexibility in adapting East Coast and European ideas, bending them in new directions, exploring new techniques and theories in fresh, innovative ways. Beyond this, generalizations about California photography become increasingly glib. The subject is simply too big, the work too varied.

This book does not pretend to present a comprehensive history of photography in California. It is, more than anything, a survey of a single collection. For nearly forty years the Oakland Museum of California has collected the work of California photographers, both celebrated and obscure. Much of the collection's strength derives from the Museum's unique fusion of three earlier institutions into a single building encompassing the art, history and environment of the state. Because all three disciplines within the Museum collect and display photographs, an unusually broad representation of the medium has emerged. Fine art, documentary, commercial, vernacular and scientific photography are all present, amounting to more than a million images in total. The result is certainly the most distinguished and extensive collection of photographic imagery relating to California anywhere.

Presenting a comprehensive survey of such a vast collection, so varied in time, technique and style is probably impossible. There is, first of all, the thorny question of which photographers to include. One of the great pleasures of working with the collection over the past ten years has been the discovery of unknown or forgotten masterpieces by artists whose names are not yet common currency, even among experts. In the following pages you will find familiar icons next to works which appear startlingly new, even though they may have been made a century ago. Having settled on the artists, there is the problem of summarizing each person's career in one or two images. Some photographers are able to make single pictures which seem to encapsulate their entire output; others can only be understood in series. These latter must be given context, using interpretive material of the sort found in the biographies and notes to the plates.

Then there is the matter of the curator's vision, or less charitably, the curator's taste. Among other tasks, museums seek to present historically balanced interpretations of their collections. That said, the selection and sequencing of artworks for an exhibition or book is unavoidably subjective, undeniably personal. This is particularly true in regard to recent work which has yet to pass through the filter of time, and about which there is little consensus. Let me state clearly: Although I have employed every effort to choose photographs based on their importance to the history of the medium, the selection is, at bottom, governed by my own eye. Another editor could have produced a completely different, but no less valid, book from the same collection.

Inevitably, there are painful omissions. California imagery by well-known photographers not usually associated with the state (Diane Arbus or Alvin Langdon Coburn, for example) have been passed over in favor of those who built careers here. Snapshots, advertising and other "vernacular" photography are largely overlooked in favor of "fine art" photography (a problematic phrase at the turn of the twenty-first century), whose primary goal is personal artistic expression. Hence the book's subtitle, "Masterpieces of California Photography," which unapologetically implies a "greatest hits" approach. Then there are the inevitable weak spots which occur in even the finest collection. I was grieved, for instance, to discover we lacked a good representation of work by Japanese-American Pictorialists. Whenever possible, we have attempted to remedy these omissions by the inclusion of work from other collections within the essays. Finally, the selection of images from the past twenty years, when so much work has been produced in such a bewildering variety of styles and media, has been more than usually difficult. Time alone will tell whether the choices made for this final section are valid, or whether we have overlooked the truly significant photography of late twentieth century California. Suffice to say that I am wholeheartedly enthusiastic about every photograph presented here; each has remained powerful during the process of editing and re-editing.

A word about the structure of the book: At the heart is a selection of two hundred color plates, arranged chronologically and interspersed with essays on California photography during the period discussed. Because the plates reproduce vintage prints, each of which possesses a unique history, notes to the plates follow. These brief notes contain technical, contextual and anecdotal information, which will hopefully prove entertaining as well as illuminate the significance of each work. Biographies of each artist follow, accompanied, whenever possible, by portraits. It is our hope that the resulting catalog will help foster a new appreciation for California photography in addition to providing a brief survey of an important collection.

I would like to thank the staff of the Oakland Museum of California for support at every stage of this project. The book itself would not have been possible without a generous grant from the Oakland Museum Women's Board. Executive Director Dennis Power took an early and active interest, as did grant writer Jerry Daviee, whose appreciation for the photographs informed our fund-raising efforts. Rich Edwards of our Board of Directors was a dynamo—his enthusiasm for the exhibition and for photography in general is truly energizing. Sandy Wolfe of the Women's Board and the Art Guild instantly understood the importance of presenting photography to the widest possible audience; her behind-the-scenes support has been valuable in too many ways to enumerate. Erin Garcia researched and wrote the notes to the plates and assisted tirelessly throughout all stages of the manuscript. Abby Wasserman was an astute and cheerful editor. Marcia Eymann and Diane Curry of the History Department provided unrestricted access to their department's photography collections. Claudia Kishler and Joy Walker offered friendship and support in their capacity as registrars, as did Bill McMorris.

Outside the Museum, many individuals provided expertise and support. Special thanks must go to our essayists, Peter Palmquist, Naomi Rosenblum, Sally Stein and Andy Grundberg. Besides contributing an essay, Peter Palmquist also wrote the artists' biographies and offered expert advice. He is a treasure. Designers Gordon and Suzanne Chun were asked to perform miracles under tight deadlines, as were John Hartz and the staff of Camera Corner, Oakland. Joan Murray contributed a large group of portraits from her *California Photographers* series, in the process donating a set of prints to the Museum. Mary Alinder helped with research questions, as did Taylor Horton of San Francisco Maritime National Historical Park. Robert Weil and Neil Giordano at W. W. Norton were patient beyond any reasonable expectation.

A number of institutions and individuals contributed photographs to the essays and biographies. Special thanks are due to Marianne Babal of Wells Fargo Bank Historical Services; Jacklyn Burns, the J. Paul Getty Museum; Jon Burris, the Brett Weston Archive; Shaula Coyl, Eve Schillo and Cheryle T. Robertson, the Los Angeles County Museum of Art; Susan Ehrens; The Fraenkel Gallery, San Francisco; Susan Friedewald of the John Gutmann Trust; Susan Haas, the Society of California Pioneers; G. Ray Hawkins and the G. Ray Hawkins Gallery, Santa Monica; Debra Heimerdinger/ Fine Art Photographs; George Hurrell, Jr. and Hurrell's Hollywood; The International Center of Photography; Deborah Irmas and the Mortensen Estate Collection; Steven Josefsberg; the Jan Kesner

Gallery; Gary Kurutz of The California State Library; Janice Madhu and Barbara Puorro Galasso, International Museum of Photography at George Eastman House; Sarah Murkett, P.P.O.W., New York; Dianne Nilsen and Denise Kramer, the Center for Creative Photography; Pace/MacGill Gallery; Elizabeth Partridge of The Imogen Cunningham Trust; Allan Rich, Creative Arts Images; Merriam Saunders, The Ansel Adams Publishing Rights Trust; Kim Schoenstadt and John Baldessari; Julie Warren, British Columbia Archives; Stephen Wirtz Gallery; and Linda Wolcott-Moore. Photographers contributing work specifically for the catalog include Marion Brenner, Jo Ann Callis, Linda Connor, Robert Dawson, Geoffrey Fricker, Lynn Hershman, Stephen Johnson, Victor Landweber, Greg MacGregor, Emily Matyas and Mark Klett, Doug Muir, Patrick Nagatani, Ted Orland, Joe Samberg, Stephen Shore, Larry Sultan, Andrée Tracey, Michelle Vignes, Lew Watts and Jo Whaley.

The late Henry Mayer first introduced me to our publisher and stimulated the editorial process during many fascinating discussions. At the time of his death, Henry had just completed research for a biography of Dorothea Lange. He is sorely missed.

M. Lee Fatherree, who produced the color transparencies for each of the plates, is in a class by himself. Lee is more than a craftsman; the care and precision he lavished on each image came from a deep involvement with and appreciation for the photographs.

Finally, special thanks must extend to Therese Heyman, Curator Emeritus of prints and photographs. The majority of images presented in this book were collected by Therese, starting in the mid-1960s. For three decades she acquired the best in California photography, often working against fashion and the prejudices of the market. Her instincts are impeccable and her choices have stood the test of time. Any distinction possessed by the collection is largely due to her efforts.

Drew Heath Johnson
Curator of Fine Art Photography
OAKLAND MUSEUM *of* CALIFORNIA

NOTES

1. There is evidence that at least one person made photographs in California prior to the Gold Rush, as Peter Palmquist relates in his essay which follows. Although the story of Epifania de Guadalupe Vallejo is intriguing, however, there is no corroborative proof of her experiments with daguerreotypy.

2. Quoted in Roger W. Lotchin, *San Francisco, 1846–1856: From Hamlet to City* (New York: Oxford University Press, 1974), p. 291–2.

3. Edward Weston, "America and Photography," quoted in Peter Bunnell, ed., *Edward Weston: On Photography* (Salt Lake City: Gibbs M. Smith, Inc., Peregrine Smith Books, 1983), 56.

4. Quoted in Therese Thau Heyman, *Anne Brigman: Pictorial Photographer/Pagan/Member of the Photo-Secession* (Oakland: The Oakland Museum, 1974), unpaginated introduction and page 3.

1850 – 1900

PORTFOLIO I

The Pioneers

The Pioneers: Landscape and Studio

PETER E. PALMQUIST

The existence of California has, at length, become a 'great fact' [of] the day. For nearly two years Europe was stupefied with the strange exaggerations and contradictory tales which were received from the unknown and mysterious Dorado, but which she feared to believe. The doubt is, however, now solved . . . several of the localities have been daguerreotyped; and from a set of these views taken in the first month of the present year at San Francisco and Sacramento City, we have selected the originals of the accompanying illustrations. To refuse the evidence of the Daguerreotype is to deny the existence of the 'prime-cheerer' light, and the Sun and his works.

– *London Illustrated News*, October 19, 1850

CALIFORNIA'S PIONEER PHOTOGRAPHERS were a wonderfully diverse and colorful group of individuals.[1] One was a certifiable lunatic with delusions of grandeur who walked the streets of San Francisco dressed as George Washington. In addition to daguerreotypes, he offered his services as a "matrimonial promoter" and proposed an elaborate and prescient scheme to drive a railroad tunnel through the Sierra Nevada mountains so that unmarried women from the East Coast could be matched with California's lonely miners (figure 1).[2] Another pioneer daguerreian invented a rat poison and became an expert in Mayan culture; unfortunately, he is also reputed to have dynamited portions of ruins that impeded his archaeological investigations.[3] Many early California photographers had simultaneous careers as midwives, journalists, sign painters, dentists, musicians or undertakers. Perhaps the most enterprising among them was the man who set up his camera at the entrance to San Francisco's largest cemetery in order to "preserve the likeness" of corpses before they were buried.[4]

In fact, two of the most famous names in nineteenth-century California photography lived lives which could serve as the basis for novels. Edward James Muggeridge was an egotistical self-promoter who immigrated from England, changed his name to Eadweard Muybridge and, at the height of his fame as a photographer, murdered his wife's lover in cold blood. After creating a superb body of work in California, Alaska and South America, he went on to become one of the inventors of the motion picture. Carleton Watkins, on the other hand, specialized in large-format landscape photographs. With almost no formal training, he rose to enjoy international recognition and, at the apex of a fifty-year career, established the largest gallery ever devoted to outdoor photography. Yet most of his professional life was spent in a state of financial despair, and in the end he not only lost his eyesight, but was abandoned by a much-younger wife who declined to care for him in his old age. He spent the final six years of his life in a mental institution, and lies buried in an unmarked grave. Perhaps most tragic, thousands of his precious landscape negatives were destroyed in the San Francisco earthquake and fire of 1906. Rediscovered in the late twentieth century, his large prints (which in his lifetime sold for $3.50, including frame) are now considered priceless masterpieces.

What better time than the new millennium to review the role of photography in documenting the ideals of the California Dream?[5] It is also a fitting moment to celebrate the accomplishments of the men and women who recorded the people, places and great events of California so long ago. Who among us would not relish an opportunity to step back in time to pay a visit to Gold Rush California? What was it like to drop in for a "likeness" at a San Francisco daguerreian studio operated by Coombs, Shew, or Vance? Photography was far more common in the nineteenth century than has previously been recognized. The sheer scale of photographic practice in California compels us to look beyond the big names, such as Watkins and Muybridge, to examine the careers of little-known image makers. It is their stories that reveal the place of photography in the lives of ordinary people, and its role in creating a visual iconography of California that would become recognized around the world.

Though the Gold Rush of 1849 dramatically focused the eyes of the world on California, the seeds of the California Dream had been sown much earlier. In 1625, for instance, English cartographer Henry Briggs published the first of many maps picturing California as an island, initiating the idea of California as a place apart, quintessentially different from mainland America. As late as the

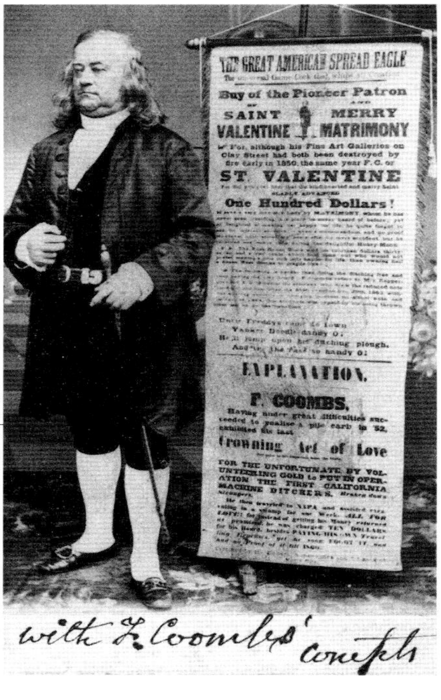

FIGURE 1.
Frederick Coombs
Untitled (Self Portrait), c. 1865
Albumen carte de visite
COURTESY OF PETER E. PALMQUIST

1840s, on the eve of the California Gold Rush, much of the western American continent remained unexplored or poorly understood. The Great Plains and Rocky Mountains were regarded as impregnable obstacles to westward travel, while vast areas of the American West were deemed a worthless desert. Rumor, myth and mystery abounded.

By the early nineteenth century the world was changing at a rapidly accelerating rate. Emigration from Europe and elsewhere, whether driven by economic hardship, famine or religious and political repression, resulted in a more adventurous global population, one that was increasingly knowledgeable of distant events. Even before 1840, in places as remote as rural Maine, local newspapers carried accounts of such far-away and exotic places as Palestine, the Sandwich Islands (Hawaii), Haiti and South America. In October 1839, the same season photography arrived in America, the *Kennebec Journal* contained a detailed plan for developing a "Panama Canal" ten years before the California gold fever would send hordes of adventurers across the Isthmus of Panama.[6] News of the world was increasingly available, especially in cosmopolitan centers such as Boston and New York.

Inevitably, readers demanded pictorial representations of such distant wonders. Moving dioramas and panoramas, forerunners of the motion picture newsreel, had been introduced in the late 1830s. Essentially illustrated lectures, panoramas consisted of large, continuous painted canvases which were slowly unrolled past an audience. In the 1840s and '50s each new panorama advertised itself as bigger and more wondrous than the one before. Paintings such as *Bayne's Gigantic Panoramic Painting of a Voyage to Europe,* viewable in Boston's Armory Hall in March 1848, or Donnavan's *Great Serial Panorama of Mexico!* could each boast more than 21,000 feet of canvas. Beyond their obvious entertainment value, this type of exhibition fueled the public imagination for exotic locales and fulfilled a public longing to see "the thing itself."[7]

Since these prodigious productions were often based on little more than the artist's own imagination, they tended to lack truthfulness. Photography, by contrast, was infinitely more reliable, a quality the general public was quick to grasp. In 1841, just two years after Americans began taking pictures, John Lloyd Stephens and his associates Frederick Catherwood and Dr. Samuel Cabot, Jr. daguerreotyped the lost cities and ruins of the Yucatán. Extremes of heat and humidity, as well as obscuring tropical overgrowth, proved daunting, yet the daguerreotypists were successful in making images remarkable for their verisimilitude. Just one year later, the explorer John Charles Frémont packed a daguerreotype apparatus on his first western expedition. From Independence Rock to the Wind River Mountains in present-day Wyoming, the future presidential candidate repeatedly tried to take daguerreian views, but failed at every attempt. On another expedition in 1853, he still considered photography essential, but this time wisely hired an accomplished daguerreian, Solomon Nuñes Carvalho (1815–1897). Despite terrible hardship, Carvalho's efforts were successful, though his daguerreotypes have been lost.

Today, thanks to several decades of research, we know the names of nearly eight hundred individuals who were involved in the photographic industry in California before the end of 1865. By 1880, this number is likely to have doubled or even tripled. Much of the latest research has centered on the relationship between technological progress and economic opportunity for photographers working in the state. The issues, however, are not merely a succession of dusty facts. Since each photographer was a unique individual, it is useful to study their biographies in order to better understand the forces that drove them west to practice the fledgling art. This is especially pertinent in California, as the state came into existence during the first flush of photography.

Who were California's first photographers? Historians have long been puzzled by the apparent lack of photography in California prior to the Gold Rush. After all, a substantial number of daguerreotypes from the Mexican War survive; why not images of Mexican California?[8] Recent evidence suggests that photography may have come to the region as early as 1842 and that the state's first identifiable photographer was a twelve-year-old girl! Epifania de Guadalupe Vallejo (1835–1905), or Fannie, as she was affectionately called, was the precocious daughter of Mariano Guadalupe Vallejo, later to gain fame as the Comandante General of Alta (upper) California. A gifted amateur painter, Fannie had the benefit of the finest tutors, many from Europe. In about 1847, according to family letters, she came into possession of a small daguerreotype camera and learned how to use it to take a tiny daguerreotype portrait of her mother. Mounted in a ring (probably by her uncle, a goldsmith), it survives today, still in family hands.[9]

Although gold was discovered in 1848, only a handful of photographers actually reached California before 1850. The first appears to have been an Englishman, Richard H. Carr (1818–1888). Carr was a former sailor who had been shipwrecked near Pensacola, Florida in August 1844, a harrowing experience that caused him to take up the safer trade of photography. After trying his hand at daguerreotypy in New Orleans, he traveled to Mexico in 1846, only to be blockaded by the Mexican War. Carr was photographing in Ecuador when news of the January 1848 gold strike in California reached him. He immediately sailed for California, arriving in San Francisco harbor on the last day of 1848. Putting ashore on New Year's Day 1849, he was operating a daguerreian portrait studio by January 25th, the first-recorded establishment of its kind in the Pacific West. In inflationary San Francisco, this first studio consisted of a twelve-by-eight foot room costing thirty-five dollars per month, an outrageous sum for 1849. Lacking a system of house numbering in the infant city, patrons were directed to the new "cream color" house of one Mr. Wetmore, "just above the Quartermaster's Office."[10]

Other 1849 arrivals included New Yorker George Howard Johnson, who first came to San Francisco but quickly established himself in Sacramento, much closer to the mines. Johnson's advertisement in a city directory of July 1850 drew the public's attention to his "Facial and Landscape Gallery." In August, Johnson made daguerreotypes of the Sacramento "Squatter's Riot," one of which was published as an engraving in the *Illustrated California News* of September 1, making him one of the first photojournalists in California. Obscure for more than a century, Johnson is now recognized as one of the finest photographers of the California Gold Rush (plate 7).[11] In June 1849, one E. Sutton took a room on Clay Street in San Francisco, where he advertised that he had "three of the best German cameras and a full assortment of superior stock." True to the transient nature of early photography, within a short time he, too, had relocated to Sacramento, where he became the lead partner in a company called Sutton & Jefrees. They offered "Daguerreotype Miniatures" in their room next door to the offices of the *Sacramento Placer Times*.[12] Another early California arrival was James W. Johnston (born c. 1812) who claimed to have opened a daguerreotype studio in San Francisco in 1849.[13]

This short list of confirmed pre-1850 photographers is doubtless incomplete, due to the overall scarcity of early newspapers and other primary documentation. California's first two newspapers, the *Californian* (published in Monterey, 1846–47) and *The California Star* (published in Yerba Buena, as San Francisco was then known, 1847–48), report no daguerreian activity at all. San Francisco's first two city directories, published in March and September of 1850, list just four daguerreotypists: Frederick Coombs, William Henry Bradley, James Pierpoint and Mrs. Julia Shannon. Mrs. Shannon apparently had been working as a daguerreian since January 1850, according to a report in the San Francisco *Alta California*: "DAGUERREOTYPES TAKEN BY A LADY—Those wishing to have a good likeness are informed that they can have them taken in a very superior manner, and by a *real live lady* too . . . on Clay Street, opposite the St. Francis Hotel. . . . Give her a call, gents." Despite the obvious professional advantage her gender offered in woman-starved California, she was forced to maintain two careers: Shannon was the daguerreotypist mentioned earlier who doubled as a midwife.[14]

Like the miners they were photographing, some daguerreians came overland to California; others took the long sea voyage around Cape Horn or utilized a shortcut across the Isthmus of Panama. Three of the pioneers spent time in South America: Carr, Robert Vance and William Rulofson. Vance is an interesting case in point. Leaving his gallery in Dover, New Hampshire, he traveled by sea to Valparaíso, Chile, where he operated a very successful portrait gallery until 1850.[15] That summer he journeyed northward along the coast to Panama City, and thence to San Francisco. Similarly, Rulofson—destined for considerable fame as a partner in the San Francisco firm of Bradley & Rulofson (plate 28)—began his photographic career in St. John, New Brunswick, at age sixteen. He worked in Boston and upper New York State before making a tour of England and France in 1846. In 1848 he married (the bride was just fourteen or fifteen), and in January 1849 he left for California, leaving his wife and young son at home, but taking a daguerreotype outfit (years later he recalled that on the voyage he had "sketched" Rio de Janeiro, Patagonia and Valparaíso, but whether this refers to daguerreotypes or drawings is unclear). He arrived in San Francisco on June 13, 1849 and proceeded directly to the southern mines.[16]

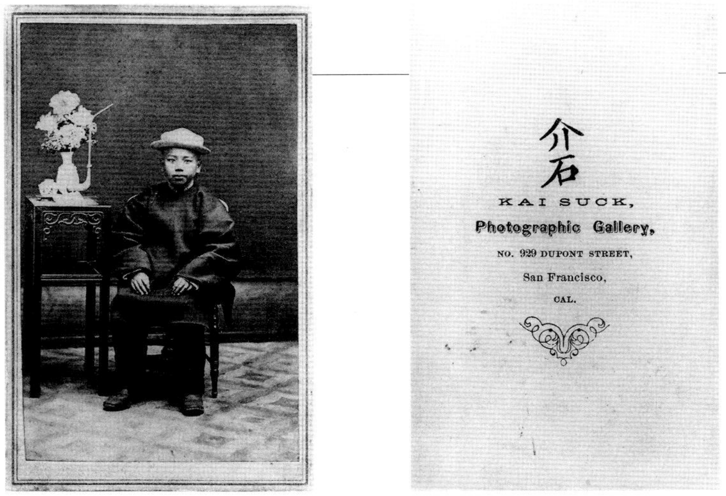

FIGURE 2.
Kai Suck Photographic Gallery
Portrait of a Young Boy, c. 1865
Albumen carte de visite (front and back views)
OAKLAND MUSEUM OF CALIFORNIA,
LENT BY MR. AND MRS. ROYAL E. TOWNS

With the exception of Miss Vallejo, all of California's pioneer photographers were immigrants to the state. While most came from the eastern United States, there were visitors from other countries as well. Joseph N. Silveira came from Portugal, his advertisements reflecting his European heritage: "The English, German, French, Spanish and Portuguese languages fluently spoken in this Gallery."[17] Despite the virulent and organized racism present in Gold Rush California, China contributed a number of photographers. As early as June 1854, the San Francisco *Daily California Chronicle* featured an account of the work of daguerreian Ka Chau, with the less than enthusiastic admission that Chau had "some beautiful specimens" of the daguerreotype on display.[18] San Francisco photographers Kai Suck and Lai Yong also enjoyed successful careers (figure 2). Proficient as a portrait painter, Yong was in the photographic portrait business until at least 1881.

By 1852 photographic activity was widespread in California. The state's special census for that year listed twelve daguerreotypists in San Francisco, as well as several others operating in rural areas. There were undoubtedly more. San Joaquin County, for instance, claimed two daguerreians, Perez M. and Benjamin P. Batchelder, and Yuba County one, Moses Hanscom (1823–1863). The first known photographic establishment in Los Angeles was in business in August 1851, operated by the partnership of Osburn & Searles. Typical of daguerreian jacks-of-all-trades, Dr. Osburn (c. 1813–1867) was a physician, pharmacist, notary public, postmaster and nurseryman who arrived in California in 1847, establishing the first pharmacy in Los Angeles in 1850. He was also fluent in Spanish. His partner, Searles, had previously traveled to California as part of a mining company, later trying his hand at various trades, including that of tailor and professional house and sign painter.[19] Monterey, California's first state capital and home of one of the state's earliest newspapers, surprisingly appears to have hosted not a single photographer during the daguerreian era.

Within a few years, portrait galleries were well-established throughout the state, many in surprisingly remote areas. Peter Britt (1819–1905), located in Jacksonville, Oregon, dominated the

Oregon-California border area from 1852 until the turn of the century.[20] In 1854, Oliver H. P. Norcross (1824–1871) began a fifteen-year tenure as a studio photographer in Weaverville, deep in the northern mountains of Trinity County. Other Northern California towns, such as Yreka, Eureka, Shasta City and Red Bluff, were served by a succession of portrait establishments. Most studios were concentrated in towns accessible by river navigation, or in areas convenient to interior mining areas, such as Sacramento, Marysville and Stockton. Gold Rush boom towns like San Andreas, Rough and Ready, Mokelumne Hill, Dutch Flat, Auburn and Dry Creek also boasted resident photographers in the early days. Unfortunately for us, the vast majority of surviving daguerreian images from California lack maker identification, thus making proper attribution of work difficult at best. In fact, less than a dozen California photographers active before 1860 actually put their names on their photographs.[21]

Towns which had no studios were visited by itinerant photographers. Generally gregarious and popular, traveling photographers provided color and excitement, in the form of the freshest gossip, to isolated communities. In 1853, Isaac Wallace Baker teamed up with Perez Mann Batchelder (1818–c. 1873) to operate a portable daguerreian van. This horse-drawn mobile studio featured large skylights and side-windows (virtually all early photography was taken with natural light) as well as a prominent sign by the door identifying it as "Batchelder's Daguerreian Saloon; walk in and examine specimens" (figures 3 and 4). During the summer and fall, this portable establishment traveled from mining town to mining town.[22] Prospectors could pose for portraits in the portable studio, or in some cases the camera was taken directly to miners in the field to record mining operations.

Characteristically, surviving outdoor views show only man-centered activity—a new building, a mining crew at work—and almost nothing of the raw California landscape in its own right. Daguerreotypes picturing California's magnificent landscape are all but nonexistent. A single daguerreian view of a redwood grove exists in the collection of the Bancroft Library. Another, in private hands, shows what appears to be a forest scene until a closer look reveals a woodland cabin as the primary focus of the image. While the lack of "scenic" or landscape daguerreotypes seems unfortunate, it is quite understandable. Since virtually all daguerreotypes were commissioned by miners or the owners of businesses, there was simply no market for purely scenic views. Why would a miner pay good money for a daguerreotype of a scene he could enjoy through his cabin window for free?

There were notable exceptions, however. Working with the sole purpose of recording California's wonders for Easterners, in 1851 Robert H. Vance created a monumental documentary work titled *Daguerreotype Panoramic Views in California.* Containing three hundred daguerreotypes in the largest (whole-plate) size, the series began with scenes of Valparaíso, Chile, then traced the trip northward to California through Panama, on to San Francisco, with at least thirty-seven views of the city before the devastating fire of May 4, 1851. Moving inland, Vance documented the southern mines, including scenes of Indian villages near John Sutter's Hock Farm. Returning to San Francisco, he re-photographed the city in the aftermath of the May fire, and again following another fire on

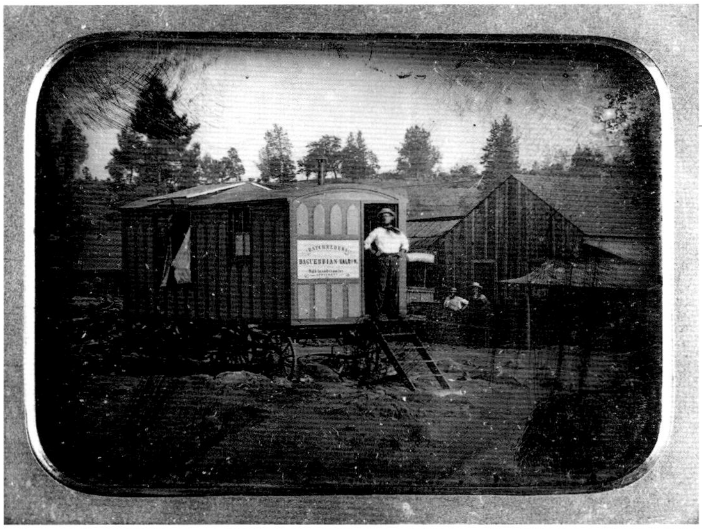

FIGURE 3.
Isaac Wallace Baker
Baker in Front of Batchelder's Daguerreian Saloon, c. 1853
Quarter plate daguerreotype
COLLECTION OF THE OAKLAND MUSEUM OF CALIFORNIA, GIFT OF ANONYMOUS DONOR

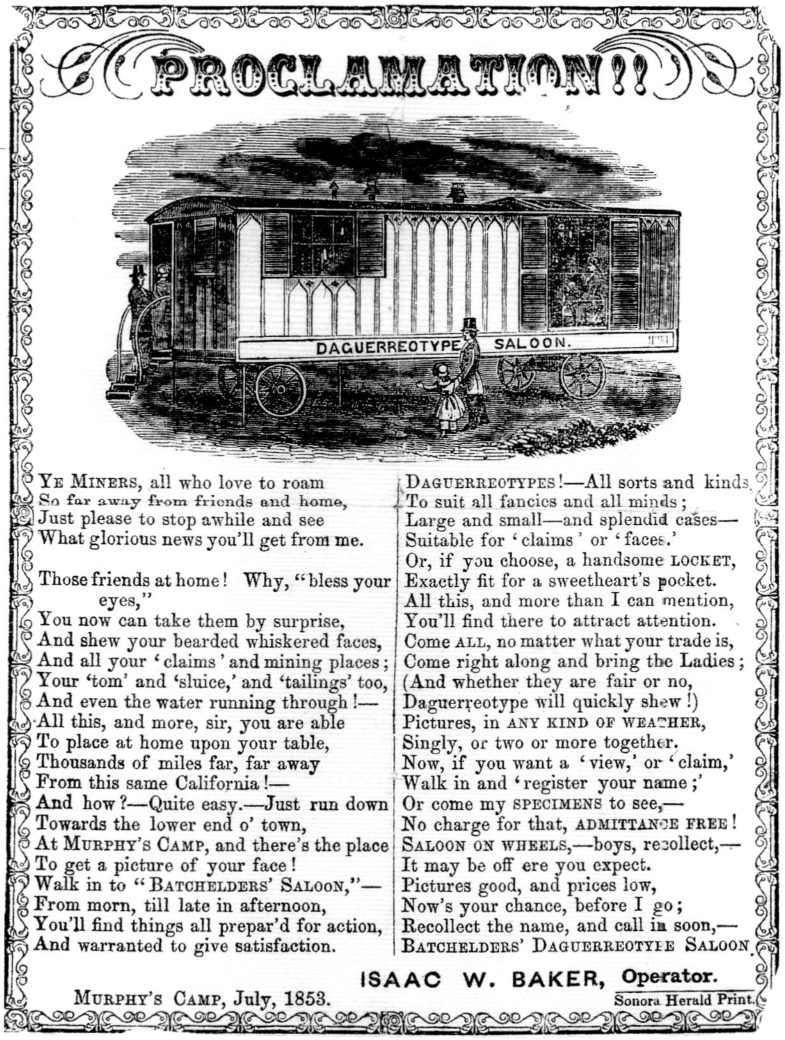

PROCLAMATION!!

DAGUERREOTYPE SALOON.

YE MINERS, all who love to roam
So far away from friends and home,
Just please to stop awhile and see
What glorious news you'll get from me.

Those friends at home! Why, "bless your eyes,"
You now can take them by surprise,
And shew your bearded whiskered faces,
And all your 'claims' and mining places;
Your 'tom' and 'sluice,' and 'tailings' too,
And even the water running through!—
All this, and more, sir, you are able
To place at home upon your table,
Thousands of miles far, far away
From this same California!—
And how?—Quite easy.—Just run down
Towards the lower end o' town,
At MURPHY'S CAMP, and there's the place
To get a picture of your face!
Walk in to "BATCHELDERS' SALOON,"—
From morn, till late in afternoon,
You'll find things all prepar'd for action,
And warranted to give satisfaction.

DAGUERREOTYPES!—All sorts and kinds,
To suit all fancies and all minds;
Large and small—and splendid cases—
Suitable for 'claims' or 'faces.'
Or, if you choose, a handsome LOCKET,
Exactly fit for a sweetheart's pocket.
All this, and more than I can mention,
You'll find there to attract attention.
Come ALL, no matter what your trade is,
Come right along and bring the Ladies;
(And whether they are fair or no,
Daguerreotype will quickly shew!)
Pictures, in ANY KIND OF WEATHER,
Singly, or two or more together.
Now, if you want a 'view,' or 'claim,'
Walk in and 'register your name;'
Or come my SPECIMENS to see,—
No charge for that, ADMITTANCE FREE!
SALOON ON WHEELS,—boys, recollect,—
It may be off ere you expect.
Pictures good, and prices low,
Now's your chance, before I go;
Recollect the name, and call in soon,—
BATCHELDERS' DAGUERREOTYPE SALOON.

ISAAC W. BAKER, Operator.

MURPHY'S CAMP, July, 1853.

Sonora Herald Print.

FIGURE 4.
Isaac Wallace Baker
Proclamation!!, July 1853
Advertising broadside
COURTESY OF TOM HORNING

June 22, before transporting his collection via the Isthmus to New York. *Views in California* was placed on display at 349 Broadway, above Jesse Whitehurst's daguerreian gallery. It received great critical acclaim but was, inexplicably, a financial disappointment. This invaluable collection was sold and resold, finally disappearing around the time of the Civil War. Collectors often refer to it today as "Vance's lost three hundred" and sorely lament the tragic loss of such a remarkable daguerreian achievement.[23]

Ever ambitious, Vance went on to establish the "First Premium Gallery" in San Francisco, creating a network of branch galleries at Marysville and Sacramento, as well as Virginia City and Carson City in Nevada. In 1860 he opened a branch in Hong Kong. He was famous for blatant and strident self-promotion, publishing extravagant advertisements in French, German and even Chinese language newspapers. In his heyday, before 1860, Vance was the dominant photographer of the American West, owning the finest galleries and hiring the best operators. He was also a great innovator, sponsoring some of California's first landscape photography. In 1858 he sent his employee, Charles Leander Weed, to the American River region, where he photographed river mining using the new wet-collodion negatives (figure 5). These large paper photographs, about thirteen by fifteen inches, were displayed in Vance's San Francisco gallery. In 1859 Vance made history by sending Weed to Yosemite to make the first photographs of that remote location, soon to become one of the world's favorite tourist destinations. The Yosemite photographs also made their public debut at Vance's establishment.[24] In 1862 Weed documented the effects of the great Sacramento Flood which had paralyzed the city (plate 16), and the following year he returned to Yosemite with a mammoth plate camera which produced negatives eighteen by twenty-two inches (plate 15).

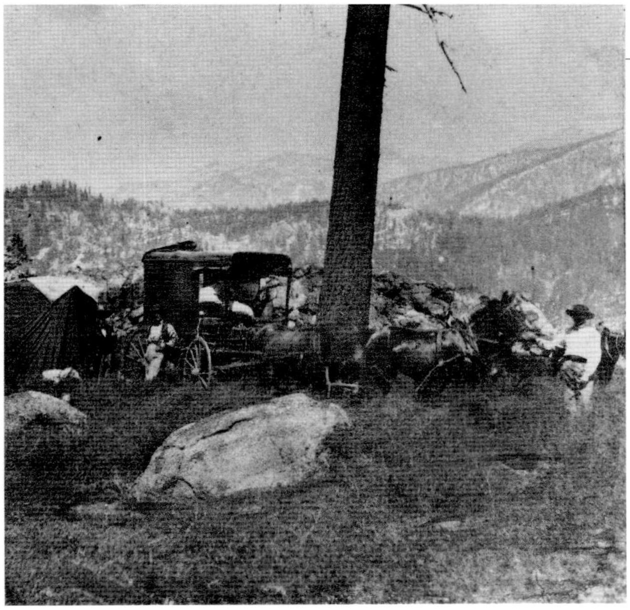

FIGURE 5.
Attributed to Charles Leander Weed
"Camp Vance" (Travelling Studio of Charles Leander Weed),
c. 1862
Albumen stereograph (detail)
COLLECTION OF THE OAKLAND MUSEUM OF CALIFORNIA, GIFT OF MARY MORGANITI

A handwritten note on the back of this stereograph reads, "Taken from the top of the Sierra Nevada's [sic] near Lake-Valley Grade. The Artist's Mules & Waggon [sic]."

Rapidly evolving technology played a significant role in the way photography was conducted as a business. Around 1854 the daguerreotype was challenged by a new process, the ambrotype, a photographic positive on glass. While cheaper, the ambrotype had an obvious flaw. In July 1858, an ambrotypist named G. S. Smith sent a view of Callahan Ranch, a small community in Siskiyou County, to the editor of *Hutchings' California Magazine* to serve as an illustration. Hutchings complained that it arrived, "broke all to pieces. . . . Can't be used. . . . Send us something else that won't break so easily."[25] Photographs on iron sheeting (tintypes), avoided this defect. Tough, cheap and easy to make, tintypes could be slipped into letters to mail to friends "in the States," but tended to look dingy when compared to the brilliance of a daguerreotype.

By far the most important advance, however, was the emergence of photographic prints on paper, made from glass plate negatives (figure 6). Unlike daguerreotypes or ambrotypes, which were unique images, paper prints could be made in any number of copies, opening the door for photographic publishing. Print formats such as the 2½-by-4-inch carte de visite dominated the portrait industry from about 1861 through 1890 (plate 21). The larger "cabinet" portrait (6½ by 4¼ inches) was first offered in 1867, remaining popular until the turn of the century (plates 26 and 27). The availability of larger portrait sizes created a need for negative retouchers and provided employment for large numbers of printers, card-mounters, overpainters and clerks. Many of these new employees were women or minorities, particularly Chinese.

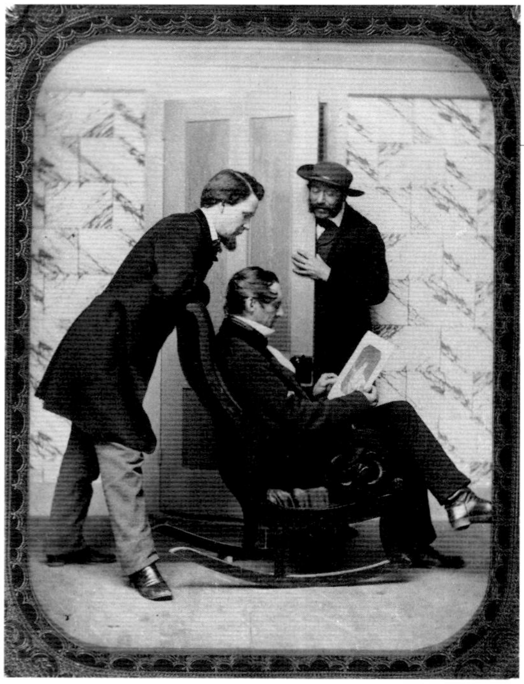

FIGURE 6.
Attributed to William Herman Rulofson
Untitled (William Herman Rulofson and Friends Looking at a Paper Photograph), c. 1856
Half plate ambrotype
COLLECTION OF THE CALIFORNIA STATE LIBRARY

The new popularity of paper prints facilitated the production and marketing of landscape views. The earliest outdoor photographs on paper appeared in California by May 1852, when two itinerant photographers named Gazan and Mazzucchelli used the calotype process to take views of San Francisco as part of a plan to produce a book of images of San Francisco and Sacramento.[26] This idea was not actually realized until 1856, when George Robinson Fardon completed his *San Francisco Album: Photographs of the Most Beautiful Views and Public Buildings in San Francisco* (plate 11).[27] In 1861, Carleton E. Watkins took a giant camera to Yosemite to make mammoth plate negatives, measuring 18 by 22 inches and weighing nearly four pounds each. Watkins transported this cumbersome apparatus to Yosemite on horseback, where he coated and processed the huge negatives in a tiny darktent (plates 12 and 13). By the 1890s, Watkins had taken outdoor views over an immense geographic region ranging from British Columbia to Mexico, from the Farralon Islands in the Pacific Ocean, to as far east as Yellowstone.

Outdoor work on this scale was fraught with dangers. In 1870 Watkins made an ascent of 14,400 foot Mount Shasta in the company of geologist Clarence King. On September 11th the party began their climb, burdened with Watkins's heavy equipment. One of the party later described the ascent as "alternations of simple slippery ice and debris slopes," with King calling it the "most dangerous kind of climbing I have ever seen." In an age of 35mm cameras, it is difficult to imagine Watkins preparing his mammoth wet plate negatives under such conditions. One of his assigned goals was to photograph the seven-mile long, slow-moving mass of ice called Whitney Glacier. At one point, Watkins pitched his photo tent on a small pond of smooth blue ice, and "when he thought he had the light all shut off, found that enough still came through the ice-floor to spoil his negatives, obliging him to cover that also"[28] (figure 7).

Although such large-scale, outdoor work forms a highly valued body of California's photographic heritage, only a handful of pre-1880 photographers could marshal the capital for such work, among them Weed, Watkins, Nathan Klain (a specialist in city views) and, after 1871, Eadweard J. Muybridge. By 1860, great economic changes were beginning to affect California's photographic fraternity. Robert Vance had invested so heavily in Nevada silver mining stock that he was forced to relinquish control of his various branch galleries. The onset of the Civil War created economic disturbances, and "prices to suit the times" were widely advertised. Payment in foodstuffs or other commodities rather than money became commonplace in rural communities: "Meacham the photographer, asks only part pay in advance . . . will trade photographs for deer horns, bear robes, wood, butter and eggs or anything else you may have."[29] In the meantime, city galleries laid off unneeded employees to trim costs. Many of these displaced photographers went into business for themselves, creating even more competition and forcing down prices across the state.

Yet there was a silver lining emerging from within the clouds of war, as the world's increasing appetite for stereographic cards unexpectedly fueled a new industry in the West. Weed's stereographs

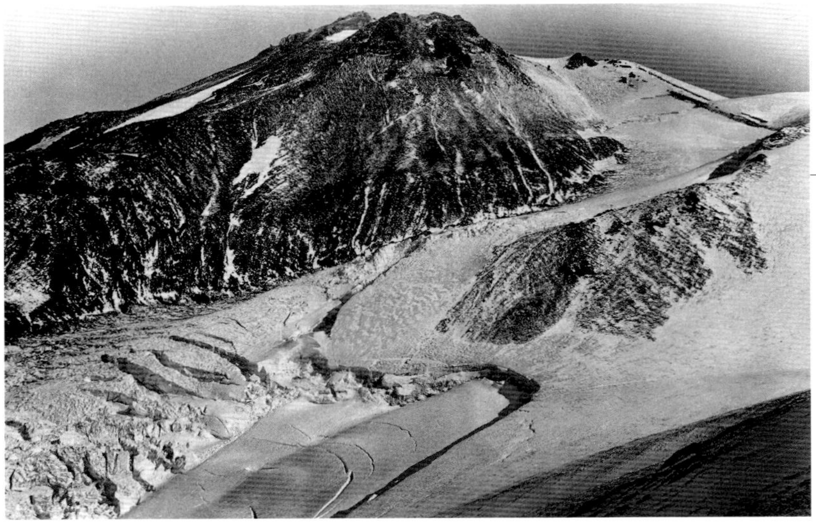

FIGURE 7.
Carleton E. Watkins
Summit of Mount Shasta, Earth Glacier, 1870
Albumen print
COURTESY OF PETER E. PALMQUIST

of Yosemite and San Francisco, virtually unmarketable in California in 1860, were sold to the huge stereopublishing firm of Edward Anthony in New York. The assorted views of San Francisco, Yosemite and the mining districts proved immediately popular and were a powerful tool for publicizing the California Dream.[30] Similarly, the San Francisco optical firm of Lawrence & Houseworth, which had stocked imported stereographs as early as 1862, began manufacturing and distributing California images on a large scale (plate 16).[31] Firms such as Lawrence & Houseworth employed a number of previously displaced studio photographers; others found work making regional stereographs.

Martin Mason Hazeltine (1827–1903) had worked in California during the 1850s, but the stereoscopic boom of the sixties gave his career a new lease on life. Hazeltine was a first-class itinerant photographer who, gypsy-like, brought his wife and six children with him on his far-ranging photographic travels. In 1867 he made beautiful photographs of the effects of a winter storm on the coast of Mendocino, including a view of the ship *Brilliant* sailing out to sea. He also made many visits to Yosemite, including annual trips during the early 1870s. During his long stereoscopic career, Hazeltine photographed in Idaho, Oregon, Washington and Alaska. He went about his business with little or no fanfare. His horse-drawn traveling wagon did not bear his name, and the great majority of his negatives were published by others. He was so self-effacing, in fact, that when photographer Charles L. Pond arrived in Yosemite it was Hazeltine who made the negatives which Pond later published as his own.

Other important stereo-photographers included Alfred A. Hart and Eadweard J. Muybridge. Hart documented the construction of the Central Pacific Railroad (C.P.R.R.) between 1864 and 1869. His images were not only important industrial documents but proved popular with the traveling public as well (plate 16). In 1869, however, his connection with the C.P.R.R. was severed and Carleton Watkins took over the publishing of Hart's negatives on behalf of the railroad.[32] The versatile Muybridge also cashed in on the stereo boom, with views published by Bradley & Rulofson in direct competition with Watkins and Thomas Houseworth & Company. Among Muybridge's more interesting contributions are a series of cloud formations and views of the Modoc War, California's only large-scale Indian conflict.[33]

One of the finest stereo-photographers of the boom days was John James Reilly. Traveling westward from New York, he photographed Colorado and Utah before arriving in Yosemite in 1870. There he erected a large photographic tent-gallery, the first photographic establishment in the valley (figure 8). Reilly worked in Yosemite every summer—specializing in stereographic views of tourists—for seven years before relocating to Marysville. His views are notable for their technical and pictorial quality (he even devised a super-proportional developer to record the spectacular clouds of Yosemite landscapes). By the 1880s, however, he was having severe financial difficulty, due to a precipitous drop in the priçe of stereographs. This downward trend was evident as early as 1874 when he wrote: "I used to get $24 per gross for stereoscopic views some eight years ago at Niagara, and two years ago $24 per gross for views of the Yosemite Valley, and today I can get barely half that." In 1894, unable to find work and increasingly depressed, Reilly committed suicide by sticking his head in an oven and turning on the gas.[34]

Throughout the nineteenth century, blatant self-promotion was common among Western photographers. Traveling artists advertised, "Coming, Coming, Pictures, 50 cents a Bushel," "Save the Shadow, ere the substance fly," or "Pictures in the finest style, on glass, metal, oil-cloth, leather, or paper!" John Oliver Welsh (c. 1840–c. 1913) was a perfect example of Yankee enterprise and ingenuity. As an itinerant photographer, he traveled over nearly a thousand square miles of Northern California, "carrying on a Bonanza King's business in the photographing line." Welsh, the entrepreneur (he was, among other things, a miner, newspaper correspondent, postmaster, merchant, dabbler in real estate, builder and operator of lumber mills, a strawberry farmer, candidate for county surveyor and Democratic party chairman), even founded a town: Mott, in Siskiyou County. Unlike others, however, his efforts actually made him rich.

Promotional gimmicks were *de rigueur* in the photographic trade. Nevada City photographer Alphonse Liebert devised a lottery, with raffle tickets at one dollar each and promises of "great prizes." Each time the drawing day approached, however, he conveniently arranged for its postponement; irate citizens eventually clamored for his head. Conflict between established photographers and "tent-men," as itinerants were called, often resulted in public advertising wars, an example of which is the following doggerel published by Ferndale gallery owner A.W. Gilfillian:

> Traveling photographers are all getting grey,
> They turn out their work in the very same way.
> The same old song they always parade,

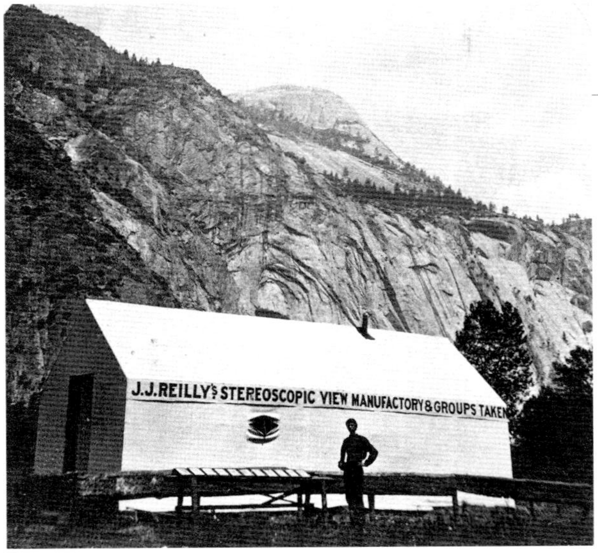

FIGURE 8.
John James Reilly
J. J. Reilly's Stereoscopic View Manufactory, c. 1870
Albumen stereograph (detail)
COURTESY OF PETER E. PALMQUIST

> And try to fool the public that their pictures don't fade.
> But they are grey and they are flat,
> So, just think of it, for time has proved that.
> So if you don't want grey pictures which will make you repent,
> The thing to do is to stay away from all tents.

Gilfillian, of course, neglected to mention that he had once been a tent-man himself.[35]

After 1870, increased competition led to a proliferation of "Cheap John" operators, who cut prices and foisted inferior quality work on the public. Many of the better operators railed at photographers who undercut their brethren in the trade. John Pitcher Spooner (1845–1917), a notoriously outspoken studio photographer from Stockton, posed this rhetorical question: "Which is the better way of photographic advertising? By 'public press,' 'circular,' 'fence post, curb, and sidewalk poster,' or 'carefully finished work' and 'discretionary conduct toward our patrons?'"[36]

There were other, more human-centered problems as well. In an example of frontier lawlessness carried over to photography, in April 1874 two studio employees resolved their longstanding feud with gunfire. When the gallery owner heard the shots, he rushed in to discover his assistants both dead on the studio floor, the result of a murder and suicide.[37] Ineptitude and fraud were also encountered. Some individuals seemed destined to cause difficulty, as we see from the following instances involving John Calvin Scripture (1828–1909). As early as 1850 a former colleague had commented: "There I found a likeness man named Scripture. I was more impressed with his name than with the quality of his work." Scripture came to California in the early 1860s, and by 1868 he had entered into a business partnership with Isaac T. Coffin. After a short time, however, the partners had a falling-out and abandoned the gallery. Coffin, who had co-signed for Scripture on the long-term lease of the gallery, was forced to make good on the debt, eventually paying out over $4,000. When he made the final installment on April 2, 1880, he noted in his diary, "Lord lead me not into temptation and save me from my friends."[38]

The completion of the Transcontinental Railroad in 1869 brought droves of tourists and excursion parties to California. San Francisco and the famous Cliff House, the California geysers and especially Yosemite and the Big Tree redwood groves were must-see attractions for these well-to-do visitors. They naturally purchased photographs for their stereoscopes and travel albums. Some photographers, such as George Fiske in Yosemite, catered almost exclusively to the burgeoning tourist trade. Fiske was widely known for his "Cloud Chasing Chariot" a steel-wheeled wheelbarrow which he used to transport his camera. "He used to push that wheelbarrow for miles," a friend recalled. Even after his hair had turned completely white Fiske remained one of Yosemite's most colorful denizens. Fittingly, he is buried in the valley he loved.[39]

Mention should also be made of Eliza Withington (c. 1824–1877) who hailed from Ione, a tiny dot of a mountain town in Amador County. A specialist in landscape photography, she frequently traveled about the region "by stage, private conveyance, or fruit wagons." Employing the wet-collodion process, she thought nothing of using her outer skirts as a darktent when the need arose. In 1876 she wrote a marvelous essay entitled "How a Woman Makes Landscape Negatives," one of our best accounts of California field photography during the 1870s; it speaks highly of her own personal courage and fortitude. After describing her travelling photographic outfit she declared: "last but *not least* in usefulness is a strong black-linen cane-handled parasol. If not absolutely necessary for a cane, and more necessary for a shade, I so use it . . . and for climbing mountains or *sliding* into ravines a true and safe alpenstock." Her surviving stereoscopic views of primitive towns and gritty mining operations are inspirational. Because of her great energy, it would be easy to assume that she was a young woman; in fact, Withington was already fifty-one years old when she penned her essay. Sadly, she died soon after, apparently of cancer.[40]

America's Centennial celebrations of 1876 served to focus attention on regional resources, and led to a ready market for photographs of local products and a chamber-of-commerce style attitude towards local self-promotion. This push for regional identity created yet another significant market for photographs. In southern California the emphasis was on agriculture: seedlings one year were seemingly full-grown fruit trees the next, grape vines and rose bushes grew as large as houses and a single squash could fill a wheelbarrow. Utopian communities, health spas and the Santa Monica beaches became not just tourist destinations but places where visitors stayed to become residents in ever-increasing numbers. With them came new photographers. Even the most isolated regions became deeply involved in photographic self-promotion, as regional photography blossomed in every district of California, with images exhibited in local and state agricultural exhibitions, as well as such national venues as the Chicago World's Fair of 1893.

By 1900 the number of professional photographers in California had exploded. Exact numbers are not easy to calculate, but the "Photographers" section of the San Francisco city directory of 1900 has some seventy-five *paid* listings. To these must be added many photographers who balked at paying a specific listing fee. A line-by-line examination of the white pages of directories from around the state generally yields two to three times as many photographers as actually appear in the classified section of city directories. Moreover, there were many individuals who were employed in various unspecified occupations within the industry. Among these were large numbers of women. By 1905 at least twenty percent of the photographic workers in California were female.[41] In San Francisco, between 1850 and 1900, there were nearly ninety women photographers and about 235 other women involved in photographically related trades. Statewide, there were no less than eight hundred and fifty women involved in some aspect of California photography before 1901. The proliferation of roll film cameras and amateur photography further contributed to the soaring number of images produced. This amateur interest also led to professional and commercial opportunity for camera sales and photo-finishing, even photographic schools.

Today, at a time when photographic images have become as common as the grains of sand on California's beaches, we must offer profound thanks to those pioneer image makers who struggled to record the evolving California Dream on daguerreotype plates and stereograph cards. Finally, we should not lose sight of the fact that those unsmiling and funny-looking people captured on yesterday's ubiquitous carte de visite or tintype so long ago are but markers for the day when our own photographs will not only be considered curious, but potentially *collectible!*

NOTES

1. This essay draws heavily on my personal research files, which have been assembled over a thirty-year period. In 1994, I joined with my colleague Thomas R. Kailbourn in compiling this collected data into nearly 1,500 biographical entries representing photographers active in the frontier West—from Hawaii to the east side of the Wyoming/Montana/Colorado border, north to Alaska, including British Columbia, and south to Panama, including Baja California and western Mexico—who were active before 1866. This manuscript (roughly 2,800 pages) will be published by Stanford University Press and should be available by October 2000. Due to the comprehensive nature of this compilation, I have chosen not to extensively footnote those photographers who are already well documented in this reference. Uncited references to photographers in this essay may be presumed to be covered in this upcoming volume.

2. Frederick C. Coombs (1803–1874), sometimes referred to as "Uncle Freddy." Coombs once advertised "Jumping Babies Daguerreotyped."

3. Augustus Le Plongeon (1826–1908). See also Lawrence Gustave Desmond and Phyllis Mauch Messenger, *A Dream of Maya: Augustus and Alice Le Plongeon in Nineteenth-Century Yucatán* (Albuquerque: University of New Mexico Press, 1988).

4. San Francisco *Alta California,* September 23, 1855. The San Francisco firm of George Howard Johnson & Silas Selleck erected a small building at Yerba Buena Cemetery for the purpose of taking daguerreian views of the deceased to send east to relatives.

5. For useful insight into the various manifestations of the California Dream see Claire Perry, *Pacific Arcadia: Images of California 1600–1915* (New York and Oxford: University of Oxford Press, 1999).

6. *Kennebec Journal,* October 1, 1839. Demonstrating an interest in both photography and exotic locales, the same newspaper described Palestine on October 29, 1839. The *Maine Democrat* related the adventures of John Mix Stanley, who took his camera to Fort Gibson, Arkansas, and photographed the local Indians in October 1841. On June 2, 1843, the *Journal* published an article concerning colored daguerreotypes, and another on September 8, 1843. Likewise, an extensive article about California appeared on September 4, 1846, and an entire column was devoted to the Talbotype process on July 3, 1846.

7. There are a number of good writings on panoramas, including Stephan Oettermann, *The Panorama: History of a Mass Medium* (New York: Zone Books, 1997). See also John Francis McDermott, *The Lost Panoramas of the Mississippi: Paintings by the Mile—the Story of the Newsreel Travelogue-Documentary "Movie" of the Nineteenth Century* (Chicago: University of Chicago Press, 1958). For an interesting around-the-world account, see Ivan Sanderson, "The Prodigious Panorama," *American Heritage* 12, no. 1 (December 1960): 55–62.

8. There are several instances where daguerreotypes were taken of Mexican inhabitants who are believed never to have left California prior to the Gold Rush. In at least one case, the individual died before gold was discovered in January 1848. Some of these portraits were in daguerreotype cases that could be dated to as early as 1842. Pre-Gold Rush society was not as backward as we might think, especially when we consider that some Californio families could afford to send their children abroad for schooling, or import tutors for home schooling.

9. The daguerreotype is about the size of a modern ten-cent piece. Details concerning the taking of this portrait were found in correspondence between Platon Vallejo (Fanny's brother) and Eve E. Dye, June 16, 1894, in the Vallejo Family Papers, Bancroft Library, University of California, Berkeley. Thanks are due to Martha McGettigan, a Vallejo descendent, for alerting me to this letter.

10. See Peter E. Palmquist, "An Account of California's First Photographer," *Photography in the West I* (Manhattan, Kansas: Sunflower University Press, 1987): 102–105.

11. For Johnson's coverage of the riot in Sacramento, see "Sacramento Squatter's Riot—G. H. Johnson Captured the Scene," *The Daguerreian Annual* (Eureka, California: Daguerreian Society, 1990): 19–20. There has never been a comprehensive article on Johnson, who must be ranked as one of California's finest daguerreians.

12. San Francisco *Alta California,* June 28–August 23, 1849, and Sacramento *Placer Times,* September 29, 1849.

13. California *Chronicle,* May 13, 1856: "The celebrated daguerrean [sic] artist, well known in this city since 1849."

14. San Francisco *Alta California,* January 29, 1850. Shannon's September 1850 notice in Kimball's *San Francisco Directory* listed her as a midwife and daguerreotypist, including as references the names of twelve physicians.

15. See also Abel Alexander, "Robert H. Vance: Pioneer of the Daguerreotype in Chile," *The Daguerreian Annual* (Eureka, California: Daguerreian Society, 1993): 11–30.

16. See Peter E. Palmquist, "William Herman Rulofson: 'The P. T. Barnum of American Photography,'" *The Daguerreian Annual* (Eureka, California: Daguerreian Society, 1993): 136–154.

17. San Francisco *Sun,* May 7, 1853.

18. San Francisco *Daily California Chronicle,* June 8, 1854.

19. *Los Angeles Star,* August 9, 1851. Another early Los Angeles gallery was operated by George Reuben, according to an advertisement in the *Star* on April 2, 1853.

20. See Alan Clark Miller, *Photographer of a Frontier: The Photographs of Peter Britt* (Eureka, California: Interface California Corporation, 1976).

21. They are: James A. Clayton, Frederick Coombs, James M. Ford, Charles F. Hamilton, George H. Johnson, J. Ruth, Silas Selleck, Shaw & Johnson, Jacob Shew, William Shew, and Robert H. Vance.

22. See Therese Thau Heyman, *Mirror of California: Daguerreotypes* (Oakland, California: Oakland Museum, 1973).

23. See Peter E. Palmquist, "The Sad but True Story of a Daguerreian Holy Grail," in Drew Heath Johnson and Marcia Eymann, eds., *Silver & Gold: Cased Images of the California Gold Rush* (Iowa City: University of Iowa Press/Oakland Museum of California, 1998), 43–73.

24. For Vance's San Francisco years, see Peter E. Palmquist, "Robert H. Vance: Pioneer Photographer," *Argonaut* (Journal of the San Francisco Historical Society) 8 (Spring 1997): 4–35.

25. *Hutchings' California Magazine* 3, no. 1 (July 1858): 48.

26. The calotype or Talbotype (named after its inventor, William Henry Fox-Talbot) was most common in England in the 1840s, whereas the daguerreotype was the dominant process used in the rest of Europe and in America. The calotype procedure employed a paper negative; because of the fibrous structure of the negative, prints generally lacked the sharpness and clarity of those produced by means of the wet-collodion glass negative.

27. See George Robinson Fardon, *San Francisco Album: Photographs of the Most Beautiful Views and Public Buildings* (San Francisco and New York: Fraenkel Gallery, San Francisco, and Hans P. Kraus, Jr., Inc., New York, in association with Chronicle Books, 1999).

28. Benjamin P. Avery, "Ascent on Mount Shasta," *Overland Monthly* 12 (May 1874): 472.

29. Redding Free Press, January 27, 1894. Mark Meacham was only one of many California photographers who sometimes traded for pictures. In fact, it was relatively common well into the twentieth century.

30. Weed's California photographs, after being sold to Edward Anthony & Company, were first announced in a New York newspaper on May 15, 1860. For information on Weed, see Peter E. Palmquist, "California's Peripatetic Photographer: Charles Leander Weed," *California History* 58, no. 3 (Fall 1979): 194–219. After 1863, Weed made many stereoscopic negatives that were published by Lawrence & Houseworth.

31. See Peter E. Palmquist, *Lawrence & Houseworth/Thomas Houseworth & Co.: A Unique View of the West 1860–1886* (Columbus, Ohio: National Stereoscopic Association, 1980).

32. See Mead B. Kibbey (Peter E. Palmquist, ed.), *The Railroad Photographs of Alfred A. Hart, Artist* (Sacramento: California State Library Foundation, 1996).

33. There are innumerable books and articles devoted to Muybridge. See, for example, Robert Bartlett Haas, *Muybridge: Man in Motion* (Berkeley, Los Angeles and London: University of California Press, 1976).

34. See Peter E. Palmquist, *J. J. Reilly: A Stereoscopic Odyssey 1838–1894* (Yuba City, California: Community Memorial Museum, 1989).

35. "Something Funny," Ferndale *Enterprise,* November 23, 1894. The remainder of the verse reads as follows: "And another thing is they make themselves funny, / Thinking their stories will bring them the money. / So the chorus comes in, now bring down your flag— / Who wants a picture taken under a rag. / So all my good friends join us in a laugh, / Come up to the Glass Gallery and get the best Cabinets for $1.50. / A. W. Gilfillian."

36. J. Pitcher Spooner, "Photographic Advertising," *The Philadelphia Photographer* 11, no. 121 (January 1874): 14.

37. "Horrible Tragedy in a Photographic Gallery," Eureka *Humboldt Times,* April 11, 1874. The studio was that of Joseph Silva's, 64 Third Street, San Francisco.

38. The first comment on Scripture was made by James F. Ryder in *Voigtlander and I in Pursuit of Shadow Catching* (Cleveland, Ohio: Cleveland Printing & Publishing Co., 1902), 86. Coffin's comment, written on April 2, 1880, is from his diary, which has been reprinted by Russell Towle as *The Dutch Flat Diary of Isaac Tibbetts Coffin Spanning the Years from 1870 to 1903* (Dutch Flat: Giant Gap Press, 1996), 121. See also Peter E. Palmquist, "California's 'Mr. Peeps,'" *The Photographic Historian* 8, no. 3 (Autumn 1987): 4, 8.

39. See Paul Hickman and Terrance Pitts, *George Fiske: Yosemite Photographer* (Flagstaff, Arizona: Northland Press in cooperation with the Center for Creative Photography, University of Arizona, 1980).

40. See Peter E. Palmquist, "Eliza W. Withington" in *Shadowcatchers: A Directory of Women in California Photography Before 1901* (Arcata, California: published by the author, 1990), 238–43, and Eliza Withington, "How a Woman Makes Photographs," *Philadelphia Photographer* 13 (1876): 357–60.

41. Since many pre-1910 photography operations were run from the home, it could well be argued that a male photographer who was married or who had female children also had female workers in his business.

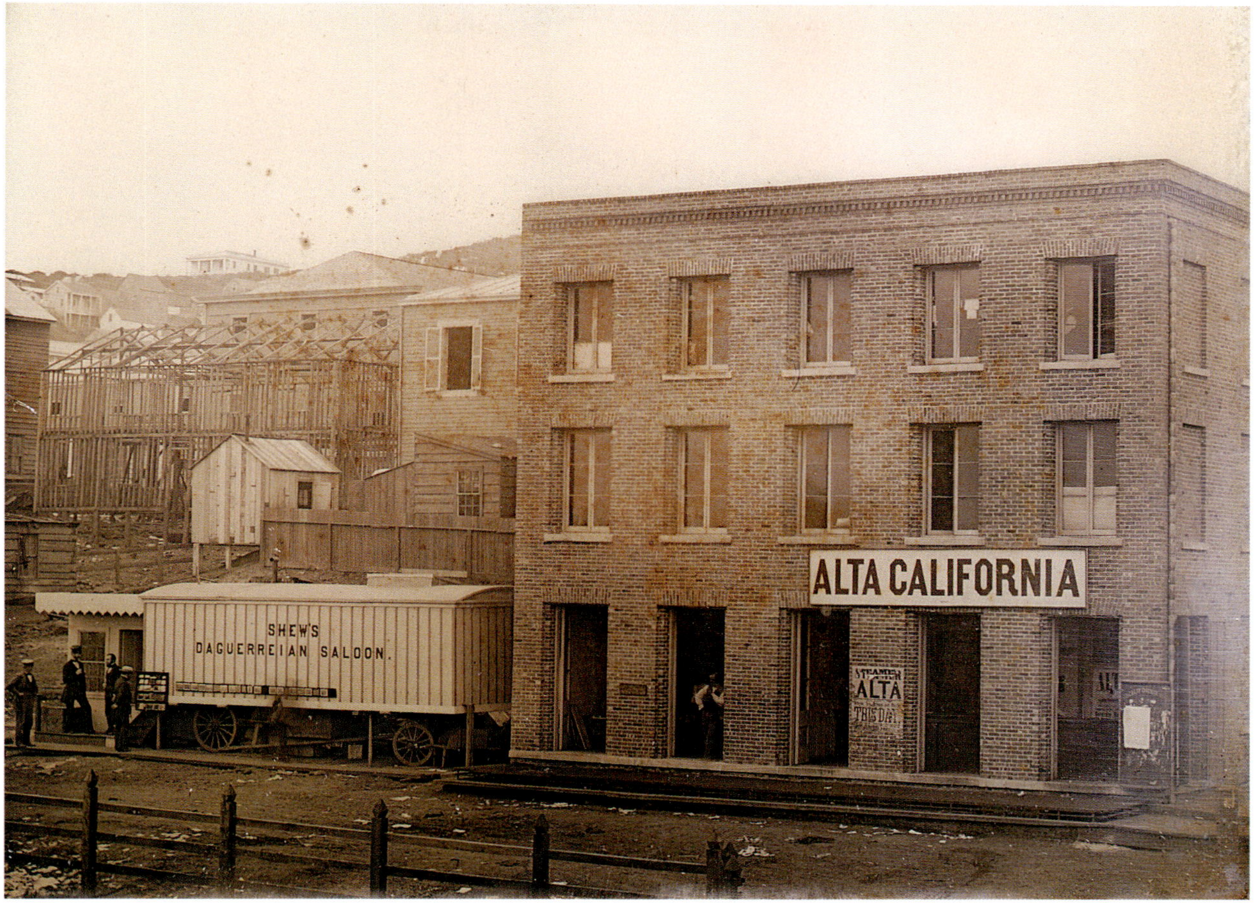

1.

WILLIAM SHEW

Untitled (Shew's Daguerrian Saloon and the Alta California Newspaper Office, San Francisco), 1851

Half plate daguerreotype

3¾ x 5 in.

GIFT OF MR. AND MRS. WILLARD M. NOTT AND DR. PAUL S. TAYLOR BY EXCHANGE

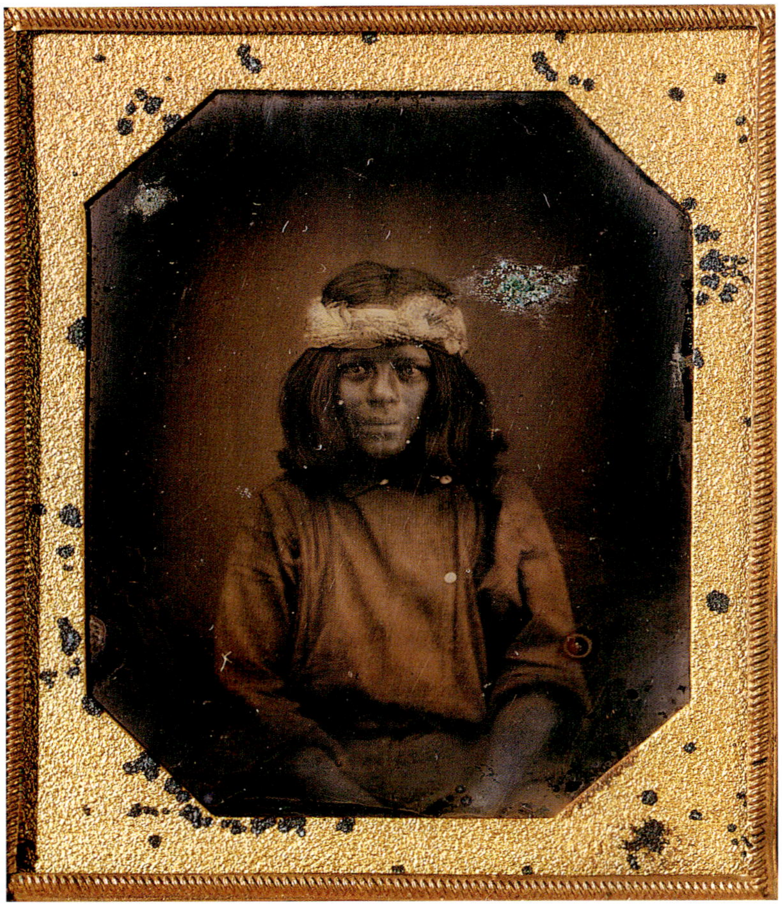

2.
ISAAC WALLACE BAKER
Native Californian, c. 1853
Sixth plate daguerreotype
3¾ x 3¼ in.
ANONYMOUS GIFT

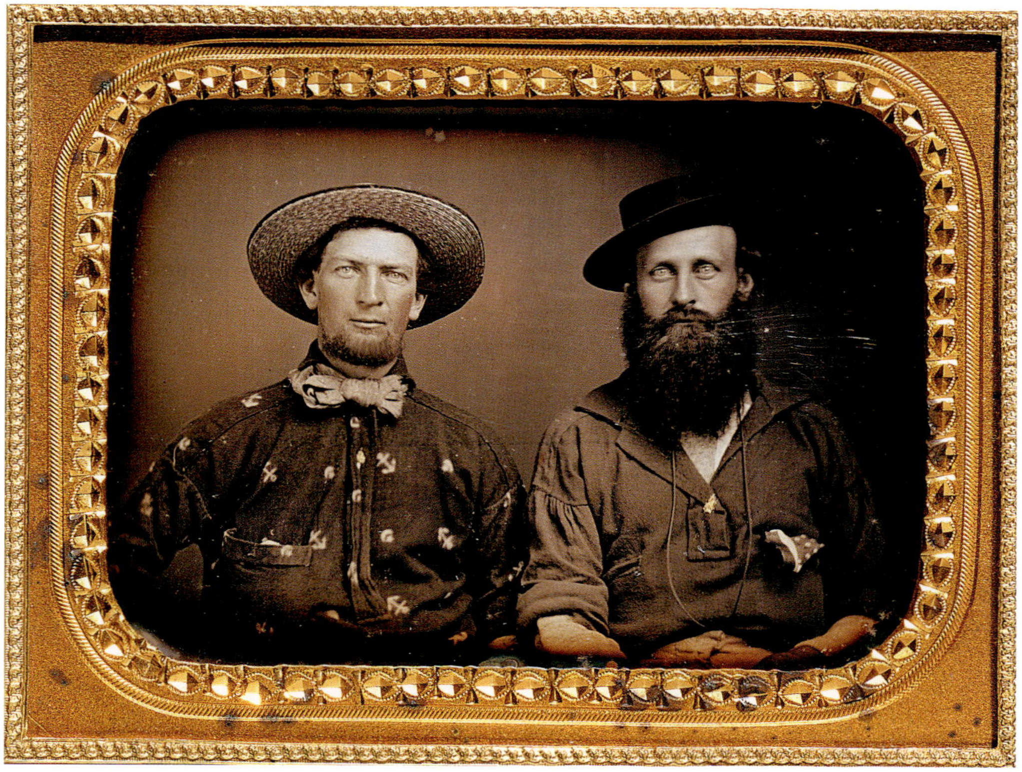

3.
UNKNOWN
Untitled (Two Miners with Gold Nugget Stick-Pins), c. 1852
Quarter plate daguerreotype
3¼ x 4¼ in.
PRINTS AND PHOTOGRAPHS FUND

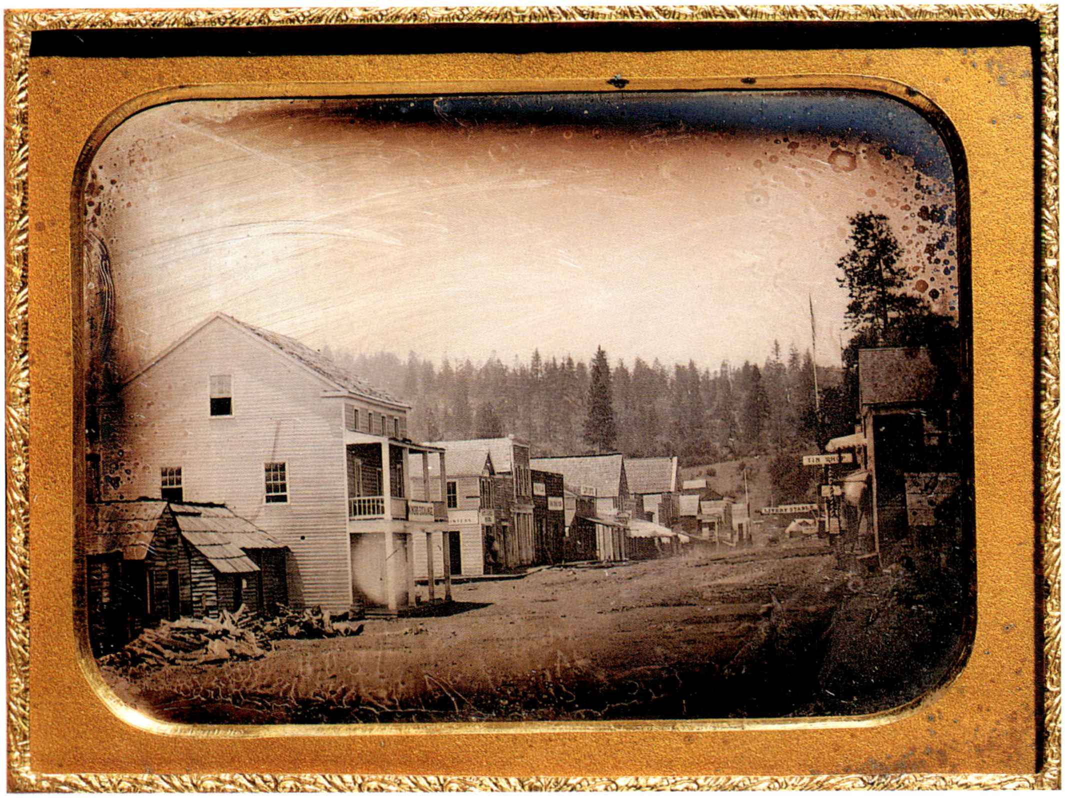

4.
ISAAC WALLACE BAKER
Untitled (Murphys, Calaveras County), July 1853
Quarter plate daguerreotype
$3\frac{3}{4}$ x $4\frac{3}{4}$ in.
ANONYMOUS GIFT

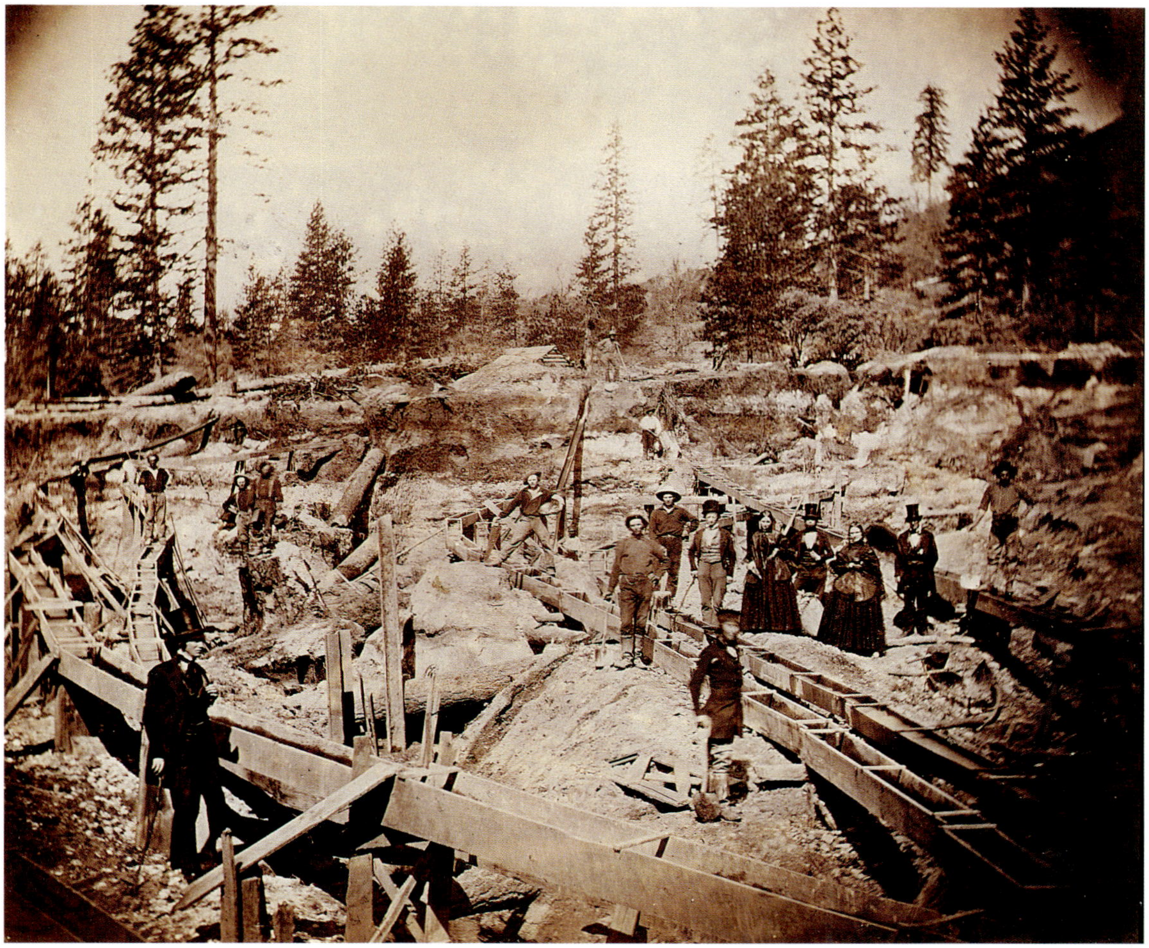

5.
UNKNOWN
Untitled (California Mining Scene), c. 1860
Albumen print
10 x 11¾ in.
GIFT OF DR. AND MRS. DUDLEY P. BELL

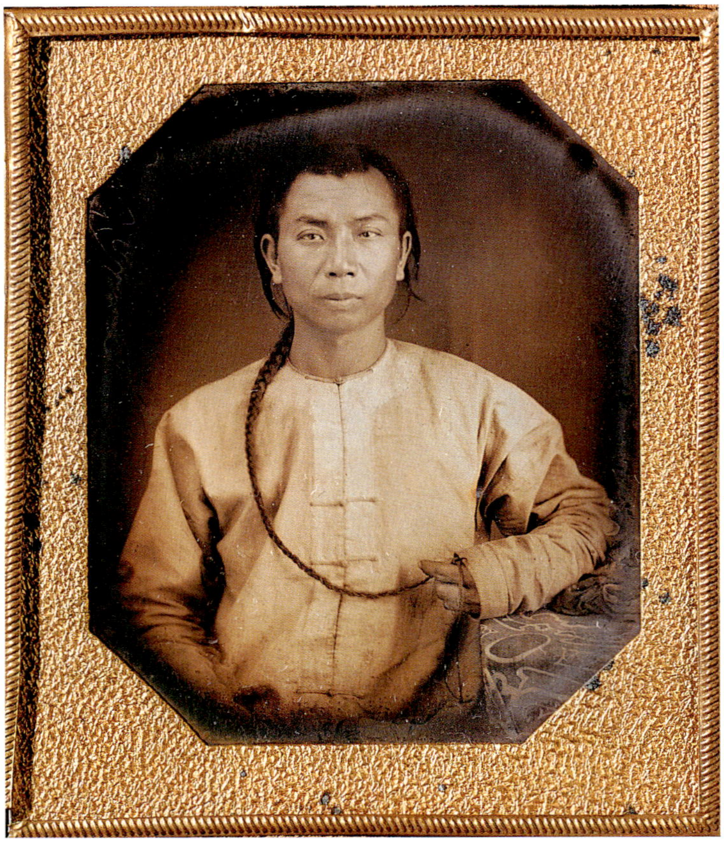

6.
ISAAC WALLACE BAKER
Untitled (Chinese Man), c. 1853
Sixth plate daguerreotype
3¾ x 3¼ in.
ANONYMOUS GIFT

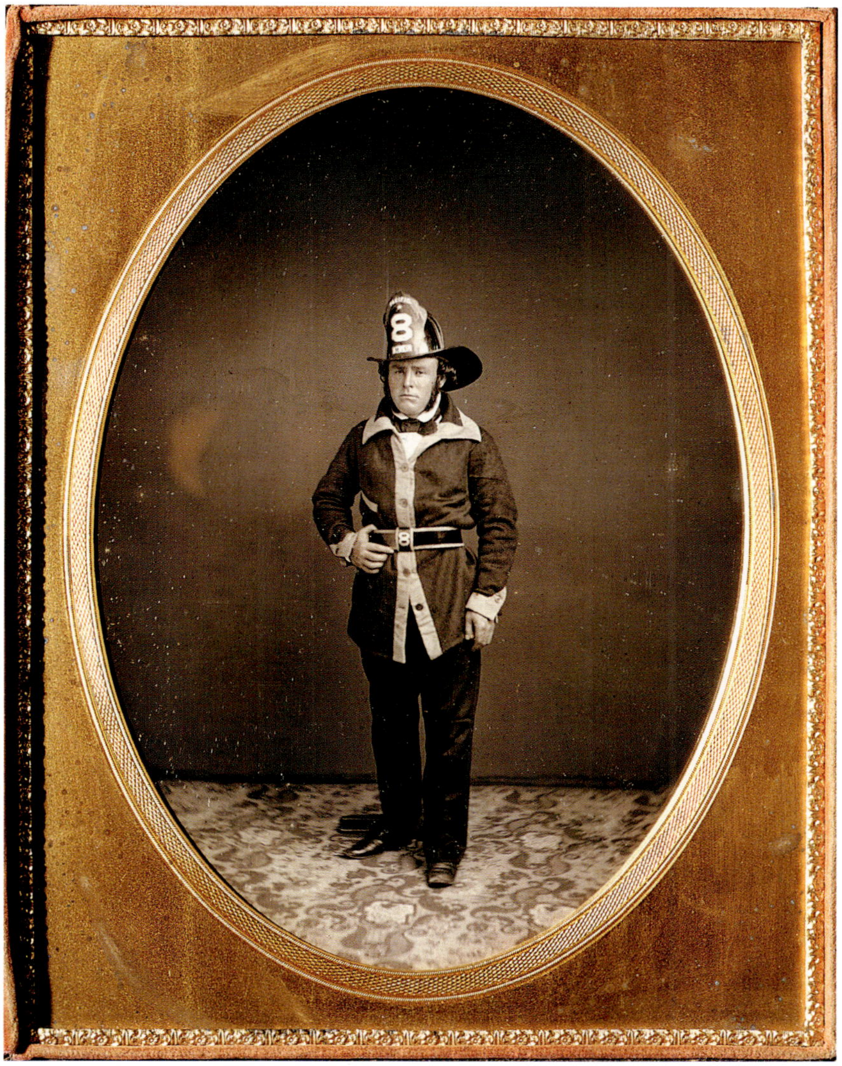

7.
GEORGE H. JOHNSON
Untitled (California Fireman), c. 1853
Whole plate daguerreotype
9 x 7 in.
MUSEUM PURCHASE

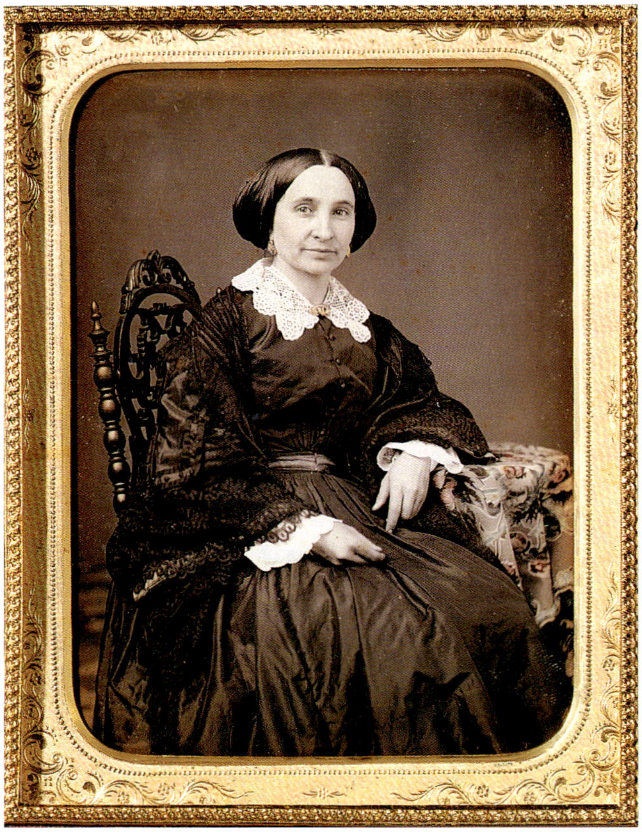

8.
ROBERT H. VANCE
Untitled (Portrait of a Woman), c. 1854
Quarter plate daguerreotype
4¾ x 3¾ in.
MUSEUM INCOME PURCHASE FUND

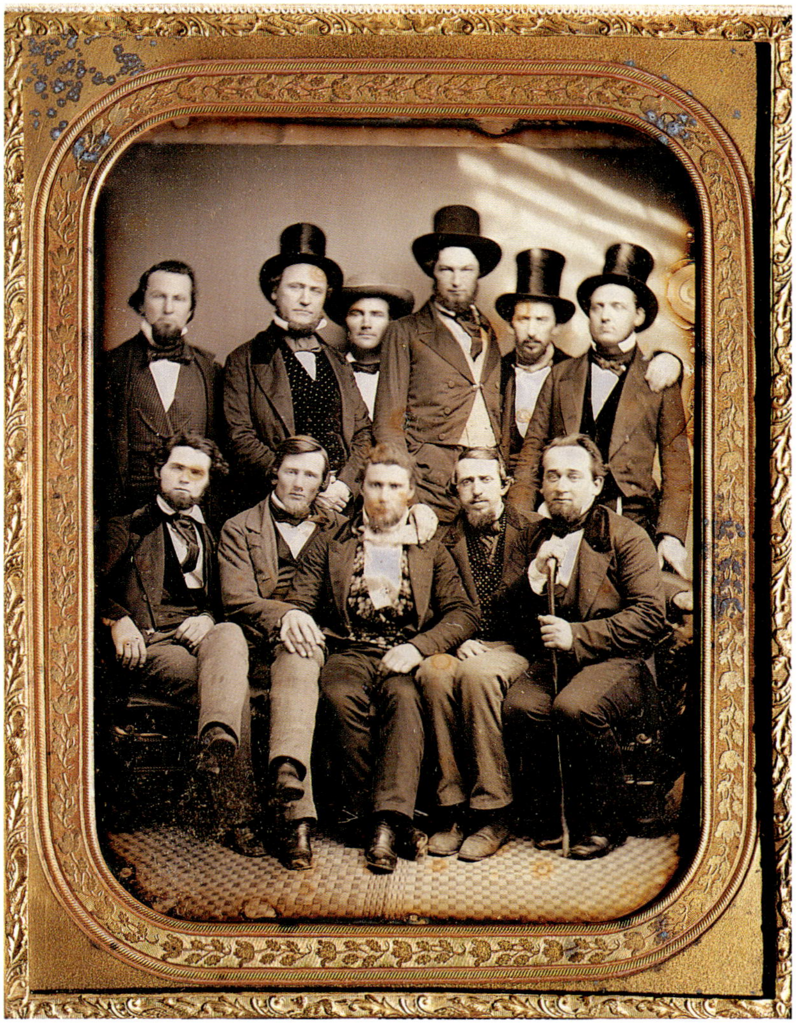

9.

ATTRIBUTED TO WILLIAM SHEW

Untitled (Eleven Men with Beards, Top Hats and Vests), c. 1853

Half plate daguerreotype

6 x 4¾ in.

GIFT OF CONCOURS D'ANTIQUES

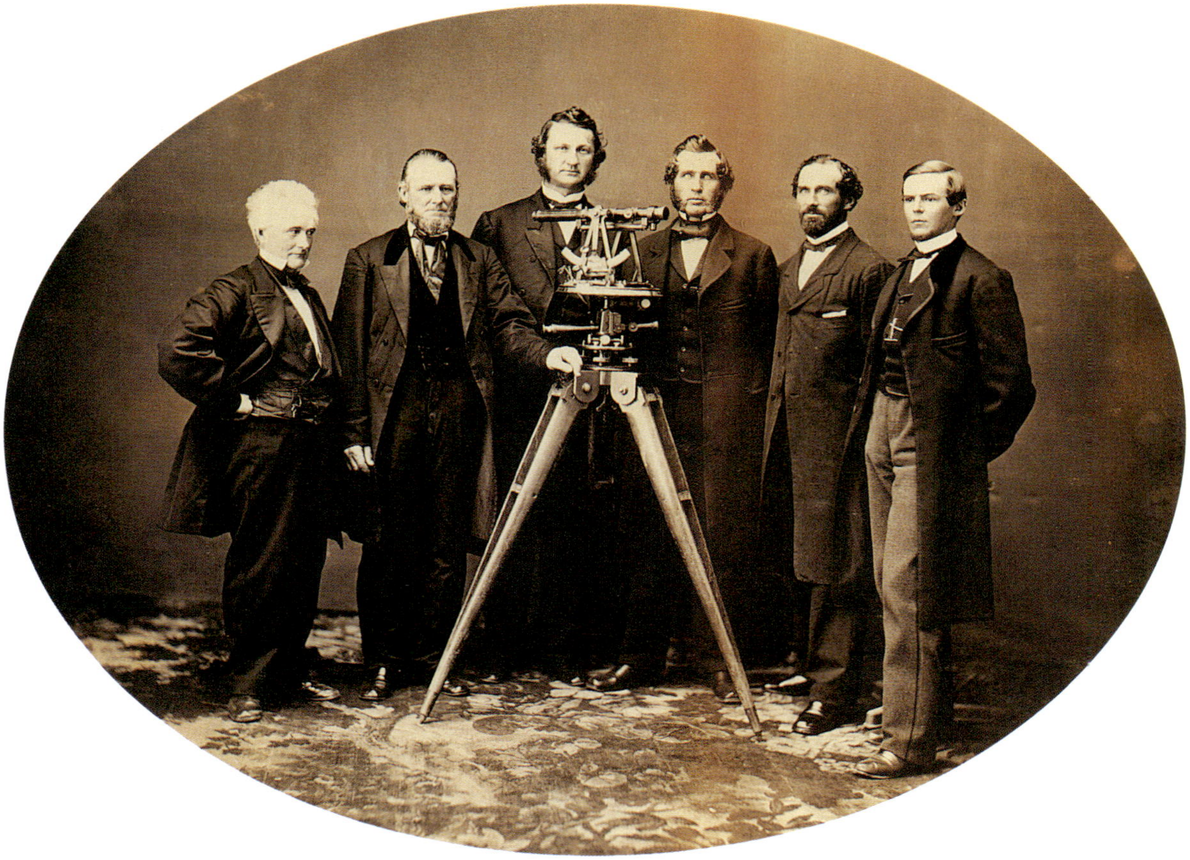

10.
ATTRIBUTED TO ROBERT H. VANCE
Untitled (William F. Boardman and Surveying Party), c. 1859
Salted paper print in vintage frame
18 x 24 in.
GIFT OF MR. WILLIAM G. BOARDMAN

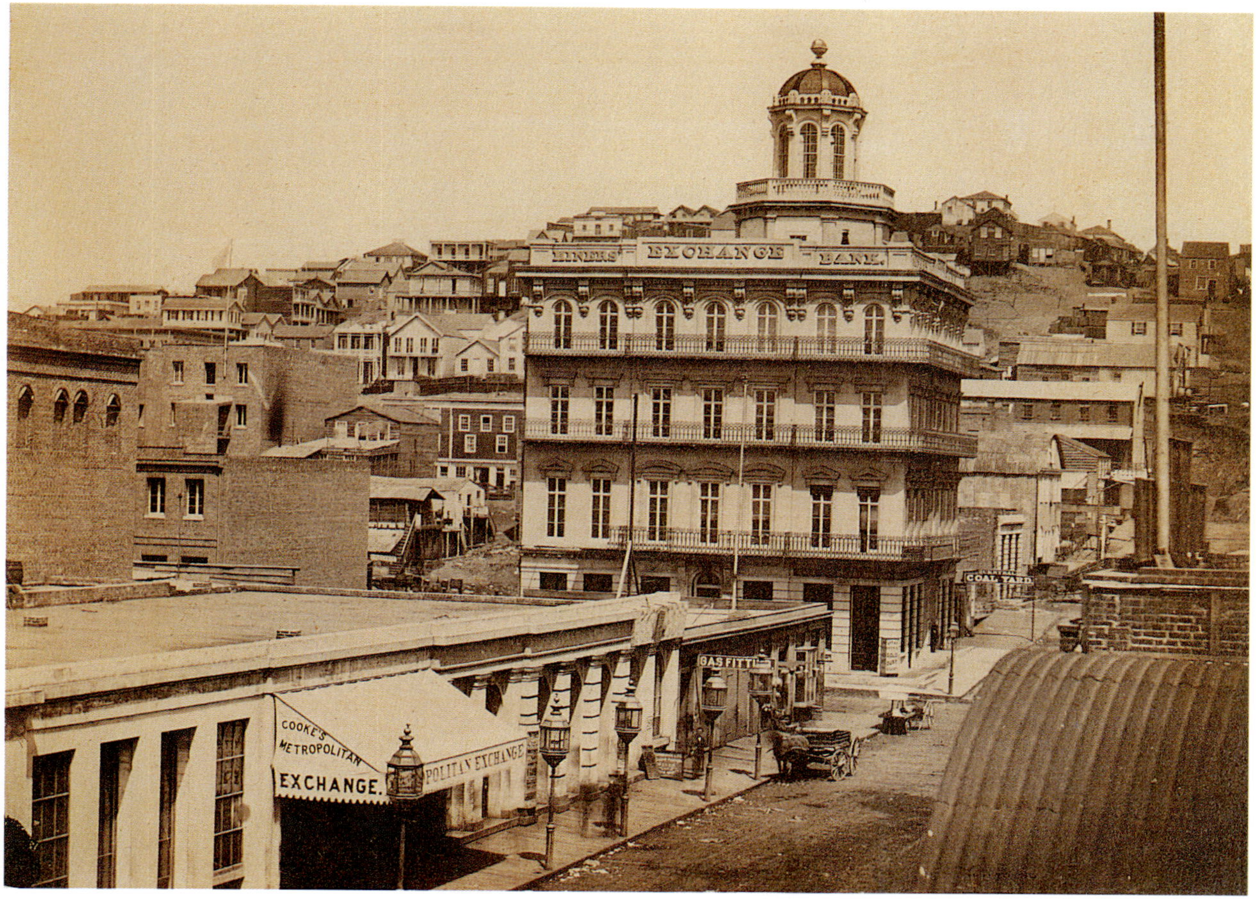

11.

GEORGE ROBINSON FARDON

View of the West Side of Montgomery Street, From Washington to Pacific, San Francisco, c. 1855

Salted paper print from a wet-collodion negative

6¼ x 8¼ in.

MUSEUM PURCHASE

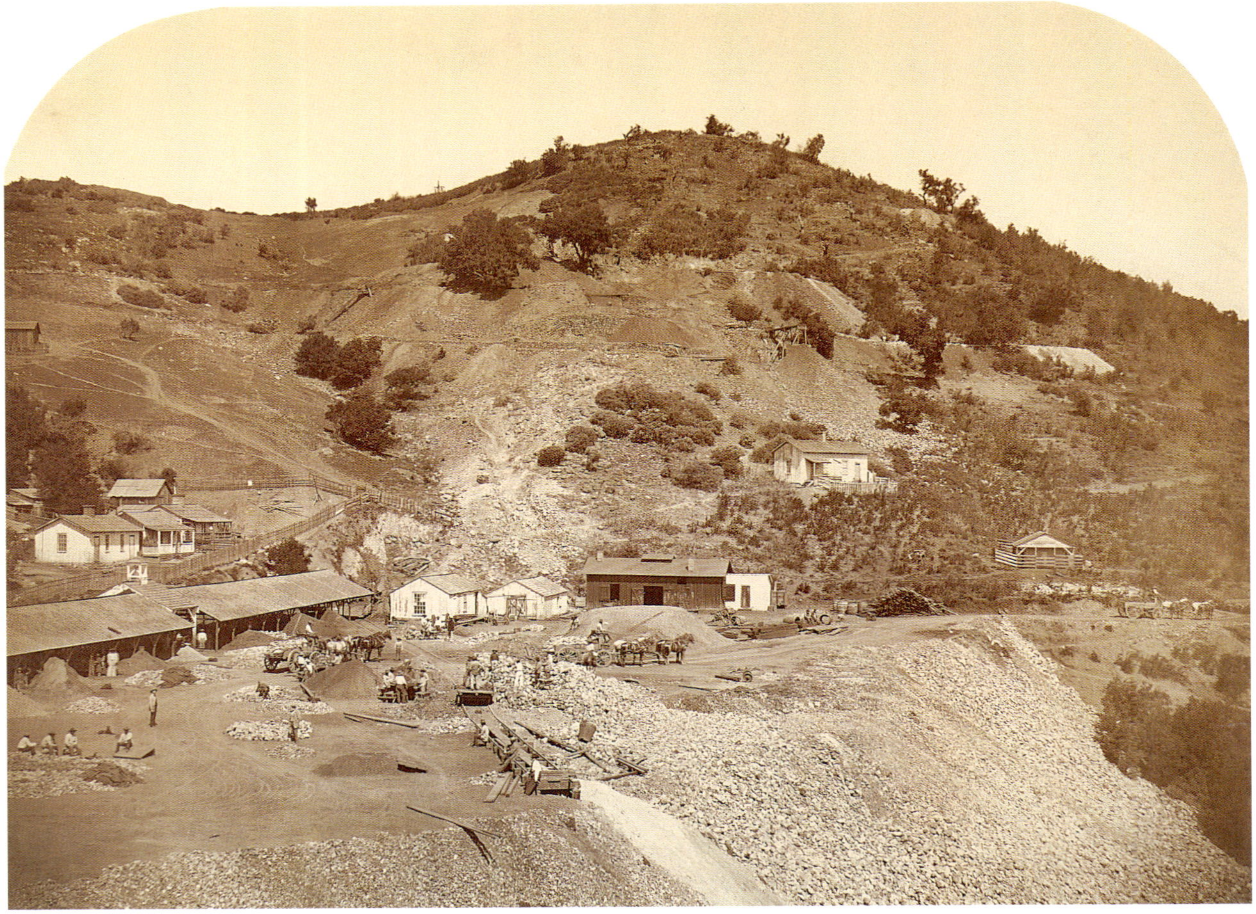

12.

CARLETON E. WATKINS

New Almaden Quicksilver Mine, 1863

Mammoth plate albumen print

15¼ x 20½ in.

GIFT OF PAUL S. TAYLOR BY EXCHANGE THROUGH OAKLAND PUBLIC LIBRARY

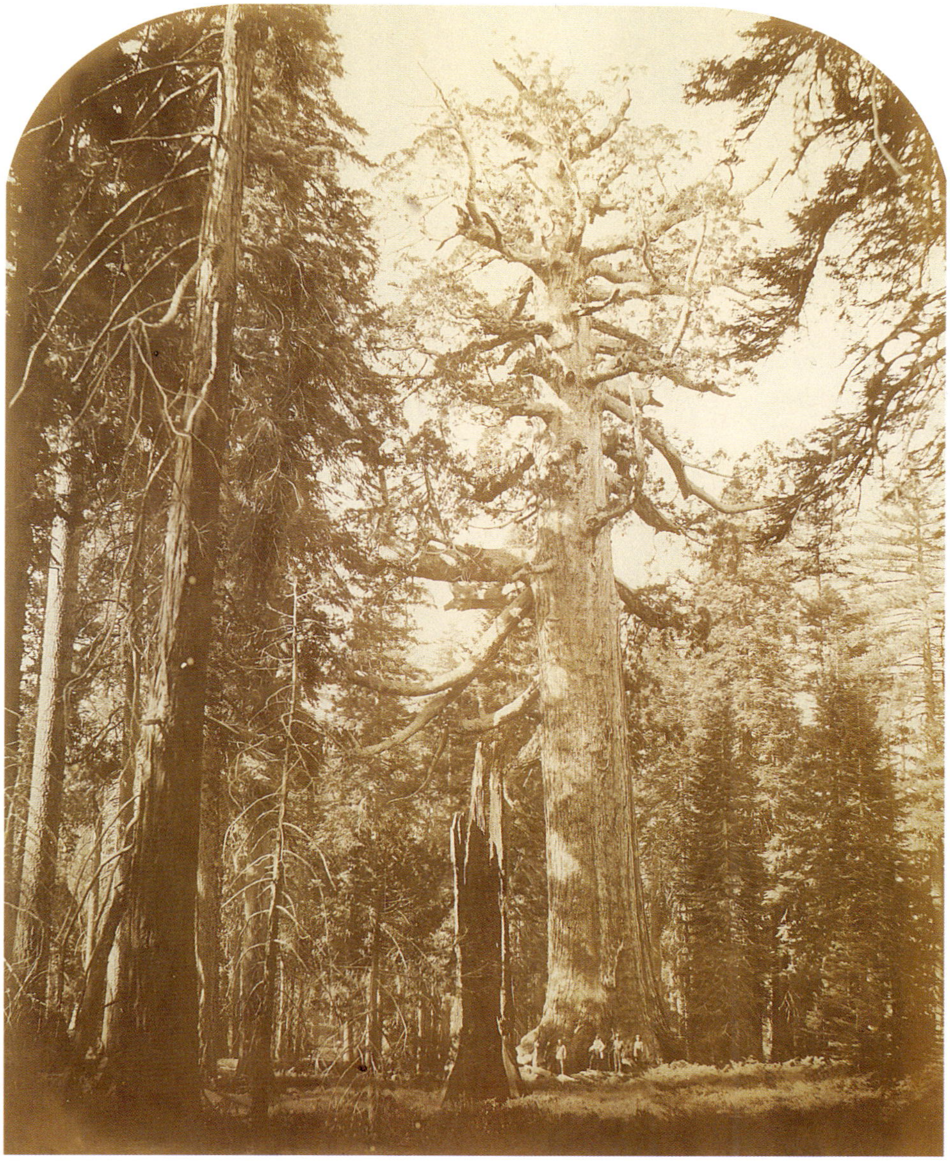

13.
CARLETON E. WATKINS
Grizzly Giant, Mariposa Grove, Yosemite, 1861
Mammoth plate albumen print
20⅝ x 16½ in.
MUSEUM PURCHASE

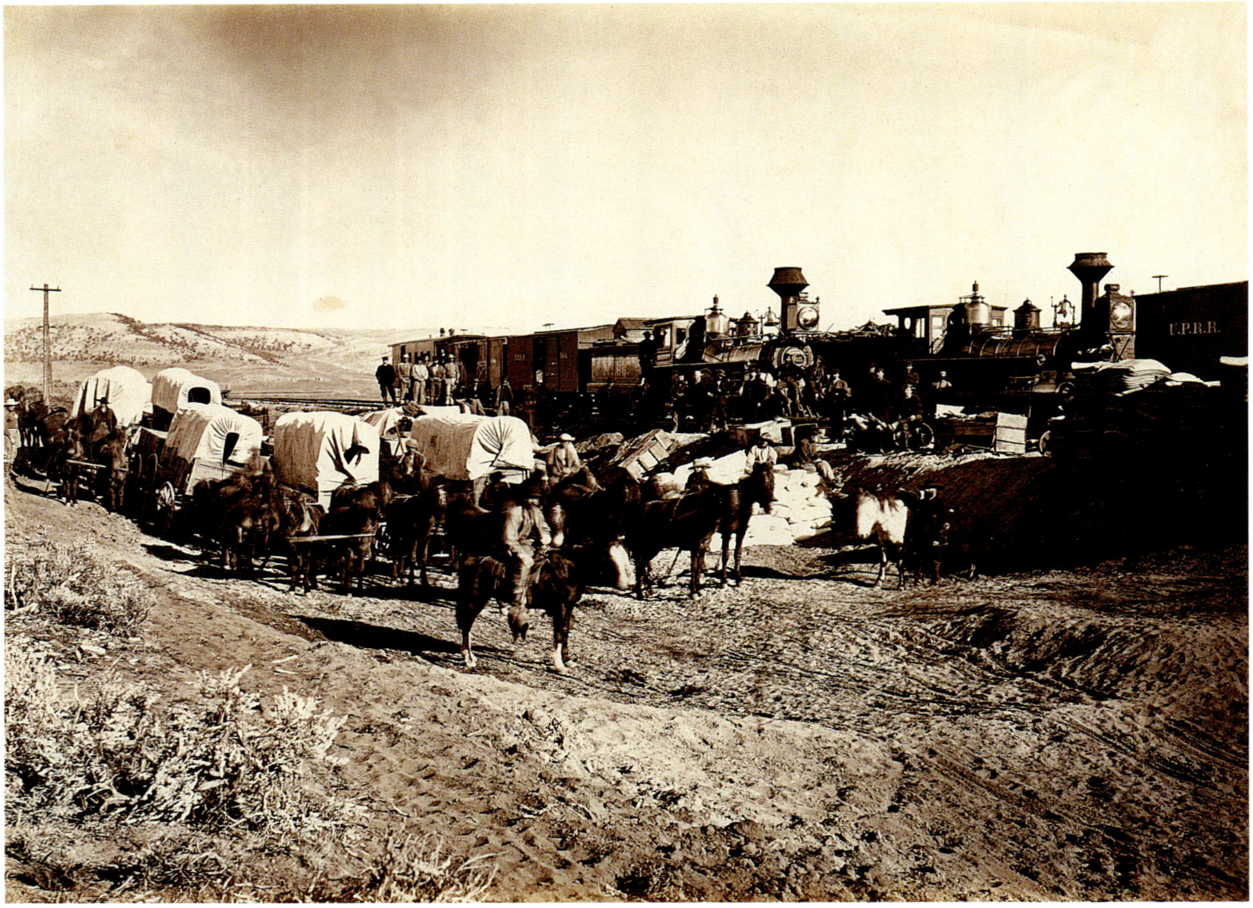

14.
ANDREW J. RUSSELL
Supply Trains at End of Tracks, Last Siding, c. 1868, from *The Great West Illustrated In a Series of Views Across the Continent*
Albumen print
9 x 12 in.
GIFT OF GEORGE E. ARNOTT

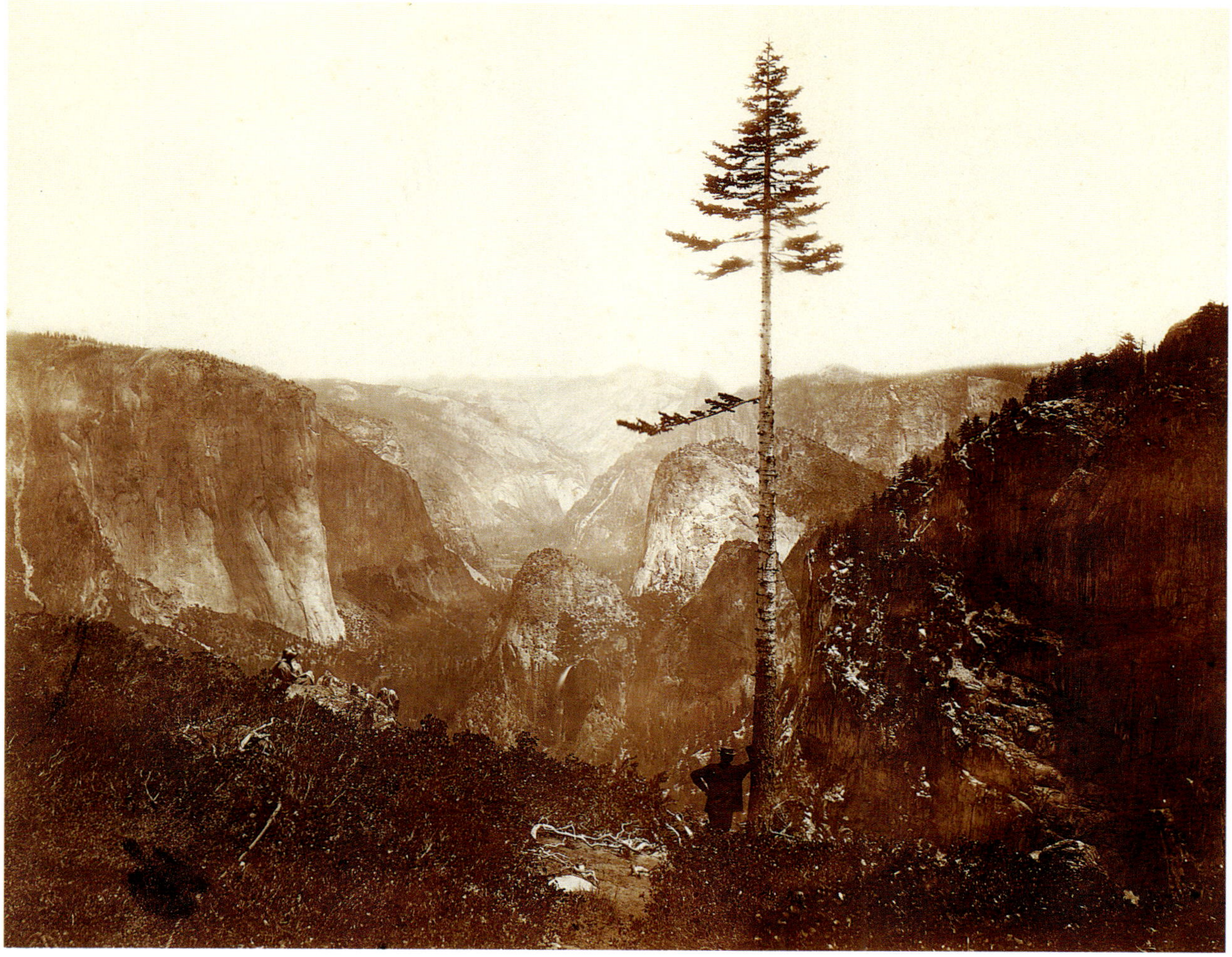

15.
CHARLES LEANDER WEED
(Thomas Houseworth & Co., publishers)
Yo-Semite Valley from the Mariposa Trail, 1864
Mammoth plate albumen print
15¾ x 20¼ in.
GIFT OF THE OAKLAND MUSEUM WOMEN'S BOARD

16.

CHARLES LEANDER WEED
Vernal Falls, 1859
Albumen stereograph
3 5/16 x 6 13/16
GIFT OF MARY MORGANITI

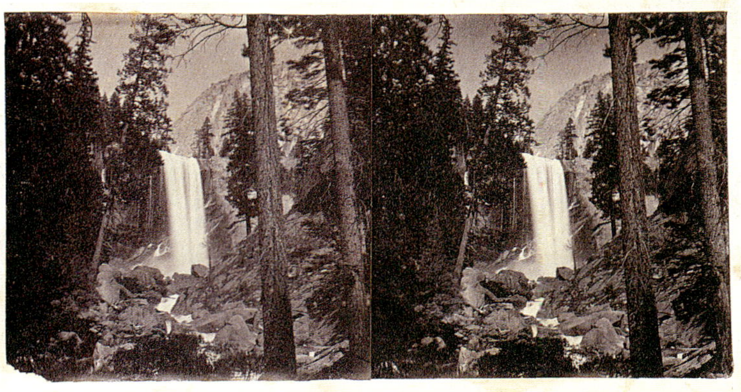

ALFRED A. HART
Infantile Glacier, 1868
Albumen stereograph
3 1/4 x 6 3/4 in.
GIFT OF LEWIS FERBRACHE

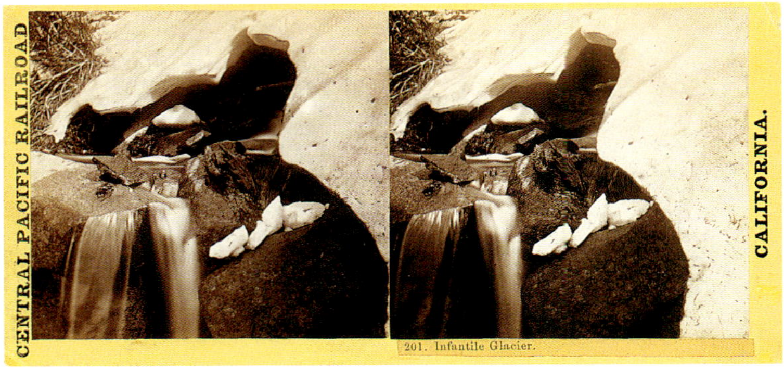

GEORGE S. LAWRENCE &
THOMAS HOUSEWORTH, Publishers
Teams Passing Through the Snow, on the Road Leading Down into Lake Valley, from Summit of Sierra Nevada, 1865
Albumen stereograph
3 1/4 x 6 3/4 in.
MUSEUM PURCHASE

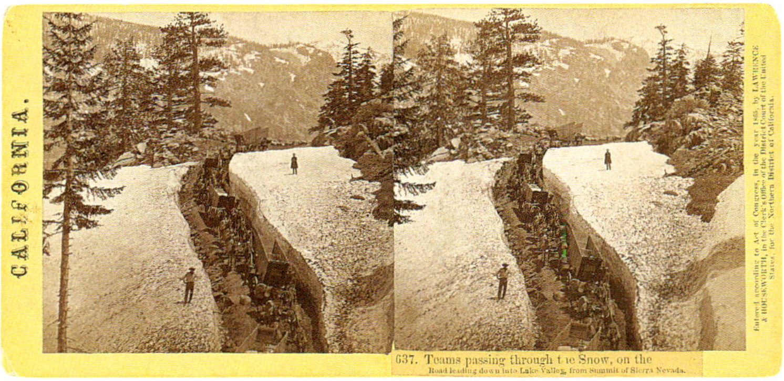

CHARLES L. POND
San Francisco, California, from Russian Hill, c. 1870
Albumen stereograph
$3\frac{7}{16}$ x $6\frac{15}{16}$ in.
MUSEUM PURCHASE

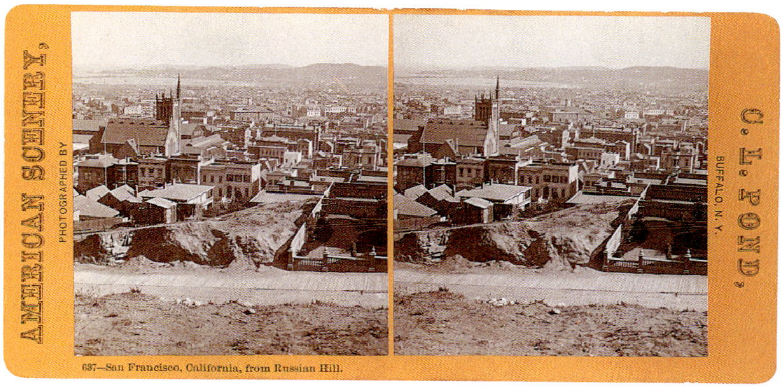

JOHN JAMES REILLY
Three Graces and Bridal Veil Fall, height of Rocks 2660 ft., c. 1875
Albumen stereograph
$6\frac{15}{16}$ x $3\frac{7}{8}$ in.
MUSEUM COLLECTION

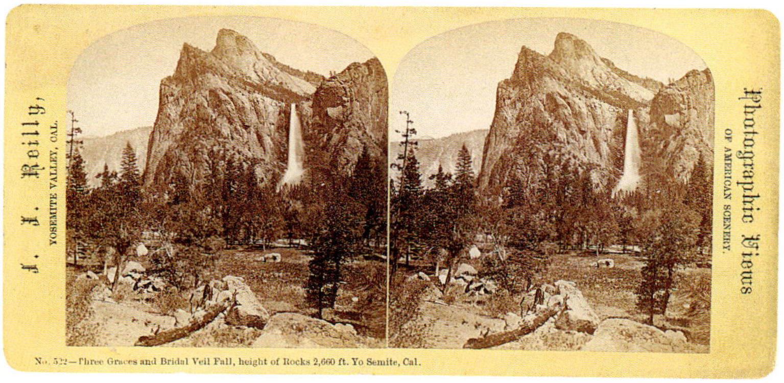

CHARLES LEANDER WEED
(Lawrence & Houseworth, publishers)
Untitled (Sacramento during the flood, K Street east from Fourth Street), 1862
Albumen stereograph
$2\frac{7}{8}$ x $6\frac{11}{16}$ in.
GIFT OF MARY MORGANITI

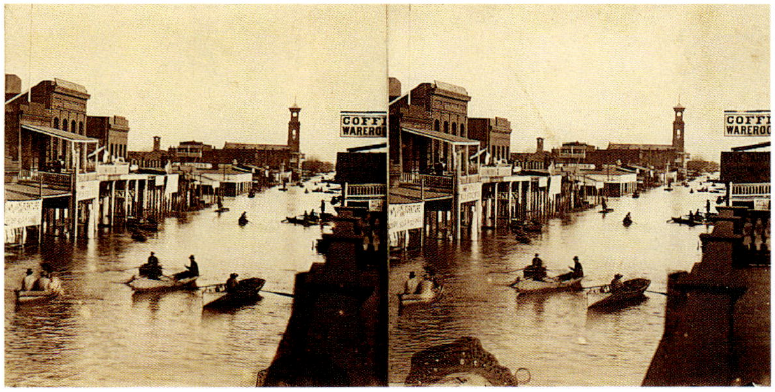

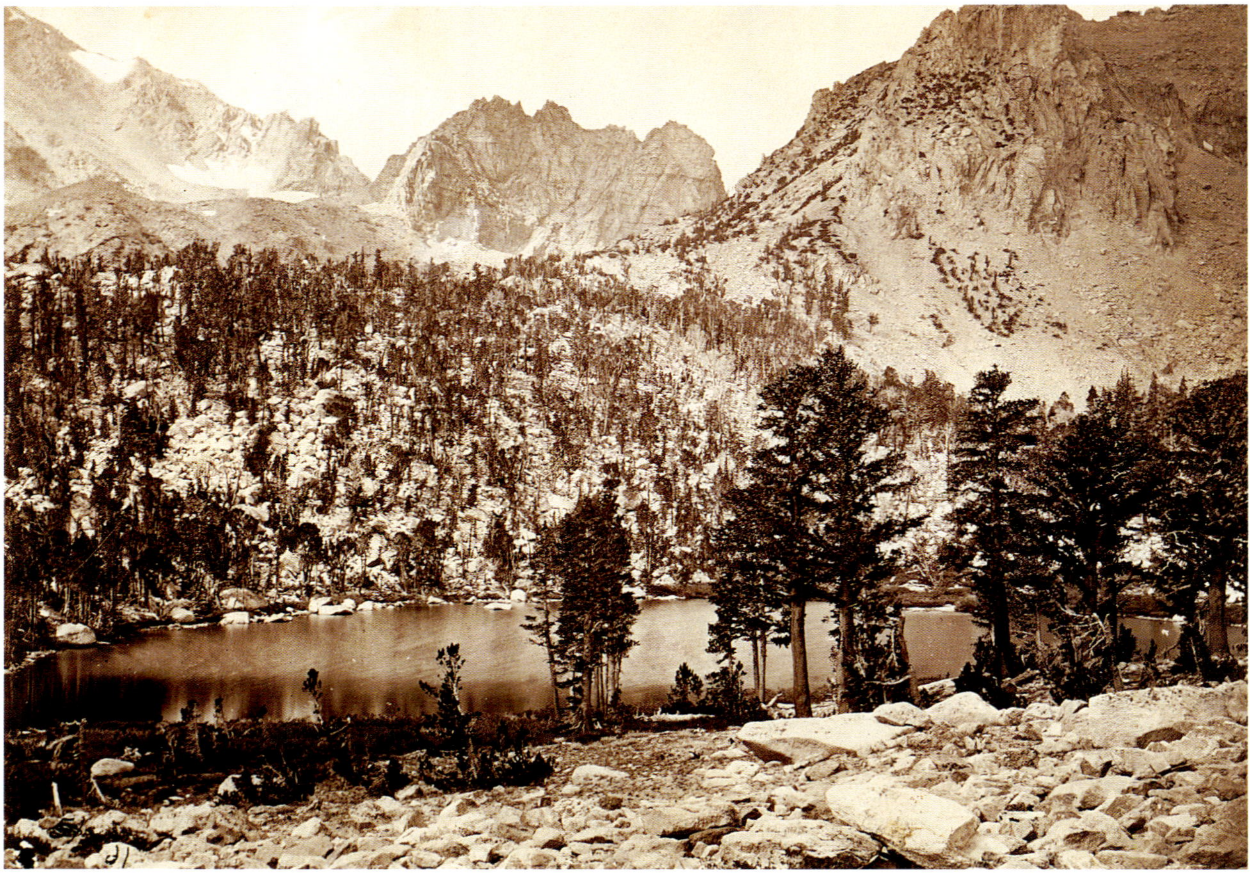

17.
TIMOTHY O'SULLIVAN
Alpine Lake, in the Sierra Nevada, California, c. 1871
Albumen print
8 x 10 13/16 in.
TIMKEN FUND

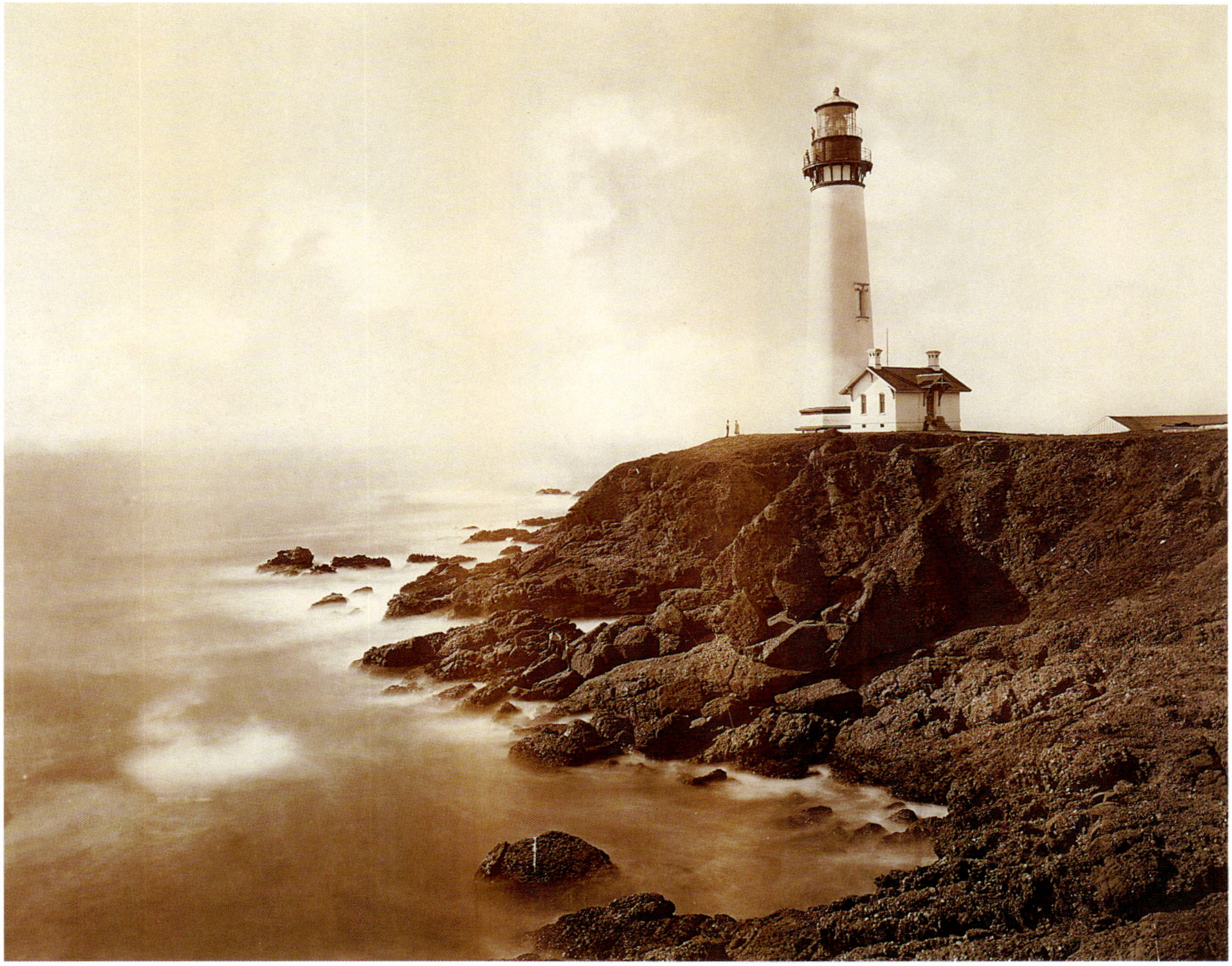

18.
EADWEARD MUYBRIDGE
(Bradley & Rulofson, publishers)
Untitled (Lighthouse), 1868
Mammoth plate albumen print
16½ x 21¼ in.
THE OAKLAND MUSEUM FOUNDERS' FUND

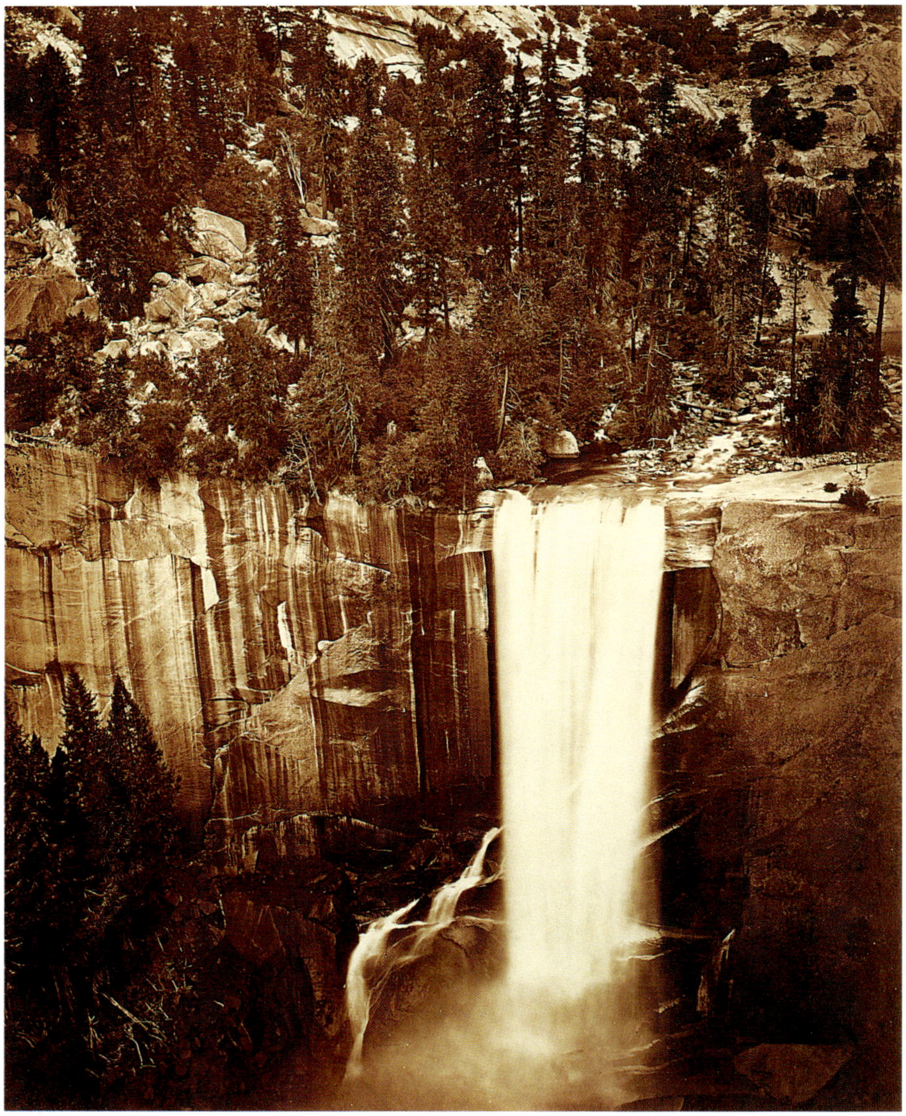

19.
EADWEARD MUYBRIDGE
(Bradley & Rulofson, publishers)
Pi-Wi-Ack, Valley of the Yosemite (Shower of Stars), Vernal Fall, 400 Feet, 1872
Mammoth plate albumen print
21 x 16⅞ in.
GIFT OF DR. AND MRS. DUDLEY P. BELL

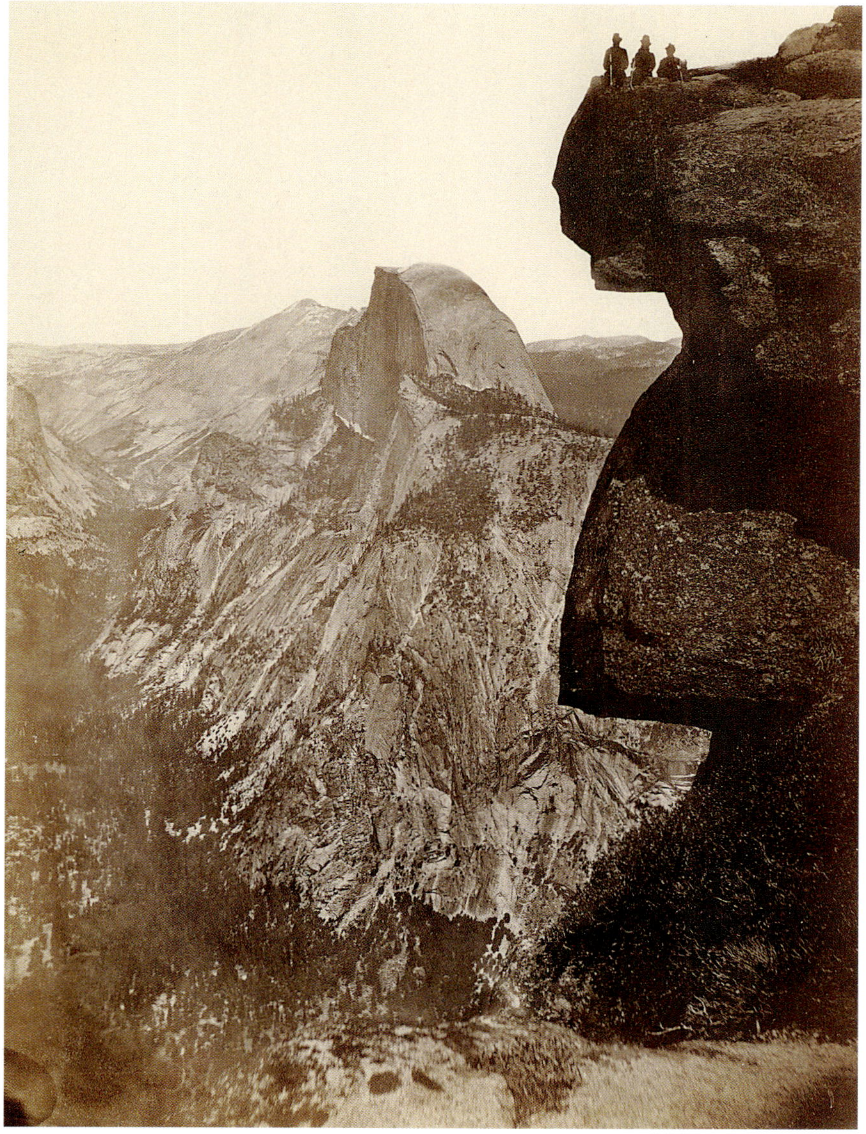

20.
GUSTAVUS FAGERSTEEN
Untitled (Overhanging Rock, Glacier Point, Yosemite), c. 1883
Albumen print
8⅝ x 6⅜ in.
GIFT OF THE OAKLAND MUSEUM WOMEN'S BOARD

21.

GEORGE S. LAWRENCE &
THOMAS HOUSEWORTH, publishers
Oakland Ferry—Steamer Washoe, San Francisco, c. 1864
Albumen carte de visite
2³⁄₈ x 3⁵⁄₈ in.
GIFT OF AMADOR COUNTY MUSEUM

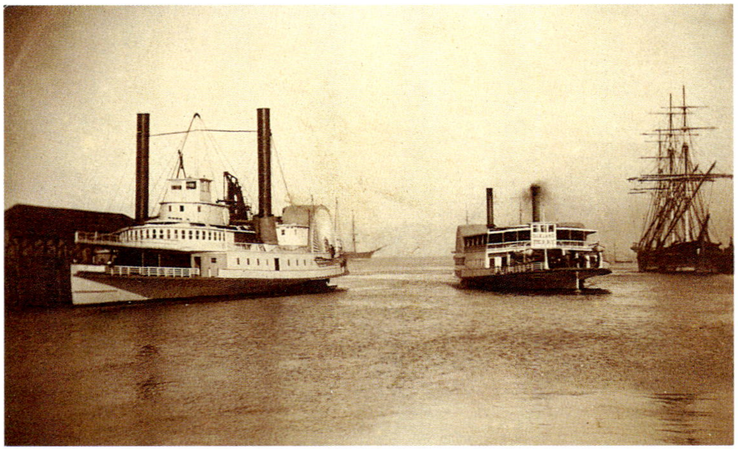

HUGH S. ANDERSON
The National Sanitary Cake, 1865
Albumen carte de visite
3⁵⁄₈ x 2³⁄₈ in.
GIFT OF PAUL S. TAYLOR AND MR. AND MRS. WILLARD M. NOTT BY EXCHANGE

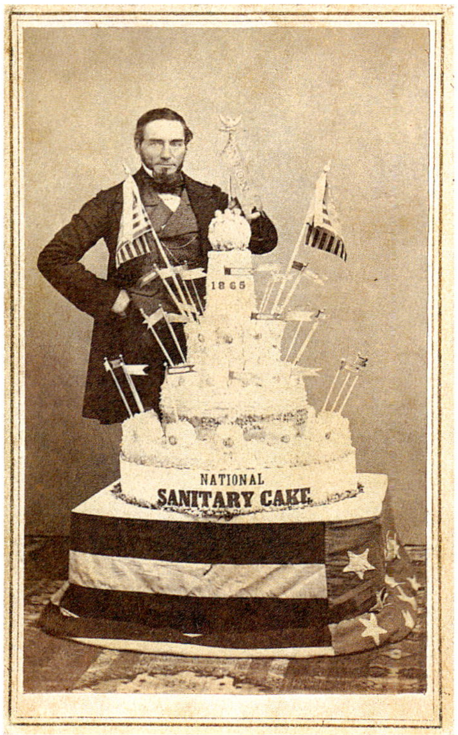

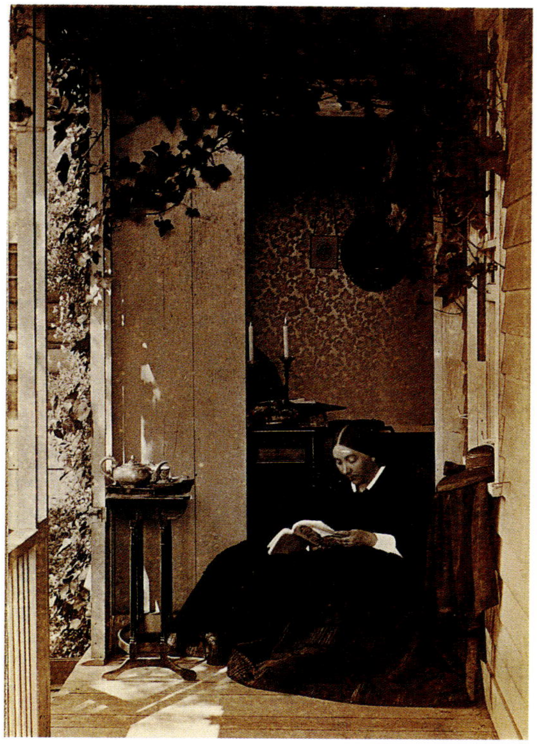

UNKNOWN
Mrs. J. C. Frémont at Marapose [sic], 1867
Albumen carte de visite
3 5/16 x 2 1/4 in.
GIFT OF MRS. CAROLYN K. LOUDERBACK

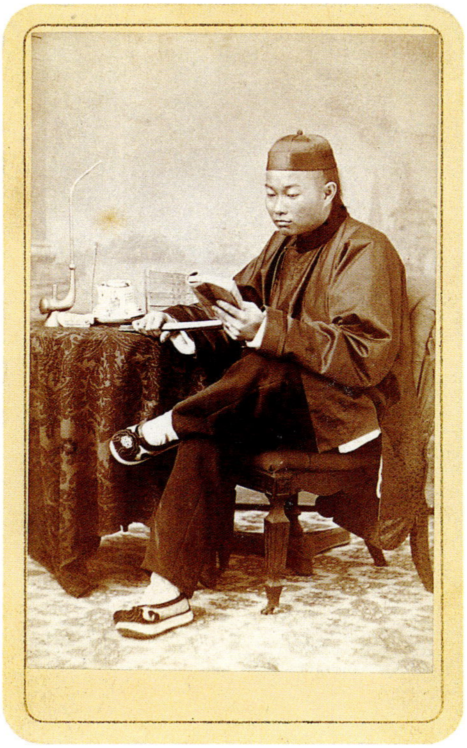

AMOS WOODS
Untitled (Chinese Man with Pipe), c. 1875
Albumen carte de visite
4 3/16 x 2 1/4 in.
MUSEUM PURCHASE

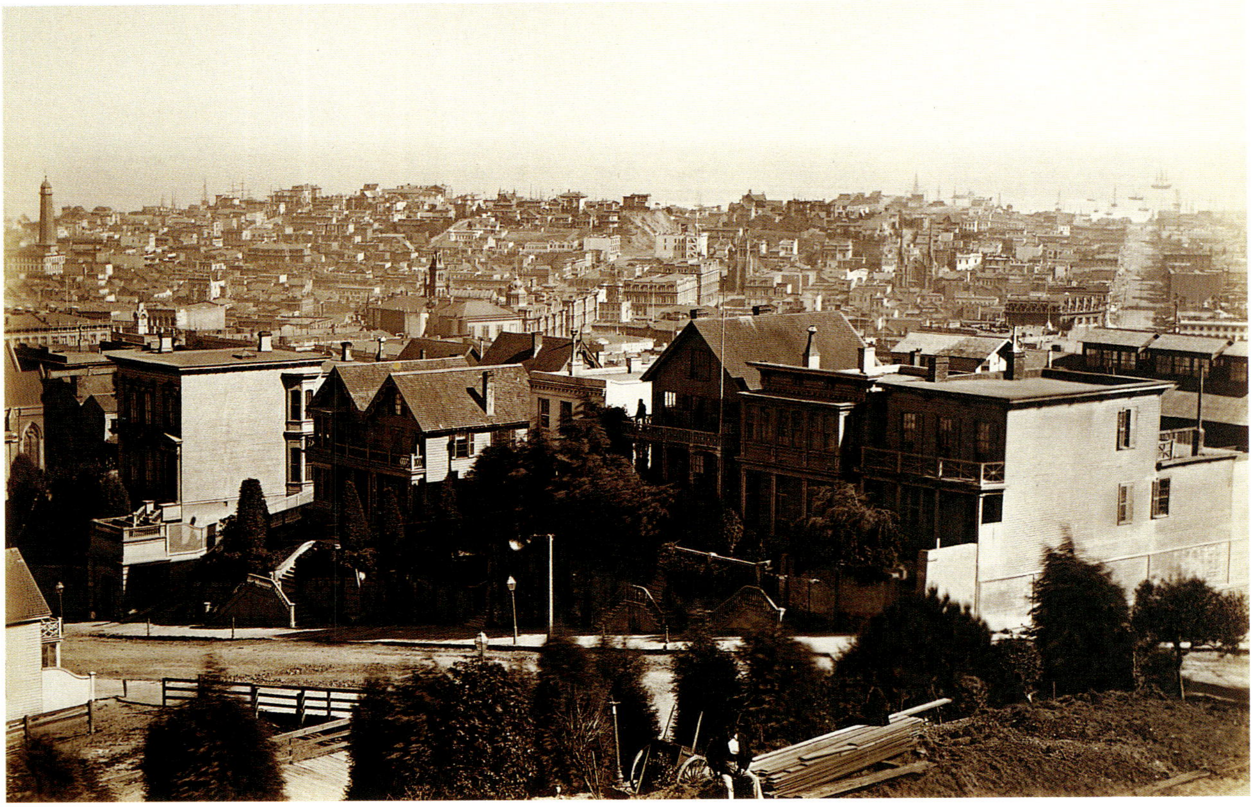

22.
CARLETON E. WATKINS
Panorama from California and Powell, San Francisco, c. 1879
Albumen print
8 1/16 x 12 1/8 in.
MUSEUM DONORS' ACQUISITION FUND

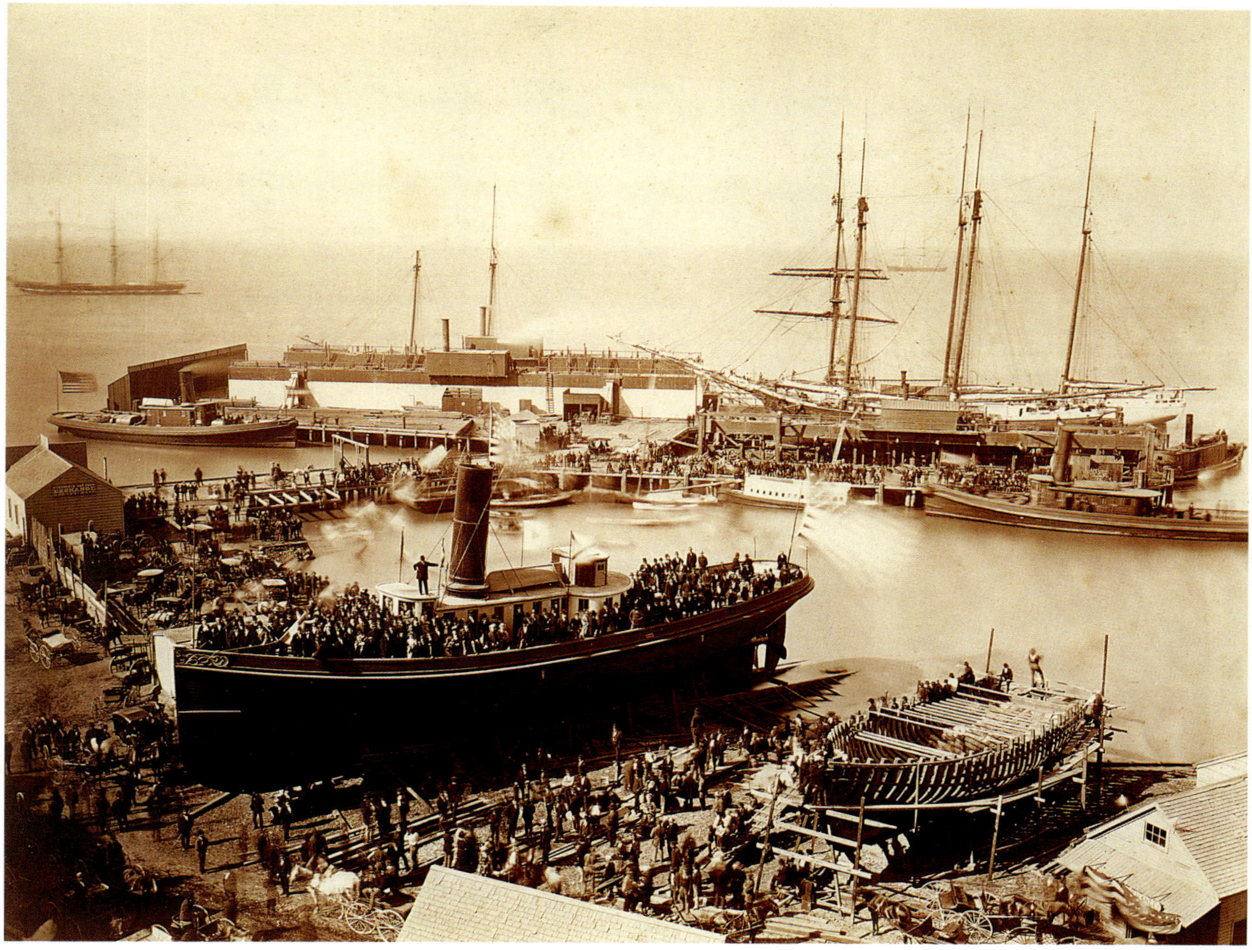

23.
THOMAS HOUSEWORTH & CO., publishers
Launch of the Monarch, San Francisco, 1875
Mammoth plate albumen print
$15\frac{7}{8}$ x $20\frac{1}{4}$ in.
THE OAKLAND MUSEUM FOUNDERS' FUND

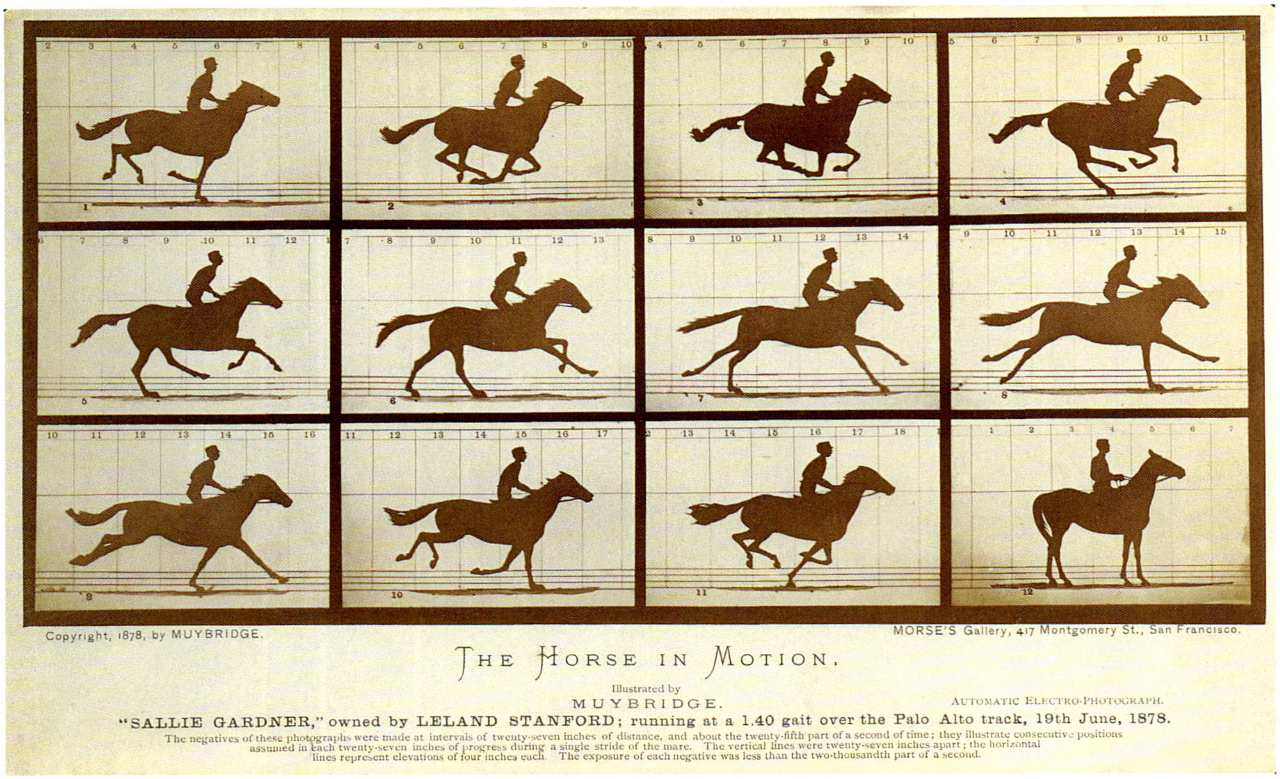

24.
EADWEARD MUYBRIDGE
(George D. Morse, publisher)
The Horse in Motion, 1878
Albumen print
5¼ x 8½ in.
MUSEUM COLLECTION

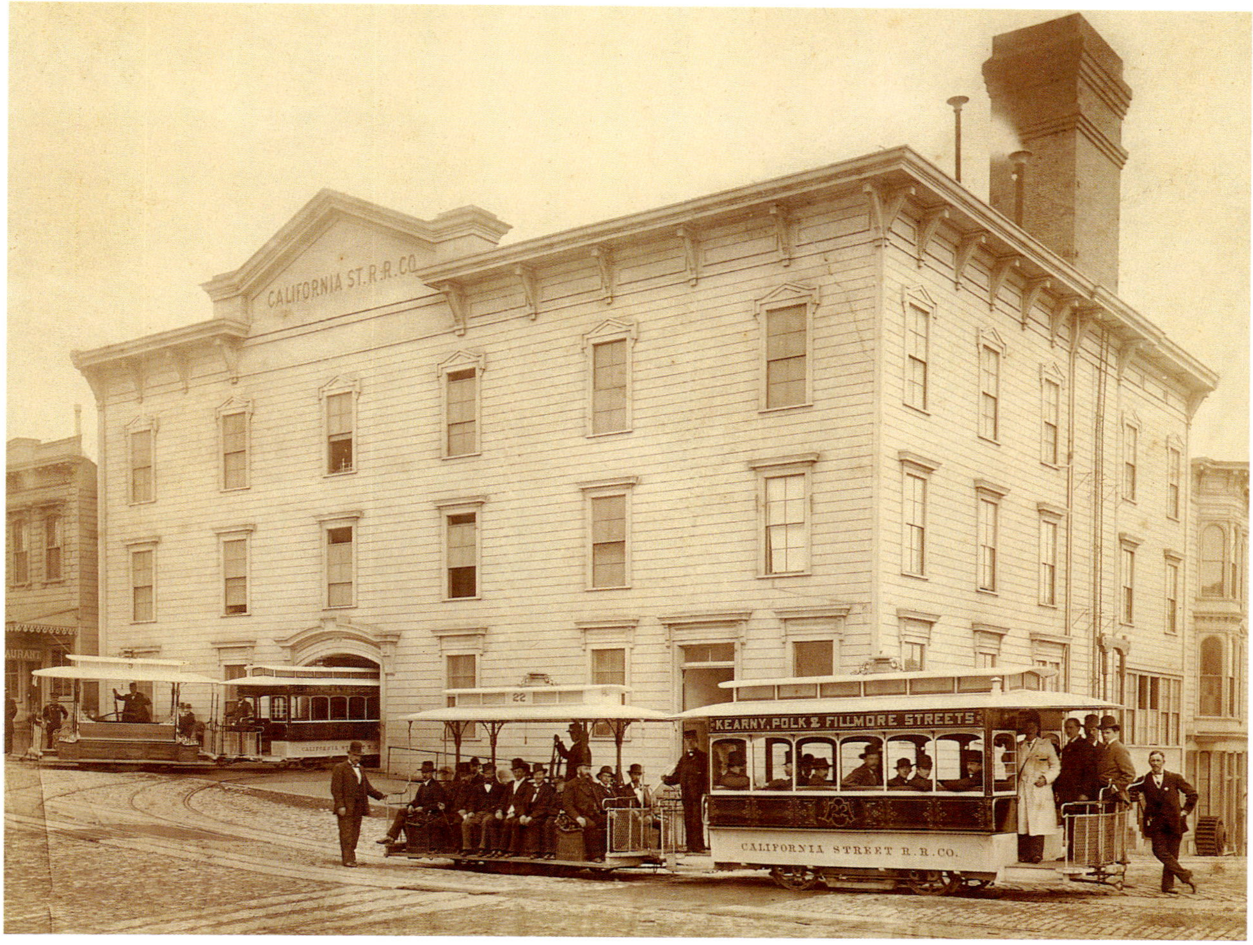

25.

EADWEARD MUYBRIDGE
(George D. Morse, publisher)
California Street Rail Road, April 10, 1878
Albumen print
$7\frac{1}{16}$ x 9 in.
MUSEUM PURCHASE

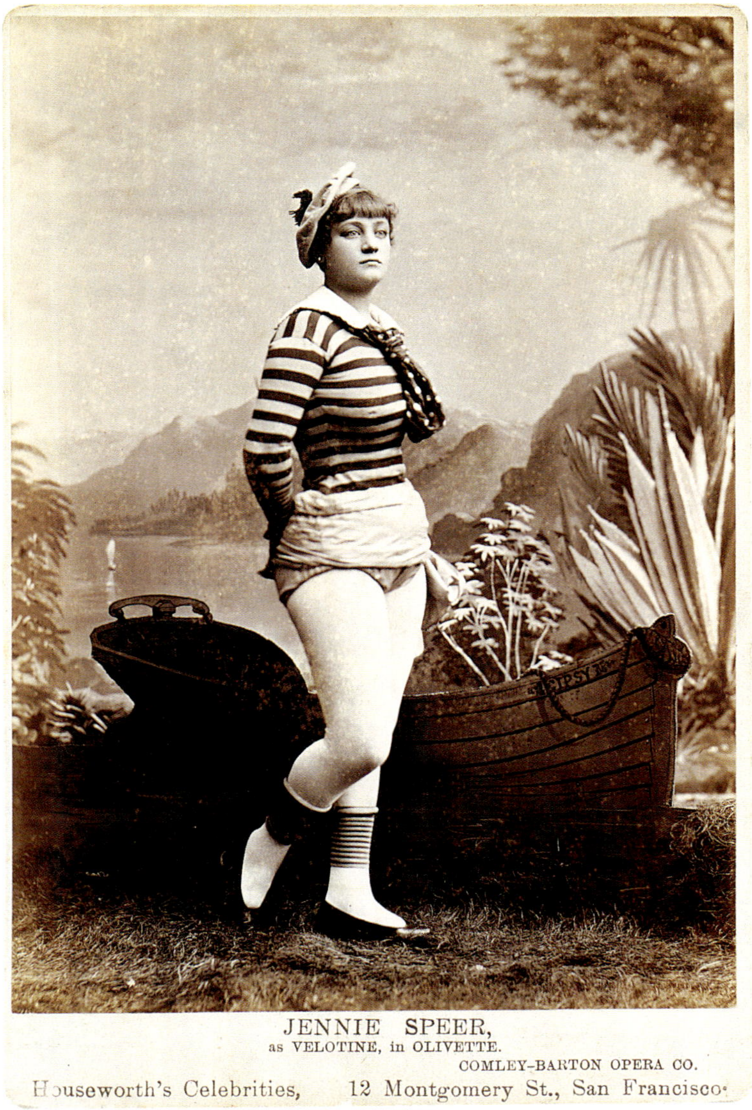

26.

THOMAS HOUSEWORTH & COMPANY

Jennie Speer as Velotine in Olivette, c. 1875

Albumen cabinet card

6½ x 4¼ in.

MUSEUM PURCHASE

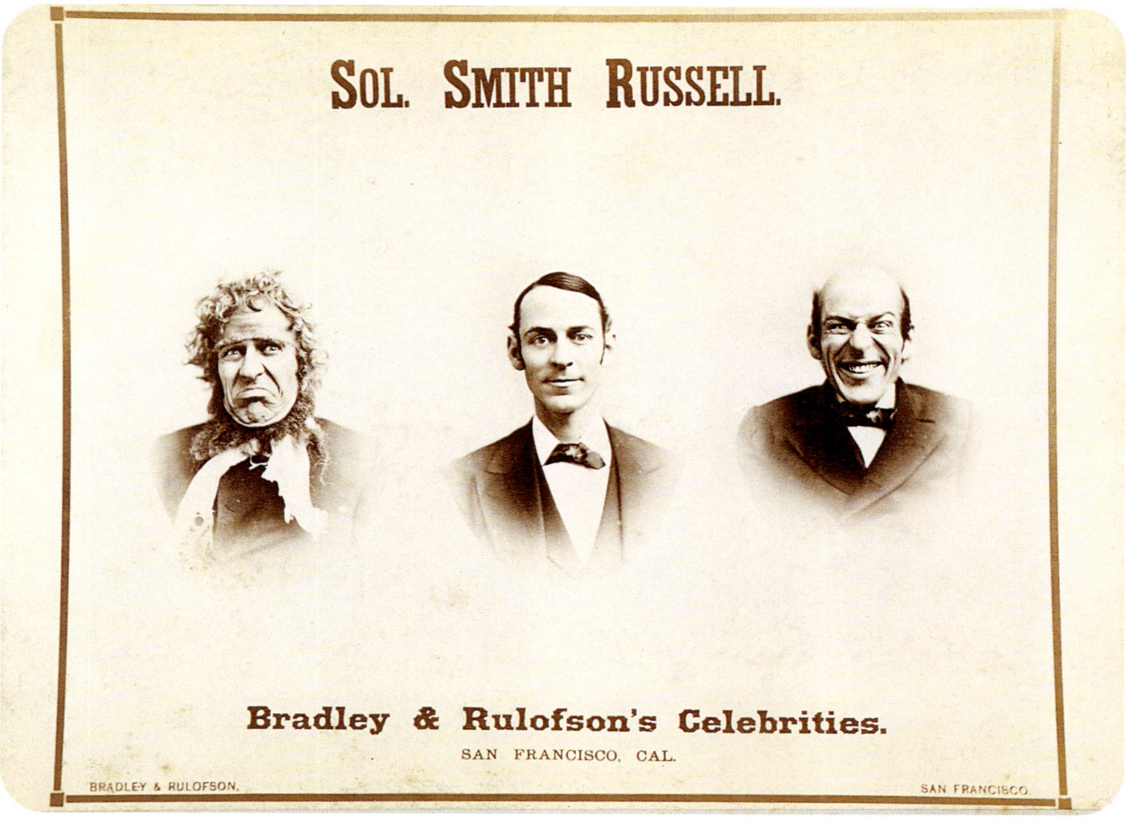

27.
HENRY W. BRADLEY and WILLIAM HERMAN RULOFSON
Sol. Smith Russell (Bradley & Rulofson's Celebrities), c. 1875
Albumen cabinet card
4¼ x 6½ in.
MUSEUM COLLECTION

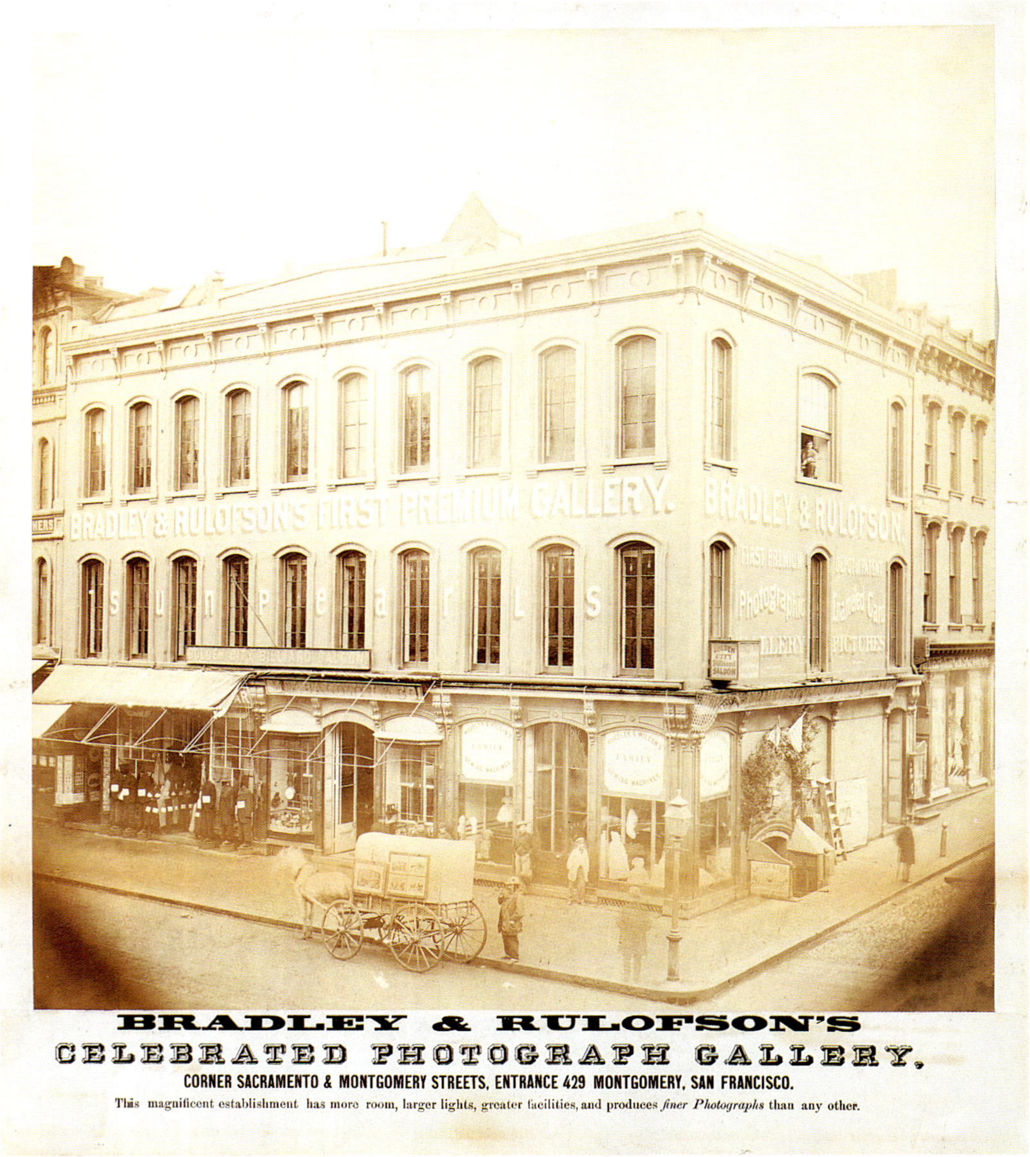

28.

HENRY W. BRADLEY and WILLIAM HERMAN RULOFSON

Bradley & Rulofson's Photograph Gallery, c. 1870

Albumen print

19 x 16¼ in.

GIFT OF DR. AND MRS. DUDLEY P. BELL

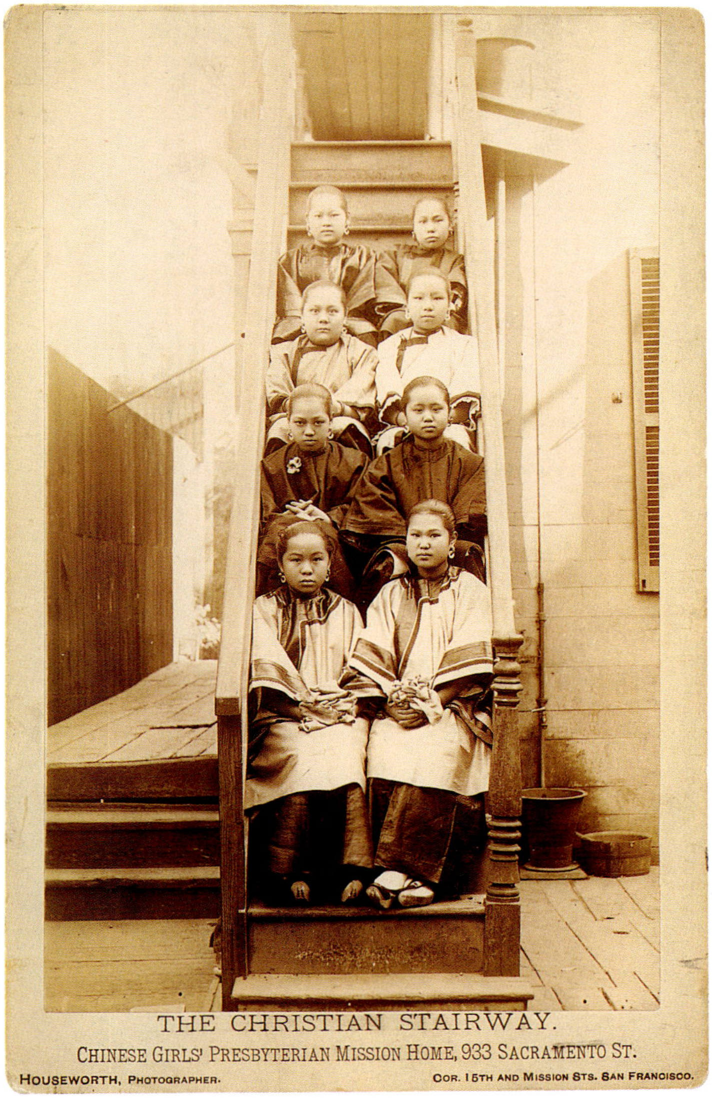

29.
THOMAS HOUSEWORTH & CO.
The Christian Stairway (Chinese Girls' Presbyterian Mission Home, 933 Sacramento Street, San Francisco), c. 1888
Albumen print
8½ x 5¼ in.
MUSEUM PURCHASE

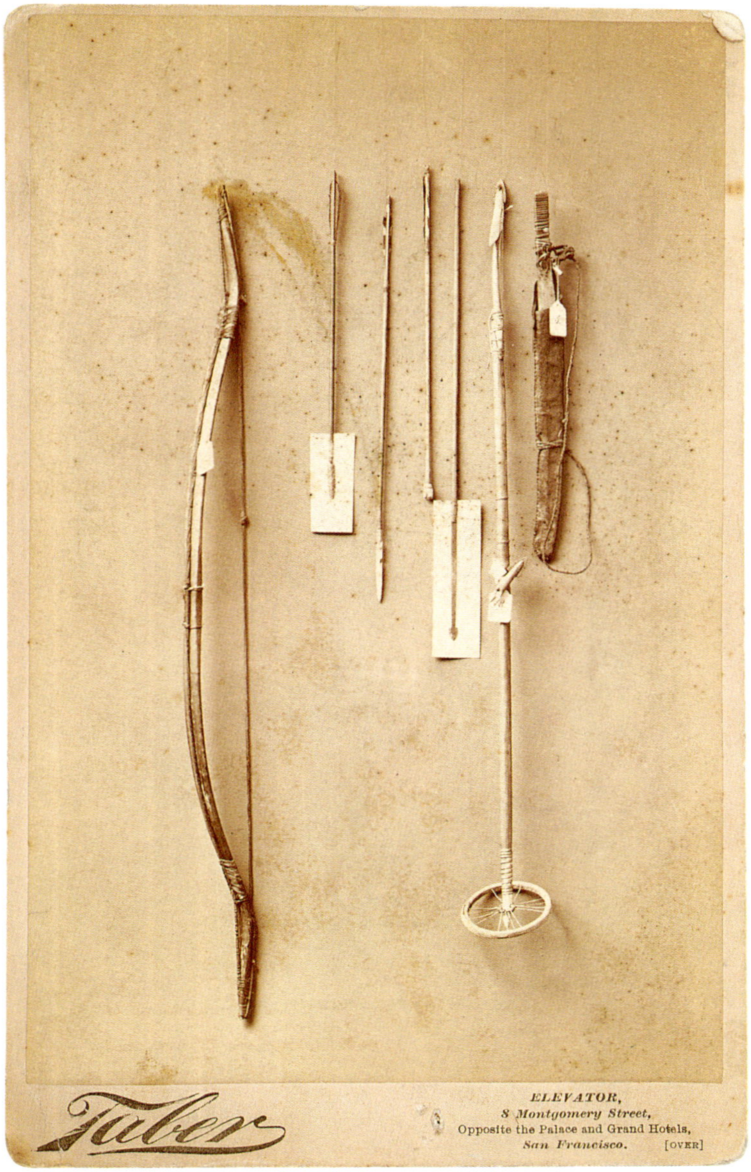

30.

ISAIAH WEST TABER

Untitled (Indian Artifacts), c. 1880

Albumen print

8½ x 5¼ in.

GIFT OF MRS. CARLOTTA E. HOOPER

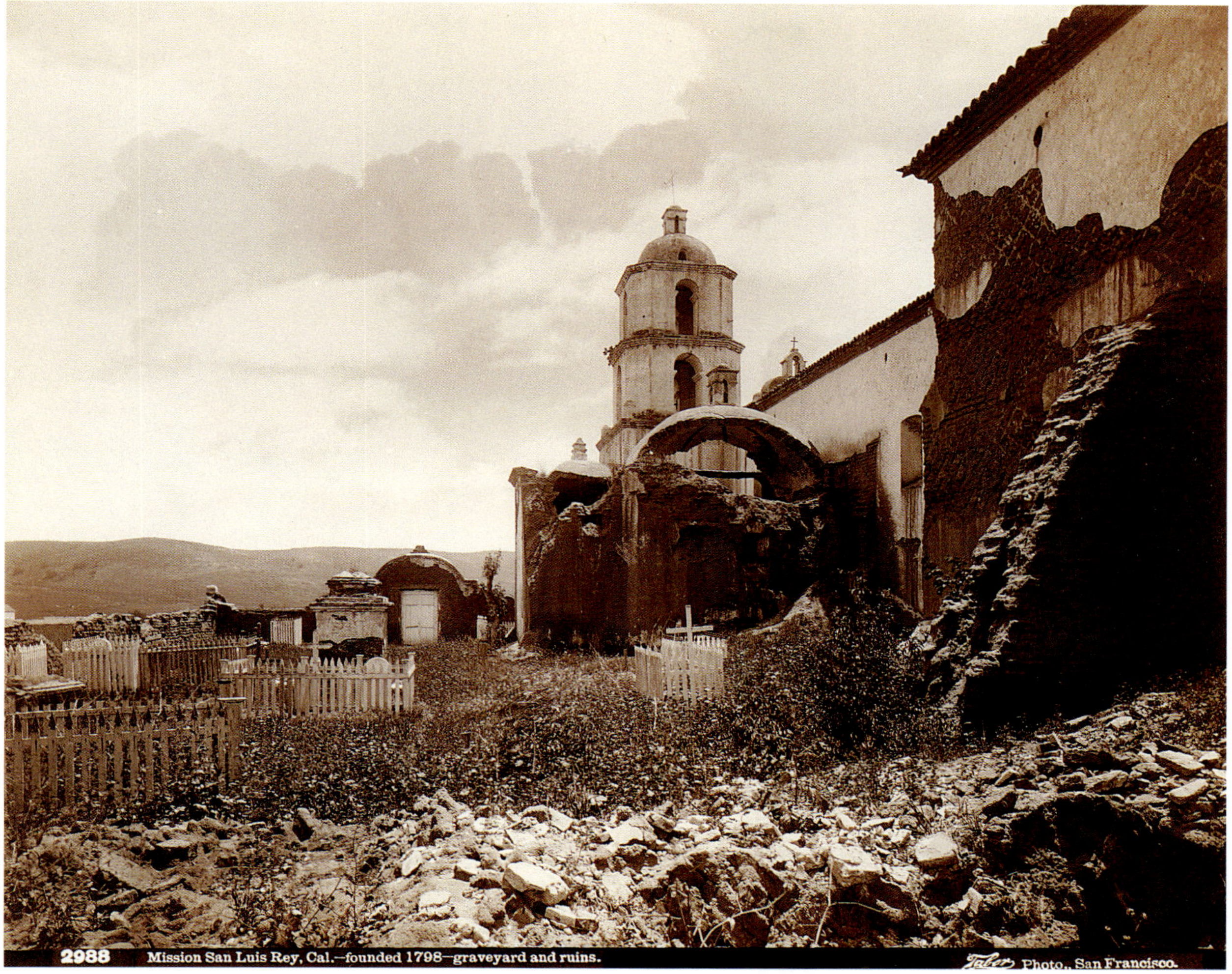

31.
ISAIAH WEST TABER
Mission San Luis Rey, Cal.—founded 1798—graveyard and ruins, c. 1880
Albumen print
$7\frac{5}{8}$ x $9\frac{11}{16}$ in.
MUSEUM PURCHASE

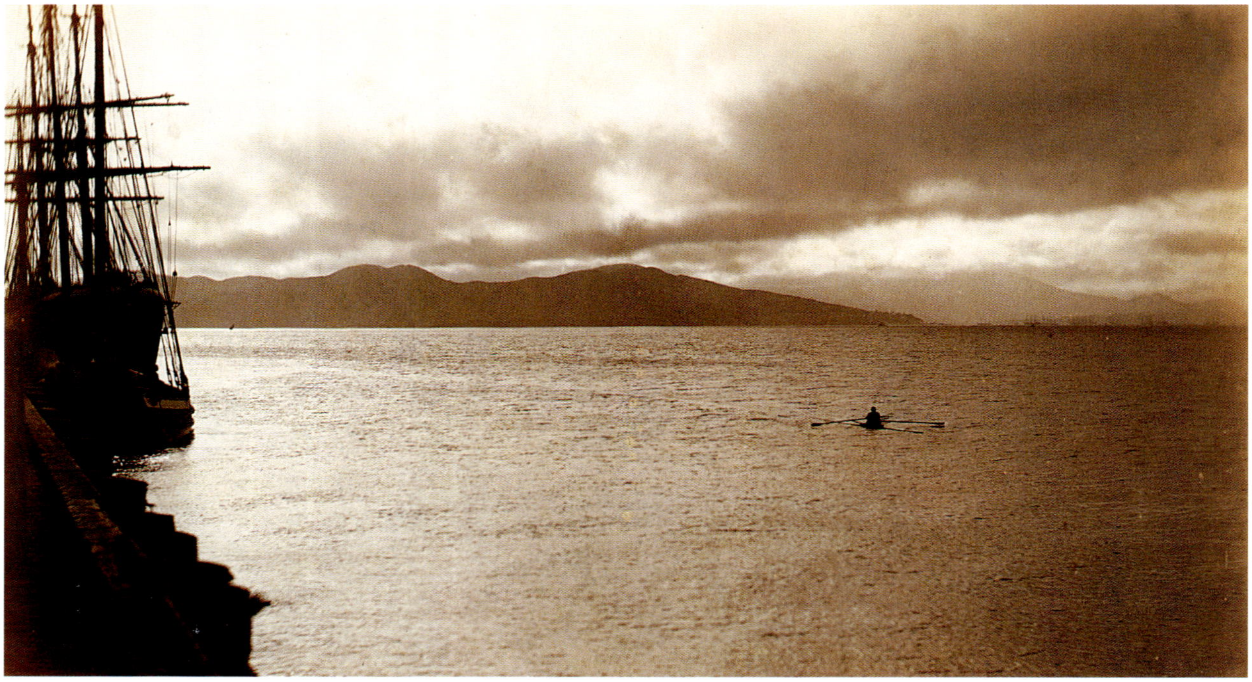

32.
GEORGE FISKE
Sunset Study, San Francisco Bay, 1884
Albumen print
4 3/16 x 7 1/2 in.
GIFT OF LEONARD BARDSLEY, JR.

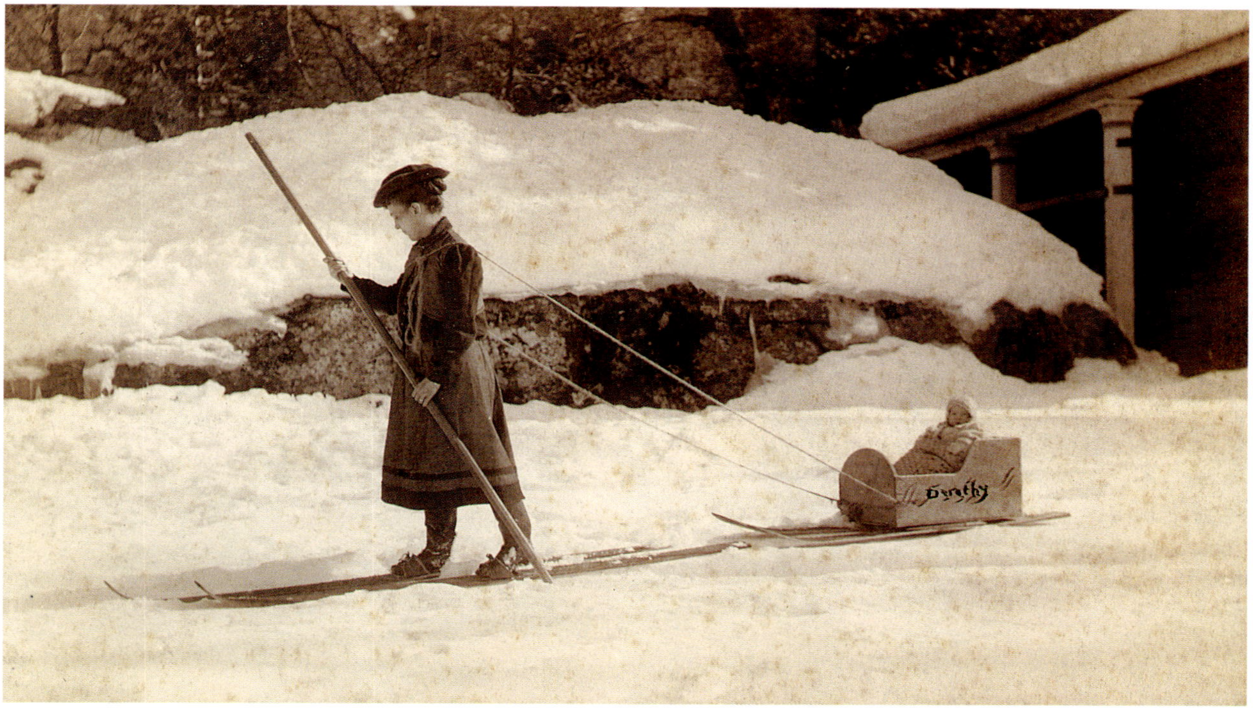

33.
GEORGE FISKE
Untitled (Nell Atkinson and her Daughter Dorothy on Skis, Yosemite), c. 1885
Albumen print
$4\frac{3}{8}$ x $7\frac{1}{2}$ in.
GIFT OF LEONARD BARDSLEY, JR.

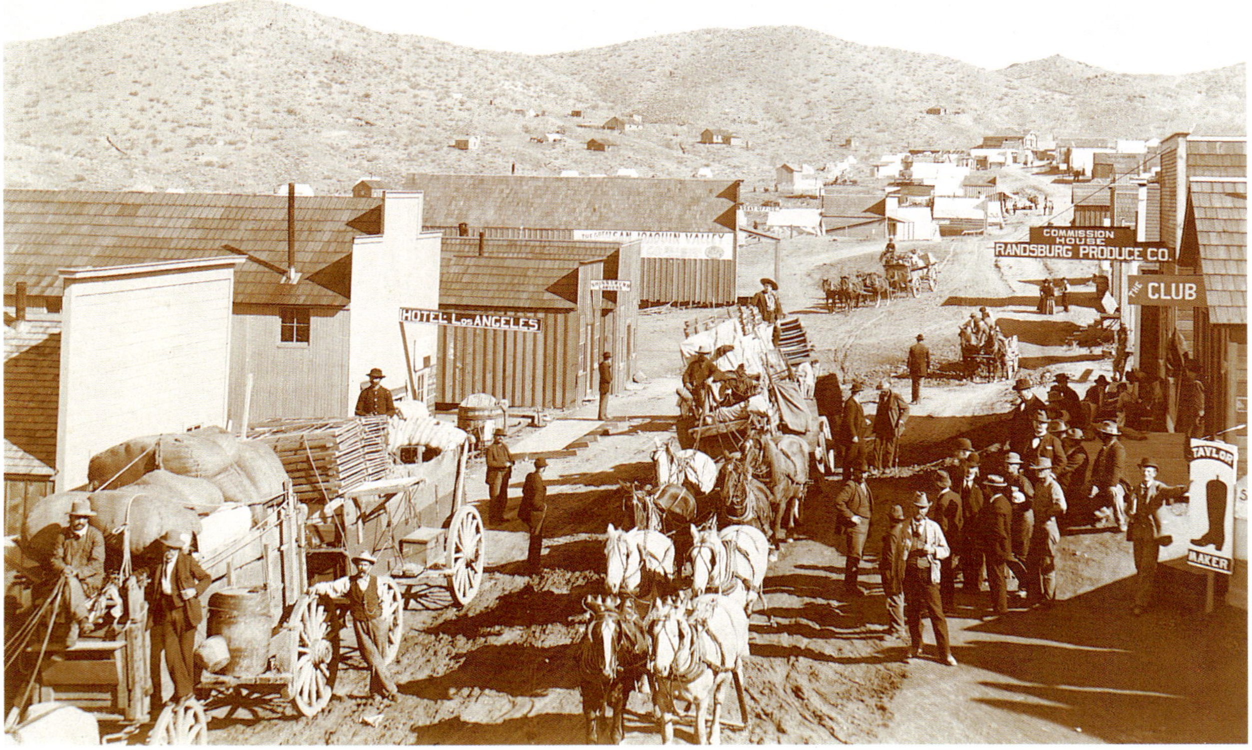

34.
STIFFLER (FRANK M. or GEORGE L.)
Randsburg, Ca., Feb. 1897
Albumen print
6⅝ x 8 in.
MUSEUM PURCHASE

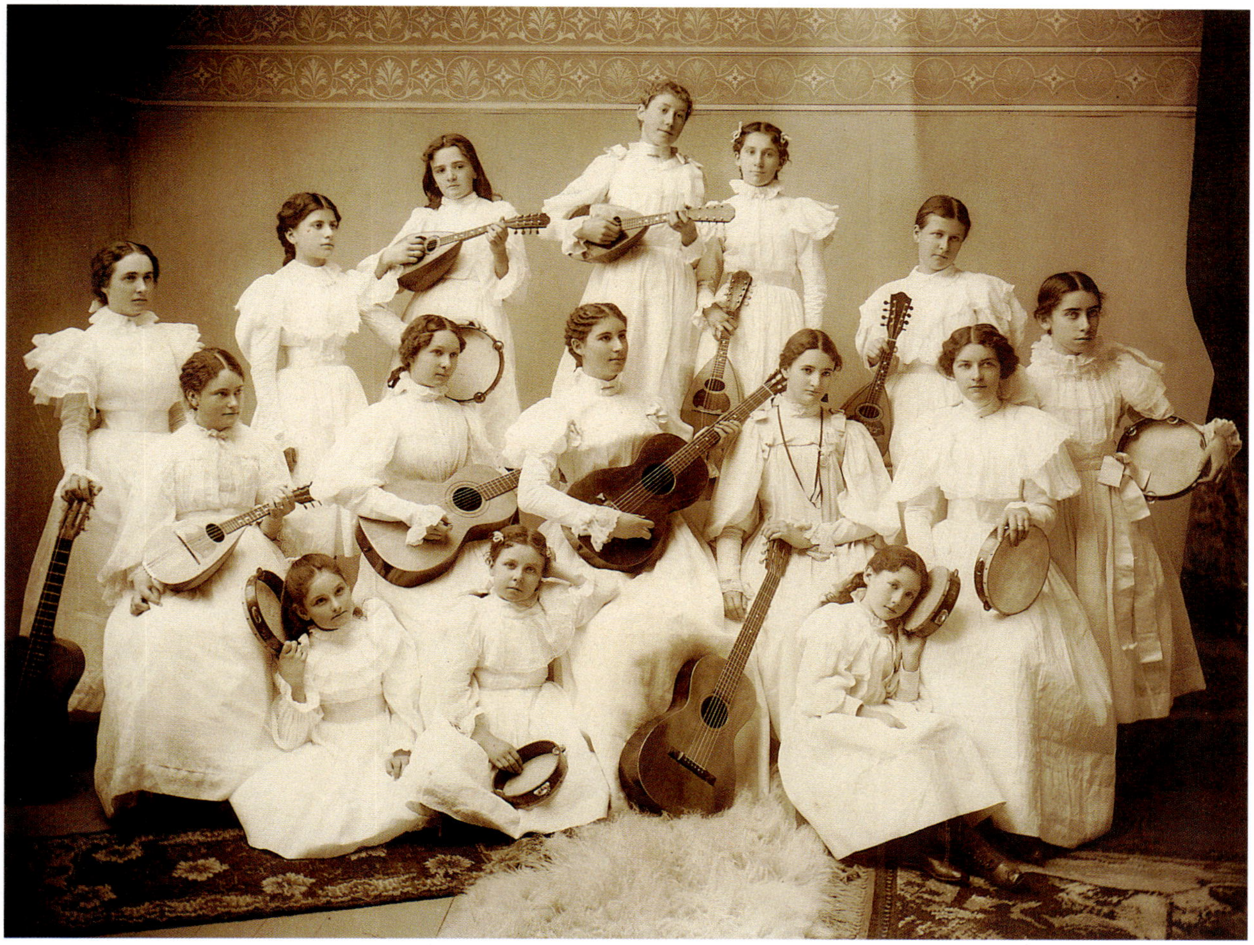

35.

UNKNOWN

Music Pupils (Petaluma Girls' Guitar Band), June 1897

Toned gelatin silver print

10⁹⁄₁₆ x 13⁷⁄₁₆ in.

MUSEUM PURCHASE

PORTFOLIO II

Mood and Symbolism

California Pictorialism

NAOMI ROSENBLUM

PICTORIALISM IN CALIFORNIA developed within a larger context of ideas about the nature of the photographic image. The dual character of the medium—its capacity to produce both art and document—had been demonstrated soon after its discovery; Louis Jacques Daguerre and William Henry Fox Talbot each had focused the camera's lens on a bit of actuality and on an artful arrangement of objects. Nevertheless, a good part of the nineteenth century was spent debating which of these directions was the medium's true function. Some mid-nineteenth-century practitioners, among them Julia Margaret Cameron and Henry Peach Robinson, were thoroughly convinced of photography's potential for imaginative expression; others felt that reality could be documented within an aesthetic framework. For those who believed that the mechanical nature of camera and lens precluded its role in art creation, photography's sole usefulness was in record-making and as "handmaiden" to the traditional arts.

As the medium's role in practical life expanded, the argument over its potential for creating art grew more insistent. Toward the end of the nineteenth century, new and less expensive equipment, in particular the Kodak, and new developments in technology—especially the separation of processing from exposing—made snapshot photography accessible to large numbers of ordinary people who wished to keep records of family, friends and events (plate 36). Commercial applications also broadened as a result of advances in printing technology, enabling publications to use greater numbers of camera images for illustration and businesses to turn to the camera for authentic depictions of their products and processes. Stereographic images, invented much earlier, remained popular for parlor entertainment and as educational tools, as did lantern slides. The public, in other words, became much more accustomed than formerly both to making and looking at photographs.

Such wide popular appeal prompted those claiming the medium for personal expression to mark off a territory for themselves under the rubric Pictorialism. This move involved the recognition that beauty and spirituality—then considered prime requisites of the hand-made arts—could also be achieved in camera images. The concept had been articulated in two earlier nineteenth century developments that, while dissimilar in their prescriptions, were each involved with aesthetics. In a widely praised 1869 publication entitled *Pictorial Effect in Photography,* English author Henry Peach Robinson had proposed a set of compositional rules based on ideas culled from precepts set forth by painters. Convinced that the hand of the artist must somehow be involved in artistic creation, he also presented a composite method of melding together sections of different camera images to create an invented whole (figure 1). While this latter prescription did not at the time gain wide adherence in

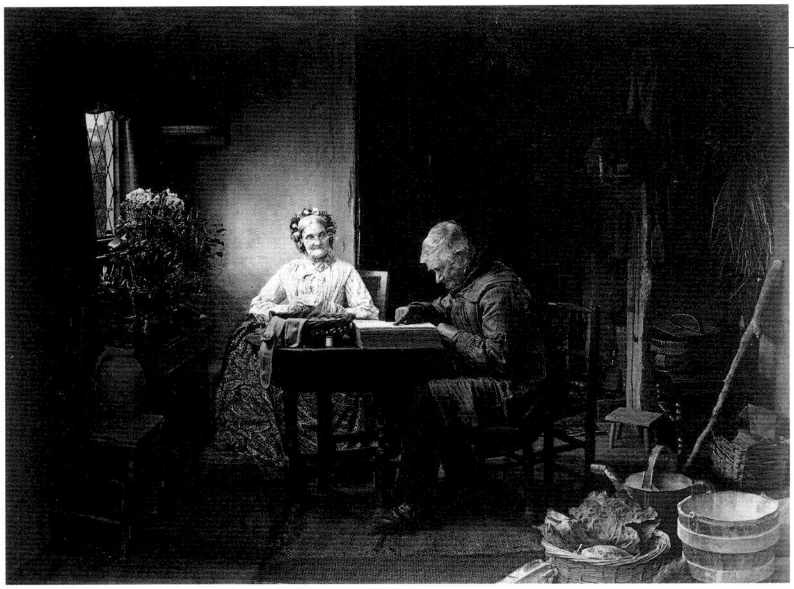

FIGURE 1.
Henry Peach Robinson
When the Day's Work Is Done, 1877
Albumen print, 22 1/16 x 29 5/16 in.
THE J. PAUL GETTY MUSEUM, LOS ANGELES

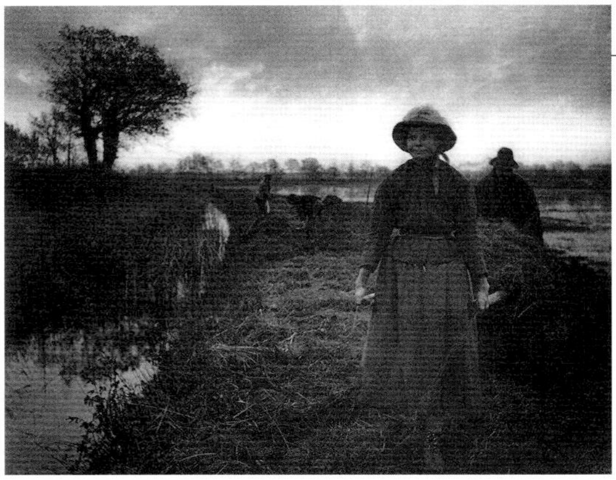

FIGURE 2.
Peter Henry Emerson
Poling the Marsh Hay, 1886
Platinotype?, 9 15/16 x 11 7/16 in.
THE J. PAUL GETTY MUSEUM, LOS ANGELES

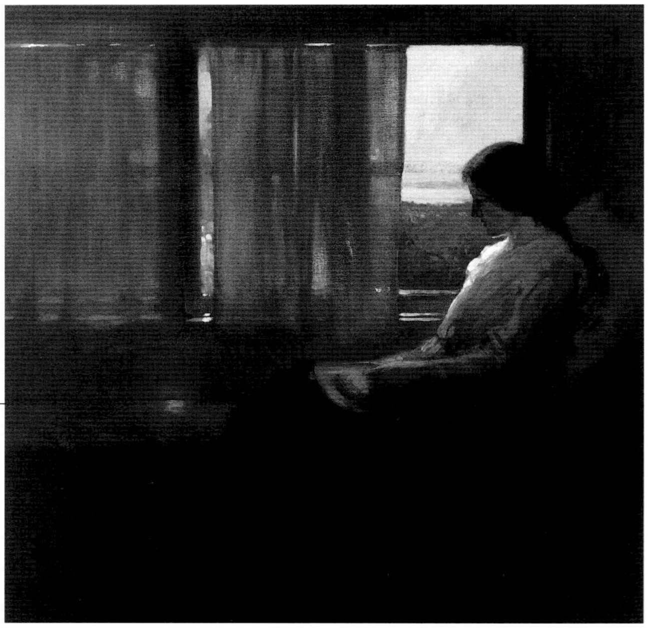

FIGURE 3.
Xavier Tizoc Martinez
Afternoon in Piedmont (Elsie at the Window), c. 1911
Oil on Canvas, 36 x 36 in.
COLLECTION OF THE OAKLAND MUSEUM OF CALIFORNIA, GIFT OF DR. WILLIAM S. PORTER

the United States, the compositional lessons gleaned from *Pictorial Effect* were heeded. Some twenty years later, *Naturalistic Photography* by Englishman Peter Henry Emerson (Robinson's opponent in artistic methodology) propounded different ways of achieving aesthetically satisfying images. With an eye on Barbizon painting, Emerson held that beauty was to be found in nature and real (invariably rural) life, and not in fanciful invention (figure 2). Images of actuality could be made pleasing to the eye by softening focus, attending to tonal matters and employing platinum paper or the gravure process for making prints. The concepts embodied in *Naturalistic Photography* had a marked influence in the United States through the book's American edition, as well as its frequent synopses in photographic magazines, and through the organization of photographic clubs devoted to pictorialist ideas. The definitive exposition of pictorialist ideology in this country appeared in 1901. In *Photography as a Fine Art,* art educator and critic Charles Caffin held that because pictorial photography conjoined natural sensitivity to beauty with an involvement in the processing aspects of photographs, it fulfilled the requirements of art.

The conviction that photographs could be art and should be accepted by the public as such, in the same manner as the traditional visual arts, initially united all American Pictorialists. Most agreed that the photographer needed to intervene manually in the processing of camera images in order to keep them from being merely mechanical. Nevertheless, many devotees were from provincial centers and were relatively unsophisticated about art. While heeding compositional rules for producing pleasurable images, many of these Pictorialists were inspired by the narrative possibilities and the sentimental nature of American genre painting. By the late 1880s, however, artistic expression in the United States was beginning to reflect a variety of influences from Europe and the Far East, which promised a more sophisticated native cultural life. The indistinct forms and muted colorations characteristic of the tonalist style created a sense of reverie and nostalgia that appealed to both painters and photographers seeking a poetic way of expressing feelings about life. To them, nature seemed at its best when its sharp edges and corners had become blurred by moonlight or twilight (figure 3).[1]

The concepts underlying Impressionism, brought back from France by American painters who had gone abroad to study, also affected photographic expression. With its emphasis on light, air, and atmosphere and its predilection for scenes drawn from middle class urban as well as country life, this movement inspired artists to confront the cityscape. Mysticism and Symbolism also found a receptive climate in late-century America, perhaps in response to evidence of the era's corruption and tastelessness, as did the restrained decorative strategies of Asian art. As a consequence of these varied influences, there emerged in urban centers a more cosmopolitan artistic climate, which offered a variety of directions and styles for photographers who wished to produce art rather than just record reality.

It is no surprise to find that as new ideas in the visual arts presented themselves, dissension surfaced among pictorial photographers. Those more comfortable with older artistic affinities remained in the pictorialist societies, which had originated in the late 1880s. Those determined to be on what they deemed the cutting edge of photographic expression gathered around Alfred Stieglitz (figure 4) and the Photo-Secession. Initiated in 1902, it was named for similar European movements that had seceded from more established groups in an effort to throw off older concepts in favor of new ideas. In the struggle for the leadership of what was sometimes called "the new school of American photography," F. Holland Day in Boston and Stieglitz in New York City vied for the allegiance of the advanced sector of camera artists, with Stieglitz eventually winning out.[2]

The Photo-Secession in reality included only a small number of the nation's Pictorialists and while its activities, gallery and journal *Camera Work* were acknowledged elsewhere,[3] its message resounded less insistently outside of New York. The far greater number of pictorial photographers who remained outside the Photo-Secession were organized loosely into camera clubs and amateur societies which prized conviviality as well as art. After a bumpy start in the 1880s, these associations became more confident of their goals. In the first years of the twentieth century and up through the 1920s, they continued to promote what they considered beauty through the selection of appropriate subjects and the use of harmonizing strategies such as soft-focus. Manipulative printing practices—sometimes referred to as "ennobling"—encouraged hand-work and enabled the introduction of coloring matter in processes using carbon, gum bichromate and gum bromoil materials. These interventions made it possible for photographers to vary tonalities from print to print, as in *Dawn, Sunset and Moonlight*—three variations of a single negative by Sigismund Blumann (plate 73).

New York's prominence and Stieglitz's superintendence of the Photo-Secession had for long obscured developments in artistic photography elsewhere in the nation during the early 1900s. On the West Coast in the same years, California was emerging as a center for pictorialist photography. Its population of descendants of Spanish settlers, treasure hunters, Chinese and Japanese immigrants, and escapees from the more rigid social conventions of the East made for a strong sense of individualism among people who often were eager for self-expression yet were novices in the arts. At the same time, the state embraced two quite different topographical regions, each with a distinctive history and cultural outlook. One result of this divided topography and culture was the establishment of two centers for the development of pictorialist expression, one in Los Angeles and another in San Francisco.

North and south, those attracted to artistic photography found their need for instruction in the realm of art addressed by the journal *Camera Craft,* which made its initial appearance in 1900 in San Francisco (figure 5). Any number of articles suggested appropriate themes and treatments, advising that whatever the subject—landscape, genre, still-life, portraits, animal studies, architecture or interiors—it was the appreciation of beauty and the expression of emotion that would transform mundane description into something that spoke to the senses.

These ideas were basic to the salon movement, which had been initiated in the 1890s by those in camera clubs and photographic societies eager for separate venues in which to show artistic work. An additional purpose was to convince the general public that they could "no longer . . . ignore the

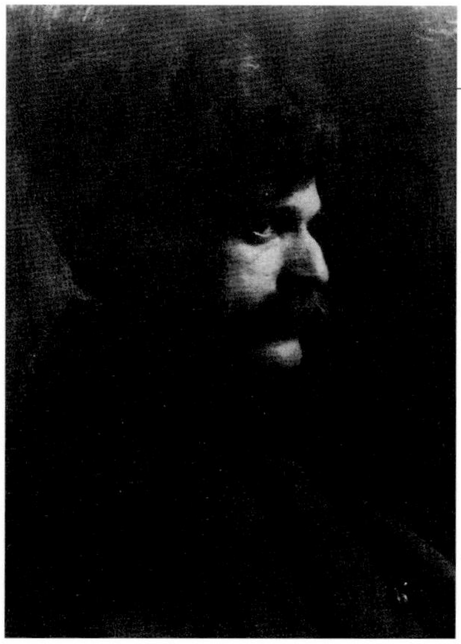

FIGURE 4.
Frank Eugene
Mr. Alfred Stieglitz, c. 1909
Photogravure from *Camera Work,* 6½ x 4 7/16 in.
COLLECTION OF THE OAKLAND MUSEUM OF CALIFORNIA,
GIFT OF MR. AND MRS. WILLARD M. NOTT

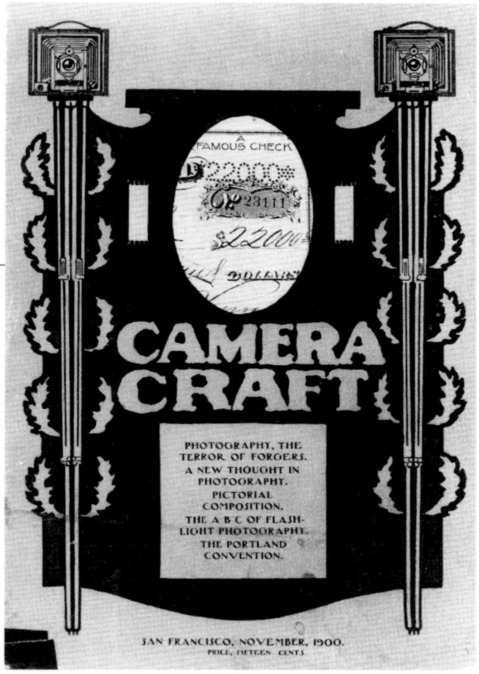

FIGURE 5.
Cover of *Camera Craft,* 1900
COLLECTION OF THE OAKLAND MUSEUM OF CALIFORNIA

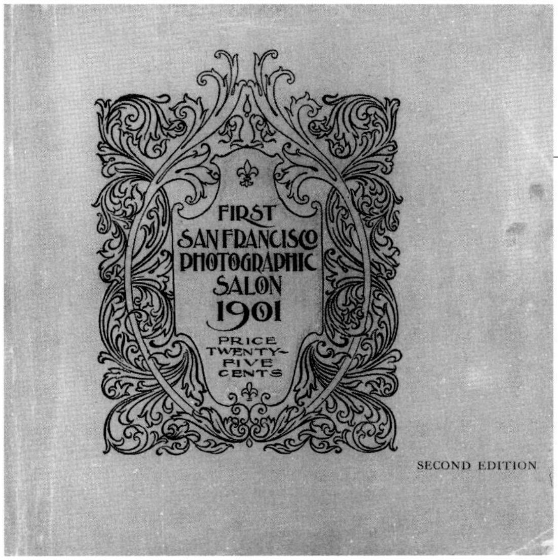

FIGURE 6.
Cover of the catalog for the First San Francisco Photographic Salon, 1901
COLLECTION OF THE OAKLAND MUSEUM OF CALIFORNIA

claims of photography as a means of artistic expression."[4] The salons—held annually or occasionally in such urban centers as Chicago, Philadelphia, Pittsburgh, Washington, D.C.—were competitive events, open to Pictorialists no matter where they resided. Judging was done initially by painters and later by photographers, and commendations were proudly affixed to the backs of the entries. By 1901, enough Californian Pictorialists had emerged to inaugurate a salon in San Francisco; a year later, Los Angeles held its first salon. These exhibitions were so successful in raising the self-esteem of California's art photographers that by 1905, the date of the First American Salon in New York City, they accounted for nineteen of the one hundred and thirty exhibitors, with only New York boasting a larger group.

California's resident photographers and critics eagerly greeted the salons held annually during the first decade not only for the opportunity they presented to exhibit, but for the chance "to view the work of modern schools" and to study "the best pictures produced by photographers throughout the United States."[5] A sense of remoteness from eastern art centers made Californians particularly eager to see what was being done in New York, but the contentiousness that soured relationships between groups in the East seems not to have divided them. Work by members of the New York Camera Club was exhibited at the First Salon (figure 6); in 1902, the San Francisco Salon invited the Photo-Secession to show a selection of its members' work; five years later, the conservative Photo-Pictorialists of Buffalo exhibited in California to high acclaim.

Exhibitions and reproductions[6] were just two of a number of strategies through which *Camera Craft* hoped to acquaint Californians with the latest concepts in the photographic arts. Descriptions of entries in salons throughout the United States, as well as articles on manipulative printing techniques and philosophical essays on the nature of beauty, appeared in issue after issue. Besides being informative, this material was designed to improve standards in what had become a popular "artistic channel open alike to the millionaire and the twenty-five dollar a week clerk."[7] The early vitality and staying power of the pictorialist movement in California was the result of factors intrinsic to the region, of which two signal elements were the absence of urban concentrations and the presence of a glorious natural landscape. This surround was not only immediately visible and accessible, but it had symbolic meaning for those arriving from less spectacularly endowed places to one of seemingly infinite promise. Nature might be given a bit of help by the photographer to improve its romantic allure, but the mountains of the Sierra Nevada range, the long Pacific coast with its beaches and peninsulas, the giant forests of the northern regions all provided entrancing subject matter. Such surroundings also turned landscape photographers into boosters for their state, for it was believed, as Edward Weston was later to claim, "everything worth photographing is in California."[8]

Landscapes by William E. Dassonville, Arnold Genthe and Oscar Maurer, reproduced in the promotional literature, suggested a brooding "spirit of romance and unrest" evoked by the state's natural scenery.[9] Indeed, even after soft-focus, highly-manipulated treatments of landscape had become outdated, the region's natural topography remained a source of inspiration for artistic photographers. While the word "Pictorial" may have irritated Weston,[10] his sharply focused depictions of the Carmel coast, as well as Ansel Adams's of Yosemite, are as idealized as those earlier versions of nature in these precincts. In fact, the soft delineation visible in Adams's early work openly declares a pictorialist lineage (plate 66).

As well as appreciating the beauties of nature, the pictorialist sensibility was attuned to what it perceived as "exotic" subject matter, which also abounded in California. San Francisco's large community of Chinese, many of whom still dressed in native garb and followed their own cultural modes, provided photographic material that was both mysterious and enticing (plate 55). Using a concealed camera, Arnold Genthe made his exposures in the Chinese quarter surreptitiously, so that his depictions might be thought to verge on documentation. The selection of what he believed to be typical incidents, however, along with the hand-work done to excise any evidences of westernization, qualify the images as pictorialist (plates 39, 40). Native American life presented a similar situation, in that the photographer might document people and events in a straightforward fashion in the manner of Californian George Wharton James,[11] or might view the same subject through a romantic scrim. Seattle photographer Edward S. Curtis brought artistic sensibility to an extensive project that resulted in a twenty-volume depiction of Native Americans, among them tribes resident in Northern California (plates 47, 48). At times, he mythologized his subjects by providing them with costumes and implements they no longer used, but which he felt would give this "vanishing race"[12] heroic stature. In a similar attempt at idealization, but with considerably less skill and far less persistence, Emma Belle Freeman produced sentimental portraits of Native Americans in her studio in Northern California (figure 7).

When coupled with a sense of the indivisible character of all organic life—animal, vegetable and mineral—California's bountiful natural envelope inspired transcendent symbolist approaches. To photographer Anne Brigman, the presence of such scenery afforded the opportunity to affirm "the spiritual through the material." Mystical experiences she claimed to have had in the Sierras inspired her to "express in the abstract the solemn majesty of the rocks," the weirdness of a tree, the joyousness of a brook and her own longing for personal and sexual freedom (plates 51, 52).[13] This marriage of the mystic and the sensual, seen as well (if less ardently expressed) in the work of easterners F. Holland Day, Gertrude Käsebier and Clarence White, recommended Brigman to Stieglitz and made her acceptable for membership in the Photo-Secession.

Brigman was one of a number of women active between 1900 and 1930 in the pictorialist movement in California; they were but a small part of the many women involved in the medium's commercial sector. Most lived in the San Francisco area and several had been trained at the Mark Hopkins Institute of Art (later the San Francisco Art Institute), which had opened its walls very early to joint exhibitions of camera images and graphic art. In California as in the East, women constituted

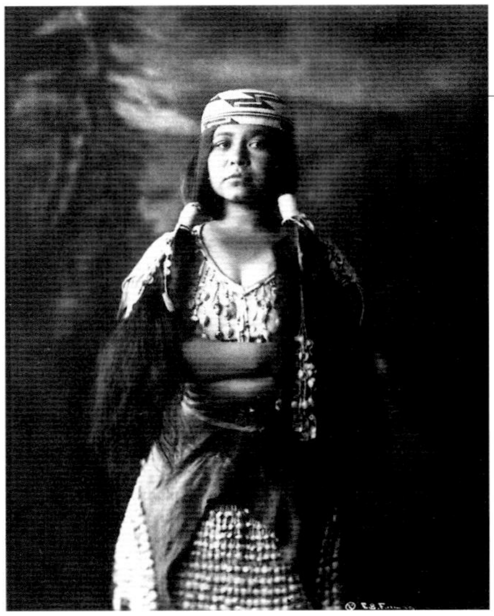

FIGURE 7.
Emma B. Freeman
Daughter of the Klamath, c. 1910
Gelatin silver print
COURTESY OF PETER E. PALMQUIST

a large part of the student body in art schools and academies, but had difficulty forging professional careers in the traditional arts. Recognizing, perhaps, that making a living as a photographer would be more feasible than as a painter, Laura Adams (later Armer) opened a portrait studio in San Francisco, which later was taken over by Adelaide Hanscom. Convinced of the difference between a likeness and a portrait, both turned out tasteful work that reflected their artistic training in the way they posed sitters, arranged hair and drapery, managed lighting, and composed the entire ensemble (plate 69).[14] From 1900 up through the 1920s, Laura Adams Armer regularly exhibited portrait work at salons throughout the United States, often gaining prizes. She was active, too, in selling work for book and magazine illustration.

Hanscom, who shared the studio first with Emily Pitchford and then with Blanche Cumming, satisfied her ambition to produce even more expressive photographic art by creating illustrations for several books of poetry. For the most notable, Edward Fitzgerald's *Rubáiyát of Omar Khayyám,* she employed a panoply of pictorialist maneuvers (plate 54). The scenes were set up, costumed and enacted by friends and associates; the negatives were retouched and the prints were manipulated, with some eventually colored by hand. As was the case with many other San Francisco photographers, a great part of Hanscom's negatives and prints were lost when the earthquake and fire of 1906 destroyed her studio.

Up through the 1920s, portraiture remained the gateway into the photographic profession for most American women, wherever they resided. Dorothea Lange's trip across the United States from New York in 1918 ended in a portrait studio in San Francisco. Her highly acclaimed artful management of light and composition soon brought well-heeled customers to her door (plate 65). Similarly, Margarethe Mather, who shared Weston's studio in Glendale, started out as a portraitist (plate 59) before enlarging her capabilities to include the taking of decorative interiors. Of course, making artistic portraits was not limited to women practitioners. It was the sole possibility for men desirous of creating art, but needing also to earn a professional livelihood. Although widely exhibited, pictorial photographs were rarely purchased. Weston, for example, continued to depend on portrait commissions for a living—as meager as it was—even after he embarked on the expressive landscapes and studies on which his reputation is based.

In the East, large industrial and media concentrations made it possible for pictorial photographers to market their work for commercial illustration. In part, this was effected through an alliance between the Pictorial Photographers of America (the "PPA" was organized in 1916 by Clarence H. White) and a group of business executives who formed the Art Center in an effort to improve the quality of camera illustration in advertising and editorial work. Even those in the business world who distrusted art were said to understand that products were "enhanced by the fine tone-spacing and the beauty of contrasted textures" that pictorial photography could provide.[15] Absent this alliance of art and industry on the West Coast, Californians had mainly to depend on income from portraits.[16]

Portraiture provided Imogen Cunningham with her entry into photography, but her work also reflects the transitions taking place in pictorialist style in the West following World War I. Before she moved from Seattle to San Francisco in 1917, Cunningham had made a name not only for her elegantly lighted portraits, but for scenes with symbolist overtones. Usually printed in platinum, these staged enactments feature gauzily costumed figures posturing in the landscape to suggest emotions associated with such indefinable ideas as "a farewell" or "clairvoyance" (plate 56). In the 1920s—still regarding herself as a Pictorialist—Cunningham's photographic art took on a different appearance. More clearly defined close-up studies of plants and the nude body avoided any suggestion of context or narrative while still retaining an aura of sensuousness (plate 60).

Reaction by Cunningham and others to the hackneyed subjects and lack of creativity represented by the salon formula assumed several directions in the late teens and on into the next decade. Fresh ideas concerning theme, focus and pictorial organization had drifted westward from Europe, where emphasis on the specific character and texture of objects was gaining a following under the banner of "the new realism." From New York, where Stieglitz, Sheeler and Strand (figure 8) had been investigating modernist ideas since 1916, came concepts involved in pictorial abstraction. These strands became interwoven with local influences deriving both from Far Eastern culture and from Hollywood cinema spectacles to effectively propel California artist photographers in new directions.

Attempts to bring together the various new ideas in artistic photography were undertaken by Pictorial Photographers of America through its salons and its well-designed and printed annual publication. Although centered in New York, the presence of John Paul Edwards (plate 68) on the selection committee assured a fair representation of West Coast work; at one point a Pacific Coast chapter of PPA was contemplated.[17] The 1920 *Annual* included work by eighteen Californians, compared with thirty-four New Yorkers; by 1929 there were fourteen works from California and nineteen from the state of New York.

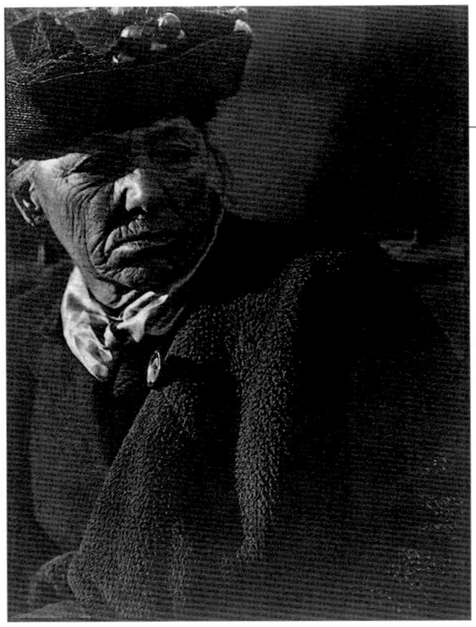

FIGURE 8.
Paul Strand
Portrait—New York, 1916
Platinum print, 13½ x 9⅞ in.
THE J. PAUL GETTY MUSEUM, LOS ANGELES

One distinctive feature of California cultural life that affected pictorialist imagery during the 1920s was the influence of Far Eastern art, in particular that of Japan. Even before 1900, American painters such as John LaFarge and Winslow Homer had taken notice of the decorative and spatial modes of representation employed by Japanese artists; by the turn of the century, similar concepts were being integrated into discourses on photographic aesthetics, most notably by art teacher and curator Arthur Wesley Dow.[18] Called *notan,* these strategies, which were derived largely from Ukiyo-e prints, avoided western perspective and treated form without recourse to chiaroscuro effects. Their integration into the photographic medium gave early work by the precocious photographer Alvin Langdon Coburn its special decorative character (figure 9). His images, along with Anne Brigman's, in the long, narrow format typical of many Japanese prints, and Dassonville's (whose portrait of Coburn is practically a lesson in how to transmute Japanese art into an American vernacular) appeared in *Camera Craft* in the early 1900s, suggesting that Japanese visual practice was of interest to a wide community of West Coast pictorial photographers.

The presence of active Japanese photographers' clubs in Los Angeles and San Francisco in the 1920s—among the largest in the United States—made Asian art precepts even more tangible. Lacking opportunities in the commercial sector, Japanese-American photographers were free to pursue the expressive aspects of photography in ways that directly reflected their visual heritage. The pronounced emphasis on pattern and geometric shape, now accompanied by greater attention to sharp focus, lent these images a superficial similarity to European modernist photographs,[19] but Japanese-American work dealt largely with organic rather than mechanical forms. The restrained tonalities and an interest in the play of light on various surfaces firmly anchor this "technically flawless work" to its Asian heritage. Landscapes, still lifes and close-ups of plant forms by Japanese-Americans were widely reproduced during the twenties in pictorialist publications and may well have influenced Cunningham and

Weston to embrace similar material.[20] To more conservative California pictorial photographers, however, these images, with their angled views and startling close-ups, seemed "queer . . . an assault on pictorial codes."[21] Much of the work by the Japanese Pictorialists, some of whom had been active in the Los Angeles area since the teens, was lost or destroyed as a result of the infamous resettlement process that took place in 1942.[22]

The older pictorialist outlook also remained alive. Although sometimes mistaken by the public for etchings or lithographs, images such as the romantic landscapes printed in gum platinum by the displaced New Yorker Karl Struss still showed up in Salon entries. Architectural monuments, in particular those associated with the Spanish Mission buildings which had been almost a stock-in-trade item for California Pictorialists since before the turn of the century, continued their allure, especially after the construction of the 1915 Panama-Pacific International Exposition buildings in San Diego and San Francisco (plate 57). Louis Fleckenstein, active since 1907 in the Salon world and leader in the 1920s of the Camera Pictorialists of Los Angeles, specialized in portraits that demonstrated decided artistry in their placement and lighting. His images of dancers were thought to express a typically pictorialist appreciation of the spiritual communion between human beings and nature. Among other Californians who continued to work in this more traditional pictorialist style were Fred Archer and Otis Williams.

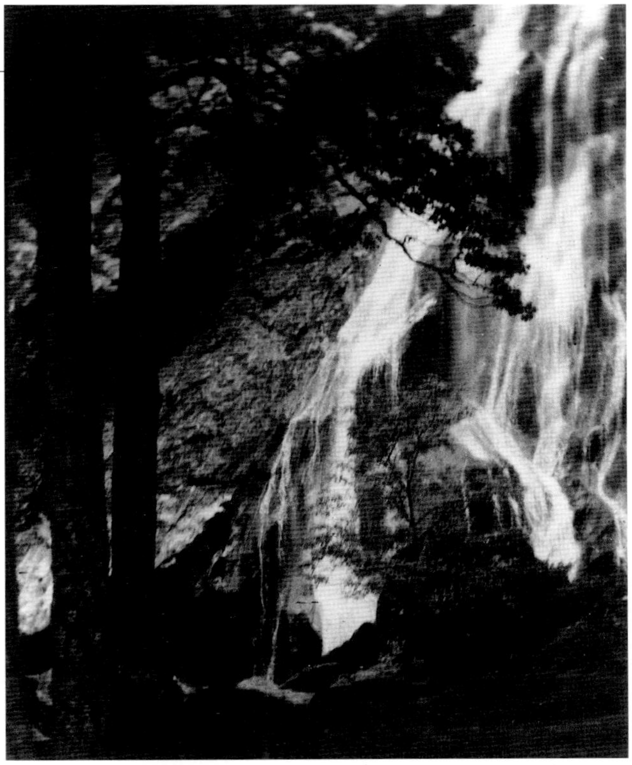

FIGURE 9.
Alvin Langdon Coburn
California, Yosemite Falls, c. 1920
Platinum print, 12 x 10 in.
COLLECTION OF THE OAKLAND MUSEUM OF CALIFORNIA, BURDEN FUND FOR PHOTOGRAPHY

City scenes were something new and fresh, however. At times, they invited conventional pictorialist soft-focus treatment of smoke, cloud or haze along with symbolic captions, but the geometry of city architecture also mandated new notions about organizing form and space. Just this conjunction of the tried and the new endows Johan Hagemeyer's images of San Francisco's buildings and street activity with an enigmatic quality of instability (plate 62).

Pictorialism found still another direction in the twenties in the work of William Mortensen and Arthur B. Kales. Indifferent to both the poetic ambitions of the earlier salon photographers and dismissive of the "brittle" stringencies of the purists (see below), Mortensen in particular desired to create what he called a "meta-realistic" direction, concerned with "a new world of beauty and fantasy."[23] To achieve this end, he took up ideas outlined much earlier in *Pictorial Effect in Photography* for creating composite images by joining together portions of various photographs and applying hand-work if necessary (plates 76, 77). Undoubtedly, this way of working, as well Mortensen's urge to create a fantasy world, reflected the then-current methods used to create motion pictures, in which filmed sequences made at different times and locations were assembled into a seemingly consistent narrative. Moreover, his highly dramatized effects mimicked the melodramatic character of early motion pictures. While this work was long regarded as "kitsch" by photographic curators and historians, it may now be seen as a forerunner of the fantastical images produced by a number of photographic artists of the 1980s, most notably Joel Peter Witkin. The arch postures (plate 71) and frieze-like arrangements of flimsily-clad, prancing or supine figures tie many of Kales's images even more firmly to the appearance and iconography of the Hollywood extravaganza; in fact, the photographer often made use of motion picture sets as backgrounds for his narratives based on ancient legends.

For almost a quarter of a century, as Will Connell noted, "the Salon was the only tool" and Pictorialism the main channel through which the California artist photographer could speak.[24] By the mid-twenties, however, its authority over artistic photography was being challenged by those interested in camera work unaided by hand-work and in themes from ordinary life. This purist branch of artistic camera imagery mandated a different approach both to visualization and processing. Its call for a sharply focused negative without modifications or handwork will be discussed in the next essay, but the new direction did not spring forth all of a sudden. It had its genesis in work done in the late teens by Edwards, Hagemeyer, Henry Hussey, and Weston. Aware of the changing scene in the arts and, indeed, in the nature of American reality, these individuals sought to incorporate concepts of photographic honesty with an appreciation of ordinary aspects of daily life (plate 81). Their images, often pre-visualized, were still realized in soft-focus, but were printed directly and cleanly. In this, they prepared the way for the even sharper purity that was to emerge. As California Pictorialists endeavored to give camera art a more modern character, they signaled their recognition that "American life is moving and changing—we must expect our arts to respond."[25]

NOTES

1. Edward Steichen mentions the "romantic and mysterious quality of moonlight" in *A Life in Photography* (Garden City, New York: Doubleday & Company, Inc., 1963), unpaginated.

2. In 1899, F. Holland Day had urged Stieglitz to establish an "American Association of Artistic Photography." When Stieglitz did not respond, Day gathered the work together and sent it to London for exhibition in October 1900, where it opened as the "New School of American Photography."

3. See, for example, Alfred Stieglitz, "The Photo-Secession—Its Objects," *Camera Craft* 7, no. 3 (August 1903): 81–3.

4. Will Sparks, "The First American Photography Salon," *Camera Craft* 10, no. 5 (May 1905): 282. Not all the salons lasted as annual events.

5. Helen L. Davie, "The Los Angeles Exhibition, Its History and Success and Those Responsible," *Camera Craft* 5, no. 2 (June 1902): 43.

6. A portfolio of sixteen well-reproduced images by the followers of Clarence H. White appeared in *Camera Craft* in 1901, accompanying an article by Emma Spencer entitled "The Work of the White School," *Camera Craft* 3 (July 1901): 85–104; the journal continued to reproduce pictorial works for two decades, usually from the various salons but also, occasionally, from abroad.

7. George Brookwell, "First International Photography Salon," *Camera Craft* 25, no. 4 (April 1918): 142.

8. Bill Barich, "Acts of Attention," in Therese Heyman, ed., *Picturing California: A Century of Photographic Genius* (San Francisco: Chronicle Books, 1989): 7.

9. Carrie Stevens Walter, "California," in *California The Beautiful by Western Artists and Authors* (San Francisco: Paul Elder and Company, 1911), unpaginated.

10. Edward Weston, "Photography—Not Pictorial," *Camera Craft* 37, no. 7 (July 1930): 313.

11. See George Wharton James, "The Study of Indian Faces," *Camera Craft* 8, no. 1 (December 1903): 12–18. Other Californians who worked in the documentary fashion were Ruth K. Roberts and Adam Clark Vroman.

12. Curtis titled one of his best-known images, of Native Americans on horseback seen from behind, *The Vanishing Race.* His photograph *The Clam Digger* received first prize for genre work in *Camera Craft* 1, no. 5 (September 1900): 268.

13. Unsigned review, "Lens Studies by Annie W. Brigman," *Camera Craft* 12, no. 1 (January 1906): 43.

14. Otto Walter Beck, "Portrait Photography and Art Education," *Camera Craft* 15, no. 2 (November 1907): 473–75. Beck also wrote *Art Principles in Portrait Photography* (New York: Baker & Taylor Publishing Co., 1907).

15. Margaret Watkins, "Advertising in Photography," *Pictorial Photography in America* Vol. 4 (New York: Pictorial Photographers of America and The Art Center, 1926), unpaginated.

16. The income from portraiture was not large; Fleckenstein was considered a highly successful portraitist in Los Angeles, but seems to have made a barely adequate living. See Dennis Reed, "Southern California: Pictorialism, Its Modern Aspects," in *Pictorialism in California: Photographs 1900–1940* (Malibu and San Marino: The J. Paul Getty Museum and The Henry E. Huntington Library and Art Gallery, 1994), 68.

17. John Paul Edwards, "Pictorial Photography in the Far West," *Pictorial Photography in America 1920* (New York: Pictorial Photographers of America, 1919): 14.

18. Arthur Wesley Dow, *Composition* (New York: Baker & Taylor Publishers, 1899). The book went through six editions.

19. Dennis Reed, *Japanese Photography in America, 1920–1940* (Los Angeles: George J. Doizaki Gallery, Japanese American Community center, 1986), 61. Reed suggests that Japanese photographers were inspired by works visible in the German photographic annuals *Das Deutsche Lichtbilder* and *Photofreund Jarhbuch*.

20. See James N. Doolittle, "The Photographic Salon—What of It?," *Camera Craft* 37, no. 4 (April 1930): 169, in which the author notes that the work of the Japanese Pictorialists "has gained a force to be contended with." Weston's first solo exhibition was sponsored by Shakudosha, a Japanese cultural society in Los Angeles. See Dennis Reed, *Japanese Photography in America.*

21. F. C. Tilney, quoted in Dennis Reed, *Japanese Photography in America,* 55.

22. In February 1942, President Franklin D. Roosevelt issued Executive Order 9066, which allowed the U.S. Government to intern 110,000 West Coast residents of Japanese ancestry—two thirds of them native born—in relocation centers. It was not until 1998 that President Clinton offered an apology for the mass internment of people not charged with any criminal or espionage activity.

23. William Mortensen, "Venus and Vulcan: An Essay on Creative Pictorialism," *Camera Craft* 51, no. 3 (March 1934): 103, and no. 6 (June 1934): 257. Mortensen refers to unmanipulated work by Weston as "hard and brittle."

24. Will Connell, quoted in Dennis Reed, "Southern California: Pictorialism, Its Modern Aspect," *Pictorialism in California,* 67.

25. Ira Martin, "Why Should Style in Pictures Change?," *Camera Craft* 37, no. 10 (October 1930): 480.

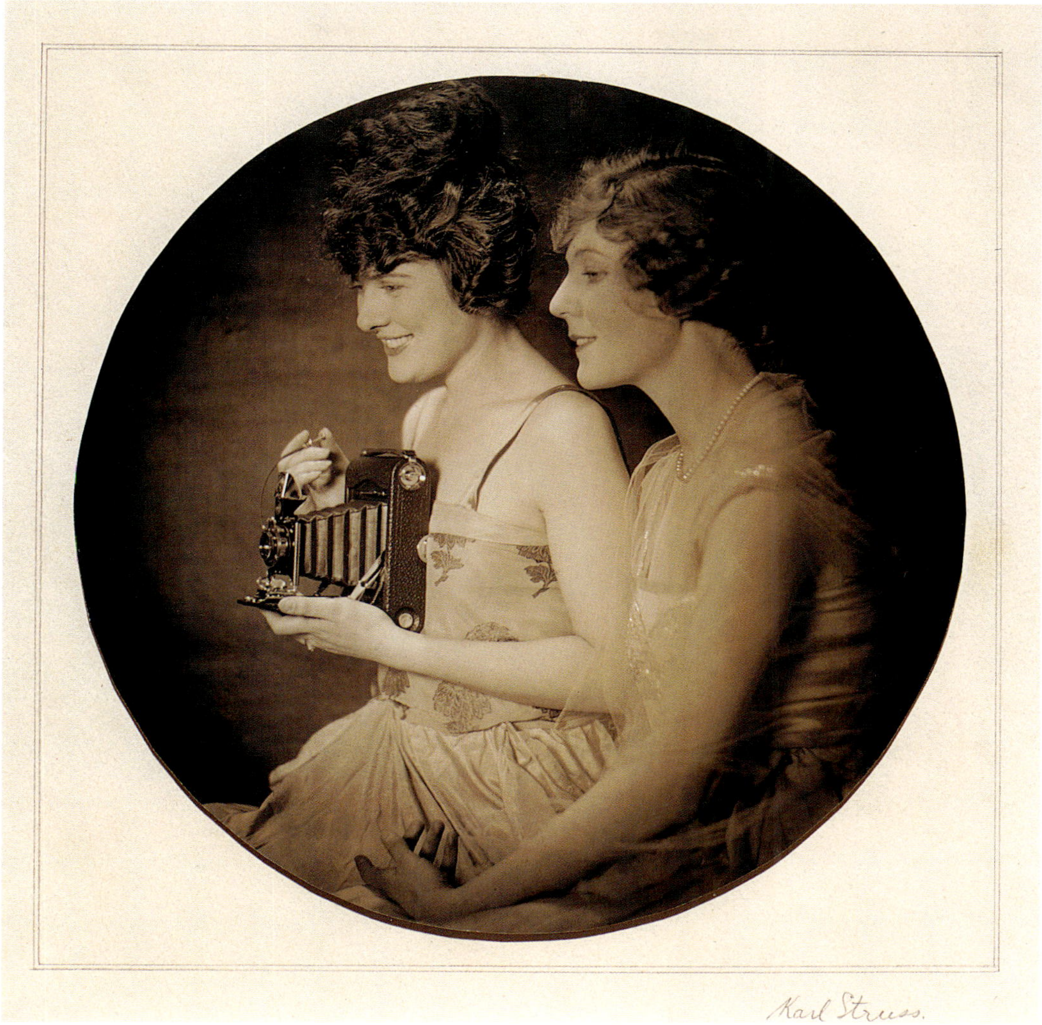

36.
KARL STRUSS
Two Women with Kodak Camera, 1914
Bromide print
8 in. diameter
THE SHIRLEY BURDEN FUND FOR PHOTOGRAPHY

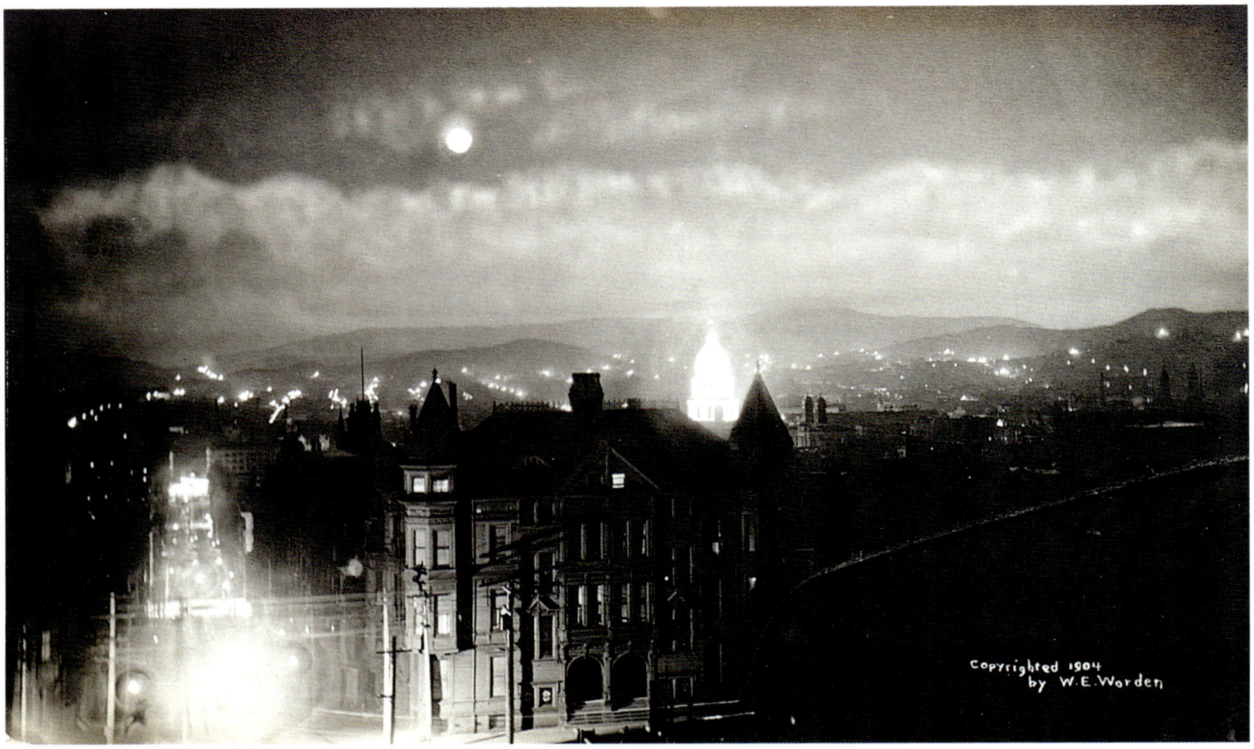

37.
WILLARD E. WORDEN
Untitled (San Francisco at Night), 1904
Gelatin silver print
4¾ x 7⅝ in.
GIFT OF DR. ROBERT SHIMSHAK

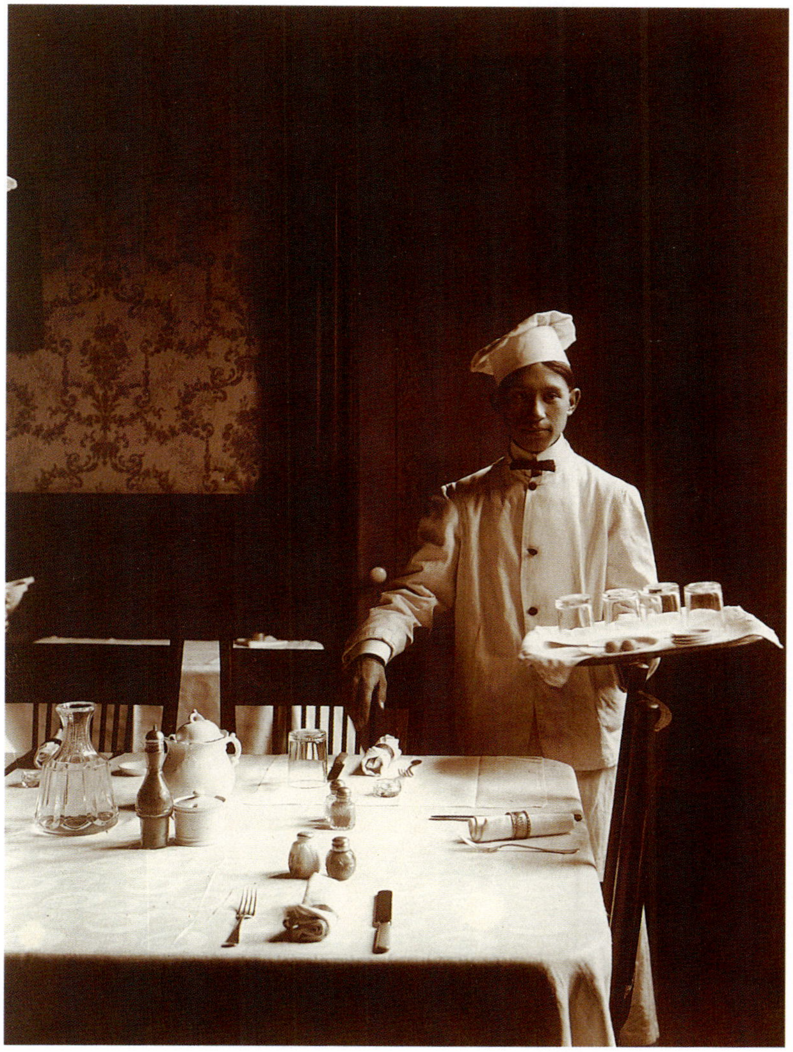

38.
THEOPHILUS HOPE D'ESTRELLA
The Perfect Table, c. 1900
Toned gelatin silver print
6 x 4 3/16 in.
GIFT OF THE CALIFORNIA SCHOOL FOR THE DEAF

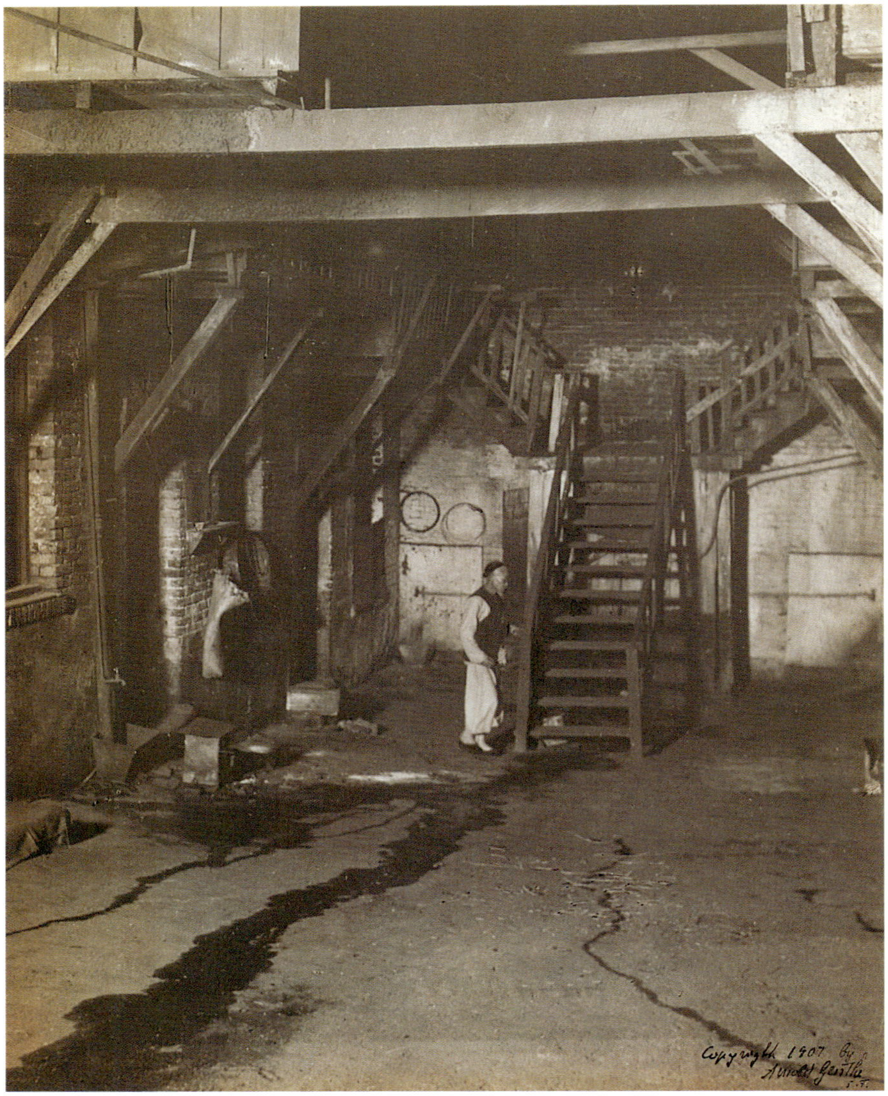

39.

ARNOLD GENTHE

The Devil's Kitchen by Night, c. 1907

Gelatin silver print

$9\frac{1}{4}$ x $7\frac{3}{8}$ in.

GIFT OF DR. AND MRS. WILLIAM FIELDER

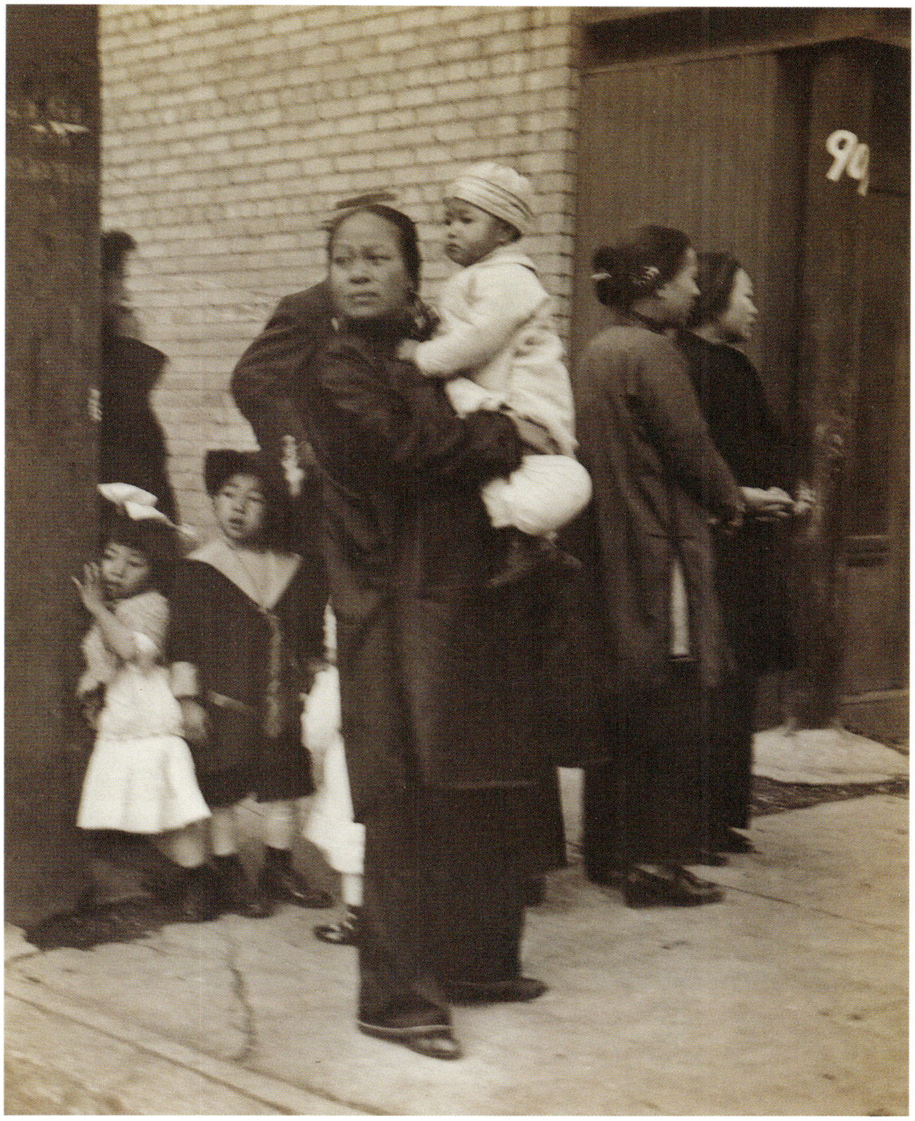

40.
ARNOLD GENTHE
Untitled (Mother and Child, Chinatown, San Francisco),
c. 1900
Gelatin silver print
9 x 7¼ in.
GIFT OF ANONYMOUS DONOR

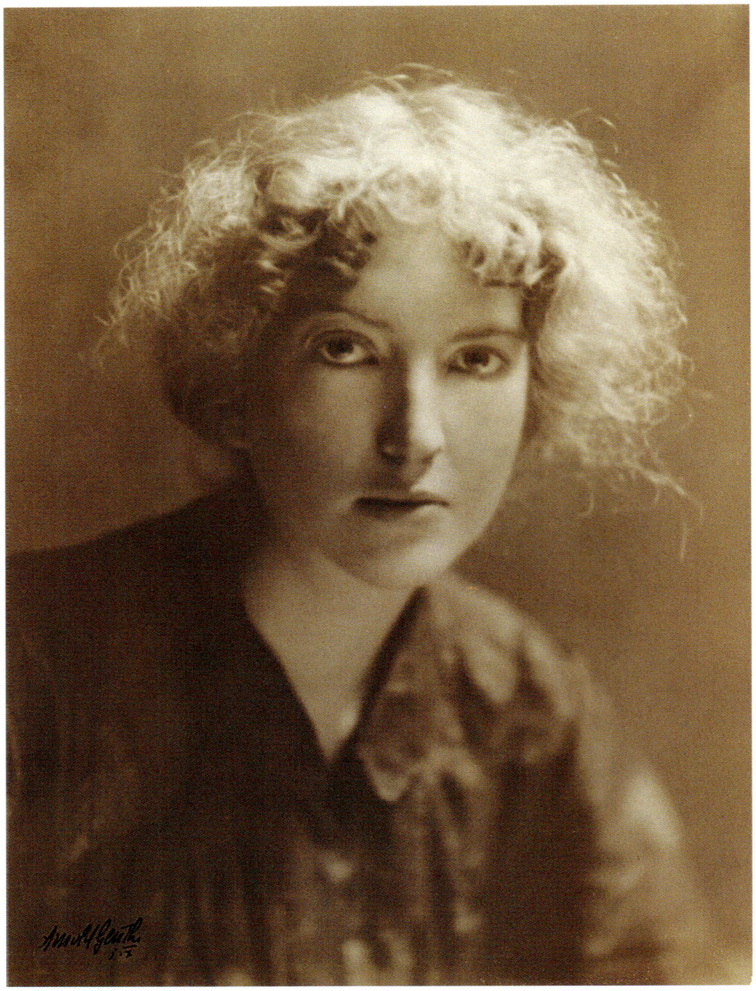

41.
ARNOLD GENTHE
Nora May French, c. 1903
Platinum print
9¼ x 6⅞ in.
GIFT OF ANONYMOUS DONOR

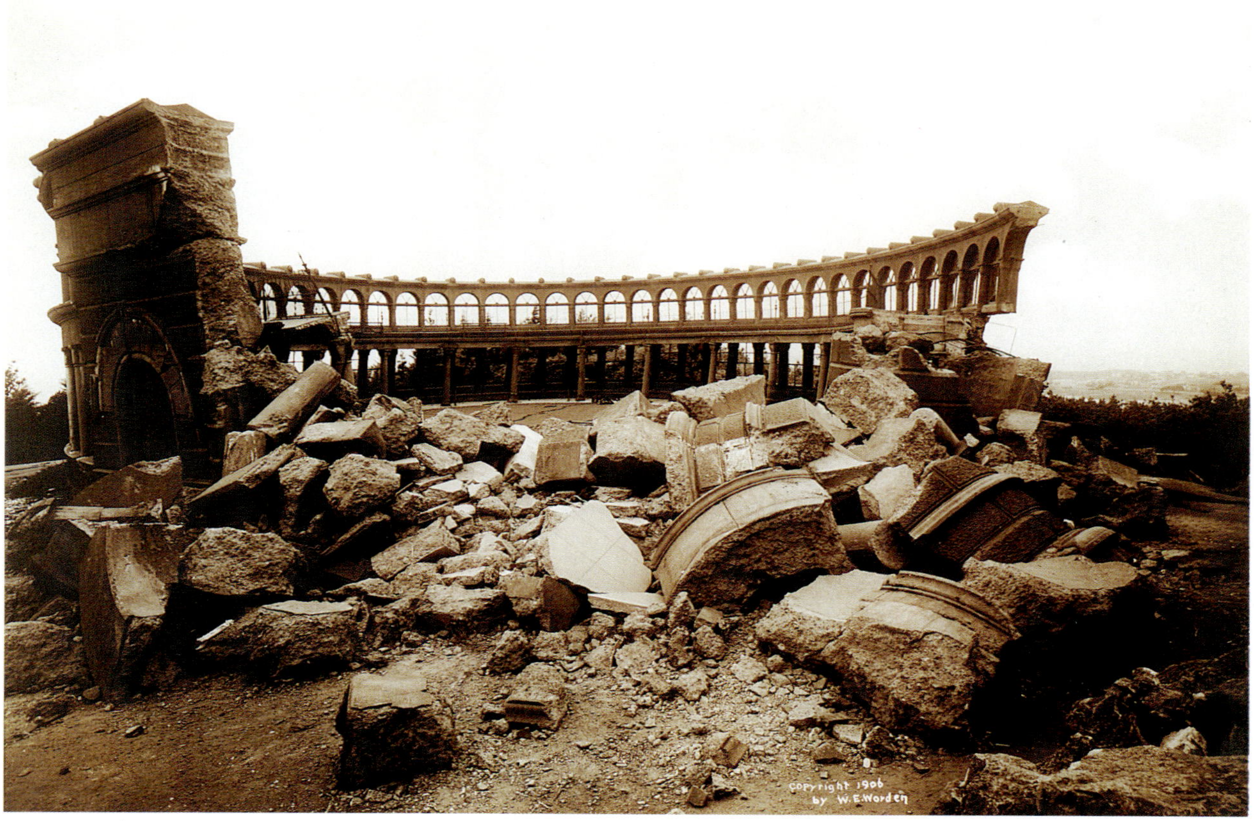

42.
WILLARD E. WORDEN
Untitled (Ruins, Golden Gate Park, San Francisco), 1906
Gelatin silver print
6 ½ x 9 3/16 in.
GIFT OF DR. ROBERT SHIMSHAK

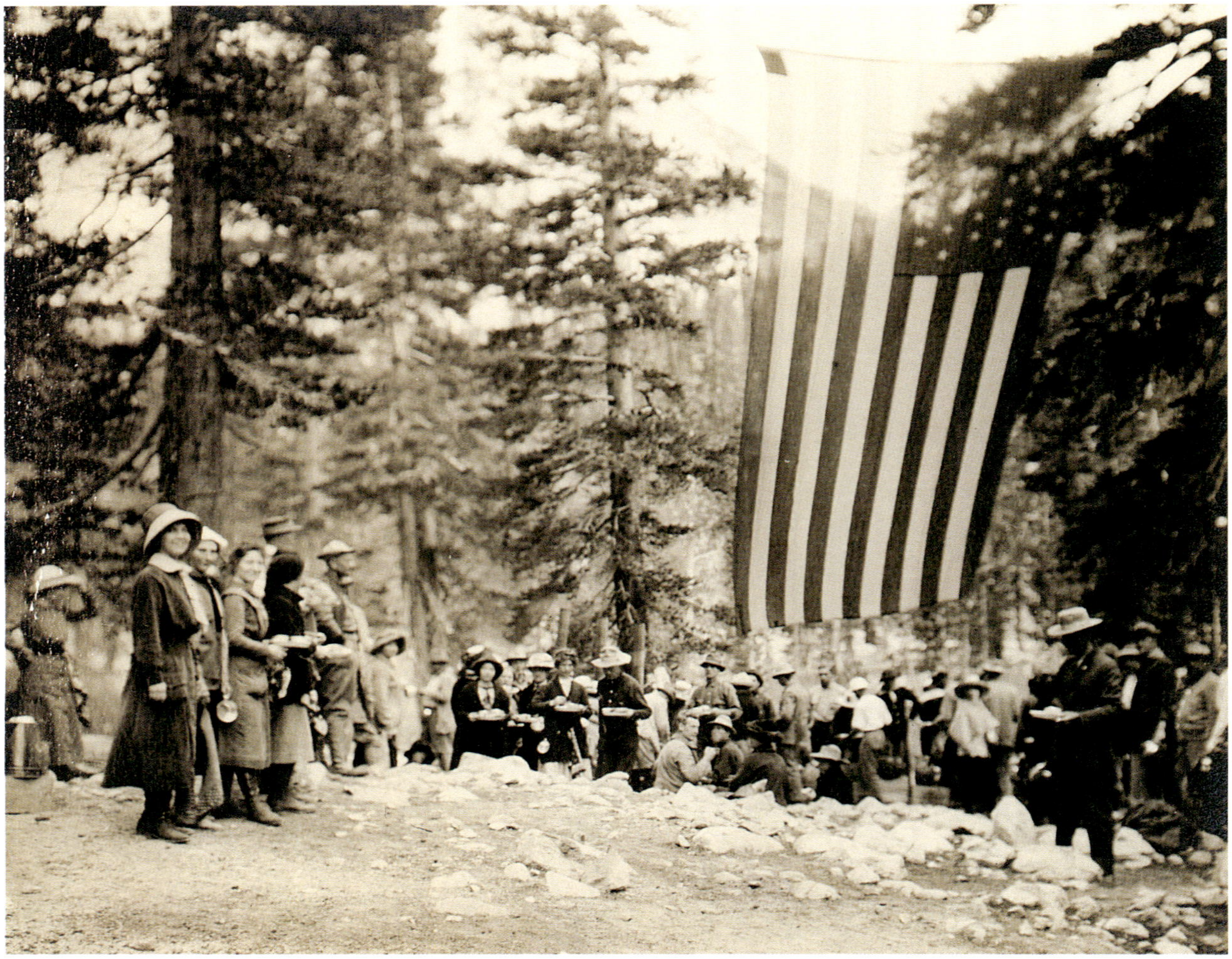

43.

ANDREW BARNABY McKINNE

Untitled (Sierra Club Outing), c. 1900

Gelatin silver print

$7\frac{3}{4} \times 9\frac{3}{4}$ in.

GIFT OF MRS. ANDREW BARNABY McKINNE

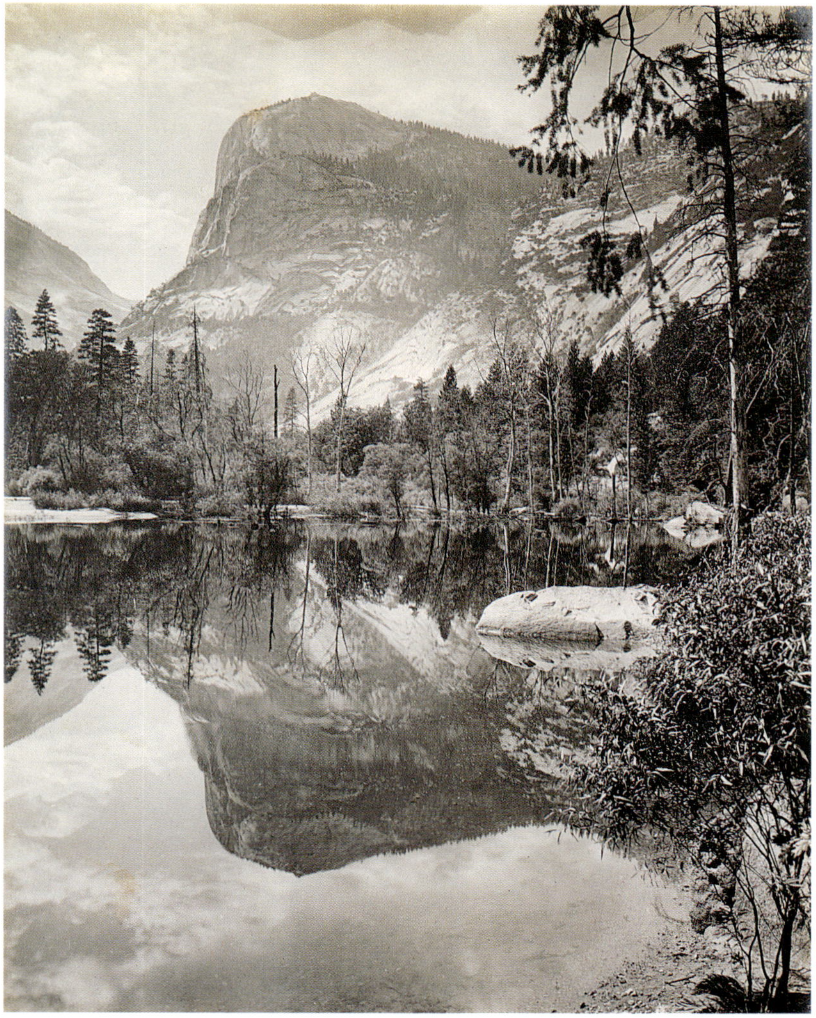

44.
JULIUS THEODORE BOYSEN
Half Dome (from *Album of Yosemite Views*), c. 1903
Gelatin silver print
7½ x 9½ in.
GIFT OF RAIDELLE HIRSCH NEWMAN AND JEROME H. NEWMAN IN MEMORY OF LEONORA E. HIRSCH AND JOSEPH J. HIRSCH

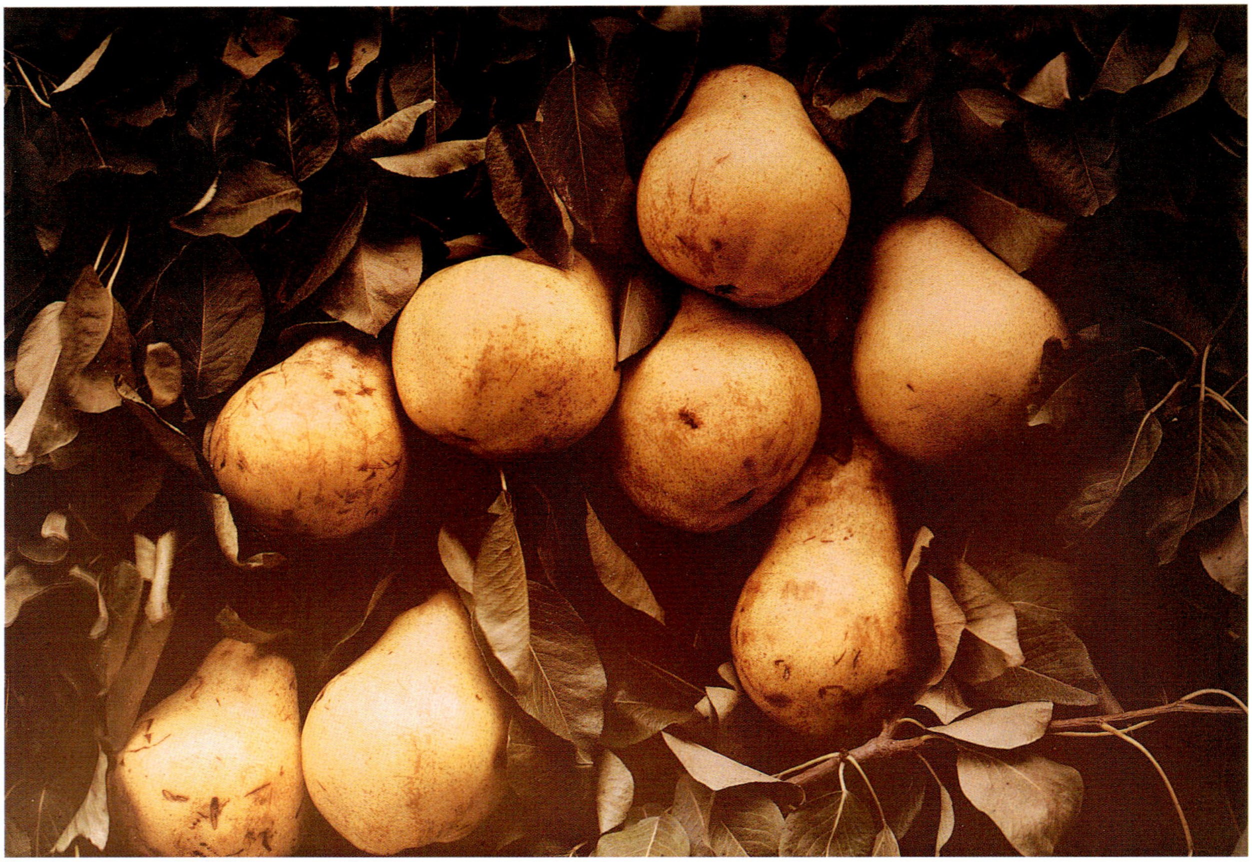

45.
UNKNOWN (DEL MONTE CORPORATION)
Untitled (Pears), c. 1920
Autochrome
7 x 10 in.
GIFT OF DEL MONTE CORPORATION

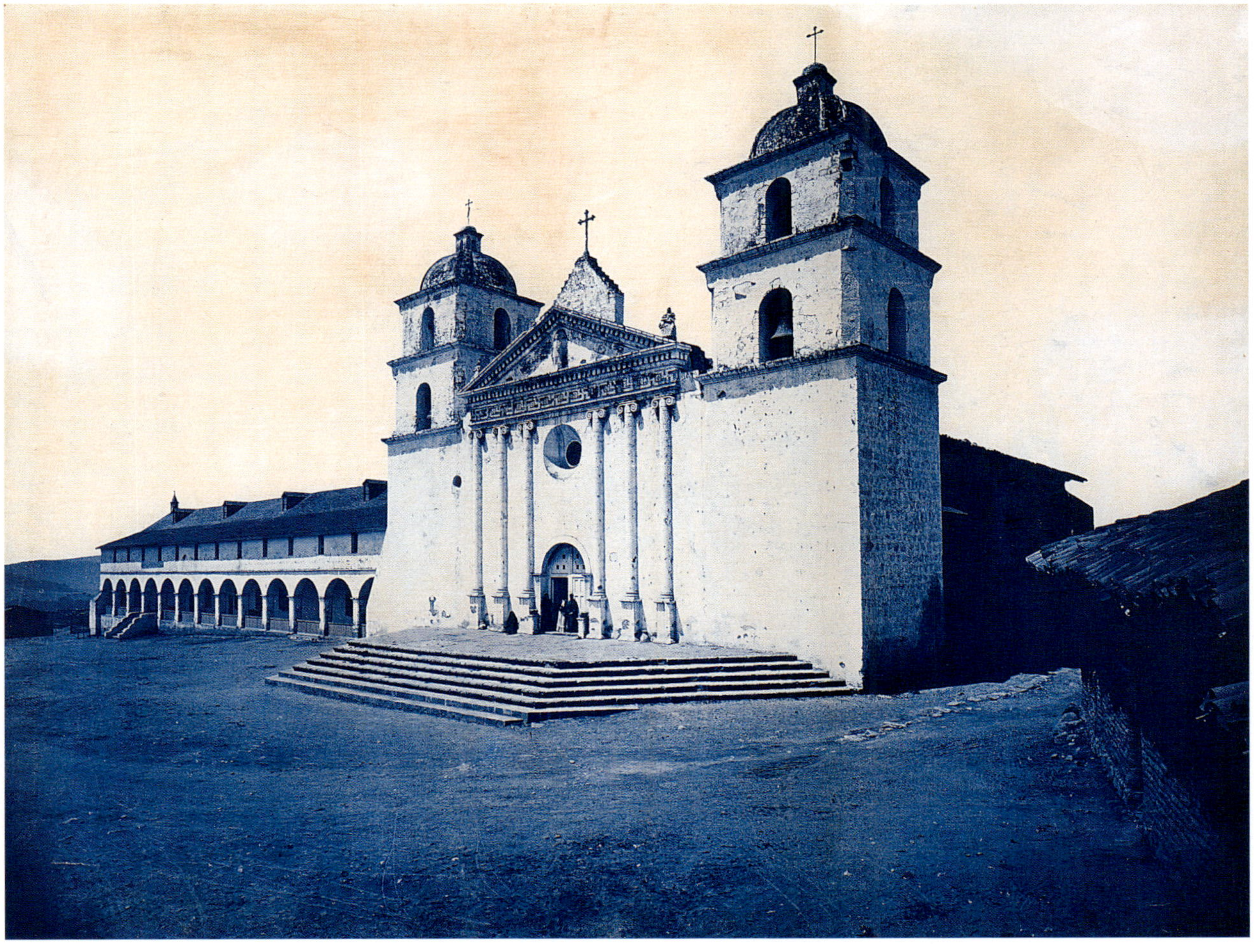

46.
SAMUEL NEWSOM, SR.
Mission Santa Barbara, c. 1904
Cyanotype
16 x 20 3/16 in.
GIFT OF MRS. L. A. MOGLICH

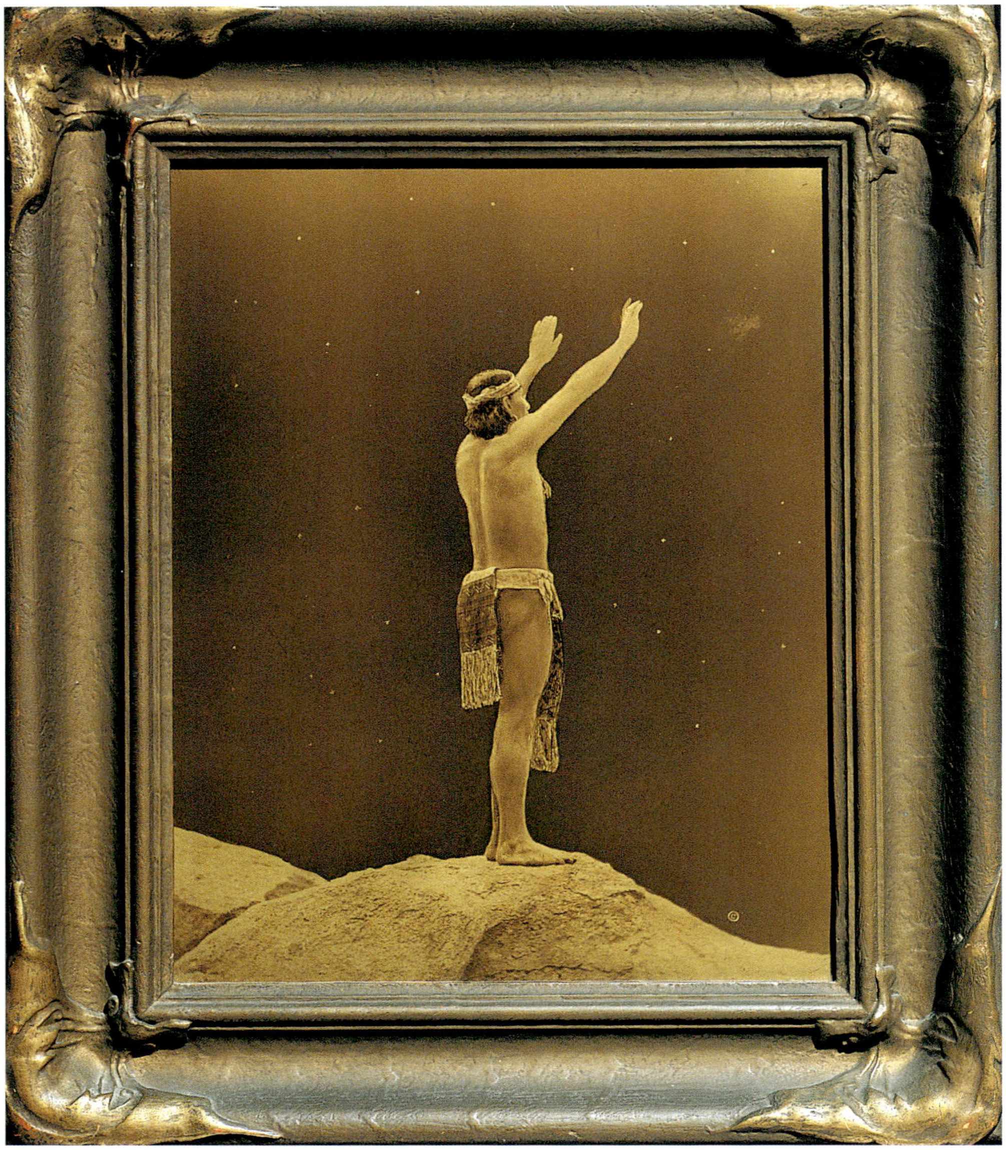

47.
EDWARD S. CURTIS
Prayer to the Stars, c. 1910
Orotone in vintage frame
18¾ x 15⅝ in.
GIFT OF MR. AND MRS. HOWARD WILLOUGHBY

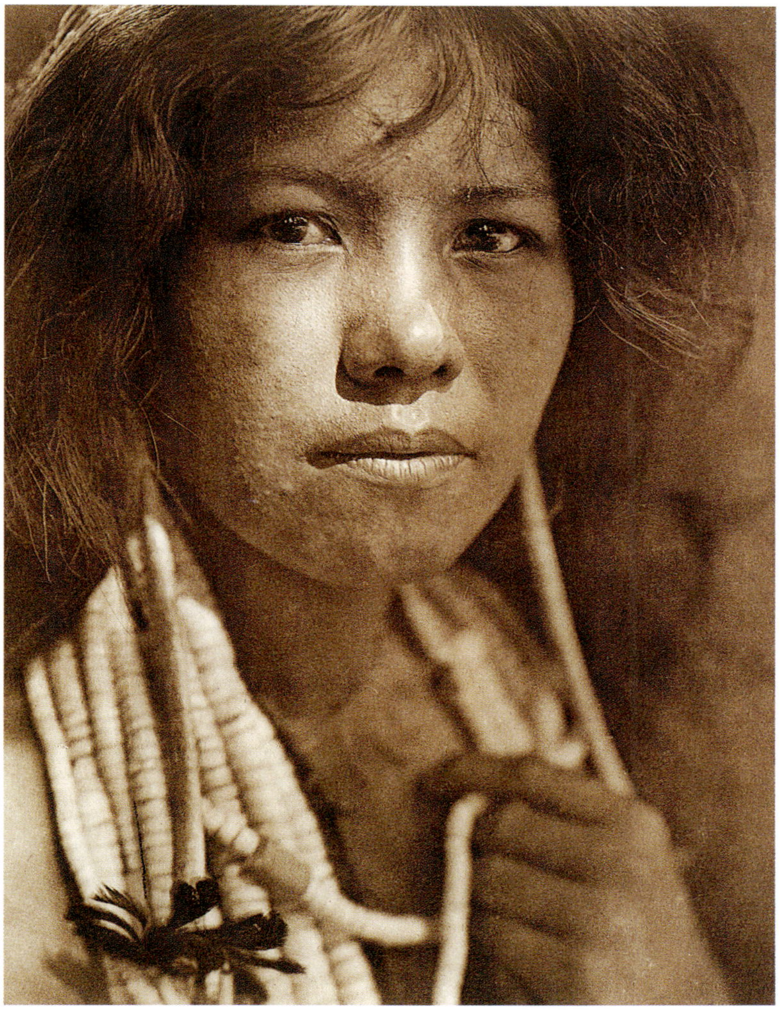

48.
EDWARD S. CURTIS
A Pomo Girl, from *The North American Indian,* c. 1924
Photogravure
15⅛ x 11⅜ in.
MUSEUM PURCHASE

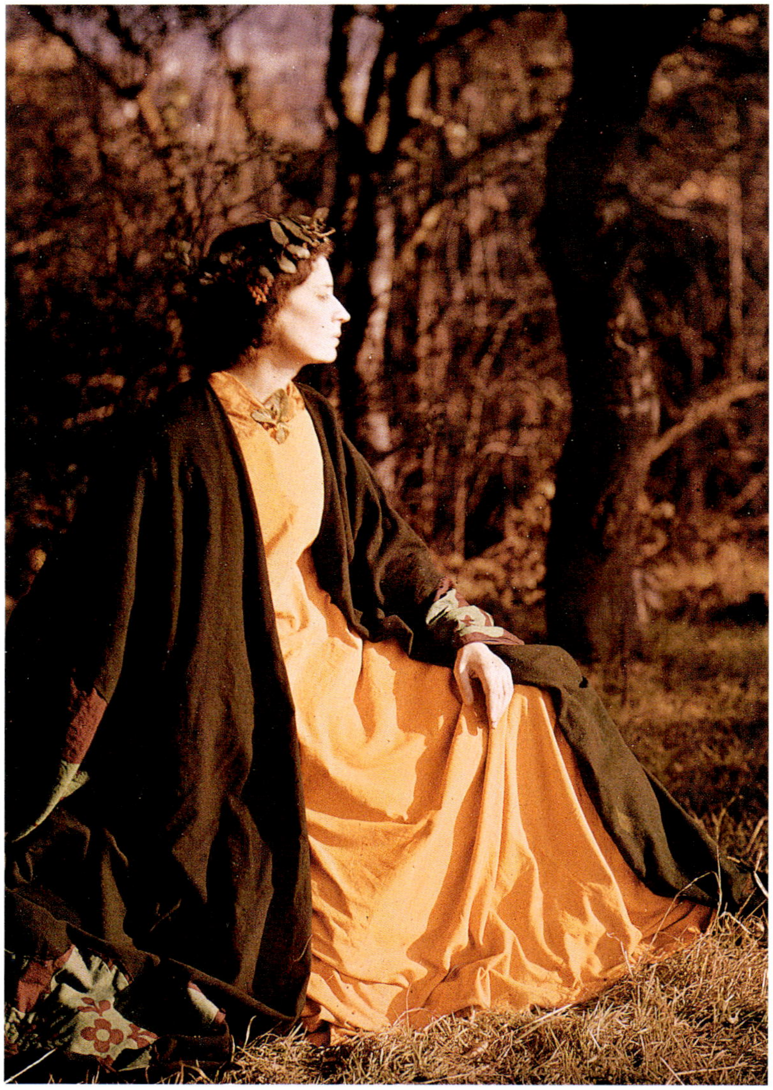

49.

LAURA ADAMS ARMER

Untitled (Self Portrait at La Honda), 1908

Autochrome

6½ x 4¼ in.

GIFT OF MR. AND MRS. AUSTIN ARMER

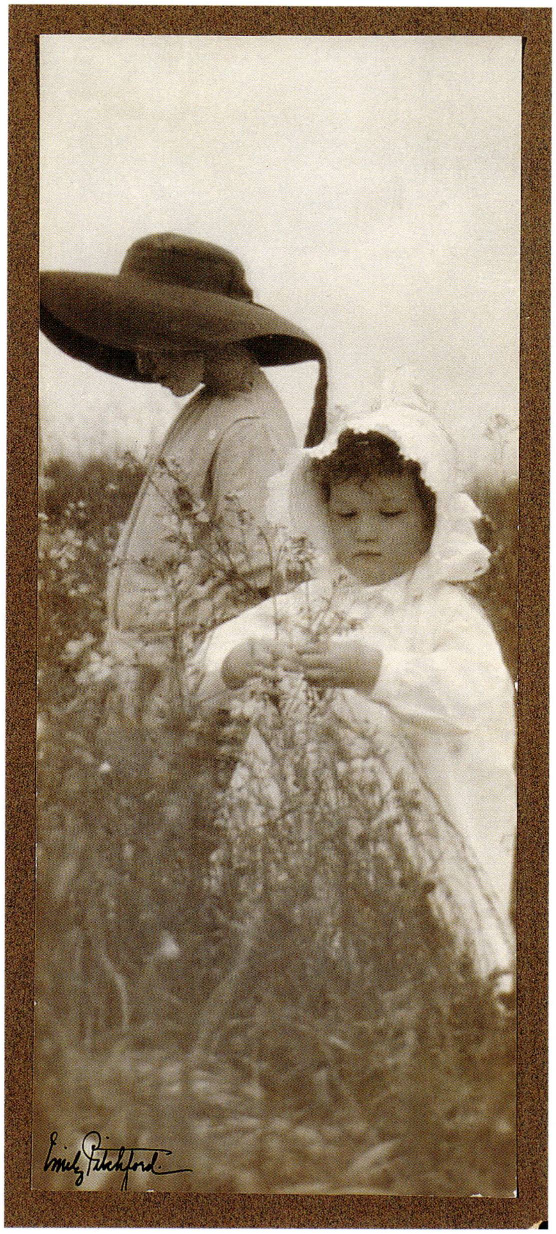

50.
EMILY PITCHFORD
Untitled (Woman and Child in a Field of Flowers), c. 1915
Gelatin silver print
11 x 4¾ in.
GIFT OF MRS. HENLEY MILLER

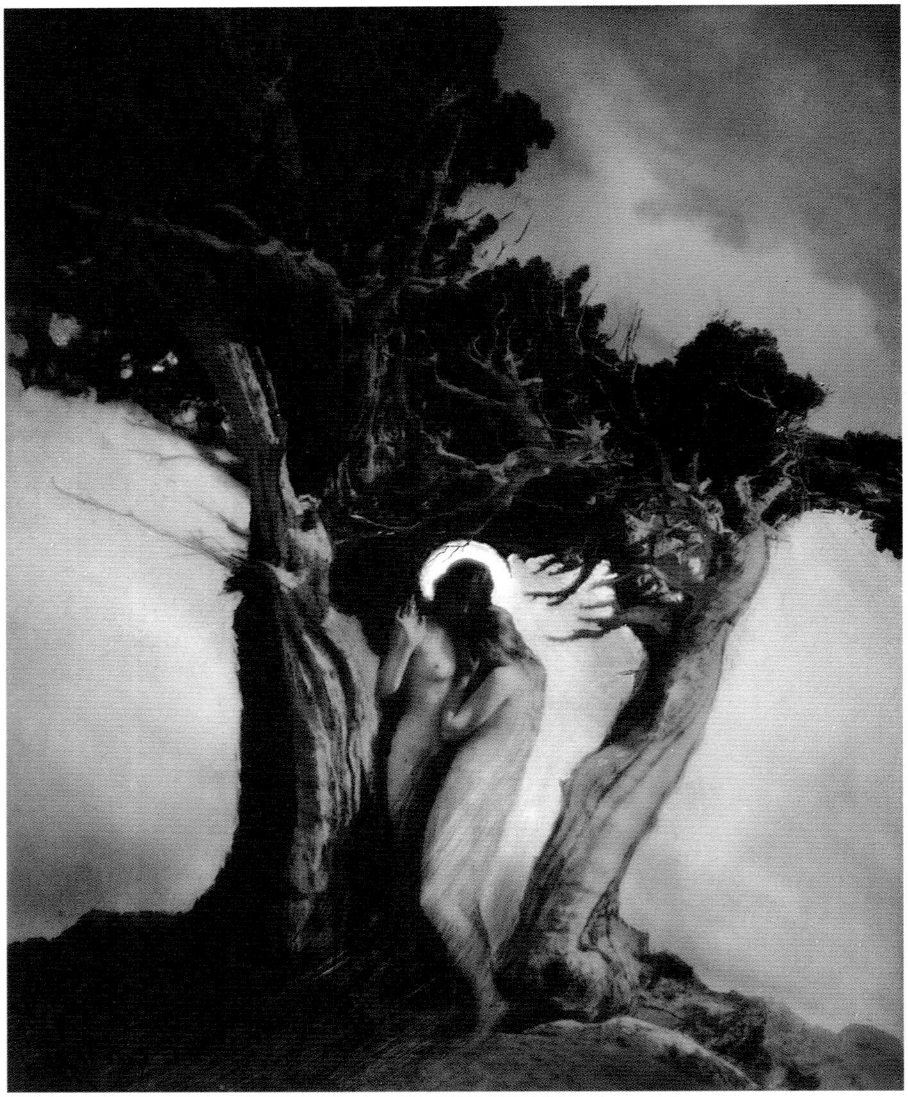

51.
ANNE BRIGMAN
Heart of the Storm, 1912
Gelatin silver print
9¾ x 7¾ in.
GIFT OF MISS MARYLES NAHL

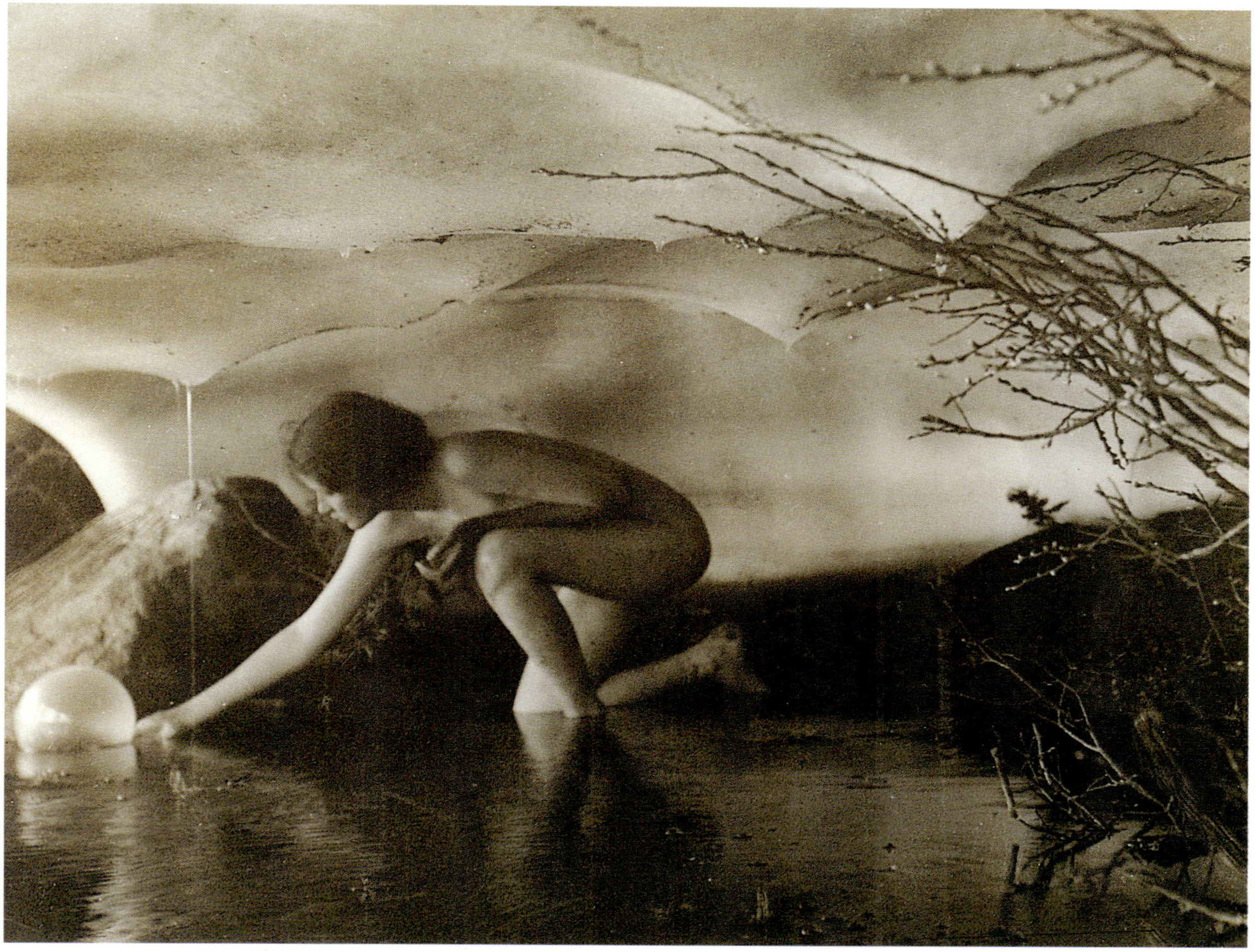

52.
ANNE BRIGMAN
The Bubble, 1905
Gelatin silver print
7¼ x 9¼ in.
GIFT OF MR. AND MRS. WILLARD M. NOTT

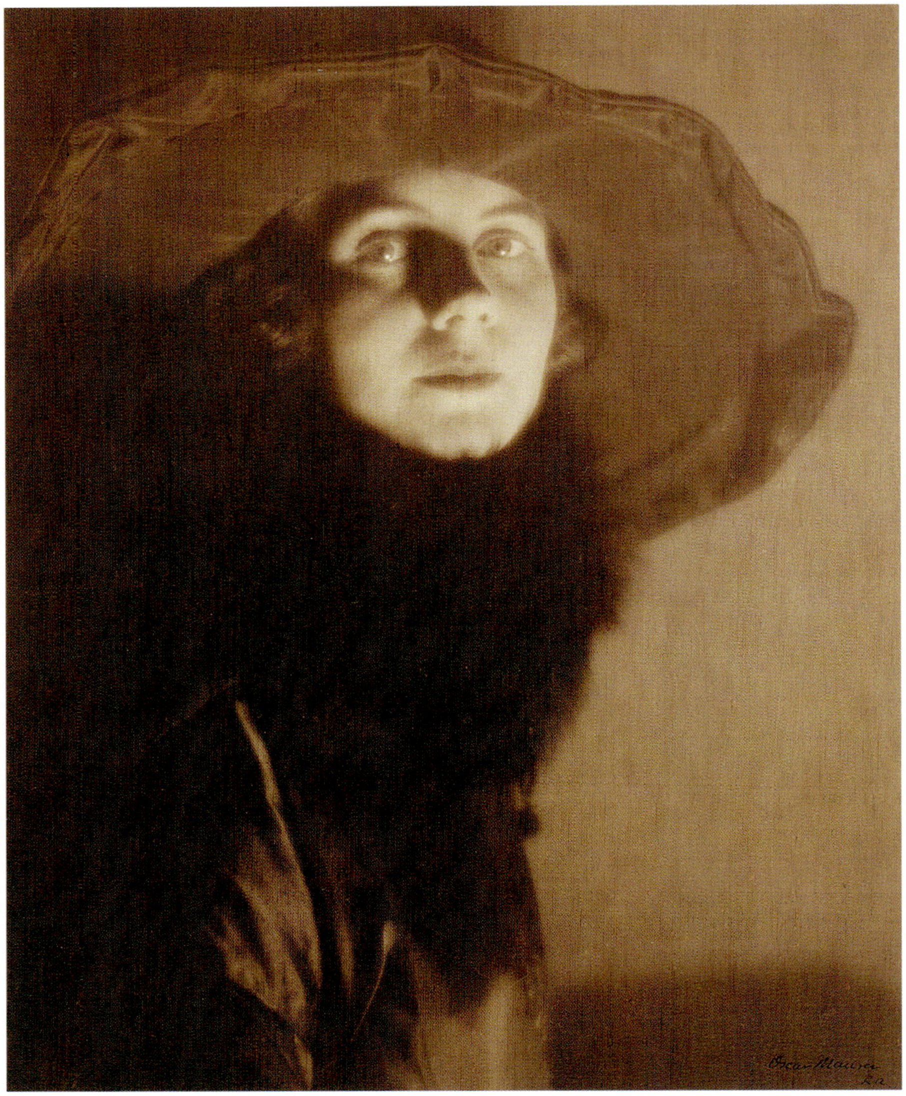

53.
OSCAR MAURER
Portrait of Mrs. Rollin Brown, c. 1918
Platinum print
13 9/16 x 10 3/4 in.
GIFT OF DAVID BOHN

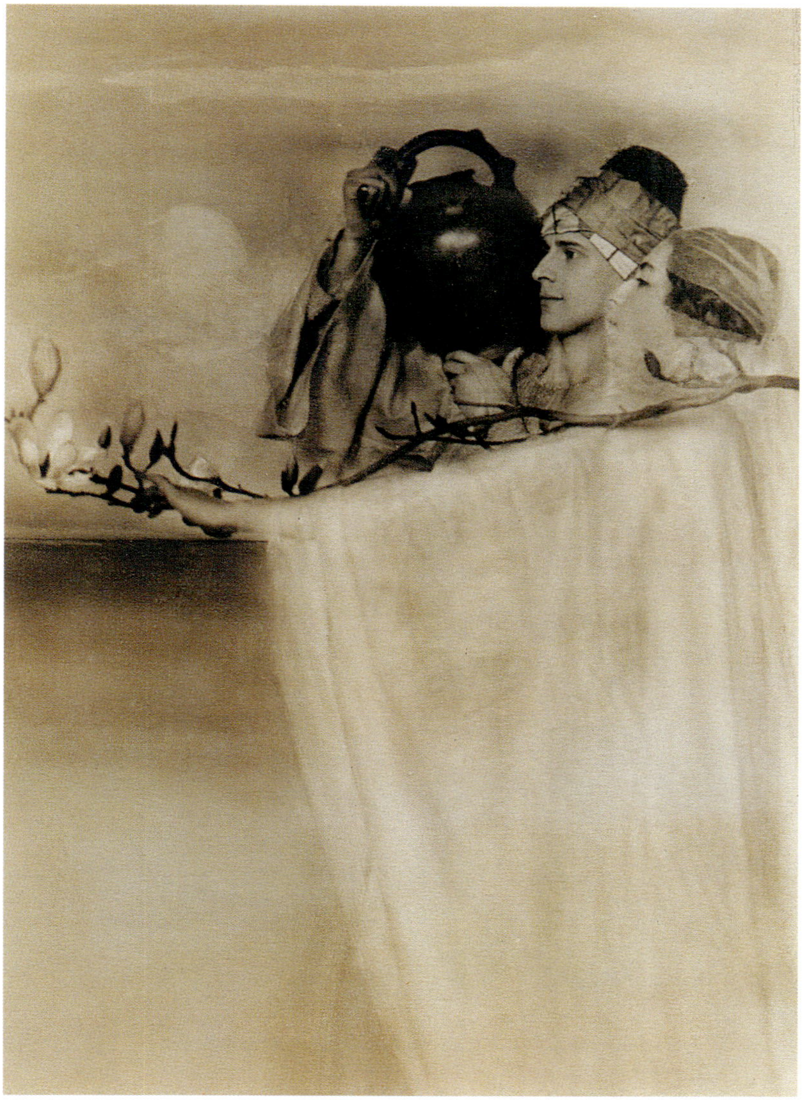

54.

ADELAIDE MARQUAND HANSCOM

Underneath the Bough (Illustration from *The Rubáiyát of Omar Khayyám),* 1905

Gelatin silver print

9½ x 6¾ in.

GIFT OF MR. AND MRS. WILLARD M. NOTT

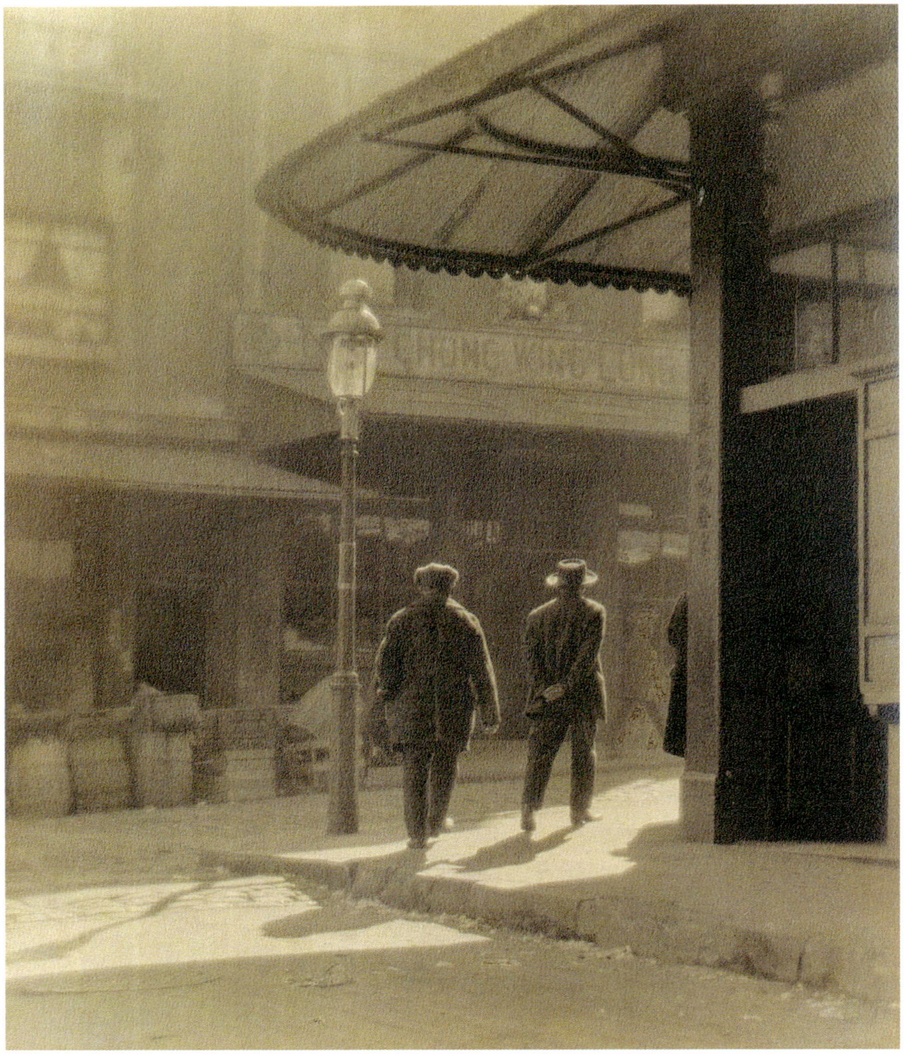

55.

P. DOUGLAS ANDERSON

A Corner in Chinatown, S.F., 1915

Gelatin silver print

11$\frac{3}{8}$ x 9$\frac{1}{2}$ in.

GIFT OF DR. ROBERT SHIMSHAK

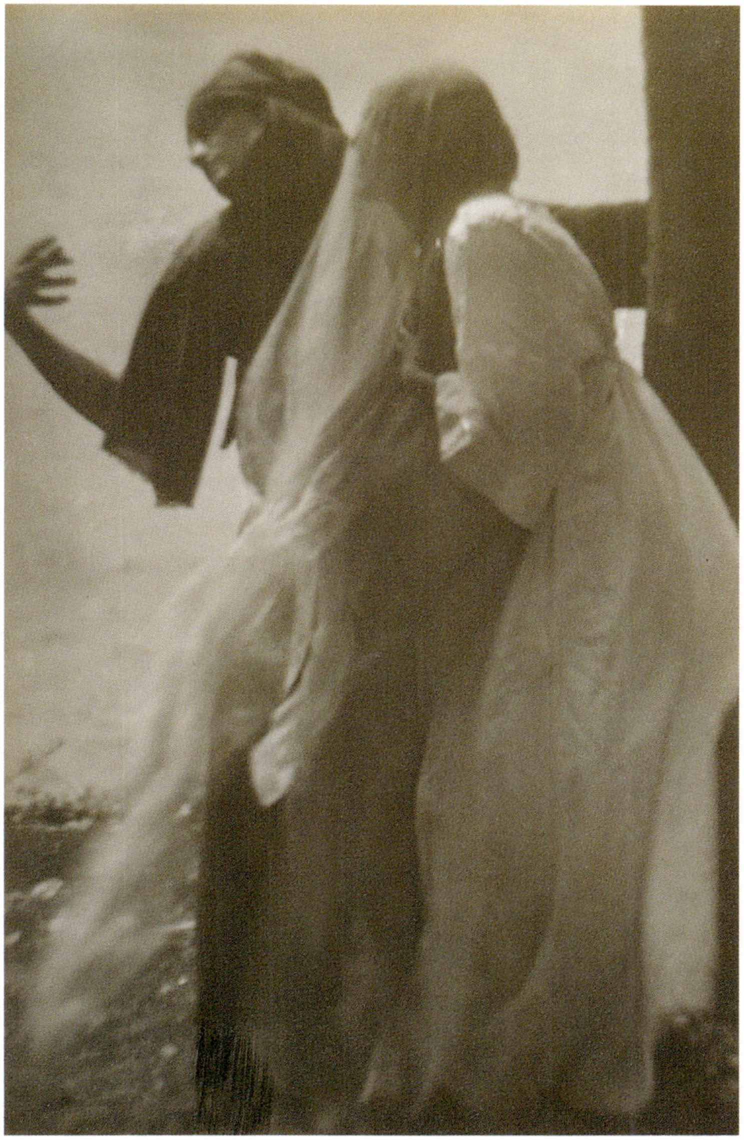

56.
IMOGEN CUNNINGHAM
The Clairvoyant, c. 1910
Platinum print
9¾ x 6 in.
GIFT OF DR. AND MRS. DUDLEY P. BELL

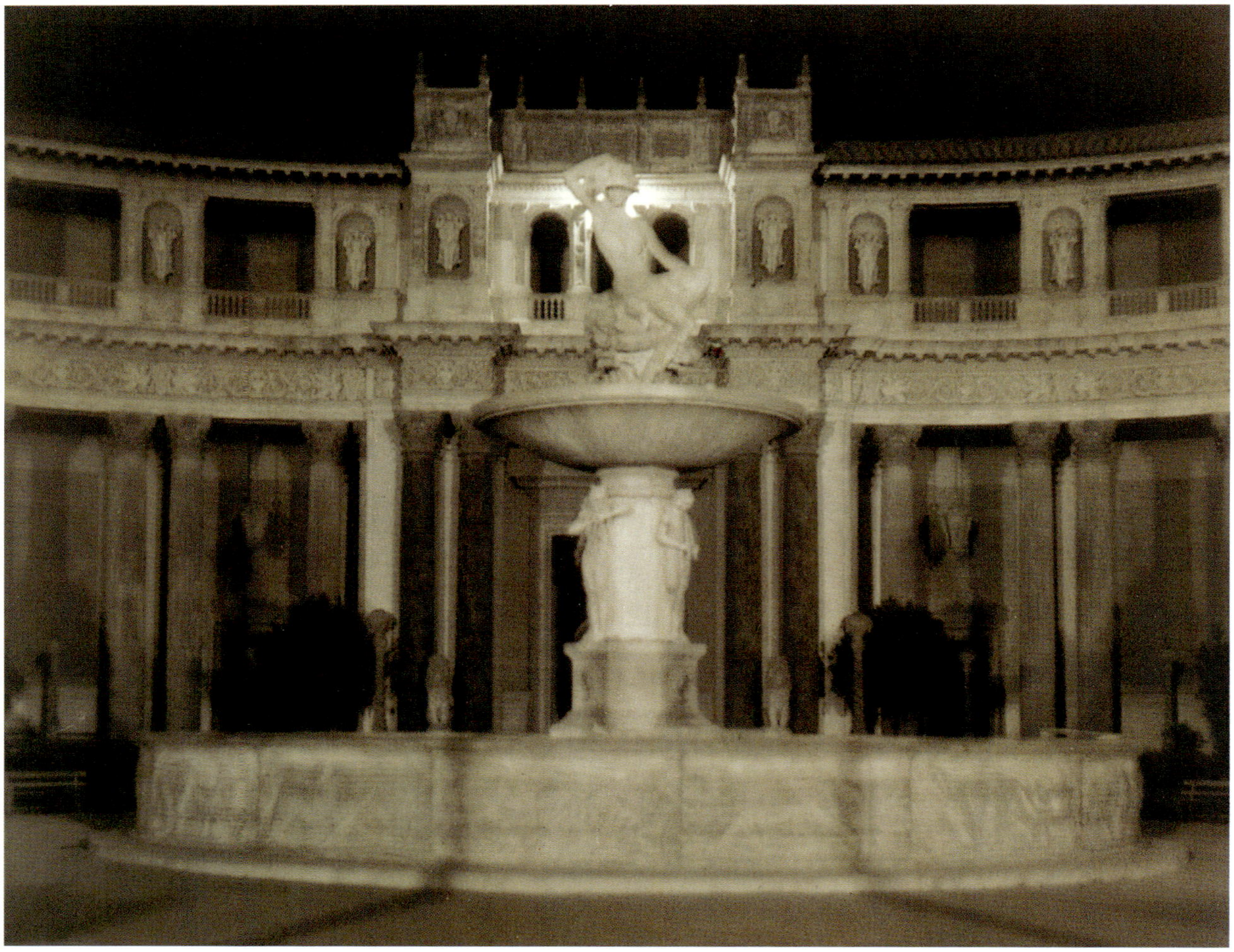

57.
FRANCIS BRUGUIÈRE
Beauty and Beast Fountain, Court of Flowers, 1915
Gelatin silver print
10⅝ x 13⅜ in.
GIFT OF ANONYMOUS DONOR

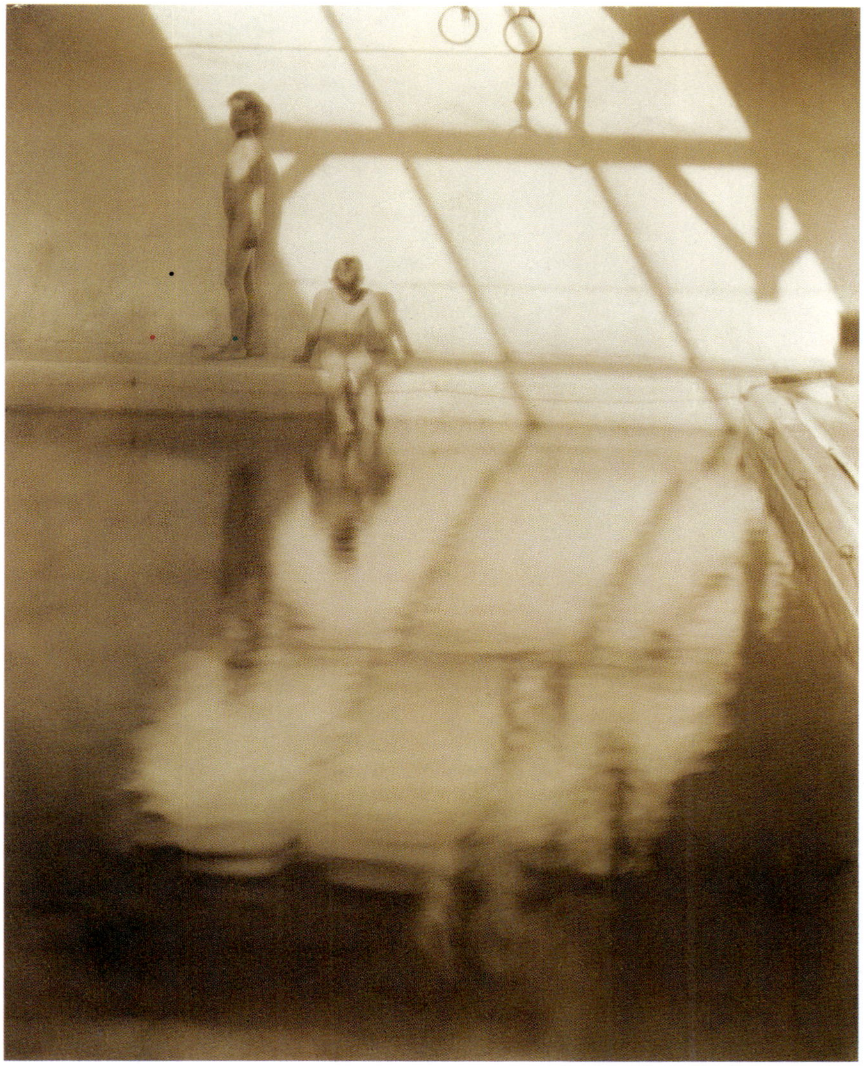

58.
EDWARD WESTON
Bathing Pool, 1919
Platinum print
9½ x 7½ in.
GIFT OF THE BELL FUND

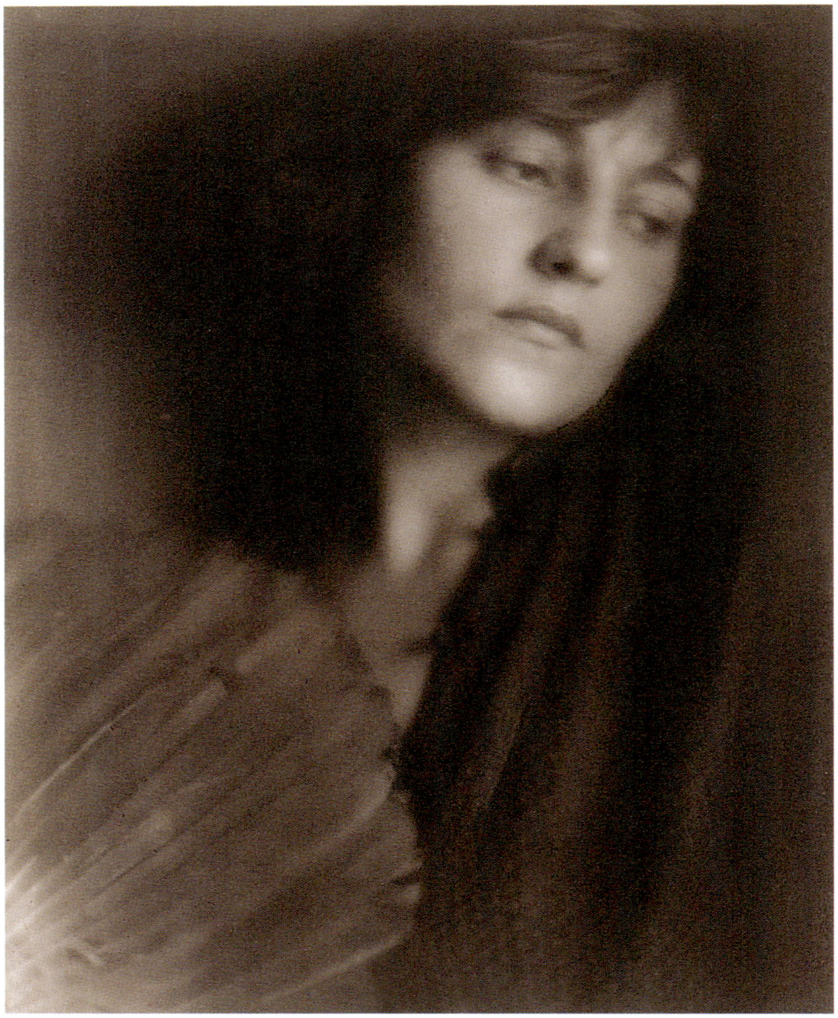

59.
MARGRETHE MATHER
Portrait of Florence Deshon, 1921
Platinum print
9½ x 7½ in.
GIFT OF DR. AND MRS. DUDLEY P. BELL

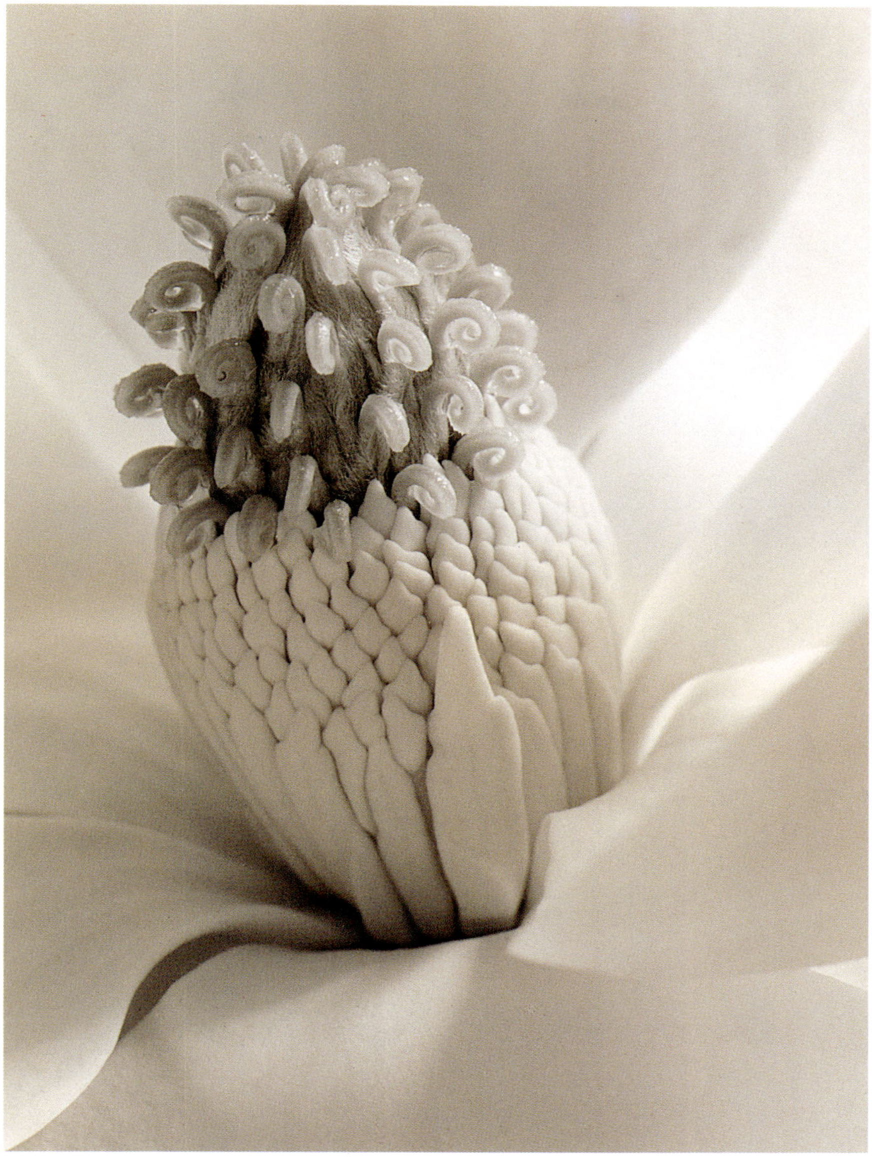

60.
IMOGEN CUNNINGHAM
Magnolia Blossom: Tower of Jewels, 1925
Platinum print
12½ x 9¼ in.
GIFT OF THE ART GUILD, OAKLAND MUSEUM ASSOCIATION

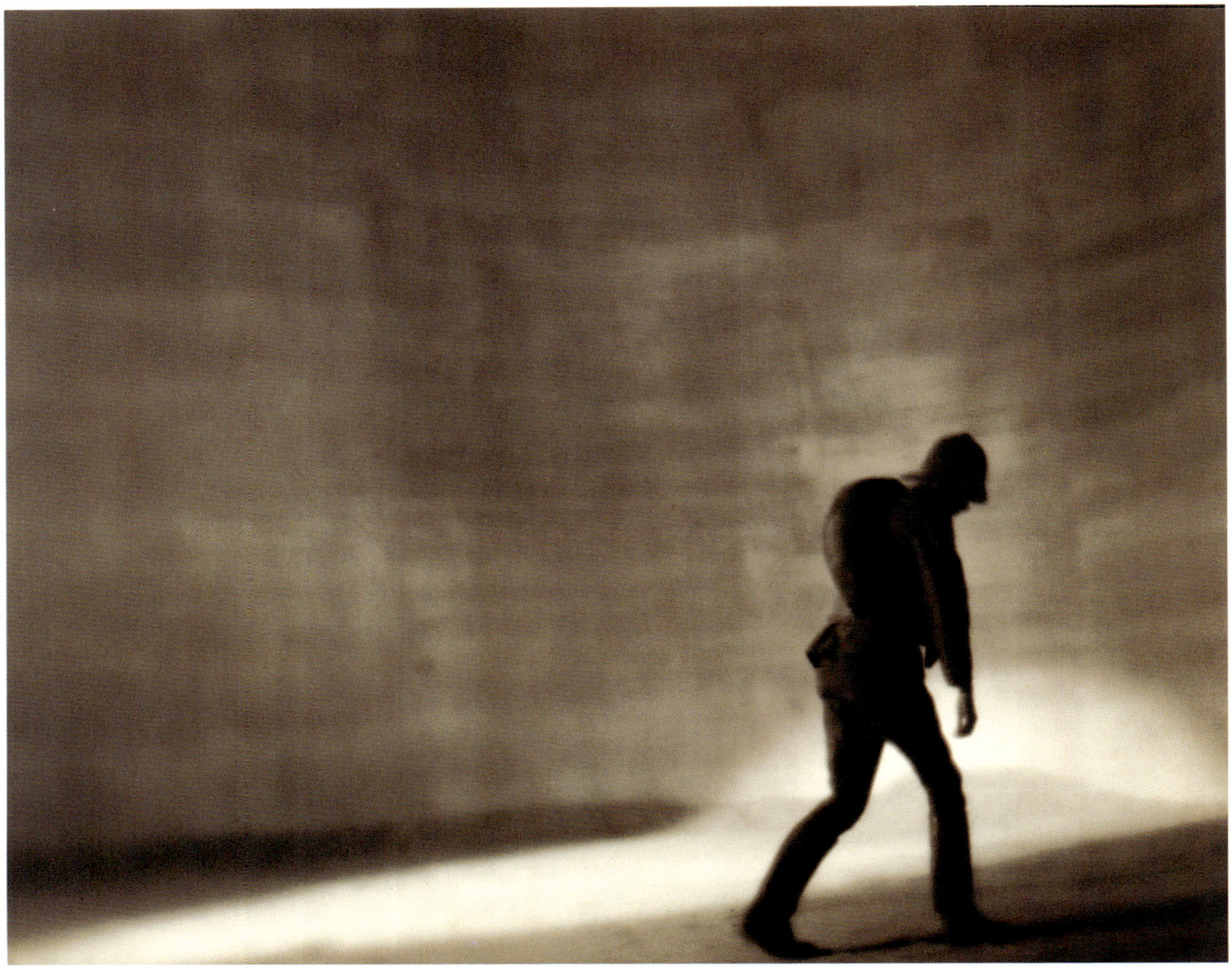

61.

JOHAN HAGEMEYER

"Boots" by Kipling (George Ball), 1924

Gelatin silver print

7⅞ x 9¾ in.

GIFT OF MRS. MABEL T. BJORGE IN MEMORY OF MRS. HORTON DENNY

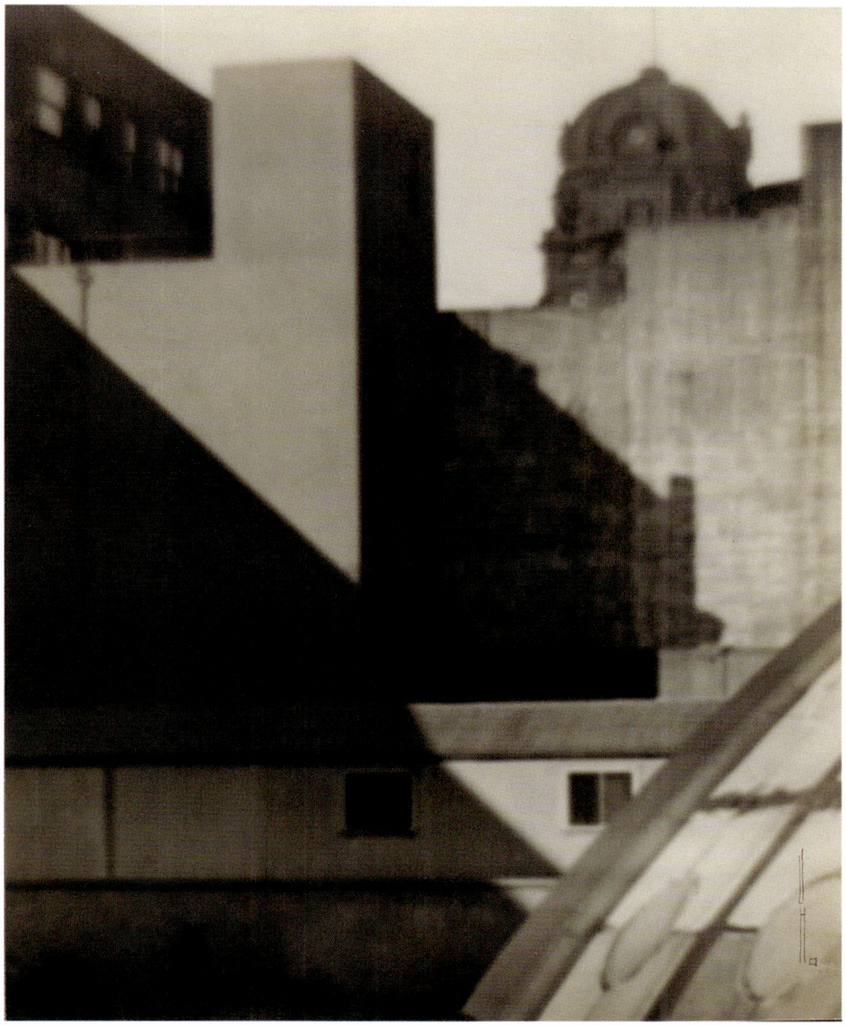

62.
JOHAN HAGEMEYER
Castles of To-day, 1922
Gelatin silver print
9¾ x 7⅞ in.
GIFT OF IMOGEN CUNNINGHAM

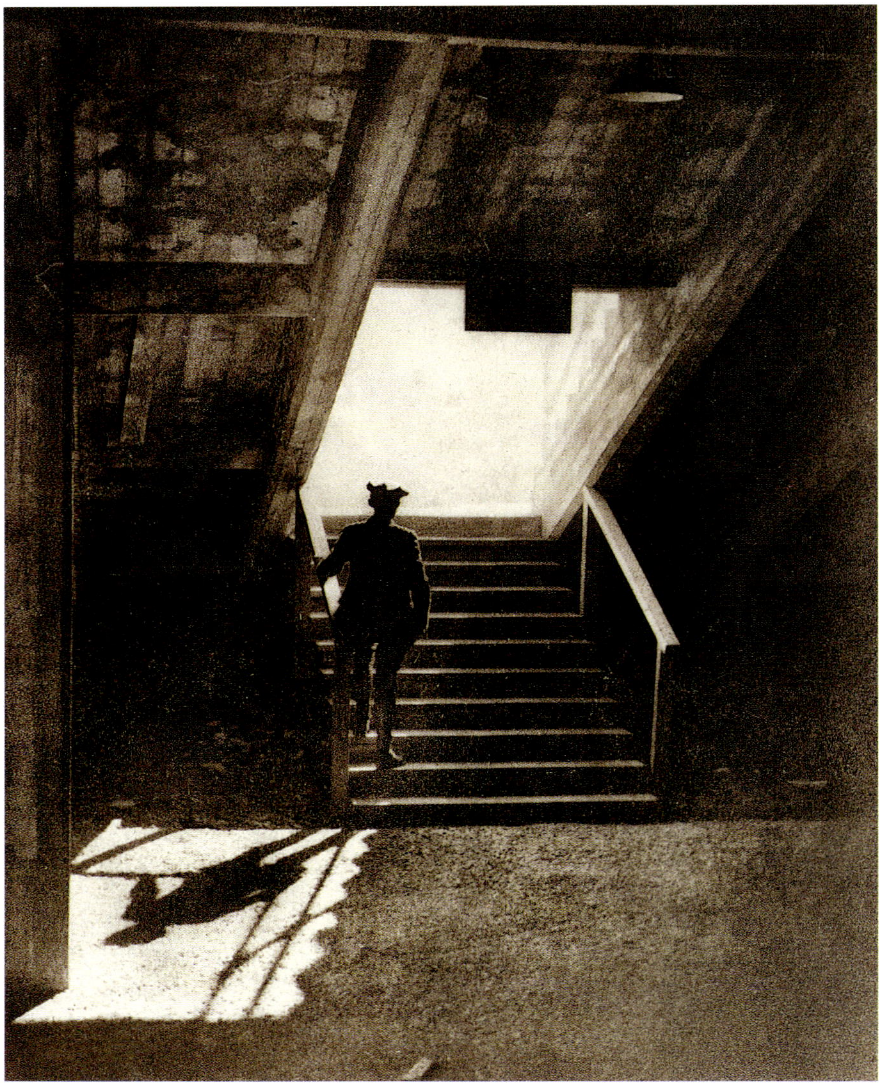

63.
HENRY A. HUSSEY
Up to the Sunshine, c. 1926
Bromoil print
9¾ x 8 in.
GIFT OF MRS. HENRY A. HUSSEY

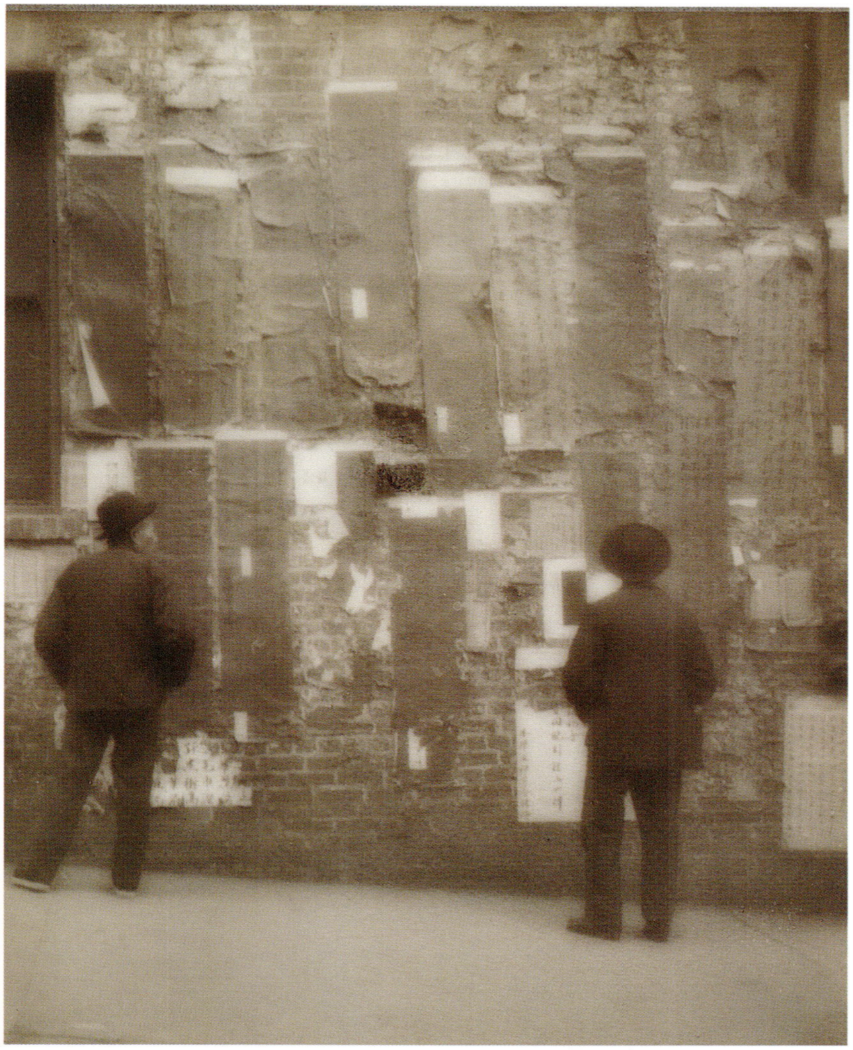

64.
HENRY A. HUSSEY
Signs of the Times, c. 1920
Gelatin silver print
$9\frac{11}{16}$ x $7\frac{7}{8}$ in.
GIFT OF MRS. HENRY A. HUSSEY

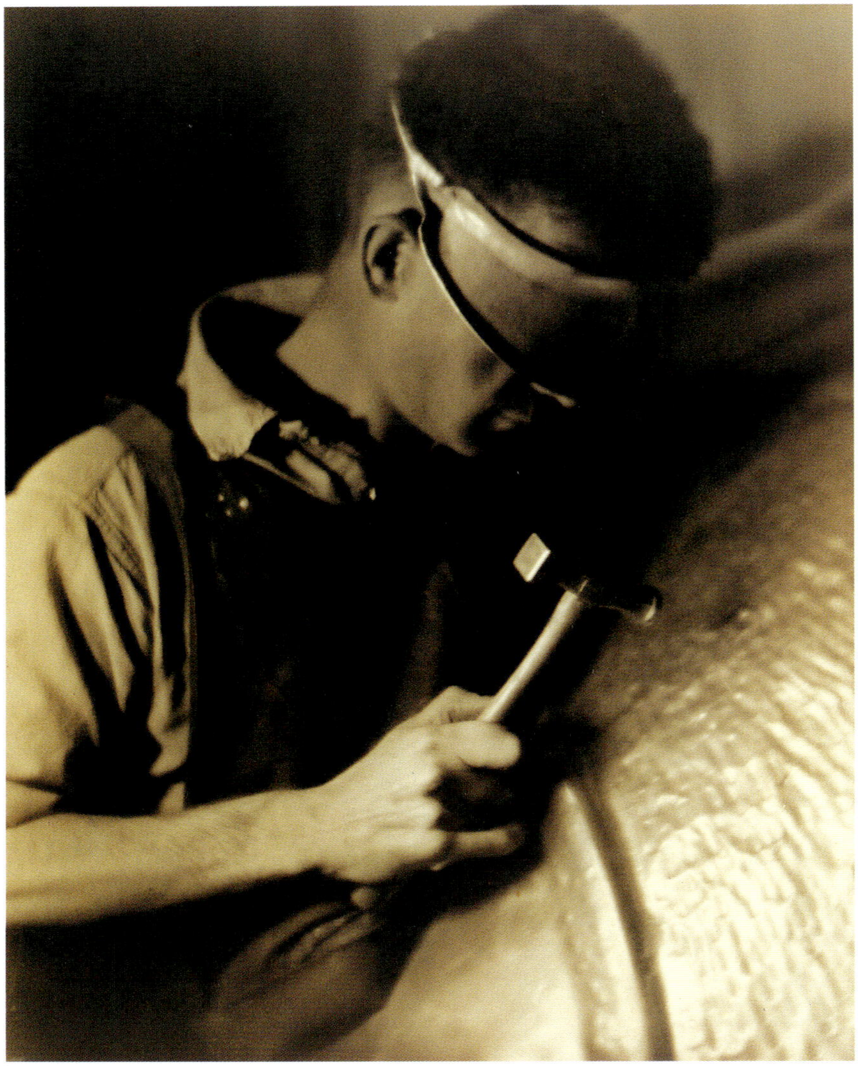

65.
DOROTHEA LANGE
Portrait of Harry St. John Dixon, 1922
Gelatin silver print
11¾ x 9¼ in.
GIFT OF FLORENCE DIXON

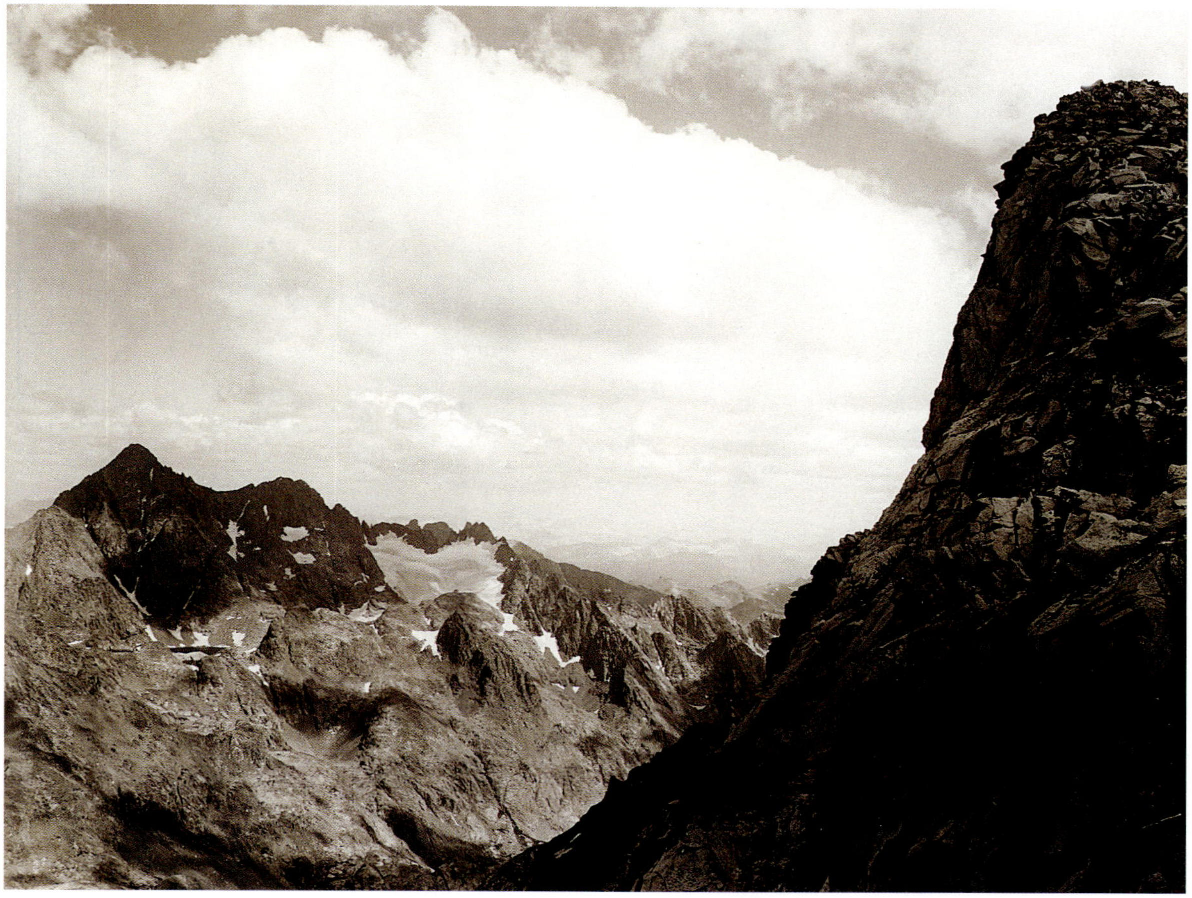

66.

ANSEL ADAMS

Mount Ritter from Electra Peak, Summer 1931

Gelatin silver print

7⅛ x 9¼ in.

GIFT OF MR. FRANCIS P. FARQUHAR

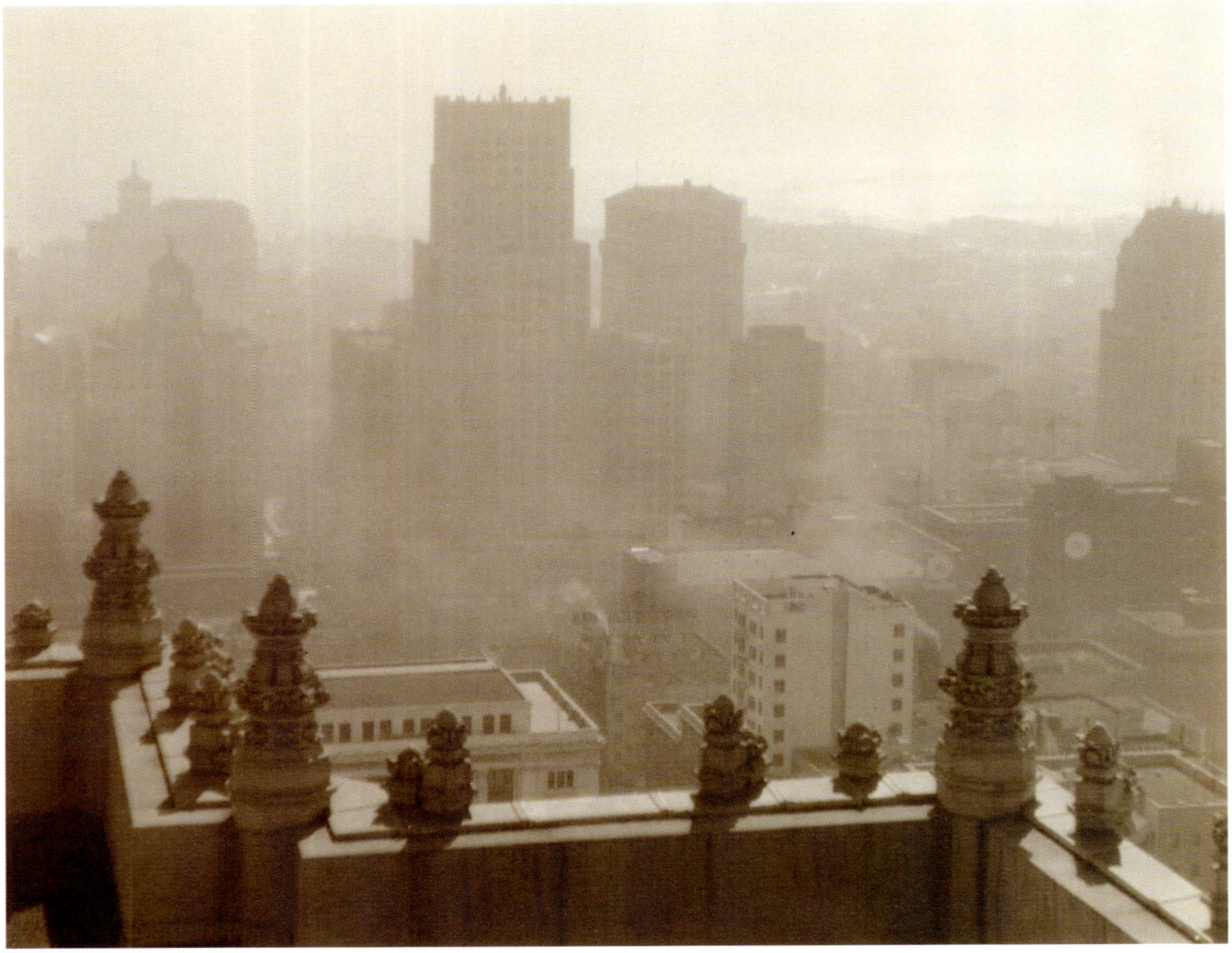

67.
WILLIAM E. DASSONVILLE
Downtown San Francisco from Mark Hopkins Hotel, n.d.
Platinum print
8 x 10 in.
GIFT OF MRS. ALMA LAVENSON WAHRHAFTIG

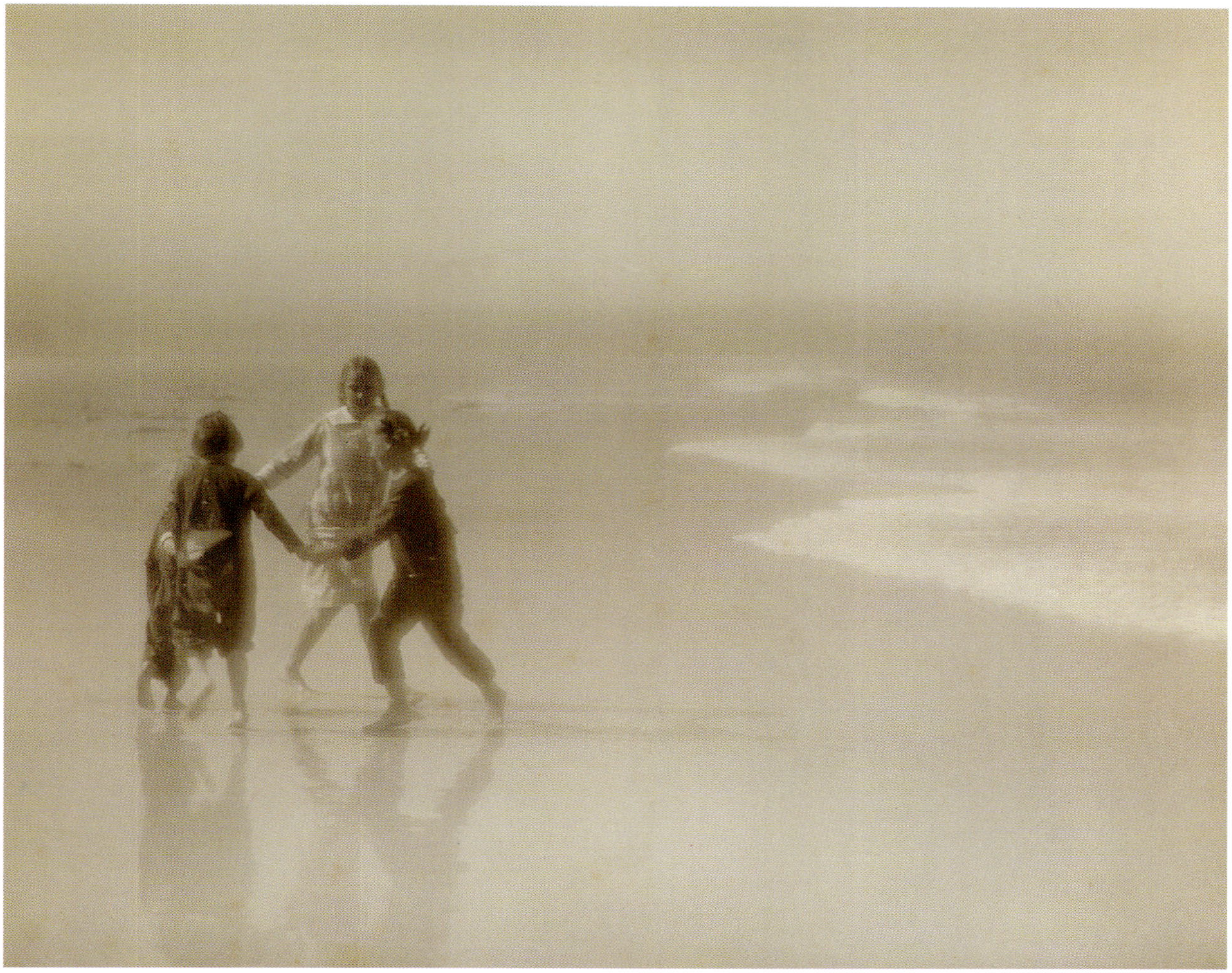

68.
JOHN PAUL EDWARDS
On the Beach at Carmel, 1924
Gelatin silver print
9 9/16 x 11 9/16 in.
GIFT OF MRS. JOHN PAUL EDWARDS

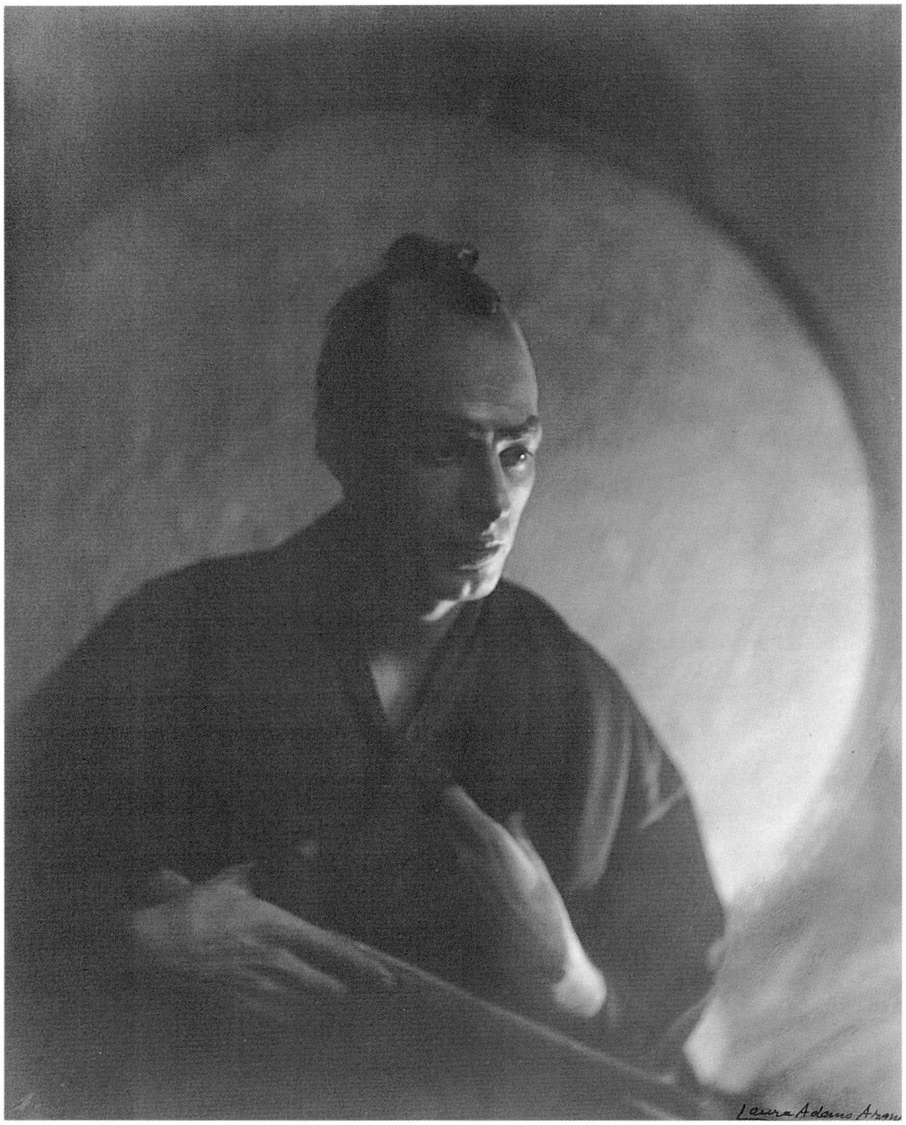

69.
LAURA ADAMS ARMER
Irving Pichel as Lord Kurano, February 1923
Gelatin silver print
$13\frac{3}{16}$ x $10\frac{1}{4}$ in.
GIFT OF MRS. HENRY A. HUSSEY

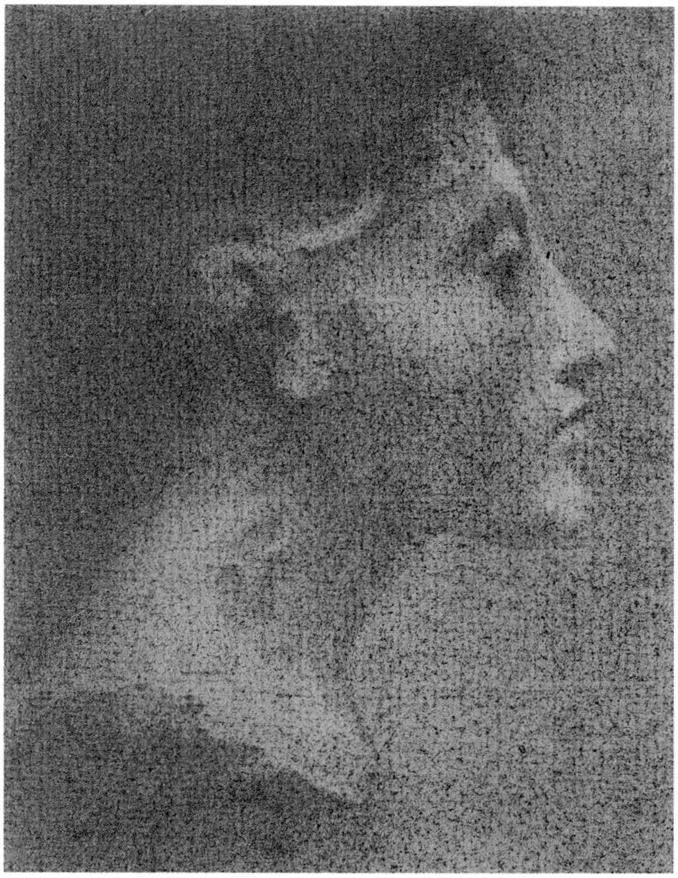

70.
ALICE BURR
Untitled (Portrait Bust of Nefertiti), n.d.
Bromoil print
10½ x 7¼ in.
GIFT OF MR. AND MRS. ANTHONY R. WHITE

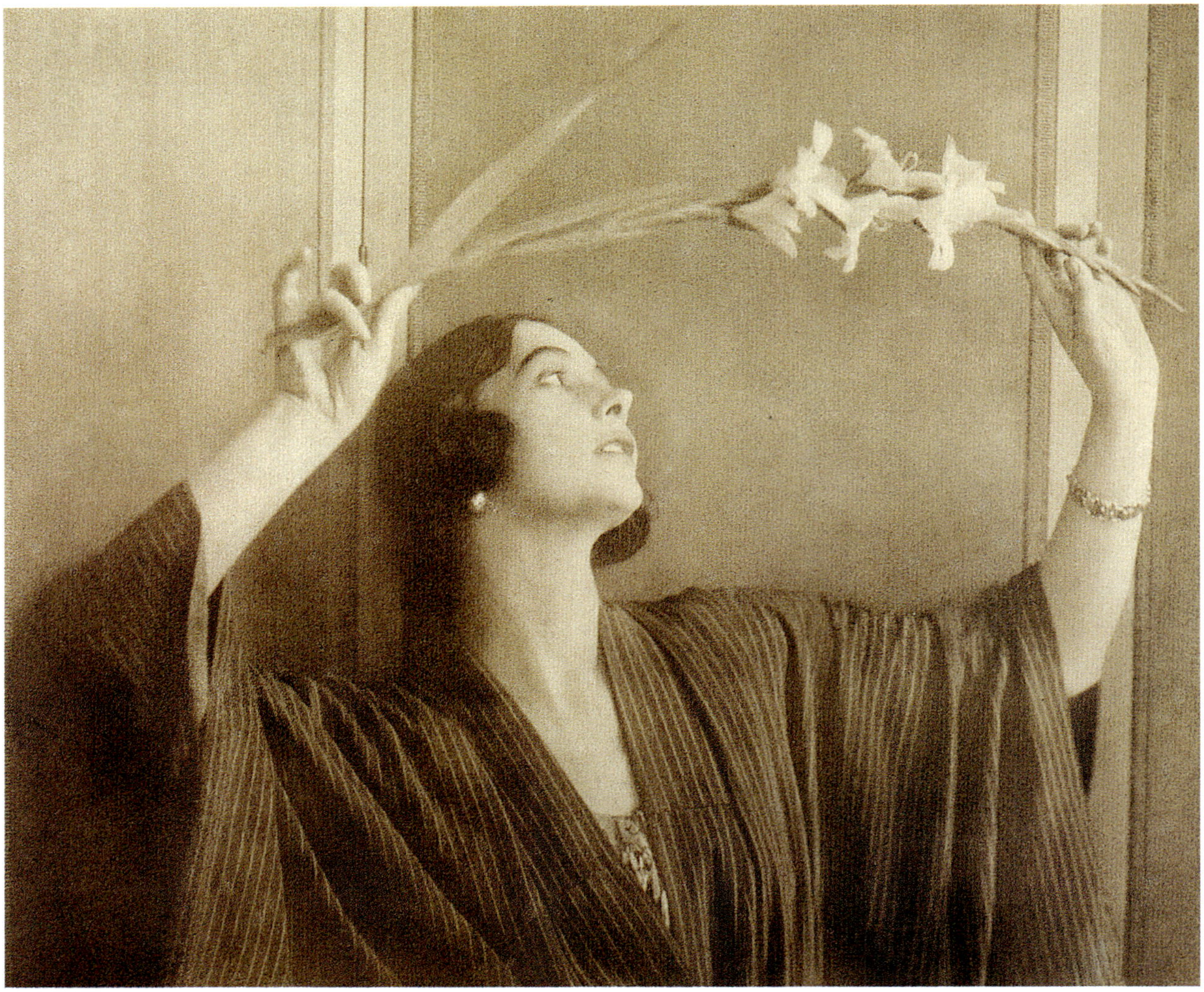

71.
ARTHUR F. KALES
Easter Blossom, c. 1920
Bromoil transfer print
10¾ x 13¼ in.
THE SHIRLEY BURDEN FUND FOR PHOTOGRAPHY

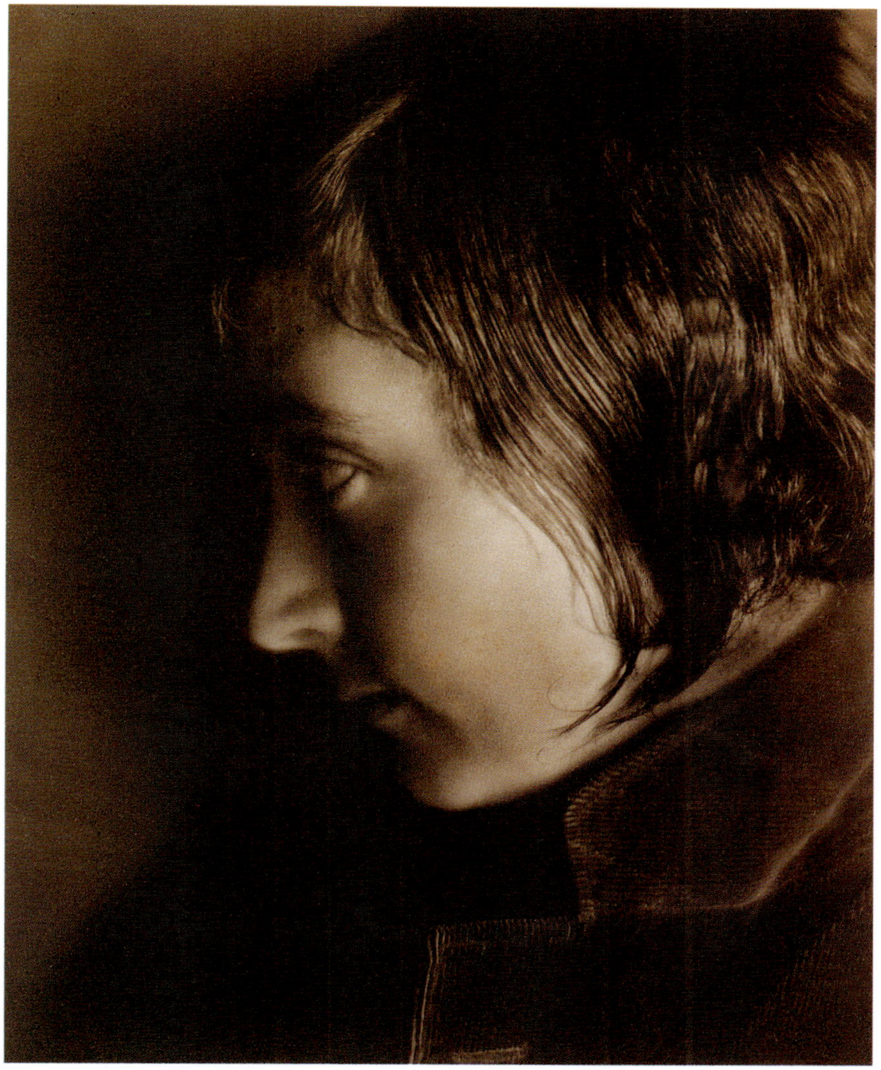

72.
EDWARD WESTON
Portrait of Jo, Glendale, 1922
Platinum print
9½ x 7½ in.
THE OAKLAND MUSEUM FOUNDERS' FUND

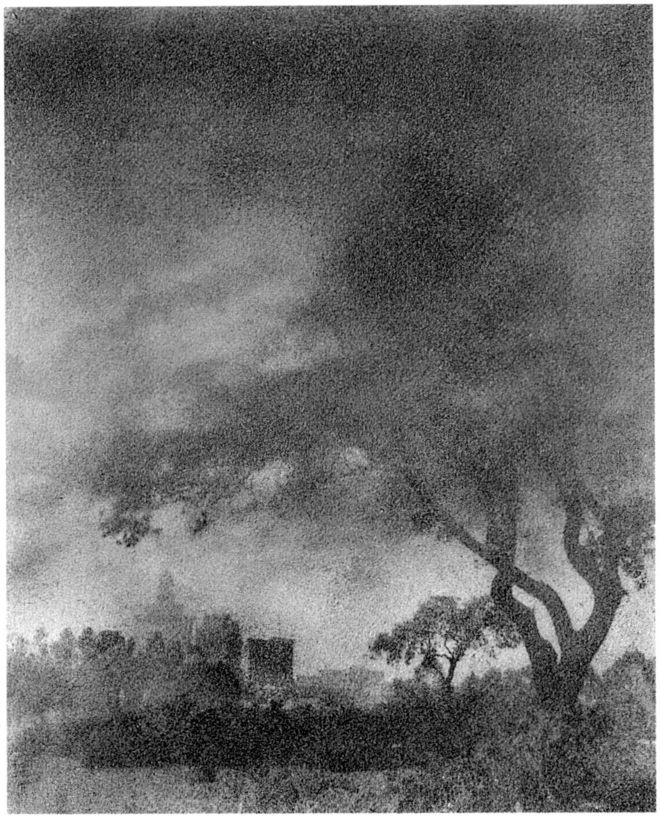

73.

SIGISMUND BLUMANN

Dawn, Sunset, Moonlight (Experiments in Contrast),

1925–1926

Bromoil prints

Each 6¾ x 8⅝ in.

GIFT OF TOM AND NANCY HIGH

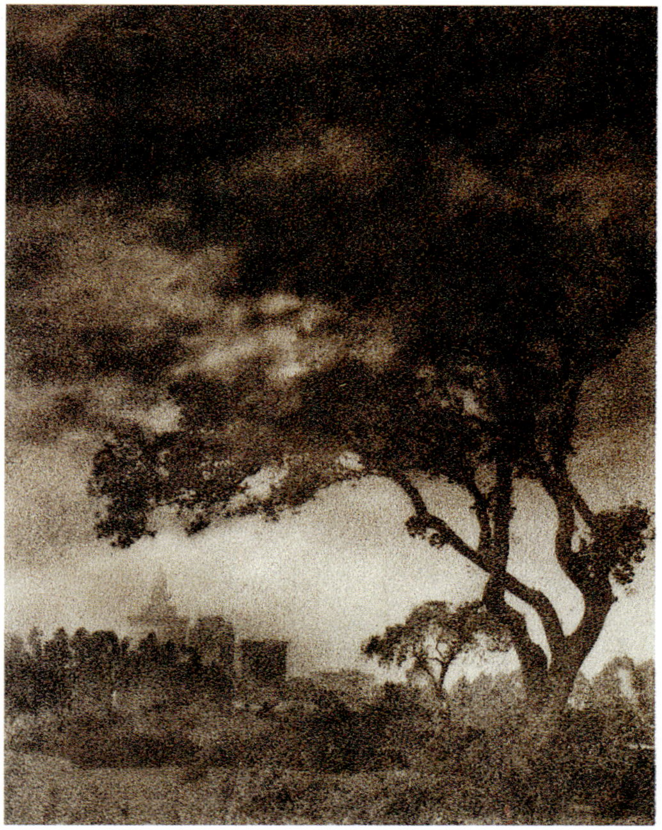

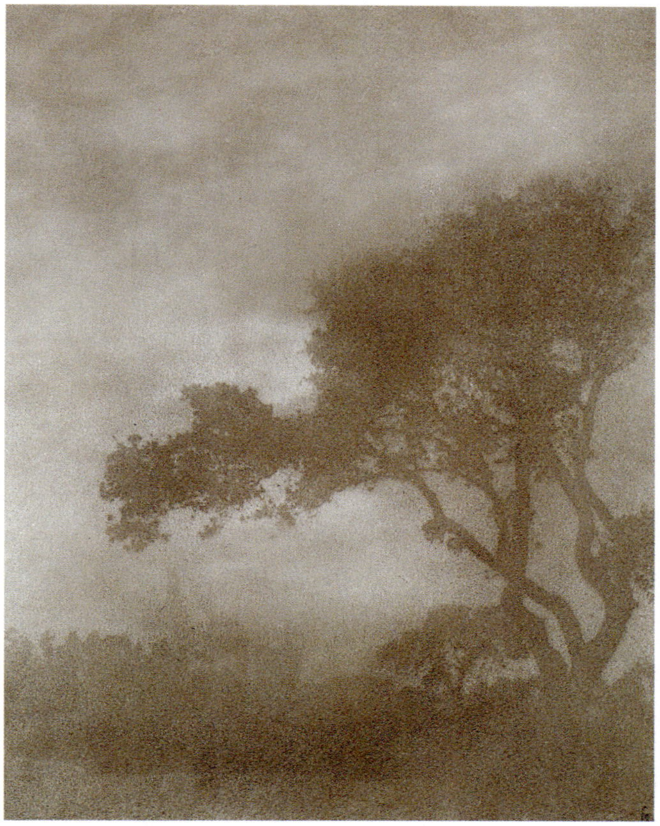

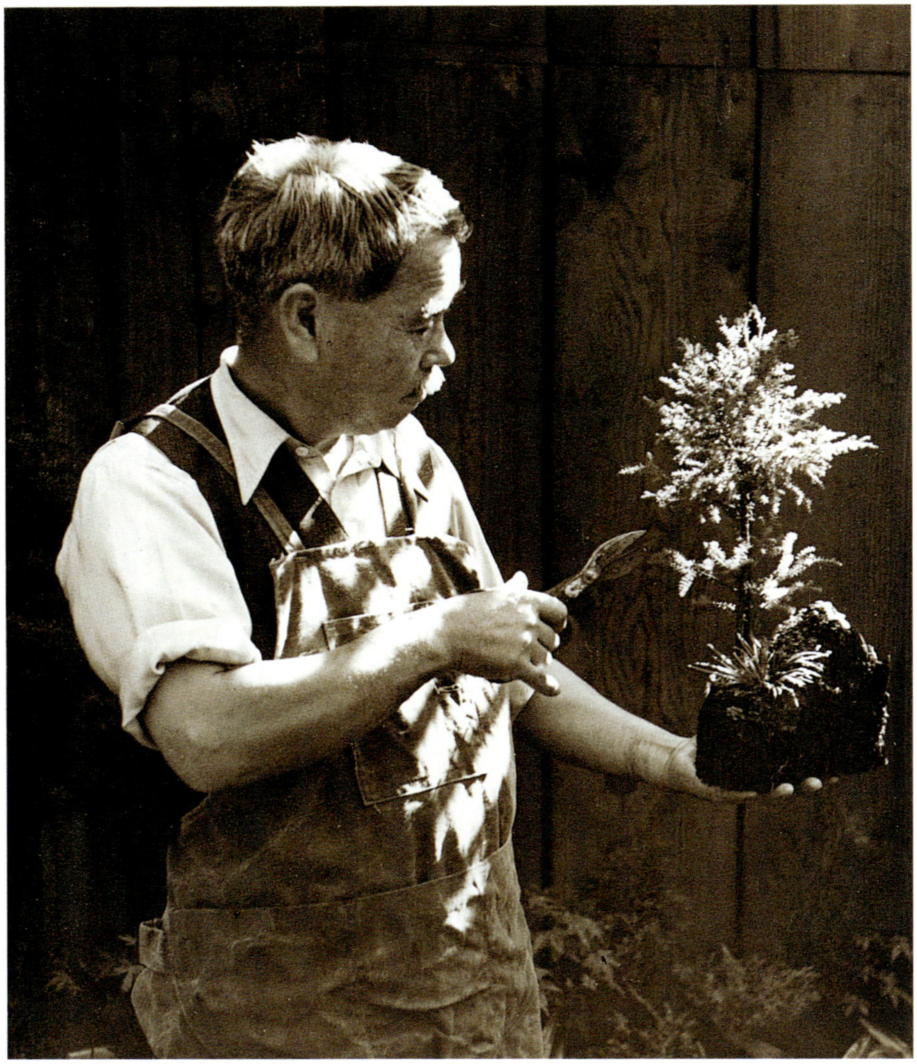

74.

HENRY M. TAKAHASHI

Spare Time, 1936

Bromide print

9½ x 7 13/16 in.

GIFT OF THE TAKAHASHI FAMILY OF BERKELEY

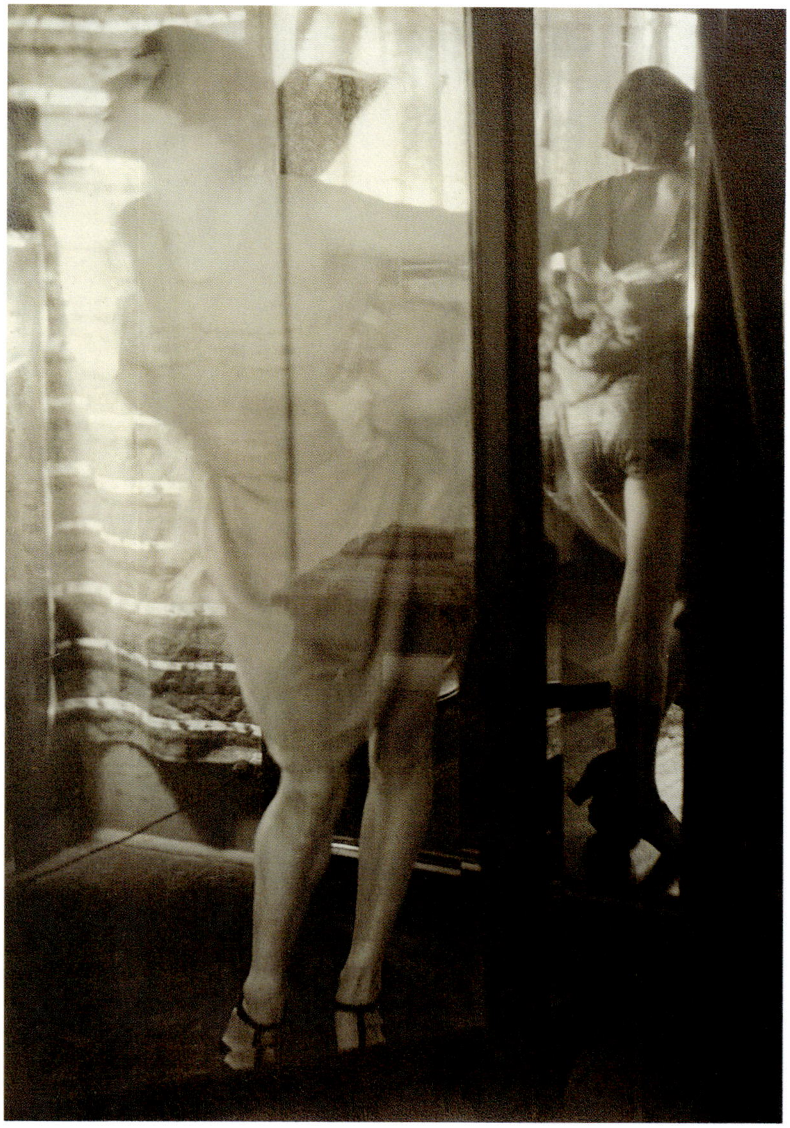

75.
ROGER STURTEVANT
Ectoplasm of the Charleston, c. 1925
Toned gelatin silver print
9½ x 6½ in.
GIFT OF THE ARTIST

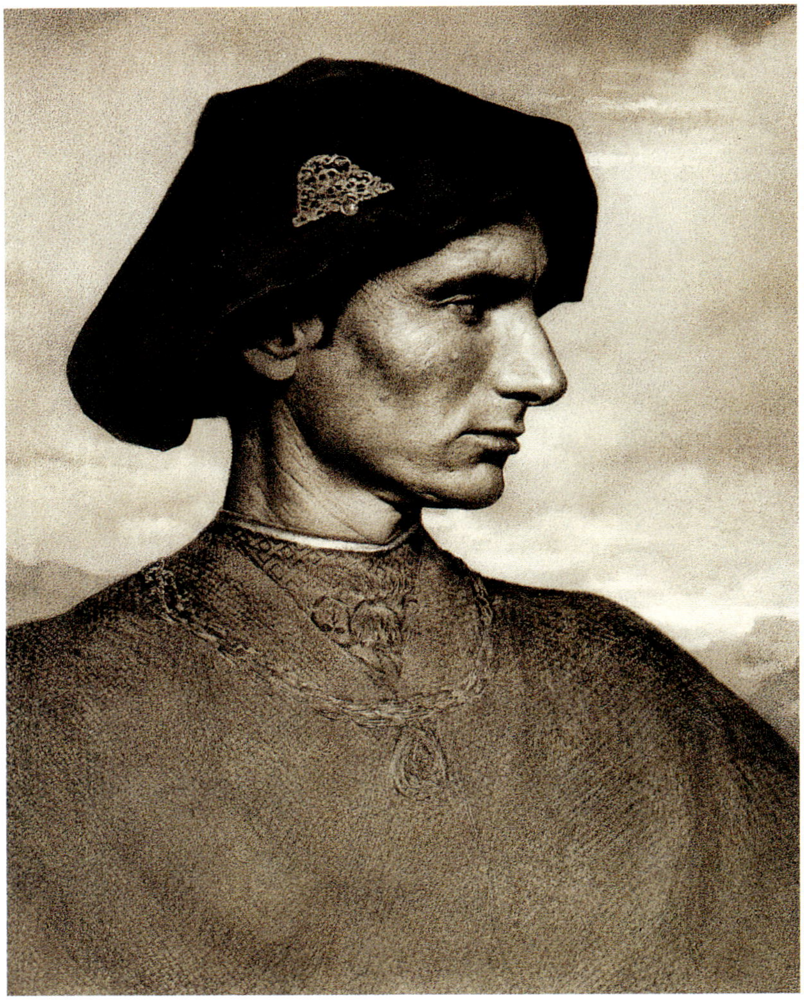

76.
WILLIAM MORTENSEN
Marco Polo, n.d.
Gelatin silver print
13½ x 10¹¹⁄₁₆ in.
THE OAKLAND MUSEUM FOUNDERS' FUND

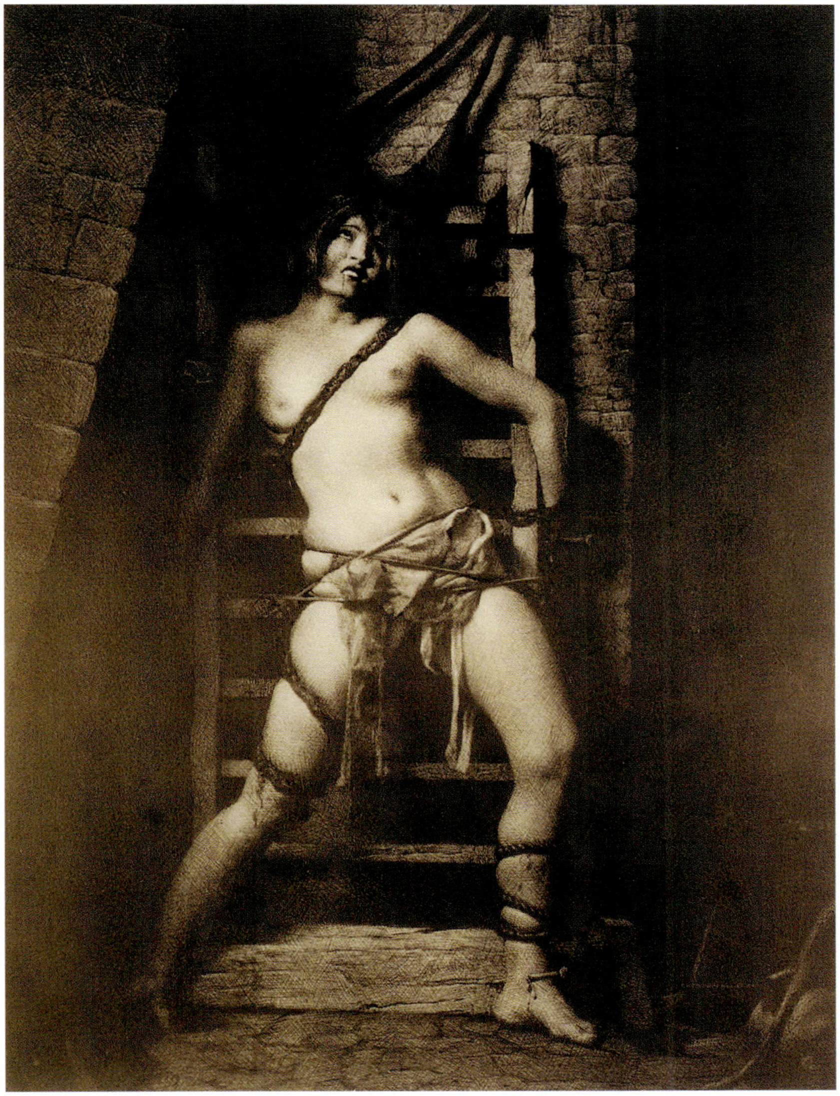

77.
WILLIAM MORTENSEN
The Spider Torture (The Heretic), c. 1934
Bromoil print
7⅝ x 5⅝ in.
GIFT OF MR. WILLARD M. NOTT

1925 – 1945

PORTFOLIO III

Seeing Straight

Starting from Pictorialism

Notable Continuities in the Modernization of California Photography

SALLY STEIN

WEIGHING THE EFFECTS of continuity and change is the fundamental task of history. Change is a hallmark of modernity, so it stands to reason that historians of the modern period are predisposed to emphasize rupture, sweeping transformations and paradigm shifts. But precisely because it has become habitual to put the stress on change, it is useful to walk the other side of the street and downplay the conventional signposts of decade markers and freshly-minted labels for artistic moves and movements.

In the case of the alleged break by modernist photographers with the pre-World War I fashion for pictorialist imagery, a new trend of scholarship fosters more serious interest in the persistence of older pictorial practices by photographers long ignored in the canonical histories. And indeed California is an apt region to explore the many decades of photography with an allegorical sensibility and soft-focus style of rendering, for Pictorialism continued to be practiced and defended arguably longer on the West Coast than elsewhere in America.[1] While that revisionist strategy contributes to a more multi-faceted picture of photography's diverse practices, sometimes coexisting and sometimes locked in battle, it leaves unchallenged the claims of the canon as the site of unequivocal invention. This essay aims to qualify those canonical assumptions by reconsidering the pictorialist residue in much twentieth century California photography that previously has been hailed as resolutely innovative.

One of the most telling visual artifacts to underscore some key differences between the West Coast and East Coast transition from Pictorialism to Modernism happens to be a photograph made in Oakland, California, between the late teens and the early twenties. The picture is not signed though it is definitively titled, *Anne of the Crooked Halo* (figure 1). Judged by any formal criteria, it's not much of a picture: slightly off-kilter, though not radically so, it records a group of robed figures assuming various melodramatic poses of supplication around a single woman whose head is framed by the eponymous crooked disk that must have been scissored out of cardboard just before the picture was taken. The lighting is so poorly orchestrated that initially I had trouble just finding all nine figures noted in the caption accompanying one recent publication of this photograph.[2] In terms of technique, it hardly meets the standards of any of the photographers identified as actors in this latter-day tableau vivant: Imogen Cunningham, Edward Weston, Johan Hagemeyer, Roger Sturtevant, Dorothea Lange, as well as the central figure of Anne Brigman. It seems safe to conclude that this was a spontaneous party picture, very casually created in communal fashion, and accept it as nothing

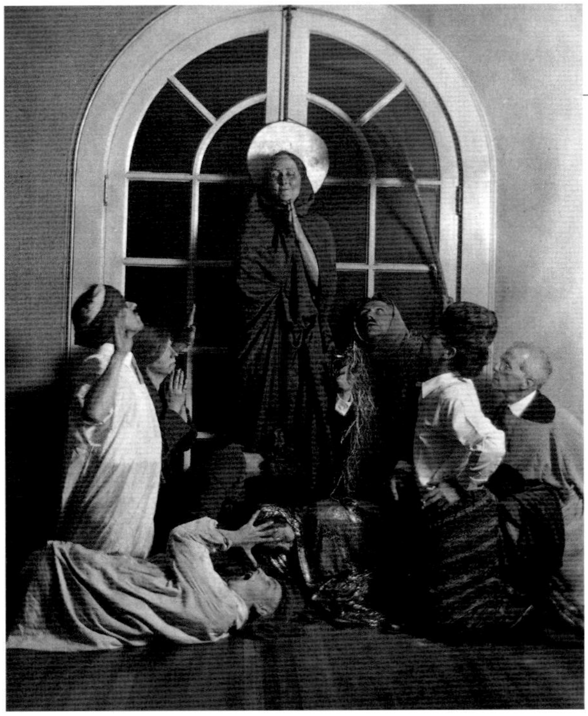

FIGURE 1.
Unknown (possibly Roi Partridge)
St. Anne of the Crooked Halo, 1925
Gelatin silver print, toned, 9 5/8 x 7 5/8 in.
THE J. PAUL GETTY MUSEUM

more than that. Even so, when I first saw it I was inclined to judge it a poor example of that snapshot genre. The party pictures that most appeal to me tend to the raucous (no doubt reflecting my own cultivated preference for modernist rule-breaking), whereas this stages a full-dress reenactment of the old reverent pictorialist formulas.

Of course, there is a considerable measure of irony in that rehearsal but, notwithstanding my feminist commitments, it took me some time to appreciate the more radical aspects of this pictorialist enactment. This after all is no standard homage to the Great Artist. Though hagiographic, the picture's honored central figure is a woman. At the risk of anachronism, we would do better to substitute the contemporary term of "femmage." But recategorizing it thus makes it far more anomalous for the early twentieth century, especially as the assembled cast of adoring figures was composed equally of men and women. Just as extraordinary, at a time in the post-World War I era when on the East Coast all young self-respecting artists were flagrantly turning their backs on the sentimental traditions of the pre-War period,[3] these figures were, at least for a moment, paying full allegiance to it.

There are numerous ways to interpret this document. We could conclude that the West Coast was such a cultural backwater that none of the characters was even aware that a full-fledged rebellion in the arts was taking place that made it *de rigueur* to reject all the old tenets of painterly art photography. Of course, some among this group exhibited little interest in new developments in art. Brigman, for one, followed her own path. Among the younger figures, Dorothea Lange at this time was hardly setting trends, for her early photography was largely confined to commercial portraiture in the still-reigning bourgeois style of soft-focus flattery. Even Johan Hagemeyer exhibited little interest in modernist experimentation, despite his extensive travels, personal contact with Alfred Stieglitz, and sustained study of the progress of self-conscious art photography as promoted in the pages of Stieglitz's *Camera Work.* But the same cannot be said of Edward Weston, Imogen Cunningham and Roger Sturtevant. By the early 1920s, all three were individually exploring ways to extend their practice of photography with results sufficiently distinctive that by the end of the 1920s each was exhibiting work in Germany alongside the leading photographic Modernists of Europe.[4] But unlike ambitious photographers on the East Coast, they felt no need to sever all ties with their local forerunners.

Perhaps because of their gender or because of their rarity, foremothers as a rule have not assumed positions of overriding authority that foster rebellion. Certainly Anne Brigman was no typical leader of old-school Pictorialism. Although many women quickly joined the ranks of photographers at the end of the nineteenth century as portable hand cameras became widely available, Brigman pursued photography and life with uncommon abandon. When her passion for photography seemed to get in the way of her marriage, she had few qualms about deciding the marriage had to end. She likewise flouted convention in the way she depicted herself and female friends shedding clothes and inhibitions in nature. To be sure, her use of unsharp lenses and extravagant handwork in printing afforded a protective veil against charges of obscenity. Even with that veil, these pictures manifestly contravened the standards of academic nudes: the naked women in her pictures, though posed, were quite evidently roughing it and relishing it.[5] It's a moot point whether a male Pictorialist could have produced comparable work; in actuality, though many male Pictorialists used naked female models, no male photographer working in the pictorialist idiom produced work that suggests a dynamic synthesis rather than a pat, patronizing equation between women and nature. Nature in Brigman's work was less a space of retreat than an allegorical setting in which to promote the idea that women would do best to turn their backs on most man-made laws.

No wonder, then, that in the early 1920s some of the pioneers of photographic Modernism on the West Coast would rise to the occasion while gathered at Anne Brigman's studio and flamboyantly pay their respects without feeling compromised. Anne of the crooked halo and of equally self-fashioned photography remained their local patron saint, and in other more material ways she figured as enabling patron to the next generation of artistically-committed West Coast photographers. At the end of the twenties, when she decided to move to Southern California, her studio at 683 Brockhurst Street was rented by Willard Van Dyke, who made it the central meeting place for photographers. Van Dyke recalled that when the barn was modestly refurbished to serve as a gallery space for western photographers, the first exhibition was devoted to work by one member of the supporting cast in the *Crooked Halo*: Edward Weston. According to Van Dyke, it was a retrospective, "displayed in chronological order . . . from 1903 when he began . . . to his most recent photographs."[6] This, too, suggests the local commitment to the principle of continuity, even in the early 1930s, when the spirit of innovative Modernism had provoked photographers to issue proclamations under the banner of a new photographic alliance: Group f.64.

If one seeks markers of change, the founding of Group f.64 in 1932 fills the bill perfectly and the small band of Bay Area photographers even went to the extreme of issuing a "manifesto" to accompany their first exhibition. The very name alluded crisply to the principle of precision, while referring literally to the smallest aperture opening on a view camera lens that permitted maximum sharpness. Stopping down the lens requires proportionally longer exposures. Stopping all the way down to f.64 (somewhat counter-intuitively, the higher the number, the smaller the aperture) effectively precluded the possibility of photographing with natural light anything in rapid motion. Accordingly, "f.64" stood for rigorous choices, using the camera only for what it did best: renderings in extremely sharp detail of subjects that ideally facilitated such close inspection by remaining still. It is no wonder that however dramatic as a rallying cry, Group f.64's conception of serious photography was too narrow to remain self-sustaining for more than a few years. The theory of pure photography in this case followed practice, and it would soon be tested anew by quite different approaches to photography inspired by the rapidly changing world of the Depression.[7]

Thus the emergence of f.64 was as much a summation as a proclamation, for the call for pure photography was sounded after a decade of slow and steady exploration by West Coast photographers to establish a new contemporary direction. Compared to the development of modernist, objective photography in post–World War I Europe or the East Coast, abstraction would develop along the axis of stylistically sharp studies of women and natural forms, with industry and the machine-made object figuring only slightly.[8] Of course, California photographers were aware that industry was a major preoccupation of self-styled Modernists in other metropolitan centers. Weston even made a composition of industrial smokestacks as early as 1922, while making a stop at his sister's in Ohio before travelling on to New York to visit Alfred Stieglitz (figure 2). The exterior view of Armco Steel was one of Weston's pictures that most impressed Stieglitz, who noted that he would have published it were he still editing *Camera Work*. Quite possibly it was made with Stieglitz in mind, for it updates Stieglitz's prior exploration of turn-of-the-century industrial spaces, notably *The Hand of Man,* his 1902 view of the converging tracks of a railroad yard. Like that tonalist study, Weston's image confronts industry while including steam and mist, though no poetic title, to soften the encounter. To be sure, the 1922 picture is more hard-edged, but the composition cleverly pushes the weighty horizontal pipes to the upper foreground, creating an archway through which can be seen the towering metal stacks lined up diagonally in the middle ground. Even Stieglitz noted that Weston did not cross that threshold to confront at closer range the industrial forms. A few years later, while working in Mexico, Weston once again engaged briefly with a few industrial motifs. One blindingly bright factory exterior and two gorgeous studies of a gleaming mass-produced porcelain

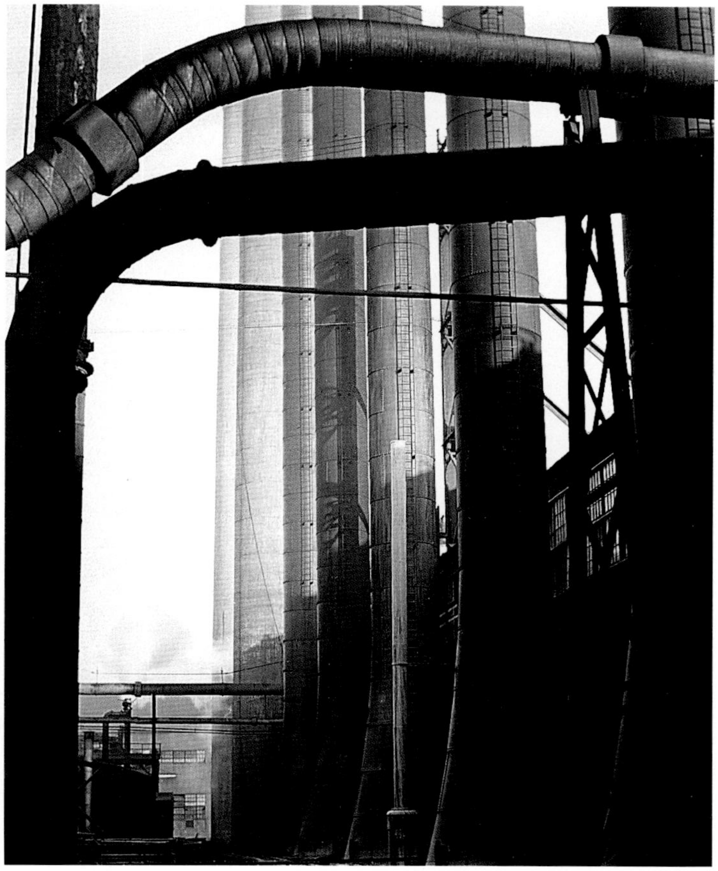

FIGURE 2.
Edward Weston
Pipes and Stacks: Armco, Middletown, Ohio, 1922
Palladium print, 23.9 x 19.1 cm.
COLLECTION CENTER FOR CREATIVE PHOTOGRAPHY, THE UNIVERSITY OF ARIZONA, TUCSON.

toilet were exceptions (and highly aestheticized ones at that), compared with his prolific photography of historic and folkloric artifacts, contemporary portraits and nudes that he produced during two extended stays in Mexico between 1923 and 1926. When Weston returned to California in 1926, the spread of industry registered hardly at all in his photography, which concentrated on increasingly abstract studies of natural forms and human figures.[9]

A relative indifference to industrial modernity could also be said to characterize that other pioneer of photographic Modernism on the West Coast, Imogen Cunningham. After learning the science of photography as part of her university education in the first decade of the twentieth century, she refined her skills by emulating the lyric technique of Pictorialism. Like Brigman before her, Cunningham in the teens tested the limits of Arts and Crafts conventions by making male figure studies that were considered quite shocking for the time. Starting in the late teens, Cunningham began to sharpen her vision, indeed earlier than Weston, though with characteristically less fanfare. Most famous are her studies of flowers, viewed at extremely close range under luminously bright light. If most have a luscious sensuality, one study from the 1920s, *Flax,* has a quite different, ascetic resonance (plate 85). In this spare set-up of reed against wall, object and soft shadow intermingle and very nearly dissolve into a chimerical, rippled tear in the light gray background. The only element that reminds us of the materiality of the slender sheath is its classical column-like central position. But in this radical abstraction that borders on drawing with light, the stress on drawing (rather than on brilliant light effects) has a languorous, even liquid feel that is reminiscent of old-style art photography.

At the end of the twenties, Cunningham briefly turned her attention to industrial forms. The few images she produced match the rigorous geometry of European contemporaries whose work she had carefully studied in magazine reproductions. Yet after demonstrating her capacity to master the lexicon of *neue Sachlichkeit* ("New Objectivity"), she quickly turned away from industrial subjects. Some, recognizing this ambivalence in her work, propose that her range would have extended beyond portraits, nudes and botanicals if she had not been tethered to the home as a mother of three young children. As Cunningham later recalled these years, her days were divided between the kitchen and the darkroom, leaving little time to explore more widely. But even after she divorced her husband when her children were close to grown, she continued for many decades to mine the same material. At the end of her life she repeatedly acknowledged that the search for beauty, for better or worse, governed her choice of, and approach to, photographic subjects. Perhaps her greatest foray into the unlovely world was the nonagenarian portrait series she produced in the ninth decade of her life, and in the main even these photographs make a point of ennobling those who traditionally slipped into obscurity. In 1968, she formulated her long view of photography's development, in which the soft and the sharp, the literal and the symbolic, had been repeatedly cycled and were bound to continue to do so. This was enunciated to students when she already was in her eighties, but her photography had consistently expressed the idea that past practice propelled all efforts at innovation.[10]

For Cunningham, the continuous reworking of established subjects and modes of depiction could always stimulate a significant enlargement of vision and expression, which was reason enough to keep at it. Her lifelong commitment to photography on this incremental basis attests to her personal perseverance, and no less to the fortifying spirit of suffrage-era feminism that prevailed in her formative years, and also, it seems, to the relatively egalitarian character of the photographic community on the West Coast. With Brigman as one leading forerunner that male and female photographers continued to consider a daring pioneer, the work of women was treated with far more seriousness on the West Coast than on the East Coast. While the figure of Stieglitz continued to command from afar, inspiring the artistically ambitious to make periodic pilgrimages to New York with portfolios in hand, Brigman remained an immediate source of encouragement, as she herself gradually began to modernize her own vision.

Edward Weston's reputation as a womanizer is the stuff of myth. The women he loved inspired him but he also reciprocally inspired them. His intense relationships with Margrethe Mather, Tina Modotti, Sonya Noskowiak and Charis Wilson Weston, led each to serve him as very pliant model but also led each to photograph or, in Charis Wilson Weston's case, to write. Reflecting on his first artistic liaison with Margrethe Mather, Weston retrospectively declared, "I will take from anyone all they can give me and try to return as much or more."[11] At a somewhat less intense heat, this avowal of interdependence characterized the entire network of art photographers on the West Coast, and unlike many other artistic groups it seemed to serve women as well as men. To be sure, the modern period of California photography produced two male figures of epic stature, Weston and Ansel Adams, and it could be said that both effectively used photography to reclaim virgin nature as the rightful terrain for masculine expression. But the same period also sustained Imogen Cunningham, who cherished her ongoing interaction with Weston, and even more, this network seemed invaluable to the emergence of that other key modern woman photographer, Dorothea Lange. For the local artistic community that congregated first around Brigman and continued to meet at Brigman's old address after Willard Van Dyke had rented her studio extended many forms of support to Lange at a critical turning point in her development.

A study of Lange that emphasizes the feminist perspective at the core of her social vision has yet to be written. When it is written, it ideally will not downplay the crucial contributions of men in her life. Reviewing the biographical details, I am struck by the key forms of support provided by Roger Sturtevant, Willard Van Dyke and Ansel Adams, in addition to her first and second husbands, painter Maynard Dixon and labor economist Paul S. Taylor. Van Dyke and Adams were principal organizers of the first Group f.64 exhibition, and they briefly considered but did not invite Lange to be part of the exhibition of the original seven members of the group—Ansel Adams, Imogen Cunningham, John Paul Edwards, Sonia Noskowiak, Henry Swift, Willard Van Dyke and Edward Weston—plus another four associate photographers—Preston Holder, Consuelo Kanaga, Alma Lavenson and Brett Weston. As documented in the *Crooked Halo*, Lange had known Cunningham and Weston since the early twenties. Notwithstanding these established relationships, in 1932 her work simply did not qualify as "pure" photography. The exclusion doubtless stung, but it also probably provoked Lange to sharpen her own conception of photographic possibilities, though on her own terms, which did not hinge upon the hyper-sharpness of f.64-view camera technique. Instead, she turned her portrait skills to the growing crowd of desperate figures filling the streets aimlessly in the first years of the Great Depression. By early 1933 she had made *White Angel Bread Line* (plate 102).

Though this oft-reproduced picture has come to stand as emblem of the early Depression years, it was for Lange very much a transitional picture, and the signs of transition are contained in the image. The choice of subject matter surely is inspired by Franklin Roosevelt's invocation of the "forgotten man" in his 1932 election campaign, but the way she framed her subject shares the general air of uncertainty that hung over the nation during the four-month transition between Hoover's defeat in November and Roosevelt's inauguration and commencement of New Deal reforms in March 1933. In Lange's photograph, a lone man turns his back on a milling crowd to rest momentarily on a temporary police barrier. Maybe one reason this figure elicits such strong identification is that the position afforded the viewer is nearly as provisional: neither truly looking down from above nor firmly on the ground. Lange had just emerged from her second-floor studio after spending much time studying the street from that safe perch. The sense of curiosity that impelled her to venture forth with a camera was mixed with some measure of hesitation. The poignancy of the image hinges on this double sense of precarious balance.

Photographs of this kind always depend on a measure of chance, this one even more so. *White Angel Bread Line* was made so tentatively that it almost failed to see the light of day. Although Lange later recalled the making of this photograph as an act of miraculous intuition,[12] its actual genesis was far less smooth and far more collaborative. The collaboration in this case was not with her photographic subjects but rather with her photographic colleague, Roger Sturtevant. Milton Meltzer, Lange's first biographer, recounts that following her first foray into the street, she removed what she thought was all the exposed sheets of film from her film holder and handed the holder to Sturtevant, with whom she shared some equipment and a darkroom. The next day, while in the darkroom, he discovered in the film holder one remaining sheet of film, which he proceeded to develop. The results so impressed him that he immediately brought it to her attention.[13]

Certainly regarding this picture, Sturtevant served as midwife; arguably his actions in this instance had more extensive influence on Lange's subsequent development as a photographer. He not only salvaged the sheet of exposed film but also immediately hailed it as something significant after taking care to develop it. When Lange put a print from the negative on her studio wall, she later recalled that her middle class portrait clients were all perplexed by the picture. "What are you going to do with this kind of thing?" they asked, if they bothered to comment at all. Yet she kept it pinned to the wall, a sign of expanding horizons, while returning repeatedly to the street with the aim of making more pictures of this kind.[14] One might wonder whether she would have continued with such determination had her initial exposures not been singled out as inspired efforts by a serious, independent photographer. Sturtevant never exhibited much personal commitment to socially-oriented photography, but in his own work he had long shown an inclination to experiment (plates 75, 89 and 120). He recognized in this image the seeds of an important new direction. His enthusiasm surely fortified Lange as she set out on a new course, albeit one that had its own consistent relation to the past. Even in this chaotic setting, she drew on her portrait-making skills to give psychological nuance to a single figure in the crowd, thereby suggesting the fearful personal experience of being alone yet nearly invisible in a growing mass of the down-and-out.

This new work was also, like her pictorialist studio portraiture, a bit fuzzy. Whether by accident or by design, the photographs Lange began making in the streets of San Francisco still lacked the crisp detail that was the trademark of Group f.64. This non-conformance to the semi-official modern technique continued to set her apart from that group, and, for some, may have served as a silent rebuke. When the world was falling apart, an overriding concern for crystal-sharp optical definition might risk missing the big picture. Willard Van Dyke, for one, apparently thought so. While still a university student in the late twenties, Van Dyke had developed a passion for photography and quickly gravitated to Weston. By the fall of 1932, Van Dyke helped instigate the formation of Group f.64 by convening a meeting at his Brockhurst Street gallery. The group's activities and his own work running the gallery, while also photographing and holding a day job, was quite enough to sustain him for the next year. Nevertheless, by mid-1934 he began to have doubts about a number of these commitments.

That was a red-letter year, particularly in the Bay Area, and the rapid succession of dramatic events would challenge all but the purest of photographic purists to reconsider how they wanted to use their skills. F.D.R.'s National Industrial Recovery Act of 1933 had endorsed the right to organize, which, combined with desperate conditions, spawned a wave of labor militancy. After failing to reach acceptable terms with shippers, longshoremen in San Francisco struck the docks in early May of 1934. Other unions in the transportation sector quickly went out in solidarity. When police and National Guardsmen tried to break the mass work stoppage, violence predictably erupted. The resulting deaths of two strikers and the wounding of scores more led to the historic General Strike that brought San Francisco to a standstill for four days in mid-July, with parts of the East Bay nearly as paralyzed. Even after the militants returned to work while awaiting arbitration of their demands, the political drama remained high while shifting to a different arena: Upton Sinclair's 1934 campaign for California governor. He had begun his campaign as an independent, finding grassroots support for his EPIC platform, an acronym standing for the radical promise to end poverty in California. When he surprised all politicians by securing the Democratic nomination in the primary, party regulars grew alarmed and all but welcomed the Republican's smear campaign. The establishment's organized opposition made the campaign a truly epic battle, while demonstrating the structural weakness of such maverick political efforts. Without the support of the local party, or of F.D.R., who likewise preferred the prospect of a Republican governor to Sinclair's populist strategy and radical rhetoric, the EPIC campaign lost, though only by a narrow margin. With Sinclair's defeat in November 1934, the political situation stabilized.[15] But for a handful of months between May and November, the old certainties briefly loosened their grip, and the resulting social fissures extended even to Group f.64.

By 1935, quite a few photographers associated with f.64 would part company. Van Dyke and Kanaga left for the East with plans to use their media skills in support of the Left. Preston Holder departed with similar plans, although he stopped short in the Midwest.[16] But as early as the summer of 1934, Van Dyke had already broken ranks. He was deeply moved by the strike—later he suggested he had even lost his day job in the general labor turmoil—but he could not immediately devise a way to express this new sense of social engagement with a camera.[17] By the end of 1934, he had begun making the transition from meticulous still photography to documentary filmmaking. But months before, he made a significant shift in his gallery work at 683 Brockhurst. In the gallery where plans for Group f.64 were first hatched, and where the work of view-camera purists had been featured, Van Dyke just after the mid-summer General Strike arranged a solo exhibition of Lange's recent photographs of people in the streets of San Francisco.

This 1934 one-person exhibition in Oakland was Lange's first public exposure of any kind, and it had major consequences for her continued development as a documentary photographer. If she was still wondering what she was doing in the street, this exhibition must have allayed her doubts, demonstrating that many different people found interest in these photographs and, even more, were moved by them. Ansel Adams, for one, took notice. When he published his first book on photography, *Making a Photograph* (Spring 1935), he relied almost exclusively on his own photographs to demonstrate that a master of technique could produce a wide range of exemplary photographs: landscapes, architectural views, portraits, advertising illustrations, and so on. But Adams stopped short of claiming to cover the entire field. Thirty-one of the book's thirty-two plates reproduced his work, but in the case of documents of "the individual in relation to civilization and social conditions," Adams stepped aside. To illustrate that genre, he arranged a fine reproduction of Lange's *Bread Line*. In his commentary about this "significant genre," Adams equivocated a bit. Just previously, he lamented the entire field of action photography, for it involved "a definite compromise with the technical principles of the medium and with certain aesthetic principles as well." The pursuit of action, Adams cautioned, risked unwelcome blur and distortion. In the following section on the photo document, Adams noted comparable risks. Work of this sort is "always dated," he wrote. Adams allowed that the same was true of the paintings of El Greco and Picasso. Even so, his warning on this count implied some private equation between the attainment of "pure" objective photography and timelessness.[18]

If Adams was inclined to champion Lange's photography while worrying about the ephemeral character of the social document, others championed the work for antithetical reasons. In October 1934, Van Dyke published an article in the California photographic periodical *Camera Craft* emphasizing the timeliness of the work by Lange he had just exhibited. Her photography was literally momentous, because it recorded the American people "in the midst of great changes." He took this occasion to note that even the most well-selected moments were necessarily taken out of context, and here he hinted at his emerging interest in the more continuous chronicle captured by documentary filmmaking. But Van Dyke had no reservations about the dated quality of Lange's imagery. Over time, he decreed, its value promised to increase, not decrease. He compared Lange's current project with Matthew Brady's Civil War photography, for both "share the passionate desire to show posterity the mixture of futility and hope, of heroism and stupidity, greatness and banality that are the concomitants of man's struggle forward."[19]

This first review of Lange's photography was remarkably prophetic. It was also notable for its leaps of faith and self-fulfilling power. Since Lange had taken this new direction only eighteen months earlier, it was rather premature to speak of this as her "life's work." But this first public response, from a key member of f.64, must have deepened Lange's resolve that it should be so. Van Dyke's championing of this work also led to an expansion of her vision of how such photographs might be used. It was through this exhibition that Berkeley economist Paul S. Taylor first encountered her work after a colleague had recommended the exhibition not far from campus. Taylor was so taken by these photographs that he quickly arranged for Lange to submit one to accompany an article on the San Francisco General Strike that he had coauthored with Norman Leon Gold for the progressive illustrated monthly, *Survey Graphic.* Just as Van Dyke's article in the October 1934 issue of *Camera Craft* represented Lange's debut in a regional photography magazine, so, too, the September 1934 issue of *Survey Graphic* represented her first exposure both in, and to, the world of organized social reform. Very soon she would be immersed in this field.

Lange and Taylor married at the end of 1935 following a year of intense collaboration. At the beginning of 1935, Taylor hired Lange to make photographs as an integral part of his state-sponsored survey of rural conditions. The reports they produced gave as much attention to her pictures as his commentary. Taylor, an amateur photographer, sincerely believed that such powerful photographs had greater potential than scholarly commentary to make people see things differently and recognize the need for reform. The highly graphic state reports they produced were so innovative that they made their way to Washington, where they impressed others intent on exploring how photographic documentation might foster support for government-initiated public programs. By mid-1935, Lange began working directly for the New Deal, initially for the Resettlement Administration which in a few years became the Farm Security Administration (FSA). This agency's widely reproduced social documentation soon influenced the ideas and techniques of serious independent photographers.[20]

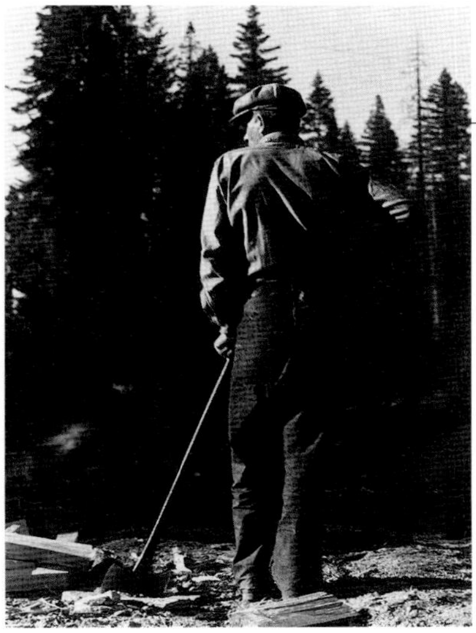

FIGURE 3.
Dorothea Lange
Unemployed Exchange Association (UXA), Oroville, California, 1934

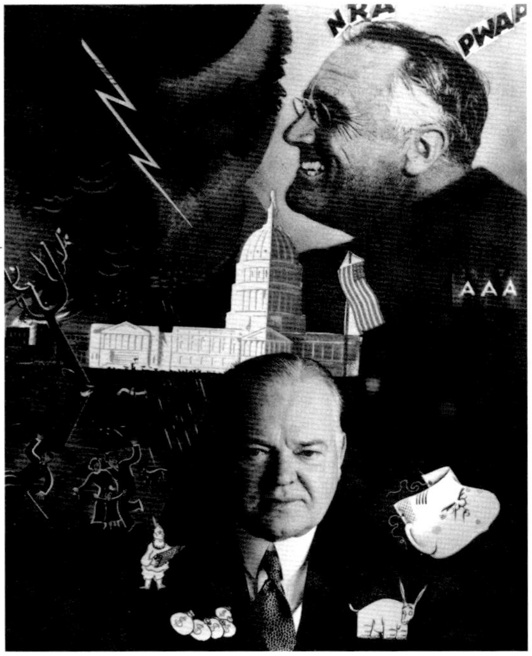

FIGURE 4.
Imogen Cunningham
Photomontage of Herbert Hoover and Franklin D. Roosevelt, c. 1935
COURTESY OF THE IMOGEN CUNNINGHAM TRUST

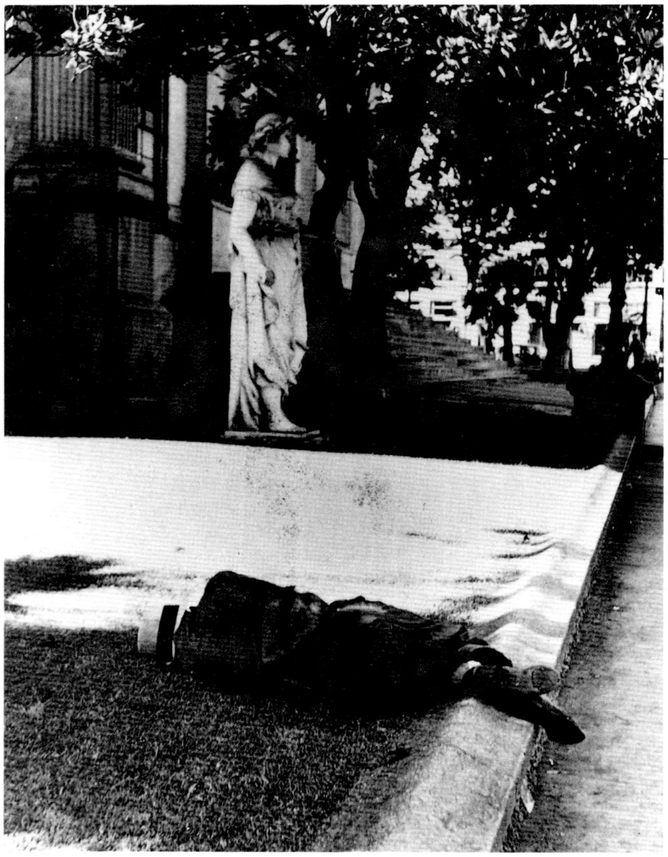

FIGURE 5.
William Simpson
Untitled (Sleeping Man), c. 1934
Gelatin silver print, 6 x 4½ in.
COLLECTION OF THE OAKLAND MUSEUM OF CALIFORNIA, GIFT OF ANITA SIMPSON

If there's some paradox in that full-circle movement, it is joined with (and possibly explained by) another. Taylor's orientation was sociological, but what initially drew him to her photography was her capacity to single out individuals. For the September 1934 *Survey Graphic*, he selected for publication no street scene but a solitary portrait of a May Day orator. Likewise, when in the fall of 1934 Taylor first accompanied a group of photographers Van Dyke had assembled to document an experimental logging cooperative, the photograph Taylor thought further demonstrated Lange's particular gift for social documentary was another single portrait of the back of one logger while he was pausing to lean on his axe (figure 3). There was something consoling in Lange's capacity to delineate distinct individuals amongst the down-and-out, with such figures occupying a central position at least in the small world of the photographic frame. Not only did Taylor find it an effective way to underscore the personal experience of privation; Adams, too, was reassured that her work seemed free of cant. At the end of 1934, Adams privately complained to Edward Weston that Van Dyke had shifted allegiance from photography to sociology. He attacked Walker Evans along similar lines. But he made a point of exempting Lange from this judgment. Lange, he noted, "strikes the middle road." Adams elaborated along traditional gender lines: "She takes contemporary material and always sees it emotionally."[21] But his first "middle road" characterization of her work may get closer to describing not only a political perspective but the formal way her concentrated, centered compositions conveyed an idea of stability that could withstand social and political polarization.

Were there any photographs from the period that, in their fundamental structure, conveyed the sense of instability that the economic crisis produced, particularly in the first half of the thirties? The overwhelming majority either avoided the subjects most redolent of despair or else they sought various ways to contain it. But not all. Imogen Cunningham made one of the relatively rare American photomontages addressing the politics of the period. Yet even this semi-satiric assemblage of fragments symbolizing the Hoover and Roosevelt administrations is structured to suggest no vacuum of leadership but rather a relatively orderly succession of power (figure 4).[22]

Cunningham's attempt at political commentary was an isolated experiment, most notable for its conspicuous departure from the narrowly prescribed conventions of the self-styled Modernists. However, a review of the Oakland Museum of California's photographic archives suggests that the rank amateur may have occasionally posed a more profound challenge to the traditional rules of composition. Photographic archives yield unexpected insights about the visual past. The obscure images prove to be in their own way quite illuminating, recording not only additional subjects but additional ways of seeing. While studying the museum's photographic collection with the aim of gauging the range of interwar photographic practice, I was struck by one photograph made by a little-known Bay Area image-maker, William Simpson.

Employed as a graphic artist for the *Oakland Tribune,* Simpson photographed on the side with enough seriousness, in the early thirties, that he had some contact with Van Dyke and the Brockhurst

Street gallery. If that suggests he had serious aspirations, there's no evidence that he either published or exhibited photographs in any venue.[23] Despite his journalistic contacts, Simpson's photography never turned professional; but like many other technically proficient amateurs in the Depression era, he apparently decided that the most interesting subject matter could be found in the street. Already in the late nineteenth century, photographers with hand cameras had combed urban areas for "picturesque bits."[24] But in one instance, Simpson pushed the picturesque to its limits. On first sight, this vertical picture appears to be composed of two different scenes stacked almost arbitrarily on top of each other (figure 5). The overall rectangle is bisected laterally by a shadow line with a man sleeping on the pavement below and a neoclassical statue standing with typical rectitude above. The lower half resembles the kind of scene Lange would have been attracted to, although Lange would have preferred softer light to concentrate attention further on the vagrant's body language. The distracting rupture at the center of Simpson's picture is intensified by the way the curb of the street that runs along the lower right edge looks like it veers sharply inward just above the central shadow line. Closer inspection shows that the curb continues straight, and this semblance of a curve is produced by the stairs leading up to the unidentified Beaux Arts building. Yet even after the illusion is recognized for what it is, the impression remains that the division between the richly shaded upper half and the barren lower half is physically bending the space to the breaking point.

How intentional was this picture? Only a small group of prints by this photographer survive in the museum's collection, and all the rest steer clear of such flagrant violations of the rules of pictorial coherence (plates 94, 107 and 116). But whether or not Simpson fully planned this ensemble of clashing elements, the results sufficiently intrigued the photographer that he went to the trouble of making and mounting a print of this image. Even if he showed it only informally to others, nobody was inspired to pursue the idea that the structure of Depression imagery might just as well suggest fracture as consolidation. All pictures rest on conventions. This one so defied prevailing conventions that it probably presented no fruitful model or direction for ongoing picture-making, even to Simpson.

Maybe only in retrospect, in light of more recent tendencies toward an art of visual dissonance, does Simpson's picture seem organized by a logic that makes any kind of sense. Likewise in retrospect, this anomalous form of social depiction helps underscore why Lange's approach proved so effective. In her photographs there was ample evidence that, recalling Yeats's poetry of modern upheaval, "things fall apart." But Lange had managed to uncouple this evidence from the modern Irish poet's linked decree: "the center cannot hold."[25] Rather, what attracted her, amazed her even, was the remarkable way the center continued to hold, or could be made to do so. Doubtless this recurring balancing act was the basis for her photography's great public appeal, first in the turbulent local context and then in the broader national context.

If even Lange's photography had a certain conservative quality in its judicious mix of the

Otto Hagel was less playful than John Gutmann, having come of age by a harder route in the streets. Largely self-educated, while still in his teens he wandered Europe with his lifelong companion Hansel Mieth before making his way to the land of Jack London. Despite their class differences, Hagel, like Gutmann, found the expanding photographic culture of Weimar Germany irresistible and he, too, acquired a camera. His hobby may have preceded any knowledge of the worker photography movement fostered by the German communists, but it quickly developed into something akin to that form of overtly polemical documentation.[30] The intense exploitation Hagel witnessed, especially in the fields of California, where he and Mieth periodically worked to subsist in the first half of the thirties, only sharpened his commitment to class struggle. In 1934–35, he concentrated on a film about the struggles of farmworkers. After that ambitious film mysteriously disappeared, he returned to still photography without amending his commitment to agit-prop imagery that contributed to labor struggles.[31]

It is no accident that the Oakland Museum's collection of Hagel photographs of the Salinas Lettuce Strike of 1936 was donated by Dorothea Lange's husband Paul S. Taylor, for it had a direct relation to the Lange archive Taylor also donated. When at the end of the 1930s Lange and Taylor were preparing their collaborative study *An American Exodus* (1939), they relied primarily on Lange's extensive documentation of the plight of migrants leaving the South and Southwest only to face intensive exploitation in the fields of California. However, they had to look beyond Lange's archive for some pictures considered crucial for this sequence. They had no photographs of the notorious dust storms that symbolized the complete exhaustion of old farm regions and the consequent need to pull up stakes, so they reproduced two borrowed from other sources: one taken by a New Deal

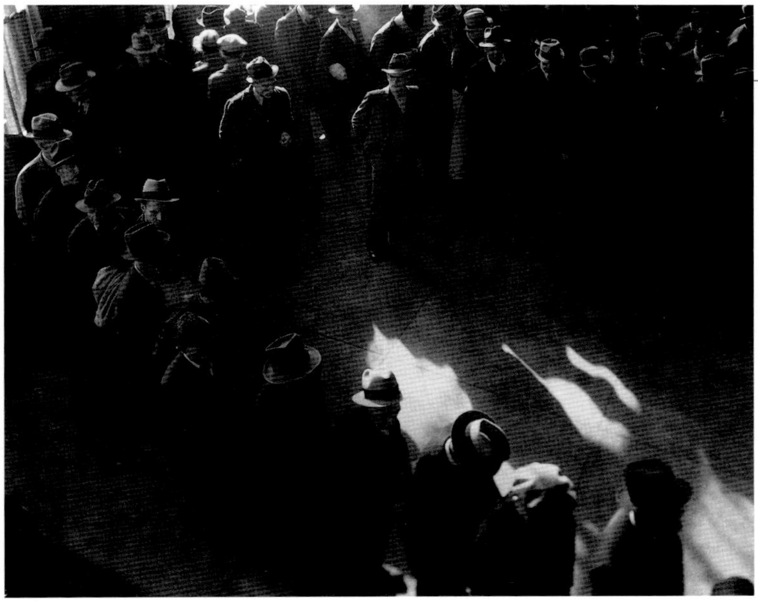

FIGURE 8.
Dorothea Lange
Unemployment Benefits Aid Begins. Line of Men Inside a Division of the State Employment Service Office at San Francisco, etc., January 1938
Gelatin silver print, 7¼ x 9⅜ in.

colleague, fellow FSA photographer Arthur Rothstein, and another taken by a small studio photographer in Colorado. Just as significant, they lacked many photographs of the pitched battles erupting regularly in the fields of California between the growers and landless poor who hired out at desperately low wages for the seasonal work of harvesting and packing the crops. To fill that gap, Lange and Taylor found what they wanted in the 1936 Salinas strike reportage of Otto Hagel. He handed over the negatives of that freelance assignment, welcoming the opportunity to circulate more widely his view of the way rural California enforced the law. They were damning pictures. In a lull during a confrontation lasting several days in September 1936, Hagel moved in relatively close with his 35 mm camera to make something akin to group portraits of the locals deputized by the sheriff (plates 105 and 106). Like most pictures, they don't tell the whole story. Yet they offer vivid evidence of the way repression depended on quite ordinary citizens who seemed to find honor and excitement in their paramilitary roles. They could not be more different from the bucolic depictions of rural communities that the New Deal promoted in popular murals. And even in the context of Lange and Taylor's study, one from Hagel's series packs a mean punch facing Lange's famous photograph of the gas station air dispenser that a small independent operator adorned with the sign:

AIR
This Is Your
Country Don't
Let The Big
Men Take It
Away
From You[32]

Reality is rarely so simple, and Lange and Taylor had the good sense to qualify that beguiling picture with Hagel's more gritty document of the way repression was enforced whenever casual laborers managed, against all odds, to begin organizing (figure 7).

Between the mid-1930s and the mid-1940s, Lange's understanding of California broadened, and so did her photography. Her contact with Hagel and his sociological orientation may have had some influence, as well as her intense collaboration with the scholarly Taylor, and she was certainly responding to the enormous changes she was witnessing in California. Doubtless her deepest instinct in making pictures remained one of simplification to a single central subject. But in this period she worked against that tendency to find ways to underscore the increasing regimentation in a society that once seemed more hospitable to free expression. Long preoccupied with depicting the individual, her photography at this point began developing a new thematic interest in groups forced into bureaucratic formations: farmworkers lined up in the fields (a subject that dominates the last portion of *An American Exodus*), applicants waiting in long lines for social security benefits (figure 8); and, a

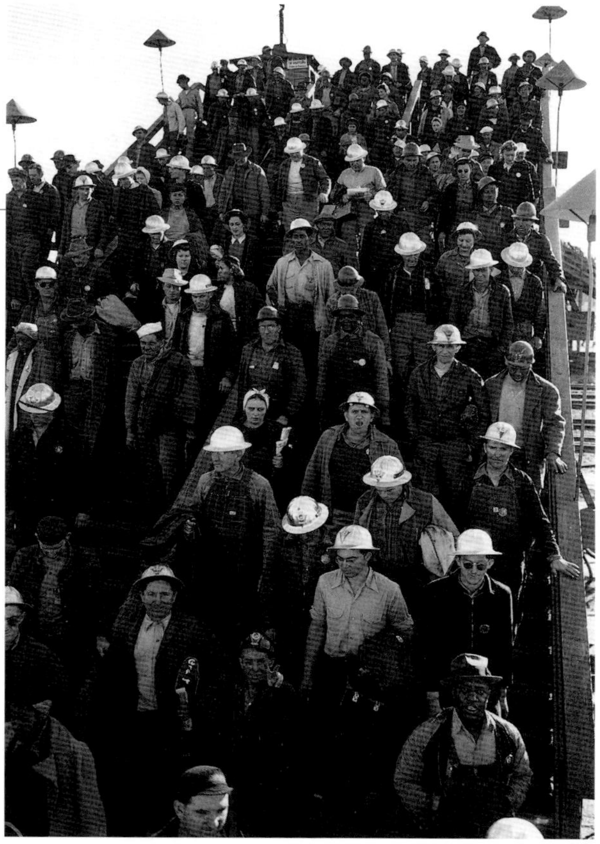

FIGURE 9.
Dorothea Lange
Shift Change 3:30 P.M.—Coming On of Yard 3—Kaiser Shipyards, c. 1943
© OAKLAND MUSEUM OF CALIFORNIA, THE CITY OF OAKLAND.
GIFT OF PAUL S. TAYLOR

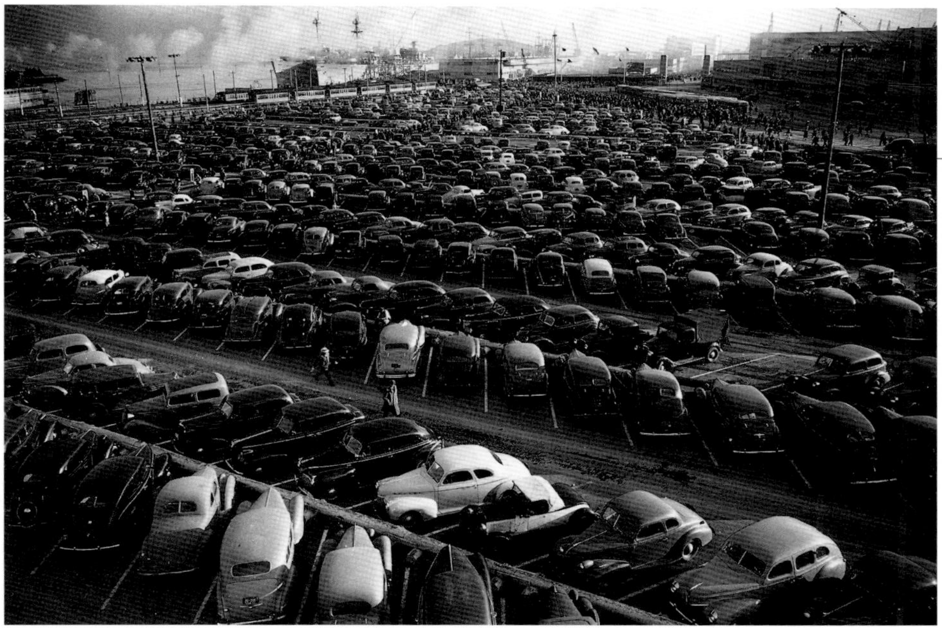

FIGURE 10.
Dorothea Lange
Auto Park—Richmond No. 1—View South, c. 1943
© OAKLAND MUSEUM OF CALIFORNIA,
THE CITY OF OAKLAND.
GIFT OF PAUL S. TAYLOR.

bit later, long-time Japanese-American residents assembled for processing and shipment to wartime internment centers (plate 122).

The decentering process in her photography is manifest when we compare the well-known *White Angel Bread Line* (1933) with urban documents she made a decade later, notably the pictures of a shift change at the Kaiser shipyard in Richmond during World War II (figure 9). *White Angel Bread Line* derives its power from the theatrical relation between a main figure and a chorus. But working from a similar overhead angle at the Richmond shipyard, there is no single figure who stands out and catches our attention. Rather, it is a crowd of small figures, of which Lange later observed: "a mass of humanity, from all parts of the country . . . all looking in different directions. They were not a group of people united on a job. It showed so plainly. . . ."[33] Neither individual nor a cohesive group, it is as if in this wartime industrial view she glimpsed the future of California. There is an even more uncharacteristic Lange photograph made while looking down on the wartime shipyard's huge parking lot filled to capacity (figure 10). It is arguably her most prescient view of postwar developments, as it includes photographic approaches shaped in response to the ever greater sprawl that

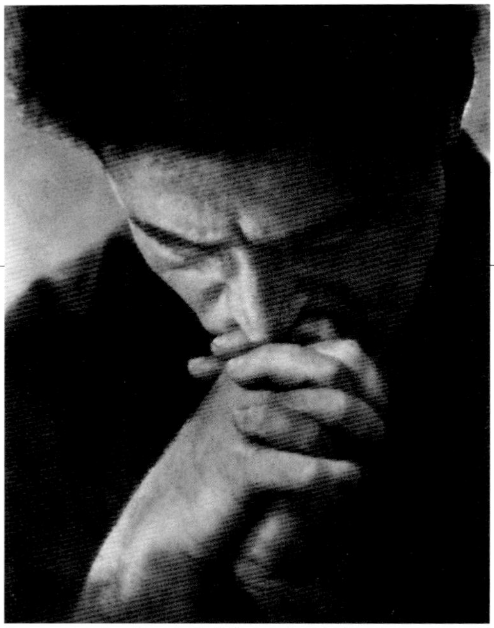

FIGURE 11.
Anne Brigman
Conflict, 1926
Gelatin silver print
9 15/16 x 7 1/8 in.
COURTESY GEORGE EASTMAN HOUSE
GIFT OF WILLARD M. NOTT

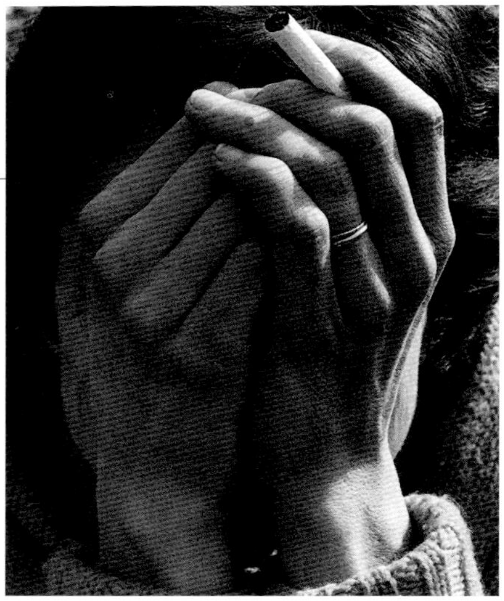

FIGURE 12.
Dorothea Lange
Bad Trouble over the Weekend, 1964
Gelatin silver print, 5 5/16 x 3 1/2 in.
© OAKLAND MUSEUM OF CALIFORNIA, THE CITY OF OAKLAND.
GIFT OF PAUL S. TAYLOR

would come to dominate the landscape, economy and culture of California. In this picture we can find genealogical links to very different work made decades later by Ed Ruscha, Lewis Baltz and Bill Owens, among others.

Lange herself did not pursue this direction, but in the last years of her life she lobbied hard for the revival of a government-sponsored documentary project to be produced by a generation of younger photographers.[34] For a variety of reasons, including health problems that grew more debilitating as she aged, Lange personally narrowed her sights, and in so doing returned to an older style of simplified, centered compositions. While concentrating on the familiar, she publicly worried that such work risked becoming mundane, or worse, too domestic in its orientation (presumably because the "domestic" would appeal only to women).[35] Despite those worries, or maybe because of them, she began to forge a new direction, using the camera to explore the politics of everyday life that feminist photographers would later pursue. Her sequential studies of her second son holding tensely his first born, and later with increasing ease his second born, seem indebted to the new discourse of photographic sequences that Minor White championed as a Bay Area photographer and teacher in the years following World War II.[36] But Lange used this form less obscurely, focusing directly on the way family members are shaped and reshaped by interpersonal family dynamics. This work anticipates a time, just a few years after Lange died in 1965, when a new generation of women were advocating "the personal is political" as part of the process of reclaiming the mantle of feminism.

Yet as much as Lange's work from the 1950s looks forward, it also looks backward, to an older generation of feminists and an older era of photography. I am particularly struck by the strong affinities between a fairly late figure study by Anne Brigman, *Conflict*, 1926, which with deceptive softness scrutinizes quite closely a pair of entwined hands pressed against the lower half of a face (figure 11) and one of Lange's last photographs, *Bad Trouble Over the Weekend,* 1964, in which a similar pair of interlocked hands covers the entire face, the only protuberance being the unlit cigarette gripped between the index and middle finger (figure 12). Made four decades apart, Lange's photograph is much sharper than Brigman's, yet it still contains the pictorialist impulse to use photography to allude to a turbulent interior world that many photographers, despite their choice of a static, surface-oriented medium, still strive to fathom and fashion anew.

NOTES

1. See Michael G. Wilson and Dennis Reed, *Pictorialism in California: Photographs 1900–1940* (Malibu and San Marino: The J. Paul Getty Museum and The Henry E. Huntington Library and Gallery of Art, 1994); see also a recent anthology of new perspectives on the photography of William Mortensen, Michael Dawson et al., *William Mortensen: a Revival* (Tucson: Center for Creative Photography, University of Arizona, 1998).

2. The photograph is reproduced with a caption identifying seven of the nine figures in Susan Ehrens, *A Poetic Vision: The Photographs of Anne Brigman* (Santa Barbara: The Santa Barbara Museum of Art, 1995), 83. In that publication it is dated approximately 1917–1923. Wilson and Reed reproduce the photograph on page 19 of *Pictorialism in California,* attaching the date of 1925. Another recent citation of this photograph makes a tentative attribution. According to Therese Heyman, photographer Roger Sturtevant recalled that printmaker Roi Partridge (and at that time husband of Imogen Cunningham) made this and a number of related photographs, while also participating as one of the models; Heyman, "Modernist Photography and the Group F.64," in Paul J. Karlstrom, ed., *On the Edge: California Modernist Art* (Berkeley: University of California Press, 1996), 257.

3. For an early, decisive call for closure and renunciation of the pictorial legacy, see Paul Strand's "Photography" which was first published in *Seven Arts* 2 (1917): 524–25, and later printed in New York in *Camera Work* 49–50 (June 1917): 3–4. The article was reprinted in Nathan Lyons, ed., *Photographers on Photography* (Englewood Cliffs: Prentice-Hall, 1966).

4. All three were included in the prestigious *Film und Foto* exhibition held in Stuttgart in 1929; for a facsimile of the original catalog, see *International Austellung des Deutschen Wekbunds, Film und Foto* (Stuttgart: Deutsche Verlag-Anstalt, 1979).

5. For a fine reappraisal of Brigman's work, see Ehrens, *A Poetic Vision.*

6. As quoted in Heyman, "Modernist Photography and the Group F.64," 258.

7. The most well-researched account of f.64, though one emphasizing the innovative character of this movement, is the multi-authored catalog edited by Therese Thau Heyman, *Seeing Straight: The f.64 Revolution in Photography* (Oakland: The Oakland Museum, 1993). This publication reprints a number of historic texts pertaining to the group, including the original "manifesto."

8. In her essay "f.64 and Modernism" in *Seeing Straight,* 40, n. 7, Naomi Rosenblum raises this important comparative point.

9. For a review of this entire period of Weston's work and for detailed entries for *Pipes and Stacks* (1922), *Plaster Works* (1925) and the two *Excusado* studies from the same year, see the invaluable catalog by Amy Conger, *Edward Weston: Photographs from the Collection of the Center for Creative Photography* (Tucson: Center for Creative Photography, University of Arizona, 1992), figs. 86, 177, and 183–84, respectively.

10. Richard Lorenz's monograph makes a strong argument for this photographer's status as a member of the avant-garde, while judiciously acknowledging some persistent pictorial strains in her work; Richard Lorenz, *Imogen Cunningham: Ideas Without End* (San Francisco: Chronicle Books, 1993).

11. As quoted in the biographic essay Amy Conger appends to her print catalog, *Edward Weston: Photographs from the Collection,* 4.

12. Interview of Lange by Richard K. Doud, May 22, 1964, page 5; transcript in the Archives of American Art, Smithsonian Institution.

13. Milton Meltzer, *Dorothea Lange: A Photographer's Life* (New York: Farrar, Straus, Giroux, 1978), 71.

14. *Ibid.*

15. These successive political dramas are deftly recounted in Kevin Starr, *Endangered Dreams: The Great Depression in California History* (New York: Oxford, 1996), 84–155.

16. Rather detailed chronologies of these artists appears in the back matter of Therese Heyman, *Seeing Straight,* 150–56.

17. In his excellent critique of f.64, Michel Oren notes these fissures, in the process citing Van Dyke's later claim to have lost his job as a gas station attendant in connection with the strike; Michel Oren, "On the Impurities of Group f.64 Photography," *History of Photography* 15 (Summer 1991): 126, n. 19. According to a careful compilation of correspondence, however, Van Dyke actually left his job months before the strike, though this slippage of memory may express the degree to which he was moved by the strike and wished to be part of it; see Leslie Squyres Calmes, *The Letters between Edward Weston and Willard Van Dyke* (Tucson: Center for Creative Photography, University of Arizona, 1992), 22–23.

18. Ansel Adams, *Making a Photograph* (London: The Studio Limited, 1935). Lange's photograph is reproduced as Plate XXIX, page 93; relevant commentary appears on pages 82 and 85–6. Lange's personal copy of the book, held by the Oakland Museum of California, bears an inscription from Adams: "For Dorothea Lange—swell human being, who helped make this book human! From Ansel Adams, April 1935."

19. Willard Van Dyke, "The Photographs of Dorothea Lange: A Critical Analysis," *Camera Craft* 41:10 (October 1934): 461–67.

20. On Lange's rapid transition from a local context to a national New Deal arena, and Taylor's role in that transition, see Meltzer, *Dorothea Lange,* 86–106.

21. Private correspondence between Ansel Adams and Edward Weston, November 29, 1934; reprinted in Mary Street Alinder and Andrea Gray Stillman, eds., *Ansel Adams: Letters and Images 1916–1984* (Boston: Little, Brown, 1988), 72–4.

22. The photomontage is reproduced in Lorenz's monograph, *Imogen Cunningham,* 40. On the comparative absence of photomontage in interwar U.S. photography, see my essay "'Good Fences Make Good Neighbors: American Resistance to Photomontage Between the Wars," in Matthew Teitelbaum, ed., *Montage and Modern Life, 1919– 1942* (Cambridge, Massachusetts: MIT, 1992), 128–89.

23. As documented in *Seeing Straight,* one 1935 article on f.64 mentions Simpson as a new associate of the group along with Dorothea Lange and Peter Stackpole. But his association seems to have been very peripheral for his name appears in no other contemporary reports, nor in any of the correspondence and memoirs by other members of the group. Therese Thau Heyman's essay "Perspective on Seeing Straight" notes Simpson's professional work as newspaper artist for the local Oakland paper; *Seeing Straight,* 28.

24. The phrase even serves as title for an early portfolio of New York photographs by Alfred Stieglitz, *Picturesque Bits of New York* (New York: R. H. Russell, 1897).

25. William Butler Yeats, "The Second Coming" (1921), from *The Collected Poems of W. B. Yeats* (New York: Macmillan, 1956), 184–85.

26. Max Kozloff's 1982 essay remains the best overview of Gutmann's photography in its bifurcated context; see Max Kozloff, "The Extravagant Depression," in Lew Thomas, ed., *The Restless Decade: John Gutmann's Photographs of the Thirties* (New York: Harry N. Abrams, 1984), 7–16.

27. See the caption underneath the top left photograph appearing in the *San Francisco Chronicle,* Friday, July 6, 1934, CCC B.

28. *Death Stalks Fillmore* (1934) is published in the monograph *The Restless Decade,* 99.

29. Starr, *Endangered Dreams,* 197–222.

30. On the worker photography movement, see Leah Ollman's catalog, *Camera as Weapon: Worker Photography Between the Wars* (San Diego: Museum of Photographic Arts, 1991).

31. For a biographic essay on the collaborative lives and works of Otto Hagel and Hansel Mieth, see Thomas Knubben's essay in the bilingual publication, *Simple Life: Hansel Mieth Otto Hagel, Photographs from America, 1929–1971* (Fellbach: Schmetterling Verlag, 1991).

32. Dorothea Lange and Paul Schuster Taylor, *An American Exodus: A Record of Human Erosion* (New York, Reynal & Hitchcock, 1939), 139.

33. From Lange's commentary in the film *The Closer for Me,* by Philip Greene, Robert Katz and Richard Moore, made for San Francisco's public television station KQED and released in 1966; as quoted in Karin Becker Ohrn, *Dorothea Lange and the Documentary Tradition* (Baton Rouge: Louisiana State University Press, 1980), 149.

34. On Lange's final advocacy of a new documentary project ("Project I"), which she envisioned deriving from and also extending the documentary efforts of the New Deal's FSA, see Ohrn, *Dorothea Lange and the Documentary Tradition,* 238–39.

35. The postwar statement she co-authored with son Daniel Dixon is particularly fraught with ambivalence about the value of focusing on the domestic scene; Dorothea Lange and Daniel Dixon, "Photographing the Familiar," *Aperture* I: 2 (1952): 5–15.

36. These family portraits from the fifties were first presented consecutively in the 1966 retrospective and accompanying monograph of Lange's photography, the preparation of which she supervised until her death in 1965; *Dorothea Lange* (New York: Museum of Modern Art, 1966), 74–75. On Minor White's practice and pedagogic advocacy of photographic sequences starting in the second half of the forties, see Walter Chappell, "The Threshold of Vision," in *Minor White: A Living Remembrance* (Millerton: Aperture, 1984), 18–21; see also David Travis, "Starting Out from Lobos: 1925–1950," in Thomas Weston Fels, Therese Heyman, David Travis, *Watkins to Weston: 101 Years of California Photography, 1849–1950* (Santa Barbara Museum of Art, 1992), 123–26.

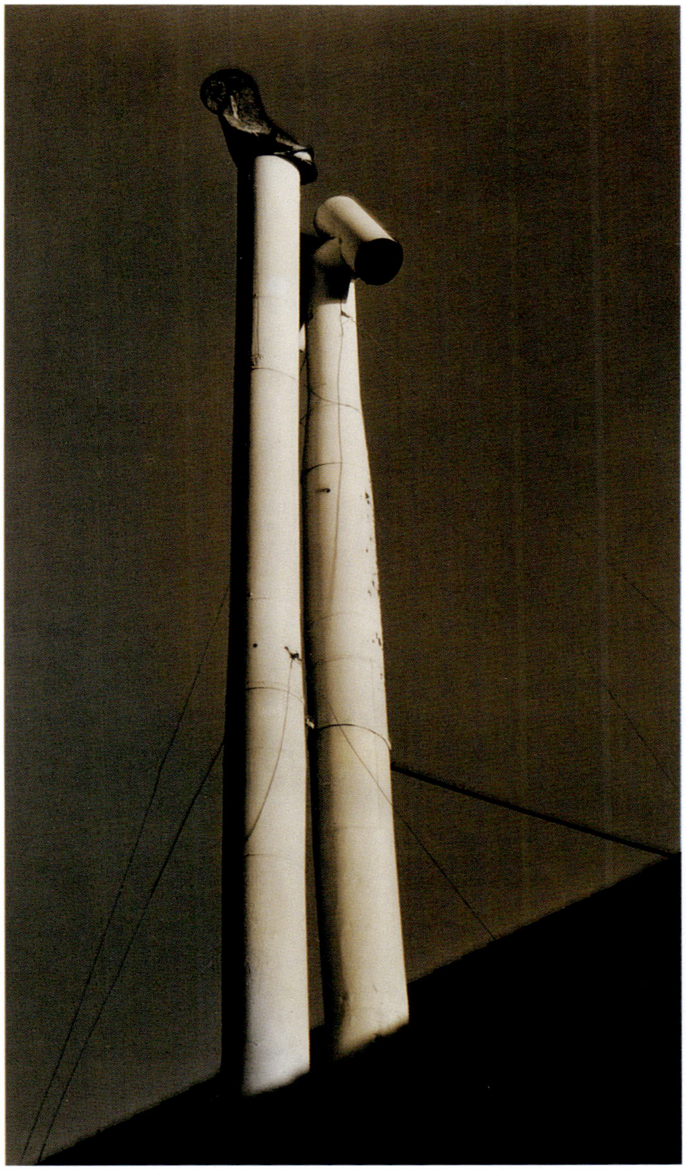

78.
WILLARD VAN DYKE
Ventilators (Telegraph Avenue), 1932
Gelatin silver print
9½ x 5½ in.
GIFT OF MRS. JOHN PAUL EDWARDS

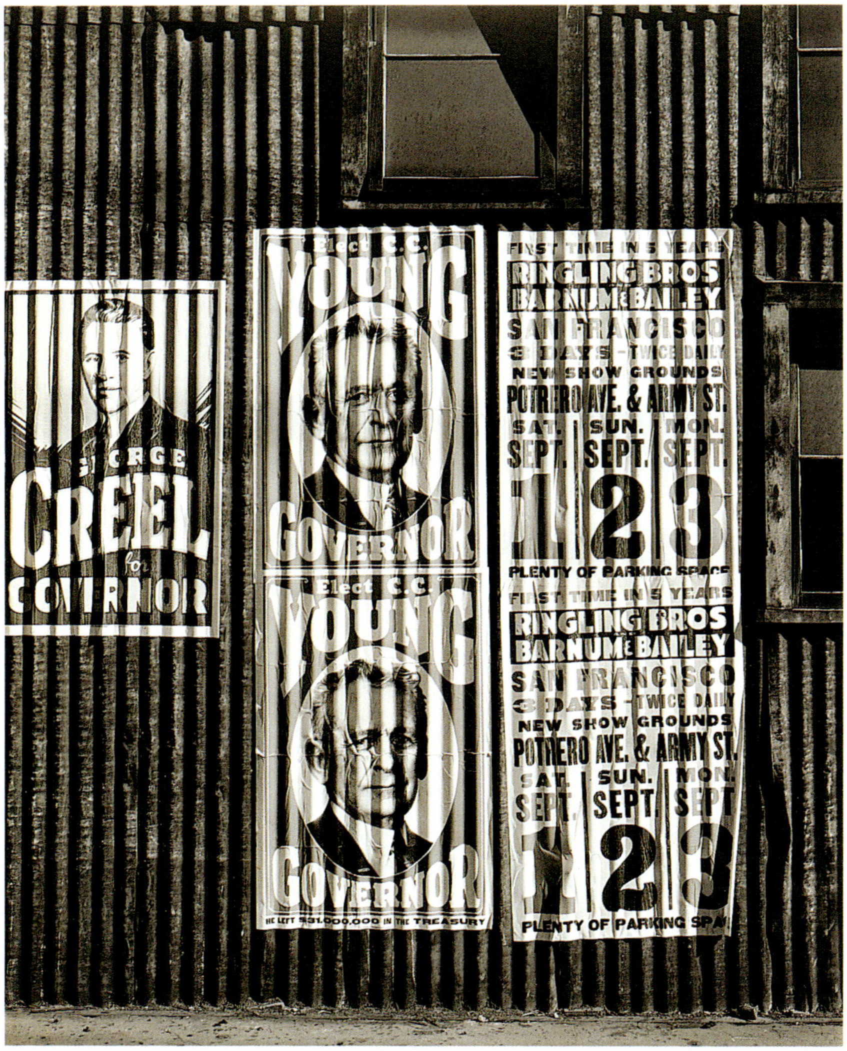

79.

ANSEL ADAMS

Political Signs and Circus Posters, San Francisco, 1931

Gelatin silver print

9¾ x 7¼ in.

GIFT OF PETER STACKPOLE

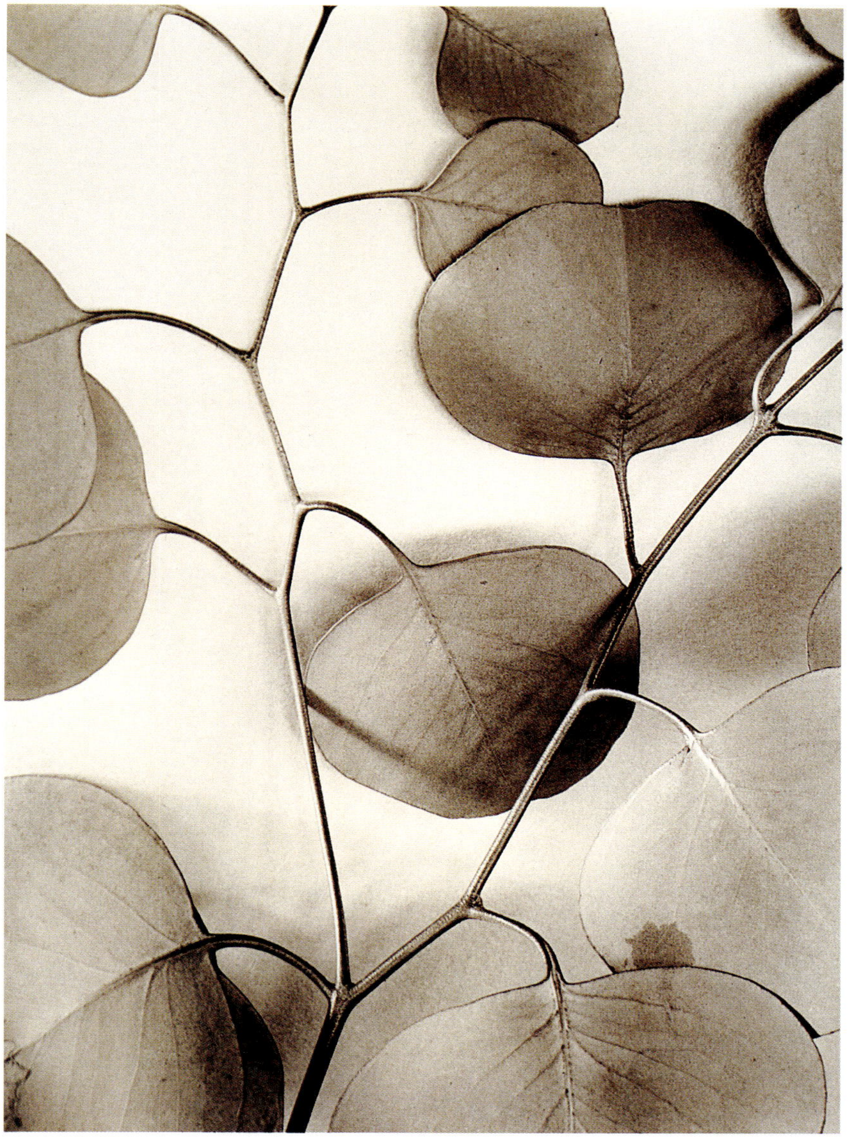

80.
ALMA LAVENSON
Eucalyptus, 1933
Gelatin silver print
9⅝ x 7⅛ in.
GIFT OF MRS. ALMA LAVENSON WAHRHAFTIG

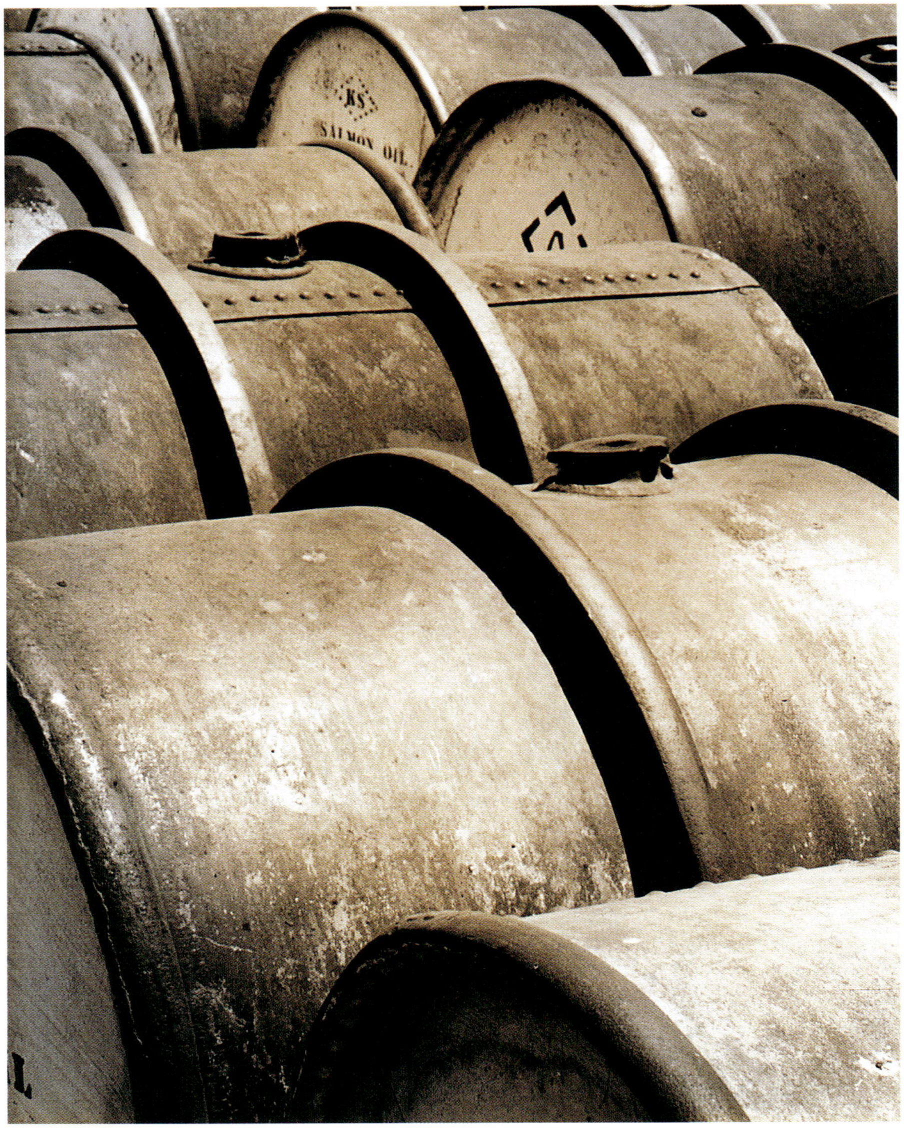

81.

JOHN PAUL EDWARDS

Oil Drums, c. 1932

Gelatin silver print

9⅝ x 7½

GIFT OF MRS. JOHN PAUL EDWARDS

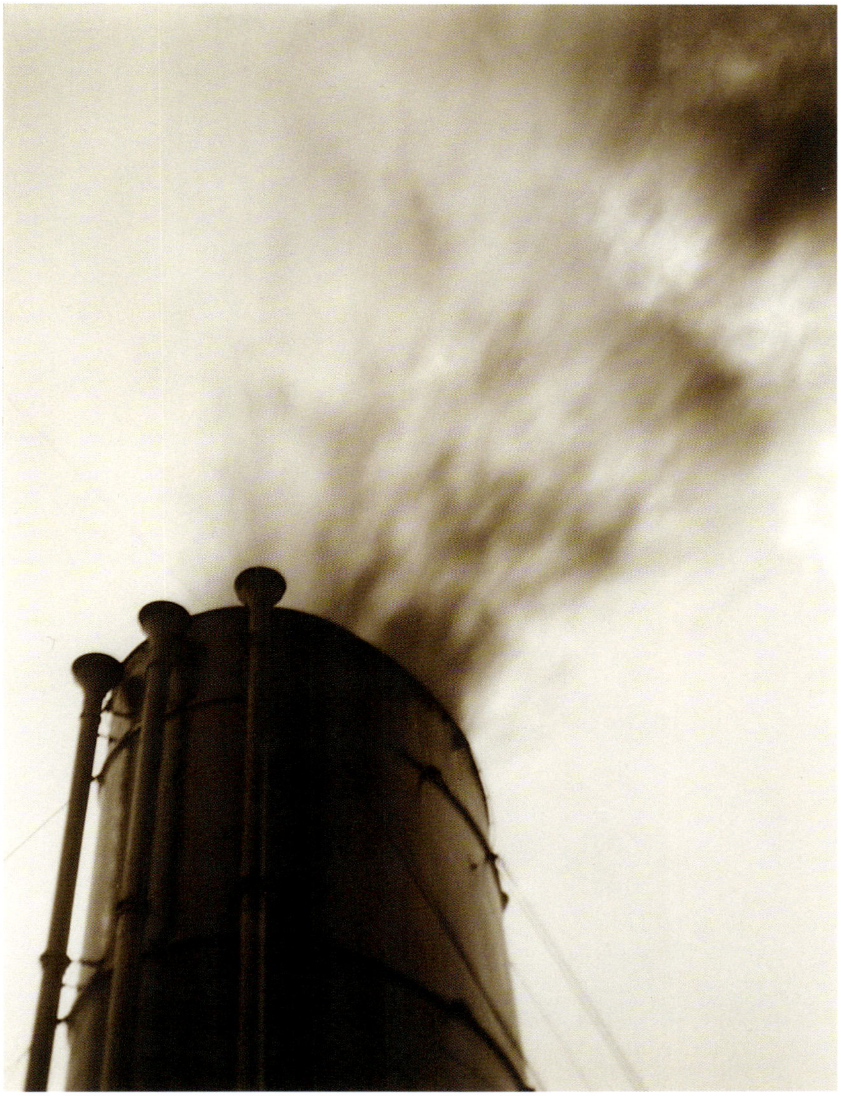

82.
JOHN PAUL EDWARDS
Roaring Stack, c. 1932
Gelatin silver print
12⅛ x 9 in.
GIFT OF MRS. JOHN PAUL EDWARDS

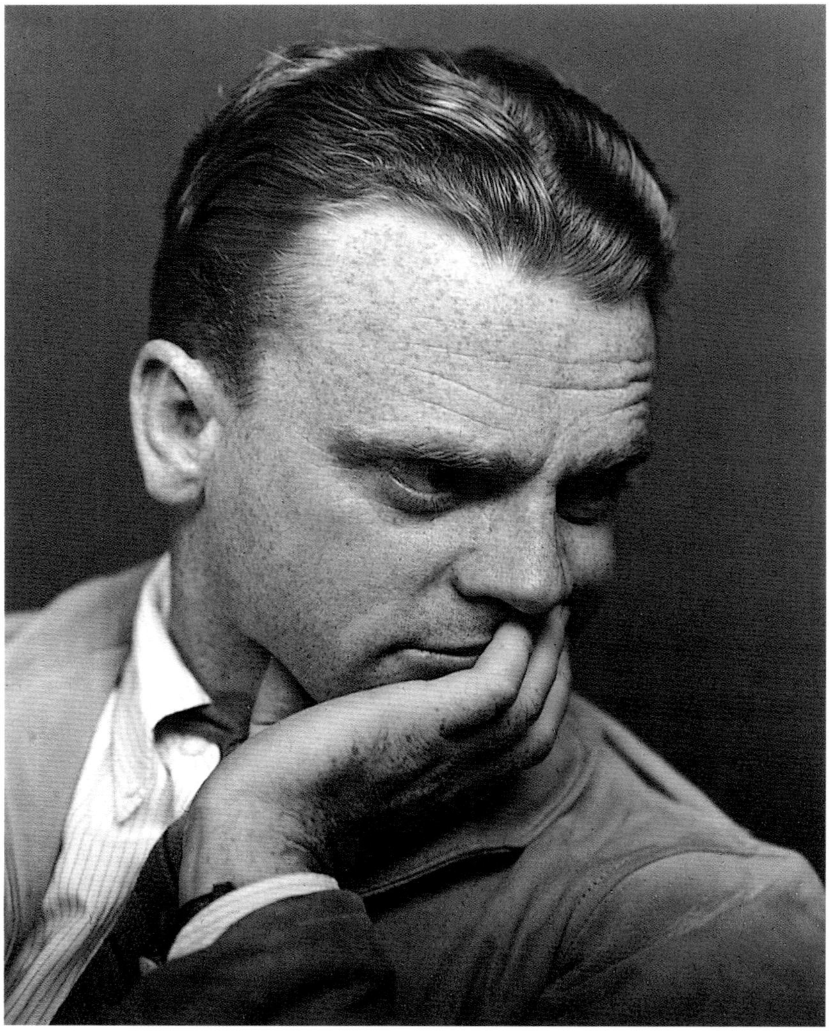

83.
EDWARD WESTON
Portrait of James Cagney, 1933
Gelatin silver print
$4\frac{5}{8}$ x $3\frac{5}{8}$ in.
THE OAKLAND MUSEUM FOUNDERS' FUND

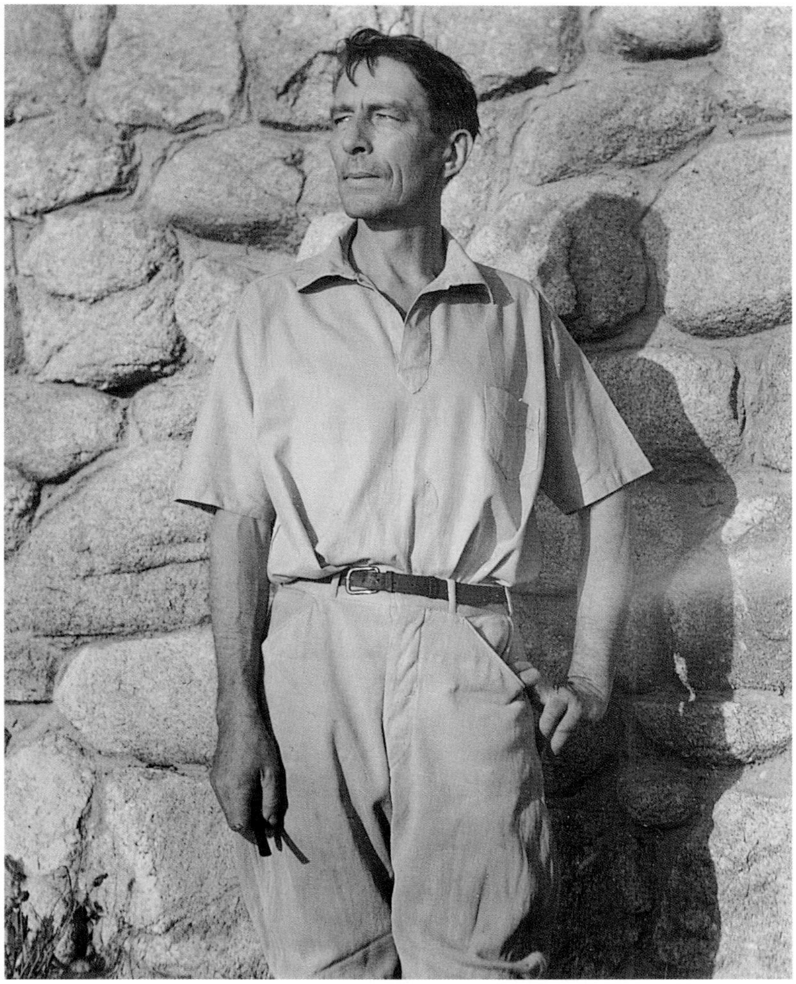

84.

SONYA NOSKOWIAK

Portrait of Robinson Jeffers, c. 1938

Gelatin silver print

3½ x 2¾ in.

THE SHIRLEY BURDEN FUND FOR PHOTOGRAPHY

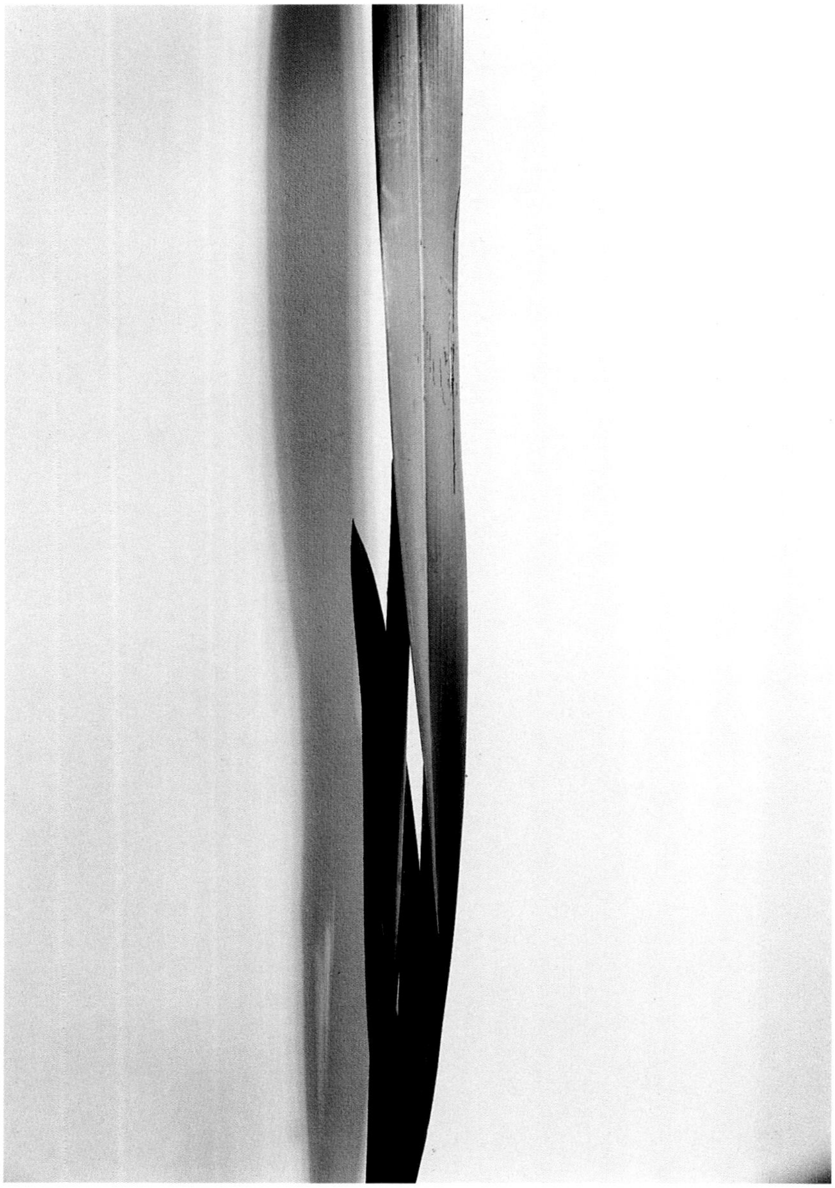

85.
IMOGEN CUNNINGHAM
Flax 2, 1920s
Carbon print
9 ¼ x 6 ⅜ in.
ACQUISITION MADE POSSIBLE BY DR. PAUL S. TAYLOR

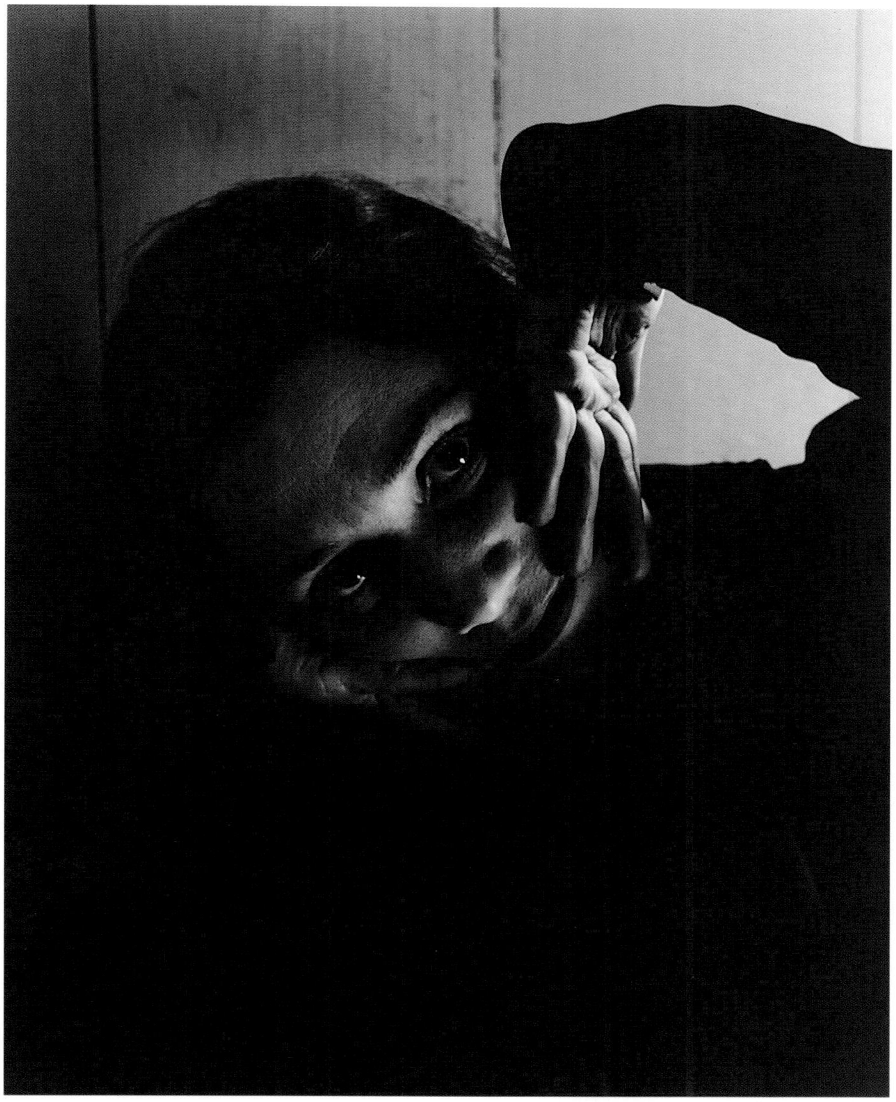

86.

IMOGEN CUNNINGHAM

Portrait of Marion Simpson, Painter, 1934

Gelatin silver print

9¼ x 7 7/16 in.

GIFT OF THE ESTATE OF MARION SIMPSON

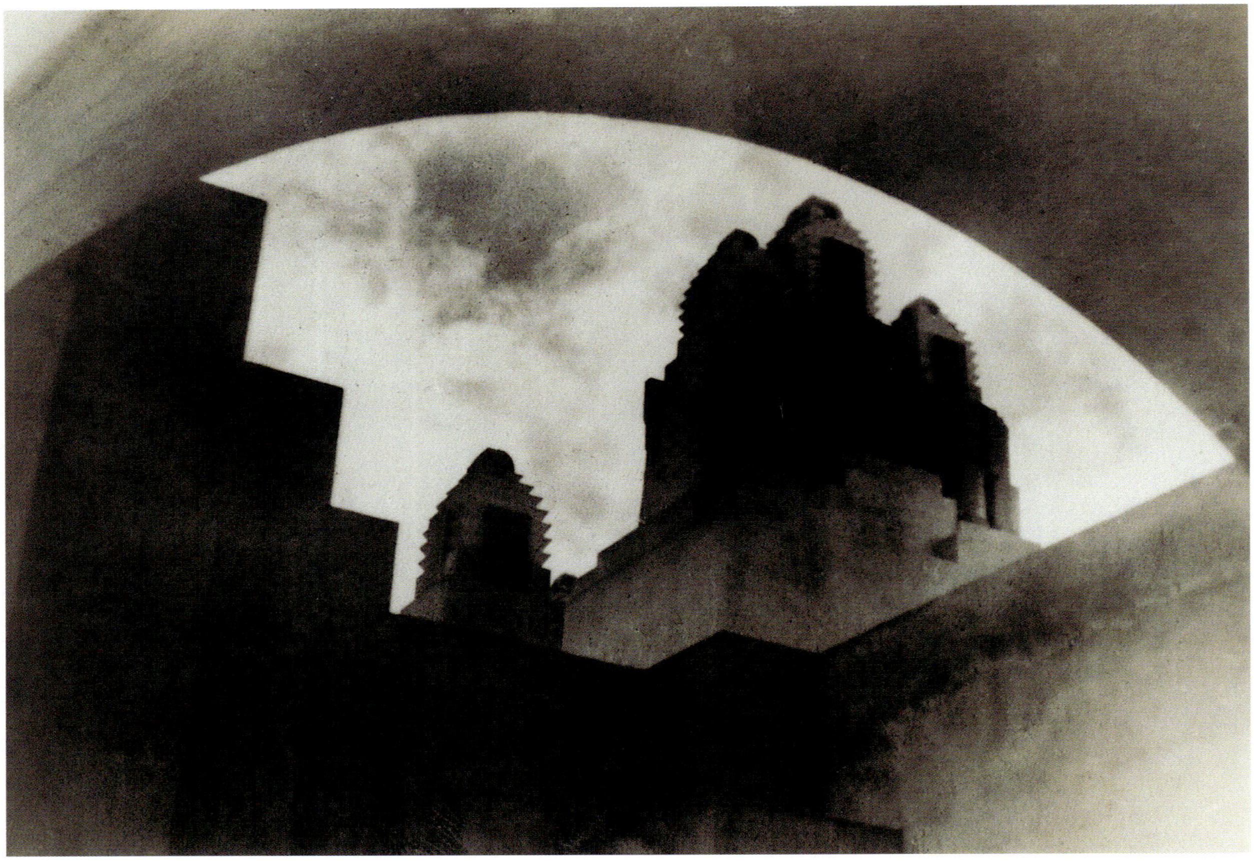

87.

ANNE BRIGMAN

West Elephant Tower, Treasure Island, 1940

Gelatin silver print

6⅞ x 9½ in.

GIFT OF MR. AND MRS. WILLARD M. NOTT

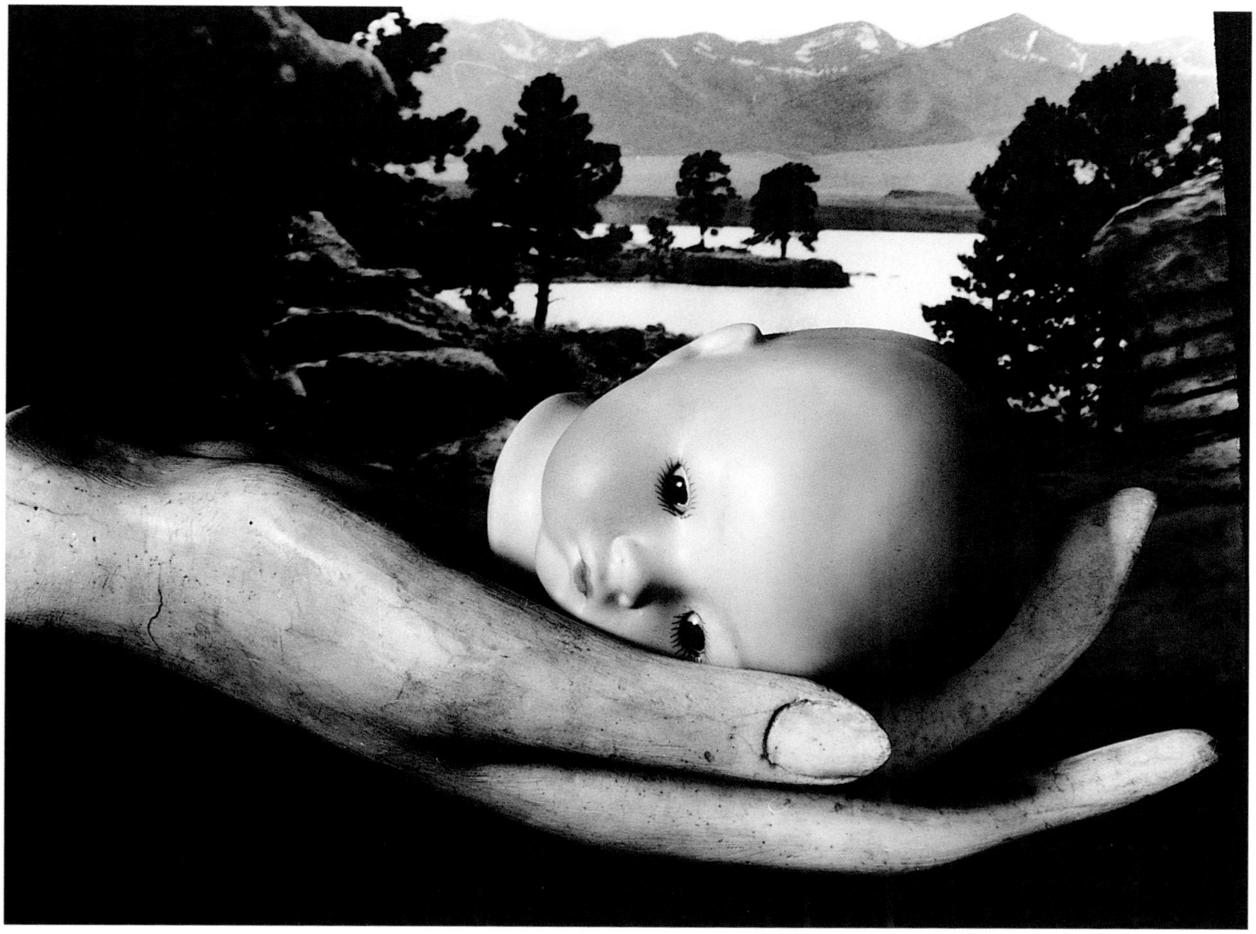

88.

RUTH BERNHARD

Creation (Doll's Head), Hollywood, California, 1936

Gelatin silver print

7½ x 9½ in.

DOROTHEA LANGE PURCHASE AWARD

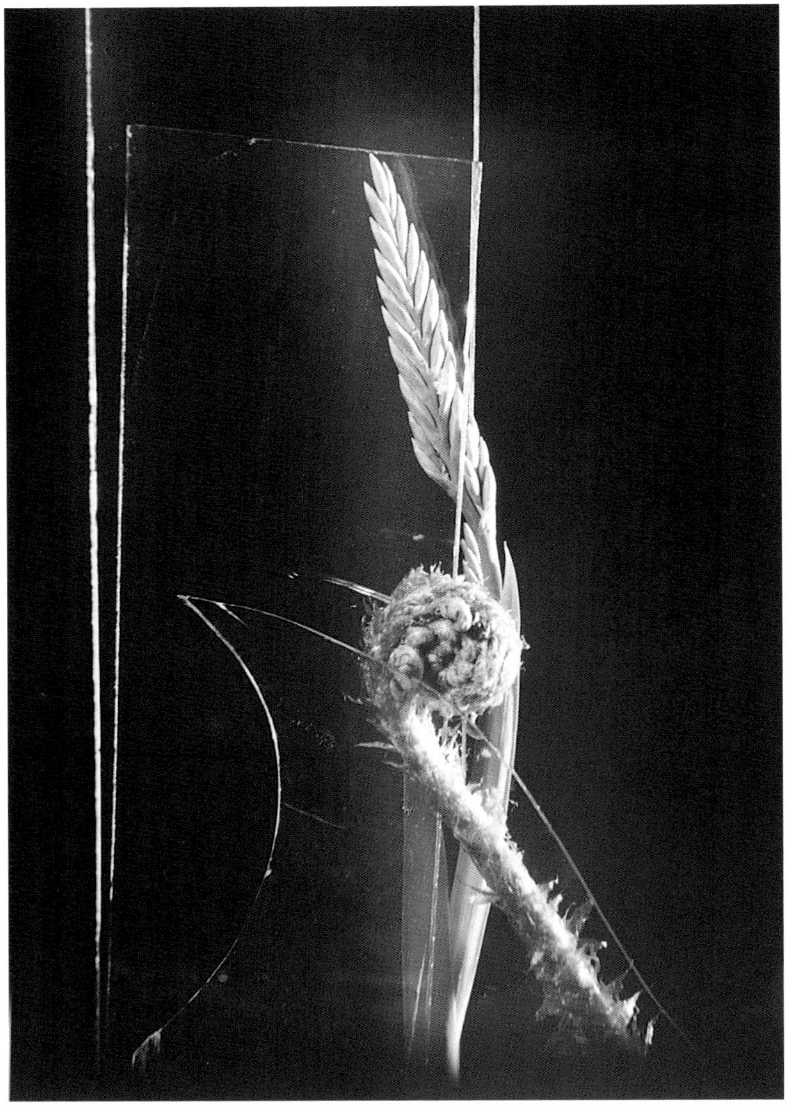

89.

ROGER STURTEVANT

Spring # 3, c. 1929

Gelatin silver print

9½ x 6½ in.

GIFT OF THE ARTIST

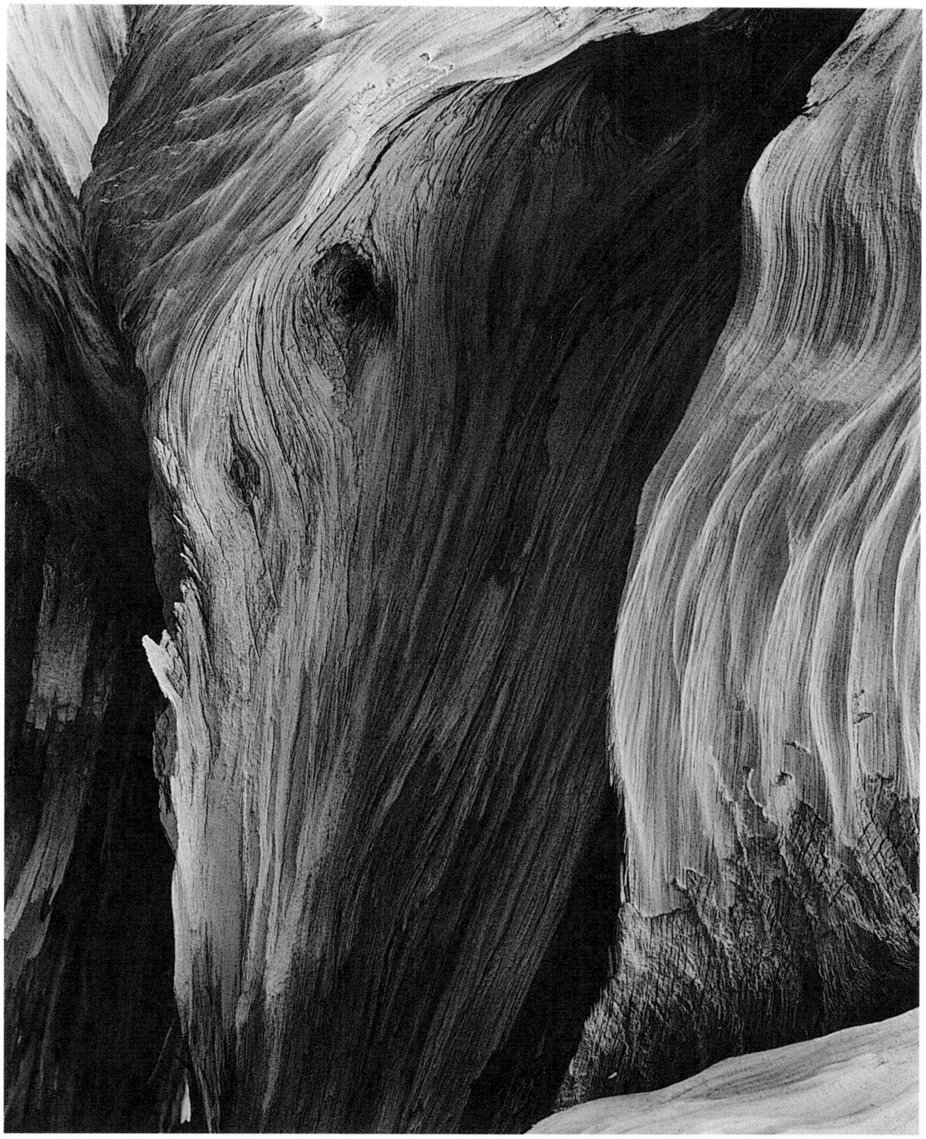

90.
CEDRIC WRIGHT
Untitled (Close-up of Wood), c. 1935
Gelatin silver print
9⅜ x 7⅜ in.
GIFT OF HELEN C. KIDDER

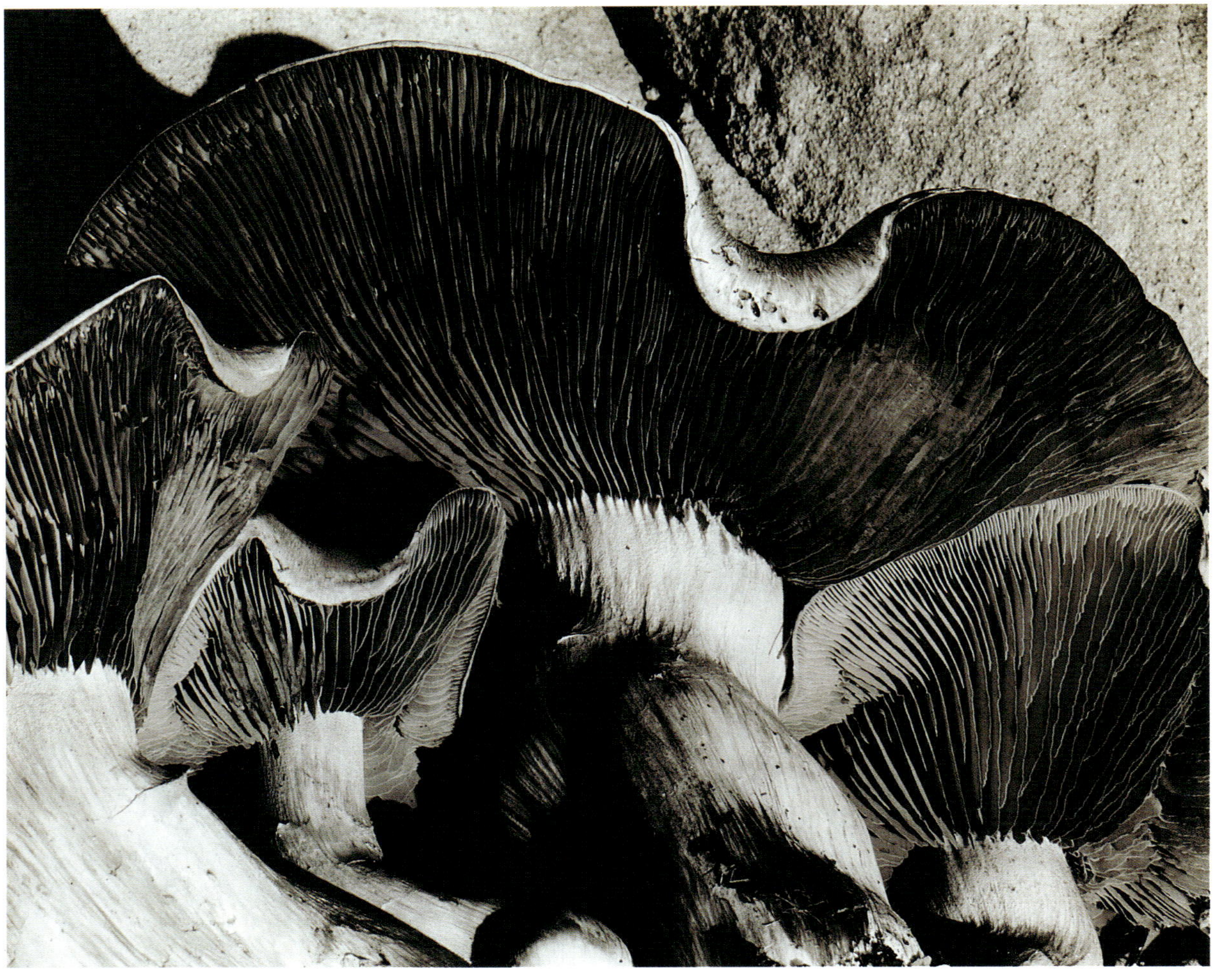

91.
WILLARD VAN DYKE
Mushrooms, c. 1934
Gelatin silver print
7½ x 8⅞ in.
GIFT OF MRS. ALMA LAVENSON WAHRHAFTIG

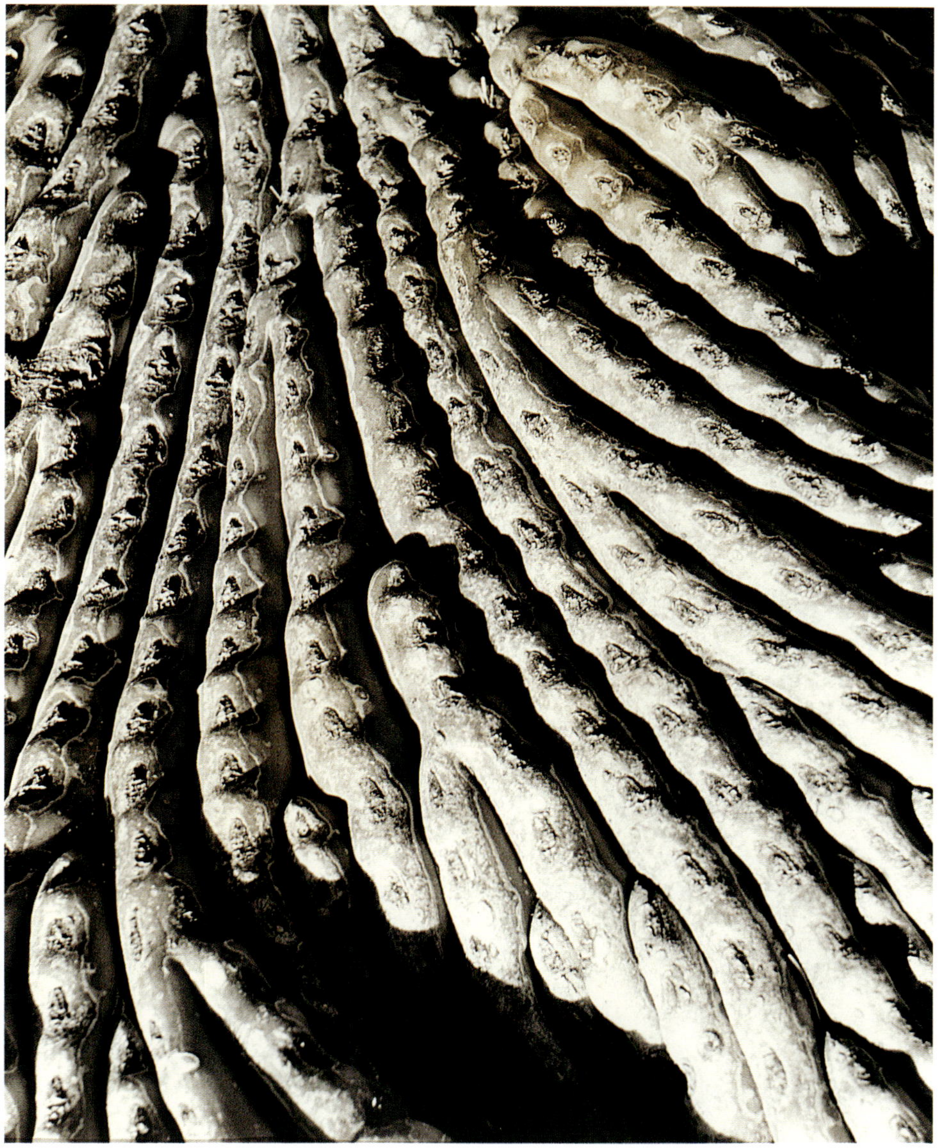

92.
SONYA NOSKOWIAK
Cactus, 1932
Gelatin silver print
9¾ x 7¾ in.
GIFT OF MR. JOHN PAUL EDWARDS

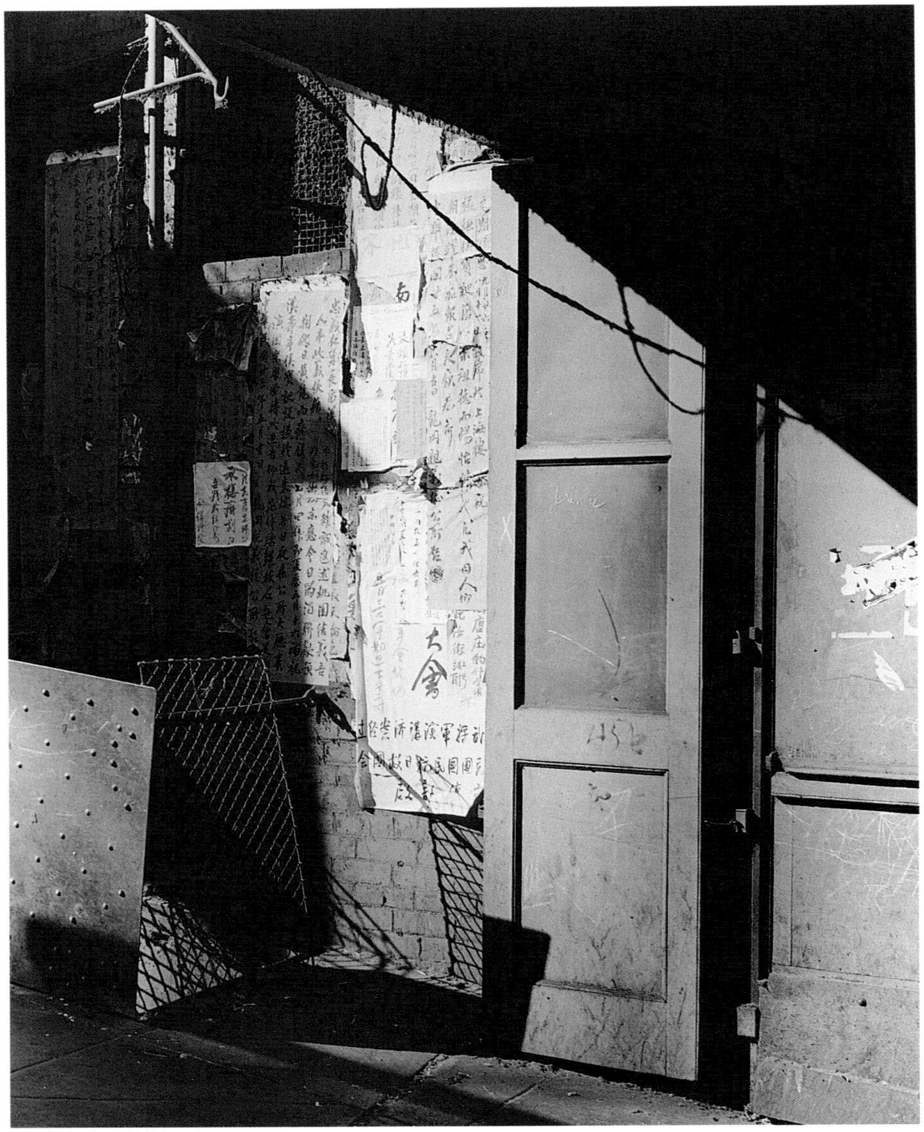

93.
WILLIAM H. ABBENSETH
Untitled (Chinatown), c. 1935
Gelatin silver print
9⅝ x 7½ in.
GIFT OF YOSHIKO KAKUDO AND JOAN ABBENSETH

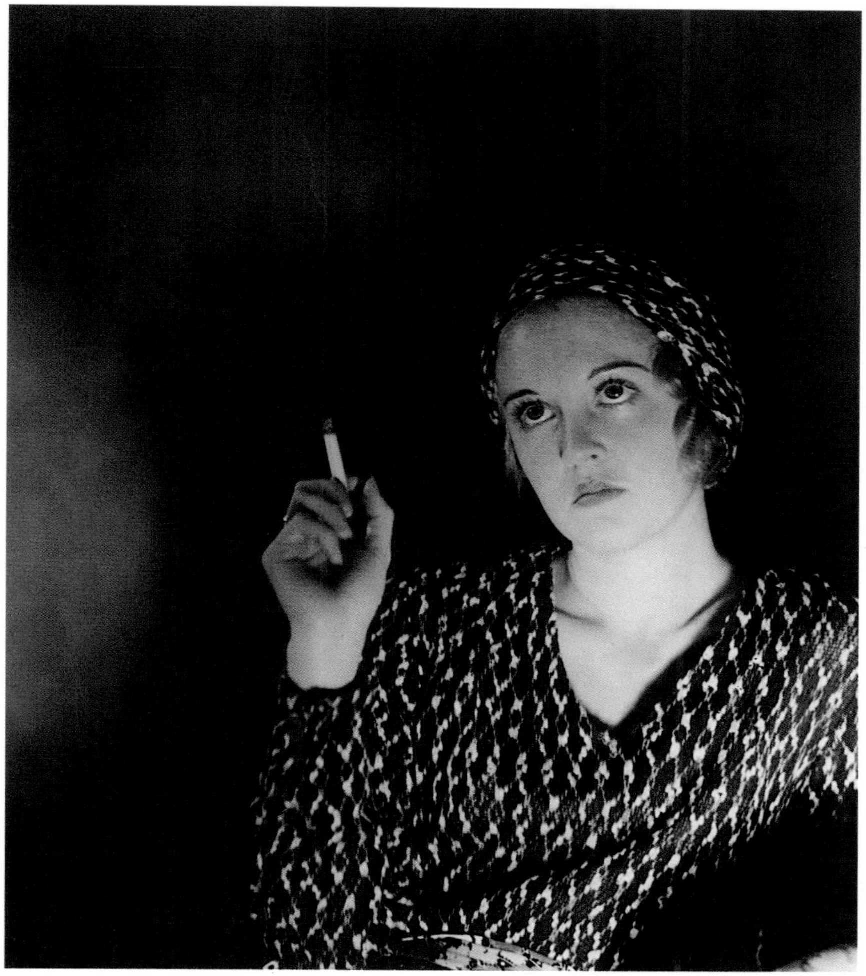

94.
WILLIAM SIMPSON
Untitled (Woman with Cigarette), c. 1935
Gelatin silver print
7½ x 6⅜ in.
GIFT OF ANITA SIMPSON

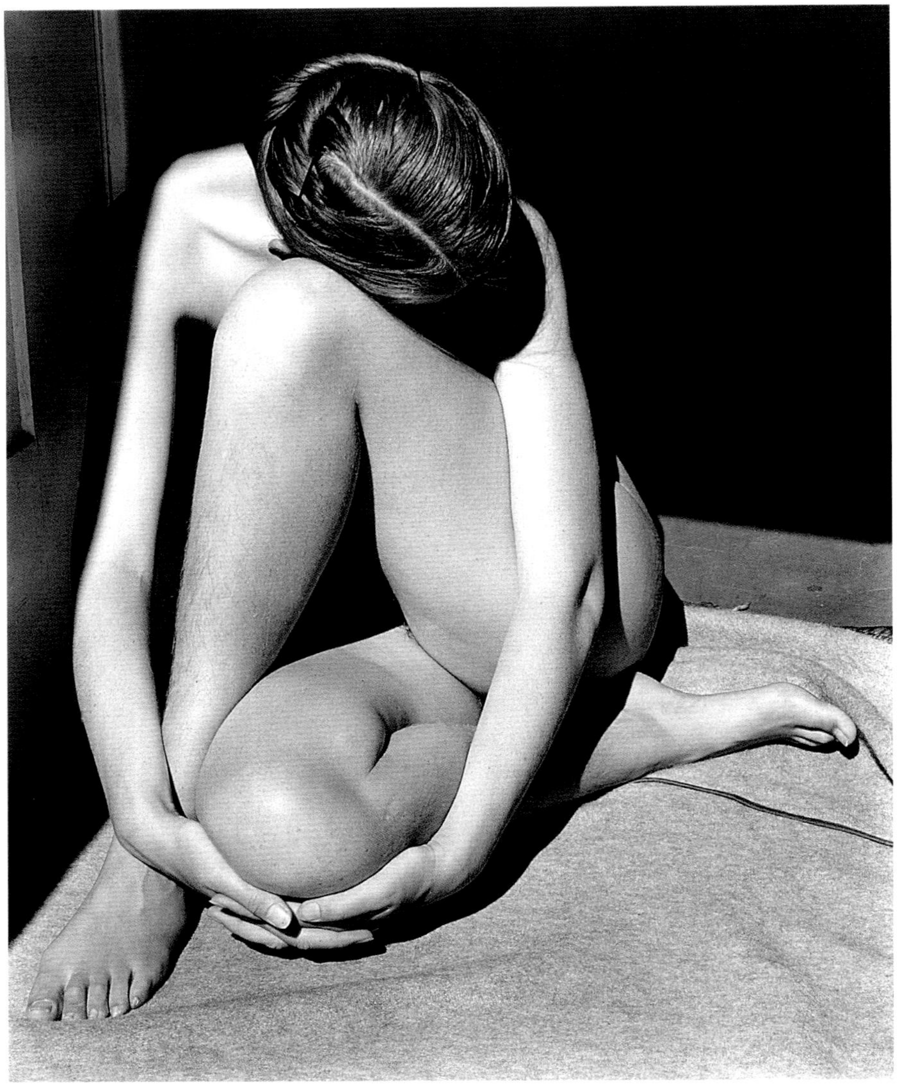

95.
EDWARD WESTON
Nude, 1936
Gelatin silver print
9½ x 7¼ in.
GIFT OF THE BELL FUND

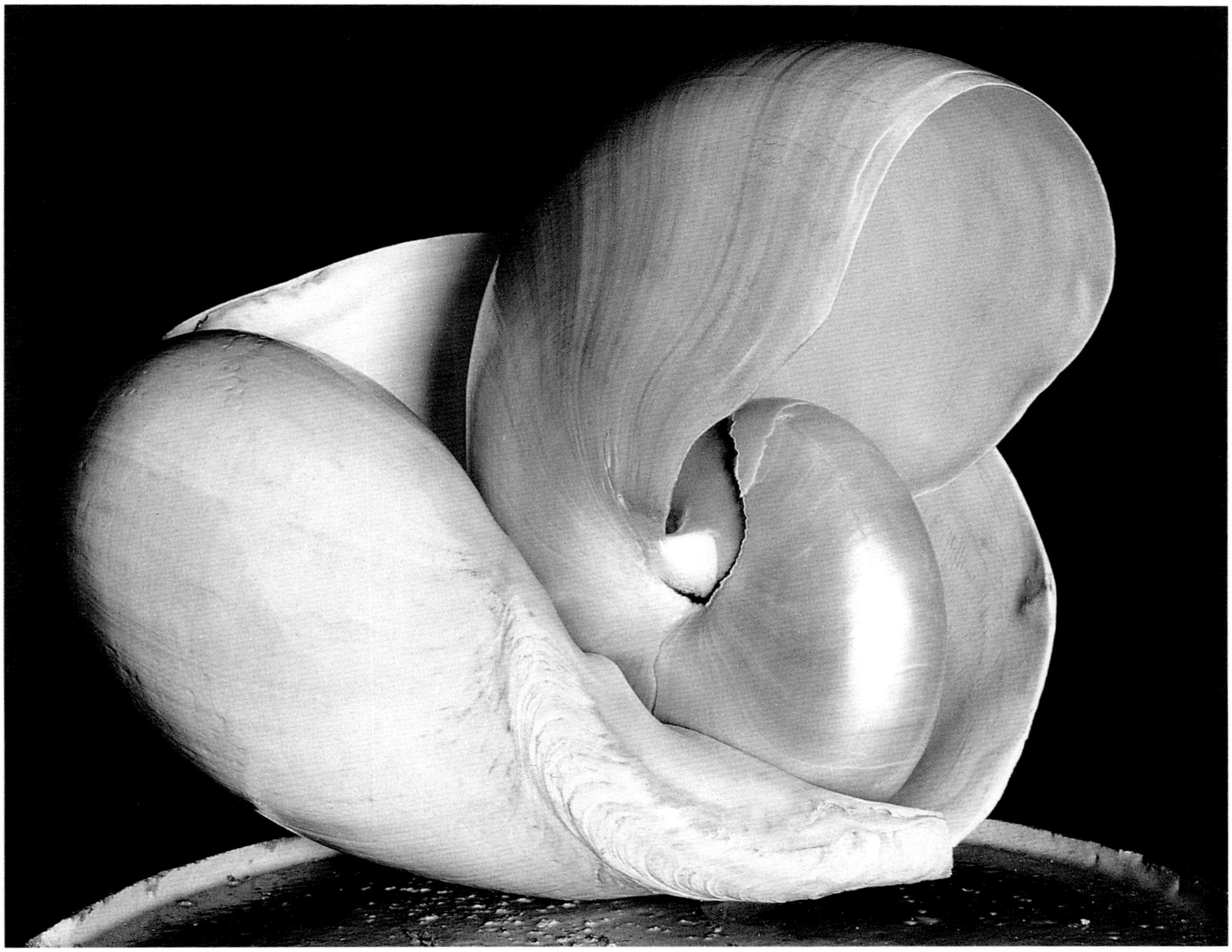

96.

EDWARD WESTON

Sea Shell, 1927 (print 1930)

Gelatin silver print

$7\frac{1}{2}$ x $9\frac{3}{8}$ in.

GIFT OF BRETT WESTON

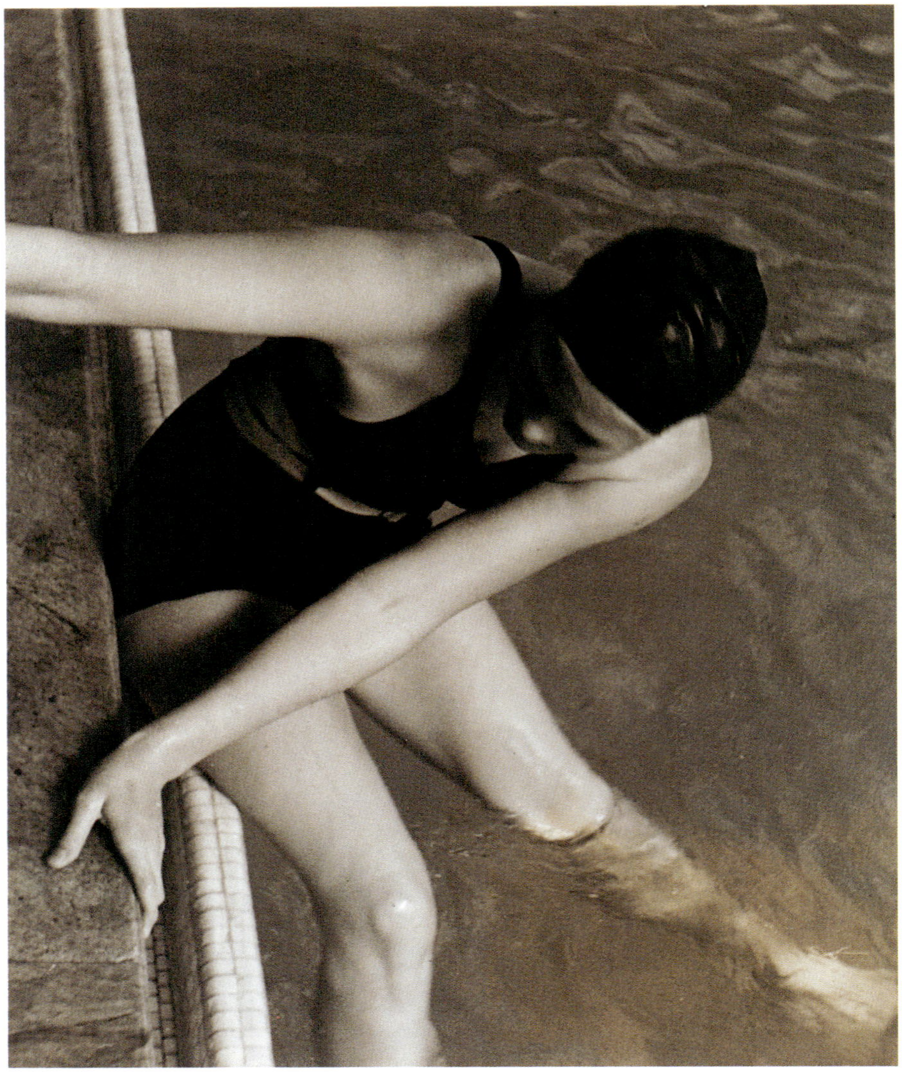

97.
PETER STACKPOLE
Dorothy Sunby Training for the Olympics, 1933
Gelatin silver print
7⅞ x 6⅜ in.
GIFT OF DOUGLAS ELLIOTT

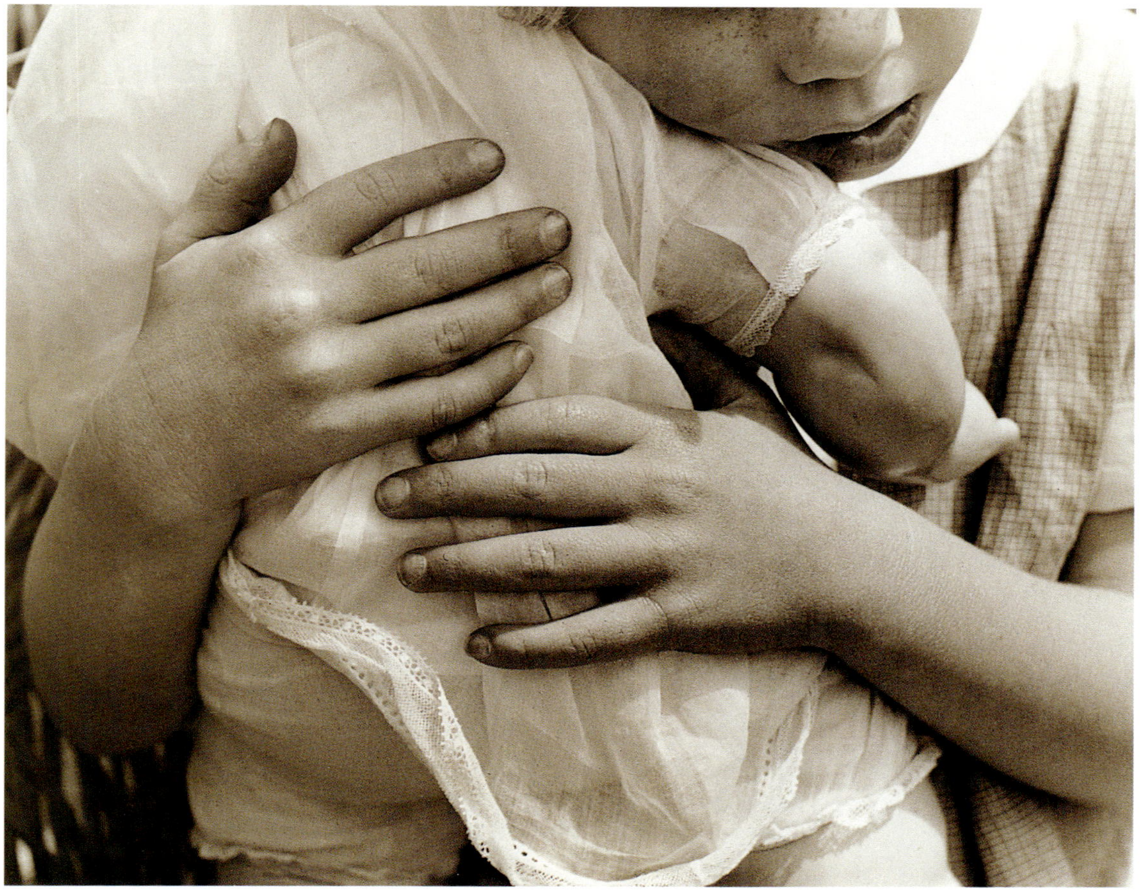

98.
ALMA LAVENSON
Child with Doll, 1932
Gelatin silver print
7½ x 9⁷⁄₁₆ in.
GIFT OF THE ARTIST

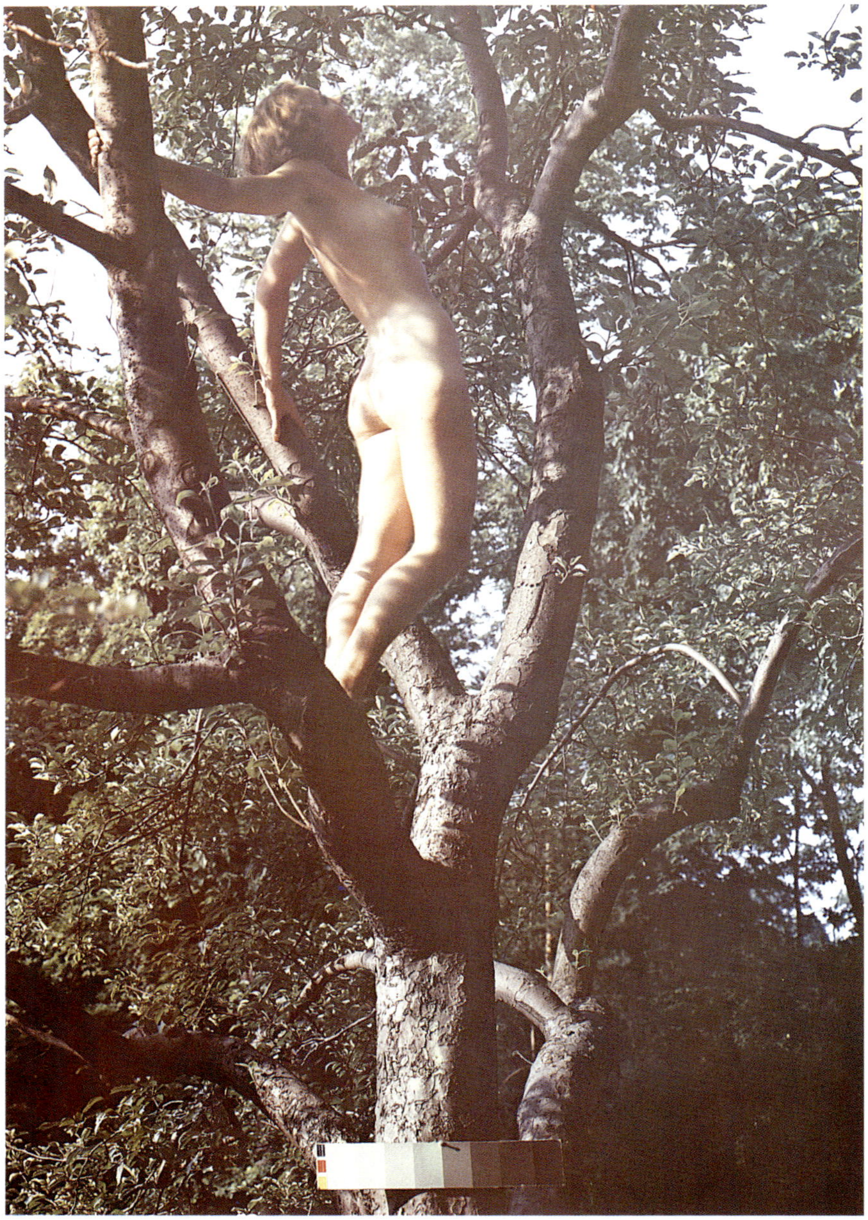

99.
PAUL OUTERBRIDGE
Nude in Tree, 1936
Tri-color carbro print
15½ x 10¾ in.
THE SHIRLEY BURDEN FUND FOR PHOTOGRAPHY

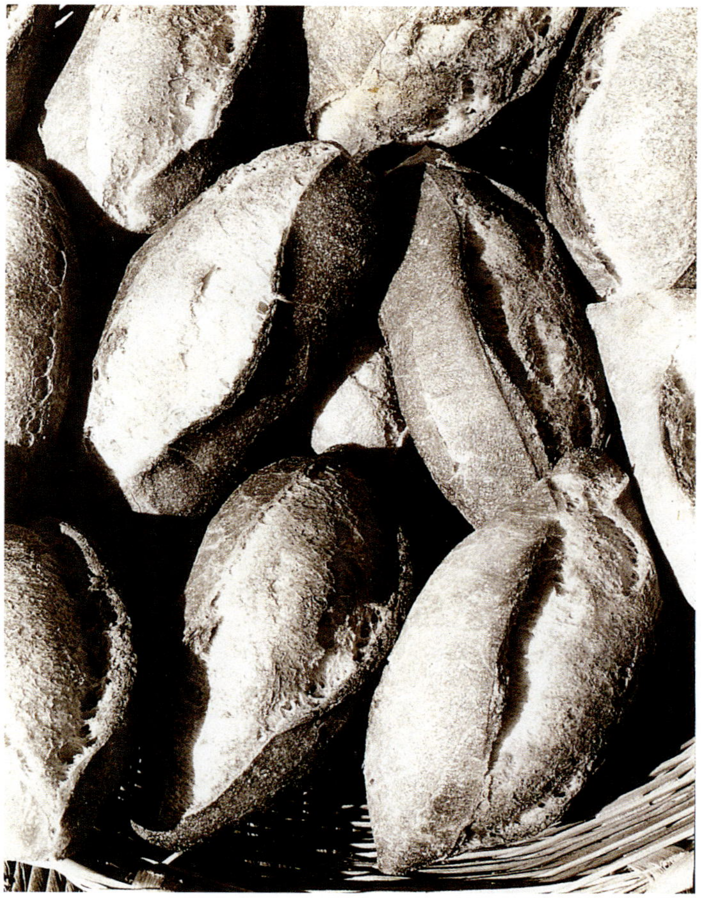

100.
BRETT WESTON
Mexico (Bread in a Basket), 1926
Gelatin silver print
3 3/4 x 2 7/8 in.
THE OAKLAND MUSEUM FOUNDERS FUND

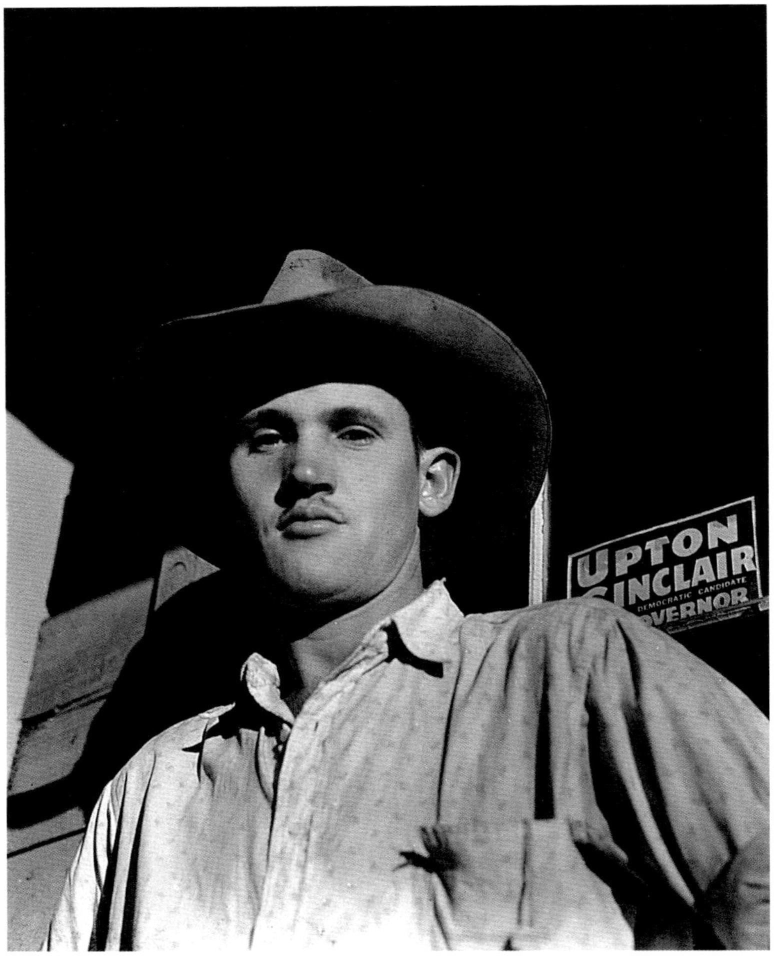

101.
IMOGEN CUNNINGHAM
Cowboy at Coonsaw, 1934
Gelatin silver print
6 x 7½ in.
GIFT OF PAUL S. TAYLOR

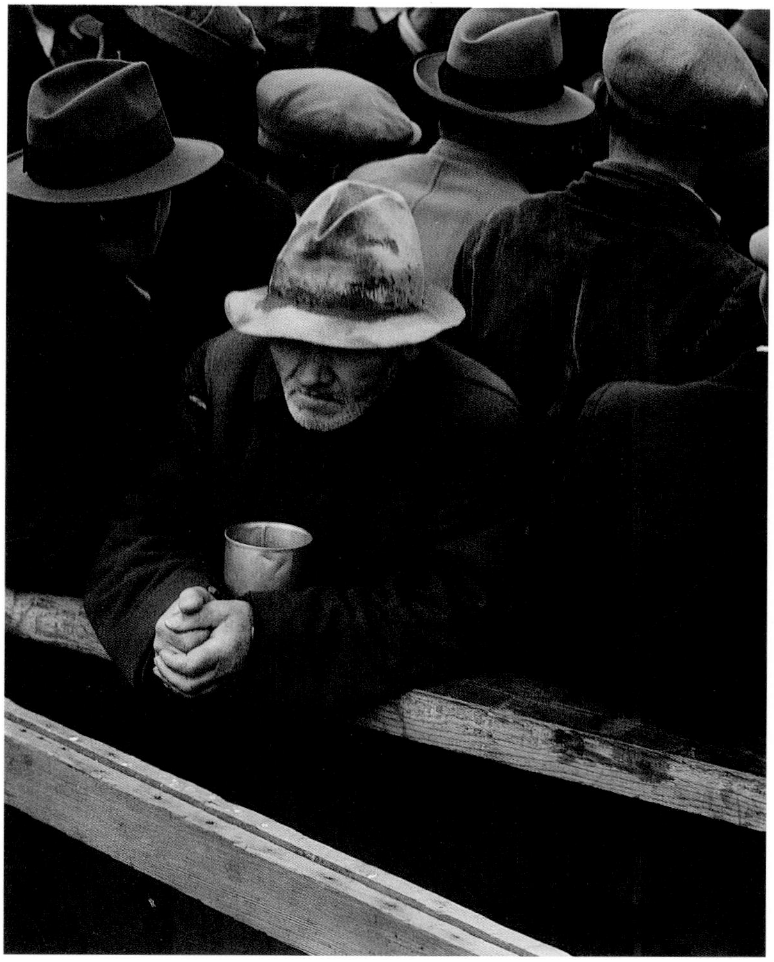

102.
DOROTHEA LANGE
White Angel Breadline, San Francisco, 1933
Gelatin silver print
7½ x 6 in.
GIFT OF PAUL S. TAYLOR

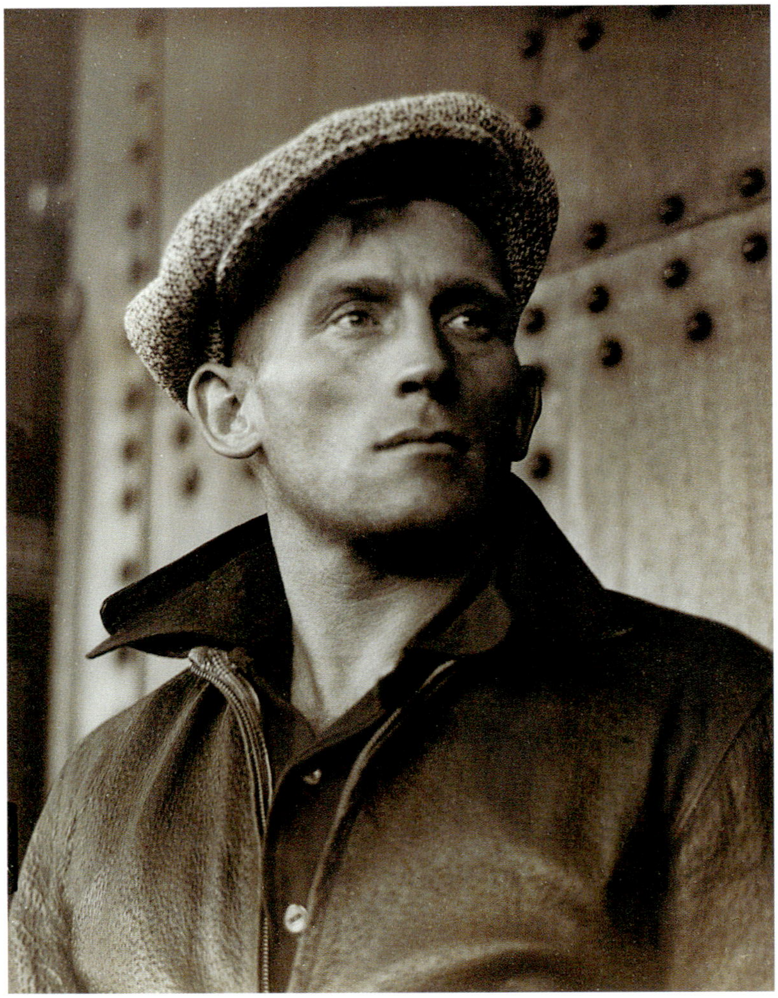

103.

DOROTHEA LANGE

Untitled (Matanuska Colonist Bound for Alaska), May 1935

Gelatin silver print

7 1/4 x 9 5/8 in.

GIFT OF PAUL S. TAYLOR

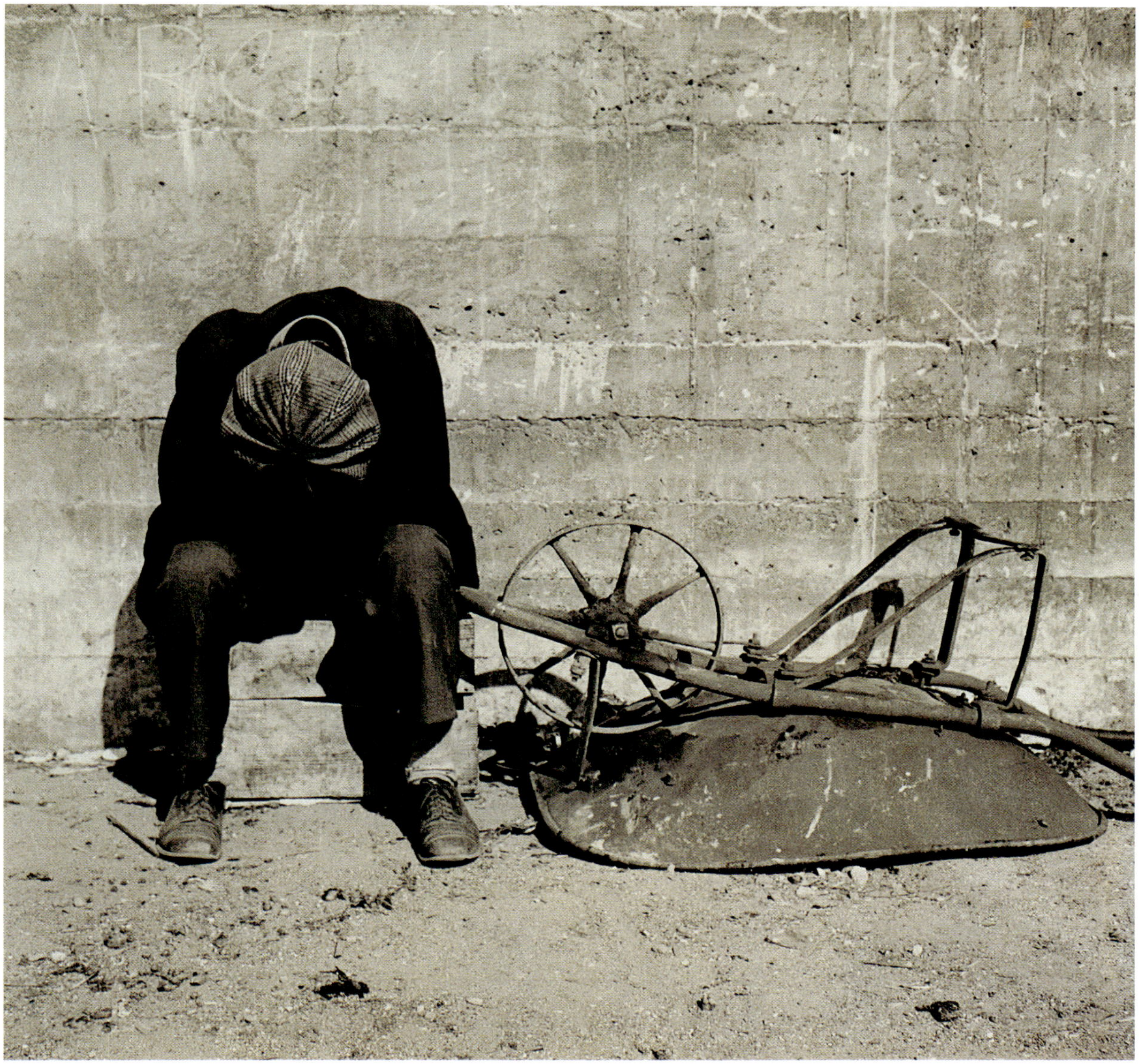

104.
DOROTHEA LANGE
Man Beside Wheelbarrow, 1934
Gelatin silver print
7 x 7⅜ in.
GIFT OF PAUL S. TAYLOR

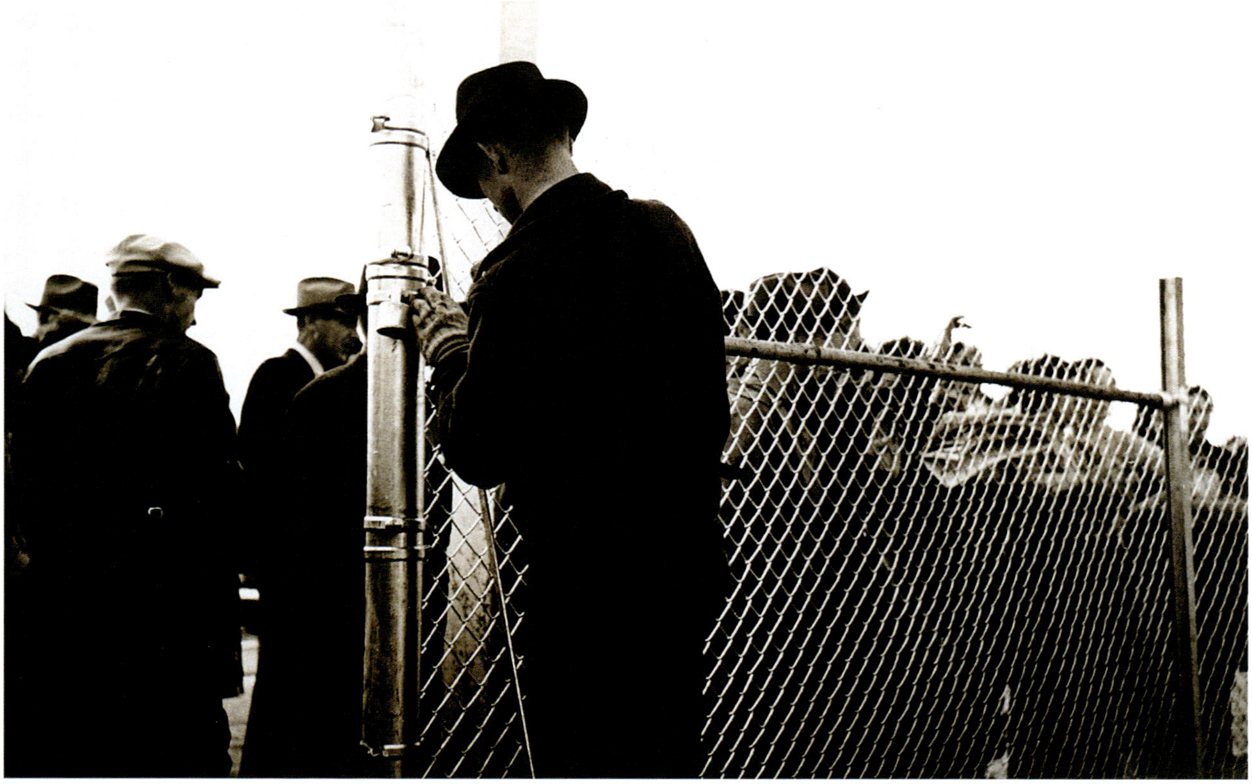

105.
OTTO HAGEL
Untitled (Salinas Lettuce Strike), 1936
Gelatin silver print
9⁹⁄₁₆ x 6⁵⁄₈ in.
GIFT OF PAUL S. TAYLOR

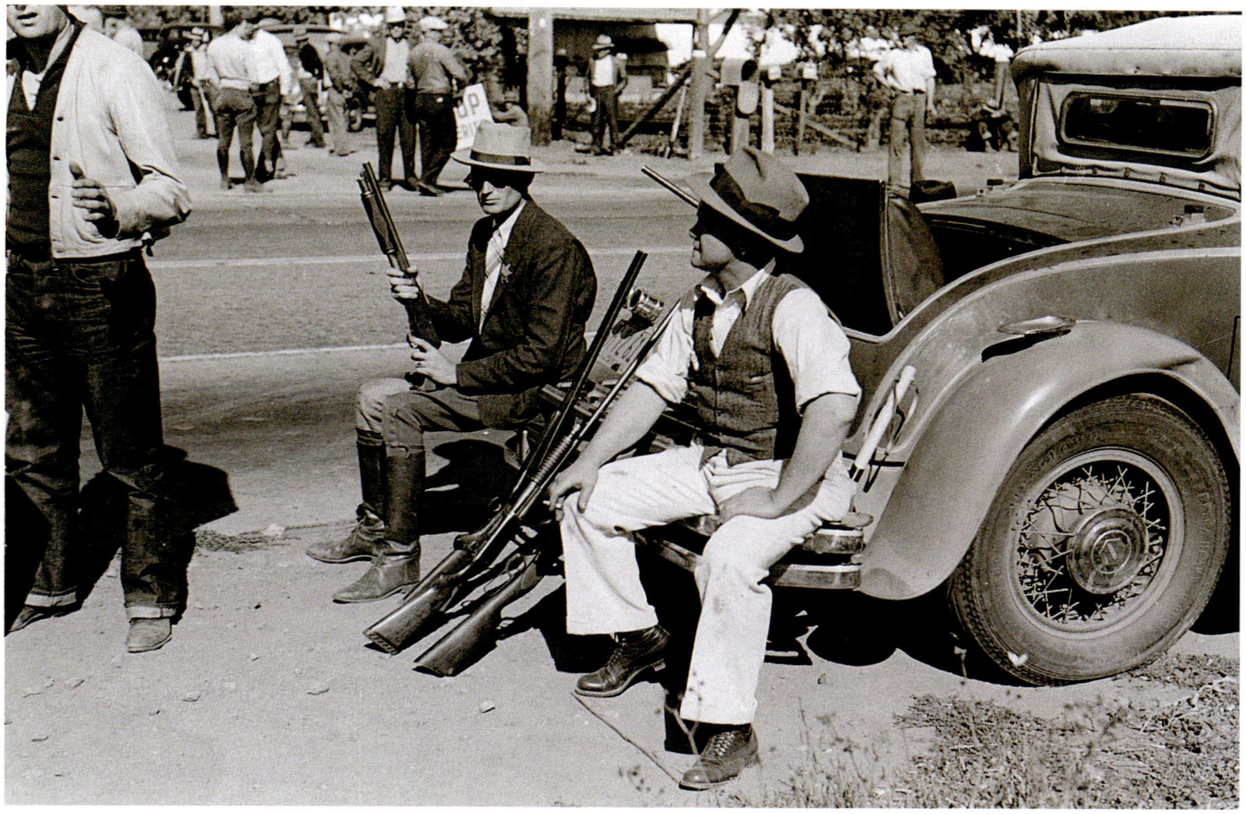

106.
OTTO HAGEL
Untitled (Salinas Lettuce Strike), 1936
Gelatin silver print
$9\frac{9}{16}$ x $6\frac{5}{8}$ in.
GIFT OF PAUL S. TAYLOR

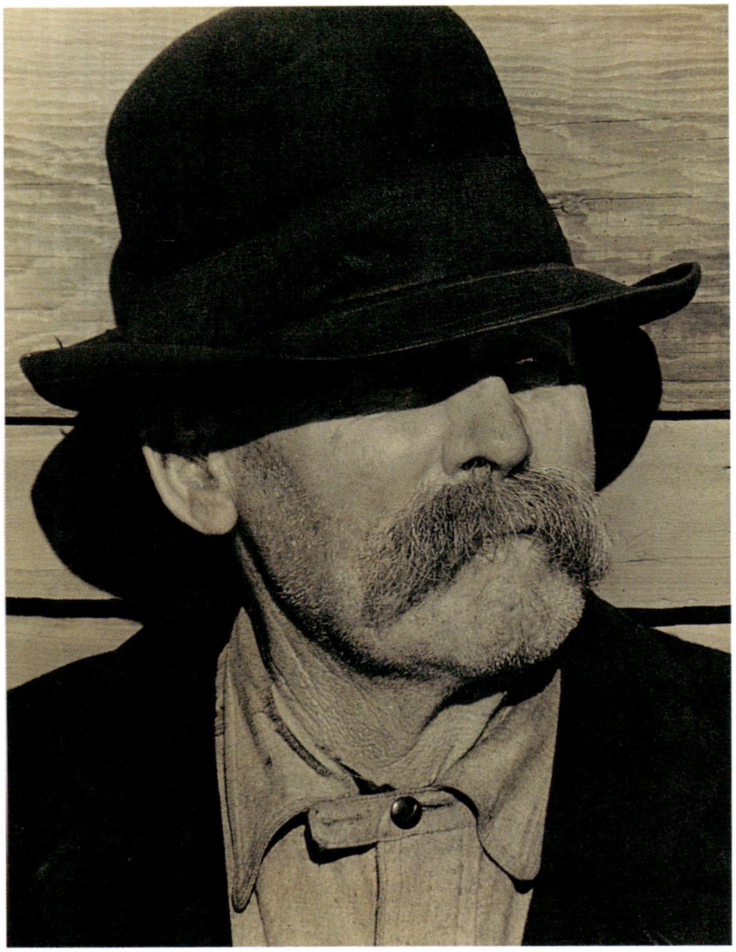

107.
WILLIAM SIMPSON
Untitled (Old Man), c. 1935
Gelatin silver print
6 x 4½ in.
GIFT OF ANITA SIMPSON

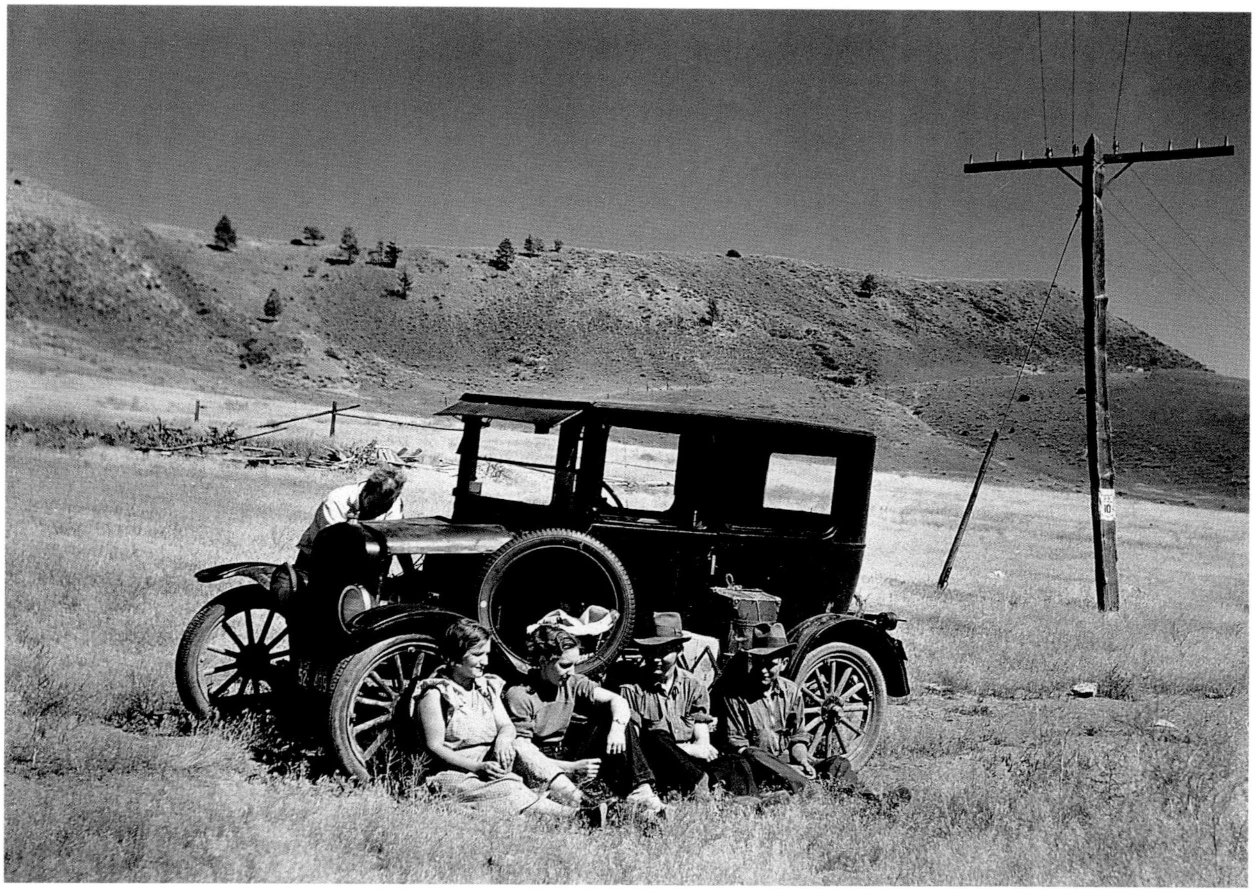

108.

ARTHUR ROTHSTEIN

Untitled (Vernon Evans and Family, Headed West from Lemmon, South Dakota), Summer 1936

Gelatin silver print

9⅝ x 7⅛ in.

GIFT OF PAUL S. TAYLOR

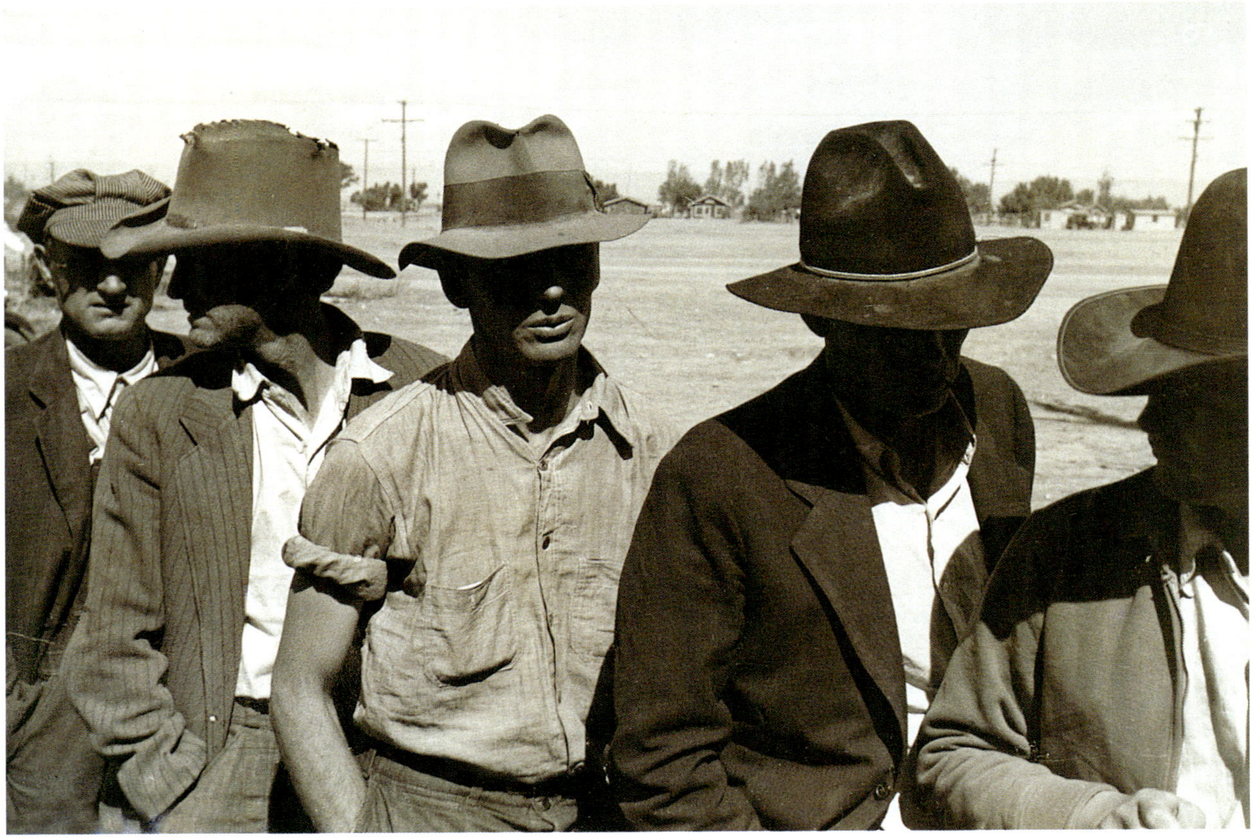

109.

RONDAL PARTRIDGE

Untitled (Men Lined Up for Relief), c. 1936

Gelatin silver print

4½ x 6½ in.

GIFT OF PAUL S. TAYLOR

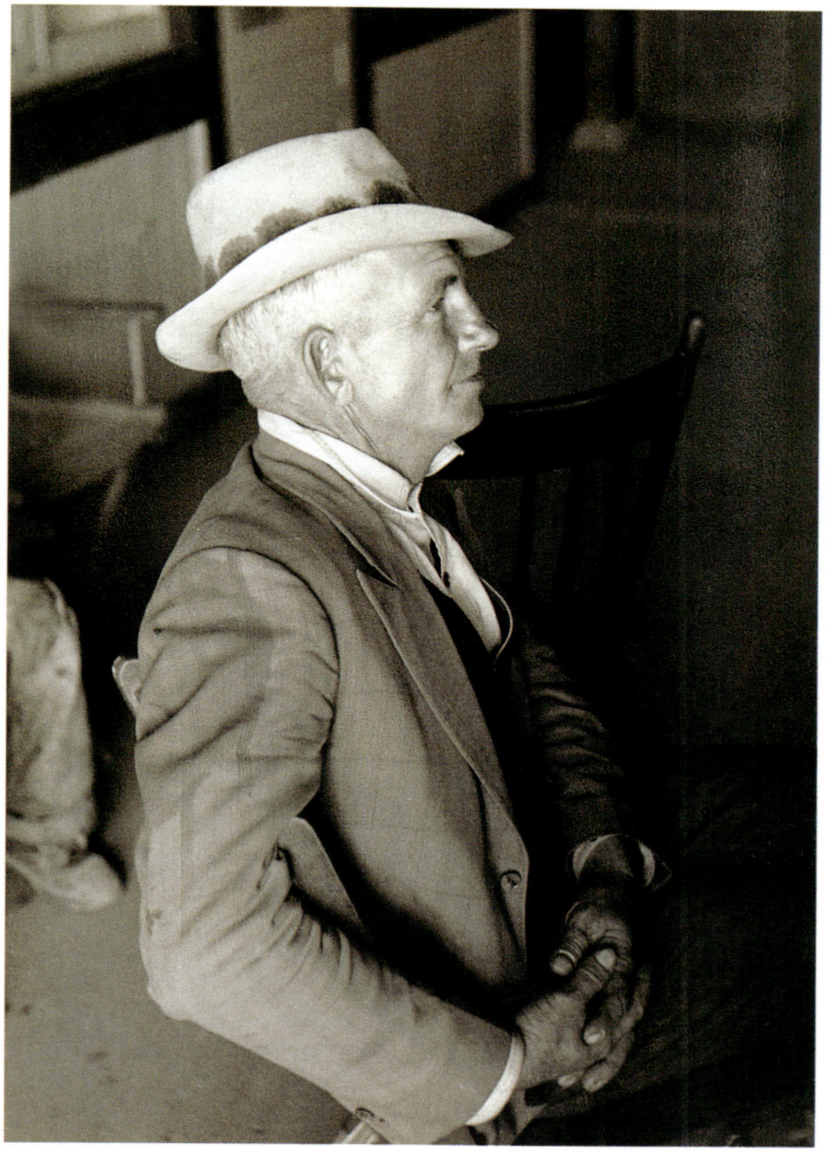

110.
RONDAL PARTRIDGE
Untitled (Unemployed Man), c. 1936
Gelatin silver print
$6^{11}/_{16}$ x $4^{11}/_{16}$ in.
GIFT OF PAUL S. TAYLOR

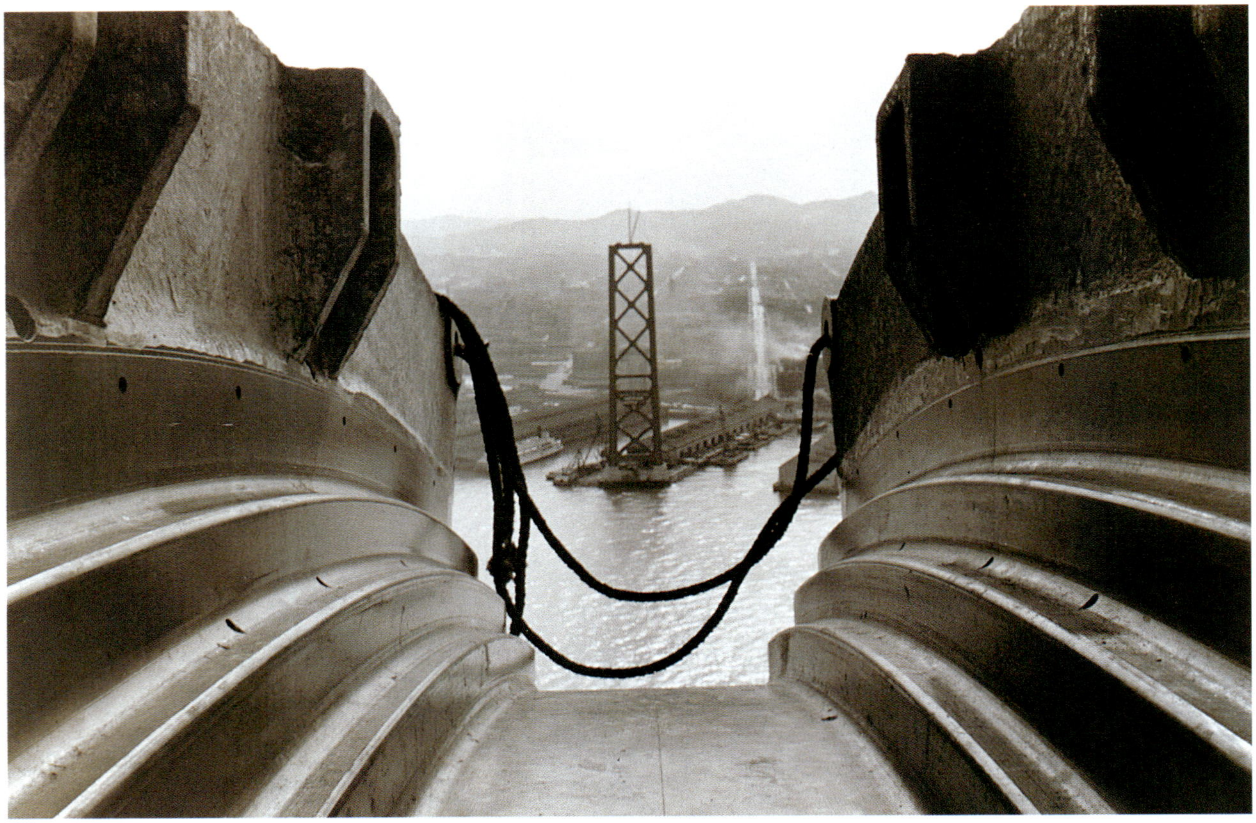

111.

PETER STACKPOLE

Cable Saddle (San Francisco–Oakland Bay Bridge), 1935

Gelatin silver print

4⅝ x 6 15/16 in.

GIFT OF THE ARTIST

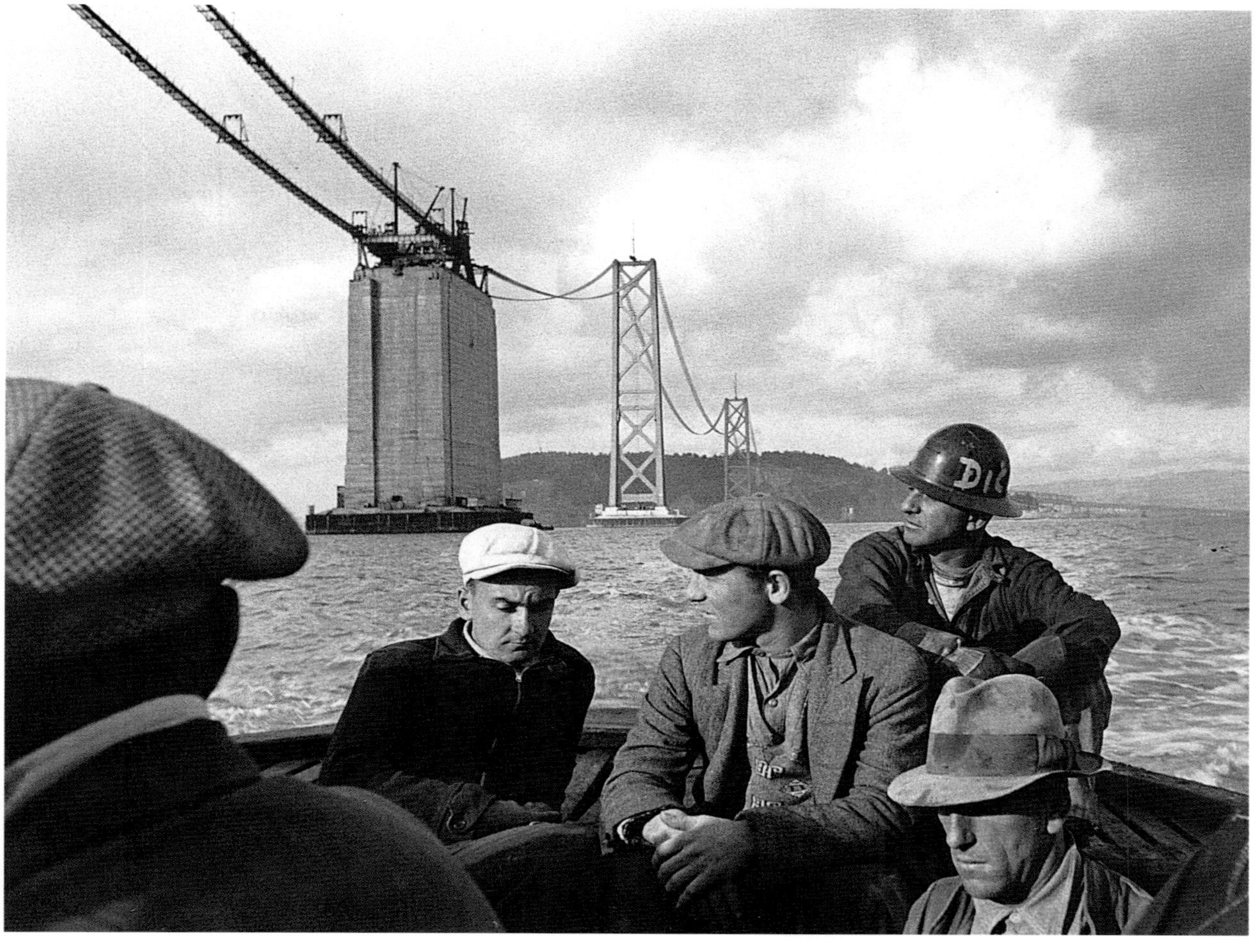

112.
PETER STACKPOLE
Quitting Time (San Francisco–Oakland Bay Bridge), 1935
Gelatin silver print
7 x 9⅛ in.
THE OAKLAND MUSEUM FOUNDERS' FUND

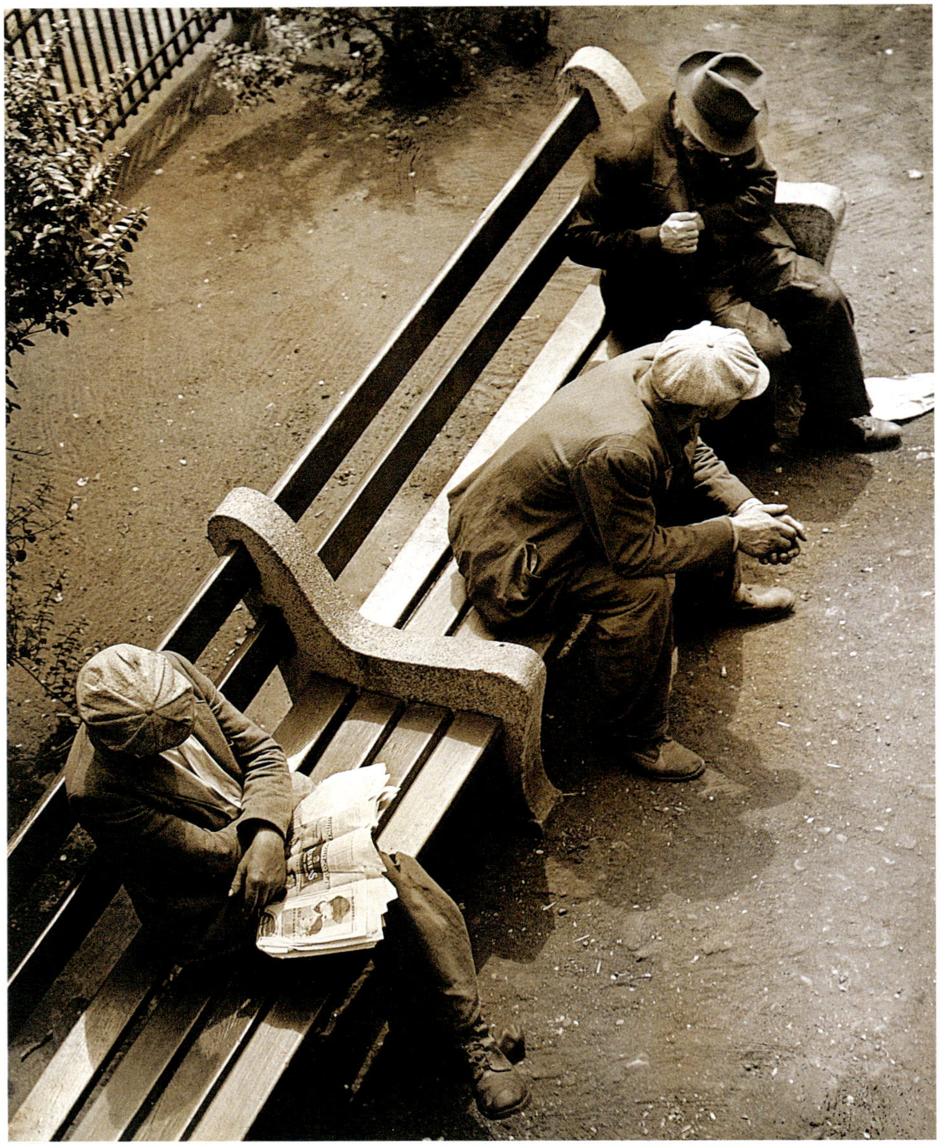

113.

WILLIAM ABBENSETH

Untitled (Men on Bench), c. 1935

Gelatin silver print

9½ x 7½ in.

GIFT OF YOSHIKO KAKUDO AND JOAN ABBENSETH

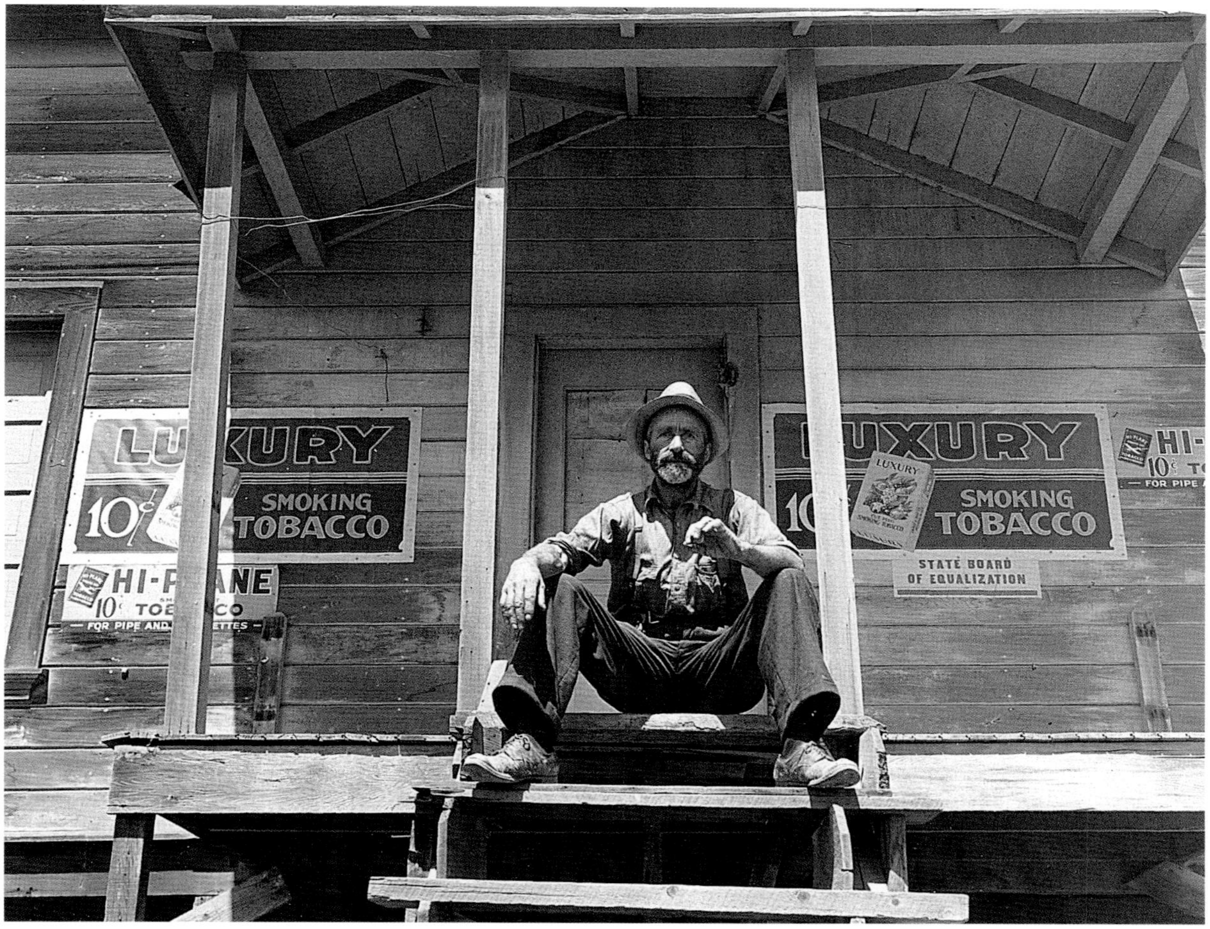

114.
WILLARD VAN DYKE
Man Sitting on Porch, c. 1935
Gelatin silver print
6 5/16 x 8 1/16 in.
GIFT OF PETER STACKPOLE

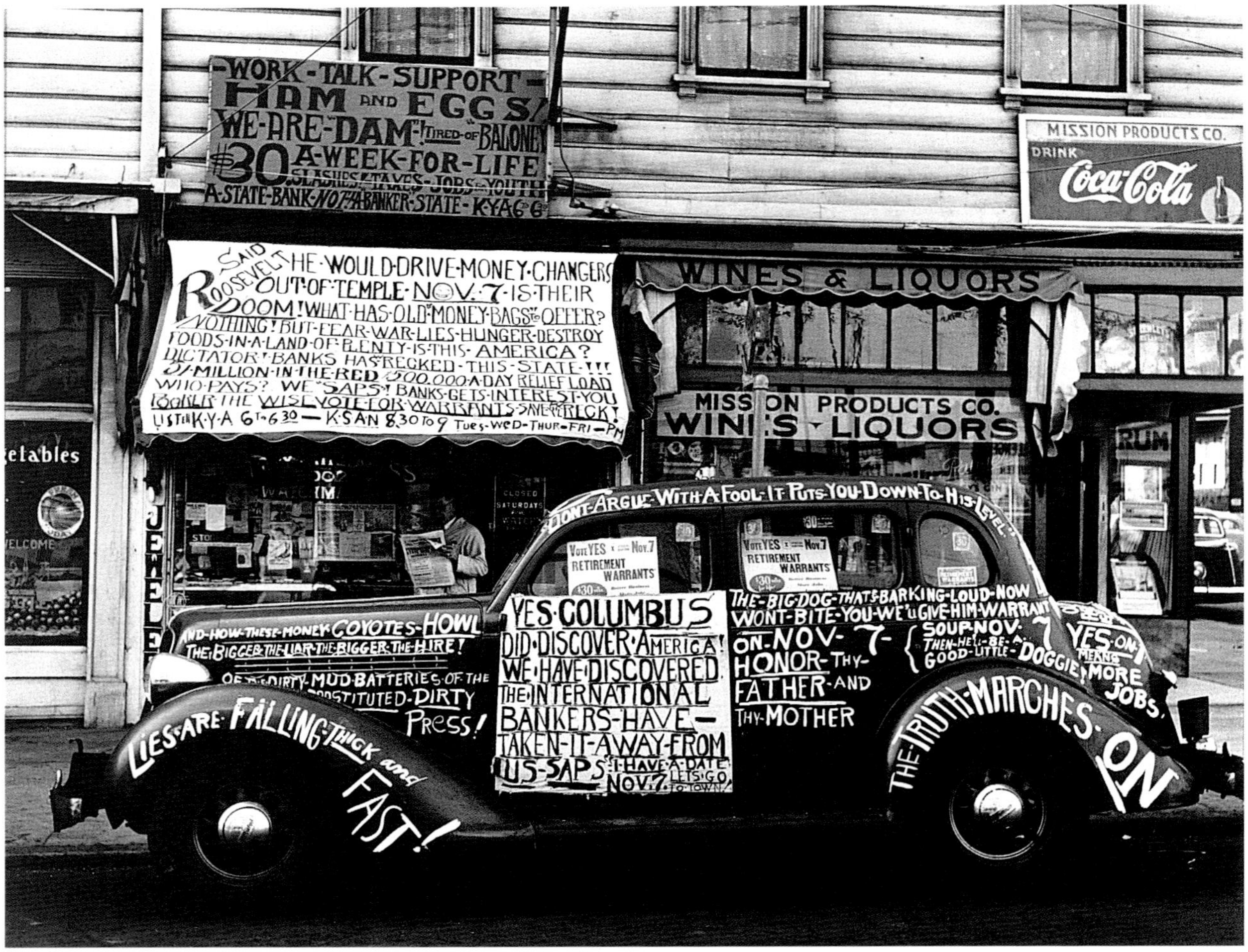

115.
JOHN GUTMANN
Yes, Columbus Did Discover America!, San Francisco, 1938
Gelatin silver print
7½ x 9½ in.
GIFT OF FRAENKEL GALLERY

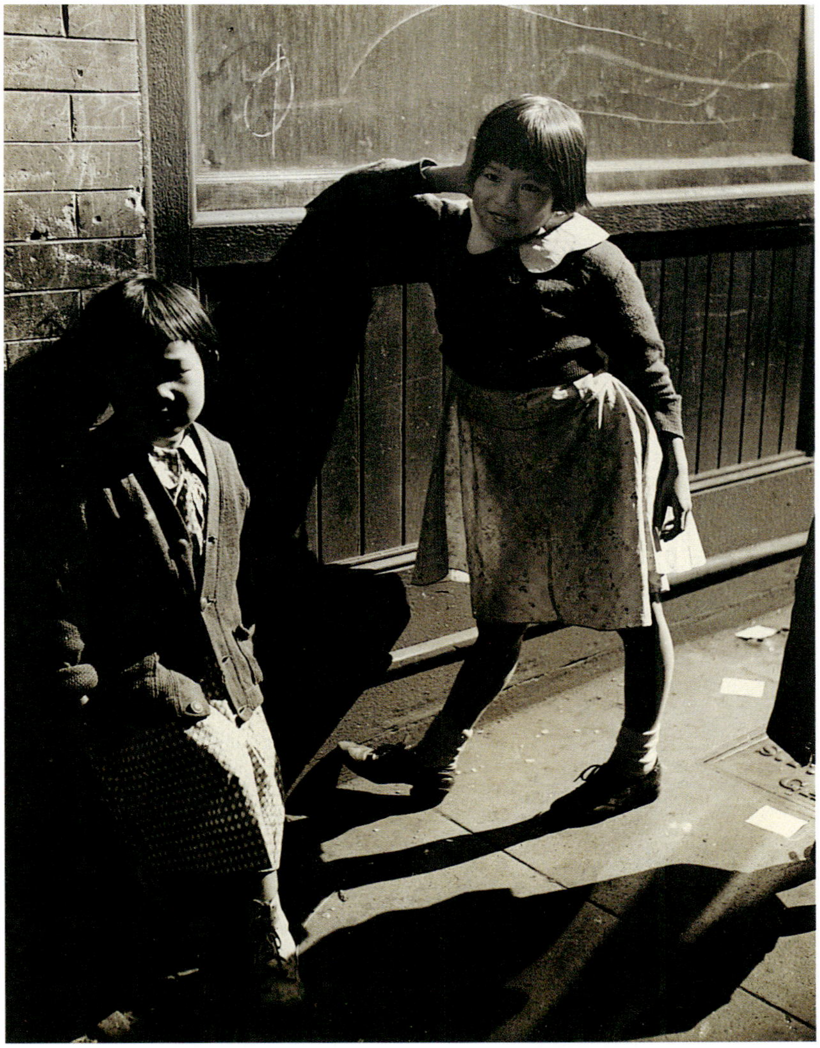

116.
WILLIAM SIMPSON
Untitled (Two Girls), c. 1935
Gelatin silver print
6 x 4½ in.
GIFT OF ANITA SIMPSON

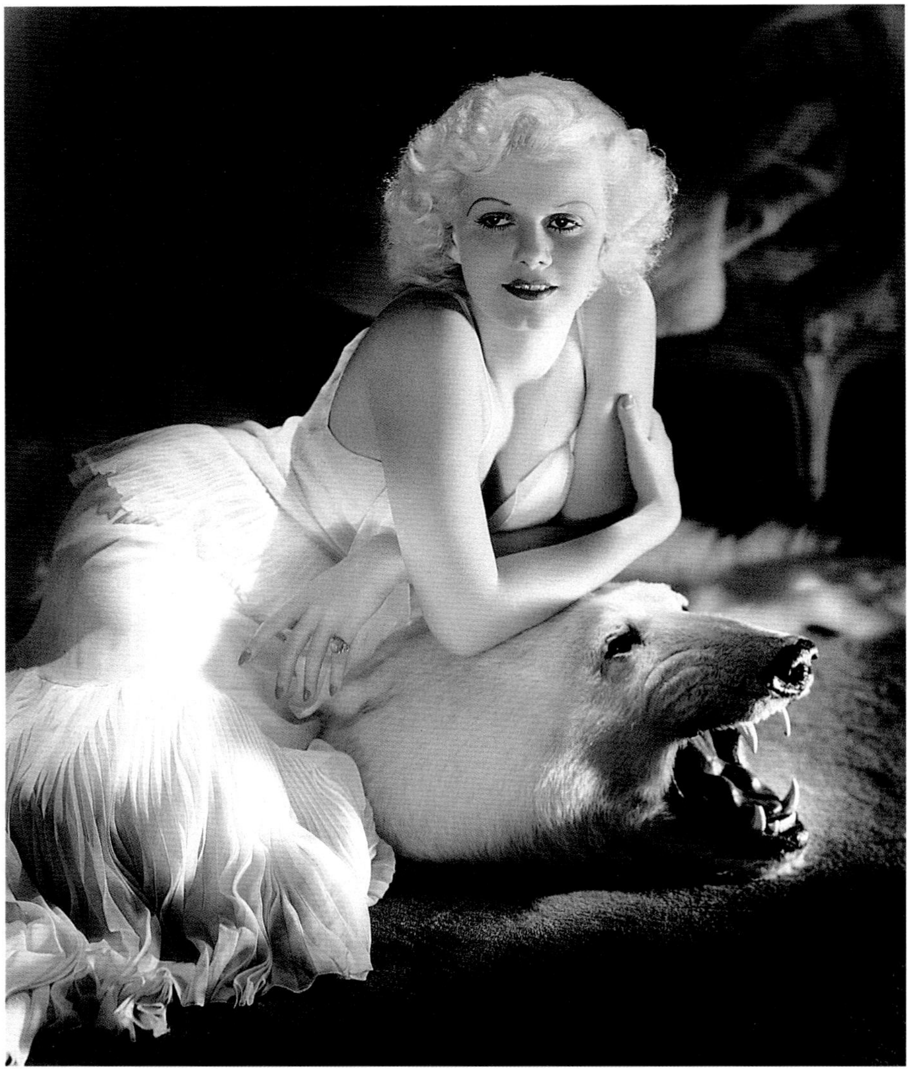

117.
GEORGE HURRELL
Jean Harlow, 1934 (printed 1980–81)
Gelatin silver print
18⅞ x 15½ in.
GIFT OF ROGER C. THOMPSON

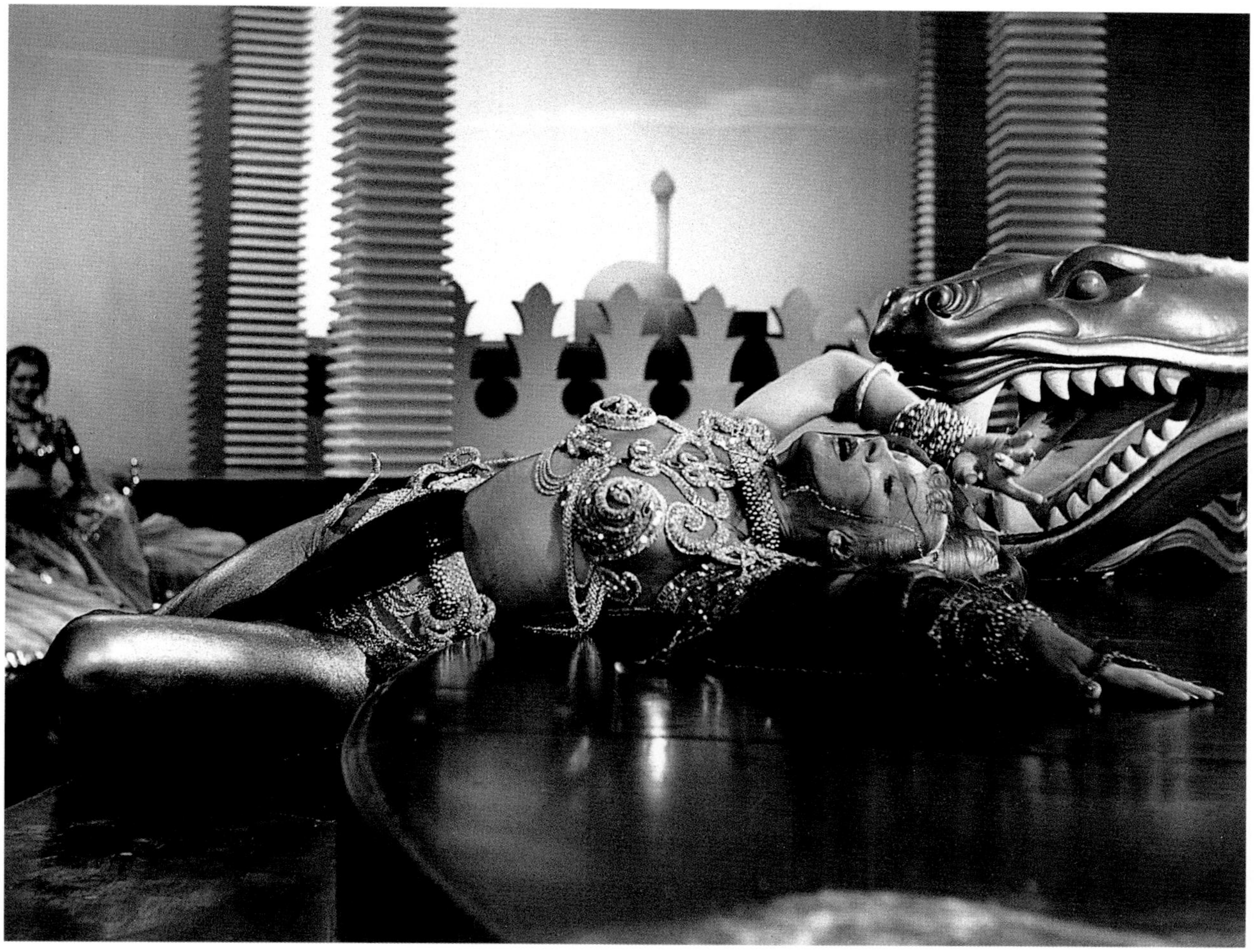

118.
PETER STACKPOLE
Marlene Dietrich, Reclining, in "Kismet," 1943
Gelatin silver print
8¼ x 10¾ in.
GIFT OF DOUGLAS ELLIOTT

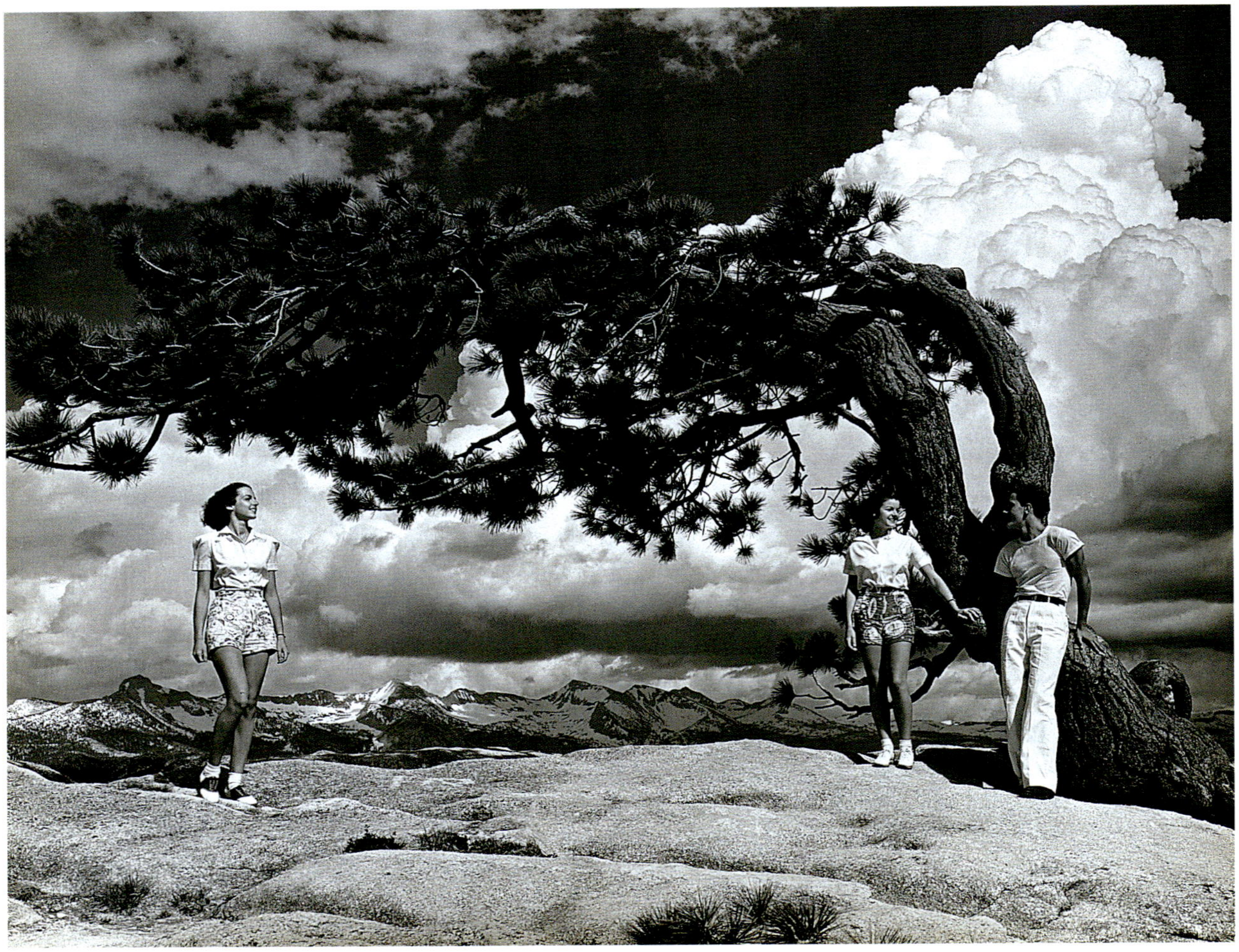

119.
ANSEL ADAMS
Sentinel Dome, Yosemite, 1936
Gelatin silver print
$7\frac{3}{8}$ x $9\frac{15}{16}$ in.
GIFT OF MR. AND MRS. ROBERT BALDWIN JR.

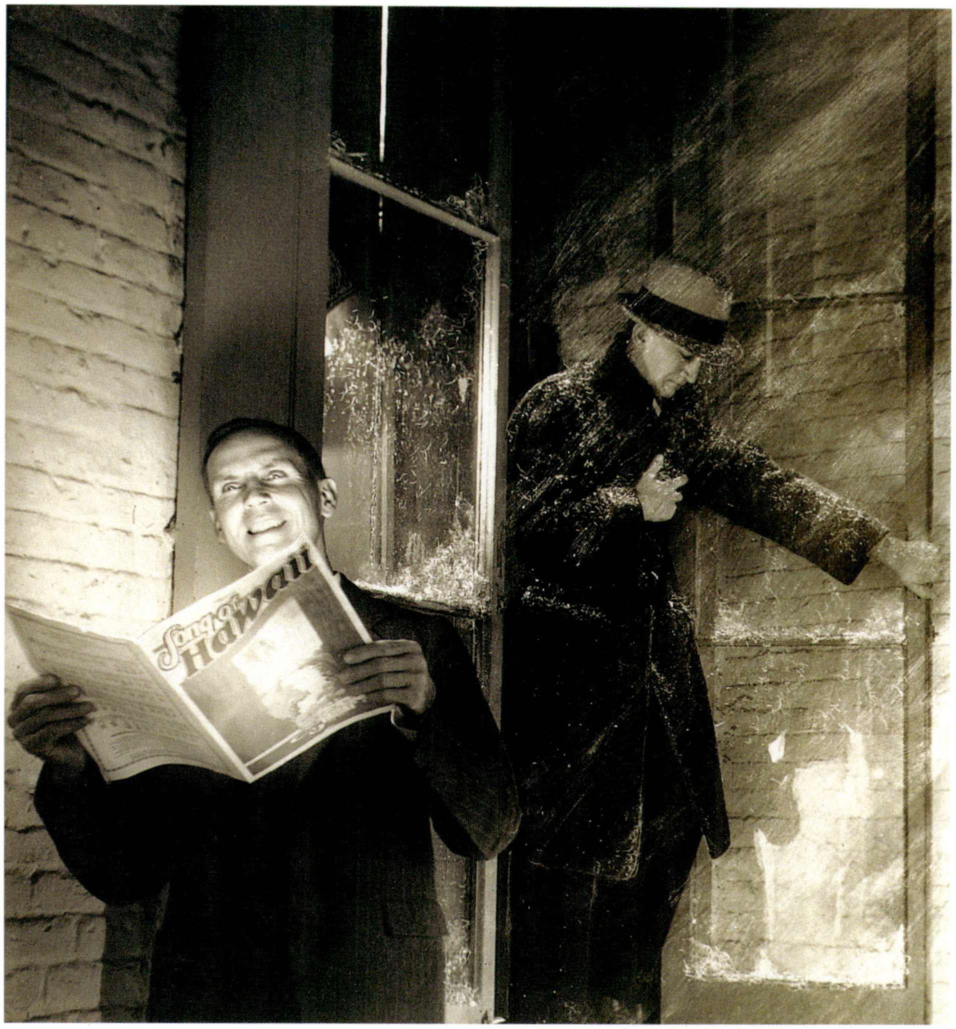

120.
ROGER STURTEVANT
Untitled (Advertising Photograph), c. 1935
Gelatin silver print
8 7/16 x 7 1/2 in.
GIFT OF THE ARTIST

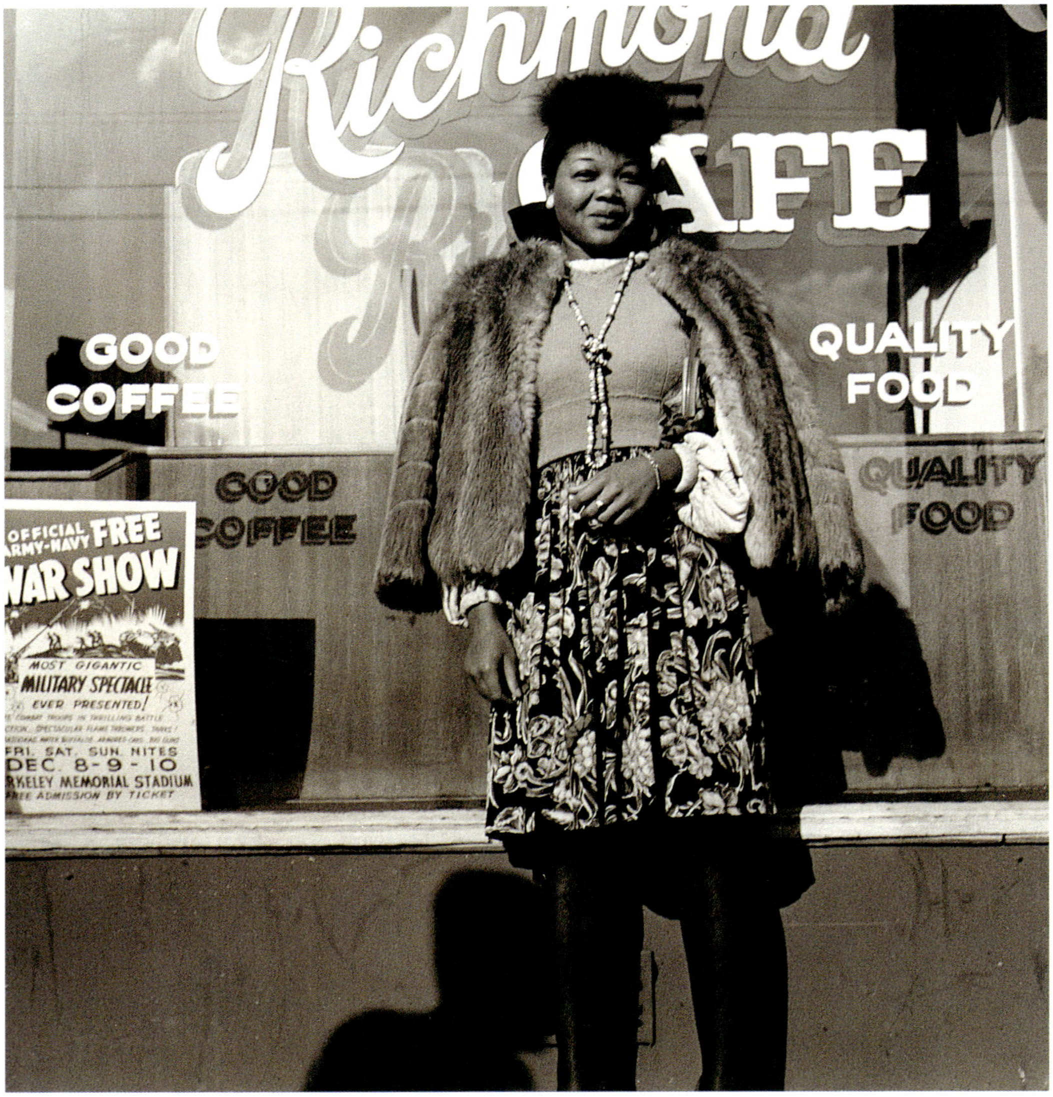

121.
DOROTHEA LANGE
Untitled (Richmond Woman), 1942
Gelatin silver print
11⅜ x 10½ in.
GIFT OF PAUL S. TAYLOR

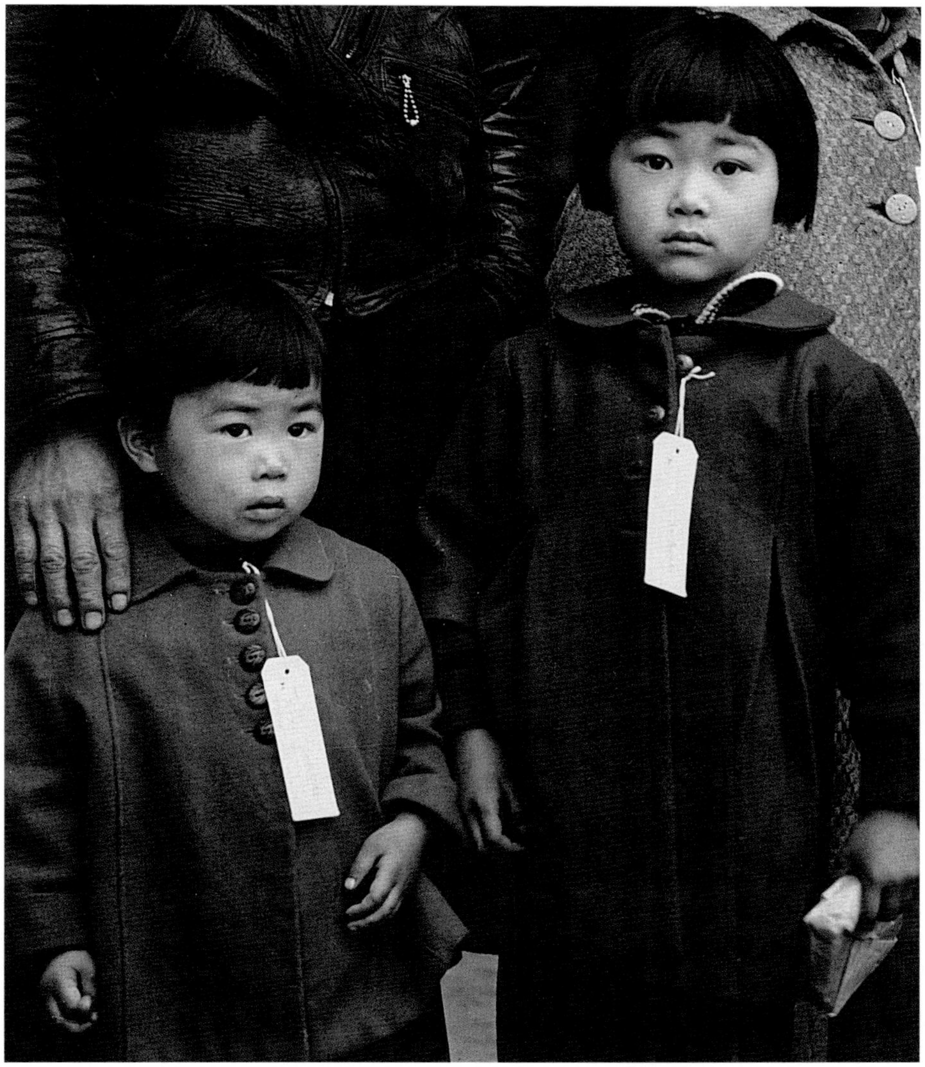

122.
DOROTHEA LANGE
Japanese Children with Tags, Hayward, California,
May 8, 1942
Gelatin silver print
10⅝ x 9 in.
GIFT OF PAUL S. TAYLOR

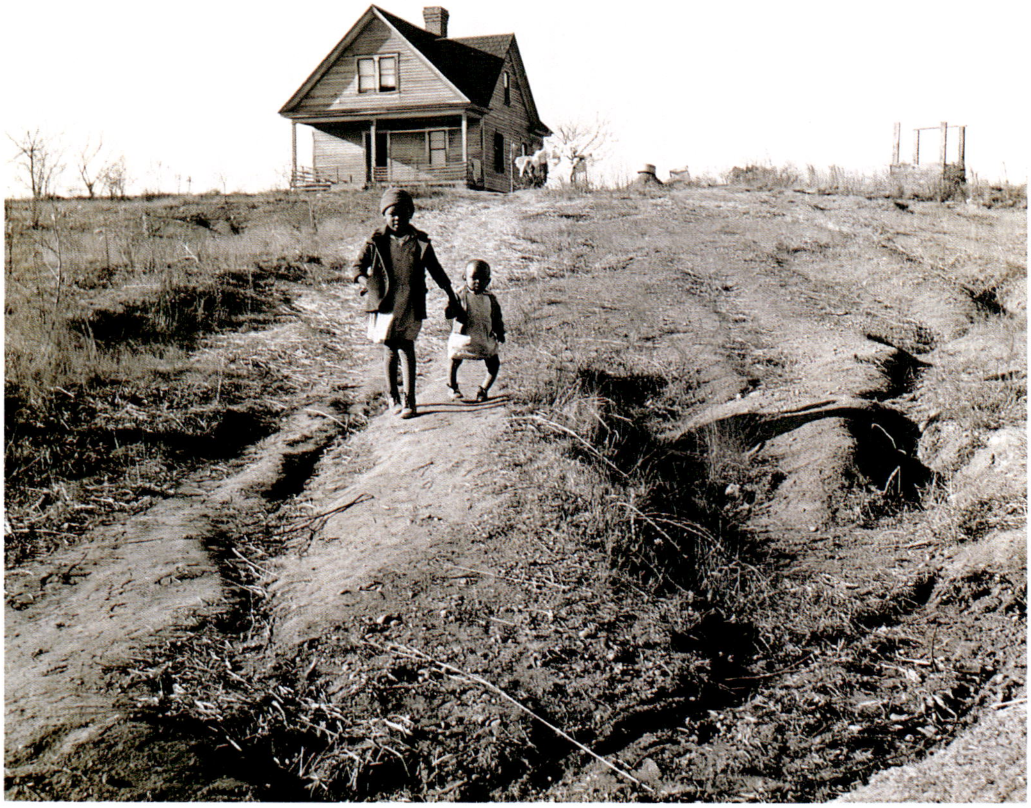

123.
MARION POST WOLCOTT
Tenant Farmer's Children, the Younger One with Rickets, Near Wadesboro, North Carolina, 1938
Gelatin silver print
7½ x 7½ in.
THE SHIRLEY BURDEN FUND FOR PHOTOGRAPHY

1945 – 1980

PORTFOLIO IV

California Dreaming

A New and Different Kind of Art

ANDY GRUNDBERG

THE THIRD QUARTER OF THE TWENTIETH CENTURY saw the fulfillment of photography's long dream to be accepted unconditionally as a means of making art. This epochal shedding of the medium's inferior status vis-à-vis painting, drawing and sculpture came about, in California as elsewhere, in the form of a double paradox. First, the new aesthetic and market interest in photographs was instigated in large part by artists and critics without any allegiance to the practice or tradition of "serious" creative photography. Second, this interest was motivated primarily by a concurrent interest in erasing the boundaries between art and everyday life, rather than by the recognition of the value of photographs as expressive, aesthetically laden objects. Much of the most radical photography of this period treats the image as a reflection of a culture that has come to be defined by camera images—an idea that contests the more traditional notion that camera images first of all reflect the intentions and inner feelings of their creators.[1] During the same quarter century, contemporary California art shed whatever last vestiges of parochialism it retained and became part of a national—and eventually international—artistic and critical network. The geographical distinctions that made California largely self-sufficient and self-defining for much of its history were dissolved in the postwar years by a number of factors, including an influx of new migrants from the East Coast and a wave of immigration from Asia and Latin America. Faster and easier travel by plane and automobile, the growth of mass communication spurred by a new television industry, and the popularity of large-circulation magazines also helped make the state a part of a global village. All conspired to make "California artist" a less appealing and useful label than "an artist living in California." Photography was a part of this transformation and, more important, a part of what propelled it.

The seeds of globalism that rooted in postwar California art were sown in part by the influx of European emigrés who arrived in the state before or during World War II. Many were linked to the Surrealist movement, the most important being Man Ray, who sojourned in Los Angeles from 1940 to 1951 (plate 127). While there, he had a direct influence on photographers like Edmund Teske, but Man Ray's openness to chance and his willingness to take photography in uncharted directions seems, in retrospect, to have informed much of what developed in Southern California decades after the artist's return to Paris.[2] In postwar Northern California, where the purist influence of Group f.64 remained in full force, internationalism was also in order. The friendship that Ansel Adams had struck with Beaumont and Nancy Newhall—two of the most influential writers and curators of the time—meant that the distance between New York and California was virtually negligible. Parkinson's disease left Edward Weston unable to photograph after 1948, but his reputation as a model of artistic seriousness continued to draw admirers and fledgling photographers to the Monterey Peninsula from around the country. And while Weston maintained something of a hermit's existence in Carmel, his reputation and outlook long had been international. Before the war he had been co-curator of the American section of the landmark 1929 exhibition, *Film und Foto,* in Stuttgart, Germany.[3]

Ironically, given this increasingly global focus, the notion of a regional California aesthetic began to blossom at the end of the period under discussion. Focused largely in and around San Francisco, where the city's Museum of Modern Art maintained an active program of exhibiting and collecting photographs, a half-dozen exhibitions were devoted to establishing a regional identity while highlighting the state's contributions to the medium.[4] This attempt to localize and distinguish the qualities of photographs being made in California continued well into the 1980s and, significantly, was not restricted to California itself. In 1982 the Museum of Art of the Rhode Island School of Design mounted a survey exhibition called *California Photography,* and the Museum of Modern Art in New York presented *California Photography: Remaking Make Believe,* in 1989.[5] Why "California photography" should take center stage at the end of this crucial period in photography's development as an art is a question of considerable interest, and one this essay will attempt to address in provisional fashion. On one hand, the reassertion of a regional character or identity can be seen as a reactionary undercurrent fighting the main drift of history—which is that in the postwar years, American culture largely lost its regional flavor. Looked at another way, however, this self-conscious focus on geographic identity reflects what was clear to many observers during the decade of the seventies: that young California photographers—many of whom wore the label "artist"—were in the vanguard in championing a new, looser, more integrated practice of photography as an art.

Conventionally, historians of photography have demarcated California photography geographically, drawing a kind of aesthetic Mason-Dixon line between the North (meaning the Bay Area as well as a hegemony of the Group f.64 aesthetic) and the South (meaning Los Angeles and vicinity, and a more open-ended, experimental approach). While this might be a useful distinction because of its simplicity, it ignores the reality that photographers failed to observe any boundary between north and south, freely commuting across this invisible aesthetic divide. Edward Weston, one remembers, was a studio photographer in the neighborhood of Pasadena (south) before he settled down in Carmel (north). Likewise, after the war, Ruth Bernhard moved from Los Angeles to San Francisco without swearing a new aesthetic allegiance, and assemblage artists like Bruce Conner, who promoted a raw, primitive use of photographic materials, moved back and forth between the two cities in the fifties and sixties. Whatever latitudinal polarities there were before the war were to become even more illusory in the period at hand.

A more useful distinction for the years from 1945 to 1980 would be to distinguish between those who practiced photography as the medium of their art and those who used photographs as a material for making art—and often as its subject matter. By convention, we tend to call the former "photographers" and the latter "artists," but there are exceptions on both sides of the rule. While photography was seen essentially as a printmaking process by both parties, those who insisted on its status as a medium preferred silver gelatin prints made by hand in the darkroom, while those for whom a photograph was simply raw material preferred cyanotypes, serigraphs (silkscreens), halftone reproductions and machine-made color prints. The latter artists also ventured into presenting their images in alternative ways—as sculpture, book works and artifacts of a performance or conceptual idea.

THE POSTWAR SITUATION

At the century's midpoint, the idea of creative freedom in the visual arts was expressed through abstraction. In painting, this took the form of Abstract Expressionism, a style centered in New York but practiced on both coasts. In photography, abstraction was more problematic but still possible. It took the form of either cameraless photograms and light studies, as encouraged by Bauhaus outposts like the Institute of Design in Chicago, or decontextualized close-ups in which the nominal subject matter was virtually unidentifiable. Both versions of photographic abstraction depended for their meaning on Stieglitz's notion of the Equivalent—of the image as a legible metaphor for the spiritual and emotional ambitions of its maker.

Ansel Adams and Edward Weston, the two most influential figures representing modernist photography on the West Coast, were reluctant to give in to abstraction completely, since they based their claims as artists on the ability of the camera to render reality in all its detail and range of tones. Still, both had produced semi-abstract sequences—of surf, in Adams's case, and of the nude, in Weston's—that would provide inspiration for a new generation of modernist photographers in the 1950s. Morley Baer, Ruth Bernhard, Wynn Bullock, Pirkle Jones and, of course, Brett Weston, the best known of Edward's sons, carried on in the tradition of metaphoric photography, producing pictures that often are mysterious, ambiguous and floating, and thus vastly open to the viewer's interpretation.

Minor White, whom Ansel Adams hired in 1946 to teach in the brand-new photography program of the California School of Fine Arts (now the San Francisco Art Institute), proved to be the most convincing postwar advocate of a purely abstract style. Although he was grounded in conventional camerawork and was an adept recorder of the urban scene in San Francisco, White became the most convincing and best-known advocate of metaphoric photography in the fifties and sixties, due both to his editorship of *Aperture* and to his teaching (after leaving California in 1953 he taught at the Rochester Institute of Technology and MIT). *Aperture,* founded in 1952 by Adams, the Newhalls and others, quickly became the leading journal for creative photography in the United States (figure 1). When White lost his job in San Francisco and moved East he took the journal with him.

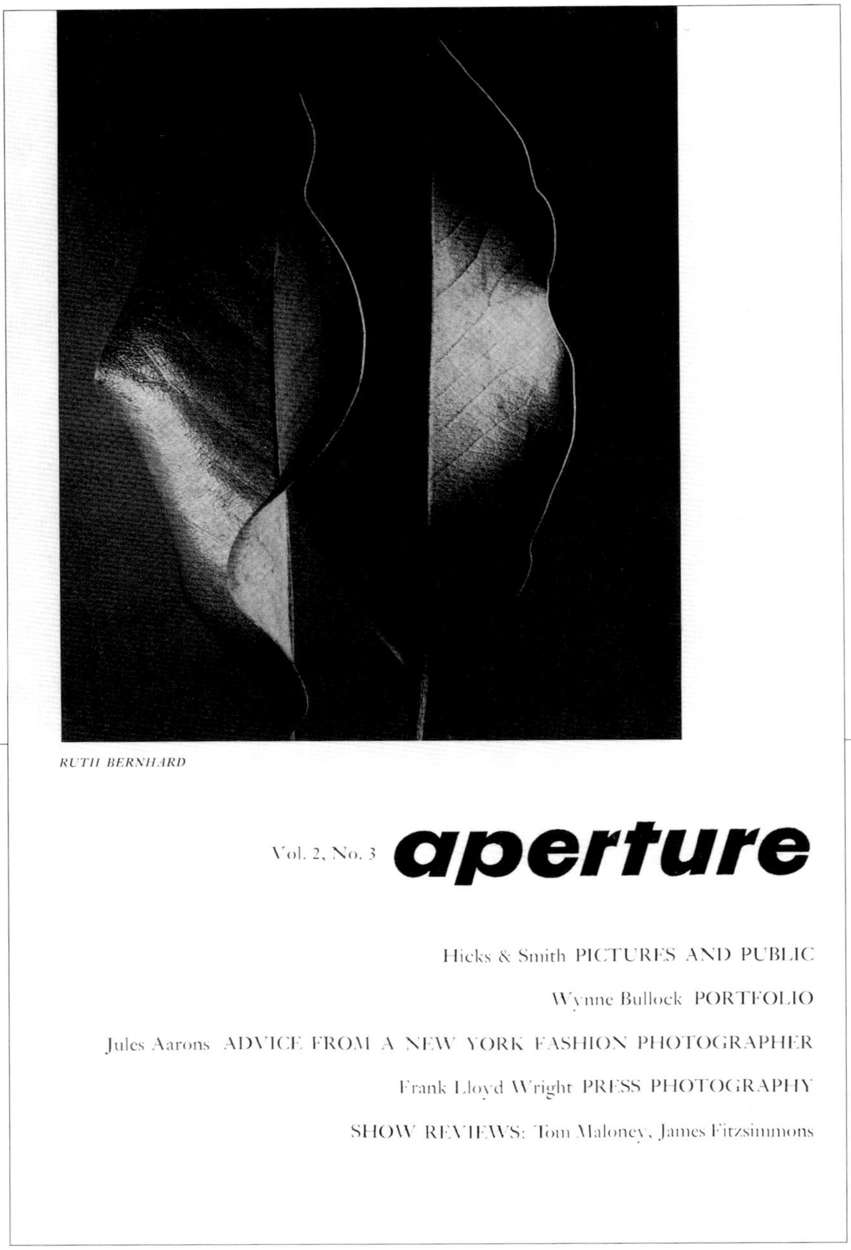

RUTH BERNHARD

Vol. 2, No. 3 **aperture**

Hicks & Smith PICTURES AND PUBLIC

Wynne Bullock PORTFOLIO

Jules Aarons ADVICE FROM A NEW YORK FASHION PHOTOGRAPHER

Frank Lloyd Wright PRESS PHOTOGRAPHY

SHOW REVIEWS: Tom Maloney, James Fitzsimmons

FIGURE 1.
Cover of Aperture, 1953
COLLECTION OF THE OAKLAND MUSEUM OF CALIFORNIA

The mystery and ambiguity of White's work was predicated on his idea of a receptive audience, one consisting of viewers sophisticated enough to be willing to meditate and ponder the various possible interpretations of the image. At the same time, however, one can read his photographs, and those of Bernhard, Bullock, and the others, as products of a surrealist temperament. A picture like White's *Driftwood and Eye, Point Lobos,* circa 1951, has the combined sense of incongruity and morbidity that characterizes much of postwar American Surrealism (plate 131). The "Eye" of the title also locates the image in the corporeal body, which is typical of French Surrealism of the 1920s. Unlike Man Ray, whose "Rayographs" are produced by the chance effects of light and shadow, White made strange and disconcerting juxtapositions issue from the physical materials of everyday life.

Surrealism within everyday life was also at play in the commercial world of photography at the time. As California's film industry became increasingly dependent on a culture of celebrity in the postwar years, photography was called upon to create exalted images of movie stars, starlets, and Hollywood itself. For every portraitist like George Hurrell (plate 117), whose mightily retouched, glossy head shots of actors and actresses were hung in theater lobbies across the country, there was a Raoul Gradwohl. Gradwohl was a practitioner of a sad and degraded genre known as cheesecake, for which aspiring actresses of uncertain talent posed in the nude with translucent balls, Japanese fans and other paraphernalia. Gradwohl's work has not entered the museum as yet, but that of Paul Outerbridge has. A semi-retired commercial photographer from New York, Outerbridge settled in Laguna Beach and produced pioneer color photographs—of nudes, mainly, but with enough fetishistic peculiarity to gain him posthumous recognition as a kind of unconscious Surrealist (plate 99).

Less surrealist than tawdry was the brand of journeyman photojournalism that sprung up around movie-fan magazines like *Modern Screen.* Part studio publicity tool and part exposé of behind-the-scenes hanky panky, these publications inspired the first paparazzi photographers to catch their film-star subjects unaware. These pictures, along with those from more respectable magazines like *LIFE* and *Look,* created a vernacular visual climate specific to Hollywood that would soon inspire artists such as John Baldessari and Robert Heinecken.

Documentary photography aspired to a higher ground, believing that unvarnished, more-or-less spontaneous pictures could penetrate stereotype and help change the world. While in the fifties veteran documentarian Dorothea Lange, who made her reputation in the thirties while working for the Farm Security Administration's photography project, continued to produce pictures that used the camera's realist powers to maximum advantage, it was becoming increasingly difficult to stake photography's claim as an art form on humanist grounds. One of the few to successfully follow in Lange's wake was Max Yavno (plate 129), who left his roots in the Photo League in New York in 1954 to run a commercial photography studio in Los Angeles. Tellingly, though, Yavno's commercial work took precedence over his documentation of Los Angeles and San Francisco, and he did not pursue exhibiting his pictures until after 1975, the year he closed his studio.[6] The popular apotheosis of the documentary idea of the art of photography was, of course, Edward Steichen's show *The Family of Man,* which opened in 1955 at the Museum of Modern Art in New York. What proved to be history's most well-attended exhibition of photographs included at least a dozen photographers from California, including Adams, Weston, Lange (as could be expected), Wynn Bullock, Shirley Burden, and Rondal Partridge. John Collier, Otto Hagel, Homer Page, and Peter Stackpole represented the state's photojournalists, while Ruth-Marion Baruch, an emigré from Germany, was chosen because her pictures were aligned with Lange's documentary aesthetic.

The defining jolt to this aesthetic, and to the optimistic sentiments behind *The Family of Man,* was the publication four years later of Robert Frank's book *The Americans* (plate 141). Frank's photographs, many of them taken in California while he was traveling on a Guggenheim Fellowship, forsook Steichen's bid for a photographic Esperanto in favor of a disaffected, ironic, and downbeat sense of the American dream gone awry.[7] Frank, an emigré from Switzerland who lived in New York, was a herald of the Beat Generation, which reacted with humor and outrage to American postwar prosperity and conformity. Many of the Beats, like the poets Lawrence Ferlinghetti, Gregory Corso and, for a time, Allen Ginsberg, were based in San Francisco. In Los Angeles, visual artists associated with the Beats included filmmaker Kenneth Anger and the assemblagist Wallace Berman.

Berman, along with Bruce Conner, George Herms (figure 2), and Ed Kienholz, began to incorporate reproductions, snapshots and other photographic images in his artwork of the fifties. All were associated with the influential Ferus Gallery in Los Angeles, opened in 1957 by Kienholz and curator Walter Hopps, and were known as assemblagists because of the way they mixed found images and found objects to create a hybrid of painting and sculpture. To a degree, their work parallels Robert Rauschenberg's "combine" paintings of the mid-fifties, like *Bed* (1955), and anticipates Rauschenberg's and Andy Warhol's photo-based silkscreen collages of the sixties. More important to the future of California photography, their work opened a Pandora's Box in which the photograph was treated not as a precious aesthetic object but as a commonplace (albeit intriguing) token of popular culture. In addition, these artists viewed the photographic image as a starting point for experimentation and transformation, an attitude that Robert Heinecken would make use of, and popularize, in the sixties and seventies.

THE SIXTIES: RADICAL TIMES, RADICAL CHANGES

In popular memory, the sixties were years of revolt, protest and anti-establishment fervor, dominated by the civil rights movement and national unrest over American involvement in Vietnam. The decade also spawned a "Love Generation" of peace signs, free love, altered consciousness, and psychedelic rock music. San Francisco was the centerpiece and central nervous system of the hippie phenomenon, and the city's unofficial "Summer of Love" in 1967 was the high-water mark of the era. Bad drugs, domestic terrorism and disillusionment followed, ending what had been, for a brief moment, an experiment in urban utopianism. Such a description, of course, belies many of the subtleties of the era, but it does suggest the climate in which the dominion of purist photography—as represented by elder statespersons Adams and Lange—could be successfully challenged. In large part, this challenge was facilitated by the growth of college-level photography programs in schools throughout the state.

In San Francisco, the program begun by Ansel Adams at the California School of Fine Arts (renamed the San Francisco Art Institute in 1961) was in transition, with Morley Baer and John Collier leading the faculty.[8] A new generation of teachers appeared in the late sixties, starting with

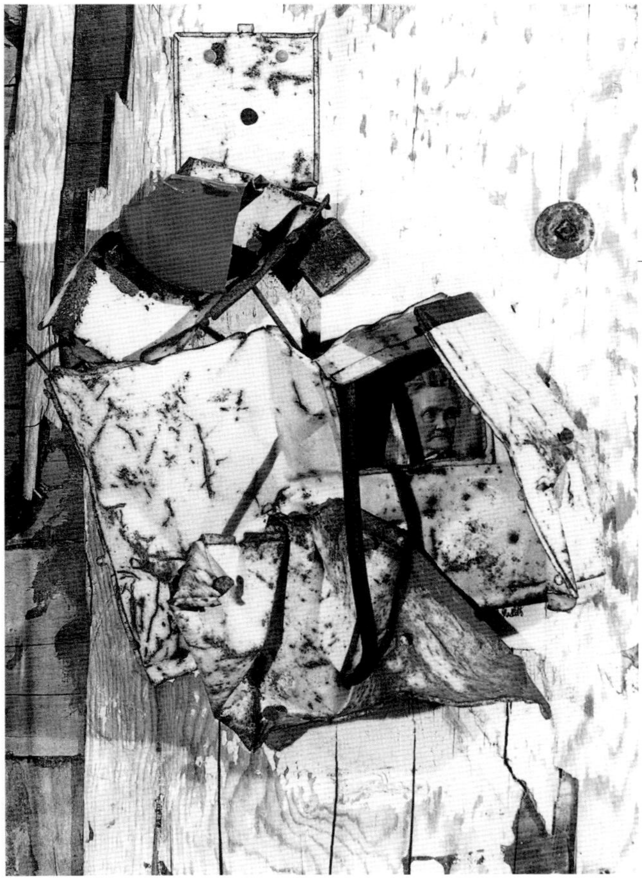

FIGURE 2.
George Herms
Lady MacBeth, 1960
Mixed media assemblage
22½ x 15¾ in.
COLLECTION OF THE OAKLAND MUSEUM OF CALIFORNIA, GIFT OF DR. REIDAR WENNESLAND

Jerry Burchard in 1966 and followed by Linda Connor and Jack Fulton two years later. Burchard's long exposures, Connor's arranged still lifes of book pages and natural objects, and Fulton's funky combination of photographs and handwritten texts (figure 3) signaled a departure both from straightforward documentary practice and the hands-off purity of the f.64 tradition. One of the original members of Group f.64, Imogen Cunningham, served as a role model for many of this new and restless generation of photographers in the Bay Area. Never one for orthodoxy, Cunningham had rebelled at the beginning of her career by photographing and exhibiting a series of male nudes, and throughout her life she maintained an insistence on creative freedom. She taught at the Art Institute and at the California College of Arts and Crafts in Oakland while continuing to make pictures well into her eighties. During the heyday of the Haight Ashbury scene, she could be seen walking the streets with her camera around her neck, a grandmotherly figure who blended in perfectly with the hippies.

Among the students at the Art Institute in the sixties were Lewis Baltz, a seminal figure in the "New Topographics" landscape movement of the 1970s; Annie Leibovitz, who became the official photographer of *Rolling Stone* magazine during its San Francisco heyday; and Mike Mandel and Larry Sultan, who collaborated on several public projects, including an enormously influential collection of found photographs called *Evidence*. The diversity of these artists' careers after leaving the school suggests how loosened the ties of traditional modernist photography had become in the sixties.

A second important center for photography in San Francisco was the photography program at San Francisco State College. Started by John Gutmann, who had taken up the camera as his livelihood after immigrating from Germany in the thirties, the curriculum was broadened by the hiring of Jack Welpott in 1959.[9] A descendant of Moholy-Nagy's Bauhaus influence, via his teacher, Henry Holmes Smith, Welpott encouraged students to consider photographs in terms of both form and content. Among his students were Michael Bishop, Judy Dater (with whom he collaborated on a series of portraits of women[10]), Joanne Leonard and Leland Rice. Rice was instrumental in founding, in 1969, a group of young photographers called the Visual Dialogue Foundation. The group organized exhibitions of its members' work and met regularly to discuss aesthetics. In 1972 Rice left the Bay Area for Los Angeles, where he became an influential curator, teacher and photographer. His move to color photography, which he used to record the walls of painting studios (the *Wall Sites Series*), established his reputation beyond the West Coast (plate 165). Similarly, Bishop gained national exposure in the early seventies when his work was shown at Light Gallery in New York (figure 4).

In Southern California, the role of photographic education initially was limited to the Art Center School in Los Angeles, where Ed Kaminski taught photography to Wynn Bullock and Todd Walker in the forties and Lee Friedlander in the fifties. But the Los Angeles scene changed substantially in 1961 when Robert Heinecken, a graduate student in UCLA's printmaking program, was

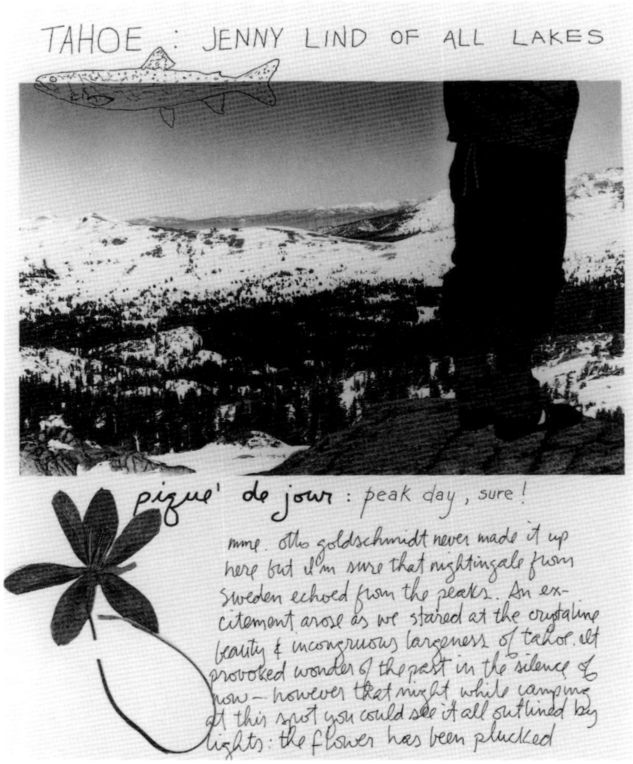

FIGURE 3.
Jack Fulton
Jennie Lind of All Lakes, 1978
Photo collage with dried flowers, 10 x 8 in.
COLLECTION OF THE OAKLAND MUSEUM OF CALIFORNIA, PRINTS AND PHOTOGRAPHY FUND

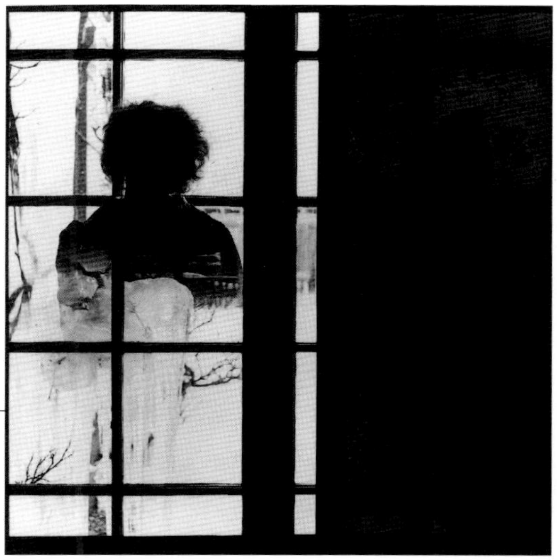

FIGURE 4.
Michael Bishop
Untitled, 1970
Gelatin silver print, 10 x 8 in.
COLLECTION OF THE OAKLAND MUSEUM OF CALIFORNIA, GIFT OF MR. AND MRS. DUDLEY P. BELL

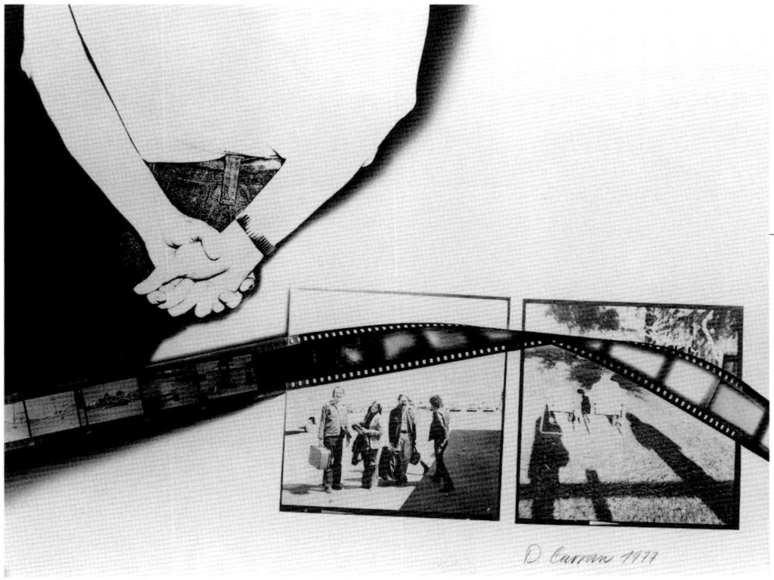

FIGURE 5.
Darryl Curran
Untitled, 1977
(from the portfolio *Silver See*)
Color Xerox on paper, 14⅞ x 20 in.
COLLECTION OF THE OAKLAND MUSEUM OF CALIFORNIA, GIFT OF MRS. PAUL WILHELM

asked to start a photography program at the school. Adding a graduate program the next year, Heinecken launched a revolution in the way photography was taught, viewing the medium in process terms as simply an extension of the possibilities of printmaking while also recognizing its functional role in popular culture (plate 163). The photographers he brought to UCLA as his colleagues, Robert Fichter, Edmund Teske, and Todd Walker, shared his interest in printmaking and his wide-open approach.[11] Heinecken's work of the 1960s is not so much photography, as traditionally understood, as it is a meditation on the pervasive presence of photography in mass media and the entertainment industry. In his *Are You Rea* series of 1964–68, he essentially made photograms of magazine pages, superimposing the imagery on both sides of the paper. Vietnam War pictures thus combined with advertising images of happy suburban homemakers. In another series, he reproduced pornographic images as silkscreens to form sinuous panoramas that resembled landscapes.

A remarkable number of Heinecken's students became important photographers and teachers, among them Ellen Brooks, JoAnn Callis, Darryl Curran (figure 5), John Divola, Robbert Flick and Victor Landweber. All were restless experimenters, producing works that ranged from three-dimensional photo sculptures to gum-bichromate prints, and all viewed the medium as open and limitless. As Callis would later remark, "Before I met Heinecken I had no idea you could make photographs of things inside your head."[12]

Such pockets of activity centered around colleges and universities in the state might have remained isolated were it not for the growth of a market for photography. The 1966 opening of Focus Gallery by Helen Johnston in San Francisco anticipated by a few years the widespread national trend toward stand-alone, commercial photography galleries. These, together with the establishment of a number of museum photography programs, helped solidify the acceptance of "fine-art photography" across the country. Most of the early collecting activity tended to be conservative, with Ansel Adams representing blue-chip territory, but museums like the San Francisco Museum of Modern Art and the Oakland Museum made a concerted effort to support younger artists in their exhibitions programs. Young California photographers, with their progressive education and expanded views of the medium, were poised to play an important role in the new photography marketplace.

OUTSIDE THE ENVELOPE: THE DEMATERIALIZED PRACTICE OF ART

As significant as was the growth and acceptance of postwar art photography, the most crucial influence on the medium's development came from outside the arena with which most photographers were familiar. Perhaps only Heinecken, with his background in printmaking and Los Angeles purview, could immediately understand and appreciate the changes that in the sixties and seventies would rewrite the way in which photography as an art was conceived and constructed.

A central figure in this reconfiguration of photography's potentials was Ed Ruscha, an artist who studied at the Chouinard Art Institute in Los Angeles from 1956 to 1960. In 1962—the very year Rauschenberg and Warhol began to silkscreen photographic images onto their canvases—Ruscha published the first of what became a series of artist's books, *26 Gasoline Stations*. The book consisted of 26 photographs by Ruscha of gas stations, each as unexceptional and unremarkable as the next, except for the fascinating ordinariness of their architecture and surroundings. Ruscha's subsequent titles—*Various Small Fires and Milk* (1964), *Some L.A. Apartments* (1965) and *Every Building on the Sunset Strip* (1966)—continued the theme, using reproductions of plain, vernacular-looking photographs to depict plain, vernacular-looking occurrences and buildings (figure 6).

In choosing to use photographs in this way, Ruscha was not advancing any claim for photography as an art. Indeed, it was the non-art, commonplace appearance of photography that attracted him. Photography functioned best for Ruscha in halftone reproduction, where its non-art status was doubled and the materiality of the photograph was negated. Although best known as a painter,

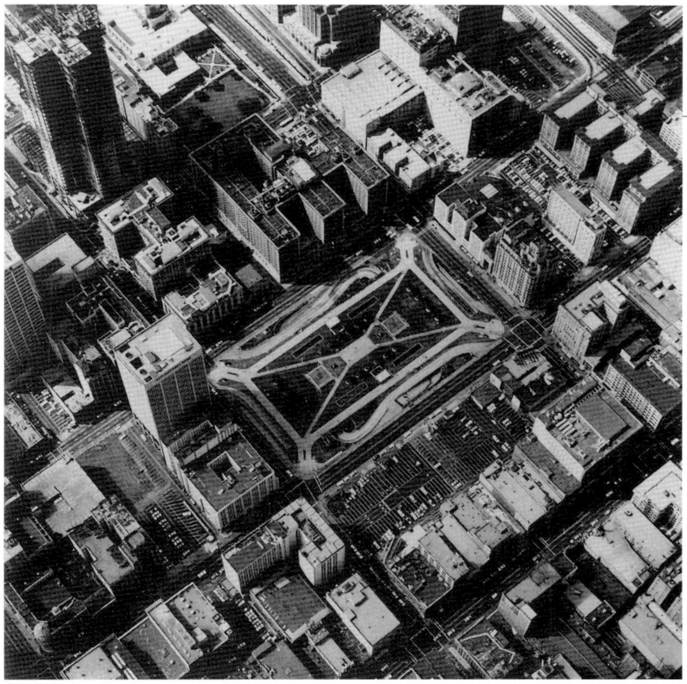

FIGURE 6.
Ed Ruscha
Thirtyfour Parking Lots in Los Angeles, 1967
Pershing Square, underground lot, 5th and Hill, photographed by Art Alanis
Gelatin silver print
10 x 8½ in.
COLLECTION OF THE OAKLAND MUSEUM OF CALIFORNIA, PRINTS AND PHOTOGRAPHY FUND

Ruscha helped launch a West Coast version of conceptual art in which photography, as a form of image-making with relatively little market value, would nevertheless become a prized means of conveying meaning.

Two other important artists in Southern California followed Ruscha's lead in the sixties. John Baldessari, trained as a painter but despairing of studio painting's remoteness from the world, produced a series of works using photographic emulsion on canvas that questioned painting's definition. The painting *Wrong,* for example, from 1967, shows a man standing in front of a palm tree so that the tree seems to grow from his head; below the photographic image is the single word "Wrong." The "wrong" is twofold: for one, composition manuals for amateur photographers warn against having a tree sprout from the subject's head; for another, the painting is not quite a painting, because it consists of a photographic image and language. Baldessari went on to stage a series of performances for the camera, making his work even more dependent on the photographic image.

Bruce Nauman, whose hybrid career includes performance, video, sculpture and holograms, used his body to stage a series of photographs taken between 1966 and 1970. Essentially illustrations of puns, like *Waxing Hot* and *Self-Portrait of the Artist as a Fountain,* these color pictures were produced for an audience that would see them as conceptual art, not as photography. This distinction between fine-art photography and photography in the service of conceptual art was reflected in the way museums, galleries, collectors and art journals treated the work of artists like Ruscha, Baldessari and Nauman. To put it bluntly, their photographs were not seen as photography. Nevertheless, their imaginative expansion of how photographs might be considered art objects would have an incalculable influence on both art and photography in the last quarter of the century.

INTO THE SEVENTIES: THE BRANCHES INTERTWINE

The decade of the seventies saw the rapid expansion of a "photography boom" across the United States. Scores of new commercial galleries were established to sell both contemporary and historical photographs, including the Weston Gallery in Carmel, the Grapestake and Fraenkel galleries in San Francisco, Susan Spiritus Gallery in Newport Beach and the G. Ray Hawkins and Stephen White galleries in Los Angeles. Photography became a special focus of support from the National Endowment for the Arts, which in 1971 established a program of fellowships for photographers and, a few years later, a grant program for photographic surveys.

Perhaps most important, in terms of photography's recognition as an art form, a number of art critics started writing about photographs. At the New York *Times,* Hilton Kramer, the newspaper's chief art critic, began reviewing photography exhibitions in 1971, and he encouraged the paper to add additional writers to cover the medium. The interest in photographs was solidified by a series of essays written in the mid-seventies by literary critic Susan Sontag and published in the *New York Review of Books.*[13] The incorporation of photography into the discourse of art inevitably led to a

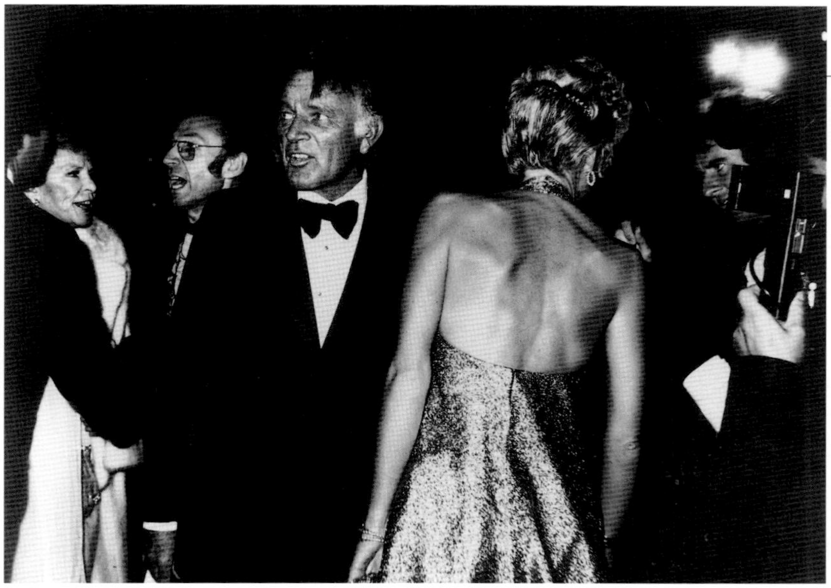

FIGURE 7.
Robert Cumming
The Burtons, Academy Awards, 1978
(from the portfolio *New California Views*)
Cibachrome print (original in color)
16 x 20 in.
COLLECTION OF THE OAKLAND MUSEUM OF CALIFORNIA, MUSEUM DONORS' ACQUISITION FUND

blurring of the distinction between photographers making art and artists making photographs. This was especially true in California, where the loosening of boundaries between the two already had occurred. Two artists who were among the first to achieve "crossover" status in this sense were Robert Cumming (figure 7) and William Wegman, both of whom came to Los Angeles to teach art at the start of the decade—Cumming at Cal State, Fullerton, and Wegman at California State University, Long Beach.

Cumming and Wegman were classmates and friends throughout their student years, having received undergraduate degrees in art from Massachusetts College of Art and M.F.A. degrees from the University of Illinois. Both artists were trained in painting and sculpture but recognized that the traditional ways of thinking about them—and about art as a whole—were subject to revision. Photography (and, for Wegman, video) served as a means to challenge art's definition and reception. Cumming's photographs were straightforward, documentary records of elaborate and often ridiculous setups fashioned for the camera. One picture shows a Coleman ice chest, its lid open, on an expanse of desert. Undoubtedly inspired by Ruscha, Cumming published his own artist's books that combined his photographs with equally fanciful narratives (e.g., *Picture Fictions,* 1971, and *Discourse on Domestic Disorder,* 1975).

Wegman made his first photographs while teaching at Long Beach, and acquired his first Weimeraner, the legendary Man Ray, there. He and Cumming were first exhibited on the West Coast as "California" artists, but Wegman's reputation was established after he moved to New York in 1972 and began showing a mix of photographs, drawings and video shorts at Sonnabend Gallery. By the decade's end his photographs, and those of Cumming, had become sufficiently well known and respected that they were embraced by photographers as well as the art world; in 1979, for example, the Friends of Photography, an organization founded by Ansel Adams and the Newhalls, published a monograph of Cumming's work.[14] Like Baldessari, Nauman and Ruscha before them, Wegman and Cumming used humor to undercut what were seen as the pretensions of modernist art, including modernist photography. Their work also aligned itself with conceptual art, a term used to describe work of the seventies in which the essence of the artwork resided not in any objects or artifacts produced by the artist, but in the procedures, performances or mental concepts that preceded them. This new way of thinking about art, which often employed photographs because of their status as believable documents, rapidly became a way of thinking about photography as well. Several California photographers, including John Divola and Victor Landweber in Los Angeles and Lew Thomas and Greg MacGregor in San Francisco, adopted the conceptual aesthetic in their pictures.

The "pluralism" of art in the seventies meant that other strains of photography flourished as well, including the experimental, process-oriented work centered around Heinecken and the program at UCLA. The most important new development of the decade, however, was a brand of environmental documentary photography that forsook both the epic grandeur of Ansel Adams's landscapes and the sentimental humanism of Dorothea Lange's social reportage. Collected in a landmark 1975 exhibition called *New Topographics: Photographs of a Man-Altered Landscape,*[15] this work looked dispassionately, but skeptically, at the ways in which human development impacted the landscape. Among the show's ten photographers were three Californians: Lewis Baltz, Joe Deal (figure 8) and Henry Wessel, Jr. They were joined by Robert Adams (figure 9), the influential German artists Bernd and Hilla Becher, and Stephen Shore, whose use of color photography was considered radical at the time. Baltz, who had studied photography in San Francisco and Southern California, was exemplary of the new aesthetic. His work from *The New Industrial Parks Near Irvine, California,* picture a landscape of Minimalist-looking functional buildings that betray no hint of their occupants or purpose. Stylistically, Baltz maintained a neutrality that even Walker Evans might envy, so that the images appear to have been taken by a remote camera of the sort recently used to record the Moon's surface. Shown at the Leo Castelli Gallery in New York, the *New Industrial Parks* pictures were also a hit in the art world, where they were viewed through the critical lens of the Bechers's and Ruscha's photographic projects.

The impact of the New Topographics aesthetic led to a general revival of interest in the landscape genre in photography, and to new work that no longer seemed constrained by the shadow of Ansel Adams. Robert Dawson, Richard Misrach, Ted Orland and Laura Volkerding were among the California photographers who found new territory in the man-altered landscape later in the seventies. Orland, who had worked in Adams's studio as an assistant, took a devilish delight in making humorous variations on the master's scenes, with pictorial spoofs like *Inspiration Point, Yosemite* (plate 168) and *Moonrise, Gonzalez.*

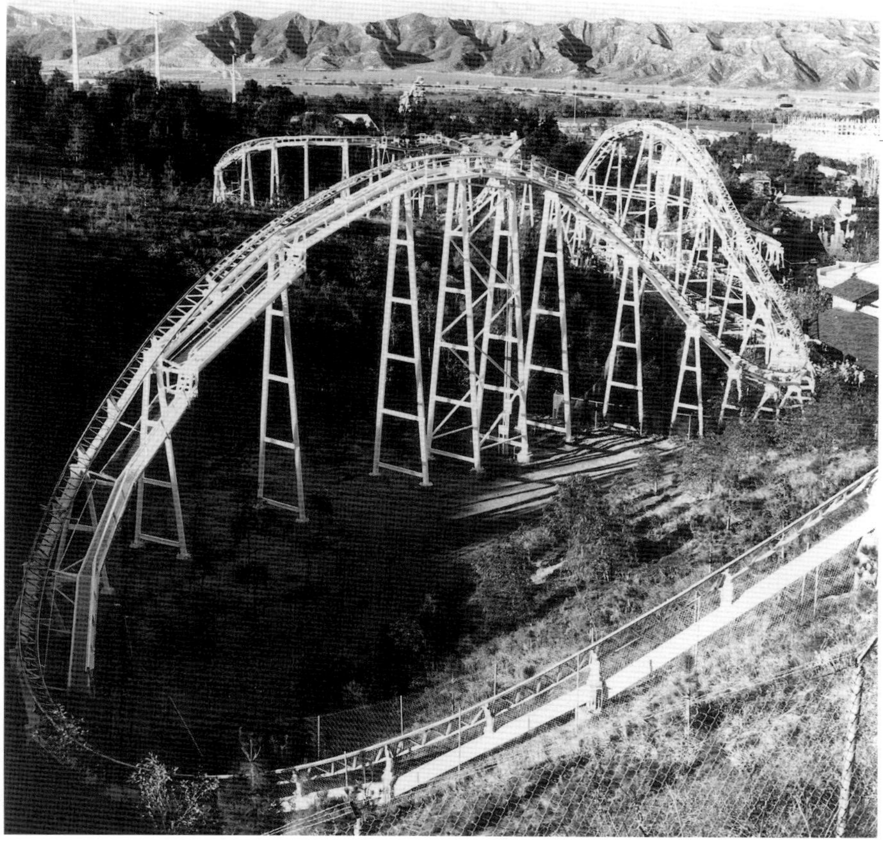

FIGURE 8.
Joe Deal
View, Magic Mountain, Valencia, California, 1977 (from the portfolio *New California Views*)
Gold toned gelatin silver print
16 x 20 in.
COLLECTION OF THE OAKLAND MUSEUM OF CALIFORNIA, MUSEUM DONORS' ACQUISITION FUND

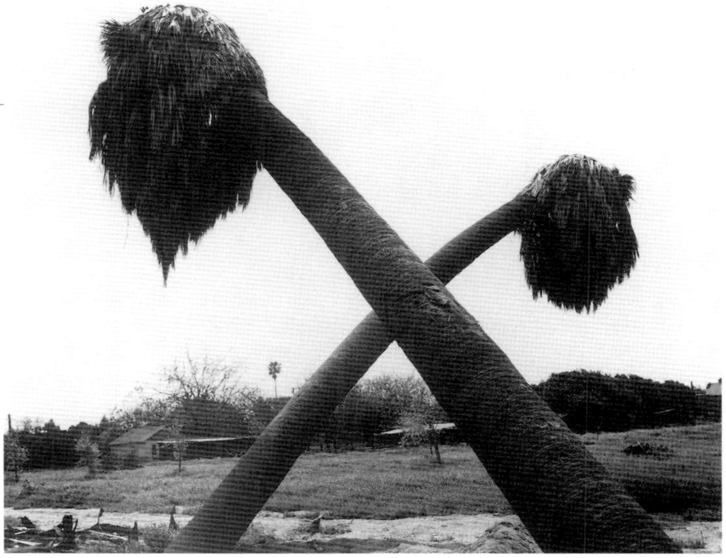

FIGURE 9.
Robert Adams
Dead Palms, Partially Uprooted, Ontario, California, 1983/1988
Gelatin silver print
11 x 14 in.
COLLECTION OF THE OAKLAND MUSEUM OF CALIFORNIA, THE SHIRLEY BURDEN FUND FOR PHOTOGRAPHY

The spirit of objectivity and consequent intentional ambiguity that characterized the pictures of New Topographics also was startlingly present in one of the decade's most interesting social documentary projects, Bill Owens's *Suburbia,* published in 1972 (plates 155, 156). Owens, at the time a newspaper photographer in the valley town of Livermore, east of Oakland, pictured the putatively happy existence of suburbanites in new housing developments. Lacing his photojournalistic report with quotes from interviews with his subjects, he maintained a balance between irony and enthusiasm. To this day commentators still argue over whether he intended to poke fun at his subjects. The success of *Suburbia* ultimately overshadowed several other social documents of the era, such as Chauncey Hare's patently bitter *Interior America.*

By the end of the decade, the role of photography within the world of art was changing yet again, as a younger group of artists came to see photography as a cultural subject and not merely as a medium for art. Later to be brought together under the banner of Postmodernism, which was to dominate critical discussion of photography and art for most of the eighties, these artists were schooled in the notion that photographs were reflections of a mass culture defined by mass media. Their teachers included some of the pioneers of Conceptualism, most significantly John Baldessari and Douglas Huebler at the California Institute of the Arts in Valencia. Often referred to as the breeding ground of Postmodernism, "Cal Arts" had a discrete photography program, led by John Brumfield, but "post-studio art" teachers like Baldessari and Huebler introduced students to photographs in the context of recent contemporary art. Among the graduates of the program are Nancy Barton, Larry Johnson and James Welling; of these, Welling produced the most provocative and critically intriguing work, most notably his small contact prints of crumpled aluminum foil.

In the mid-seventies, two recent graduate students at the San Francisco Art Institute, Mike Mandel and Larry Sultan, collaborated on a project involving "found" photographs retrieved from corporate and government archives without regard to their original contexts. *Evidence,* as the 1977 book was called, was a meditation on the ambiguity of photographic meaning and on the marvelous possibilities of camera vision that emerge in pictures despite (and outside of) the photographer's intention. Perhaps without knowing it, Mandel and Sultan demonstrated how Jacques Derrida's method of critical deconstruction could be applied to photographs as well as literary texts.

California also proved central in the development of the tableau aesthetic that would come to characterize much of eighties photography. Artists such as Ellen Brooks, JoAnn Callis, Eileen Cowin and Patrick Nagatani were living and working in California in the seventies when they first began to substitute arranged situations—sometimes with human surrogates—for the more common "candid" approach. This allowed them to control not only the formal qualities of their pictures but also the emotional resonances that they sought. In Callis's case these resonances usually evoked subconscious dream states (plate 178); in the pictures of Brooks, Cowin and Nagatani, they evoked soap operas and sit-coms.

In short, one can argue that as a result of the overthrow of the modernist aesthetic in California during the years 1945 to 1980, a new wave of camera practices were able to flourish in the state, that in the process blurred the once-strict lines between photographers and artists working in other mediums. As a result, California became a national, and by extension international, center for many of the new developments in art using photographs. Blessed with a number of schools where photographers and artists could interact and learn from one another, and with progressive faculty members interested in teaching students to express themselves in unique and innovative ways, the state incubated a great and often confusing variety of approaches to the medium.

This may explain why, in the seventies and into the eighties, the interest in positing and defining a "California photography" remained so high. According to Susan Kismaric, the curator of *California Photography: Remaking Make Believe,* one of the last exhibitions to attempt such a definition:

> The photograph's inability to describe the increasing derangement of daily experience precipitated a deliberate, radical reconsideration of conventional ideas about what a photograph might look like. The reliability of the straight photograph as a purveyor of fact, and the reliance on the purist aesthetic as a guiding principle of fine-art photography, were eventually undermined. . . . This contemporary interrogation began, among other places, in California, where there developed a distinct movement in contemporary photography, one based on an open exchange of techniques and materials between artists.[16]

Kismaric went on to argue that, "The application of photography to other artistic endeavors and the combining of photography with images from other mediums created a primarily synthetic photographic style that has come to define the essence of California photography." Whether one accepts this "synthetic style" as the sign of what developed in the state by the end of the seventies, it is clear that California's unique and lasting contribution to the art of photography—and to the photograph in art—was recognized by 1989 even in that most parochial of precincts, New York City. This is a legacy that continues to inform photography in California today.

NOTES

1. For a fuller discussion of this transformation, see Kathleen McCarthy Gauss and Andy Grundberg, *Photography and Art, Interactions Since 1946* (New York: Abbeville Press, 1987).

2. Another direct descendent of European Surrealism, Vilem Kriz, arrived in California from Prague, by way of Paris, the year after Man Ray departed. Kriz, whose work was rediscovered in the 1970s, taught at the California College of Arts and Crafts in Oakland while pursuing his own photography of bizarre still life arrangements (plate 128). See David Featherstone, *Vilem Kriz, Surrealist* (Carmel: The Friends of Photography, 1979).

3. Keith Davis, *An American Century of Photography: From Dry Plate to Digital* (New York: Hallmark/Harry N. Abrams, 1999), 134.

4. Among the exhibitions devoted to California photography and organized in California in the 1970s were *California Photography 1970* at the University of California, Davis (1970), *24 From Los Angeles* at the San Francisco Museum of Modern Art (1973), *Emerging Los Angeles Photographers* at the Friends of Photography (1977) and *Contemporary California Photography* at S.F. Camerawork (1979).

5. *California Photography,* at the Museum of Art, Rhode Island School of Design, 1982, was organized by Deborah J. Johnson and included two dozen contemporary artists, including John Baldessari, Lewis Baltz, Ellen Brooks, Linda Connor, and Judy Dater. *California Photography: Remaking Make Believe,* at the Museum of Modern Art in New York in 1989, was organized by Susan Kismaric and included seven artists: Baldessari, Robert Heinecken, Larry Sultan, John Divola, Jo Ann Callis, Nancy Barton and Larry Johnson. The most comprehensive and influential attempt to define California photography was shown at the San Francisco Museum of Modern Art in 1984: *Photography in California, 1945–1980.* This traveling show was organized by Louise Katzman and featured a book-length catalogue published by Hudson Hills Press.

6. Katzman, *Photography in California, 1945–1980* (New York: Hudson Hills Press, 1984), 24.

7. The disaffected irony of Frank's pictures did not prevent Steichen, ironically, from including them in *The Family of Man.*

8. Katzman, 17.

9. Katzman, 46.

10. Judy Dater and Jack Welpott, *Women and Other Visions* (Morgan and Morgan, 1975).

11. Gauss and Grundberg, 108–111.

12. Jo Ann Callis, quoted in Susan Kismaric, *California Photography: Remaking Make Believe* (New York: Museum of Modern Art, 1989), 50.

13. Davis, *An American Century of Photography,* 390–391. Sontag's essays were collected as *On Photography* (New York: Farrar, Straus and Giroux, 1977).

14. *Robert Cumming Photographs,* edited and with an essay by James Alinder (Carmel: Friends of Photography, 1979).

15. *New Topographics* was organized by William Jenkins, curator, at the International Museum of Photography at George Eastman House, Rochester, N.Y.

16. Kismaric, 10.

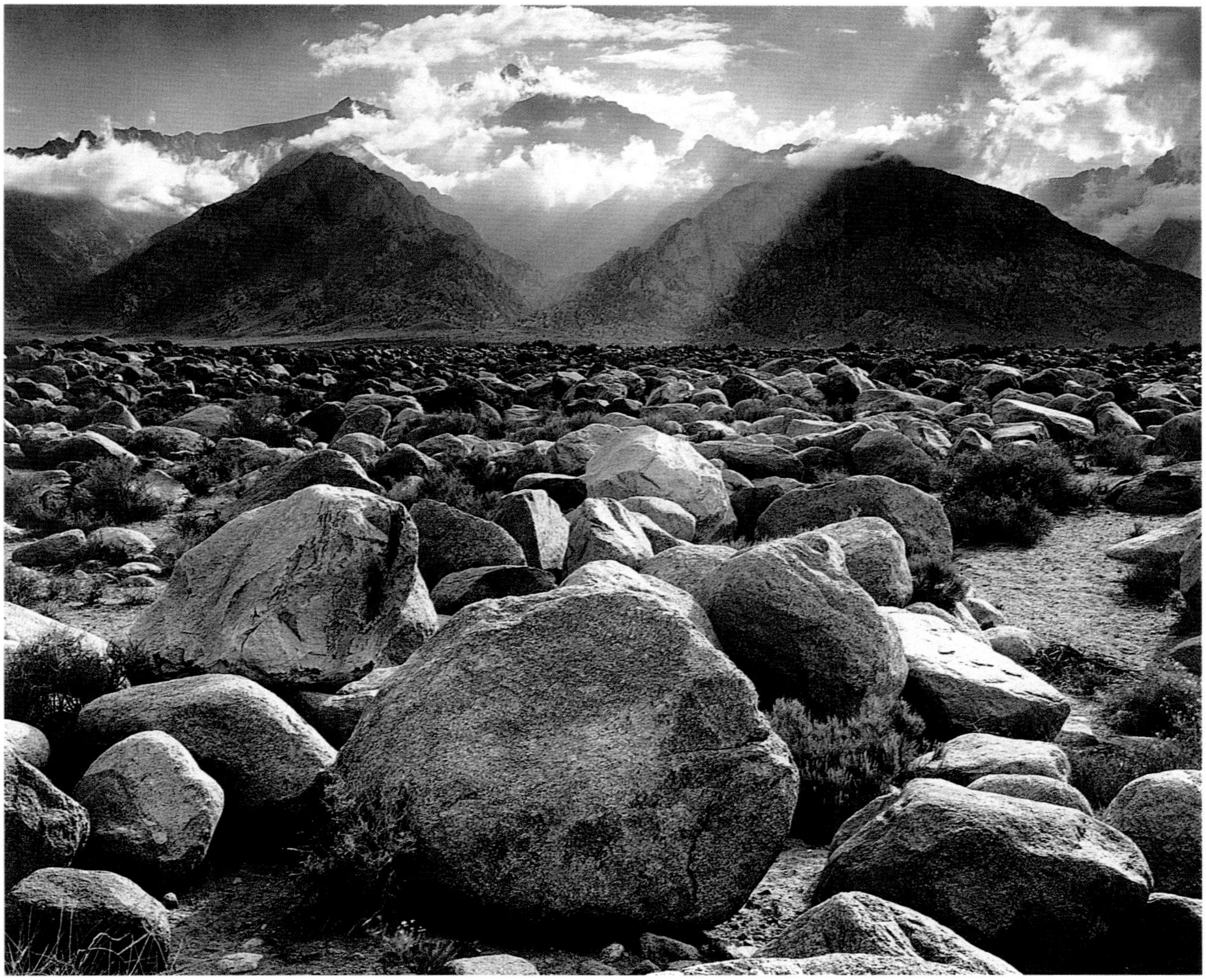

124.
ANSEL ADAMS
Mount Williamson from Manzanar, California, 1945
Gelatin silver print
15⅛ x 18¾ in.
DUDLEY P. BELL FUND

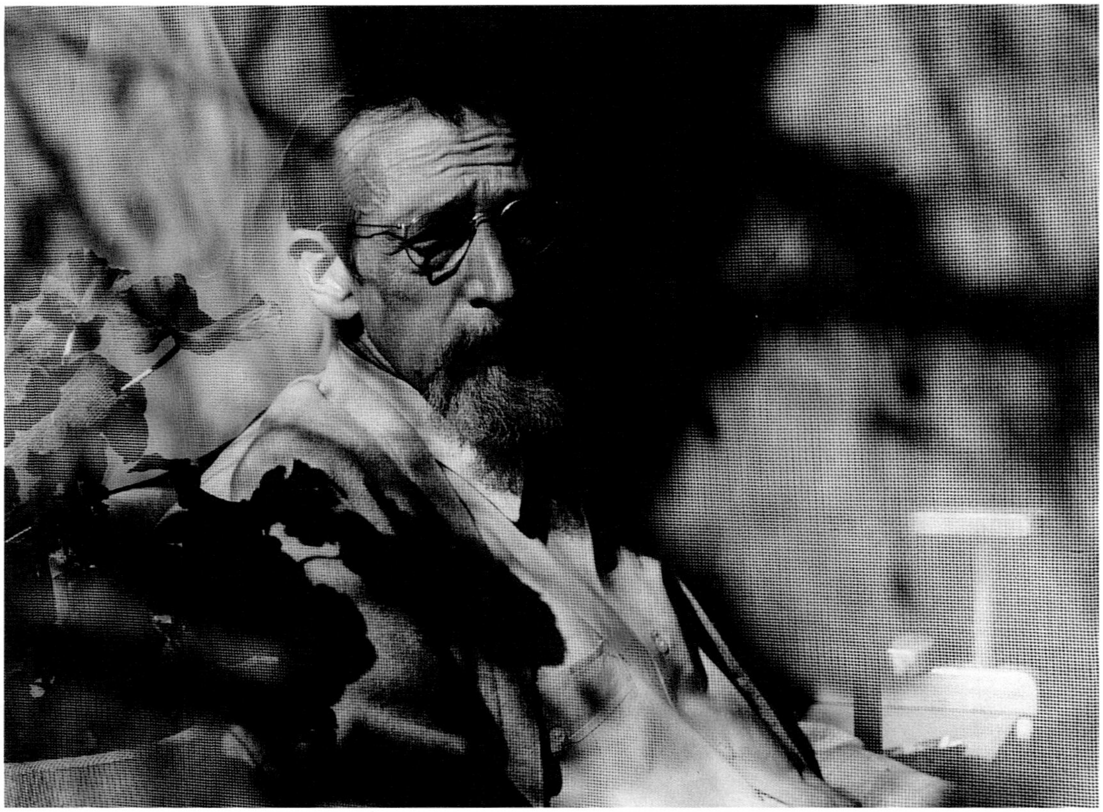

125.
ANSEL ADAMS
Portrait of Maynard Dixon, 1945
Gelatin silver print
7 x 9⅛ in.
GIFT OF EDITH HAMLIN

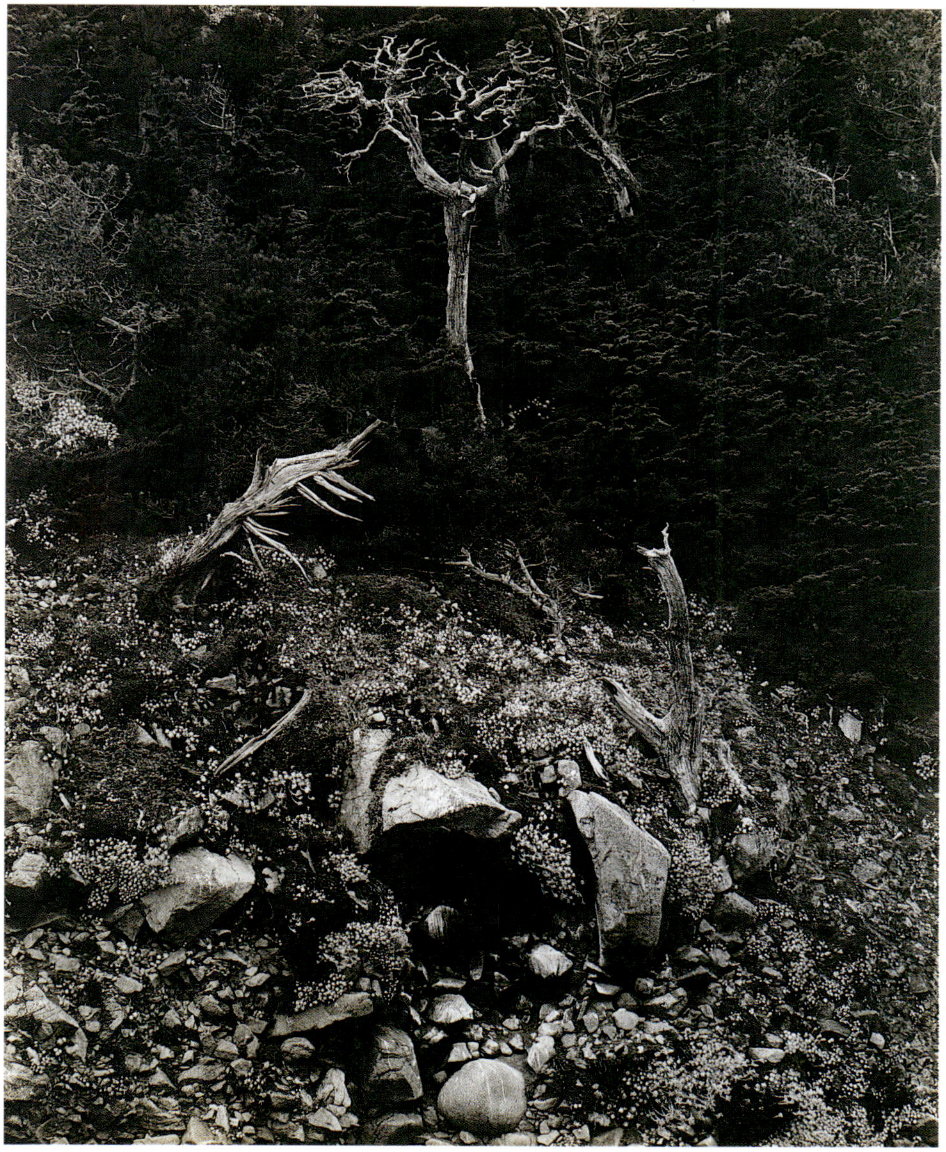

126.
EDWARD WESTON
Cypress and Stone Crop (Point Lobos), 1946
Gelatin silver print
9⁹⁄₁₆ x 7⁹⁄₁₆ in.
GIFT OF GERALD D. WRIGHT

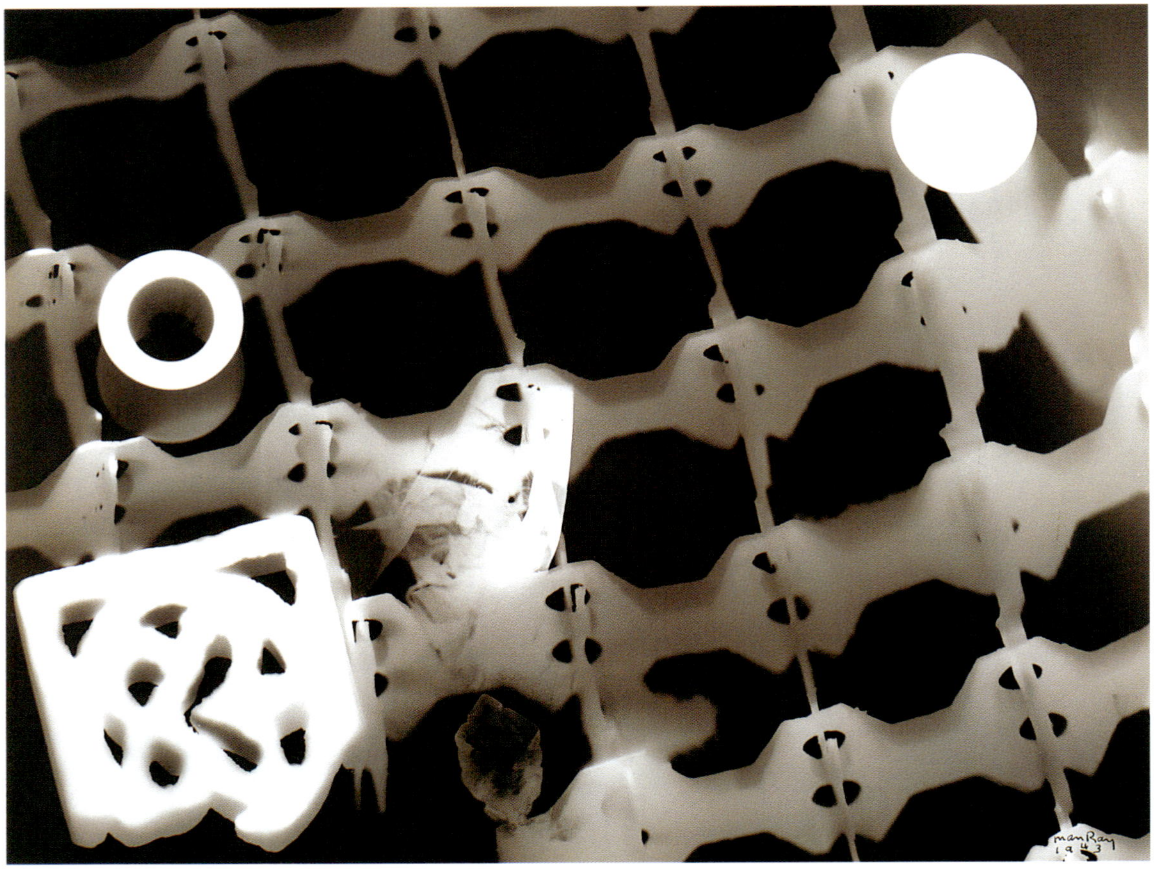

127.

MAN RAY

Rayograph, 1943

Solarized gelatin silver print

10⅞ x 13⅞ in.

MUSEUM DONORS' ACQUISITION FUND

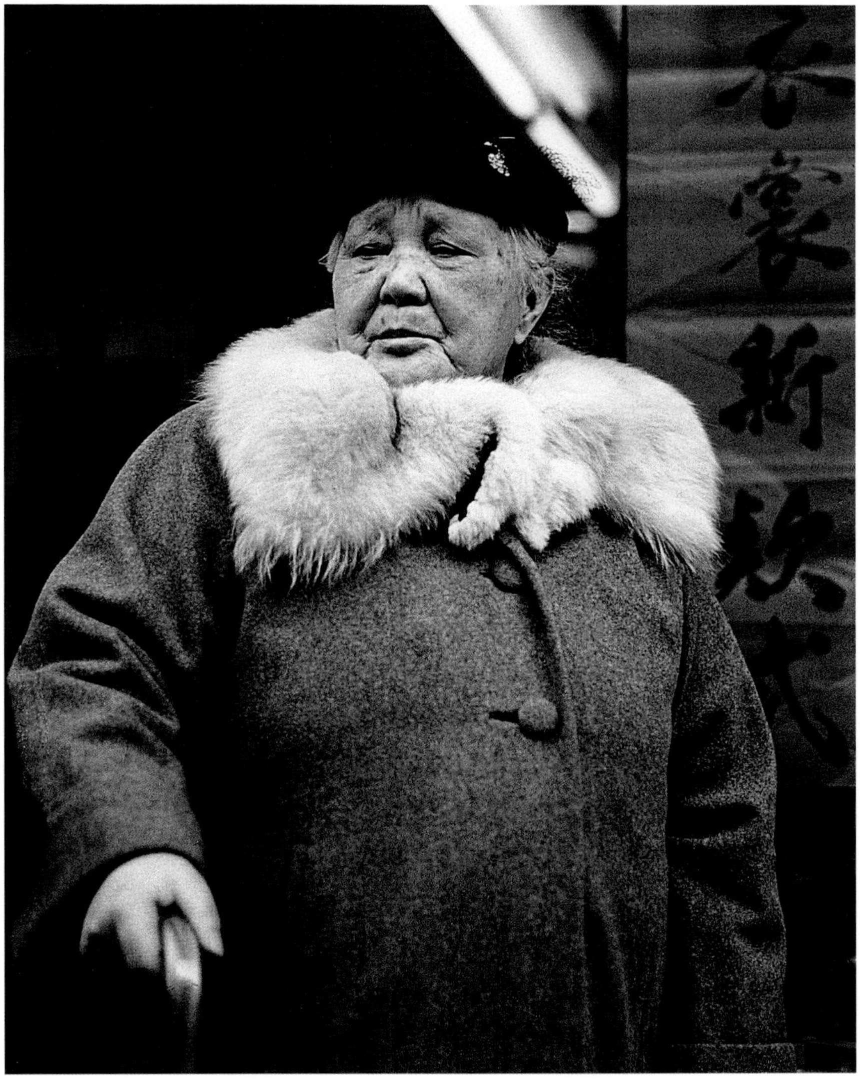

130.
RUTH-MARION BARUCH
Elderly Chinese Woman, Chinatown, San Francisco, 1955
Gelatin silver print
9¼ x 7¼ in.
GIFT OF THE ART LEAGUE OF THE EAST BAY

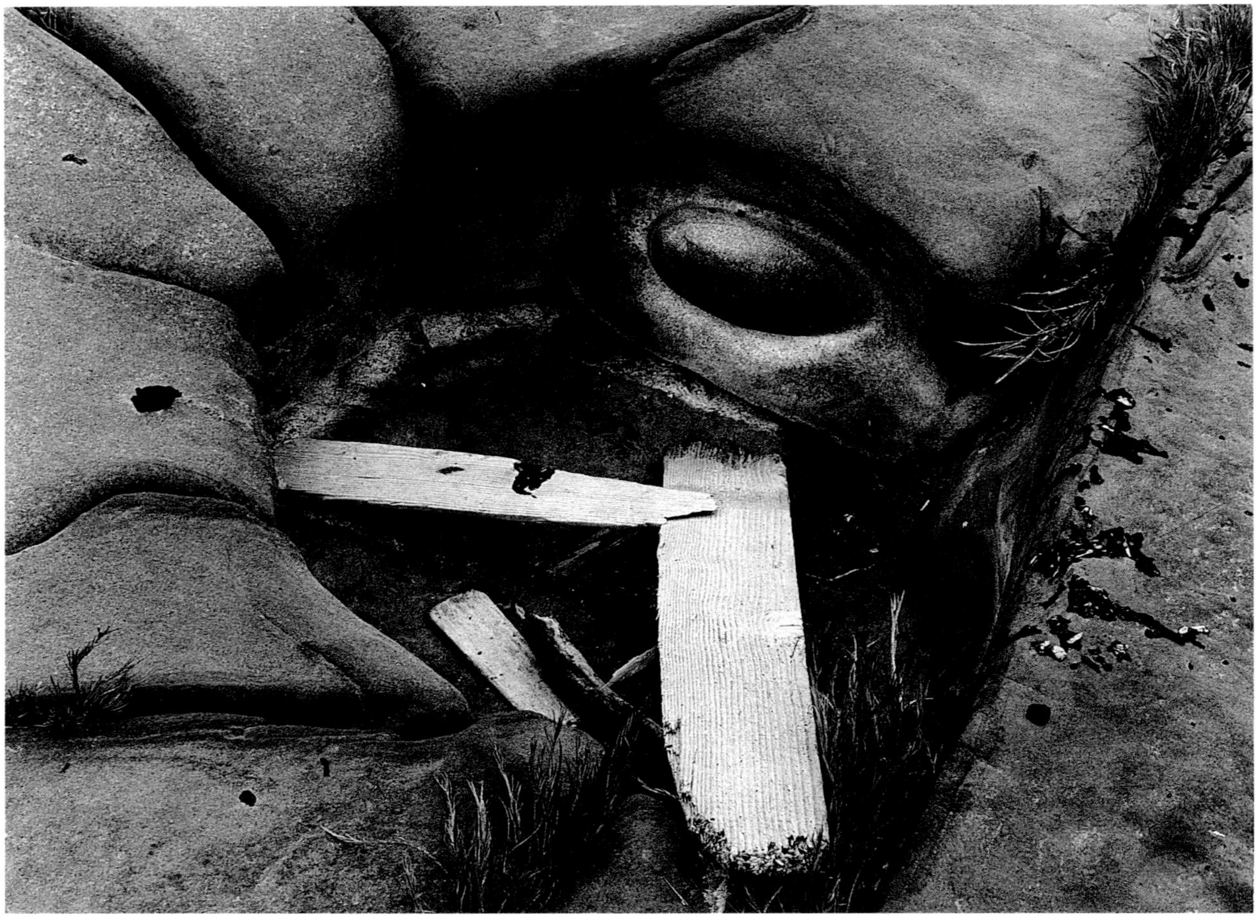

131.

MINOR WHITE

Driftwood and Eye, Point Lobos, California, 1951

Gelatin silver print

8⅛ x 10¾ in.

THE SHIRLEY BURDEN FUND FOR PHOTOGRAPHY

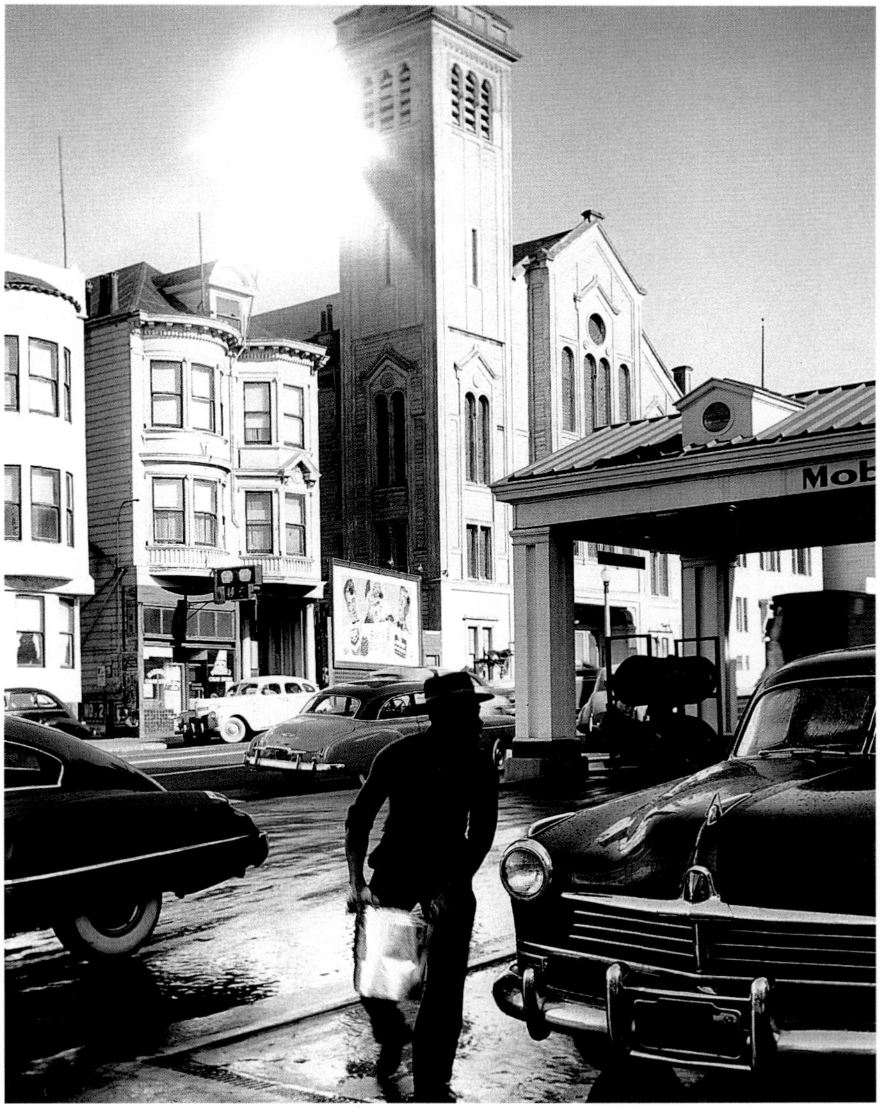

132.
MINOR WHITE
Japanese Church, San Francisco, 1949
Gelatin silver print
11 x 14 in.
THE OAKLAND MUSEUM FOUNDERS' FUND

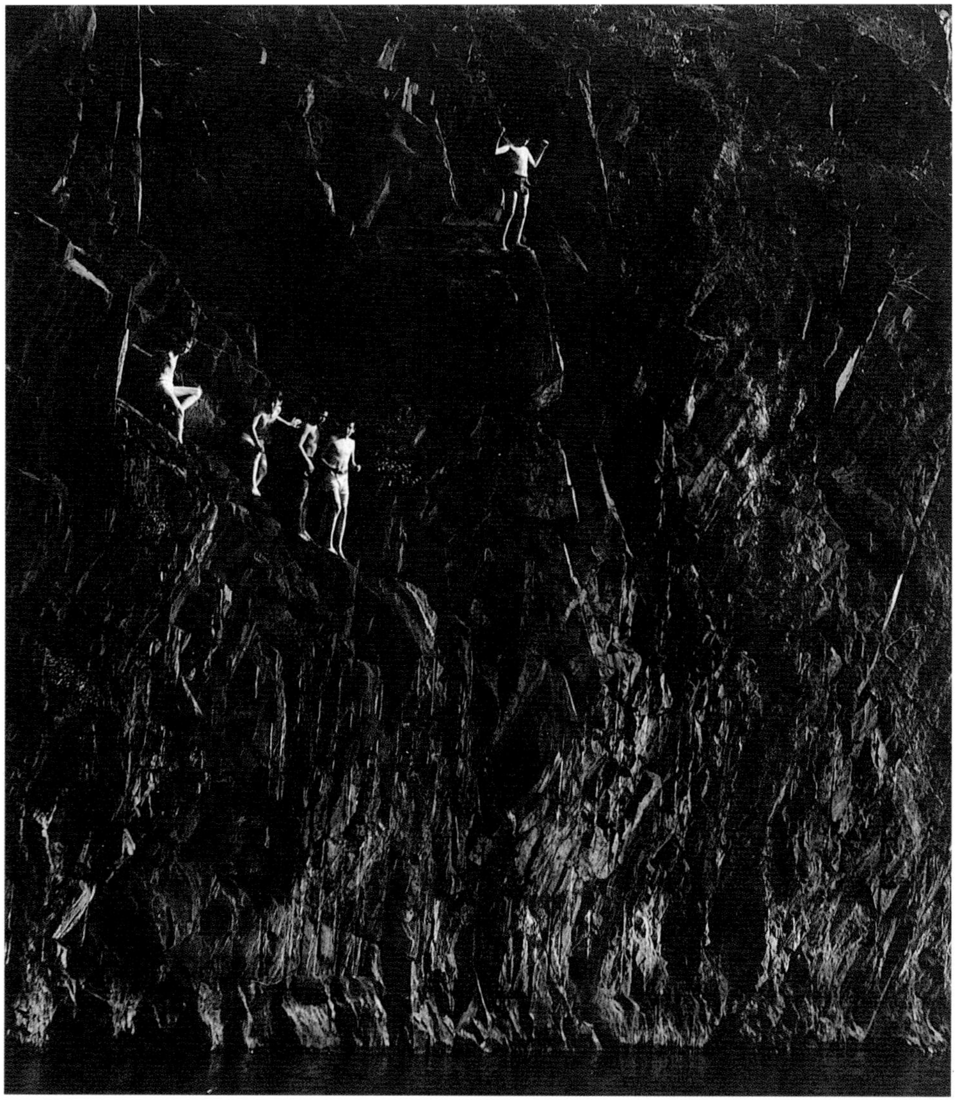

133.

SHIRLEY C. BURDEN

Untitled (Boys on Cliff over Pool), n.d.

Gelatin silver print

$6\frac{5}{16}$ x $5\frac{5}{16}$ in.

GIFT OF THE ARTIST

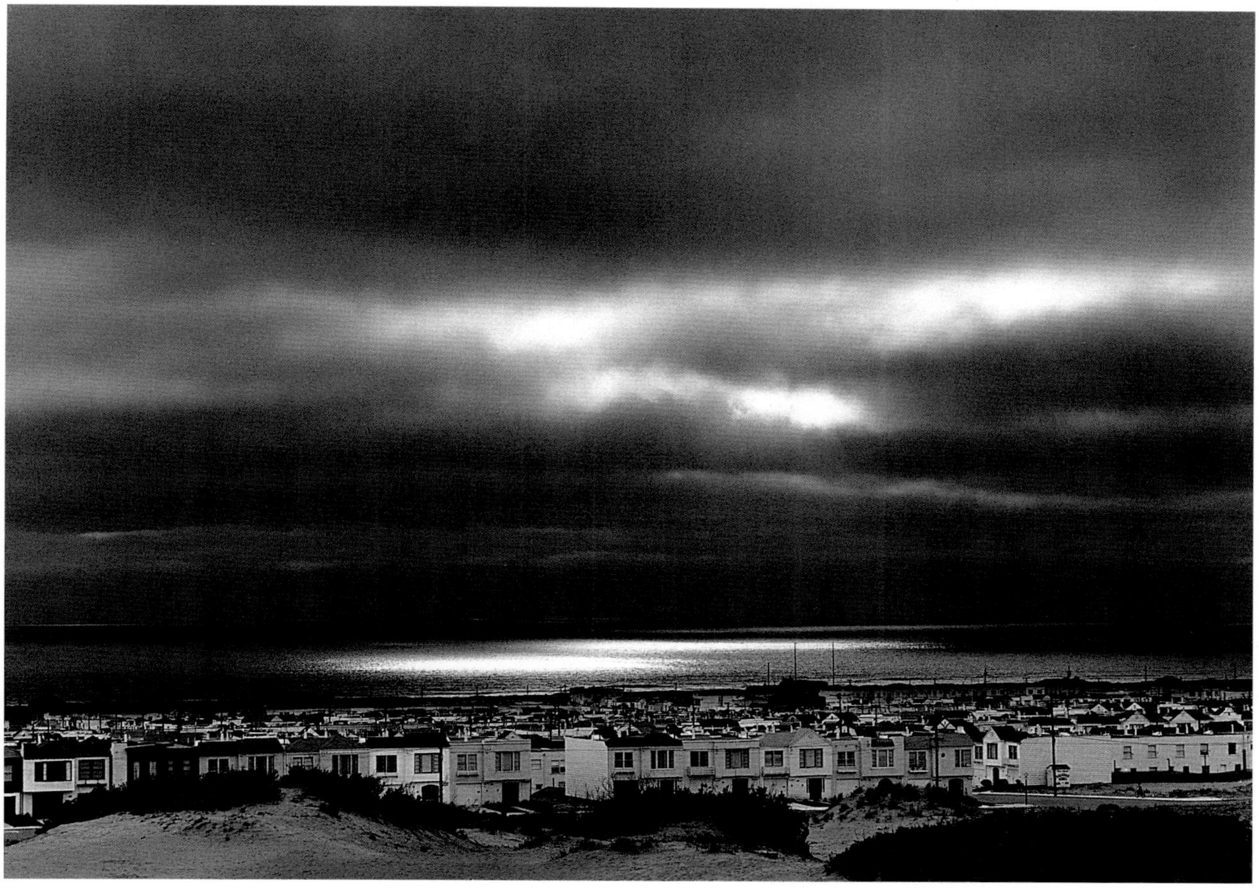

134.
PIRKLE JONES
Sunset District and Pacific Ocean, San Francisco, 1951
Gelatin silver print
9½ x 13$^{5}/_{16}$ in.
GIFT OF JOSEPH M. BRANSTEN

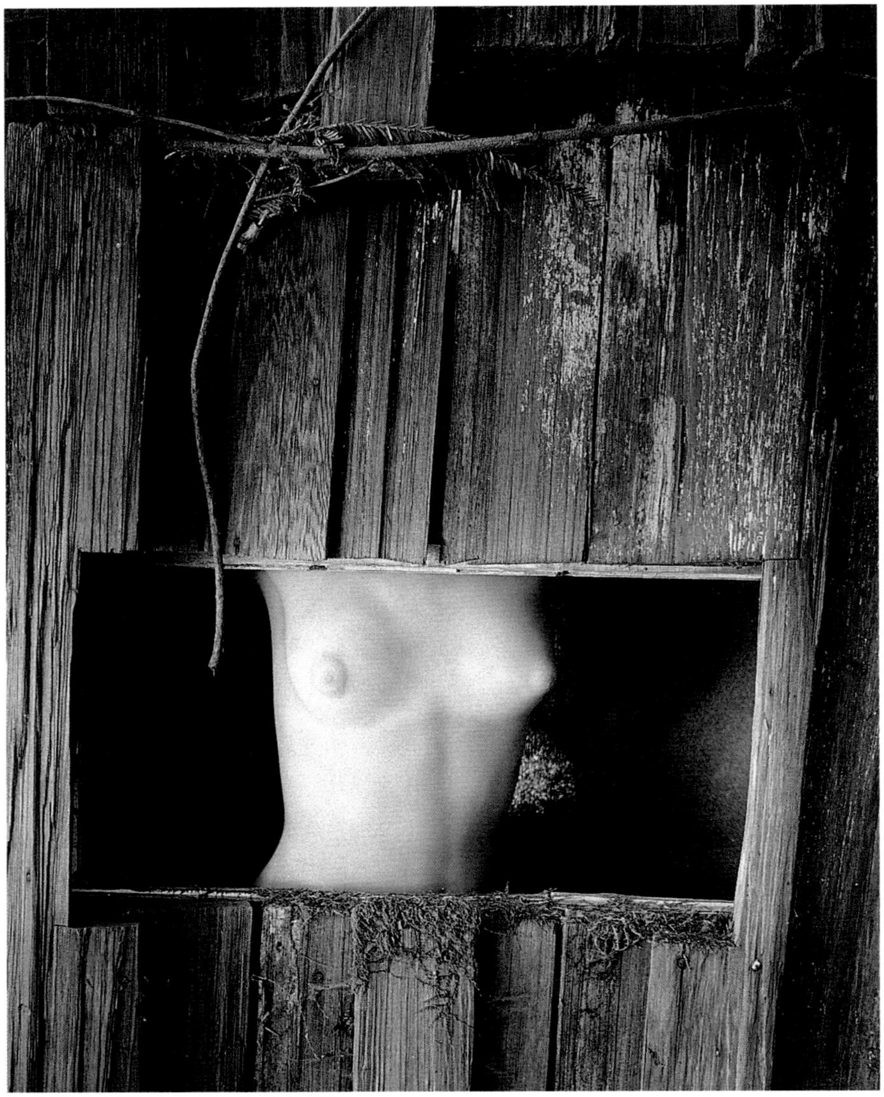

135.
WYNN BULLOCK
Torso in Window, 1954
Gelatin silver print
9 9/16 x 7 5/8 in.
GIFT OF THE 20-30 CLUB, OAKLAND

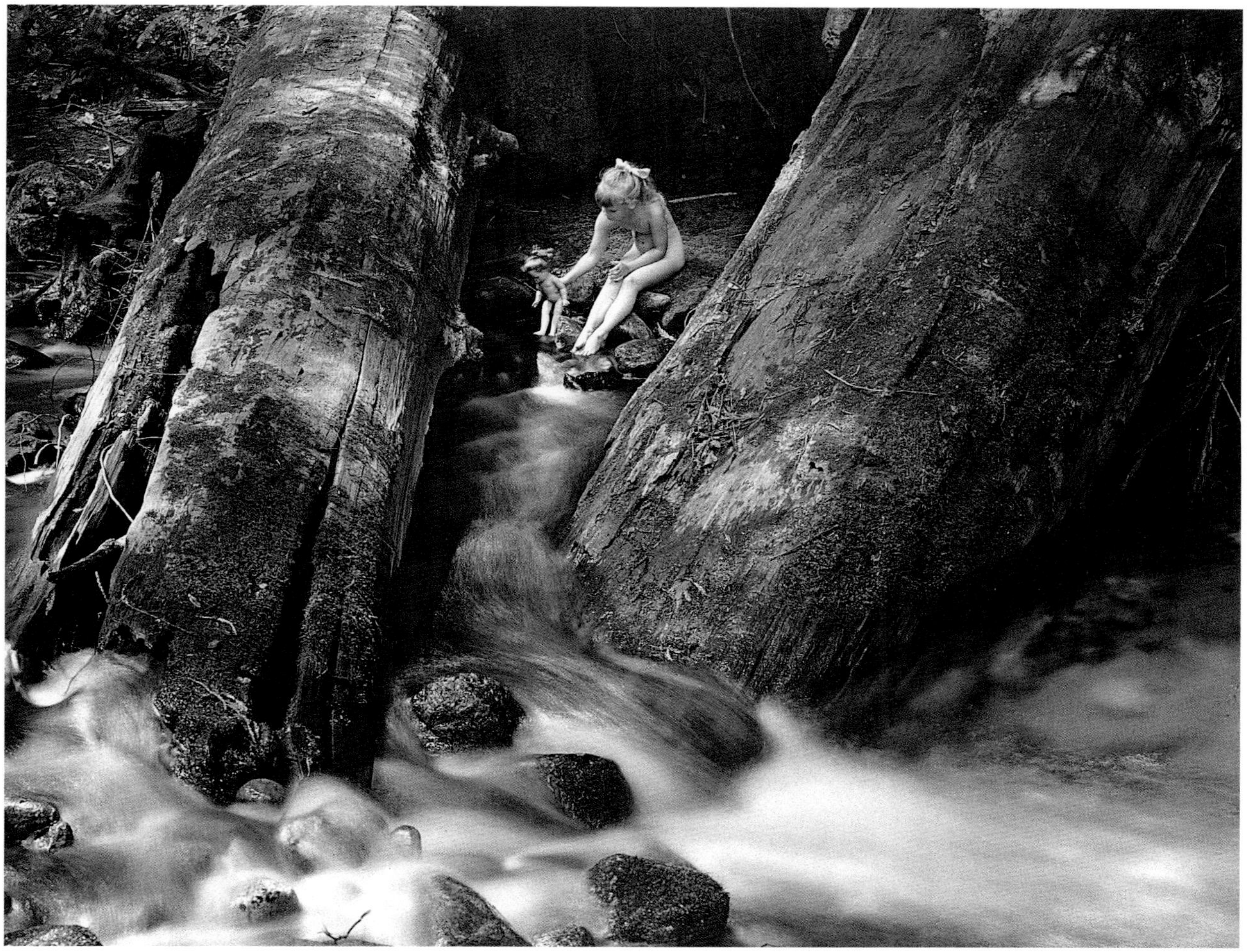

136.
WYNN BULLOCK
Untitled (Girl with Doll and Logs), 1950s
Gelatin silver print
$7\frac{5}{16}$ x $9\frac{1}{2}$ in.
GIFT OF THE ESTATE OF HELEN JOHNSTON

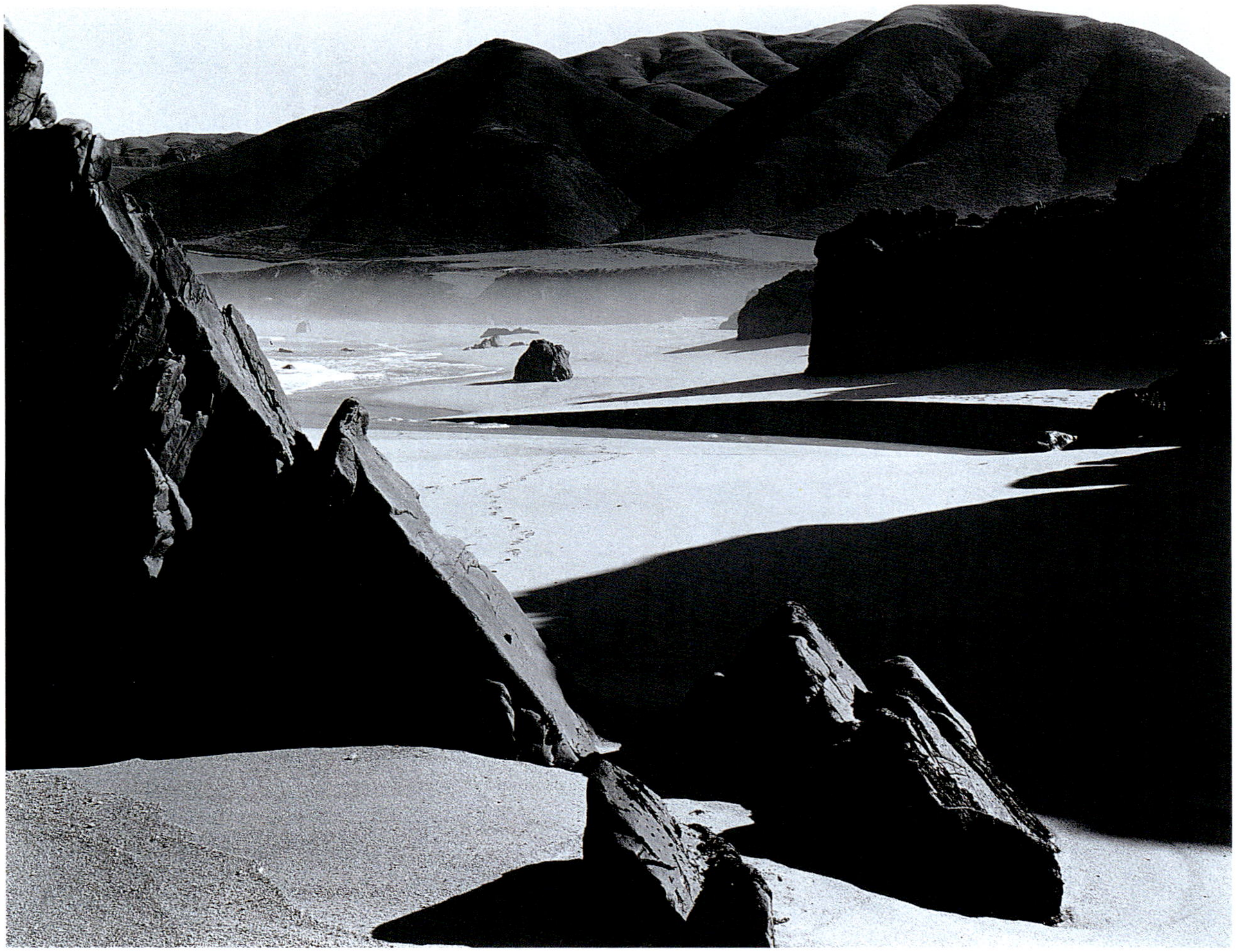

137.
BRETT WESTON
Garrapata Beach, California, 1952
Gelatin silver print
7⅝ x 9 9/16 in.
GIFT OF THE ARTIST

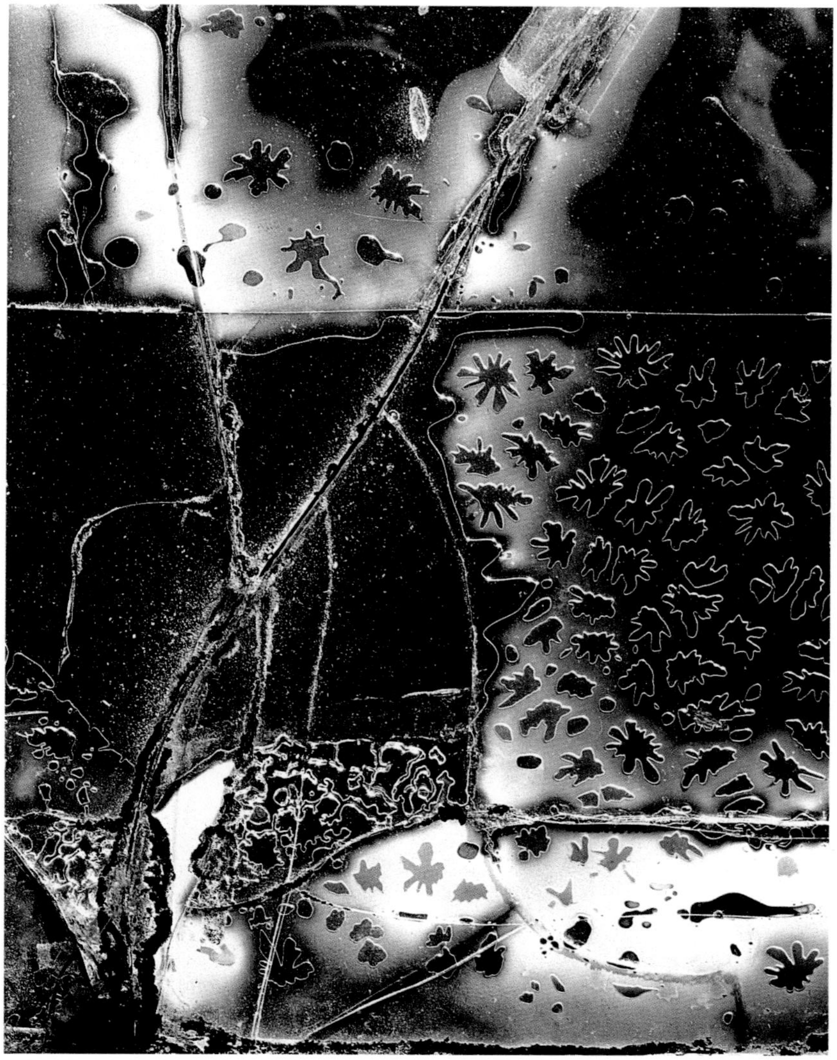

138.
BRETT WESTON
Untitled (Abstraction), 1954
Gelatin silver print
13½ x 10¼ in.
GIFT OF THE GALLERY SHOP, WOMEN'S BOARD

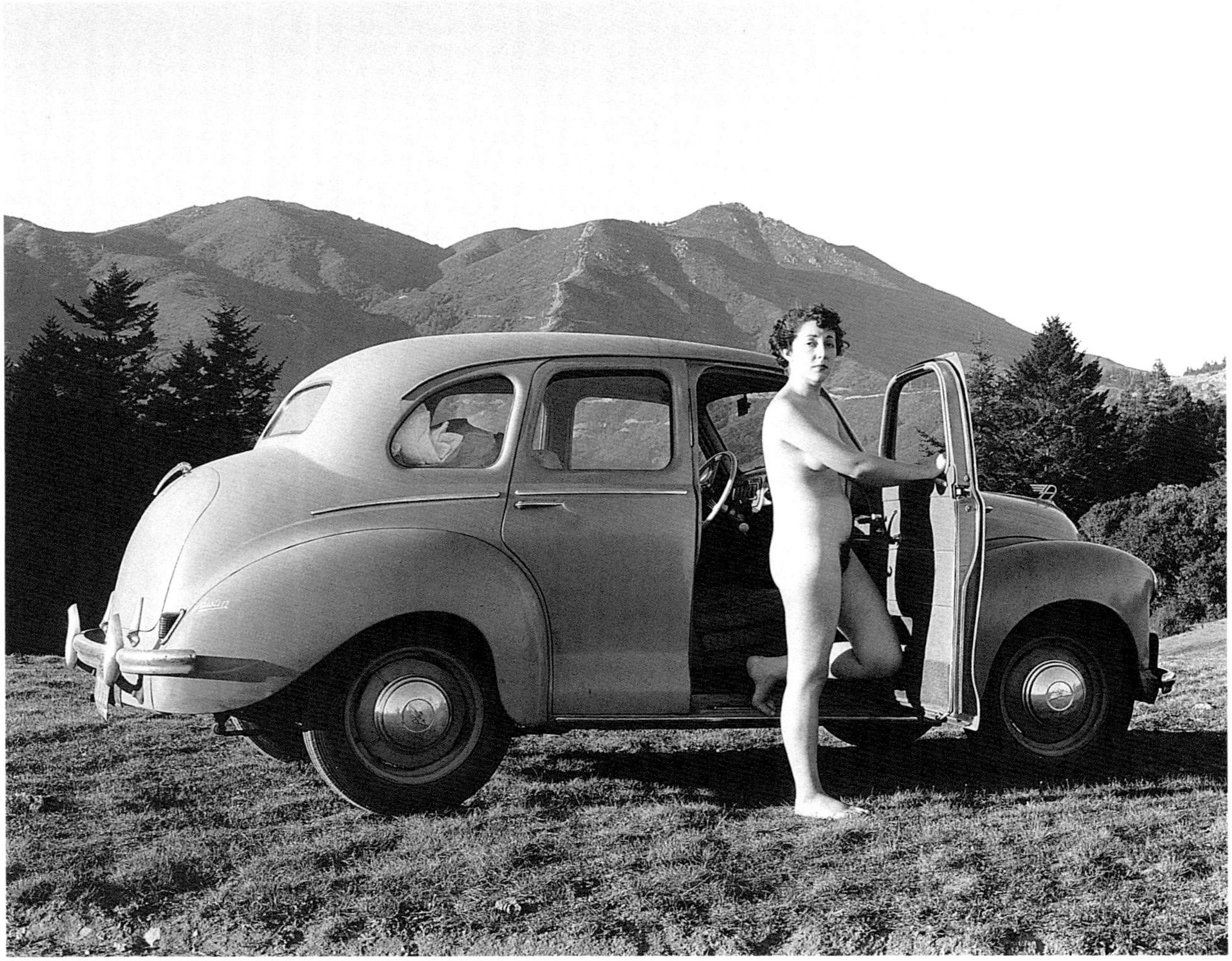

139.
HARRY BOWDEN
E.R. and Austin, October 1953
Gelatin silver print
$7\frac{5}{16}$ x $9\frac{1}{4}$ in.
GIFT OF CHARLES CAMPBELL

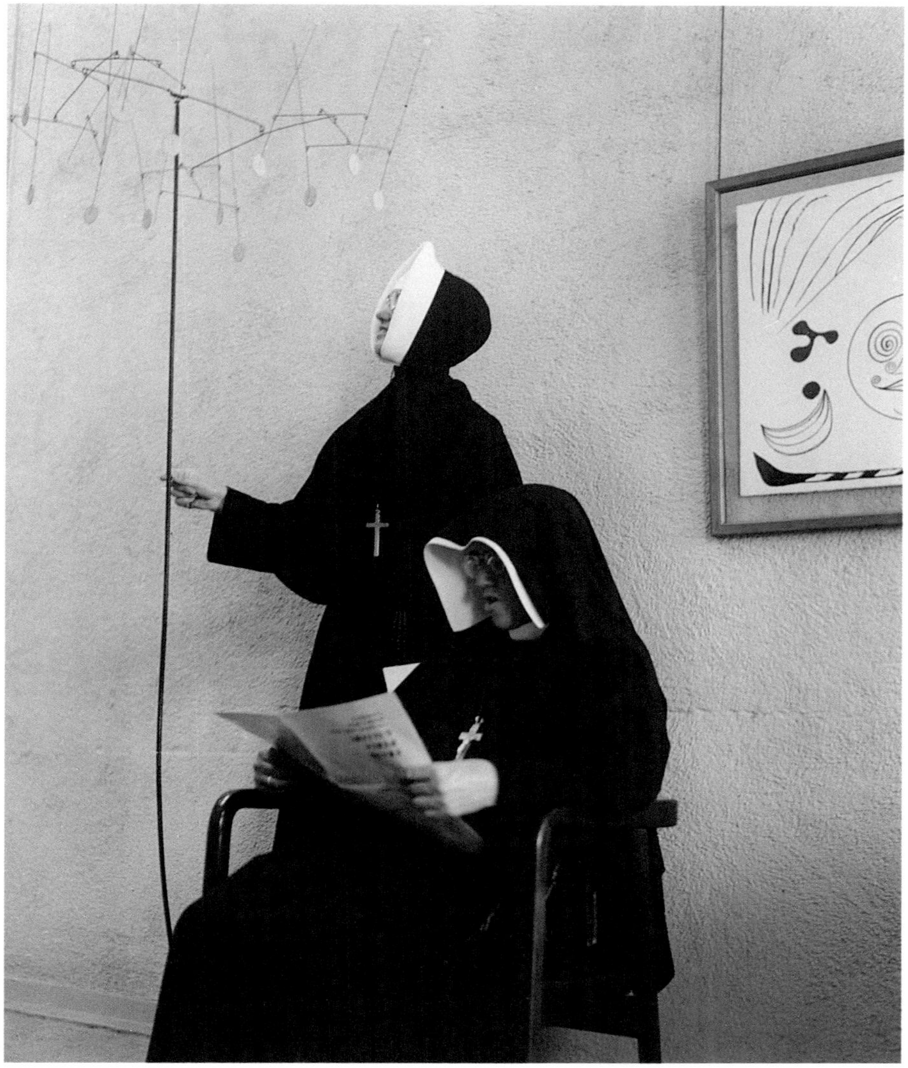

140.
IMOGEN CUNNINGHAM
Nuns at a Calder Show, Los Angeles, 1953
Gelatin silver print
$7\frac{5}{8}$ x $6\frac{9}{16}$ in.
GIFT OF THE ARTIST

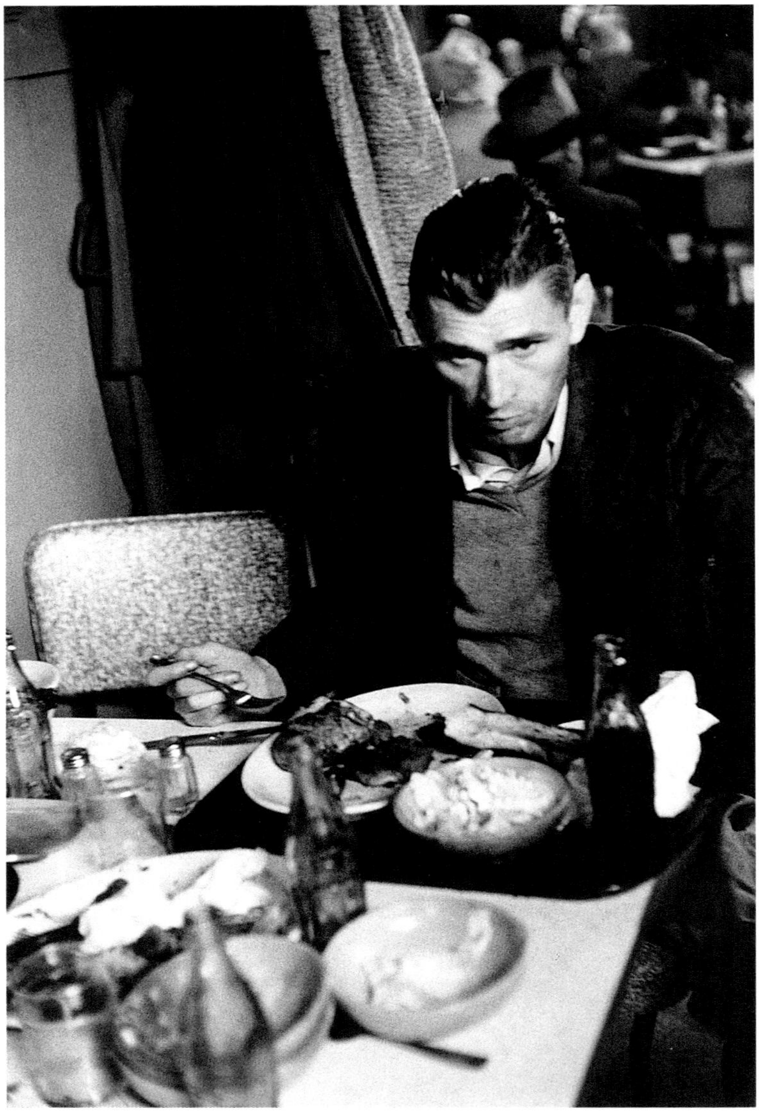

141.

ROBERT FRANK

San Francisco, 1956 (from *The Americans*)

Gelatin silver print

12½ x 8⅜ in.

THE SHIRLEY BURDEN FUND FOR PHOTOGRAPHY

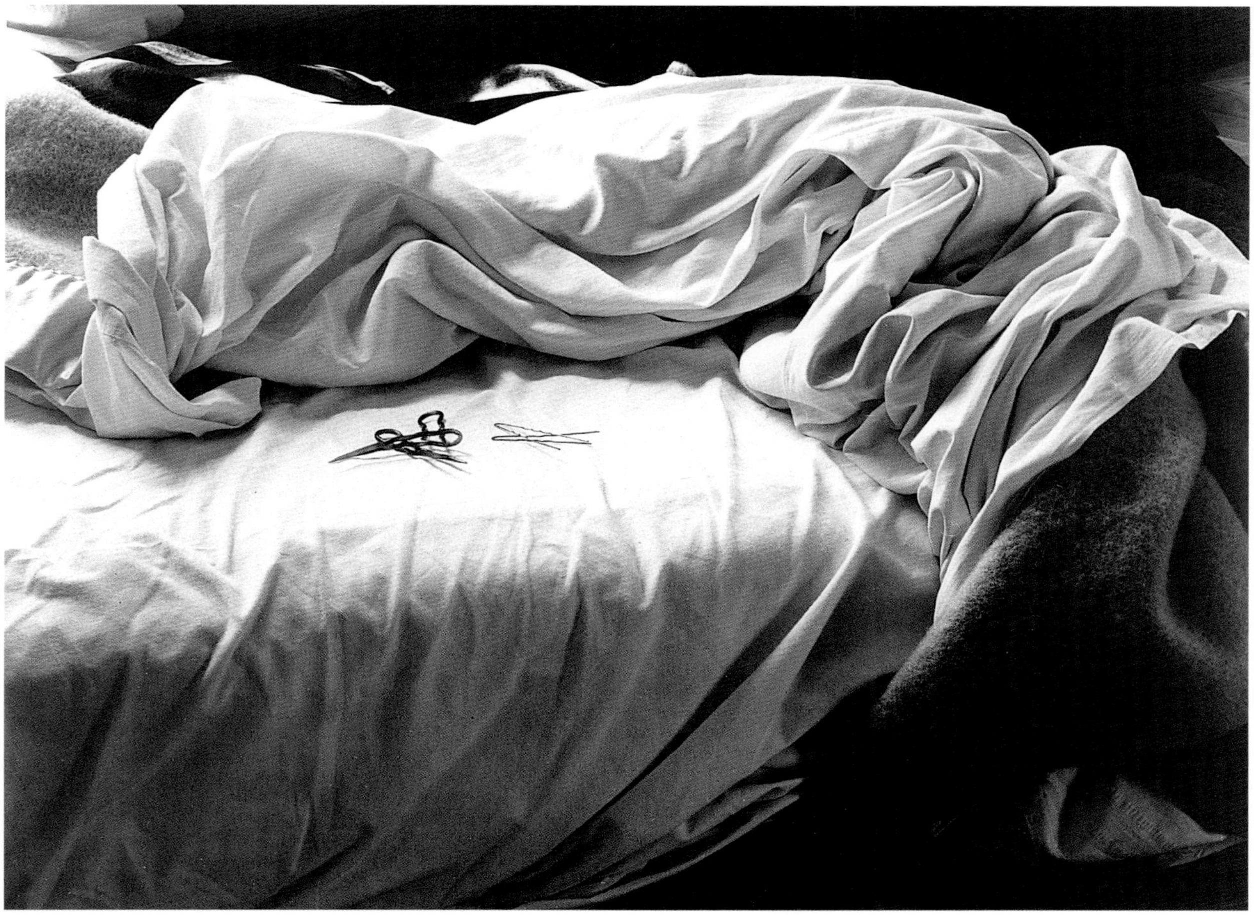

142.
IMOGEN CUNNINGHAM
The Unmade Bed, 1957
Gelatin silver print
7¾ x 9³⁄₁₆ in.
GIFT OF THE ART GUILD OF THE OAKLAND MUSEUM ASSOCIATION

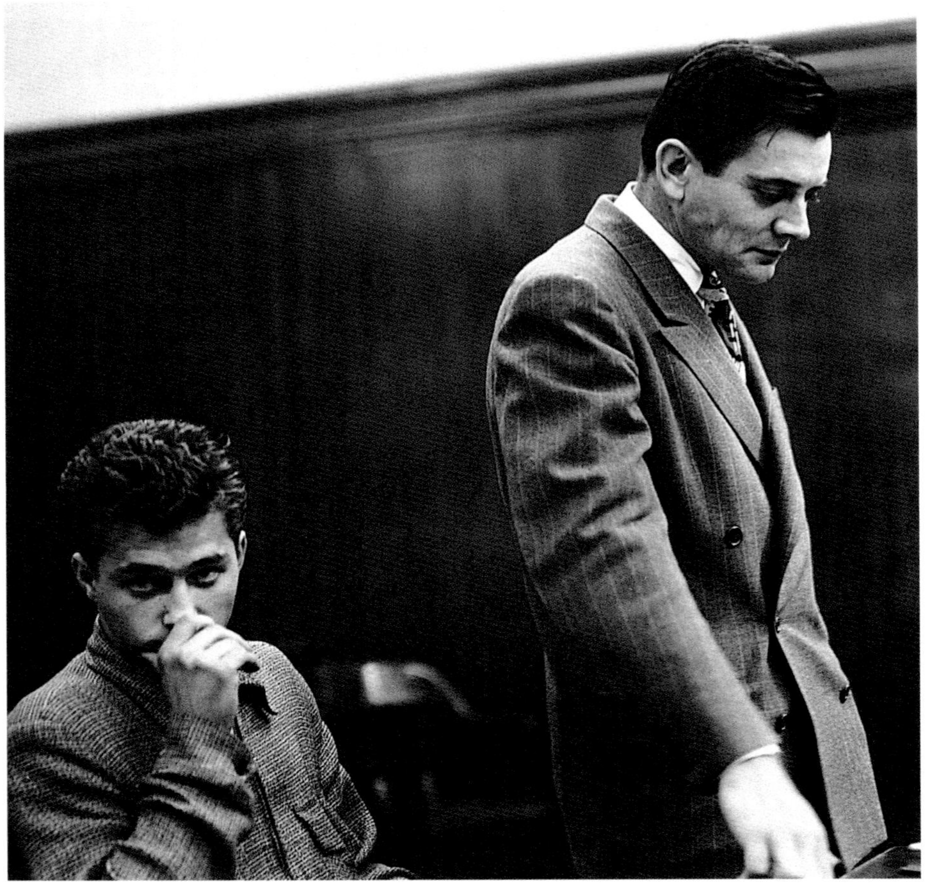

143.
DOROTHEA LANGE
Untitled (Defendant and Attorney), Public Defender series, 1957
Gelatin silver print
$7\frac{1}{2}$ x $7\frac{1}{2}$ in.
GIFT OF PAUL S. TAYLOR

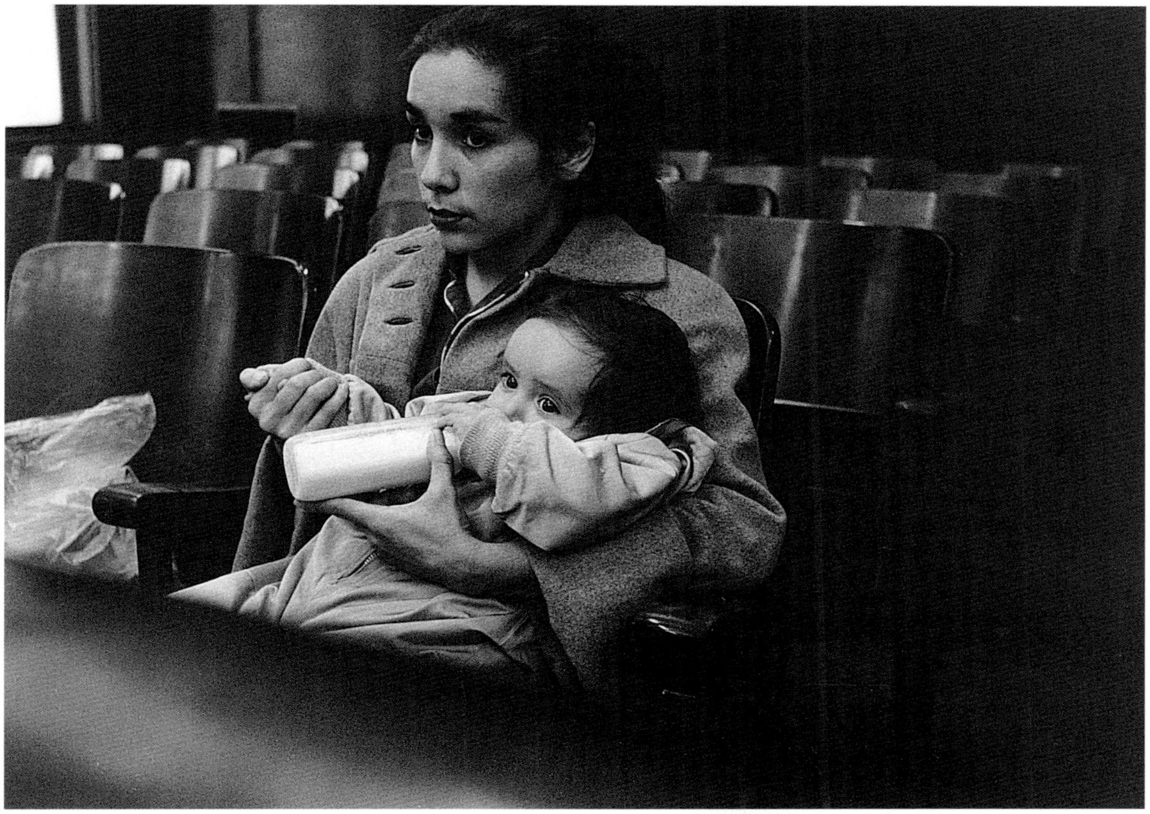

144.
DOROTHEA LANGE
Untitled (Defendant's Wife and Baby), Public Defender series, 1957
Gelatin silver print
8 7/16 x 6 13/16 in.
GIFT OF PAUL S. TAYLOR

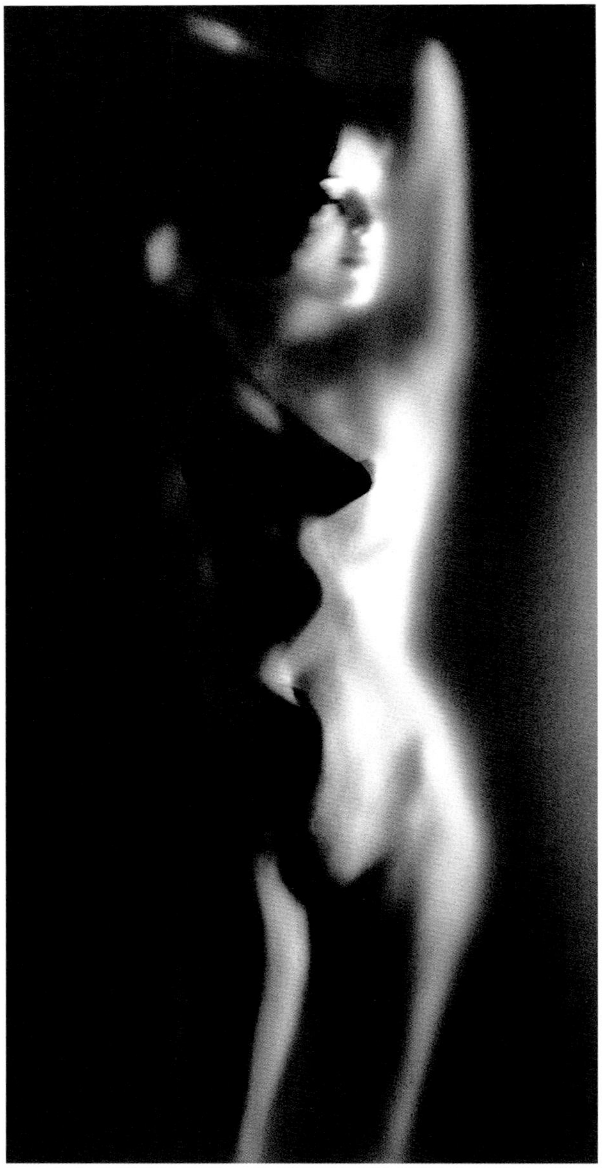

145.
RUTH BERNHARD
Luminous Form, 1962
Gelatin silver print
13¾ x 6⅞ in.
GIFT OF DOROTHEA LANGE PURCHASE AWARD

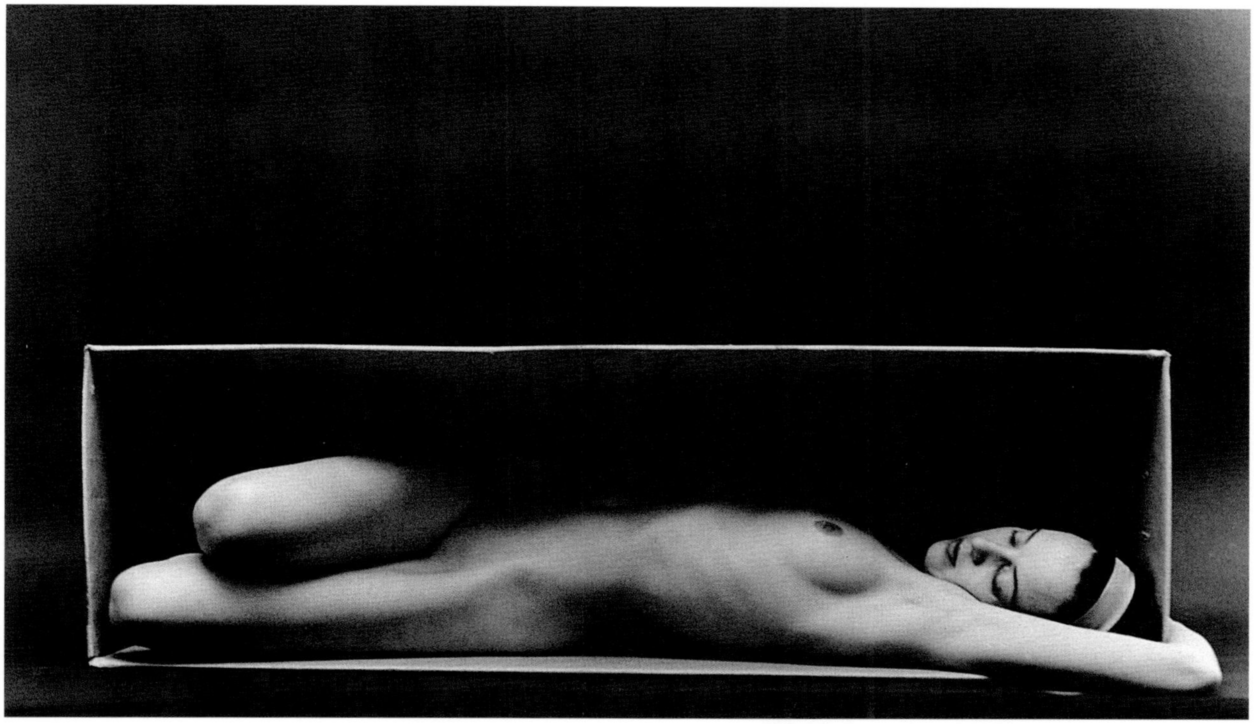

146.
RUTH BERNHARD
Nude in Box Horizontal, 1962
Gelatin silver print
5¾ x 9½ in.
GIFT OF THE ARTIST

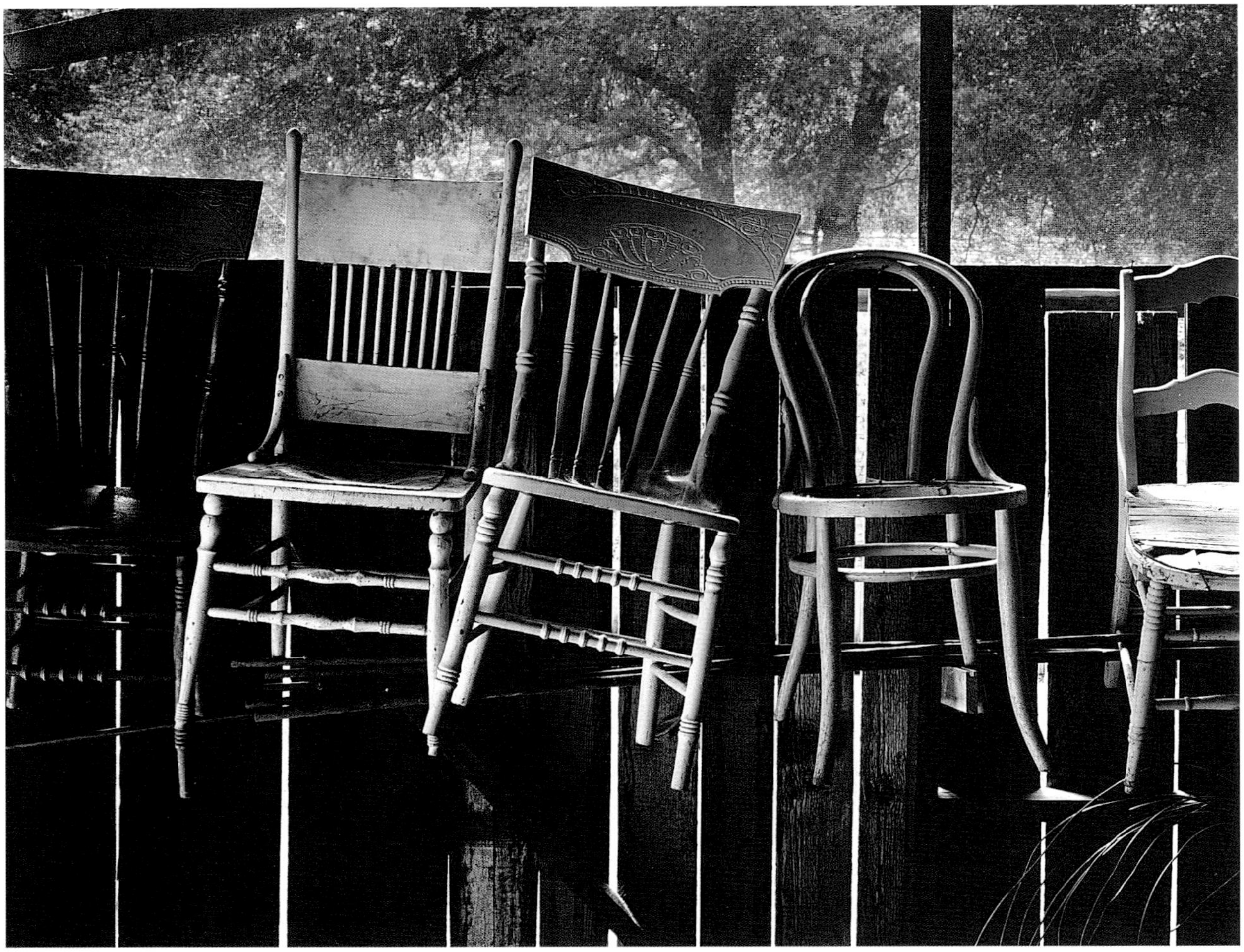

147.
MORLEY BAER
Chairs, Tassajara Hot Springs, 1959
Gelatin silver print
7⅝ x 9⅝ in.
GIFT OF THE ARTIST

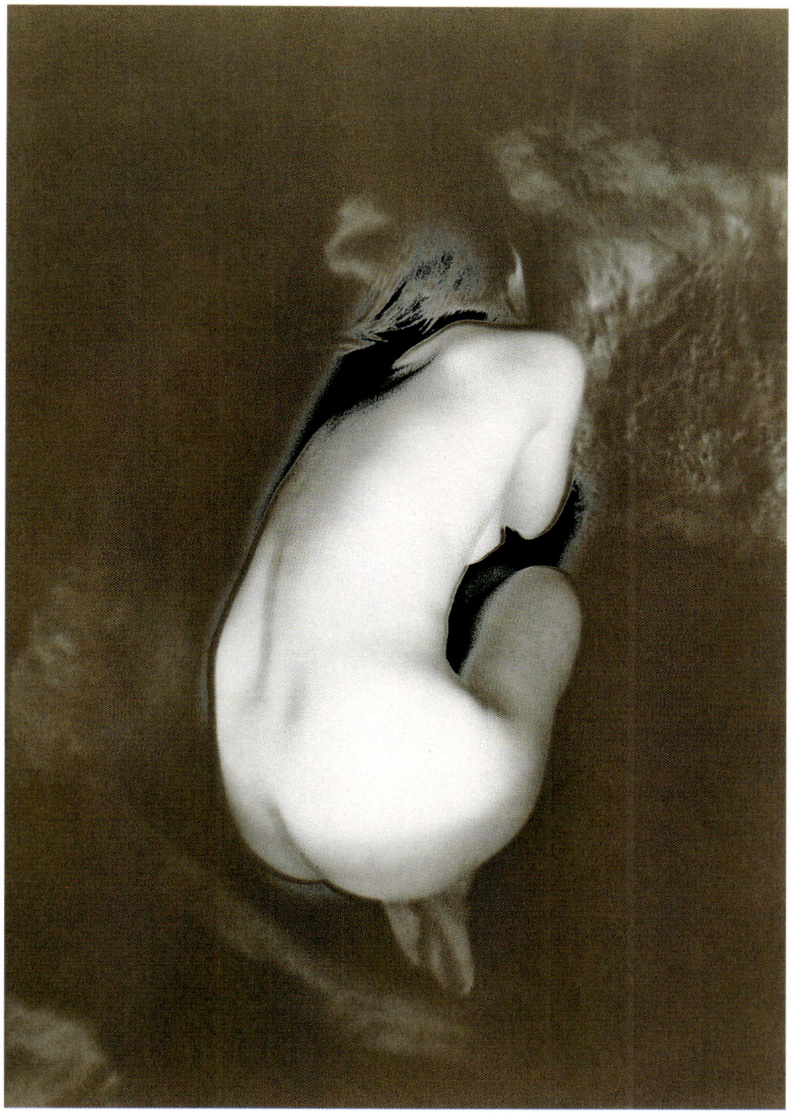

148.
TODD WALKER
Untitled (Nude), 1969
Gelatin silver print, Sabattier effect
9½ x 6½ in.
GIFT OF DR. AND MRS. DUDLEY P. BELL

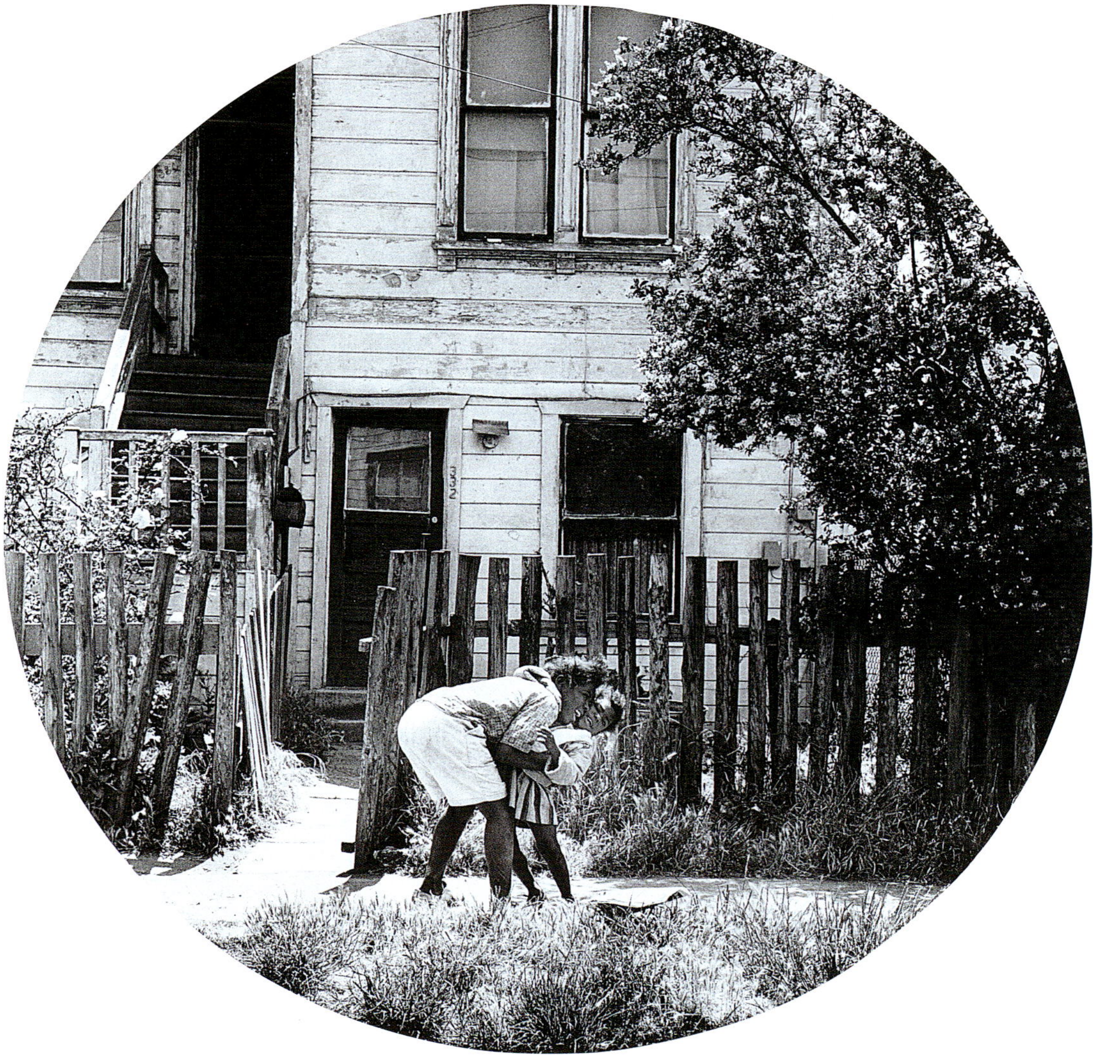

149.

JOANNE LEONARD

My Next Door Neighbors, West Oakland, 1965

Gelatin silver print

9⅝ in. diameter

GIFT OF THE ARTIST

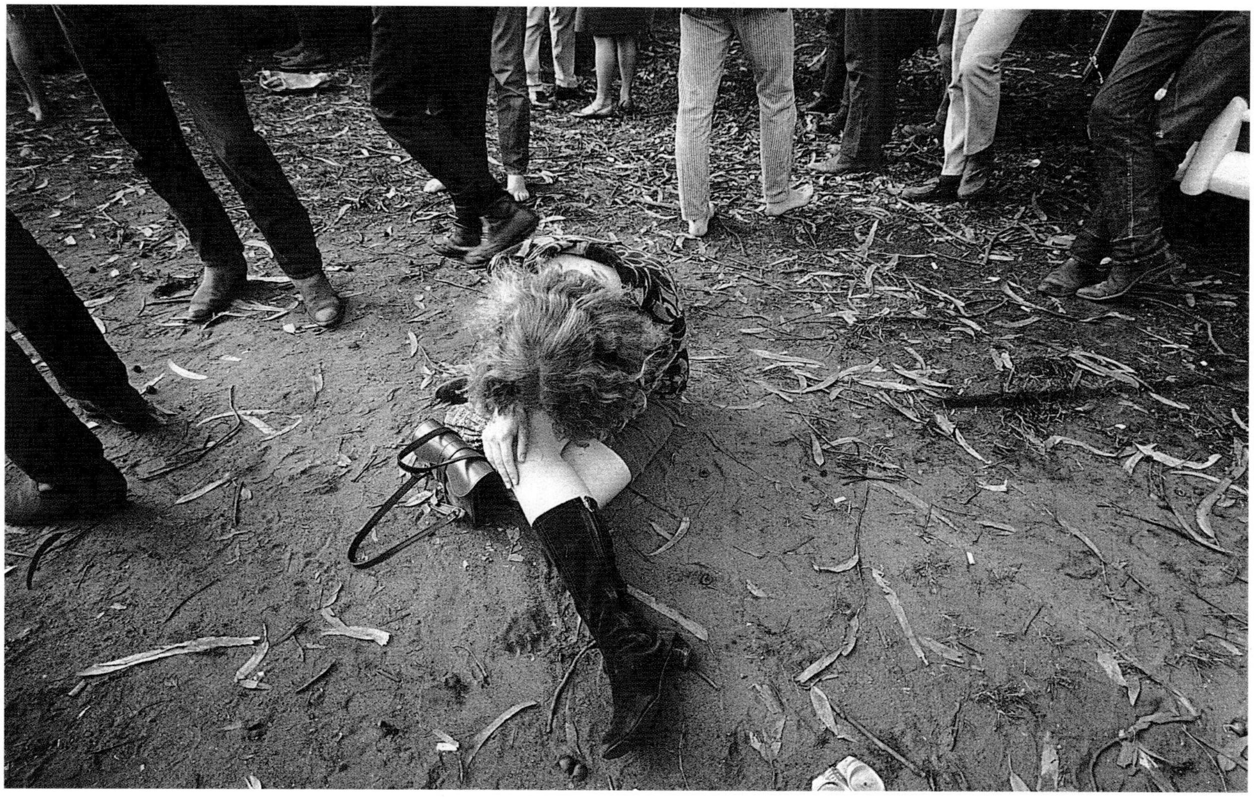

150.

HELEN NESTOR

Sadie Hawkins Day #4 (from the *Haight/Ashbury* series), 1968

Gelatin silver print

8¼ x 12½ in.

GIFT OF THE ARTIST

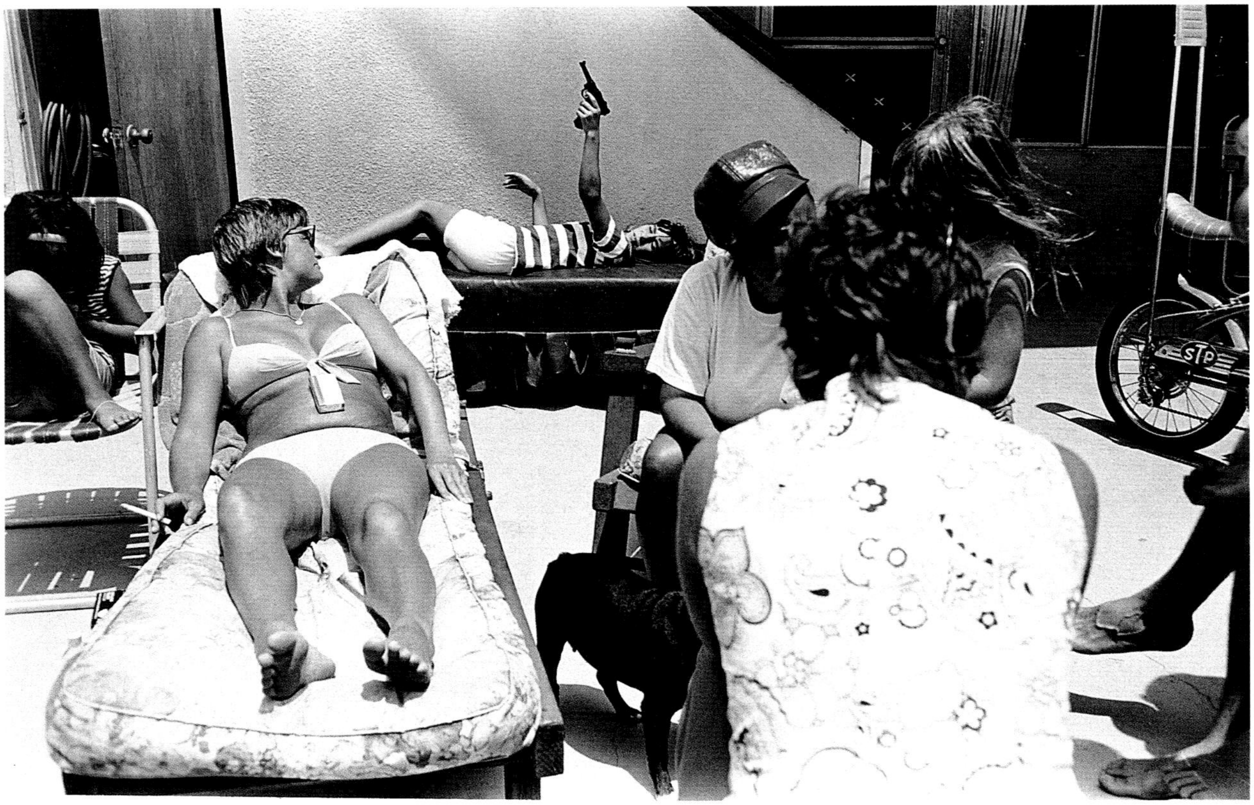

151.
WILLIAM DOHERTY
Untitled (Balboa Beach, California), 1969
Gelatin silver print
8½ x 12⅞ in.
THE SHIRLEY BURDEN FUND FOR PHOTOGRAPHY

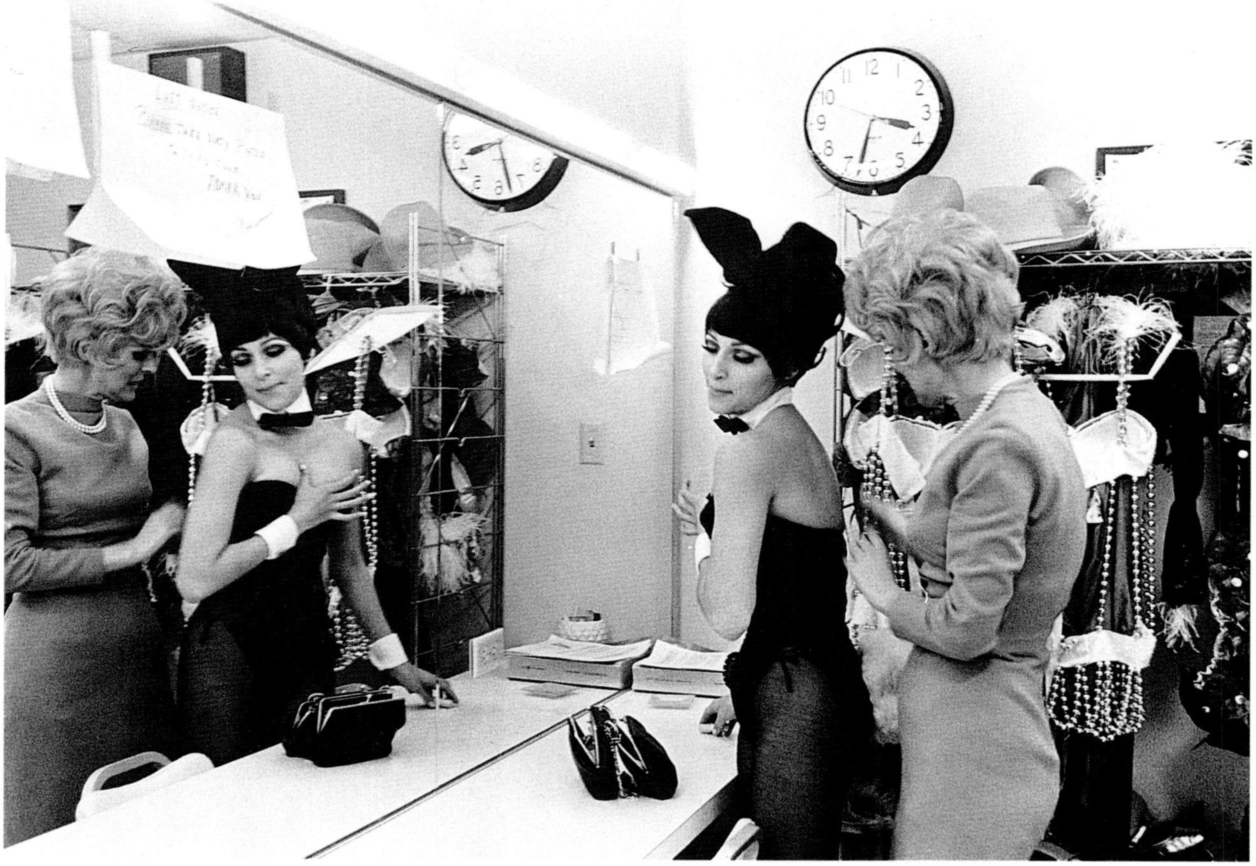

152.
MICHELLE VIGNES
Untitled (Dressing Room at the Playboy Club), c. 1967
Gelatin silver print
6¾ x 9½ in.
GIFT OF THE ESTATE OF HELEN JOHNSTON

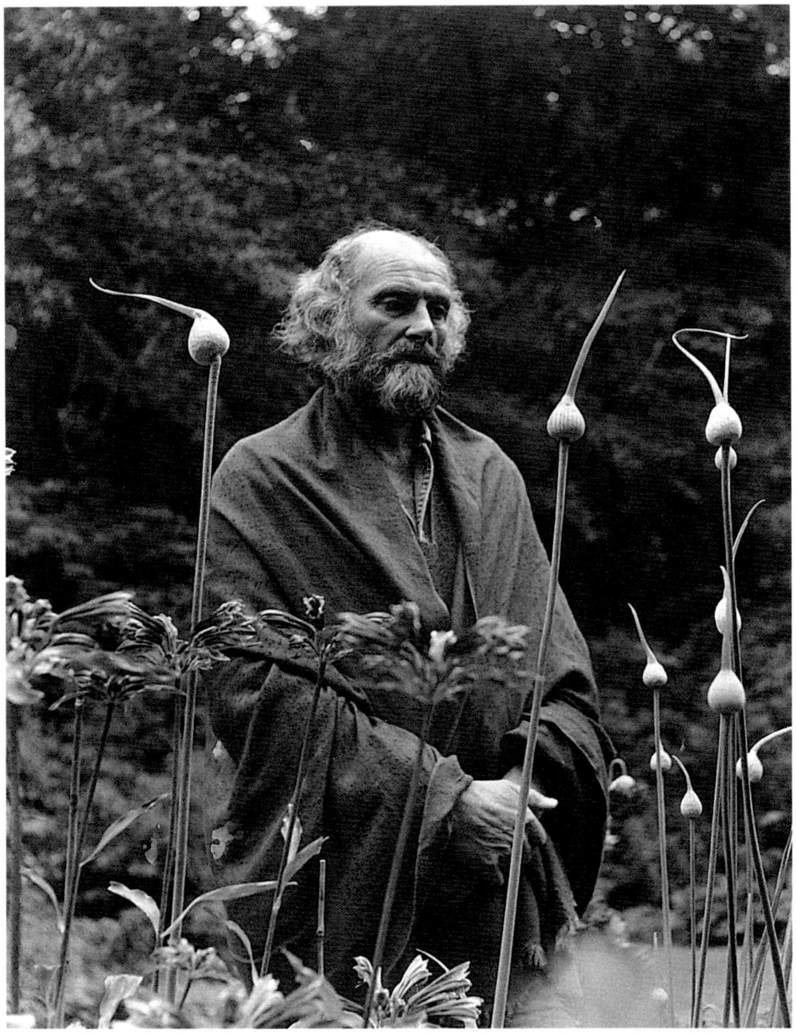

153.
IMOGEN CUNNINGHAM
Morris Graves in His Leek Garden, 1973
Gelatin silver print
9 9/16 x 7 7/8 in.
GIFT OF THE ARTIST

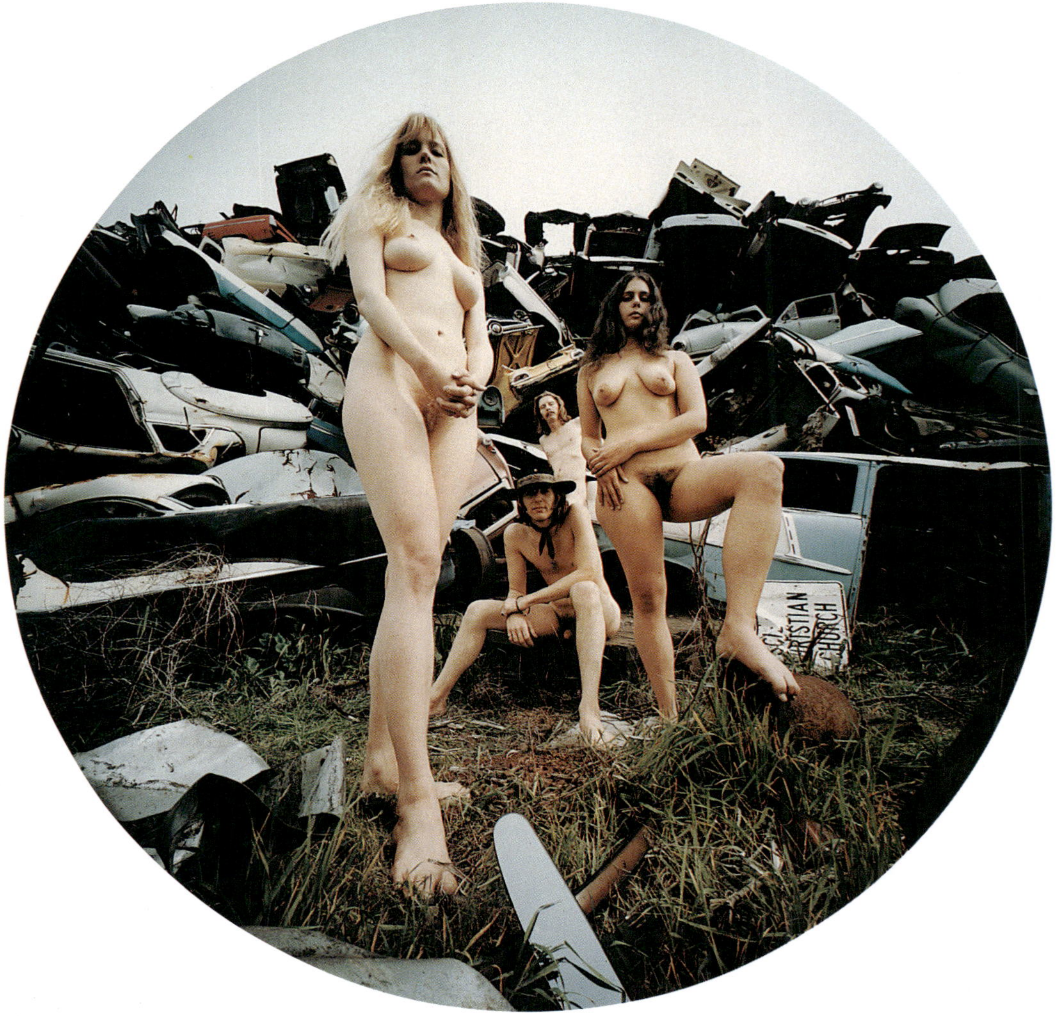

154.

THOMAS WEIR

The Diggers, c. 1968

Type C print

10 in. diameter

THE OAKLAND MUSEUM FOUNDERS' FUND

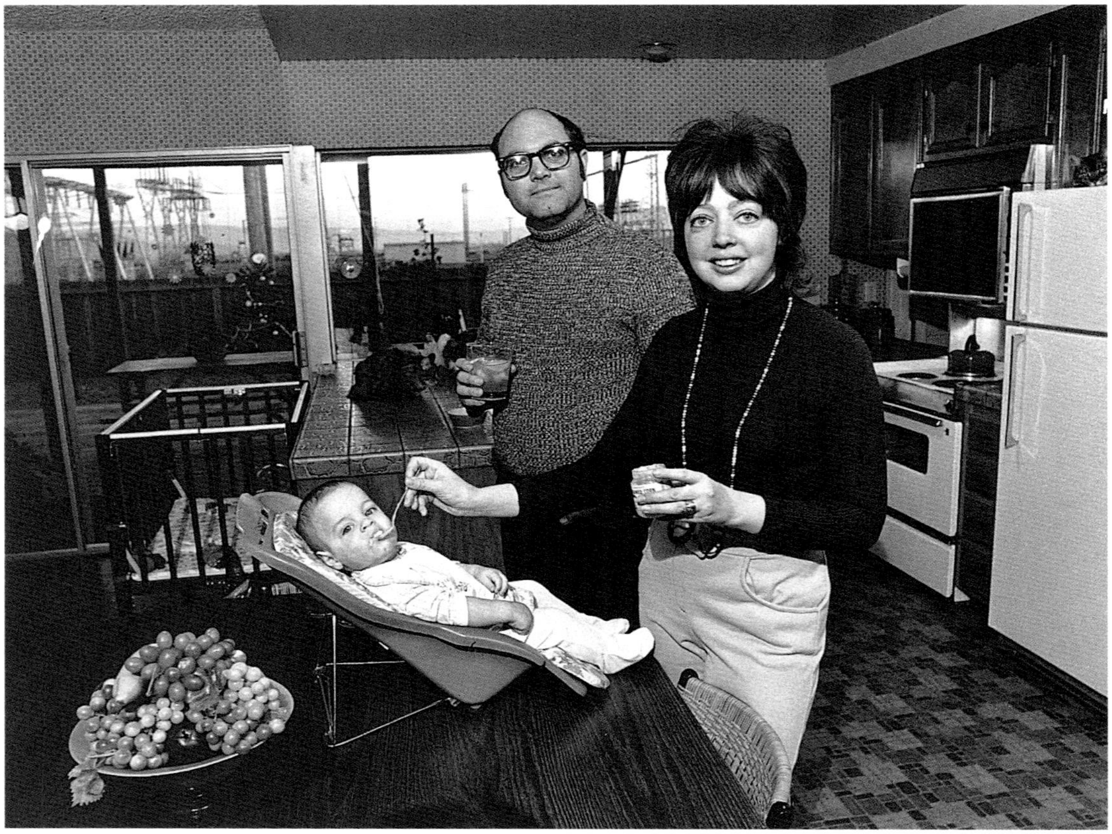

155.
BILL OWENS
We're really happy. Our kids are healthy, we eat good food and we have a really nice home (from *Suburbia*), c. 1970
Gelatin silver print
7¼ x 9⁷⁄₁₆ in.
GIFT OF THE JOHN BERGGRUEN GALLERY

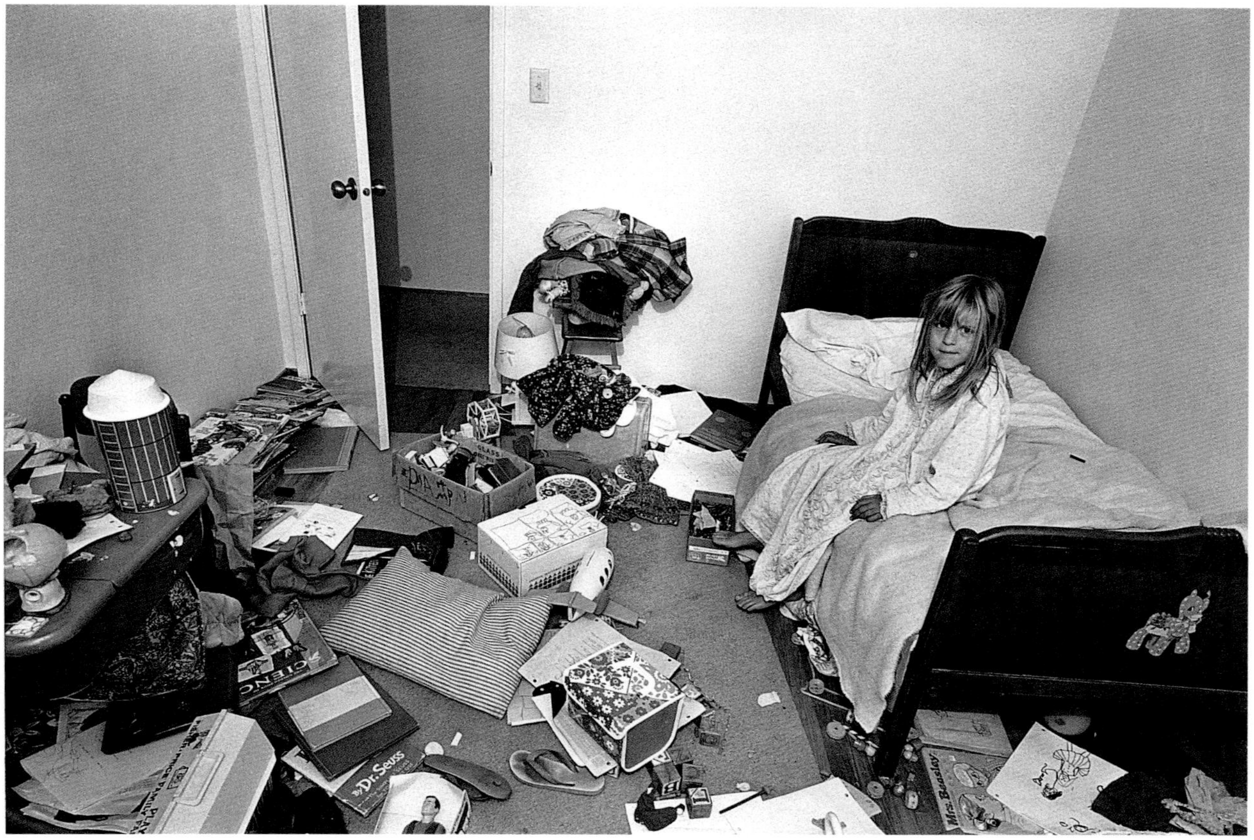

156.
BILL OWENS
I wanted Christina to learn some responsibility for cleaning her room, but it didn't work (from *Suburbia*), c. 1970
Gelatin silver print
$6\frac{3}{8}$ x $9\frac{1}{16}$ in.
GIFT OF THE JOHN BERGGRUEN GALLERY

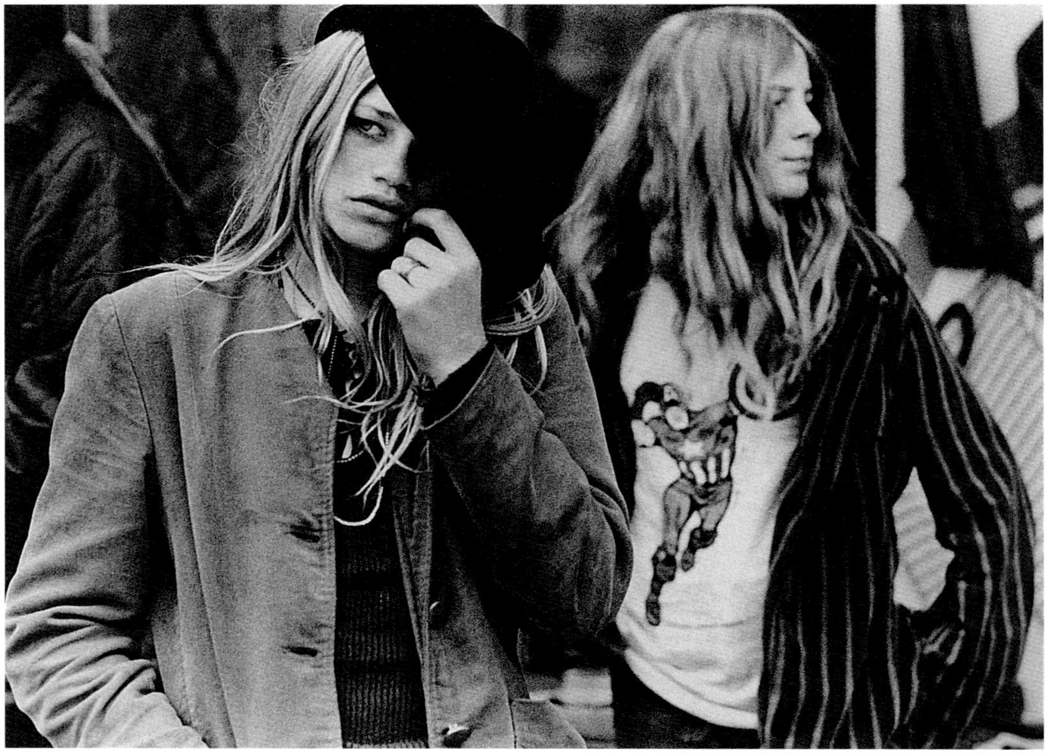

157.

JOE SAMBERG

Cindy and Vanessa, c. 1971

Gelatin silver print

7 5/16 x 9 3/4 in.

PURCHASE WITH FUNDS FROM THE COLLECTORS GALLERY

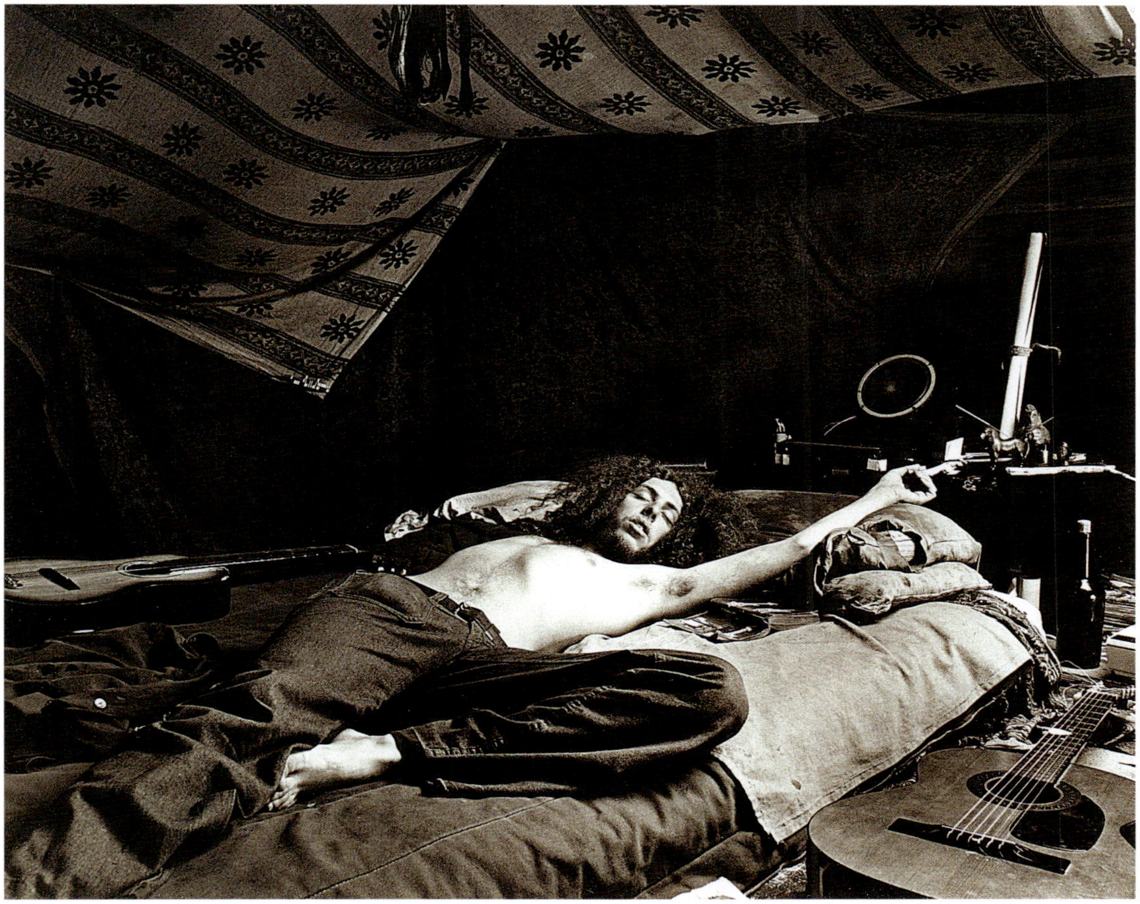

158.
RICHARD MISRACH
Tumbleweed, 1973
Gelatin silver print
9¼ x 11⅜ in.
GIFT OF THE ARTIST

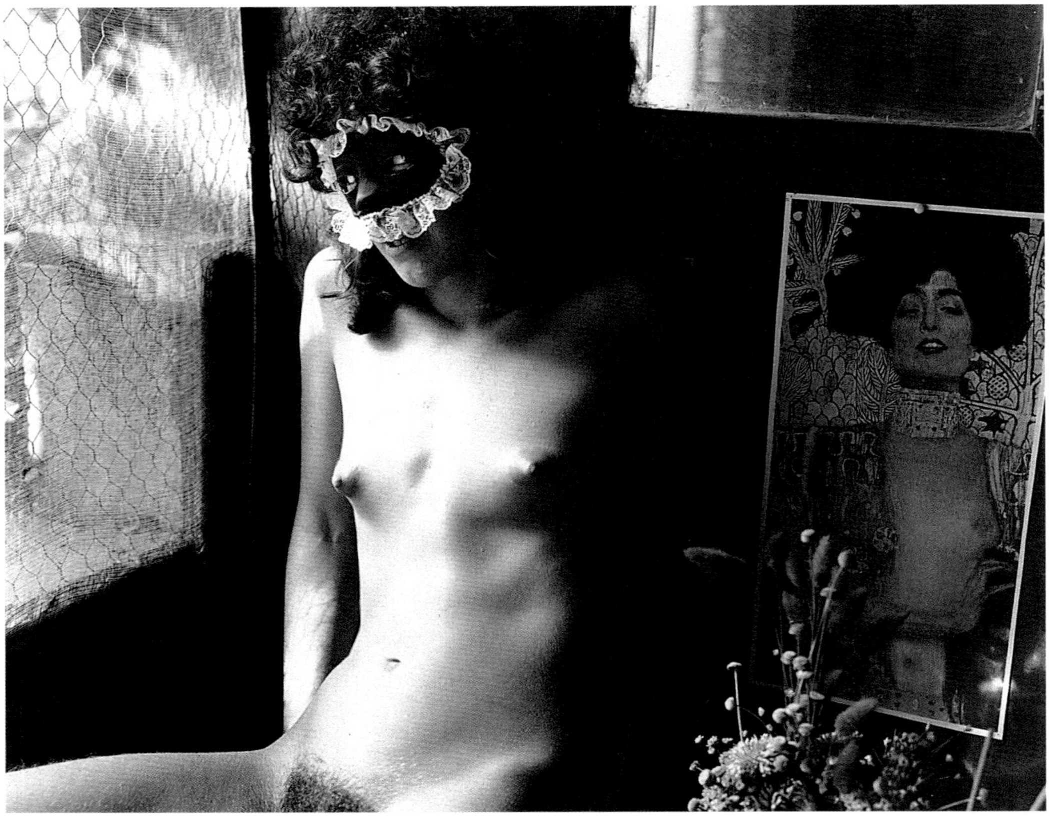

159.
JACK WELPOTT
Untitled (Girl at Window with Mask), 1972
Gelatin silver print
6½ x 8¼ in.
GIFT OF THE ESTATE OF HELEN JOHNSTON

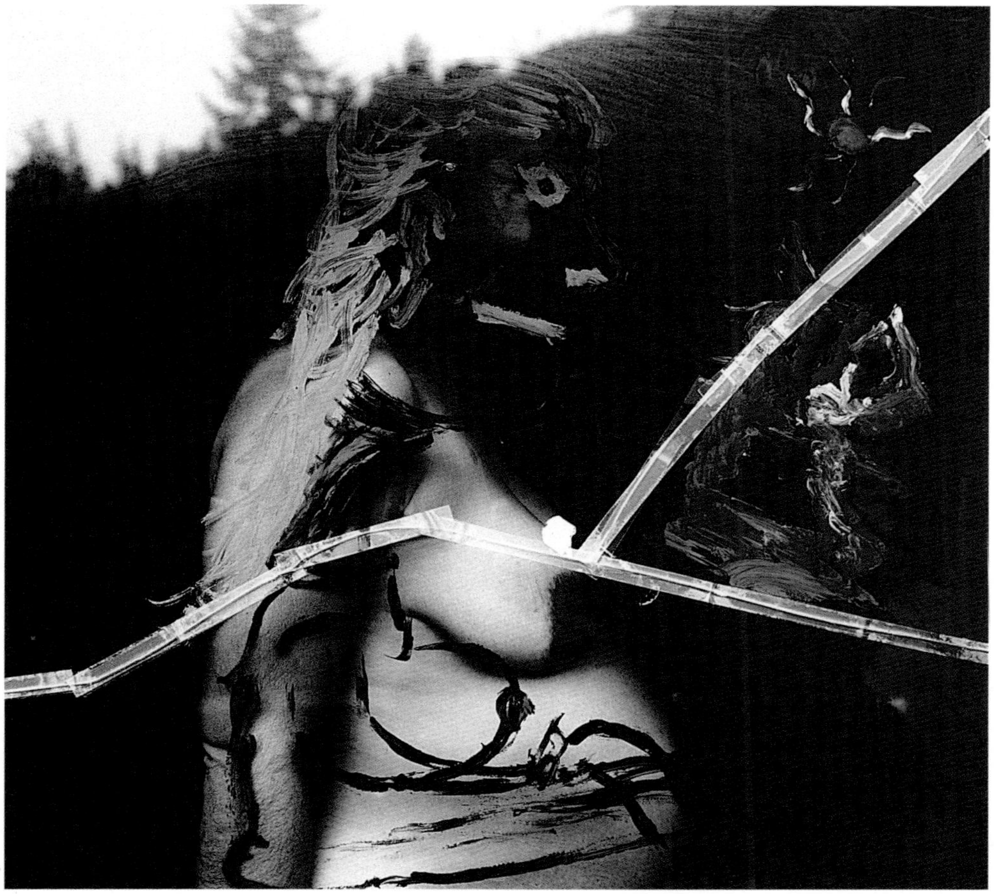

160.
JACK WELPOTT
Taped Window, 1966
Gelatin silver print
7½ x 8 in.
THE OAKLAND MUSEUM FOUNDERS' FUND

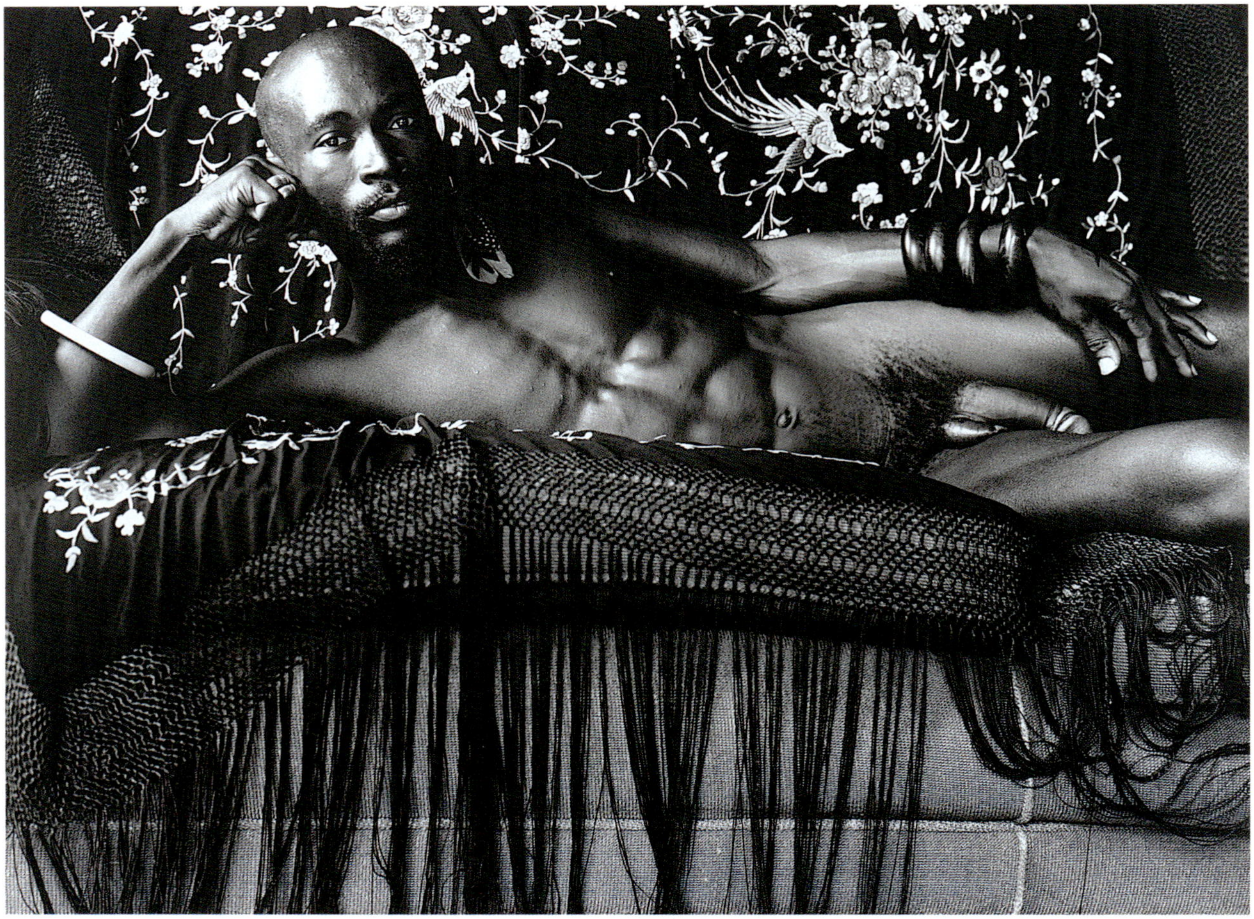

161.
JUDY DATER
Nehemiah, 1975
Gelatin silver print
10¼ x 13½ in.
GIFT OF ARTHUR SHARTSIS

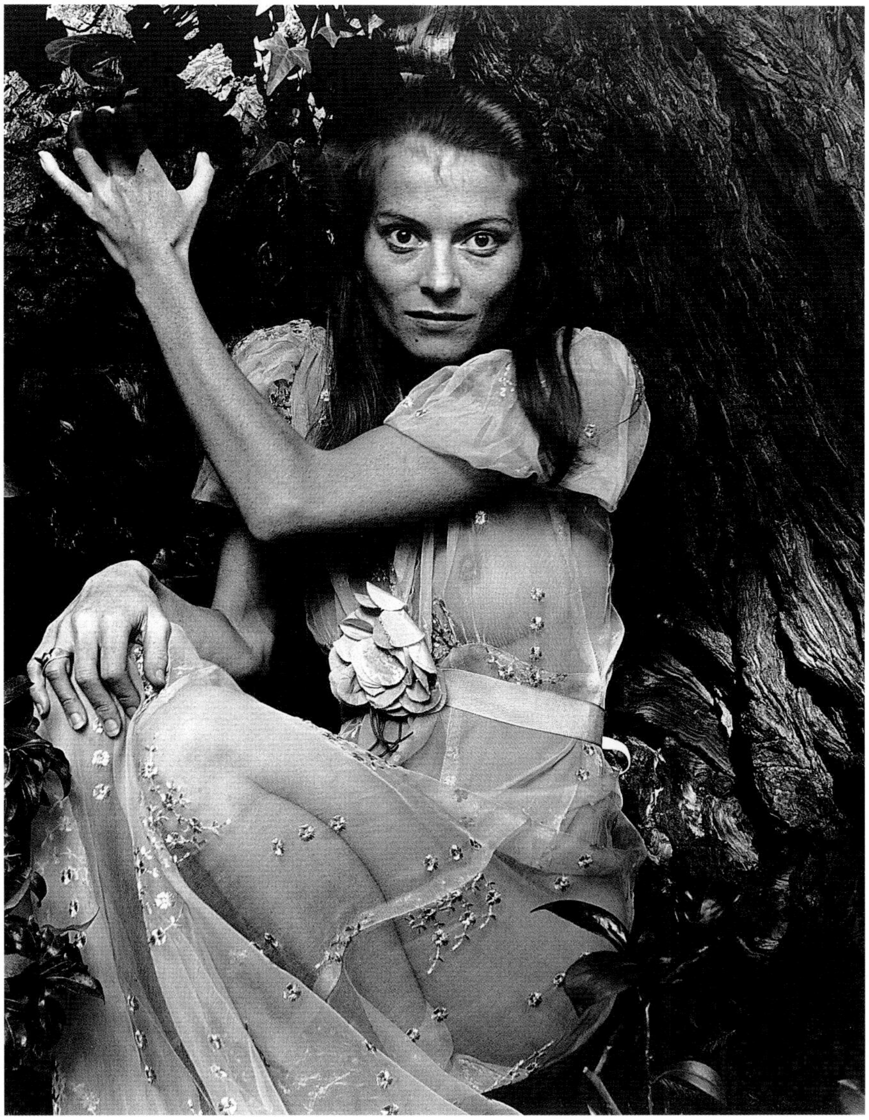

162.
JUDY DATER
Twinka, 1970
Gelatin silver print
12⅝ x 9⅞ in.
GIFT OF DR. AND MRS. DUDLEY P. BELL

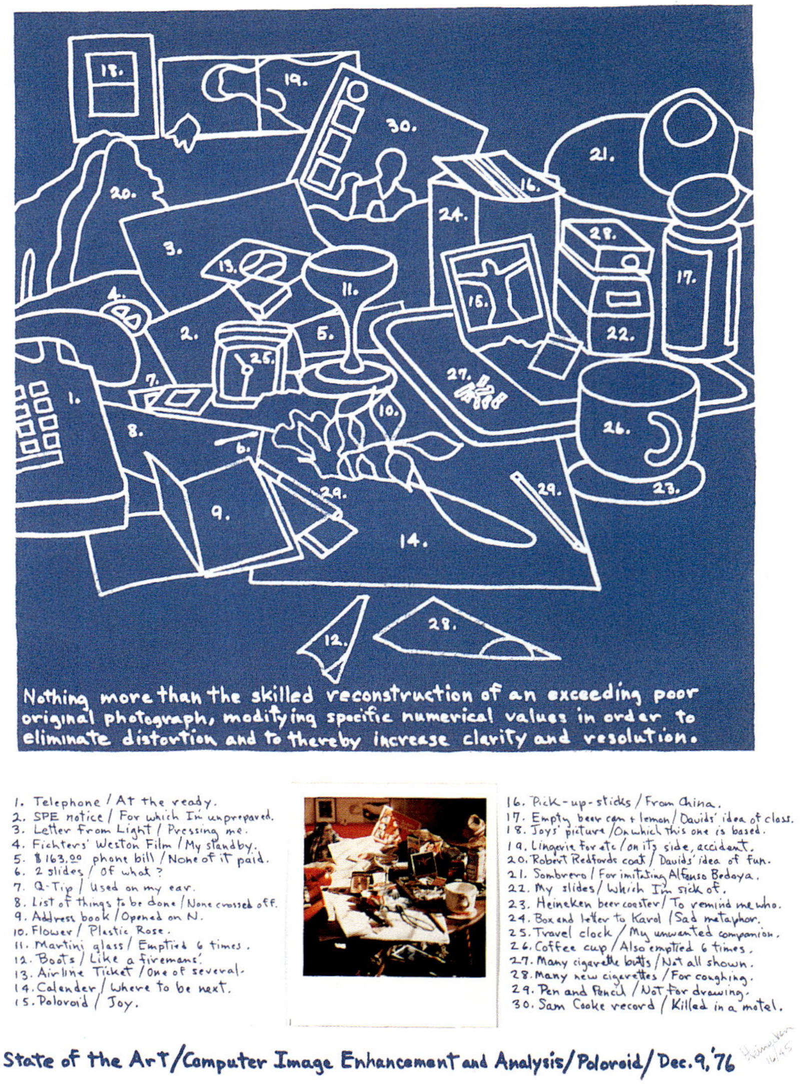

163.

ROBERT HEINECKEN

State of the Art/Computer Image Enhancement and Analysis,
December 9, 1976
Serigraph with color Polaroid collage
20 x 16 in.

GIFT OF DR. AND MRS. PAUL WILHELM

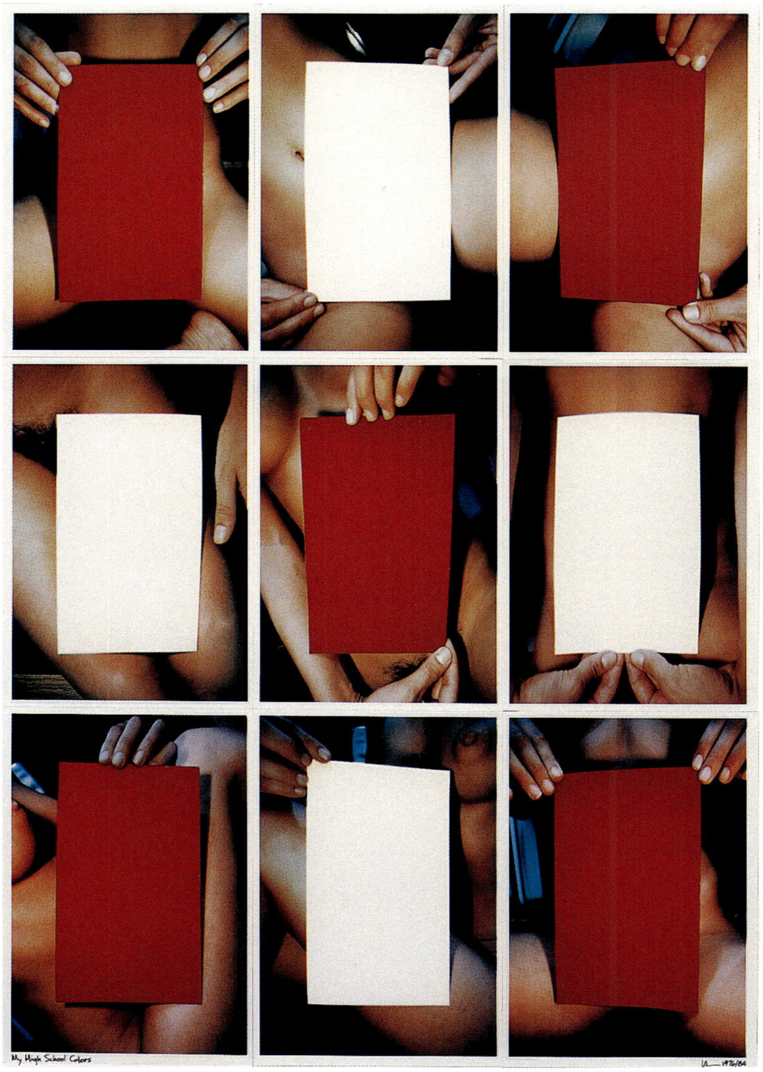

164.

VICTOR LANDWEBER

My High School Colors, 1976

Nine Ektaflex prints

$28\frac{7}{8}$ x $22\frac{1}{4}$ in.

GIFT OF THE ARTIST

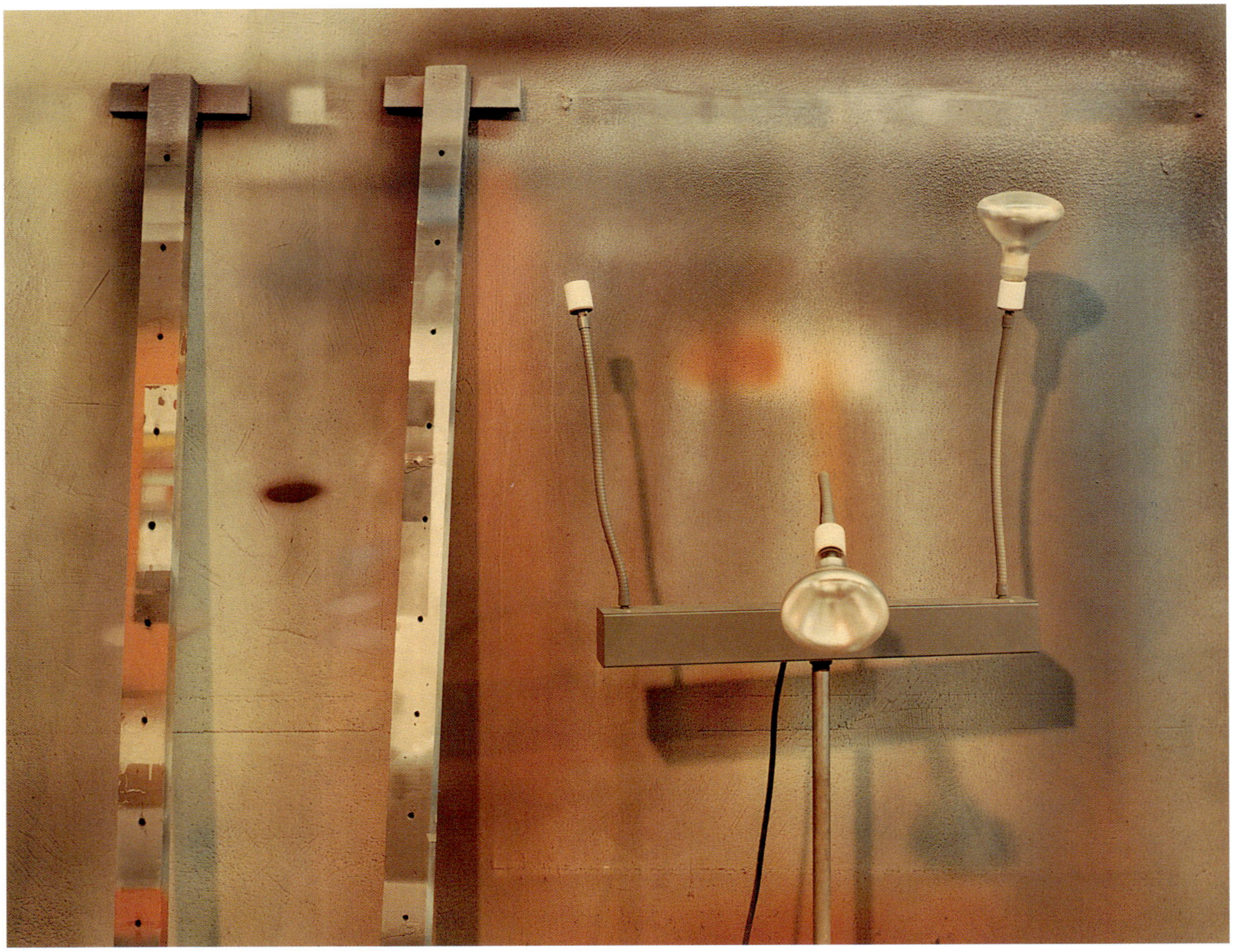

165.
LELAND RICE
Wall Site Series (Spot lights, stretcher bars), 1977
Type C print
8 x 10⅛ in.
GIFT OF THE ARTIST

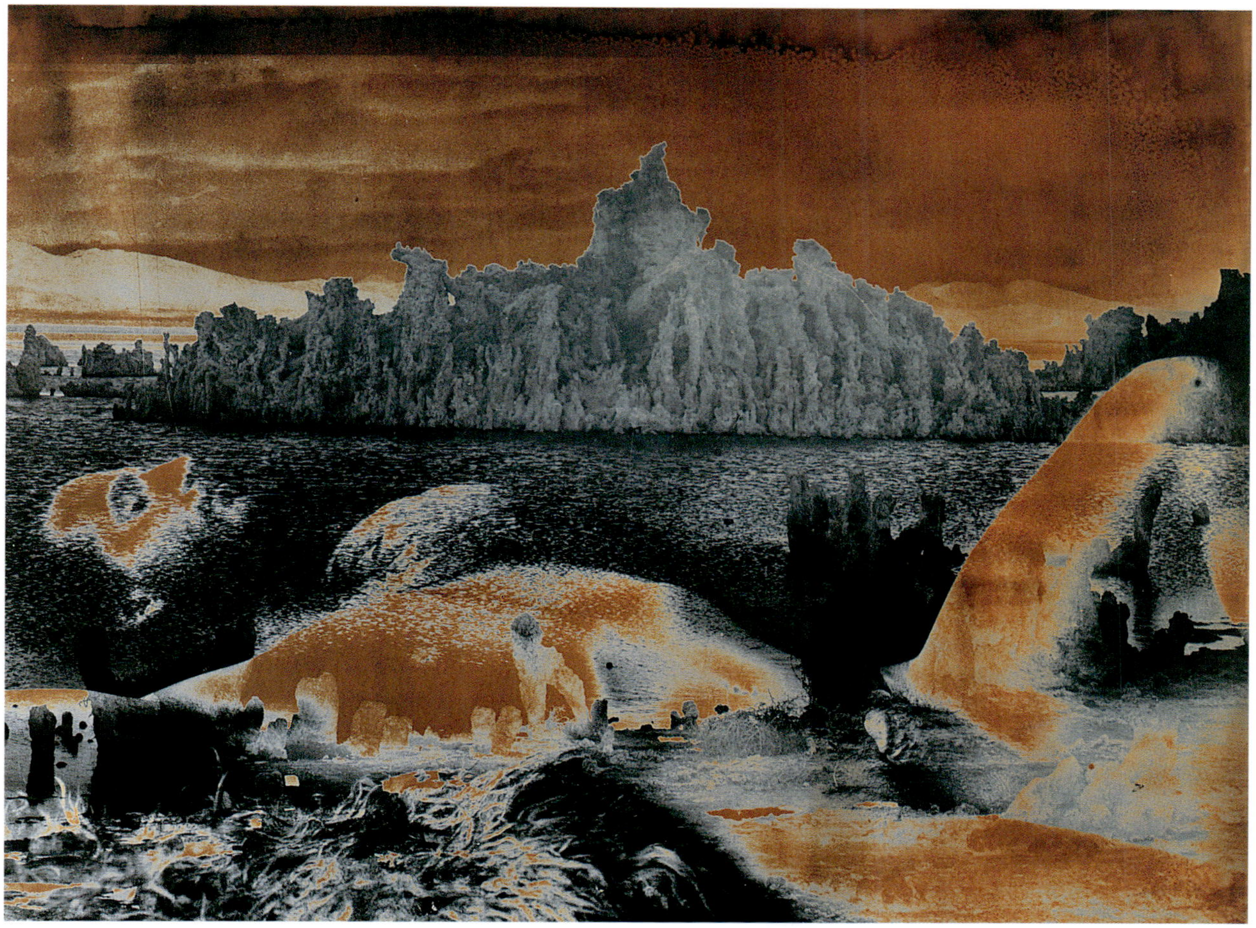

166.
EDMUND TESKE
Mono Lake, 1977
Composite, solarized gelatin silver print
$10^{15}/_{16}$ x $13^{3}/_{4}$ in.
GIFT OF DAVID DEVINE

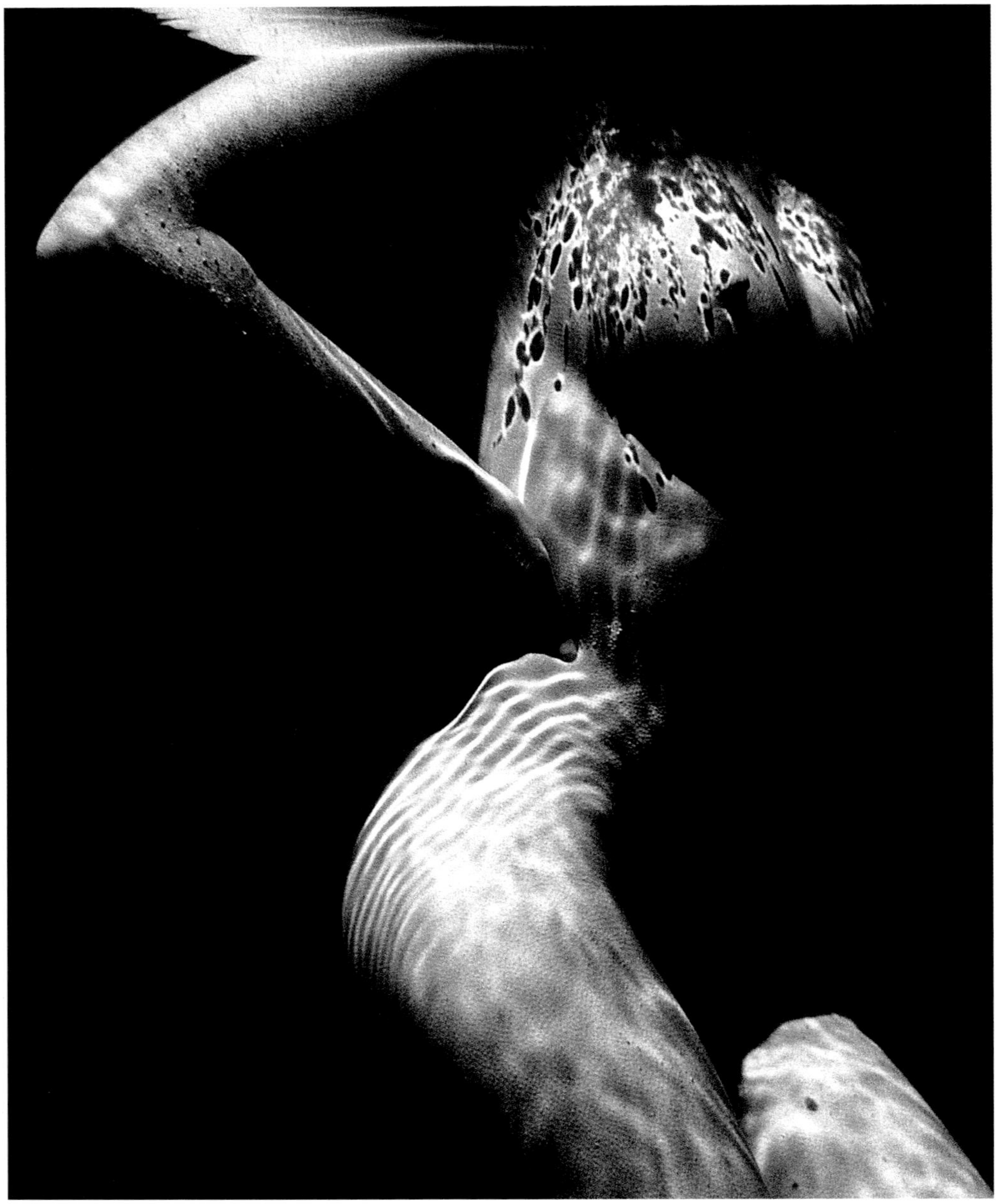

167.
BRETT WESTON
Underwater Nude, 1979
Gelatin silver print
$13\frac{5}{8}$ x $10\frac{3}{4}$ in.
GIFT OF DR. AND MRS. DONALD ABELSON

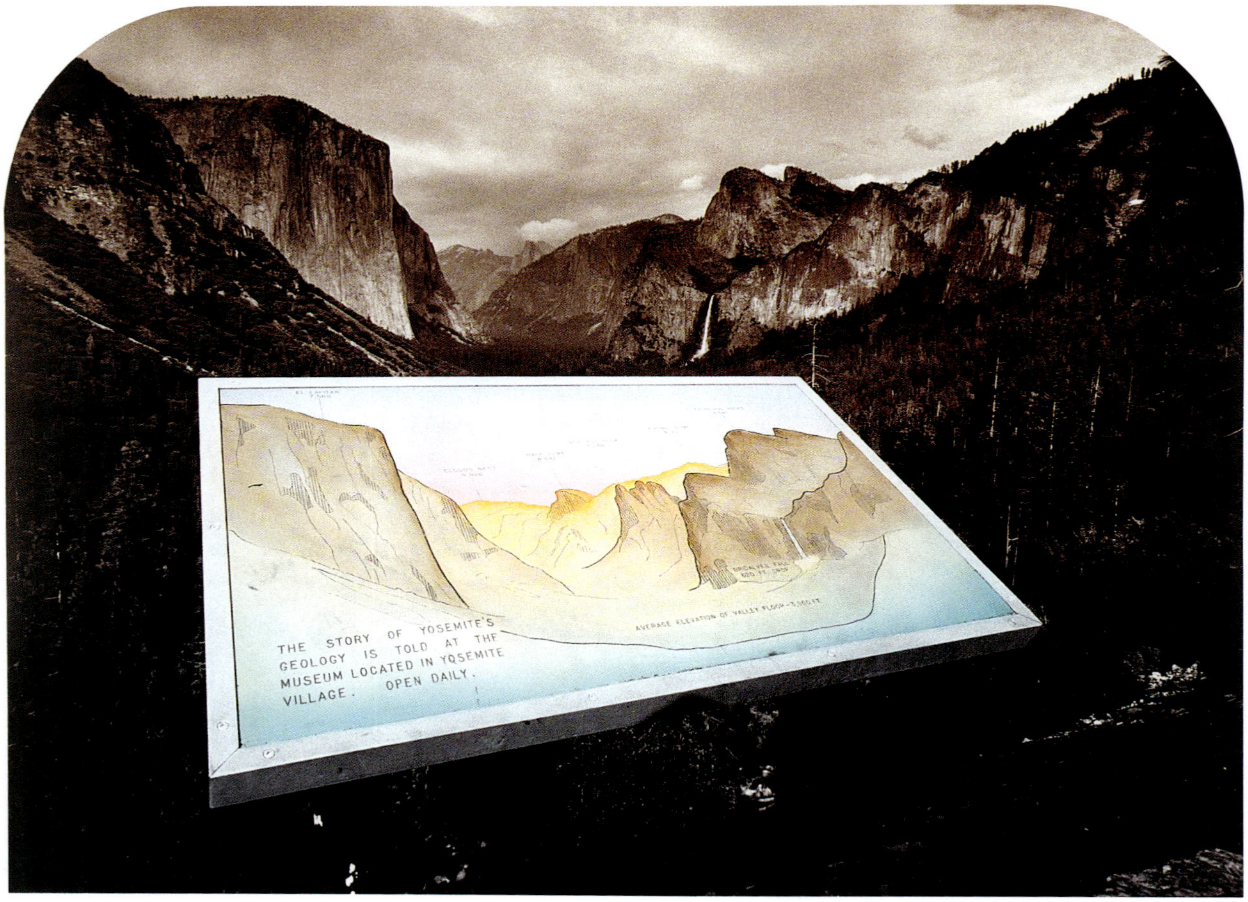

168.

TED ORLAND

Inspiration Point, Yosemite, 1975

Hand-tinted gelatin silver print

$9\frac{9}{16}$ x $12\frac{7}{8}$ in.

GIFT OF DR. AND MRS. PAUL WILHEM

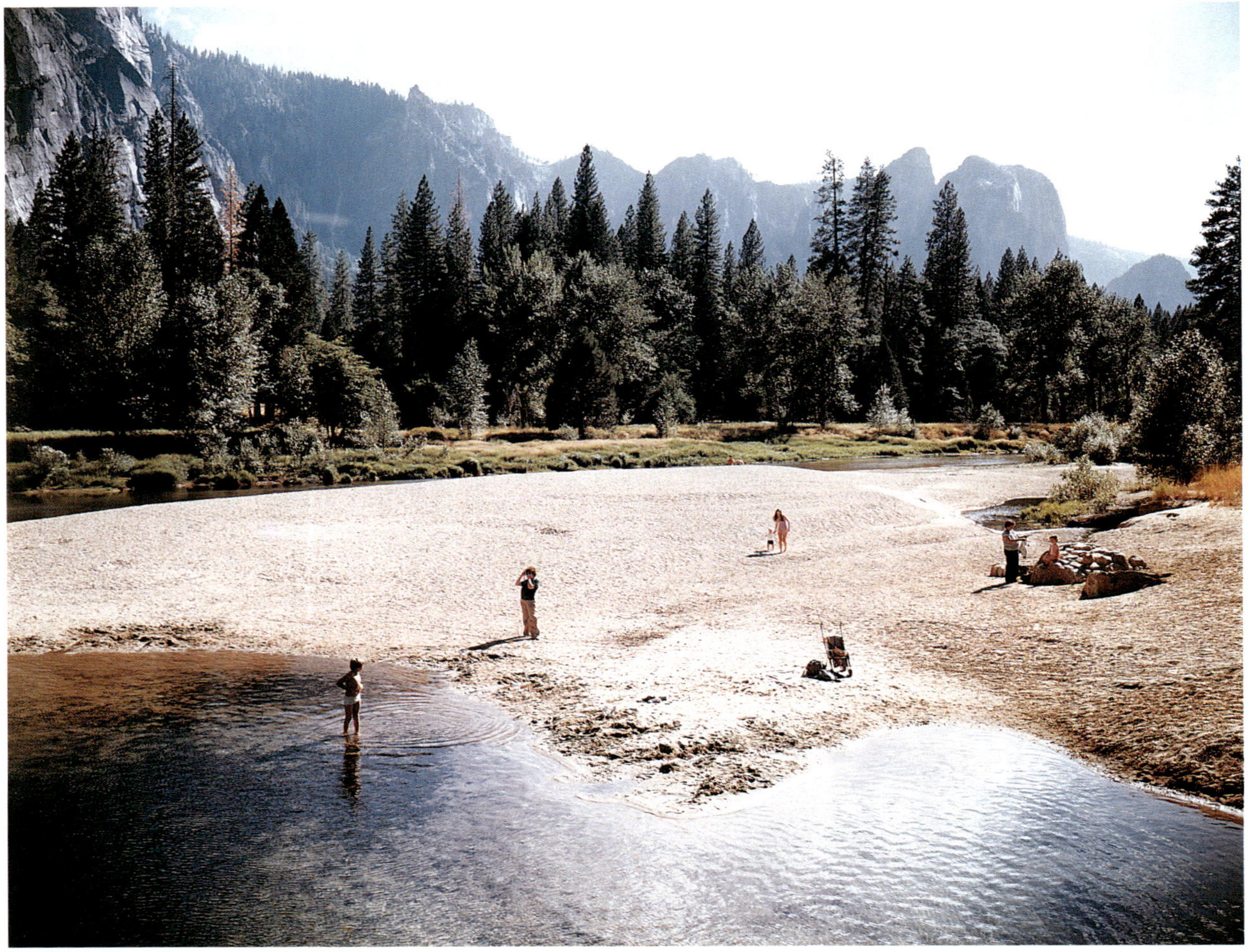

169.

STEPHEN SHORE

Merced River, Yosemite National Park, 1979

Dye coupler print

$11^{15}/_{16}$ x $15^{1}/_{16}$ in.

ANONYMOUS GIFT WITH MATCHING FUNDS FROM THE NATIONAL ENDOWMENT FOR THE ARTS

1980 – 2000

PORTFOLIO V

Toward the Millennium

EPILOGUE

SINCE 1980, California photography has witnessed an enlargement of trends mentioned in the previous essay—a decline in regionalism, concern with photographs as defining objects of our culture, and a growing acceptance of photography in the fine art market. In the past decade, these tendencies have become tangled with an explosion of computer imaging technology. The recent proliferation of digital effects, characterized by programs such as Photoshop, is fundamentally transforming our perception of what, exactly, constitutes a photograph. The possibilities for altering images digitally are virtually limitless; the notion of "making photographs of things inside your head" has never held such literal meaning. Artists are using the new capability to manipulate images in ways Pictorialists a century ago would have envied. At the turn of the millennium photography, perhaps even more than other arts, may be characterized by the phrase "all bets are off."

At the same time, the spread of new technology has been accompanied by a renewed interest in traditional photographic techniques. Artists such as Geoffrey Fricker, Robert Dawson, Mark Klett and Richard Misrach use traditional materials and a high degree of craftsmanship to create images which, on the surface at least, may be described as "straight." Reversing years of dominance by lightweight, miniaturized equipment, the view camera, with its large negatives and deliberate technique, has made a comeback. Antique processes, such as the daguerreotype, the cyanotype and the photogravure have also seen a revival.

Not surprisingly, the two camps are polarized. Much of the debate over photography now centers around the expressive qualities of digitally manipulated images versus those produced by traditional photographic chemistry and optics. The argument is as rancorous as that conducted in the 1930s between Pictorialists and supporters of modernist photography, and gives the impression of a battle for the very soul of photography as a creative medium. But this, perhaps, is the continuing legacy of California's role in photography—a place, and an idea, where diversity and innovation are taken for granted, and a multiplicity of approaches overcomes orthodoxy. In the end, this type of inquiry into the nature and meaning of photography simply argues for the continuing power and flexibility of the medium.

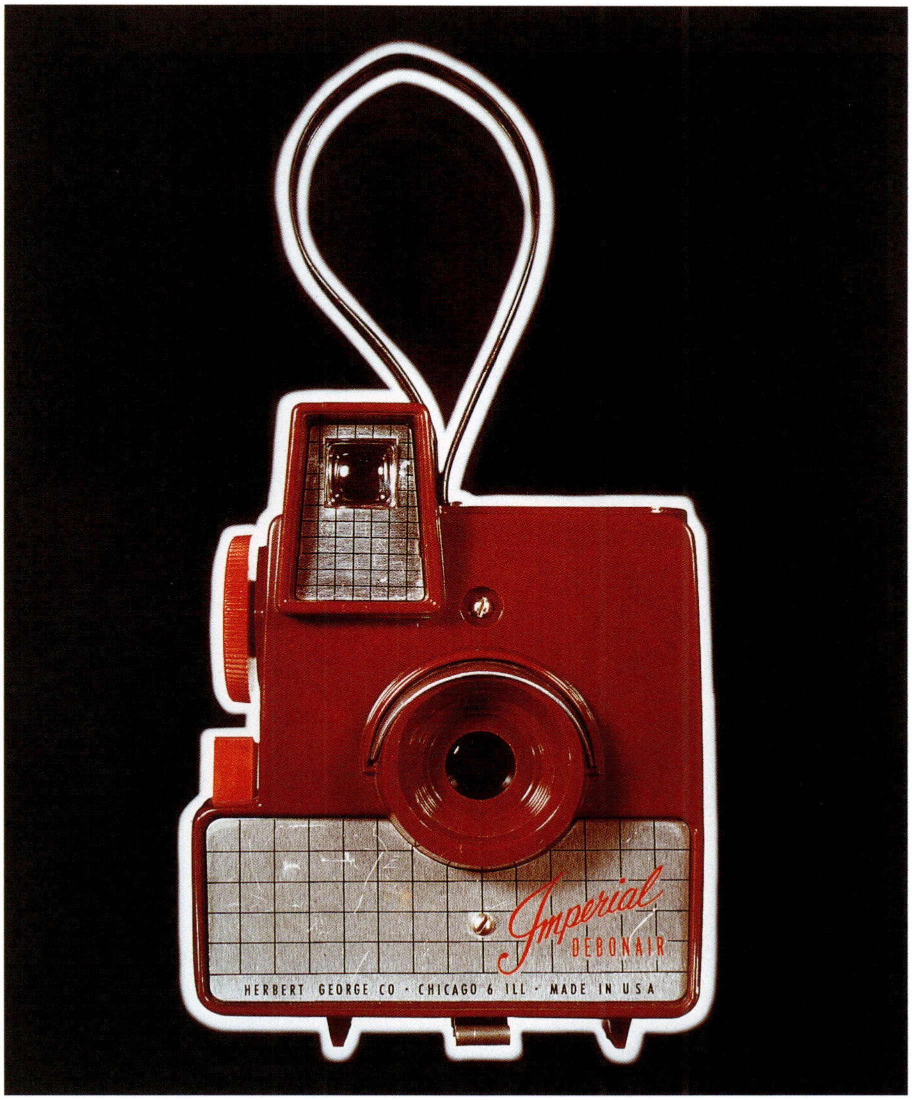

170.
VICTOR LANDWEBER
Imperial Debonair, from *American Cameras,* 1981
Cibachrome print
20 x 16 in.
THE SHIRLEY BURDEN FUND FOR PHOTOGRAPHY

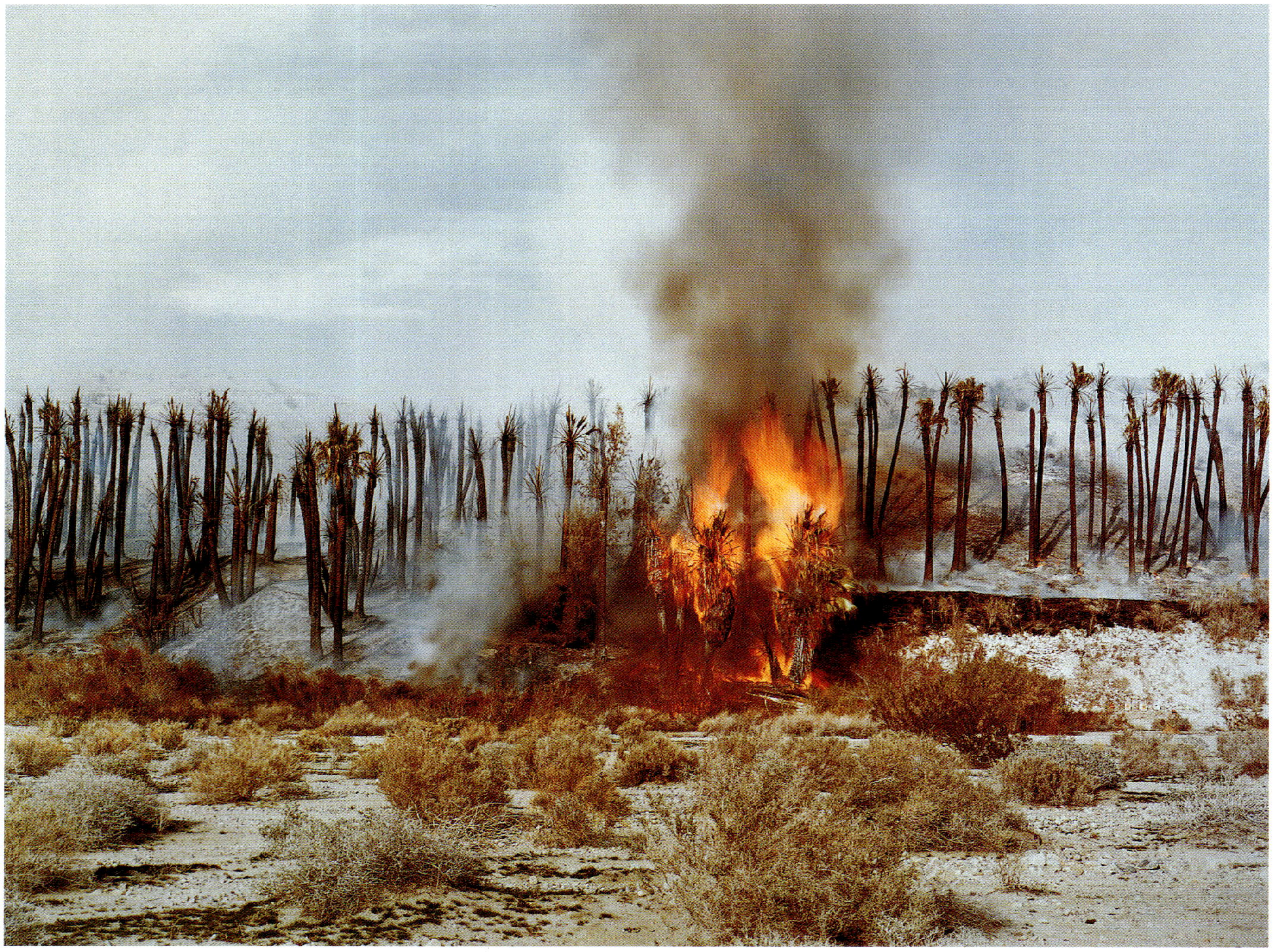

171.
RICHARD MISRACH
Desert Fire # 1, Burning Palms, 1983
Cibachrome print
28 x 36¼ in.
GIFT OF THE COLLECTORS GALLERY

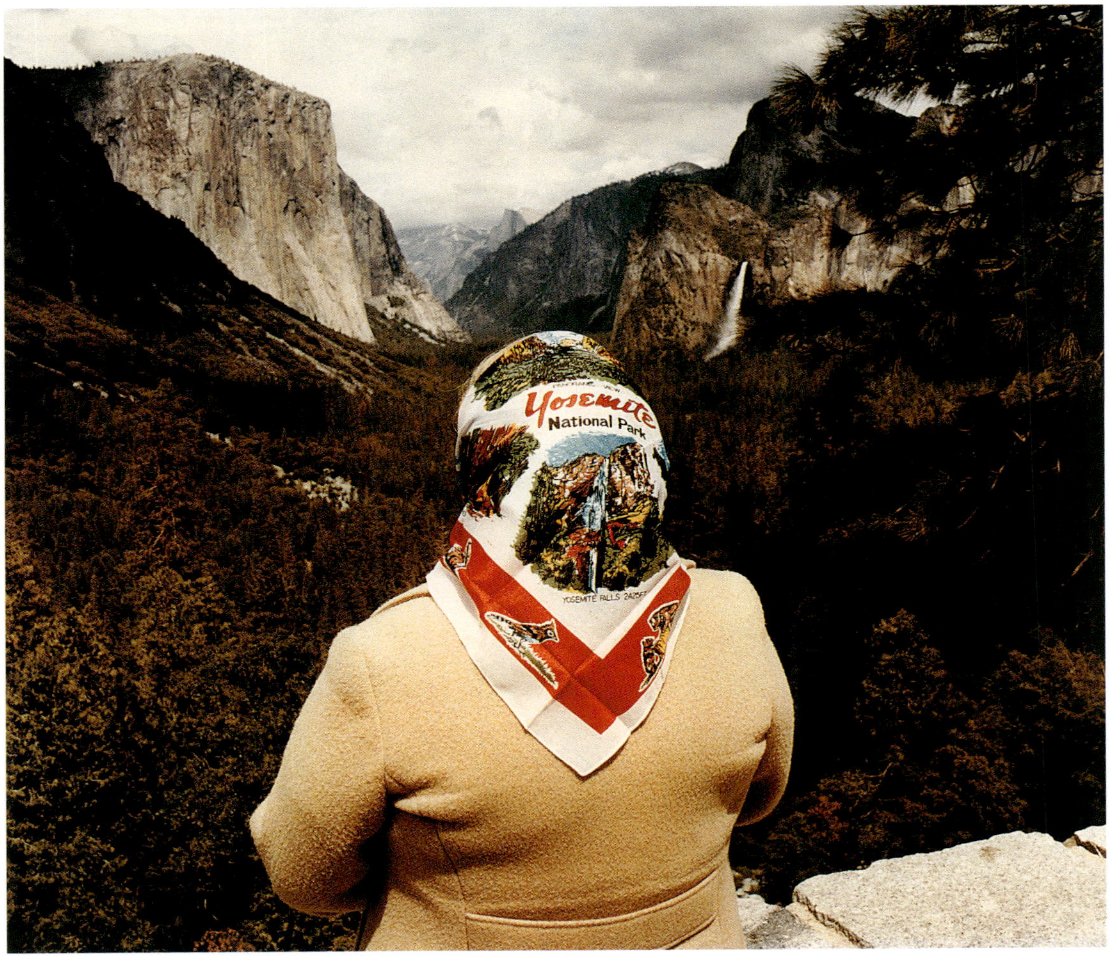

172.
ROGER MINICK
Woman With Scarf, Yosemite (from the *Sightseer* series), 1980
Dye coupler print
16 x 20 in.
PRINTS AND PHOTOGRAPHS FUND

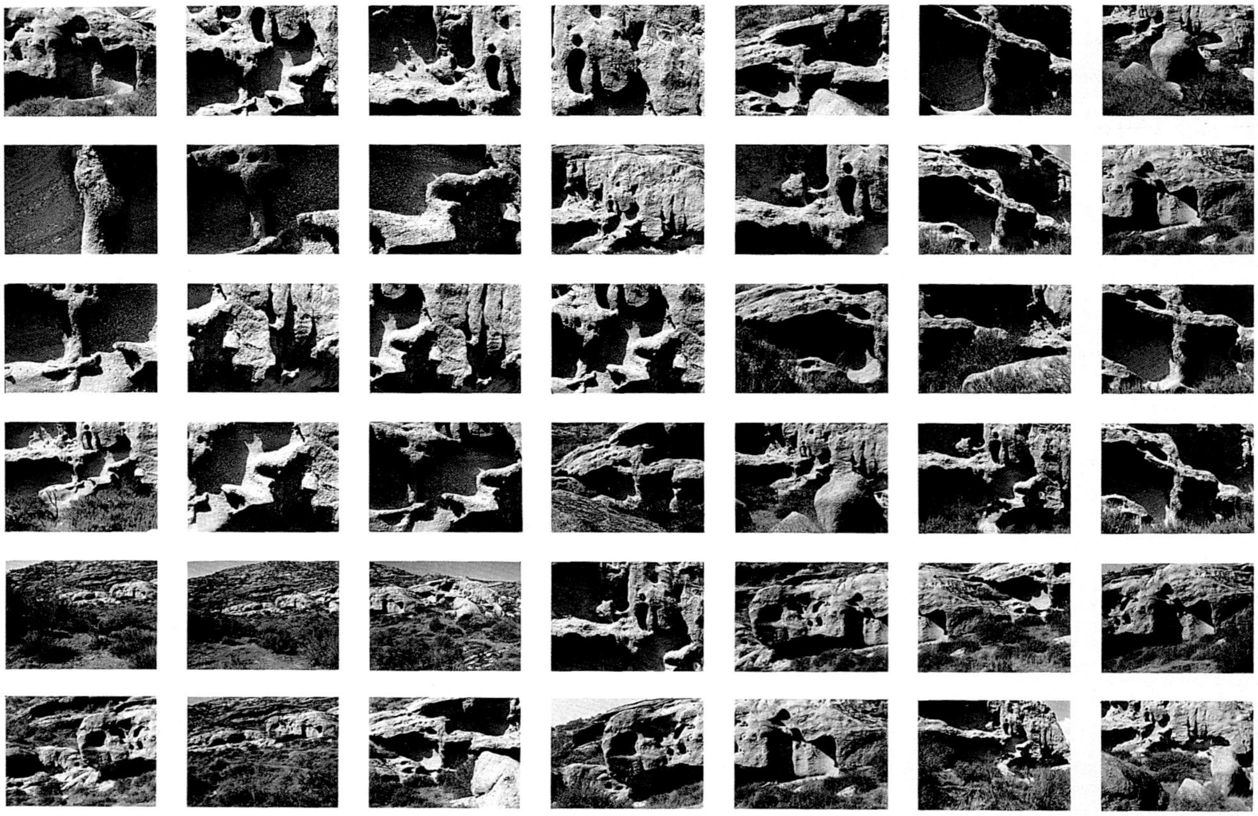

173.

ROBBERT FLICK

At Vasquez Rocks #6, 1983–85

Gelatin silver print

16 x 20 in.

THE SHIRLEY BURDEN FUND FOR PHOTOGRAPHY

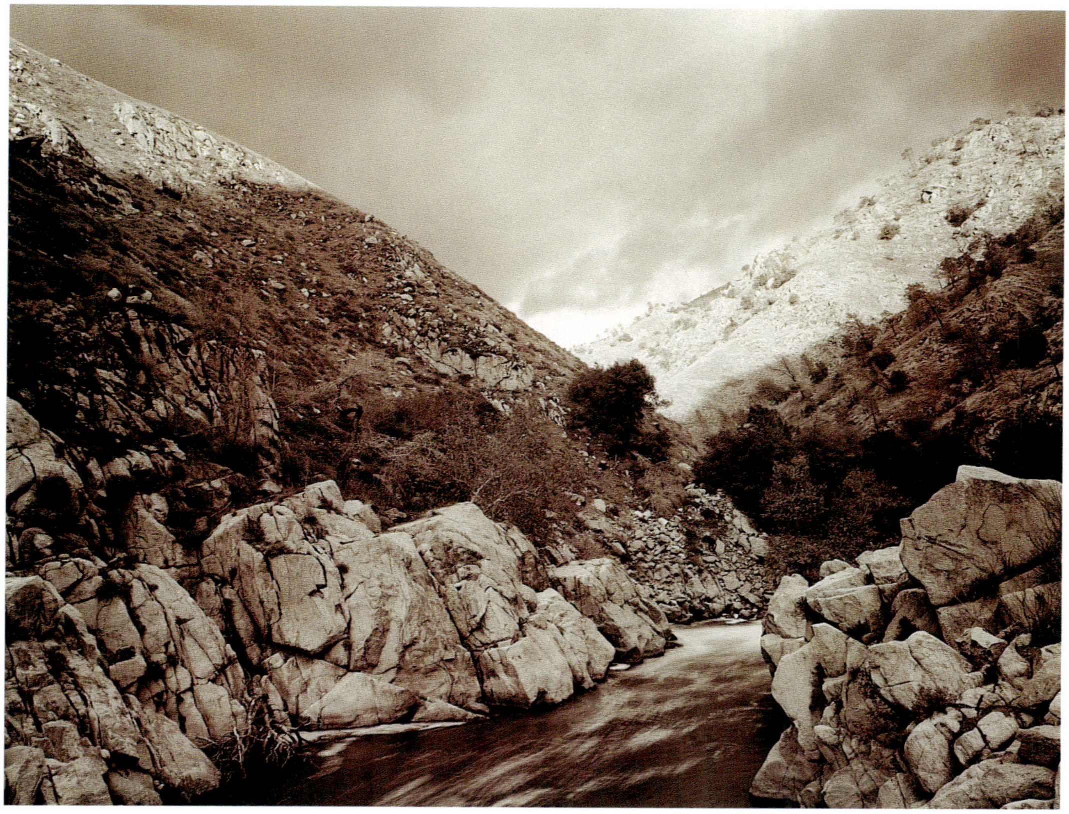

174.
LINDA S. CONNOR
Walker Pass, 1983
Gelatin silver print
7⅞ x 10 in.
PRINTS AND PHOTOGRAPHS FUND

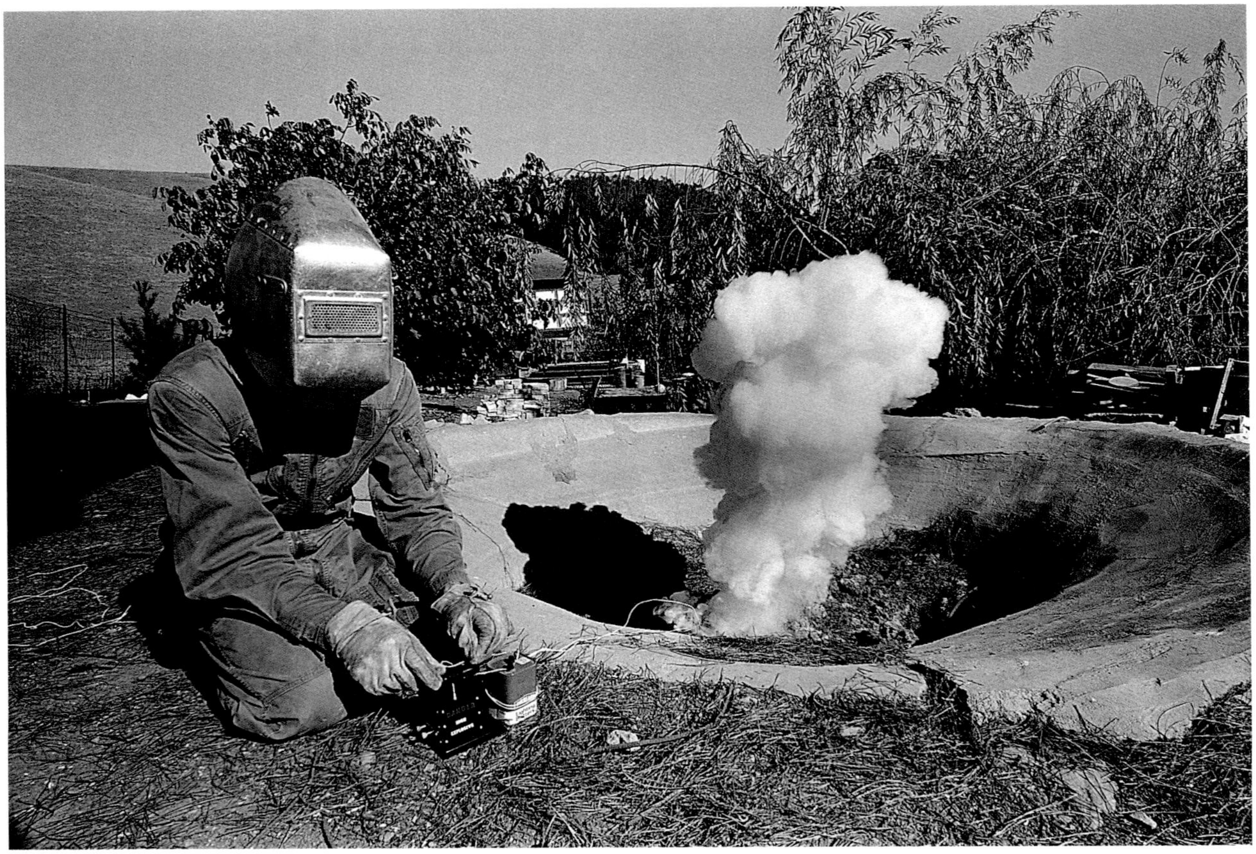

175.
GREG MACGREGOR
Testing Electric Detonator, Crockett, California, 1980 (from *Minor Explosions* series, 1978–93)
Gelatin silver print
13 x 18½ in.
GIFT OF THE ARTIST

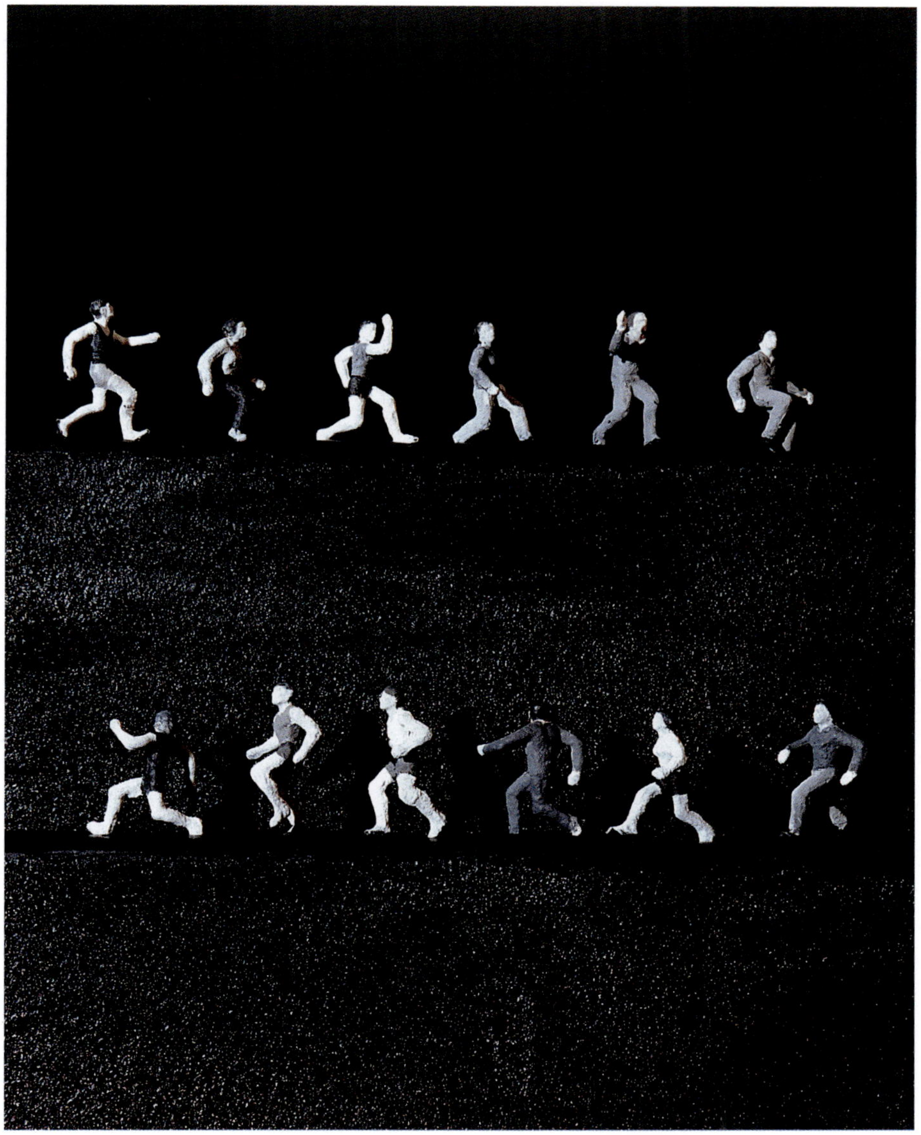

176.
ELLEN BROOKS
Untitled, 1984
Type C color print
20 x 16 in.
THE SHIRLEY BURDEN FUND FOR PHOTOGRAPHY

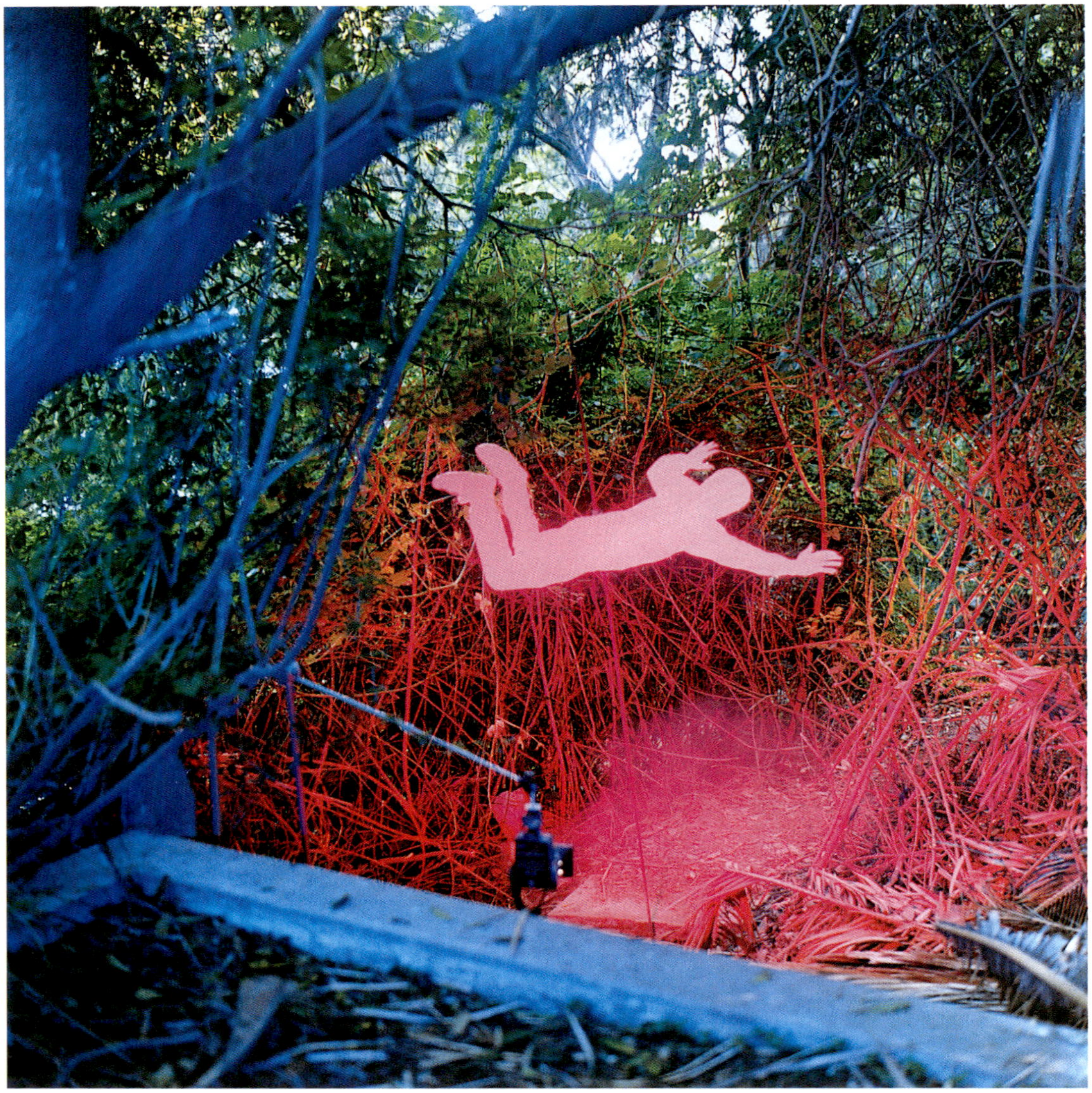

177.
JOHN DIVOLA
Falling/Flying, 1984, printed 1987
Dye transfer print
19⅜ x 19¼ in.
THE SHIRLEY BURDEN FUND FOR PHOTOGRAPHY

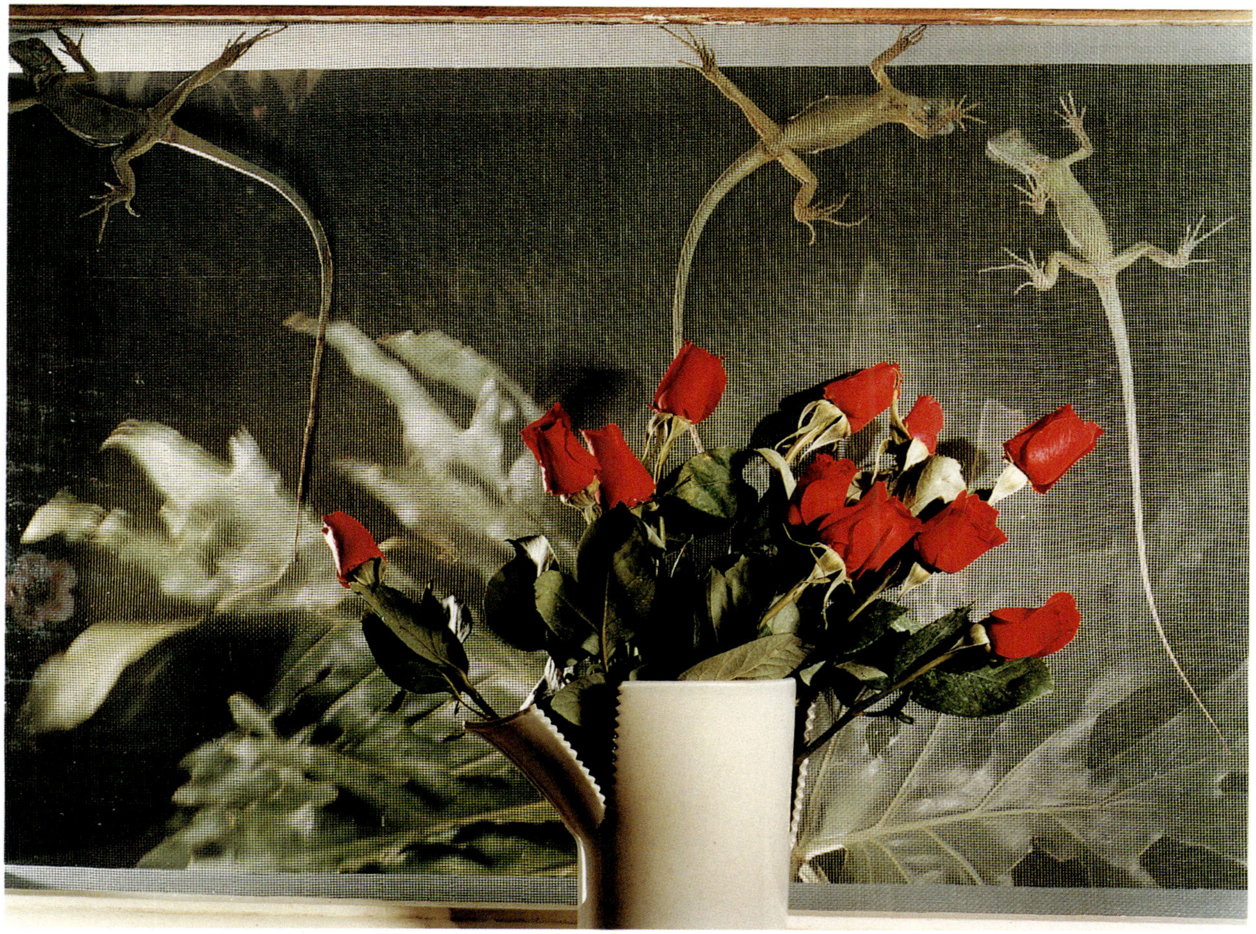

178.
JO ANN CALLIS
Lizards and Roses, 1980
Cibachrome print
$17\frac{5}{8}$ x $22\frac{3}{4}$ in.
GIFT OF ANONYMOUS DONOR

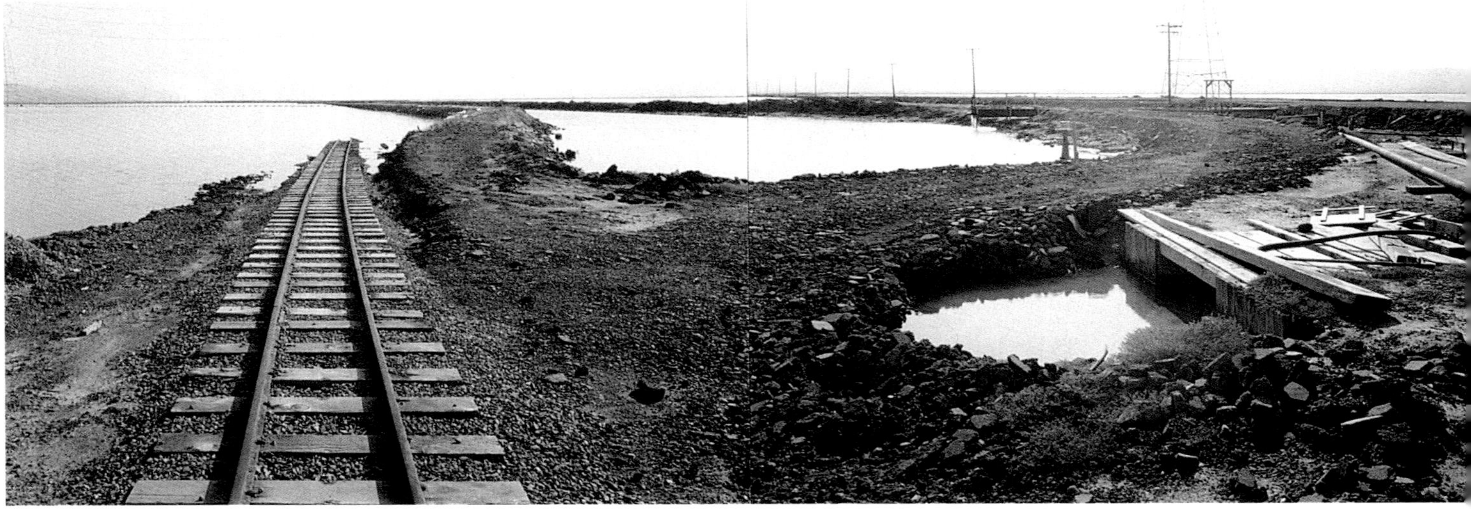

179.
LAURA VOLKERDING
Salt Ponds, 1982
Gelatin silver print
4½ x 26¼ in.
GIFT OF PHILLIPPE BONNAFONT

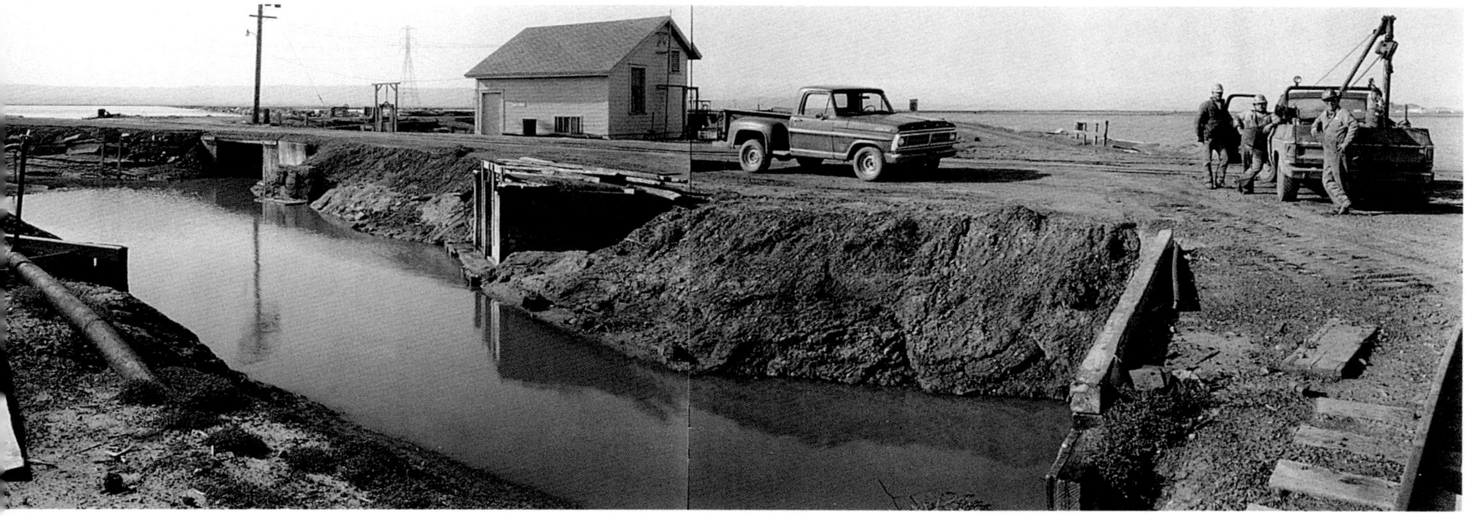

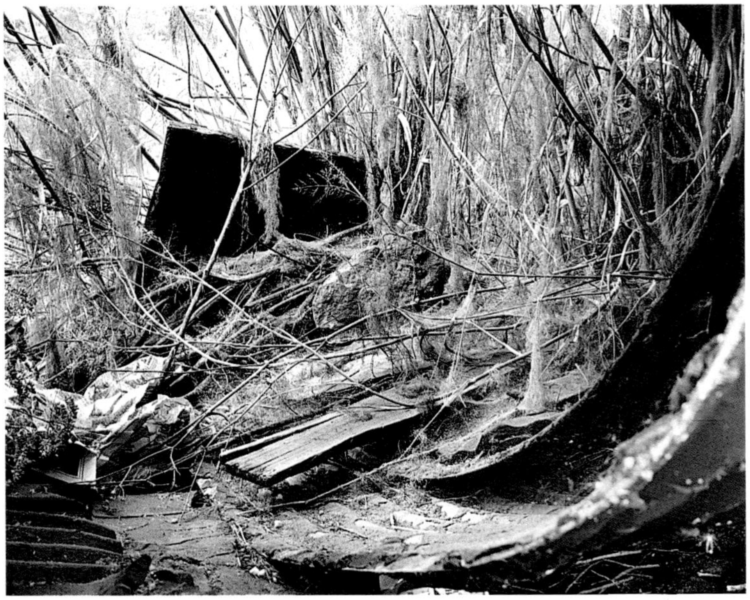

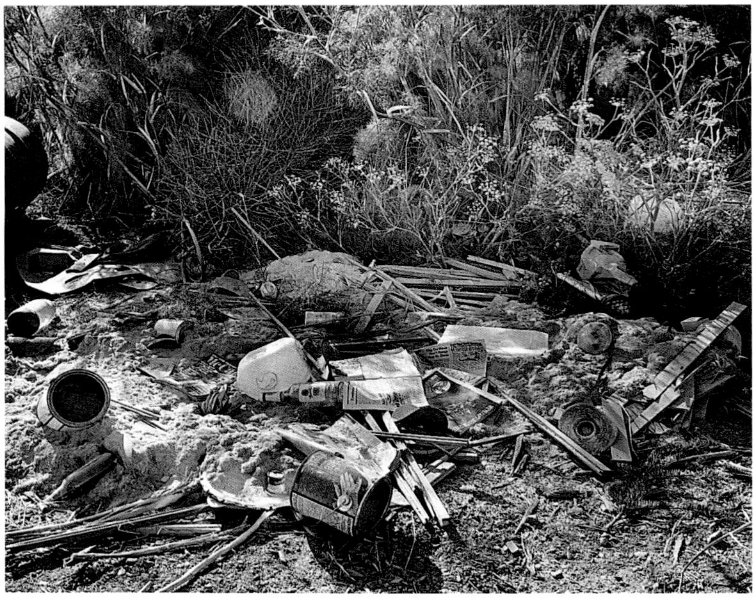

180.

LEWIS BALTZ

Four photographs from *San Quentin Point,* 1985

Gelatin silver prints

7 3/8 x 9 in. each

GIFT OF SUSAN HUNTER

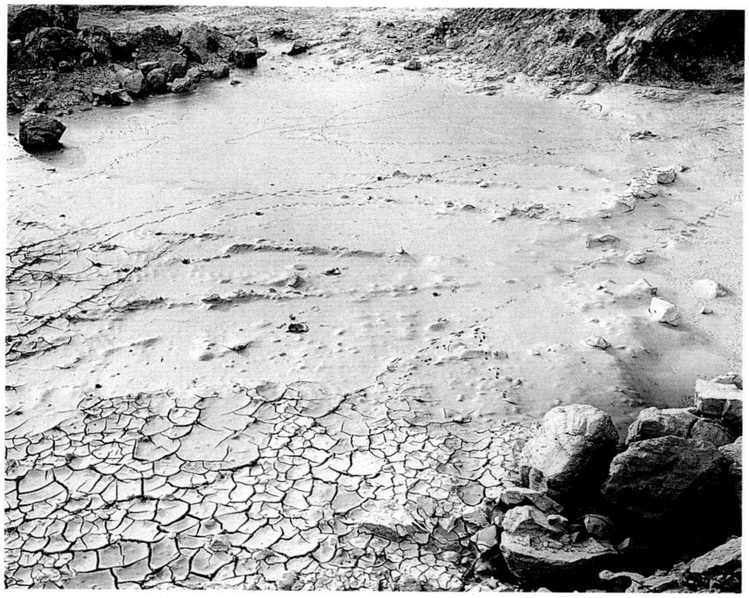

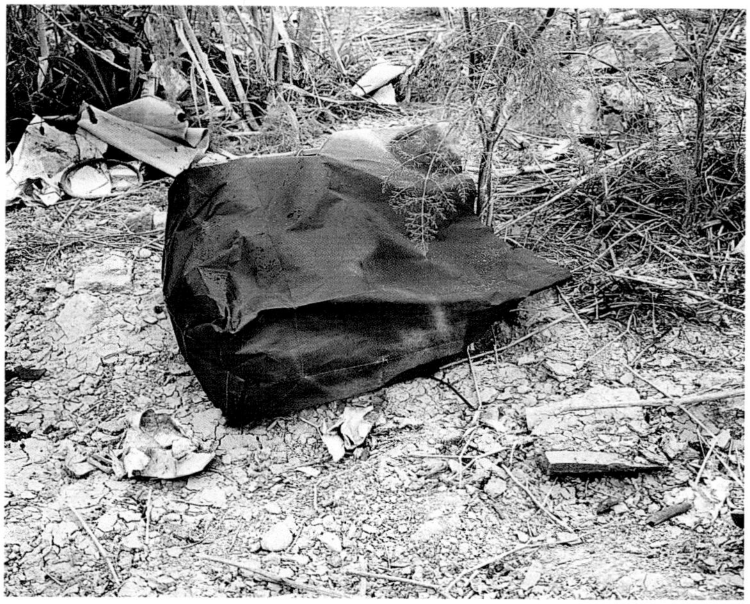

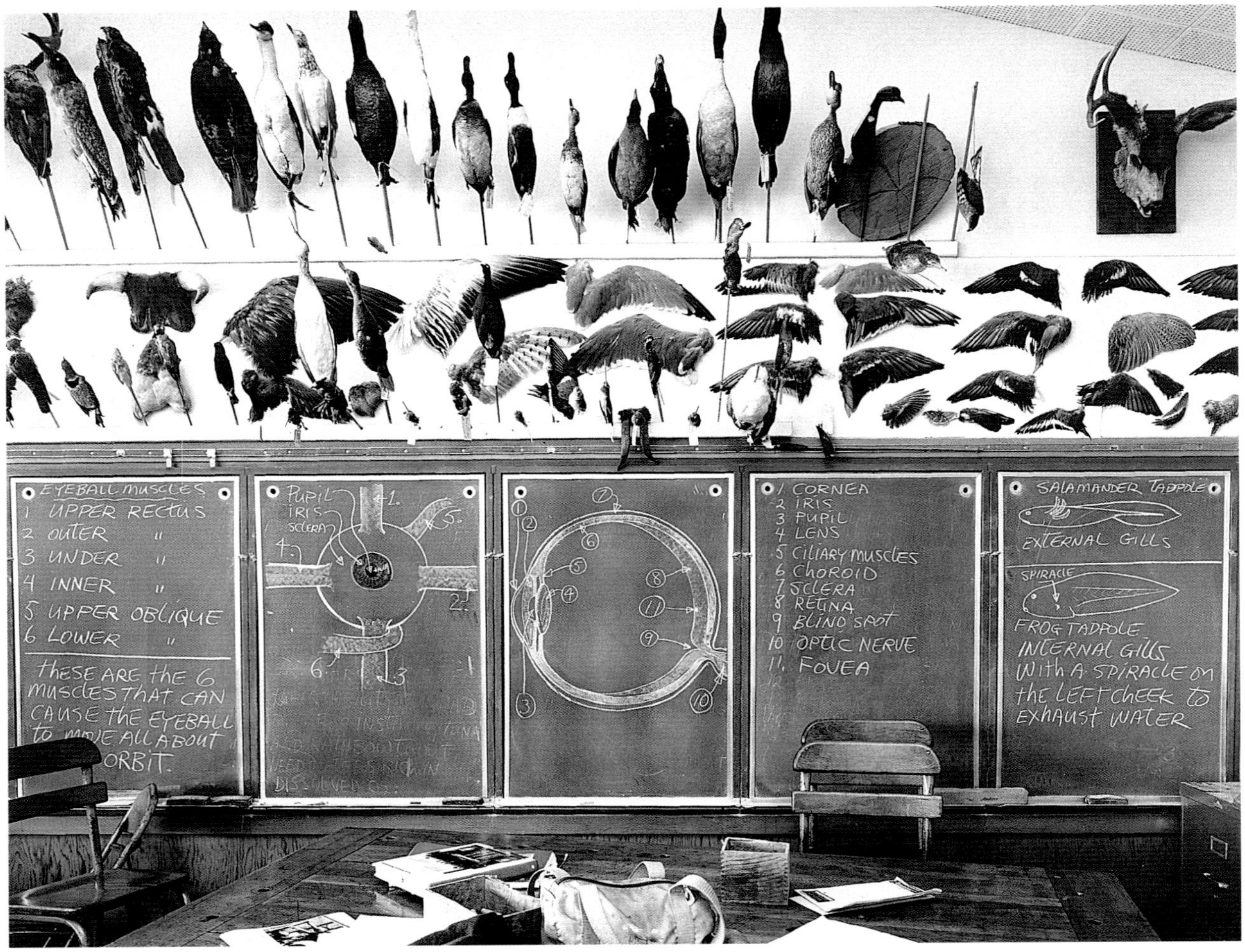

181.

CATHERINE WAGNER

Untitled (from *American Classroom* series), 1984

Gelatin silver print

14⅜ x 18¼ in.

THE SHIRLEY BURDEN FUND FOR PHOTOGRAPHY

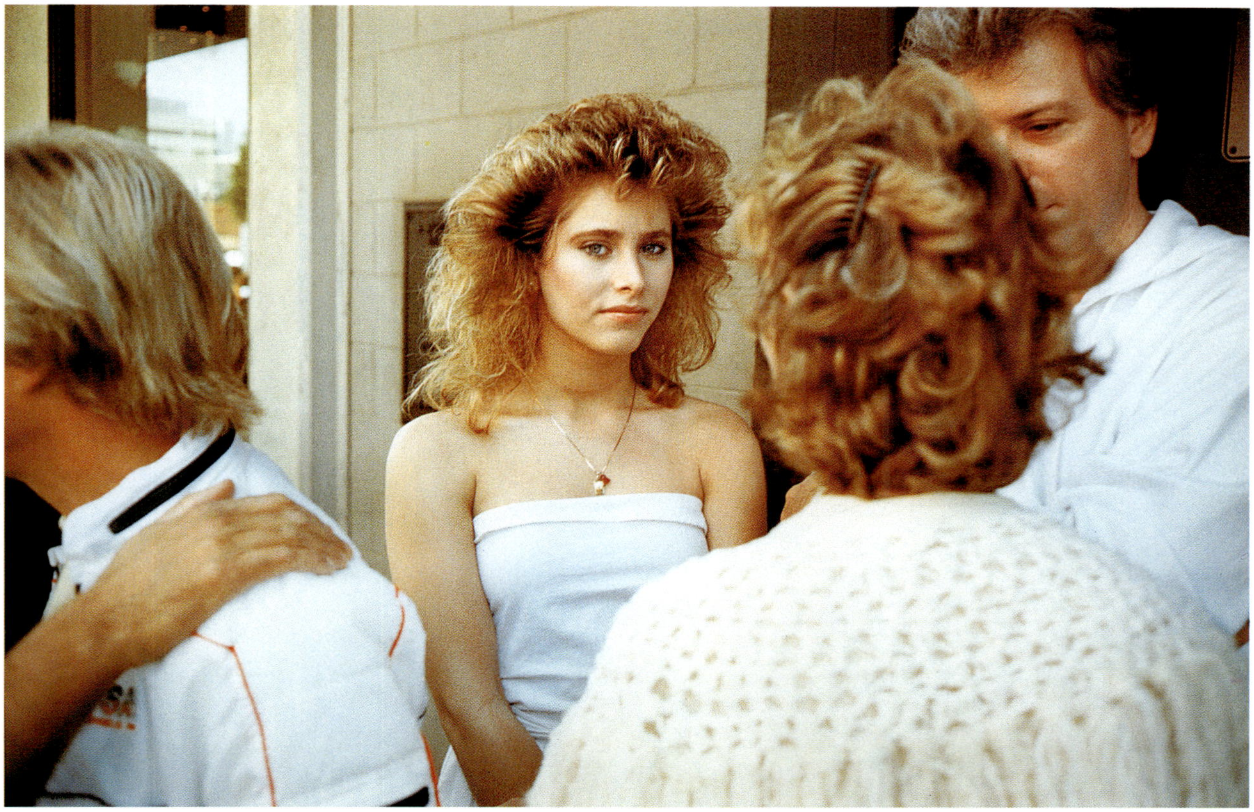

182.
ANTHONY HERNANDEZ
Beverly Hills # 2, 1984
Cibachrome print
16 x 20 in.
THE SHIRLEY BURDEN FUND FOR PHOTOGRAPHY

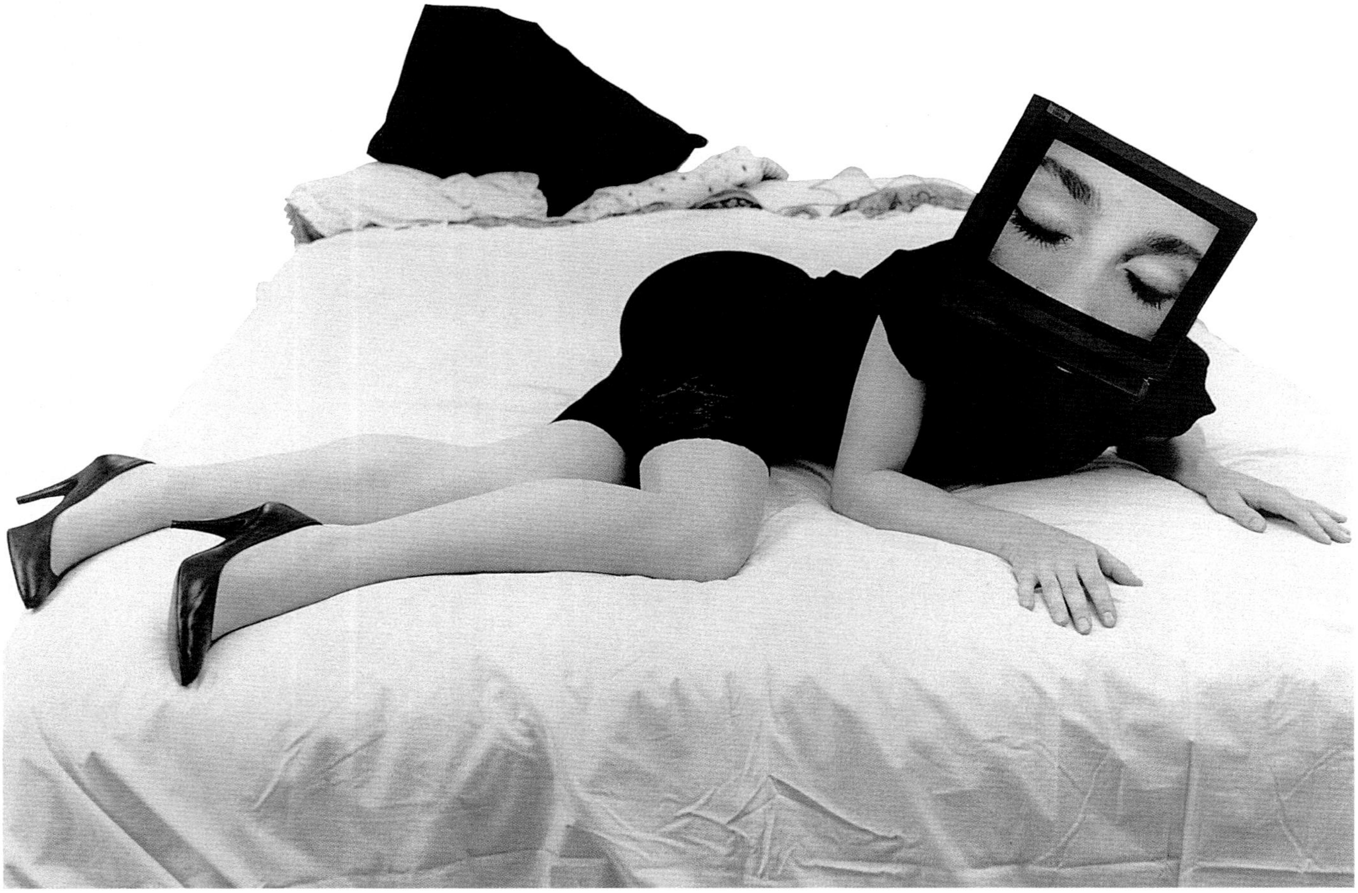

183.
LYNN HERSHMAN
Phantom Limb # 1, 1989–90
Gelatin silver print
30 x 40 in.

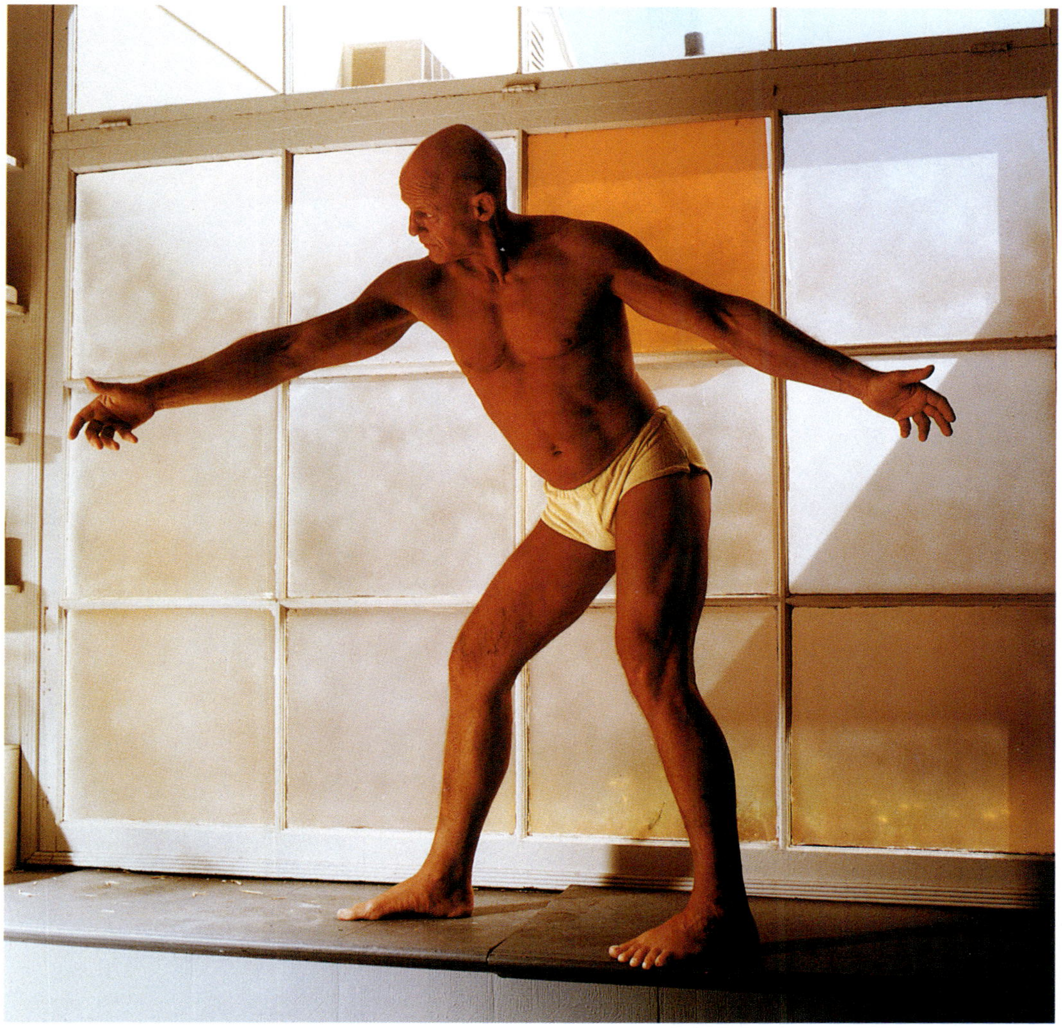

184.
KENNETH McGOWAN
Man Near Window, 1983
Cibachrome print
11⅞ x 11⅞ in.
THE SHIRLEY BURDEN FUND FOR PHOTOGRAPHY

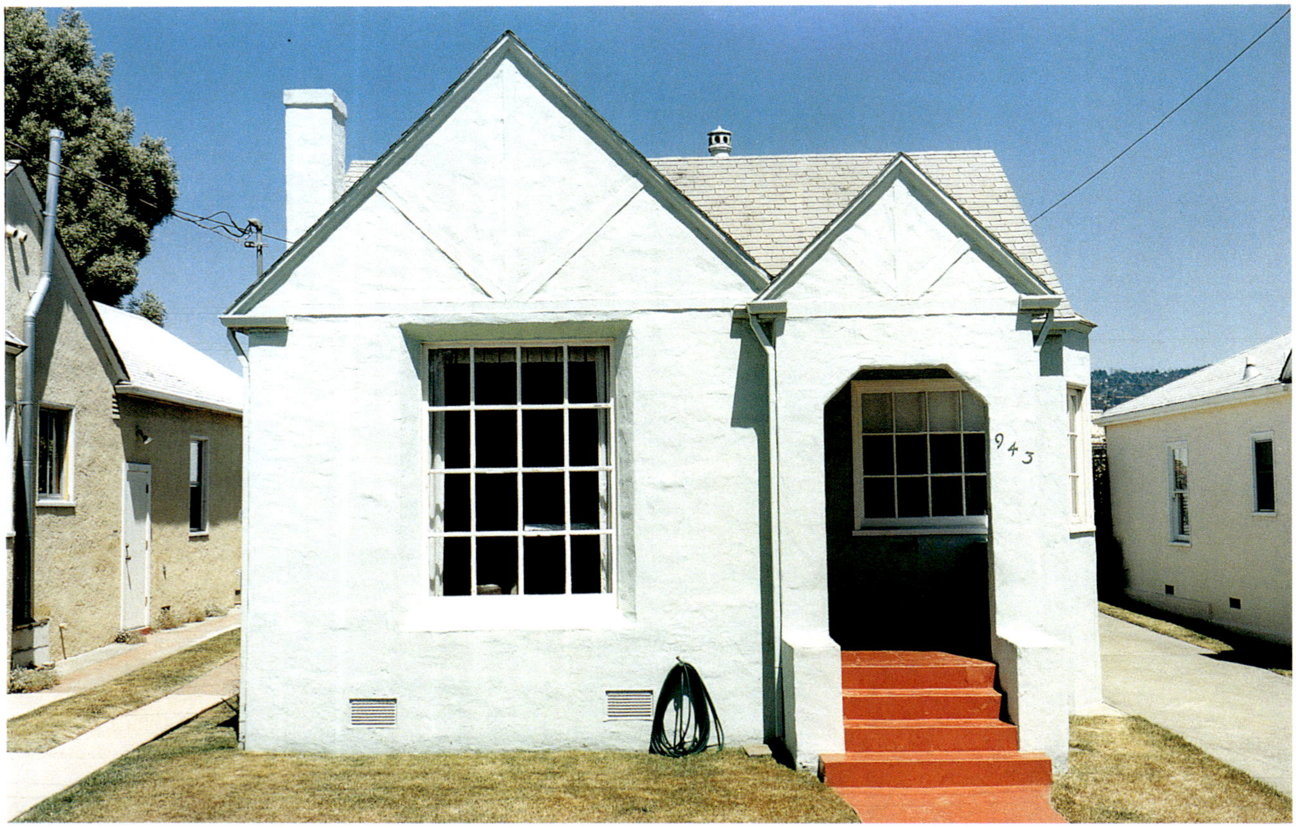

185.
HENRY WESSEL
Real Estate Photograph No. 91167, 1990–91
Chromogenic print
27 x 39½ in.
PURCHASED WITH FUNDS FROM THE COLLECTORS GALLERY

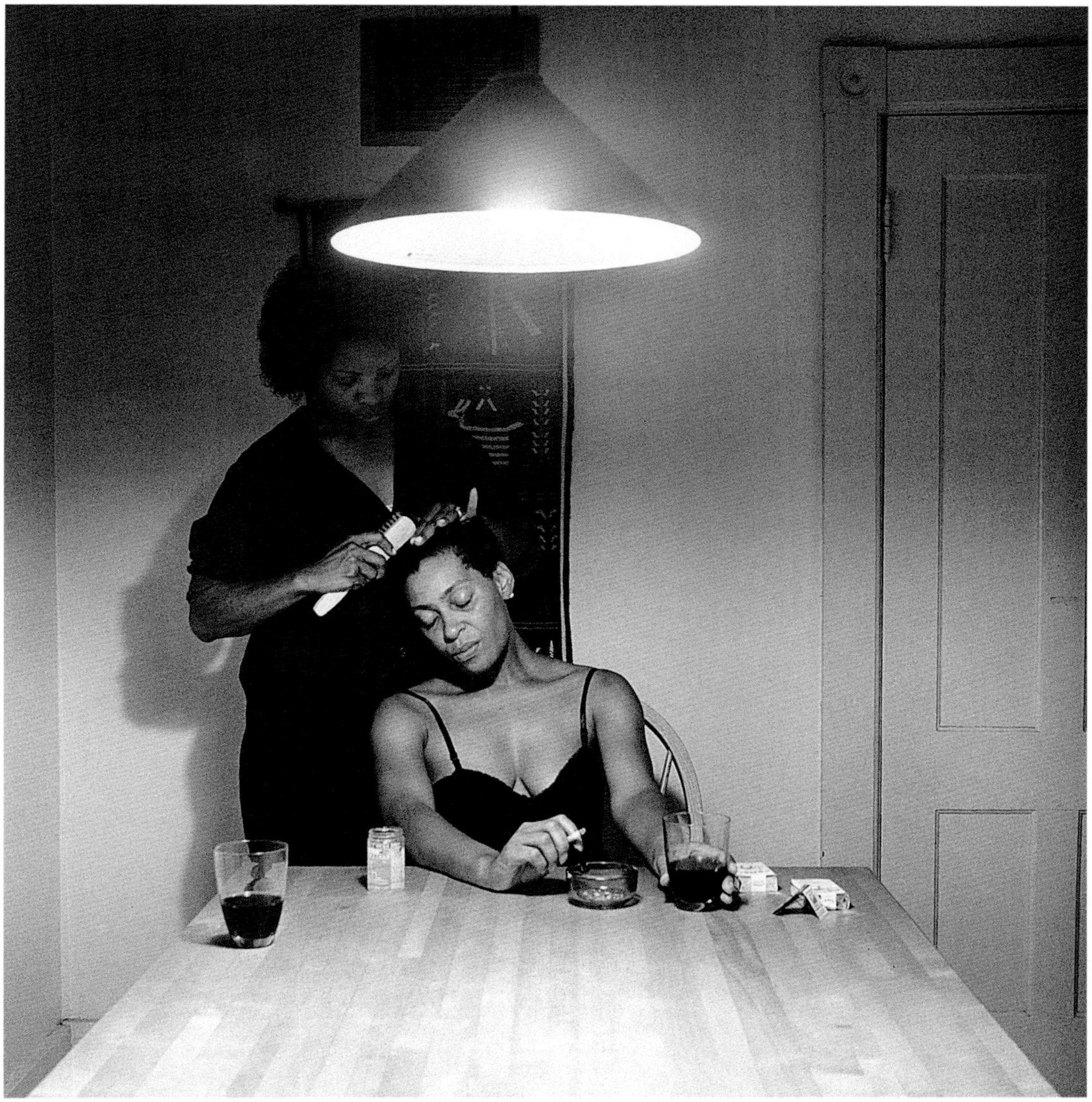

186.

CARRIE MAE WEEMS

Untitled (Woman Brushing Hair), 1990

Gelatin silver print

27½ x 27 3/16 in.

GIFT OF THE ESTATE OF MARJORIE EATON BY EXCHANGE

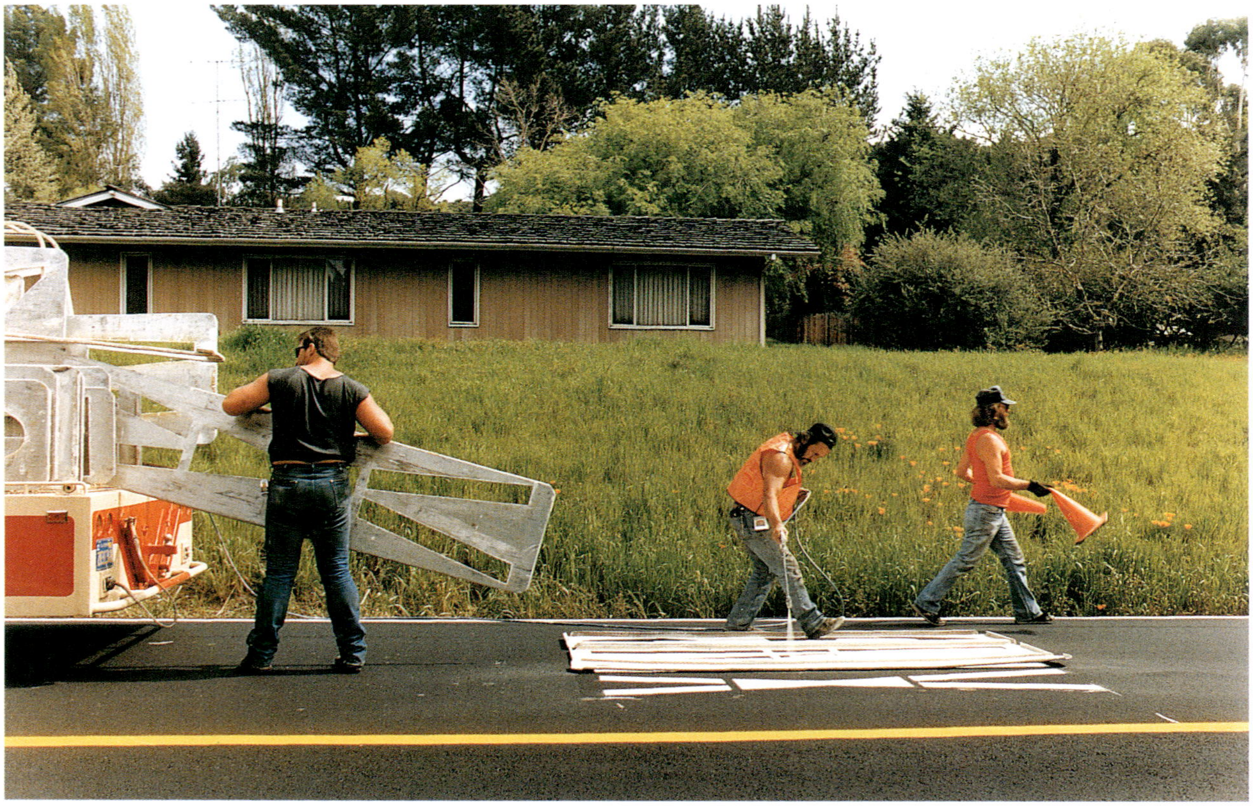

187.
DOUGLAS MUIR
Painting the Hiway, 1987 (printed 1992)
Dye coupler print
12¾ x 19½ in.
ANONYMOUS GIFT

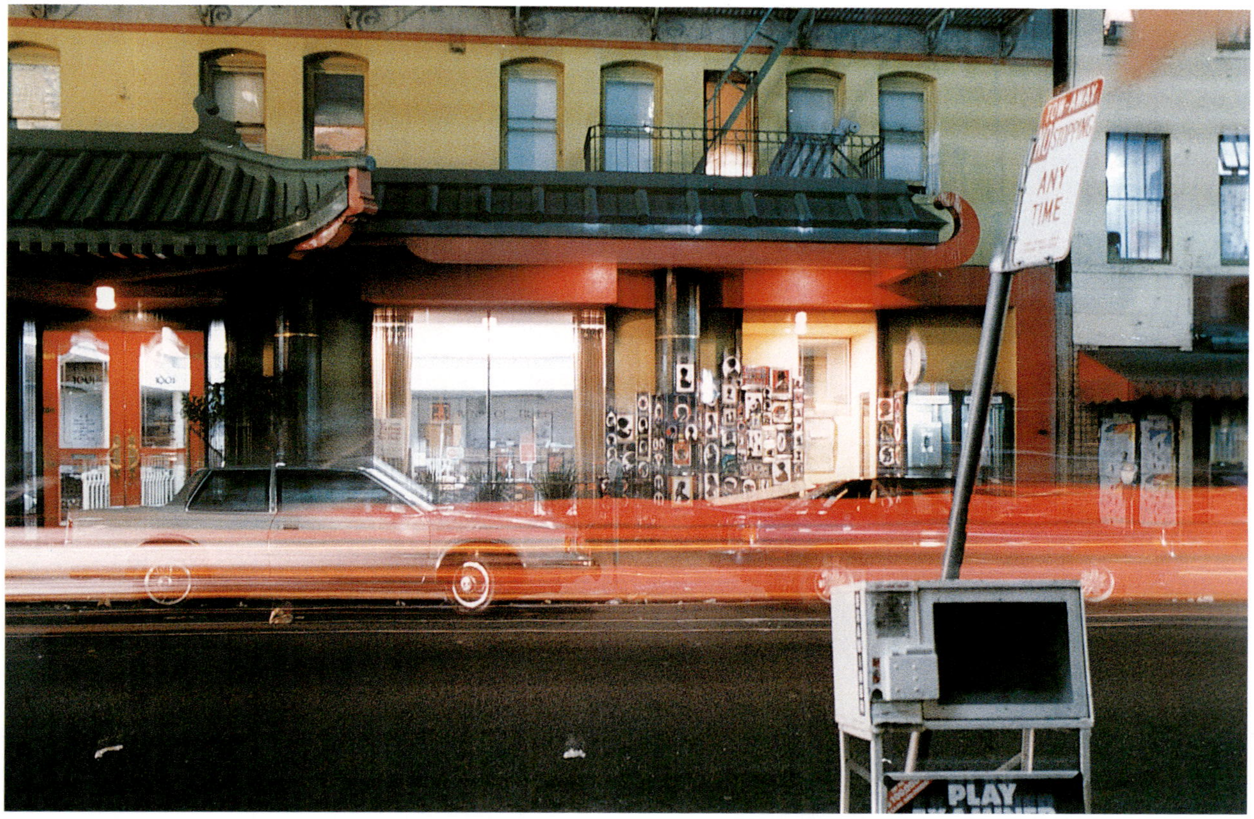

188.
JERRY BURCHARD
Grant Avenue, USA 87, 1987
Type C color print
12$\frac{15}{16}$ x 19$\frac{1}{8}$ in.
GIFT OF RON JEHU

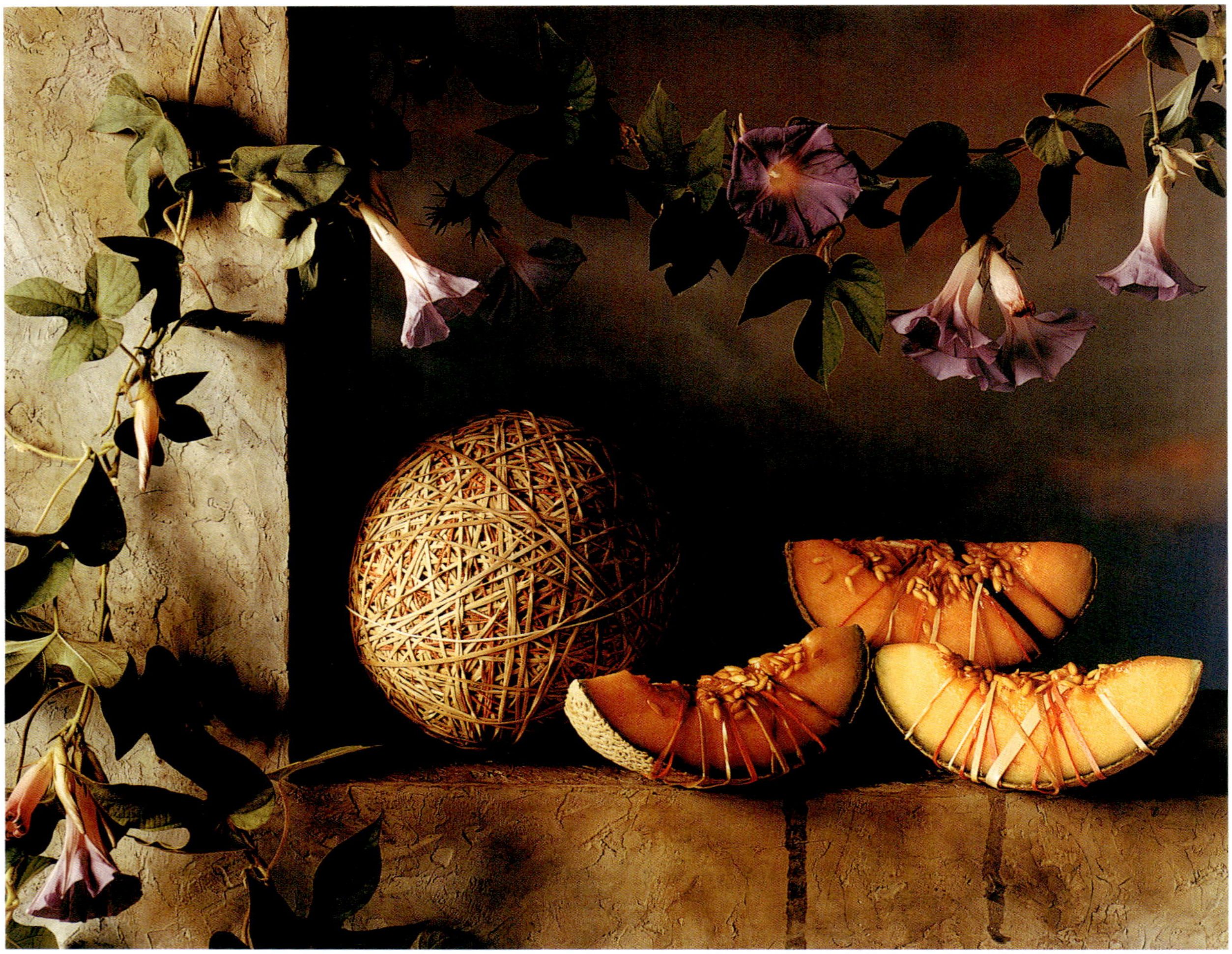

189.
JO WHALEY
Rubberloupe, 1992, printed 1999
Fuji Crystal Archive print
24 x 30 in.
GIFT OF THE ARTIST AND THE ROBERT KOCH GALLERY

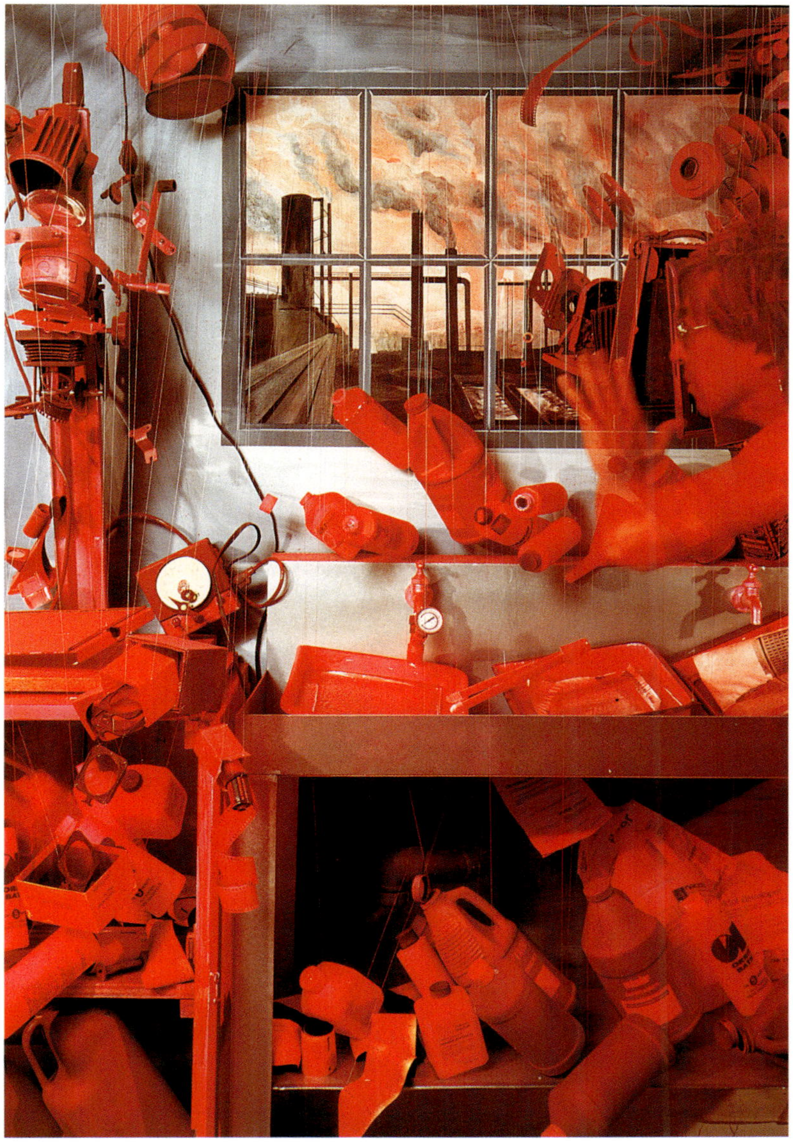

190.
PATRICK NAGATANI & ANDRÉE TRACEY
Unsafe Light, 1985
Cibachrome print
19½ x 13½ in.
THE SHIRLEY BURDEN FUND FOR PHOTOGRAPHY

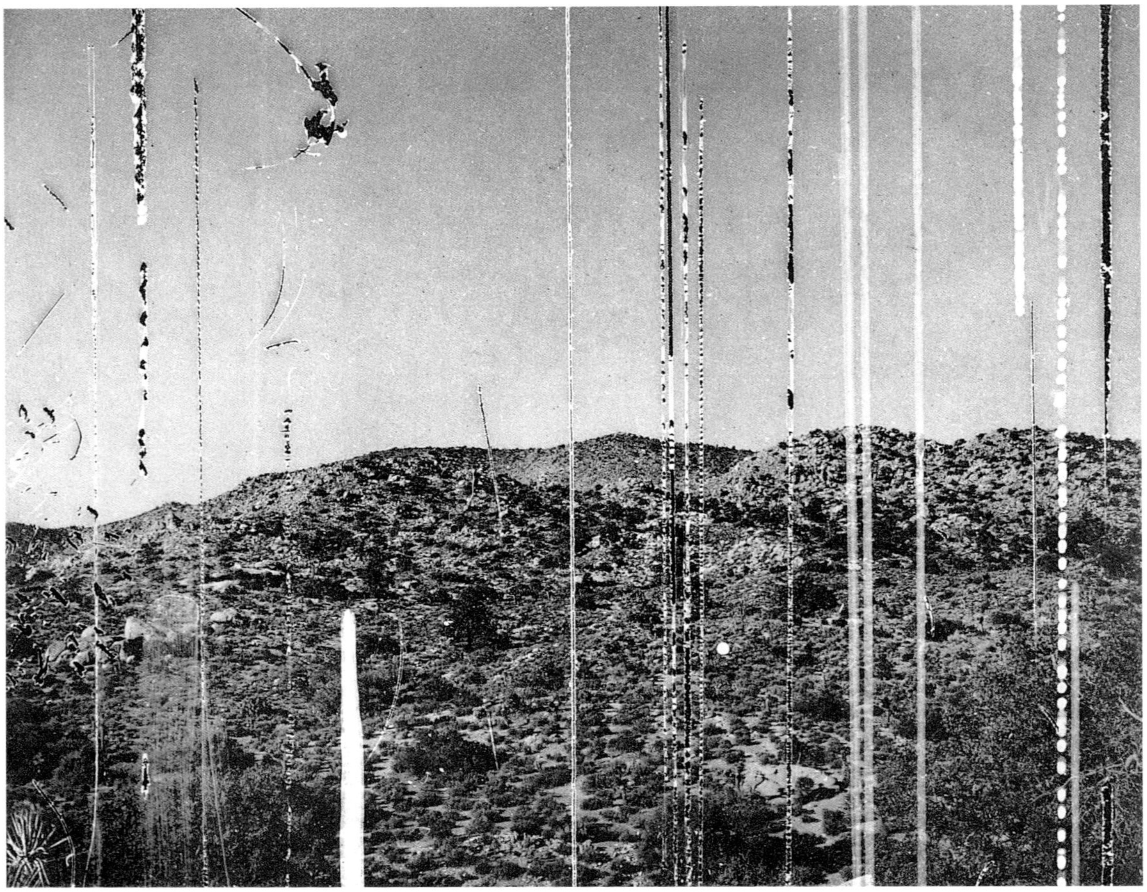

191.
ED RUSCHA
Section 22, 1995
Photogravure with etching
10⅛ x 13⅝ in.
GIFT OF THE ART GUILD

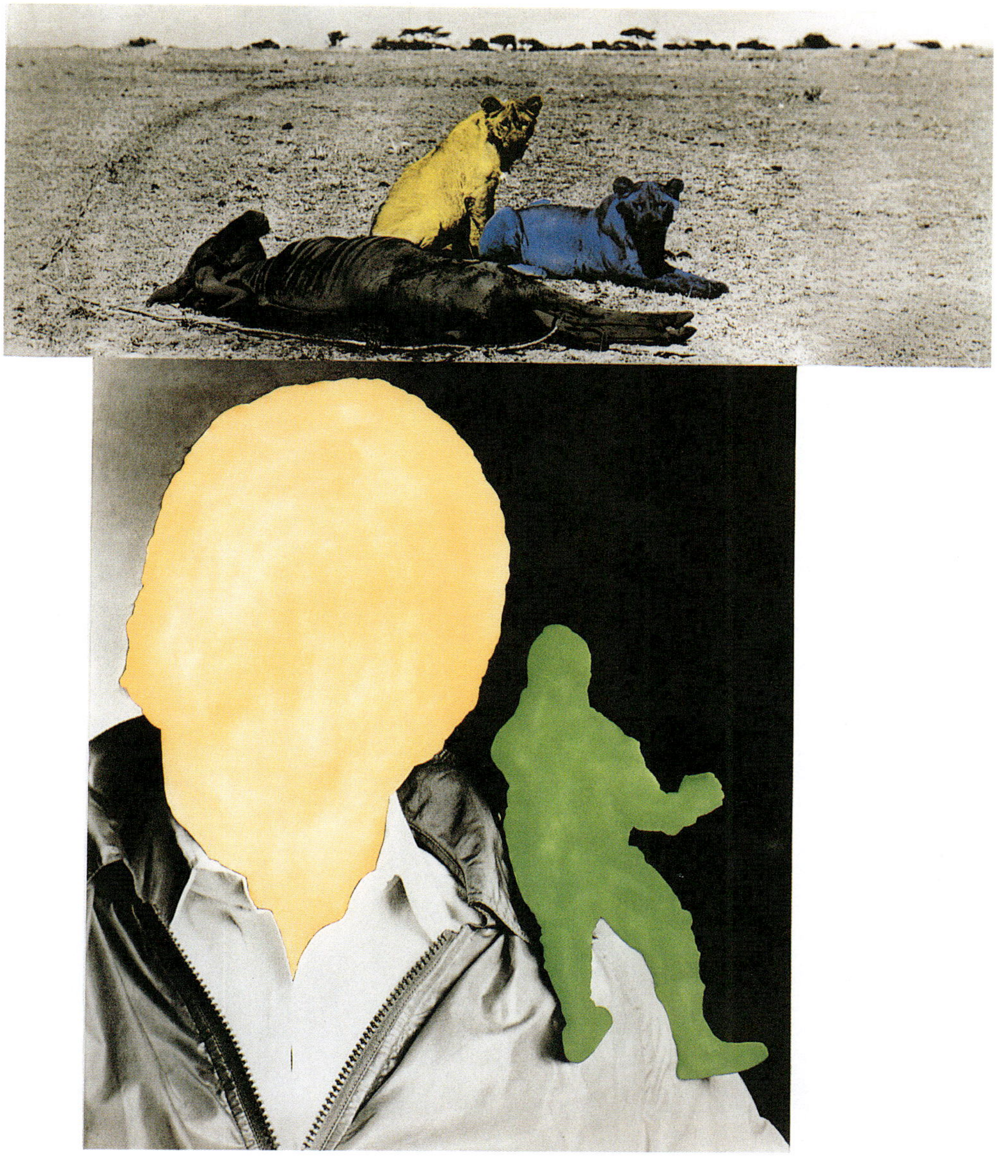

192.
JOHN BALDESSARI
Person with Conscience (Green)/Animals Quiescent (Yellow),
1991
Photogravure
41 x 35 in.
REICHEL FUND PURCHASE

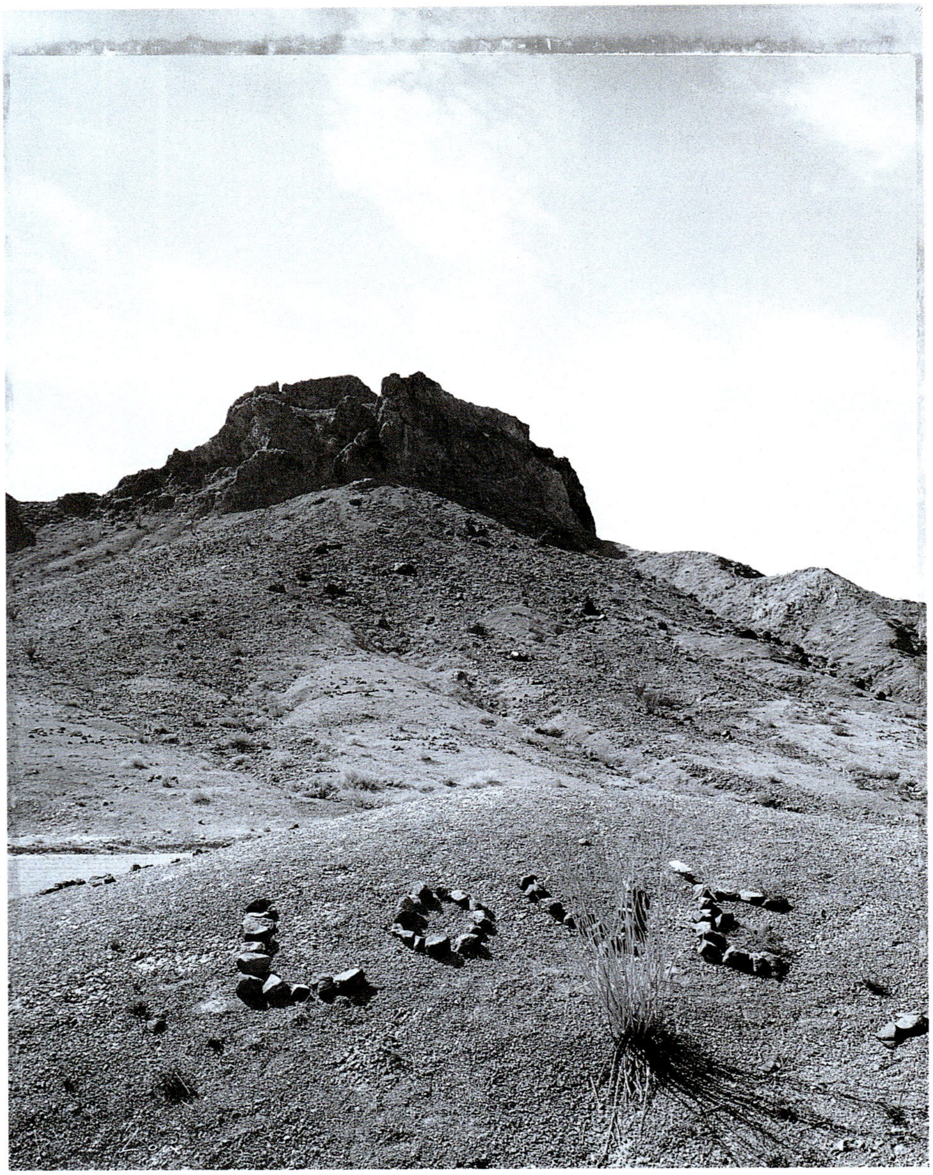

193.
MARK KLETT
"Love"—"Haight," Picacho Road, CA, 2/25/89, 1989
Two gelatin silver prints
20 x 16 in. each
GIFT OF THE COLLECTORS GALLERY

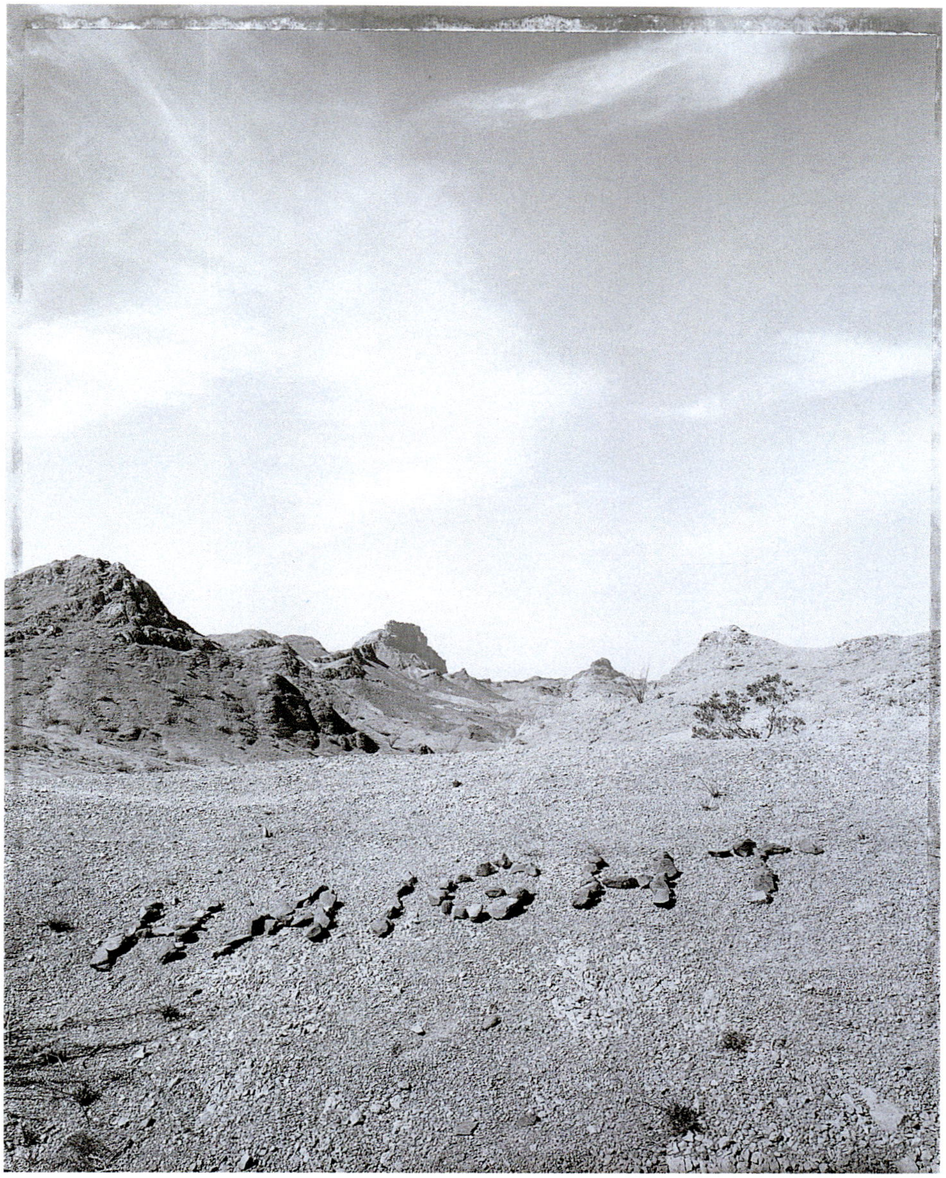
HAIGHT

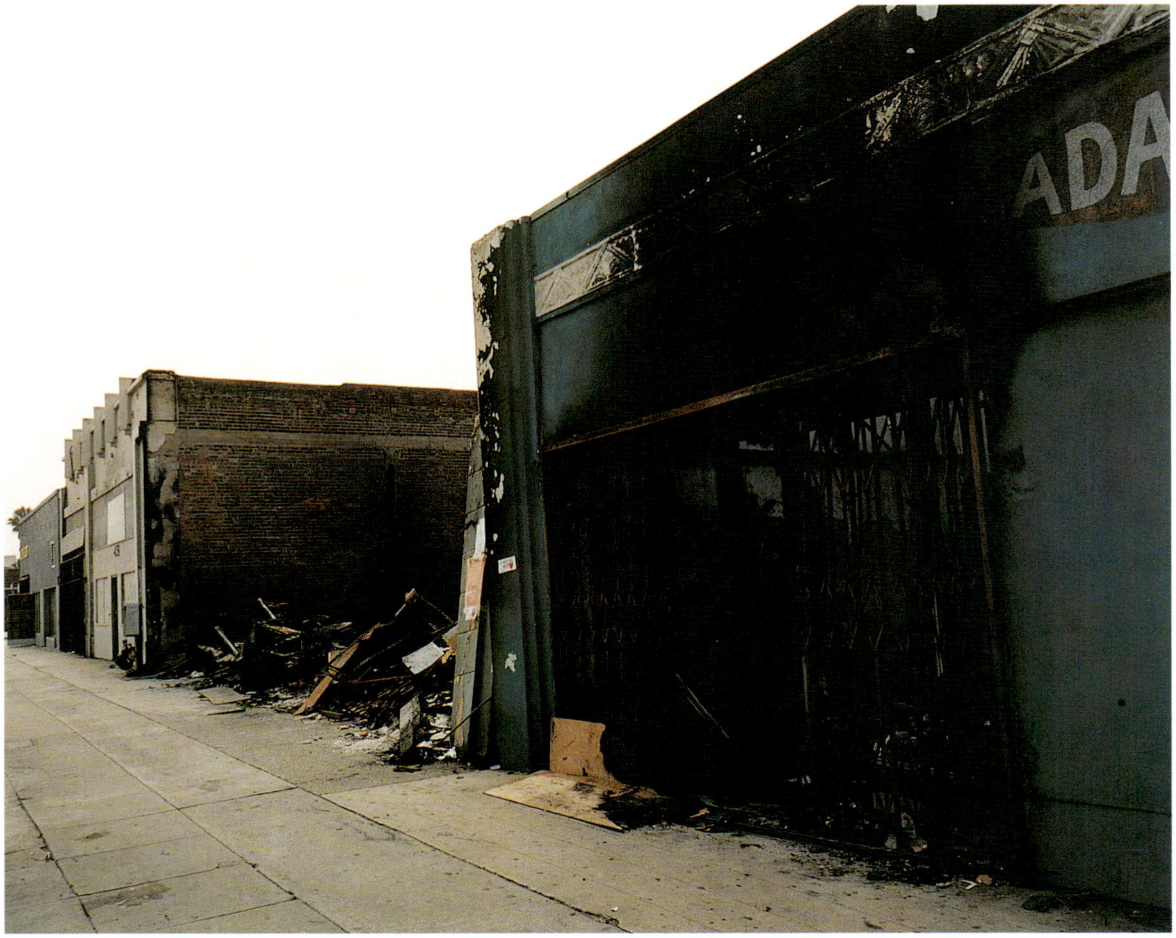

194.

REAGAN LOUIE

South Central, Los Angeles, 1992

Type C color print

20 x 24 in.

GIFT OF THE ESTATE OF MARGORIE EATON BY EXCHANGE

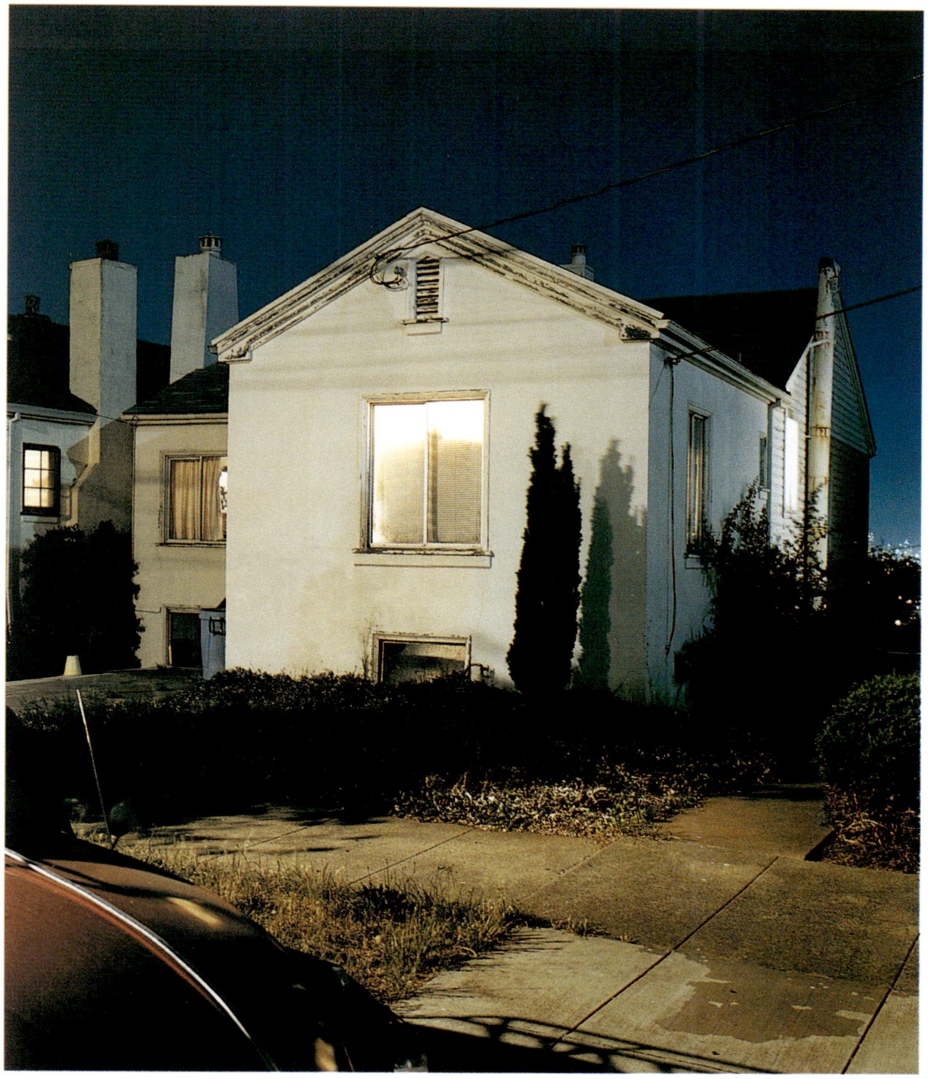

195.
TODD HIDO
Untitled (#1937) from the series *"House Hunting,"* 1997
Chromogenic print
24 x 19¾ in.
GIFT OF THE WALLACE ALEXANDER GERBODE FOUNDATION

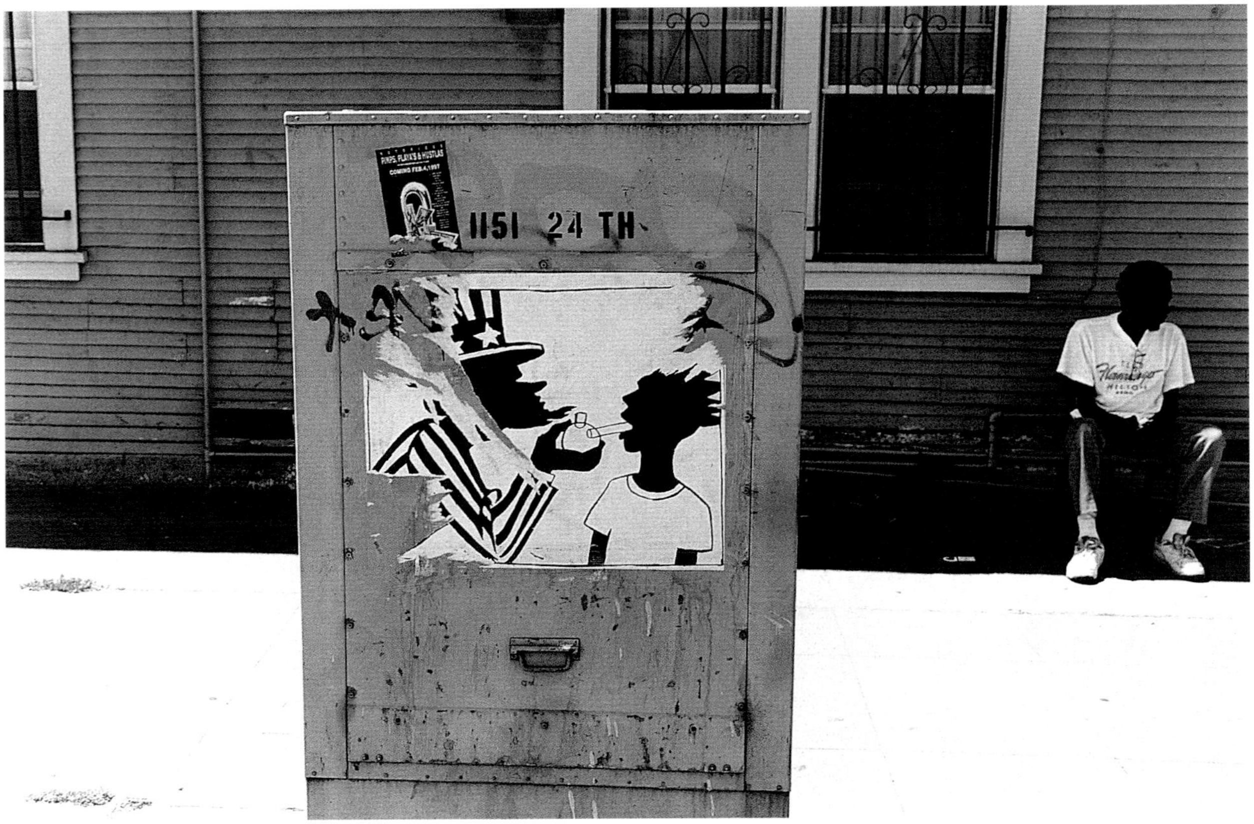

196.
LEWIS WATTS
24th Street, West Oakland, 1997
Gelatin silver print
$12\frac{3}{8}$ x $18\frac{1}{4}$
GIFT OF THE WALLACE ALEXANDER GERBODE FOUNDATION

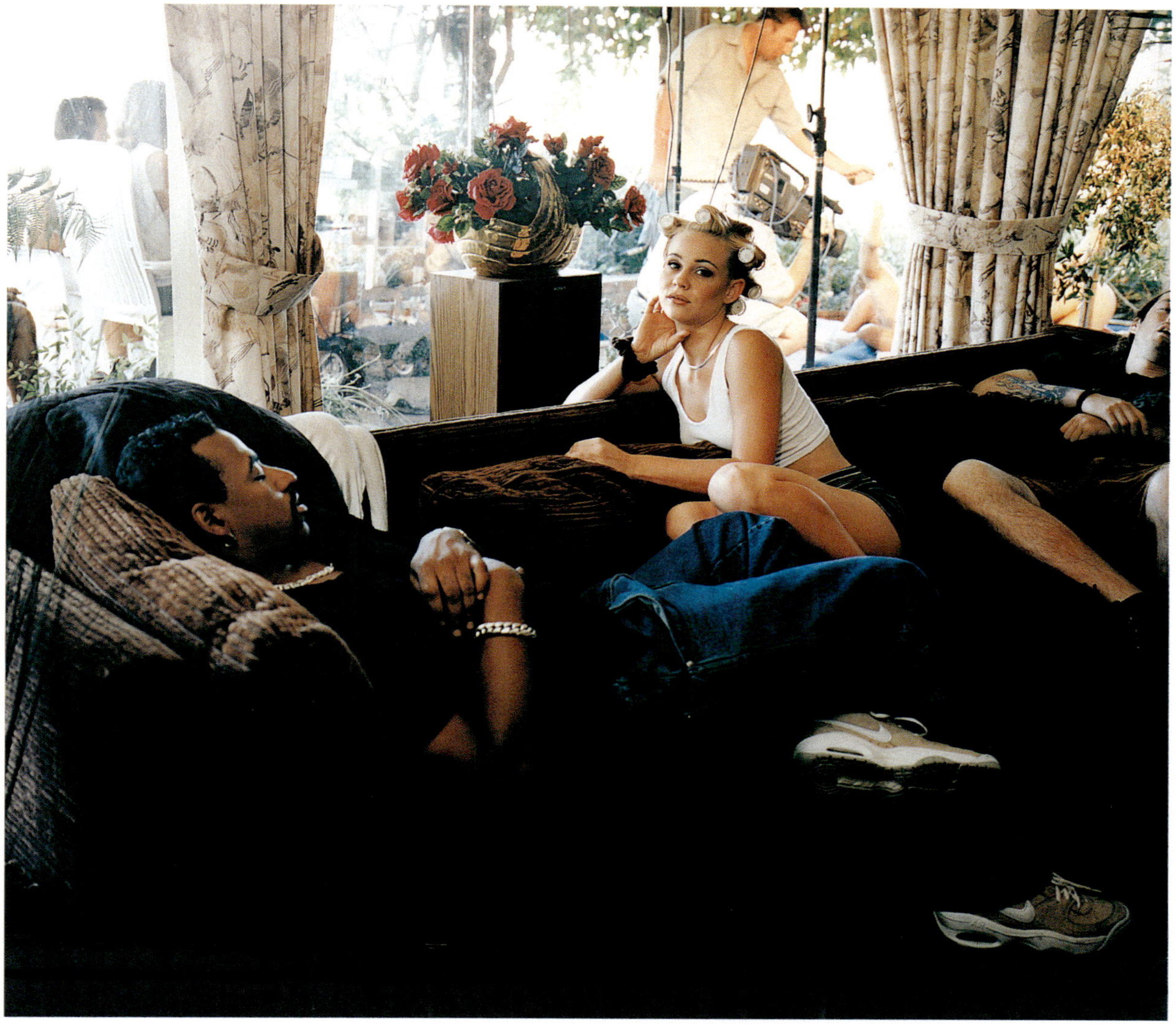

197.
LARRY SULTAN
Tasha's Third Film, 1998
Chromogenic print
30 x 40 in.
PURCHASED WITH FUNDS FROM THE COLLECTORS GALLERY

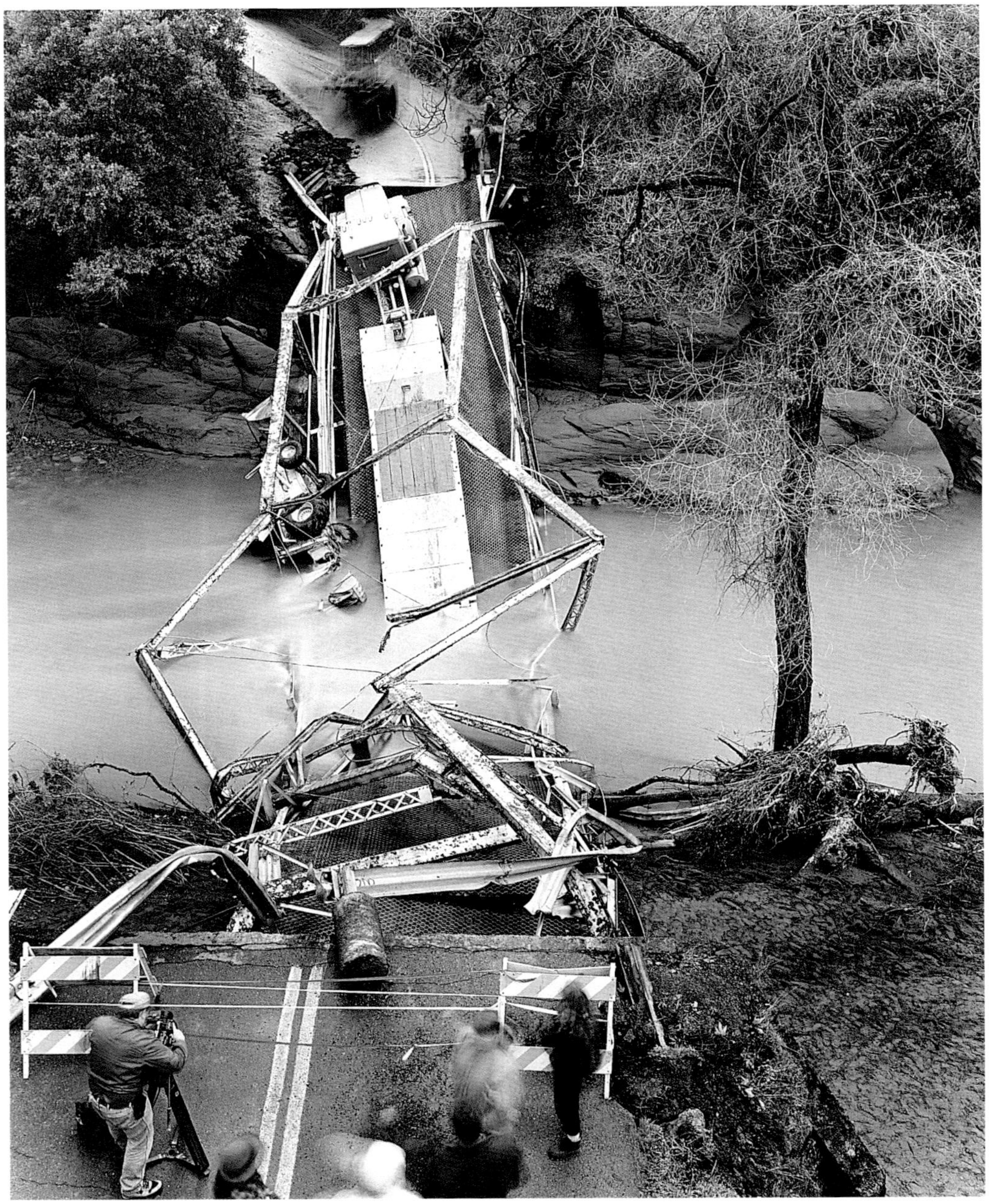

198.

GEOFFREY FRICKER

Centerville Bridge—Butte County Bridge # 17, 1907–1997,
1997 (printed 1999*)*
Gelatin silver print
32 x 26 in. (image)
PURCHASED WITH FUNDS FROM THE COLLECTORS GALLERY

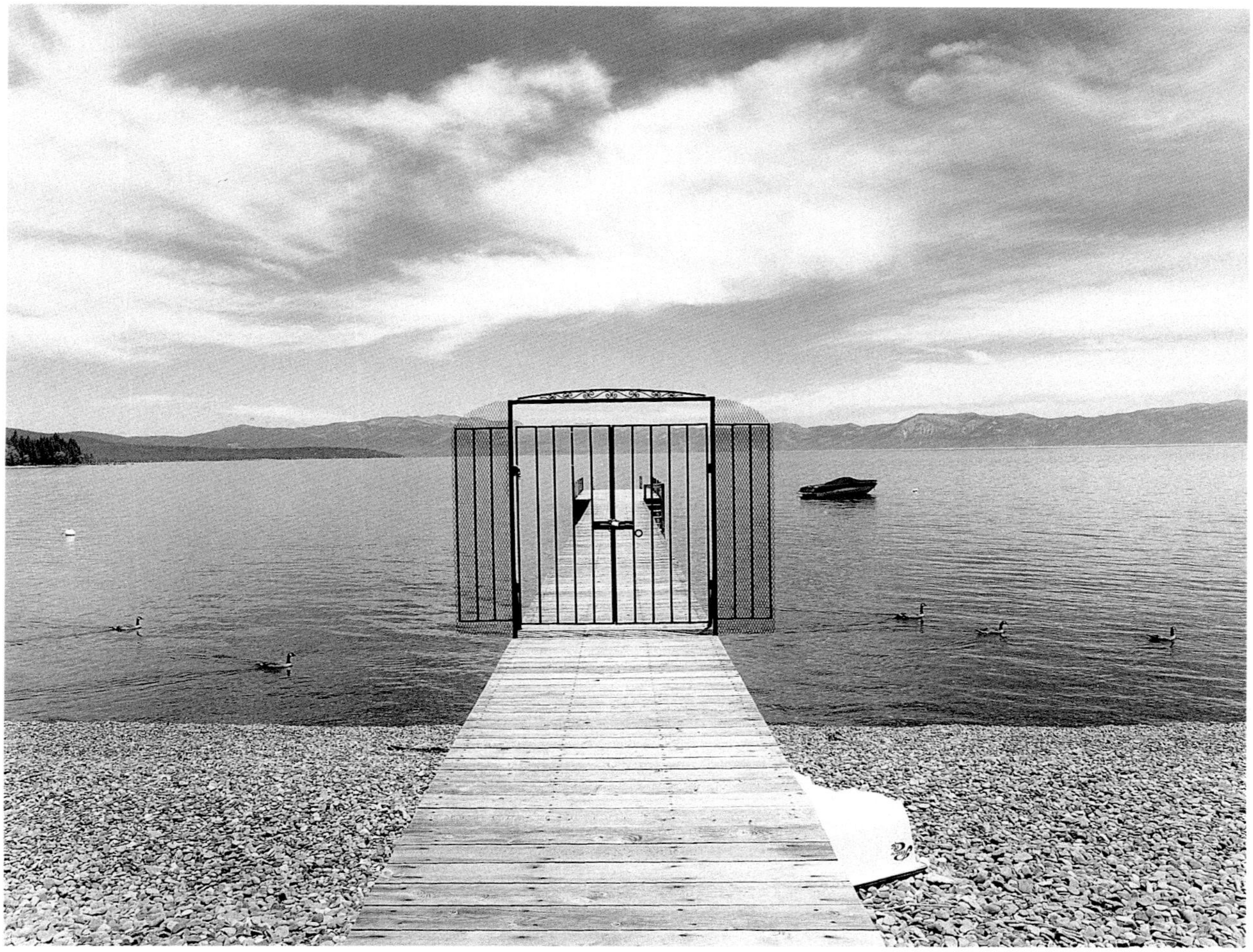

199.

ROBERT DAWSON

Private Property, Lake Tahoe, California (from the *Farewell, Promised Land* Project), 1988

Gelatin silver print

14⅜ x 18½ in.

GIFT OF STEVEN AND SANDRA WOLFE

200.
STEPHEN JOHNSON
Dune and Brush, Death Valley National Park, 1995
Modified Dicomed digital scanning camera image
(6000 x 7520 pixels)
Display print 27 x 34 inches
GIFT OF RICH AND ROBIN EDWARDS

NOTES TO THE PLATES

1.

WILLIAM SHEW

Untitled (Shew's Daguerrian Saloon and the Alta California Newspaper Office, San Francisco), 1851

> A good deal of curiosity has been expressed in regard to the object and intention of the big wagon which fills up a large portion of the Plaza. . . . Some suppose that "the elephant" which so many people come here to see was to be caged up in it and exhibited to greenhorns at a quarter a sight—others that it was to be a travelling rum mill, and a variety of other things. It seems, however, that it is to be a travelling daguerreotype establishment, with which the proprietor intends to travel around the city and country, taking views and portraits.
>
> – San Francisco *Alta California,* 1851

Immensely popular in the decades before the Civil War, daguerreotypes were the first commercially viable photographs. A daguerreotype consists of a highly polished, silver-coated copper plate, sensitized and exposed in a camera. Developed with mercury vapors which form a frostlike coating on the exposed areas, the resulting image is a one-of-a-kind positive with a remarkably high level of pictorial detail. Daguerreotypes have extremely fragile surfaces, requiring protection behind glass in ornate miniature cases.

Shew's mobile studio, unlike the permanent establishments of his competitors, escaped destruction from the many fires that ripped through San Francisco in the late 1840s and early 50s. "The elephant" referred to in the quote above was a popular metaphor for California gold fever.

2.

ISAAC WALLACE BAKER

Native Californian, c. 1853

The Oakland Museum of California holds all known daguerreotypes taken by Baker on his California travels. The handful of surviving images shows a remarkable documentary breadth for the time: mining, gambling, the photographer with his studio, Chinese, and this haunting image of a young California Indian. We know that Baker lectured about his California experiences upon returning to Beverly, Massachusetts; perhaps these daguerreotypes, passed down through his descendants, were intended to illustrate the exotic nature of the state to Eastern viewers. One of the earliest surviving photographs of a California Indian, the sitter's tribe is difficult to identify because of his western clothing.

3.

UNKNOWN

Untitled (Two Miners with Gold Nugget Stick-Pins), c. 1852

> Californians were so anxious that their friends in civilized countries should see just how they looked in their mining dress . . . when sitting for a daguerreotype to send to the States! They were proud of their curling moustaches and flowing beards; their bandit-looking sombreros; and our old friend [the daguerreotypist] accumulated much *oro en polvo* and many yellow coins from private mints.
>
> – Daguerreotypist Henry W. Bradley

Lest they be overlooked, the large gold nuggets these miners wore on their shirts when they had their portrait taken were highlighted with gold paint. The daguerreotype is housed in a Halvorson case, an unusual metal case with molded leather insets, which may have been designed for the rigors of traveling.

4.

ISAAC WALLACE BAKER

Untitled (Murphys, Calaveras County), July 1853

One of the earliest and richest gold camps in California, Murphys was a thriving community of several thousand when this daguerreotype was made. The town was named for John and Daniel Murphy, who found 1.5 million dollars in gold in 1849, the first year of the Gold Rush.

5.

UNKNOWN

Untitled (California Mining Scene), c. 1860

This albumen print shows signs of having been copied from a daguerreotype. The mining operation, the miners' clothing and the vignetting of the camera's lens are characteristic of an earlier, more primitive era, both in California and in photography.

6.

ISAAC WALLACE BAKER

Untitled (Chinese Man), c. 1853

The earliest known photographic portrait of a Chinese American, this daguerreotype exhibits a dignity belied by the Chinese experience in California. Considered a threat to white economic ambition, the Chinese were segregated into ghettos, barred by the new state government from many occupations, and subject to vigilante violence and harassment. Persisting despite this, the Chinese prospered and many whites, such as the photographers who advertised in Chinese-language newspapers, were eager to accept their money.

7.
GEORGE H. JOHNSON
Untitled (California Fireman), c. 1853

Although Johnson's imprint identifies this portrait as coming from his Sacramento studio, the unknown fireman has been identified as belonging to a San Francisco company. Fire was a continual threat in early San Francisco. From 1848 to 1851 six major fires devastated the city, and more than twenty volunteer fire brigades operated there by 1855. Organizations of great social status, San Francisco's fire brigades were also highly competitive, occasionally fighting battles with one another over the privilege of extinguishing a blaze.

8.
ROBERT H. VANCE
Untitled (Portrait of a Woman), c. 1854

An advertisement for Vance's "Premium Daguerrean Galleries" in San Francisco, Sacramento and Marysville has been cleverly worked into the red velvet lining of the daguerreotype's case. Indeed, the Vance galleries offered a high-quality product, complete with careful hand-painting to accentuate the woman's pink cheeks and gold jewelry.

9.
ATTRIBUTED TO WILLIAM SHEW
Untitled (Eleven Men with Beards, Top Hats and Vests), c. 1853

The unusually patterned carpet visible in this unattributed image matches that found in daguerreotypes known to have been taken by William Shew in his San Francisco studio. The close huddle of the men and the pattern of light from a nearby window suggest the image was made in a narrow space, perhaps the mobile "Daguerrian Saloon" pictured in plate 1.

10.
ATTRIBUTED TO ROBERT H. VANCE
Untitled (William F. Boardman and Surveying Party), c. 1859

The Oakland Museum of California holds William F. Boardman's personal papers, including an intimate set of letters written to his wife during the Gold Rush. This photograph has been attributed to Vance based on the distinctive carpet pattern which matches that in photographs known to have been taken in Vance's studio.

11.
GEORGE ROBINSON FARDON
View of the West Side of Montgomery Street, From Washington to Pacific, San Francisco, c. 1855

G. R. Fardon's salt prints of San Francisco are among the earliest paper photographs made on the West Coast. Published in 1856, his book *San Francisco Album* contained thirty views of the burgeoning Gold Rush metropolis and was the first published photograph album of any American city. Only nine copies of Fardon's album are known to have survived. This print comes from the copy originally owned by Jacob Gundlach, a pioneer brewer and winemaker.

In this view, Fardon recorded the towering Miners' Exchange Bank on Montgomery Street. Built in 1854, the Exchange was one of the first banks erected in what is today the center of San Francisco's financial district. Unfortunately, due to a financial crisis at the end of the Gold Rush, the Exchange went broke just a year after opening its doors.

Salt prints were made from ordinary writing paper saturated with a solution of table salt and silver nitrate, creating a light-sensitive emulsion embedded in the paper's fibers. Prints were made by exposing the sensitized paper to sunlight in contact with a glass plate negative. Unlike daguerreotypes, which were unique images, any number of salt prints could be reproduced from the same negative, making published albums such as Fardon's feasible for the first time.

12.
CARLETON E. WATKINS
New Almaden Quicksilver Mine, 1863

Quicksilver, or mercury, was indispensable to the process of extracting gold from its ore. Named after Almaden in Spain, a center of cinnabar (mercury ore), the New Almaden was one of the most successful mines in California's history. During the Gold Rush it was the primary source for this highly valued substance.

13.
CARLETON E. WATKINS
Grizzly Giant, Mariposa Grove, Yosemite, 1861

Carleton Watkins became nationally known with the spectacular mammoth plate photographs he took of Yosemite in 1861 on his first of eight trips to the valley over a twenty-year period. He commissioned a cabinet maker to build an immense camera capable of exposing negatives eighteen by twenty-two inches. These large, unwieldy glass plates, which required coating with photo-sensitive chemicals in the field and processing immediately upon exposure, would be worth the trouble. Watkins captured the vast, breathtaking scale of the valley with exceptional detail. Still hampered by imperfect lenses which darkened the corners, he was compelled to trim the top corners of his prints, resulting in the characteristic arched top of his 1861 photographs. This was remedied in later trips to Yosemite by newer lenses with improved optics.

14.
ANDREW J. RUSSELL
Supply Trains at End of Tracks, Last Siding, from *The Great West Illustrated In a Series of Views Across the Continent,* c. 1868

Russell was the official photographer of the Union Pacific Railroad. In 1869 the company published *The Great West Illustrated,* containing fifty original photographic prints by Russell of the railroad's westward progression, including this view of a train unloading supplies to be carried in freight wagons to men laying tracks ahead. The Oakland Museum of California holds a large collection of Russell's collodion glass plate negatives, including this exceptional image. This vintage albumen print is from a copy of *The Great West Illustrated* held by the museum.

15.
CHARLES LEANDER WEED
Yo-Semite Valley from the Mariposa Trail, 1864

Charles Leander Weed was the first person to photograph Yosemite, producing small prints and stereo views in 1859. He returned in 1864 with a "mammoth plate" camera which took glass plate negatives eighteen by twenty-two inches, including this "best general view" of the valley. Despite the importance of his accomplishment, the photographs were published without credit to Weed, a common practice in nineteenth-century photography.

16.
Stereographs

CHARLES LEANDER WEED
Vernal Falls, 1859

Weed took this view in June of 1859 on the first photographic expedition ever made to Yosemite. He accompanied James M. Hutchings, an illustrator who had been invited to Yosemite to attend the grand opening of the first two-story hotel in the valley. Weed was to make a panoramic series of photographs that would be sold through Robert Vance's San Francisco gallery and serve as the basis for engravings by Hutchings. Under the most primitive conditions, Weed produced at least twenty large glass plate negatives and forty stereo views, the first images of what would become one of the most photographed locations in the world.

ALFRED A. HART
Infantile Glacier, 1868

As the official photographer for the Central Pacific Railway, Hart was the West Coast counterpart to Andrew J. Russell. While Russell followed the Union Pacific's tracks westward, Hart recorded the construction of the Central Pacific eastward from Sacramento as the two companies raced toward their junction point at Promontory, Utah. To the Central Pacific fell the onerous task of laying tracks over the Sierra Nevada mountains, and Hart was the only photographer who recorded construction at the summit. His fascination with the infamous, year-round cold of the summit, which had taken the lives of the Donnor Party, is apparent in this stereo view. The same image is alternately titled *Melting of a Snow Bank, Scene on the Summit in August.*

CHARLES LEANDER WEED
(Lawrence & Houseworth, publishers)
Untitled (Sacramento during the flood, K Street east from Fourth Street), 1862

Built on low-lying ground, the city of Sacramento was afflicted with a series of disastrous floods in its first decade. Those that struck in December of 1861 and January of 1862 were by far the worst, causing one newspaper to declare, "Sacramento is a doomed city." An expensive project to improve levees and raise the city's streets eventually prevented a recurrence.

Weed's fascinating series of flood views is among the first large-scale records of a natural disaster in California.

17.
TIMOTHY O'SULLIVAN
Alpine Lake, in the Sierra Nevada, California, c. 1871

Although O'Sullivan is not thought of as a California photographer, his travels with the Wheeler Expedition brought him to the state in 1871. This photograph, made during the expedition, bears the insignia of the U.S. Army, War Department, Corps of Engineers. After the Civil War the U.S. Army returned to its peacetime mission of surveying the vast, uncharted West. Lieutenant George M. Wheeler was an Army engineer assigned to map the West with an eye for routes and resources that might be useful to troops traveling in the area.

18.
EADWEARD MUYBRIDGE
Untitled (Lighthouse), 1868

In 1868 the Lighthouse Board commissioned Eadweard Muybridge to photograph lighthouses along the Pacific Coast. A government agency, the Lighthouse Board was set up to safeguard the burgeoning shipping industry by installing navigation aids such as buoys, fog signals and lighthouses from Alaska to Southern California. Muybridge's photographs recorded the perilous cliffs, rocky coastlines and rough waters with which ships had to contend.

19.
EADWEARD MUYBRIDGE
Pi-Wi-Ack, Valley of the Yosemite, (Shower of Stars), Vernal Fall, 400 Feet, 1872

In May 1872, San Francisco photographer Eadweard Muybridge sent a prospectus to potential subscribers describing his latest project. He proposed to make a series of large-sized views of Yosemite Valley, which subscribers could purchase in groups of forty for one hundred dollars. Muybridge's proposal was ambitious. The twenty-by-twenty-four-inch glass negatives needed to obtain such magnificently detailed images had to be carried in and out of the valley by mules, coated with light-sensitive chemicals, exposed while still wet and developed before the chemicals dried. After many months of intense work under primitive conditions, a weary Muybridge returned to San Francisco with commitments from subscribers amounting to more than twenty thousand dollars and several of the city's leading galleries fighting for the right to publish his work.

20.
GUSTAVUS FAGERSTEEN
Untitled (Overhanging Rock, Glacier Point, Yosemite), c. 1883

Fagersteen's scene of Overhanging Rock at Yosemite is an early view of a location which would become a favorite with photographers. Throughout the late nineteenth and early twentieth centuries, dozens of fearless individuals posed atop the precarious perch, a thousand feet above the valley. Somersaulting acrobats and dancing ladies were photographed on the rock; in one case, a Model T Ford was driven to the edge of the precipice. Not surprisingly, the location is now closed to such stunts.

21.
Cartes de visite

In the 1860s portrait photographers found a new market in the enormously popular carte de visite. These small, visiting card-sized images were widely collected in albums and exchanged as keepsakes in the United States and Europe. Compared to the cased images that preceded them, cartes were inexpensive to make and purchase. Cameras equipped with sliding plate-holders and multiple lenses allowed photographers to expose eight to ten frames of a sitter on a single plate. The prints were cut apart and individually mounted on card stock, often imprinted with ornate advertisements for the studio on the back. In addition to private portraiture, studios often mass-produced carte de visite images of celebrities, public figures and scenic views for sale to the public.

GEORGE S. LAWRENCE & THOMAS HOUSEWORTH, publishers
Oakland Ferry—Steamer Washoe, San Francisco, c. 1864

In 1864, the year she was built, Captain G. W. Kidd's ill-fated *Washoe* collided with another steamer, killing one passenger. Later that same year, she exploded and sank in a narrow passage of the Sacramento River called Steamboat Slough. She was carrying more than 150 passengers and crew, many of whom died in the accident. The following year she was salvaged and rebuilt by the San Francisco and Oakland Ferry and Railroad Company. Lawrence & Houseworth's view of the *Washoe* may be the only photograph of the steamer before the explosion.

HUGH S. ANDERSON
The National Sanitary Cake, 1865

During the Civil War, the National Sanitary Commission was the equivalent of today's Red Cross. A number of creative fund raising schemes were concocted to support the Commission, including this elaborate cake. Two and a half feet in diameter, the cake bore flags from each state in the union. Pieces were auctioned to the highest bidder, with proceeds going to the Sanitary Commission. In Eureka on the North Coast of California, the cake sold for more than one thousand dollars, with photographer Hugh Anderson himself purchasing the pieces representing Iowa and Michigan.

UNKNOWN
Mrs. J. C. Frémont at Marapose [*sic*], 1867

The extraordinary Jessie Benton Frémont was the daughter of Missouri Senator Thomas Hart Benton and the wife of California Senator John C. Frémont. Her husband was an important figure in the American conquest and development of California. With Jesse by his side, he became a Gold Rush millionaire in the 1840s, won fame with best-selling accounts of his western explorations and ran unsuccessfully as the first presidential candidate of the newly formed Republican party in 1856. Formidable in her own right, Jesse Frémont was a well-known author and behind-the-scenes politician. She participated in many of the major social movements of her day, devoting her greatest energy to the anti-slavery cause. When her husband went bankrupt in 1873, she supported the family with her writing.

23.
THOMAS HOUSEWORTH & CO., publishers
Launch of the Monarch, San Francisco, 1875

The *Monarch* was a one-hundred-ninety-five-ton tug boat built for Millen Griffith, pictured standing atop the pilot house. As the Gold Rush transformed San Francisco's harbor, the many ships carrying cargo and passengers to and from the bustling port were served by craft like the *Monarch*. Tugs were particularly useful in guiding less maneuverable sailing vessels to sea via the Golden Gate, a passage dangerous to navigate due to notoriously foggy weather, strong currents and a rocky shoreline.

24.
EADWEARD MUYBRIDGE
The Horse in Motion, 1878

In 1872 Eadweard Muybridge began a series of photographic studies of motion when Leland Stanford, president of the Central Pacific Railroad and former California Governor, commissioned him to prove that a horse running at top speed has all four feet off the ground at some point in its stride. Muybridge captured the silhouette of a trotting "Sallie Gardner" by lining up a series of still cameras spaced twenty-seven inches apart at Stanford's Palo Alto training track. As the horse passed, trip cords triggered each camera. A white sheet draped over the track's back fence was numbered and marked with lines to follow the horse's progression. In 1882 Muybridge's studies were published by Stanford in the landmark book, *The Horse in Motion.*

Muybridge went on to develop the "zoopraxiscope," a device in which a sequence of photographs was projected in rapid succession to create the illusion of motion. His invention was an important step in the development of motion pictures.

25
EADWEARD MUYBRIDGE
California Street Rail Road, April 10, 1878

The first of San Francisco's famous cable cars was introduced by Andrew S. Hallidie just five years before this photograph was taken. Pulled by miles of underground wire rope, cable cars replaced horse-drawn rail cars which had served for years as San Francisco's primary means of public transportation. Hallidie, a manufacturer of cables used in mining, was inspired to find a new method of transportation when he witnessed a horse-car accident that mutilated the animals. Though it was costly and there were many skeptics, most of San Francisco's horse-drawn lines were eventually converted to cable cars, which were well-suited to the city's steep hills.

26.
THOMAS HOUSEWORTH & COMPANY
Jennie Speer as Velotine in Olivette, c. 1875

The Thomas Houseworth gallery maintained an extensive collection of photographs of notables known as *Houseworth's Celebrities.* Containing more than three-thousand images, the collection included politicians, literary figures, representatives of "exotic" cultural groups and theatrical personalities. "Cabinet cards" such as this one, bearing the image of an actor in character, were particularly popular sellers. Not much is known about the actress Jennie Speer, other than she played in at least two productions, *Manola* and *Olivette,* produced by the Comley-Barton Opera Co. which toured the United States in the 1870s.

27.
HENRY W. BRADLEY AND WILLIAM HERMAN RULOFSON
Sol. Smith Russell (Bradley & Rulofson's Celebrities), c. 1875

Sol. Smith Russell was an actor who presumably toured San Francisco in the 1870s. Typically, actors in theatrical groups played multiple roles. In this composite photograph, Russell demonstrates his range by posing as three different characters.

28.
HENRY W. BRADLEY AND WILLIAM HERMAN RULOFSON
Bradley and Rulofson's Photograph Gallery, c. 1870

As an advertisement found on the back of many photographs by Bradley and Rulofson proudly notes, their studio had "the only elevator connected with a photograph gallery in the world." The thoroughly modern gallery at 429 Montgomery Street in downtown San Francisco, pictured here, previously had been occupied by photographers Robert H. Vance and Charles L. Weed.

29.
THOMAS HOUSEWORTH & CO.
The Christian Stairway (Chinese Girls' Presbyterian Mission Home, 933 Sacramento Street, San Francisco), c. 1888

Little is known about the Chinese Girls' Presbyterian Mission Home. An unusual pamphlet titled *Dragon Stories* provides a colorful, if biased, account of the home's history. It tells of a suicidal young Chinese girl, sold into slavery in China by her father and held captive by a Chinese family in San Francisco:

> Thousands of Chinese lived in San Francisco's Chinese Quarter at the time when this story happened, in the days before the earthquake and fire. Then, as now, on the Sacramento Street Hill stood the Presbyterian Mission Home. . . . The Mission was a home to all the little slave girls who could be rescued from their owners with the aid of policemen and the laws of America which do not allow even Chinese girls to be sold into slavery. About forty Chinese girls lived in the Home and were taught to read, write and speak English, to sew and to cook, to study the bible and to commit its verses to memory.
>
> – *Dragon Stories: The Bowl of Powfah and The Hundredth Maiden, Narratives of the Rescues and Romances of Chinese Slave Girls* (with photographs by Arnold Genthe and R.E. Wales, Oakland, California: The Pacific Presbyterian Publishing Group, 1908).

30.
ISAIAH WEST TABER
Untitled (Indian Artifacts), c. 1880

The origin or purpose of this arresting still-life is unknown. The orderly, scientific arrangement of the artifacts, however, suggests that it may have been intended as an anthropological record.

32.
GEORGE FISKE
Sunset Study, San Francisco Bay, 1884

Although described as a sunset view, the effect was probably achieved by underexposing a negative in daylight.

33.
GEORGE FISKE
Untitled (Nell Atkinson and Her Daughter Dorothy on Skis, Yosemite), c. 1885

George Fiske lived year-round in Yosemite Valley, where he owned and operated a photographic studio from 1883 to 1918. Nellie Atkinson, who also lived in the valley with her family, was Fiske's assistant and friend. The Oakland Museum of California holds more than three hundred photographs by Fiske, many of which picture the Atkinson and Fiske families socializing. Perhaps in a gesture of familiarity, Fiske captioned this image by scratching the name of Atkinson's little girl into the negative on the side of the sled.

34.
STIFFLER (FRANK M. or GEORGE L.)
Randsburg, Ca., Feb. 1897

The very picture of a raucous mining town, Randsburg in Kern County sprang up when gold was discovered in the area in 1895. The name is a reference to the Rand mines of South Africa.

36.
KARL STRUSS
Two Women with Kodak Camera, 1914

Made as an advertisement for Eastman Kodak, this image carefully accentuates the fun and simplicity of photography. It is also aimed squarely at women, whom the company had made the target of a major advertising campaign. Just when Kodak was emphasizing the ease with which anyone could take a picture ("you press the button, we do the rest"), Pictorialists, including Struss, set out to prove that photography, like painting or drawing, could be a handcrafted art capable of individual creative expression.

37.
WILLARD E. WORDEN
Untitled (San Francisco at Night), 1904

Worden captured an impressive night view of a thriving San Francisco just over a year before the city's devastating earthquake and fire of 1906.

39.
ARNOLD GENTHE
The Devil's Kitchen by Night, 1907
and

40.
ARNOLD GENTHE
Untitled (Mother and Child, Chinatown, San Francisco), c. 1900

In his biography, Arnold Genthe writes of one of his many explorations of San Francisco's old Chinatown:

> In the dark alleys and courtyards rickety staircases led up to tenement hovels where the derelicts of the underworld found cover. The most sinister of these was the 'Devil's Kitchen,' an evil smelling courtyard where drug addicts and suspicious characters of all sorts cooked on charcoal burners the scraps of food they had picked up in the streets, and came out only at night to squat on doorsills or to pursue their insidious ways.
>
> – Arnold Genthe, *As I Remember* (New York: John Day in association with Reynal & Hitchcock, 1936).

In fact, the area was not nearly as sinister or romantic as Genthe claimed. Like many photographers of his time, Genthe was more concerned with creating a mood or effect than with the literal recording of fact. In the case of his Chinatown photographs, this ambition was overlaid with the preconceptions of his white audience, who demanded exotica when dealing with such subjects. Nevertheless, Genthe was quite capable of an eloquent simplicity such as this tender portrait of a mother and child.

41.
ARNOLD GENTHE
Nora May French, c. 1903

Nora May French (1881–1907) was a poet and member of Genthe's Bohemian circle. She committed suicide in Carmel.

42.
WILLARD E. WORDEN
Untitled (Ruins, Golden Gate Park, San Francisco), 1906

Following the earthquake and fire of April 18, 1906, San Francisco's Golden Gate Park became home to thousands of refugees who set up camp in tent cities. Though it offered temporary shelter from the destruction of the rest of the city, the park itself had been damaged. Worden's photograph shows the ruins of Sweeney Observatory, which used to sit on Strawberry Hill in the Park.

45.
UNKNOWN (DEL MONTE CORPORATION)
Untitled (Pears), c. 1920

The autochrome was the first popular color process. Dyed starch grains were sifted on to sticky glass plates and coated with a panchromatic (sensitive to the full spectrum of visible light) emulsion. The screen of colored grains selectively exposed the emulsion producing a positive image of tiny colored specks.

Del Monte is one of the largest fruit and vegetable canners in California.

46.
SAMUEL NEWSOM, SR.
Mission Santa Barbara, c. 1904

Samuel Newsom was a San Francisco architect known for his playful Victorian houses and public buildings. Interested in the restoration of California's old Spanish missions, Newsom began studying the Santa Barbara Mission on a vacation in the area. He later published an article about its history and design in *Overland Monthly* (October 1907). His passion for mission architecture is evident in many of his designs as well as in watercolor sketches and photographs such as this one.

Also known as "blueprints," cyanotypes are made from paper saturated with light-sensitive iron salts that produce blue pigments. Though cyanotypy was invented by Sir John Herschel in the 1840s, it was used infrequently in the nineteenth century because of its bright blue color. The process gained popularity among amateurs around the turn of the century, however, due to its low cost and simple processing. The materials used to make cyanotypes are essentially the same as those used to reproduce architectural or technical drawings—which would have been familiar to Newsom.

47.
EDWARD S. CURTIS
Prayer to the Stars, c. 1910

Curtis began producing orotones in 1916 as a specialty item for his Seattle studio. The images were printed on glass, which was then backed with a mixture of gold pigment and banana oil, yielding the characteristic iridescent gold finish. Specially designed art nouveau frames held the images.

The original Curtis Studio label adhered to the back of this frame reads:

> PRAYER TO THE STARS
> This picture was made for one of the illustrations to Marah Ellis Ryan's novel "Flute of the Gods," showing the devotee as he reaches out his hands in supplication to his brothers the stars.

48.
EDWARD S. CURTIS
A Pomo Girl, from *The North American Indian,* c. 1924

Unlike conventional photographs, photogravures are made by an intaglio printing process from plates that have been chemically etched from a photographic image. The plate distributes ink on paper corresponding to the darkest areas of the original photograph or the most deeply etched areas of the plate. The complete set of Curtis's twenty-volume epic, *The North American Indian,* includes approximately 1,500 photogravures.

Before settlers came to California, the Pomo occupied an area extending from the Russian River Valley northward to Clear Lake and westward to the coast. By the 1860s, with the influx of miners and ranchers, the Pomo were forced onto reservations at Round Valley and Mendocino.

51.
ANNE BRIGMAN
Heart of the Storm, 1912

> Are we not living in an age in which we are free reasonably to do so as we please? Who is going to limit himself to one tool when two or more will make his workmanship more beautiful? I claim the right to run the gamut from lens to show-brush to gain a desired effect.
>
> – Anne Brigman, quoted in Susan Ehrens, *A Poetic Vision: The Photographs of Anne Brigman* (Santa Barbara: Santa Barbara Museum of Art, 1995).

Subscribing to a philosophy that photography need not be limited by its accuracy, Brigman altered her negatives in the darkroom to create the mysterious, atmospheric qualities of her prints. Using etching tools, pencils and paints, she selectively added or erased elements according to her imagination and vision. In this photograph, the light emanating from behind the nude's head has been enhanced for symbolic effect.

52.
ANNE BRIGMAN
The Bubble, 1905

Brigman tipped this photograph onto a mount of three successively larger layers of watercolor papers, in a style exemplary of the Photo-Secessionists, suggesting she intended the piece for exhibition.

54.
ADELAIDE MARQUAND HANSCOM
Underneath the Bough (Illustration from *The Rubáiyát of Omar Khayyám*), 1905

> A Book of Verses Underneath the Bough, A Jug of Wine, a Loaf of Bread—and Thou Beside me singing in the Wilderness—Oh, Wilderness were Paradise enow.
>
> – Omar Khayyám (Verse XII of *The Rubáiyát,* translated by Edward Fitzgerald).

Adelaide Hanscom made this image for her photographically illustrated edition of *The Rubáiyát of Omar Khayyám.* Hanscom's symbolist interpretation of the twelfth-century, Persian poem, which had become one of the most popular books of her day, featured prominent Bay Area authors and artists as models, including Joaquin Miller, George Sterling and Xavier Martinez.

56.
IMOGEN CUNNINGHAM
The Clairvoyant, c. 1910

Miniature painter Claire Shepard occupied a Seattle studio adjoining Cunningham's and often modeled for the photographer. Shepard, who considered herself clairvoyant, influenced Cunningham in her interest in theosophy and mysticism. Cunningham's ethereal images of Shepard, such as this one, can be seen as a reflection of her friend's spiritualism.

Platinum prints are made from light-sensitive iron salts, which form a metallic platinum image upon exposure to light and development. Despite the expense of materials, the process has long been popular among artists who admire platinum prints for their matte surfaces and subtle range of tonal gradations.

57.
FRANCIS BRUGUIÈRE
Beauty and Beast Fountain, Court of Flowers, 1915

This is one of a series of photographs Bruguière made of the various pavilions at San Francisco's Panama-Pacific International Exposition of 1915. Bruguière was one of the photographers in charge of the photographic section of the fair. Like many of his colleagues who championed photography as a true art form, however, he ended up boycotting the Exposition because photography was exhibited in the Department of Liberal Arts rather than Fine Arts.

58.
EDWARD WESTON
Bathing Pool, 1919

Only two other prints of this image are known to exist, along with a handful of related photographs Weston made of the pool. As he began to embrace modernist aesthetics, Weston disavowed the soft-focus, atmospheric style of his earlier work and destroyed a great deal of it. Like the other surviving prints of this image, this print was a personal gift, inscribed in this case to Weston's friend and colleague Imogen Cunningham. The two boys pictured are probably Weston's first son, Chandler, and his boyhood friend Llewellyn Bixby-Smith. The photograph was likely taken at the Bixby-Smiths' indoor pool in Irvine, California.

59.
MARGRETHE MATHER
Portrait of Florence Deshon, 1921

Florence Deshon was a close friend of Mather.

60.
IMOGEN CUNNINGHAM
Magnolia Blossom: Tower of Jewels, 1925

This is an early print of one of Cunningham's signature pieces; she was to print the negative the rest of her life. The print shown here was exhibited in the Third International Salon of the Pictorial Photographers of America, held in New York City.

61.
JOHAN HAGEMEYER
"Boots" by Kipling (George Ball), 1924

Boots is the title of a verse in English writer Rudyard Kipling's (1865–1936) *The Five Nations,* a book of poems reflecting on war. The verse appears as a "service song":

> We're foot—slog—slog—slog—sloggin' over / Africa! / Foot—foot—foot—foot—sloggin' over Africa— / (Boots—boots—boots—boots, movin' up and / down again!) / There's no discharge in the war! / Seven—six—eleven—five—nine-an'-twenty mile / to-day— / Four—eleven—seventeen—thirty-two the day / before— / (Boots—boots—boots—boots, movin' up and / down again!) / There's no discharge in the war! / Don't—don't—don't—don't—look at what's in / front of you / (Boots—boots—boots—boots, movin' up and / down again!)
>
> – Rudyard Kipling, *The Five Nations* (Garden City, New York: Doubleday, Page & Company, 1919).

62.
JOHAN HAGEMEYER
Castles of To-day, 1922

Hagemeyer inscribed this print to fellow photographer and friend Imogen Partridge (Imogen Cunningham's married name). Note his highly stylized initials in the lower right corner of the print. The image was made in San Francisco and shows the *Call* newspaper building and the Liberty House department store.

63.
HENRY A. HUSSEY
Up to the Sunshine, c. 1926

A bromoil photograph is a silver print that has been bleached with a solution that removes the dark areas of the image, allowing oil pigments applied with brushes to be absorbed in their place. Bromoil photographs can be produced in any color. Hussey noted the process on one of the many exhibition labels adhered to the back of this print. Technical experimentation was a subject of great interest and discussion among camera club members.

64.
HENRY A. HUSSEY
Signs of the Times, c. 1920

A warm-gray, layered paper mount picks up the delicate tones of the image. Adding a decorative quality to the piece, the paper mount has a deckled edge. Hussey's attention to detail apparently won him acceptance with at least one exhibition selection committee; the piece was included in John Wanamaker's Annual Exhibition of Photographers in Philadelphia in 1920.

65.
DOROTHEA LANGE
Portrait of Harry St. John Dixon, 1922

Harry Dixon, metalsmith and artist, was the younger brother of Dorothea Lange's first husband, painter Maynard Dixon.

66.
ANSEL ADAMS
Mount Ritter from Electra Peak, Summer 1931

Adams is believed to have made this photograph on a 1931 Sierra Club outing. The image was reproduced in the February 1932 issue of the *Sierra Club Bulletin.* Francis Farquhar, who gave this print and others to the Oakland Museum of California, was the editor of the *Bulletin* for many years. Like much of Adams' early work, the reverse of this print carries a decorative label with the artist's full name, Ansel Easton Adams.

68.
JOHN PAUL EDWARDS
On the Beach at Carmel, 1924

This print was exhibited at the London Salon of Photography in 1924.

69.
LAURA ADAMS ARMER
Irving Pichel as Lord Kurano, February 1923

Irving Pichel (1891–1954) was a versatile actor and director who appeared in such films as *Jezebel* (1938), *Dracula's Daughter* (1936), and *Cleopatra* (1934). His films as a director include *She* (1935) and *The Most Dangerous Game* (1932).

As an exhibition label on the back of the mount notes, this piece won an honorable mention in the Fourth Annual Frederick & Nelson Exhibition of Photographs.

71.
ARTHUR F. KALES
Easter Blossom, c. 1920

A bromoil transfer print is a variation on the bromoil process in which the still-wet bromoil print is transferred to another sheet of paper in a press.

73.
SIGISMUND BLUMANN
Dawn, Sunset, Moonlight (Experiments in Contrast), 1925–26

Originally four in the series, this group of photographs was shown in a July 1927 exhibition of The Camera Club of New York. A member of the exhibition's print committee typed a critique of the series:

> Here is a determined, even aggressive, attempt to use a fine lead of nature in the hope of bettering it for art's sake. Your attempt at simplification has reduced good material to the service of a silhouette pattern. . . . If you could find some element of sequential interest connecting the base of the tree with the distant building and see that the foreground was differentiated in its tone from the tree (made lighter) you would land the plate a higher class than it now is.

The building in the distance is Oakland's city hall, still standing today.

74.
HENRY M. TAKAHASHI
Spare Time, 1936

Amateur photographer Henry M. Takahashi was a Berkeley resident and member of the Japanese American Camera Club of San Francisco, formed in 1930. As the patchwork of exhibition labels on the back of this print testifies, his efforts were seen at camera club exhibitions across the country, from San Francisco to Philadelphia, Chicago and Indianapolis. Though taken at a time when most serious photographers had embraced modernist aesthetics, the photograph harkens back to the soft-focus pictorial style of a decade earlier. Pictorialism persisted among amateur photographers in camera clubs across the country.

75.
ROGER STURTEVANT
Ectoplasm of the Charleston, c. 1925

A brief note in the photographer's hand on the back of the print gives a sense of the Bohemian world of 1920s San Francisco:

> Miss Jill Saergent former Charlestoner at the Aladdin Nite Club—San Francisco—swore the Charleston would never die when along came the St. Souir hop and Valencia. The materialization of the now deceased conventions thru my medium kamera.

76.
WILLIAM MORTENSEN
Marco Polo, n.d.

This print was exhibited at the 1937 London Salon of Photography.

77.
WILLIAM MORTENSEN
The Spider Torture (The Heretic), c. 1934

In a series of articles published in *Camera Craft* magazine, William Mortensen argued the merits of his highly manipulated, allegorical imagery by railing against the increasingly popular "straight" photography:

> Truth in art lies in the rendering of experience—or rather in the rendering of things-as-they-are-experienced, not of things-as-they-are. Psychological truth, not scientific accuracy, is the species of veracity with which art is concerned—conformity not to fact, but to the mind's way of apprehending fact. . . .
>
> –William Mortensen, "Venus and Vulcan," *Camera Craft,* June 1934.

78.
WILLARD VAN DYKE
Ventilators, (Telegraph Avenue), 1932

One of the main thoroughfares of the East Bay, Telegraph Avenue runs from downtown Oakland to Sproul Plaza at the University of California, Berkeley. Van Dyke's recognition of the beauty to be found in such common, industrial subject matter is typical of Group f.64 photographers.

80.
ALMA LAVENSON
Leaf Decoration, 1933

Lavenson's plant studies reflect the influence of her friend and teacher Imogen Cunningham. Though they chose similar subject matter, their approaches were quite different. Lavenson's plant forms tend toward the abstract, exhibiting flattened patterns playing across shallow spaces, whereas Cunningham's plant images emphasize their sculptural qualities.

81.
JOHN PAUL EDWARDS
Oil Drums, c. 1932

The reverse of this print carries exhibition labels from the Orange Camera Club, Brooklyn Institute of Arts and Sciences.

83.
EDWARD WESTON
Portrait of James Cagney, 1933

After seeing the portraits taken of him by Edward Weston, actor James Cagney wrote to the photographer on December 28, 1933:

> I've gone over the proofs and find it very difficult to make a choice. The "ham" comes through so often—and usually wasn't trying, believe me—that I fear we'll have to content ourselves with a few of the least "actorish" ones.
>
> – Quoted in Amy Conger, *Edward Weston: Photographs from the Collection of the Center for Creative Photography* (Tucson: Center for Creative Photography and The University of Arizona, 1992).

84.
SONYA NOSKOWIAK
Portrait of Robinson Jeffers, c. 1938

Robinson Jeffers (1887–1962) was a poet and member of the Carmel avant-garde with whom Noskowiak and her companion, Edward Weston, associated. Like Weston, Jeffers found inspiration for his art in the Carmel coastline, writing:

> . . . for the first time in my life I could see people living—amid magnificent unspoiled scenery—essentially as they did in the Idyls or the Sagas, or in Homer's Ithaca. Here life was purged of its ephemeral accretions. Men were plowing the headland, hovered by white sea-gulls, as they have done for thousands of years.
>
> – Robinson Jeffers, quoted in James D. Hart, *A Companion to California* (Berkeley: University of California Press, 1987).

86.
IMOGEN CUNNINGHAM
Portrait of Marian Simpson, Painter, 1934

Marian Simpson was a Berkeley painter and friend of Cunningham.

87.
ANNE BRIGMAN
West Elephant Tower, Treasure Island, 1940

Late in her career Brigman made a series of photographs at the 1939 Golden Gate International Exposition in San Francisco, where her work was being shown in an exhibition of California artists. The quality of fantasy exhibited in the Exposition's architecture apparently inspired her.

88.
RUTH BERNHARD
Creation (Doll's Head), Hollywood, California, 1936

Though Bernhard is not generally thought of as a surrealist, in this photograph she juxtaposes logically unconnected elements, creating an image evocative of subconscious thought. In keeping with a surrealist interpretation of the image, Bernhard's account of its evolution shows an intuitive approach:

> Everyday, while living in Hollywood, I browsed on Hollywood Boulevard. Because I loved dolls, I would visit this doll hospital. I saw a doll's head in the window. I went inside and asked the man if I could buy the head. He asked me what kind of body I wanted with it. I told him that I didn't want a body, only the head. He asked what I was going to do with it, and I told him that I didn't know yet. I took the little head home with me. The next day I went browsing on Hollywood Boulevard again and I passed a cigar store. In the window of this store was a hand holding Turkish cigarettes. I bought the hand and took it home to my studio. I put the whole thing together as if I had known

all my life that this was what I was supposed to do: put the head in the hand and put a landscape photograph I took while I was in Colorado, behind it. This was the first photograph I made after I met Edward Weston. So you see, it all fell into place as it always does for me: I don't plan, I just do it. When you get this kind of message, you are not allowed to say no to it.

– Quoted in Ilee Kaplan, *Ruth Bernhard: Known and Unknown* (Long Beach: University Art Museum, California State University, Long Beach, 1996).

89.
ROGER STURTEVANT
Spring # 3, c. 1929

This image, or another from the same series, was exhibited in the influential modernist exhibit *Film und Foto* which took place in Stuttgart, Germany in 1929. The checklist for the show lists its title as *Pflanzenstudie mit Glass* (Plant Study with Glass).

90.
CEDRIC WRIGHT
Weathered Stump, Timberline, c. 1935

The mountain photographer is interpreting the face of nature—that mysterious infinity; eternally a refuge, a reservoir, an amplifier of the spirit, a mother of dreams, a positive though elusive voice in whose depth lies its subtle power. Those who interpret best are never so content as when under the influence of mountain surroundings, where silence is rich in mute assurance and beauty. Here the quality of emotional knowing is most clear. . . .

– Cedric Wright, "Mountain Photography," *Sierra Club Bulletin,* February 1941.

In 1960 the Sierra Club published *Words of the Earth,* a posthumous collection of photographs by Cedric Wright. Editor Nancy Newhall sifted through hundreds of Wright's poetic writings, inspired by the Sierras, to create captions for the images. For this photograph, she chose the simple phrase, "intense beauty is liberation."

The reverse of the mount contains a label for the San Francisco International Salon, California Camera Club.

92.
SONYA NOSKOWIAK
Cactus, 1932

Noskowiak likely made this image on an outing with her companion and teacher, Edward Weston, to a friend's cactus garden in Monterey on November 8, 1932. Weston made a similar close-up of the same type of cactus that day, describing the outing in his *Daybooks.* Noskowiak's *Cactus* was probably one of the photographs she showed at the auspicious first exhibition of Group f.64 at the M. H. de Young Memorial Museum in San Francisco in 1932.

95.
EDWARD WESTON
Nude, 1936

I sat in the bedroom doorway [to the sunroof] with the room in a shadow behind me. Even then the light was almost overpoweringly bright. When I ducked my head to avoid looking into it, Edward said, "Just keep it that way." He was never happy with the shadow on the right arm, and I was never happy with the crooked hair part and the bobby pins. But when I see the picture unexpectedly, I remember most vividly Edward examining the print with a magnifying glass to decide if the few visible pubic hairs would prevent him from shipping it through the mails.

– Charis Wilson, *Edward Weston: Nudes* (Millerton, New York: Aperture, 1977).

96.
EDWARD WESTON
Sea Shell, 1927 (print 1930)

Edward Weston always insisted his still-lifes of sea shells and vegetables were created with purely aesthetic and formal motives. Those viewing the photographs often saw other subtexts, such as Tina Modotti's reaction upon seeing the first of his sea shell images:

Edward—nothing before in art has affected me like these photographs. I cannot look at them long without feeling exceedingly perturbed, they disturbed me not only mentally but physically. There is something so pure and at the same time so perverse about them. They contain both the innocence of natural things and the morbidity of a sophisticated, distorted mind. They make me think of lilies and embryos. They are mystical and erotic.

– Quoted in Thomas Weston Fels, et al., *Watkins to Weston: 101 Years of California Photography, 1849–1950* (Santa Barbara and Niwot, Colorado: Santa Barbara Museum of Art and Roberts Rinehart, 1992).

98.
ALMA LAVENSON
Child with Doll, 1932

Lavenson made very few studies of the human body and only rarely photographed people. She made this photograph for a 1932 exhibition at the M. H. de Young Memorial Museum entitled *Showing of Hands.*

100.
BRETT WESTON
Mexico (Bread in a Basket), 1926

Brett Weston took this photograph at age fifteen when he lived briefly in Mexico with his father, Edward Weston, and Tina Modotti. Brett was taking lessons from his father in composing and printing photographs.

101.
IMOGEN CUNNINGHAM
Cowboy at Coonsaw, 1934

In the depths of the Great Depression, the Unemployed Exchange Association (UXA) near Oroville, California, received a federal grant to convert a failed sawmill into a cooperative. Cunningham knew Paul S. Taylor, a University of California, Berkeley, professor of economics who was studying self-help cooperatives. Taylor invited Cunningham and several other Bay Area photographers, including Dorothea Lange (whom he later married), to provide photographic documentation for his research. The resulting images, including this picture, were some of Cunningham's earliest documentary photographs.

102.
DOROTHEA LANGE
White Angel Breadline, San Francisco, c. 1933

The White Angel Jungle was a soup kitchen close to Lange's studio on San Francisco's Embarcadero. It was established by Lois Jordan, a working-class widow who relied solely on unsolicited contributions to feed the Depression's hungry. Jordan's "roll up your sleeves" response to the suffering she saw on the street is partly credited with inspiring Lange to abandon studio work and photograph what was happening in the world around her. Lange made this image on her first outing as a street photographer, well before she began working for the government. The Oakland Museum of California holds the original negative.

103.
DOROTHEA LANGE
Untitled (Matanuska Colonist Bound for Alaska), May 1935

In May 1935, sixty-seven families passed through San Francisco as they left their homes in northern Minnesota for the Matanuska Valley, Alaska. They represented the first attempt of the Division of Rural Rehabilitation, a Federal agency, to resettle distressed people into newly established colonies. As part of her work for the Federal Emergency Relief Administration, Lange documented the migration of the Matanuska colonists. The Oakland Museum of California holds the original negative.

104.
DOROTHEA LANGE
Man Beside Wheelbarrow, San Francisco, 1934

> The photograph of the man with his head on his arms, for instance—five years earlier, I would have thought it enough to take a picture of a man, no more. But now, I wanted to take a picture of a man as he stood in his world—in this case, a man with his head down, with his back against the wall, with his livelihood, like the wheelbarrow, overturned.
>
> – Dorothea Lange, quoted in Daniel Dixon, *Modern Photography,* December 1952.

Lange made this image, like *White Angel Breadline,* before she began working for the government. The Oakland Museum of California holds the original negative.

105 and **106**
OTTO HAGEL
Untitled (Salinas Lettuce Strike), 1936

> For two days the air in downtown Salinas was thick with tear gas, sulfur gas, nauseating gas, the sound of shotgun blasts, the cries of strikers, the wail of sirens, and the groans of men whose heads had been cracked open by police billy clubs.
>
> – Richard Steven Street, "Salinas on Strike," *History of Photography* 12, no. 2 (April–June 1988).

In the fall of 1936, packing shed workers at lettuce fields near Salinas, California, went on strike. In response, growers brought in strikebreakers, armed deputies and machine gun towers. The conflict turned bloody on September 15 and 16, with pitched battles waged on the streets of Salinas.

Press photographers came from all over Northern California, only to face arrest and harassment from police sympathetic to the growers. Burdened with heavy press cameras, which took four-by-five-inch negatives, photographers were easy targets for the authorities. Moving among the crowds was Otto Hagel, a freelance photographer from Germany. Hagel was carrying the latest instrument favored by German photojournalists: a small, lightweight camera using 35mm film. Inconspicuous and mobile, he was able to move swiftly, capturing action missed by other photographers.

The Oakland Museum of California holds Hagel's original negatives from the Salinas Lettuce Strike, found among Dorothea Lange's estate.

108.
ARTHUR ROTHSTEIN
Untitled (Vernon Evans and Family, Headed West from Lemmon, South Dakota), Summer 1936

Found among Dorothea Lange's papers, Rothstein's photograph is typical of those taken for the Farm Security Administration (FSA), an agency for which both Lange and Rothstein worked. An inscription on the back shows the level of detail FSA photographers were expected to record:

> Vernon Evans and family, of Lemmon, S.D., leaving the grasshopper-ridden and drought-stricken area for a new start in Oregon or Washington. Expects to arrive at Yakima in time for hop-picking. Makes about 200 miles a day in Model-T Ford. Lives in tent. Picture taken near Missoula, Montana, on Highway 10.

109.
RONDAL PARTRIDGE
Untitled (Men Lined Up for Relief), c. 1936

and

110.
RONDAL PARTRIDGE
Untitled (Unemployed Man), c. 1936

Ron Partridge, the son of Imogen Cunningham and Roi Partridge, was Dorothea Lange's apprentice and darkroom assistant for many years. These photographs, found in Lange's estate when she died, bear the inscription "Credit Ron Partridge" in her hand, evidence of their close working relationship.

111.
PETER STACKPOLE
Cable Saddle (San Francisco–Oakland Bay Bridge), 1935

> The bridgemen were all in their safety helmets. One of them saw me and said, "Hey kid, why don't you come out with us? You'll get some good pictures." That was the invitation I wanted. . . . He took me out to where he was working, kept an eye on me and taught me how to climb ladders without blacking out. We went up maybe 150 feet over the towers. After about the third day, I got my bridgemen's legs.
>
> – Peter Stackpole, quoted in L. Thomas Frye and Therese Heyman, *Peacetime, Wartime & Hollywood: Photographs of Peter Stackpole* (Oakland: The Oakland Museum, 1992).

112.
PETER STACKPOLE
Quitting Time (San Francisco–Oakland Bay Bridge), 1935

In the 1930s Peter Stackpole photographed the building of both the Golden Gate and Bay Bridges. His images captured not only the dizzying perspectives from atop the towers but the men who risked their lives to connect the shores of San Francisco Bay. In this image Stackpole captured the solemn faces of a bridge crew quitting early after learning that one of their own had fallen to his death.

115.
JOHN GUTMANN
Yes, Columbus Did Discover America!, San Francisco, 1938

This piece exemplifies two themes consistently apparent in Gutmann's work: An interest in the automobile as a symbol of American culture, and signs as both pictures and captions.

117.
GEORGE HURRELL
Jean Harlow, 1934 (printed 1980–81)

In a style epitomizing the carefully controlled glamour of the studio system, Hurrell captured the sexy playfulness that made Jean Harlow one of the biggest stars in Hollywood. Three years later the actress was dead of uremic poisoning at the age of twenty-six.

118.
PETER STACKPOLE
Marlene Dietrich, Reclining, in "Kismet," 1943

> I think she liked the way she looked in this outfit. She didn't think I could get any bad angles on it, but she didn't demand to see the photographs like she had in an earlier meeting.
>
> – Peter Stackpole, quoted in L. Thomas Frye and Therese Heyman, *Peacetime, Wartime & Hollywood: Photographs of Peter Stackpole* (Oakland: The Oakland Museum, 1992).

Stackpole was one of the first four staff photographers hired by *LIFE.* In the fifteen years he worked for the magazine, his primary beat was the motion picture industry. His portrait of Marlene Dietrich was taken on the set of *Kismet,* an "Arabian Nights" fantasy for MGM.

119.
ANSEL ADAMS
Sentinel Dome, Yosemite, 1936

The Jeffrey Pine on the top of Sentinel Dome was a well-known Yosemite landmark. Carleton Watkins pitched his darktent under it in the nineteenth century, and countless sightseers hiked to the tree, which has since fallen, to have their pictures taken beside it. Adams likely made this advertising image for his most important client of the 1930s: The Yosemite Park & Curry Company, which ran the valley's concessions. The woman in the center is probably Patricia (Patsy) English whom Adams hired in 1936 to model and to assist him in the darkroom.

121.
DOROTHEA LANGE
Untitled (Richmond Woman), 1942

World War II brought major changes to the Bay Area's social makeup. The population grew by thirty-five percent in just five years, with thousands of people, particularly African Americans, drawn to the region by the booming defense industry. Traditionally barred from industrial jobs, women and minorities were now welcomed into the defense industry, thanks to wartime labor shortages. The black population of Richmond, home to Kaiser shipyards, multiplied twenty times during the war. Lange recorded the social transformation happening just a few miles from her home in Berkeley. The Oakland Museum of California holds the original negative of this beneficiary of the wartime boom.

122.
DOROTHEA LANGE
Japanese Children with Tags, Hayward, California, May 8, 1942

In addition to documenting the Bay Area's economic boom, Lange captured the darker side of the war at home. As droves of minorities spilled into the Bay Area for better jobs, the War Relocation Authority (WRA) forcibly relocated people of Japanese descent to internment camps on President Roosevelt's orders. Although she was opposed to the relocation, Lange worked for the WRA, using her access to document what she believed was a shameful process. Not surprisingly, the WRA, Intent on controlling the image of relocation presented to the public, impounded many of Lange's photographs.

123.
MARION POST WOLCOTT
Tenant Farmer's Children, the Younger One with Rickets, Near Wadesboro, North Carolina, 1938

Wolcott made this photograph for the Farm Security Administration on a trip to North Carolina.

124.
ANSEL ADAMS
Mount Williamson from Manzanar, California, 1945

Manzanar was the site of one of the War Relocation Authority's internment camps, where Japanese Americans were confined for the duration of World War II. Though Adams, like Dorothea Lange, had photographed internees of the Manzanar Relocation Center just a few years earlier, in this image he characteristically presents the area as a pristine wilderness, untainted by political or social realities.

125.
ANSEL ADAMS
Portrai˙ of Maynard Dixon, 1945

Although he considered them trivial compared to landscapes, Adams produced some remarkable portraits. This melancholy portrait of Maynard Dixon was made a year before the painter's death.

126.
EDWARD WESTON
Cypress and Stone Crop (Point Lobos), 1946

> Point Lobos! I saw it with different eyes yesterday than those of nearly fifteen years ago. And I worked, how I worked! And I have results! And I shall go again—and again!
>
> – Edward Weston, 1924, quoted in Thomas Weston Fels, et al., *Watkins to Weston: 101 Years of California Photography 1849–1950* (Santa Barbara and Niwot, Colorado: Santa Barbara Museum of Art and Roberts Rinehart, 1992).

Point Lobos, near Carmel, provided inspiration for Edward Weston for more than twenty years. In contrast to his early work there, his later images at Lobos are darker, more sober and less sensuous.

127.
MAN RAY
Rayograph, 1943

During the war, French emigré Man Ray left his home in Paris and returned to the United States. He lived and worked in Hollywood from 1940 to 1951. Rayographs are actually photograms, images made without the use of a camera or lens by placing objects directly on the surface of sensitized paper or film and exposing them to light. The oldest method of creating images photographically, photograms are negative traces of the outlines of objects.

128.
V LEM KRIZ
Amour d'Autrefois, 1945

The title translates to *Love of the Bygone.*

135.
WYNN BULLOCK
Torso in Window, 1954

This excerpt from Bullock's writings precedes a selection of his nudes from the 1950s, including *Torso in Window:*

> One of the ways to emphasize both space and time is to develop your sense of opposites. If you skillfully photograph an older object together with a younger one, the qualities of each are enhanced by their contrasting characters. As soon as I became aware of this, I became aware of the difference between seeing and perceiving. Seeing is an automatic

> process, perceiving is a mental, more complex process. Out of perceiving begins growth.
>
> – Wynn Bullock, in *The Enchanted Landscape: Photographs 1940–1975* (New York: Aperture Foundation, Inc., 1993).

139.
HARRY BOWDEN
E.R. and Austin, October 1953

Bowden maintained a close friendship with his model Edith R., who appears in many of his photographs.

140.
IMOGEN CUNNINGHAM
Nuns at a Calder Show, 1950

> Last July I was at the Perls Gallery in Los Angeles when there were a lot of nuns visiting the Calder show. I assure you that was a sight—so without reading my meter or speaking to anyone, I quickly set my Rollei down on a desk and shot a little unpremeditated scene of one young nun putting a mobile in motion and an old one sitting trying to find out all about it from the brochure.
>
> – Imogen Cunningham to Minor White, July 7, 1954, quoted in Richard Lorenz, *Imogen Cunningham: Ideas Without End: A Life in Photographs* (San Francisco: Chronicle Books, 1993).

141.
ROBERT FRANK
San Francisco (from *The Americans*), 1956

In 1955 Swiss-born photographer Robert Frank became the first European to receive a Guggenheim Fellowship. He used the grant to travel across the United States photographing scenes of ordinary American life. Frank documented the highways, diners, parades, juke boxes and flags that spoke of American culture. But as an outsider he was able to look beneath the surface of 1950s American wholesomeness to reveal humor, sadness, alienation, racism, and malaise. The body of work that resulted from his travels was first published in France as *Les Américains* in 1958. The second edition was published in the United States in 1959, with an introduction by Jack Kerouac.

142.
IMOGEN CUNNINGHAM
The Unmade Bed, 1957

Cunningham always claimed to have made this photograph for her friend Dorothea Lange. Lange had instructed her photography students to make "portraits" of their own environments. Intrigued, Cunningham decided to do the assignment herself, with this result.

143.
DOROTHEA LANGE
Untitled (Defendant and Attorney), Public Defender series, 1957

Late in her career, chronic illness restricted Lange to working close to her Berkeley home. Driven to find subject matter with social content, she made a series of photographs examining the criminal courts in Alameda County. Always sympathetic to the poor and disenfranchised, Lange chose to follow the cases of those in need of public legal assistance. Here, newly appointed public defender Martin Pulich (later an Alameda County Superior Court judge) is seen defending a client. The Oakland Museum of California holds the original negative.

144.
DOROTHEA LANGE
Untitled (Defendant's Wife and Baby), Public Defender series, 1957

> Her husband got a sixteen-year-old babysitter who . . . advanced herself sexually beyond what you would expect from some kids. He took the kid to San Bernardino, and then when the parents attempted contact he gave false information about it, and got sent to prison. The only man I ever represented who—charged with statutory rape—went to state prison, and that poor woman [his wife] was loyal to that absolute animal. She was there all the time.
>
> – Public Defender Martin Pulich, quoted by Therese Thau Heyman in *Celebrating a Collection: The Work of Dorothea Lange* (Oakland: The Oakland Museum, 1978).

The Oakland Museum of California holds the original negative.

145.
RUTH BERNHARD
Luminous Form, 1962

Bernhard was known to manipulate her photographs of nudes for expressive effect by making double exposures and printing multiple negatives. This image, however, appears to have been taken through rippled glass.

148.
TODD WALKER
Untitled (Nude), 1969

The Sabattier effect (also known as solarization) refers to a partial tonal reversal caused by re-exposing prints or film to light during development. The phenomenon was named for Frenchman Armand Sabattier, who first noted it in 1862.

150.
HELEN NESTOR
Sadie Hawkins Day # 4 (from the *Haight/Ashbury* series), 1968

The Panhandle is a long, narrow strip of Golden Gate Park extending into the Haight-Ashbury district of San Francisco. Scene of many impromptu happenings, the Panhandle was the location of "Sadie Hawkins Day," a hippie burlesque of the old high school theme dance. The Oakland Museum of California holds the original negative of this image.

153.
IMOGEN CUNNINGHAM
Morris Graves in His Leek Garden, 1973

Following her ninetieth birthday in 1973, Cunningham made this photograph of Morris Graves for a series on elderly people called *After Ninety.* Graves was a Northwest painter who had been denied conscientious-objector status and was imprisoned for refusing to serve during World War II. Cunningham photographed Graves in 1950 after his release, but subsequently he was reluctant to pose for her. The reclusive artist had apparently felt tormented during that first session, but in 1973 he allowed Cunningham to photograph him at his Loleta, California, home. She made separate images of the artist and the land, which she later printed as multiple exposures to suggest Graves's spiritualism.

154.
THOMAS WEIR
The Diggers, c. 1968

In San Francisco's Haight-Ashbury district of the 1960s, the Diggers were the conscience of the counterculture movement. The radical collective sought to transform staid American values by questioning accepted mores of property, sexuality, family, freedom and money. Far from a traditional activist group, the collective promoted its ideology through what can only be described as a form of street theater. An early participant in the collective, actor Peter Coyote (pictured here wearing a hat), recalls his first encounter with the group:

> I remember vividly the first day in 1966 that I went to the Panhandle with Emmett [Grogan] to visit the Digger Free Food. Hearty stew was being ladled out of large steel milk cans and dispensed to a long line of ragged street people. . . . The line of waiting people, clutching their ubiquitous tin cups, passed through a large square constructed of six-foot-long bright yellow two-by-fours: the "Free Frame of Reference." In order to receive a meal, one stepped through and received a tiny yellow replica about two inches square, attached to a cord for wearing. . . .
>
> – Peter Coyote, *Sleeping Where I Fall: A Chronicle* (Washington, D.C.: Counterpoint, 1988).

In addition to giving away free food, the Diggers ran a Free Store at Cole and Carl streets in the Haight. Merchandise was free, and so was the role-playing: customers could choose to be manager and rearrange the store as they pleased.

155.
BILL OWENS
We're really happy. Our kids are healthy, we eat good food and we have a really nice home (from the series *Suburbia*), c. 1970

and

156.
BILL OWENS
I wanted Christina to learn some responsibility for cleaning her room, but it didn't work (from the series *Suburbia),* c. 1970

Bill Owens's series *Suburbia,* a two-year project begun in 1968, was published in a book of the same name in 1973. In the introduction Owens writes:

> This book is about my friends and the world I live in. In the fall of 1968 I began working as a photographer for the Livermore (California) *Independent.* My daily routine took me into the homes of hundreds of families and into contact with the social life of three suburban communities.
>
> The people I met enjoy the life-style of the suburbs. They have realized the American Dream. They are proud to be home owners and to have achieved material success.
>
> To me nothing seemed familiar, yet everything was very, very familiar. At first I suffered from culture shock. I wanted to photograph everything, thousands of photographs. Then slowly I began to put my thoughts and feelings together and to document Americans in Suburbia. It took two years.
>
> – Bill Owens, *Suburbia* (San Francisco: Straight Arrow Books, 1973).

158.
RICHARD MISRACH
Tumbleweed, 1973

In 1972 Richard Misrach received a grant from the National Endowment for the Arts to document Berkeley's notorious Telegraph Avenue, a bastion of sixties counterculture. In the afterword to the resulting book, *Telegraph 3 A.M.*, he wrote:

> The Avenue had gone through many sobering changes since the flower children era: street people were crashing in parking lots, filthy streets and condemned buildings, and the idealistic and spirited rebellion of the late sixties had been all but destroyed by the "system's" unresponsiveness. A bitter, disheartened mood pervaded the Avenue. Yet, there remained the spark of defiance and endurance that persists as a reminder of a noble struggle.
>
> – Richard Misrach, *Telegraph 3 A.M.* (Berkeley, California: Cornucopia Press, 1974).

159.
JACK WELPOTT
Untitled (Girl at Window with Mask), 1972

This print was given to Helen Johnston by Jack Welpott and his then-wife and colleague Judy Dater with the inscription, "Xmas—1972." Johnston's Focus Gallery on Union Street, which opened in 1966, was one of San Francisco's earliest and most important fine art photography galleries. In 1972 Johnston won the Oakland Museum's Dorothea Lange Award for outstanding contributions to photography.

161.
JUDY DATER
Nehemiah, 1975

This photograph is from a larger body of work by Dater known as *Men and Women.* The print is from her 1981 portfolio *Men/Women, Portfolio II.*

162.
JUDY DATER
Twinka, 1970

Twinka, a favorite model of Dater's, is painter Wayne Thiebaud's daughter. She is the subject of Dater's most famous photograph, *Imogen and Twinka* (1974), which depicts the impish ninety-year-old Imogen Cunningham peering around a tree at the nude Twinka. Both images are published in *Women and Other Visions: Photographs by Judy Dater and Jack Welpott* (Dobbs Ferry, New York: Morgan & Morgan, Inc. 1975).

163.
ROBERT HEINECKEN
State of the Art/Computer Image Enhancement and Analysis, December 9, 1976

Though he has never owned his own camera, Heinecken is concerned with the way photography is used and manipulated. Rather than concentrate on superior camera and printing techniques, he appropriates imagery from television, advertising and magazines.

165.
LELAND RICE
Wall Site Series (Spot lights, stretcher bars), 1977

Rice uses the camera to crop the world into colorful, almost painterly, abstractions. The illusion of flattened space is disrupted only by the inclusion of a few recognizable objects.

166.
EDMUND TESKE
Mono Lake, 1977

Scene of many environmental battles, the dying Mono Lake near Yosemite becomes apocalyptic in Teske's vision. Influenced by Man Ray, Teske used multiple negatives and solarization (a technique in which a partially developed photograph is re-exposed to light before the image has been fixed) to achieve expressive effects.

167.
BRETT WESTON
Underwater Nude, 1979

Weston made this image and other underwater nudes at his Carmel Valley home, where he had installed a custom-designed black pool. An underground viewing chamber with a window to the pool allowed him to shoot underwater.

168.
TED ORLAND
Inspiration Point, Yosemite, 1975

One of the most photographed places in the world, Yosemite's breathtaking views are familiar even to those who have never visited. Here, Orland makes subtle reference to one of his many predecessors, Carleton Watkins, whose mammoth plates of the valley are characterized by their arched tops. But unlike Watkins, whose photographs celebrated Yosemite's majesty, Orland emphasizes the signposts of tourism in the valley, where the experience of visiting the park is mediated by reproductions.

170.
VICTOR LANDWEBER
Imperial Debonair, from *American Cameras,* 1981

> During the 1940s and 50s, while cameras of German and Japanese manufacture brought new ease and versatility to photography, the American photographic industry found its best shot at domestic competition to be a baroque elaboration of the non-adjustable camera in which style was substituted for function and glib packaging became the principal consumer draw. These cameras, incapable of any but the simplest modes of operation . . . were, like many American goods, designed more to be sold than used.
>
> – Victor Landweber, quoted in *Victor Landweber Photographs: 1967–1984* (San Diego: Museum of Photographic Arts, 1985).

Beginning in the late 1970s, Victor Landweber began a series of formal "portraits" of inexpensive American cameras. Brightly colored, architectural, each camera surrounded by a halo, the images recall the slick technique found in advertising photography.

171.
RICHARD MISRACH
Desert Fire # 1, Burning Palms, 1983

In the desert, land and sky extend for miles in every direction, a vastness which dwarfs even a forest of towering palms. Photographic ambiguity, even in an oversized print, heightens this distortion of scale and creates the illusion of a more compacted space.

172.
ROGER MINICK
Woman With Scarf, Yosemite (from the *Sightseer* Series), 1980

Nineteenth-century photographers of Yosemite often used tiny human figures, set in the distance against soaring peaks, to emphasize the sublime, awe-inspiring scale of the valley. Minick fills a good portion of his frame with the back of a sightseer obstructing our view, her souvenir kerchief revealing the extent to which Yosemite's famous vistas have been transformed into tourist attractions.

173.
ROBBERT FLICK
At Vasquez Rocks # 6, 1983–85

Flick shatters the traditional oversized landscape view into a patchwork of small fragments. The grid suggests the way civilization imposes logical, man-made systems upon the earth in order to bring its untamed vastness under human control. It also mimics the way we parcel land, transforming it into a commodity with monetary value and the potential to become property.

174.
LINDA S. CONNOR
Walker Pass, 1983

Printing-out paper is so named because the photographic image "prints out" or reveals itself beneath a negative upon exposure to light, without development. Common in the nineteenth century, it is generally used today only for photographic proofs. Prints made with printing-out paper are usually toned and tend to possess a reddish or purplish hue.

175.
GREG MACGREGOR
Testing Electric Detonator, Crockett, California (from *Minor Explosions* series), 1980

A former physicist, MacGregor spent fifteen years creating and photographing small explosions in a variety of locations. The figure detonating the bomb in this photograph is the whimsical sculptor Clayton Bailey.

178.
JO ANN CALLIS
Lizards and Roses, 1980

In 1980 Callis began a series of photographs inhabited by animals, fish and birds.

> Callis's animals are placed in situations that emphasize their physiognomic strangeness and their psychological unknowability. We empathize with these creatures as we recognize the ambiguity (and possible peril) of their settings . . .
>
> – Buzz Spector, *Jo Ann Callis: Objects of Reverie* (Des Moines: Des Moines Art Center/Black Sparrow Press, 1989).

179.
LAURA VOLKERDING
Salt Ponds, 1982

Laura Volkerding's panorama is made from four view camera negatives placed side-by-side in succession, a technique used by Eadweard Muybridge and other nineteenth-century landscape photographers.

180.
LEWIS BALTZ
Four photographs from San Quentin Point, 1985

An exponent of "topographical" photography, Baltz strives, in his words, to convey "sterile information with no emotional content" (Naomi Rosenblum, *A World History of Photography,* New York: Abbeville Press, 1989). These four images are from his *San Quentin Point* portfolio, containing twenty-five unmounted eight-by-ten-inch prints. Published by Hyperion Press in an edition of thirty-five, the portfolio is housed in a simple, black wooden box.

181.
CATHERINE WAGNER
Untitled (from *American Classroom* series), 1984

Catherine Wagner's photographs visually investigate the influence of science in contemporary culture. Seeing, often aided by devices like microscopes, telescopes and x-rays, is central to modern scientific inquiry. Using photography, itself an instrument of science, Wagner records the inside of an eerily uninhabited science classroom.

183.
LYNN HERSHMAN
Phantom Limb # 1, 1989–90

> We've become a society of screens, of layers that keep us from knowing the truth, as if the truth were unbearable; too much for us to deal with—like our feelings. So we deal with things through replications, through copying, through screens, through facsimiles, through fiction and faction.
>
> – Lynn Hershman, quoted in Tory Dent, "First Person Plural: The Work of Lynn Hershman," *Arts Magazine,* Nov. 1990.

185.
HENRY WESSEL
Real Estate Photograph No. 91167, 1990–91

Henry Wessel's series *House Pictures* was inspired by the photographs he saw as a boy in his mother's New Jersey realty office. Like the images realtors use to sell homes, Wessel's photographs are straightforward, close-up and uninhabited, a kind of vernacular portraiture.

186.
CARRIE MAE WEEMS
Untitled (Woman Brushing Hair), 1990

This photograph is from Weems's 1990 *Untitled (Kitchen Table Series),* a fictional story about an African American woman's struggles with love, loss, fidelity, politics, money, self-worth and raising children. The photographic narrative unfolds within the spare confines of a kitchen table, the place where families gather to find both emotional and physical nourishment. The series was originally accompanied by panels of text, written with an ear for the spoken word, that loosely parallel the images:

> Seeking clarity and purpose, she spoke about the problems with her momma who said, "There's a difference between men and women. I can't tell ya what to do. But I can tell you that I sided with men so long I forgot women had a side. Truth slapped me so hard up-side my head, I cried for days, got so I couldn't wash my own behind. Shonuff blue. Biggest fool in the world. Turning my back on friends for a piece of man. Oh sure, I've had a man or two—I mean with a capital "M"—but like a good friend, hard to come by. But look, ya got a good man, man puts up with mo a yo mess than the law allows. If he loves ya, ya best take yo behind home, drop them guns on the floor and work it out. Ya gotta give a little to get a little, that's the story of life."

188.
JERRY BURCHARD
Grant Avenue, USA 87, 1987

Grant Avenue is in San Francisco's Chinatown.

189.
JO WHALEY
Rubberloupe (from the series *Natura Morta*), 1992 (printed 1999)

> Under the guise of the traditional still-life genre, the *Natura Morta* series reflects the anxieties that arc between our technological civilization and the natural environment. . . . Historically, a perfect display of the earth's bounty was celebrated through paint. My still life's echo those compositions, but may feature fruit that is half-eaten and abandoned to mold as a metaphor for our culture's use of natural resources. The purely beautiful . . . is intruded upon by quirky elements that indicate that something is amiss. . . .
>
> Although [the prints] are all straight, unmanipulated color photographs, they are infused with a painterly sensibility. I construct and paint a theatrical environment for the still life elements, which provides a condition poised between the imaginary and the real.
>
> – Jo Whaley

190.
PATRICK NAGATANI & ANDRÉE TRACEY
Unsafe Light, 1985

In the 1980s Nagatani and Tracey collaborated on a series of tableaux concerned with nuclear disaster. Taking cues from Hollywood, the artists meticulously constructed scenes that integrate painting, installation and photography. The real and unreal combine to create frightful yet humorous projections of the apocalypse. In an ironic pun, the title of this piece recalls both the red "safelight" conditions of the darkroom and the destructive radiation of an atomic blast.

191.
ED RUSCHA
Section 22, 1995

This piece is from *Gravure Group,* a portfolio published by Crown Point Press in San Francisco. The image pictures an area of land in Southern California known officially as Geological Survey Section 22. The artist scratched the negative before the image was transferred to the etching plate.

192.
JOHN BALDESSARI
Person with Conscience (Green)/Animals Quiescent (Yellow), 1991

Like *Section 22* by Ed Ruscha, Baldessari's take on the photogravure was published by Crown Point Press in San Francisco.

193.
MARK KLETT
"Love"—"Haight," Picacho Road, CA, 2/25/89, 1989

Recording timeless views of ancient western landscapes, Klett follows in the footsteps of nineteenth-century predecessors, occasionally duplicating their vantage points with great precision. Like them, he surveys the land with an almost geological interest. But rather than presume an invisible, scientific objectivity, Klett literally writes himself into his photographs with handwritten titles in the margins of his prints. He tells us exactly where and when he made each photograph, as if casually captioning snapshots.

194.
REAGAN LOUIE
South Central, Los Angeles, 1992

Reagan Louie photographed South Central Los Angeles in 1992, just a week after white police officers were acquitted for the brutal beating of African American suspect Rodney King. In the civil unrest following the verdict, Korean-owned businesses, such as the burned-out grocery pictured here, were targets of racially motivated violence. The photograph is part of a larger body of Louie's work documenting both natural and man-made disasters.

195.
TODD HIDO
Untitled #1937 (from the series *House Hunting*), 1997

The eerie photographs in Hido's *House Hunting* series were obtained on night walks in residential Bay Area neighborhoods. Using a medium-format camera and tripod, Hido makes long exposures that emphasize the stillness and loneliness of the scene.

196.
LEWIS WATTS
24th Street, West Oakland, 1997

> West Oakland is a neighborhood that is usually ignored or reflected only negatively by the media. . . . While poverty, crime and the fruits of racism are present here, there is also a strong sense of family and pride in the community, which is reflected in its institutions: churches, community gardens, parks, businesses and homes. There is also a tradition of improvisation as people use the materials and resources at hand to suit their needs.
>
> – Lewis Watts

For more than two decades, Lewis Watts has used his camera to explore the culture and history of urban environments across America, seeking the "footprints" which describe a community's culture and heritage. His work combines elements of architecture and everyday objects with searching images of people.

197.
LARRY SULTAN
Tasha's Third Film, 1998

Tasha's Third Film is one of a series by Sultan on the pornographic film industry in Southern California.

198.
GEOFFREY FRICKER
Centerville Bridge—Butte County Bridge #17, 1907–1997, 1997

Fricker printed the following caption directly below the image:

> Residents are of course concerned about the bridge going out, . . . glad that nobody was injured, and that there wasn't a schoolbus going over at the time. Residents plan to meet to discuss carpooling, issues related to propane, mail delivery, and school bus service for the children. In Butte Creek Canyon, I am Linda Watkins-Bennett, Channel 12 News.

Using a large-format camera and hydraulic lift, Fricker hoists himself well above the land and its inhabitants. His wide-reaching, omnipotent vantage point, similar to that of many nineteenth-century painters, suggests man's harmonious dominion over nature. Yet Fricker's choice of subject tells us otherwise. Here a wrathful nature proves her dominance by destroying a town's lifeline, leaving bystanders helpless.

199.
ROBERT DAWSON
Private Property, Lake Tahoe, California (from the Farewell, Promised Land Project), 1988

> With wonder and despair, respect and anger, humor and humility, Robert Dawson's photographs ask us to bear witness to our actions and to question our personal and collective attitudes toward the land. Dawson photographs with the eye of a cultural geographer and the heart of an environmentalist. His pictures reach back through history, and simultaneously catapult us into the future with frightening clarity.
>
> – Ellen Manchester, *Robert Dawson, Photographs* (Tokyo: Gallery Min, 1988).

200.
STEPHEN JOHNSON
Dune and Brush, Death Valley National Park, 1995

Although the subject is traditional and the photographer employs what appears to be a "straight" landscape technique, this image was actually made without the use of film or photographic chemistry. Johnson uses a digital scanning camera to capture scenes electronically, on disc. The files can then be manipulated at will and printed with an ink-jet printer, achieving a higher-resolution image than is possible with ordinary film and paper.

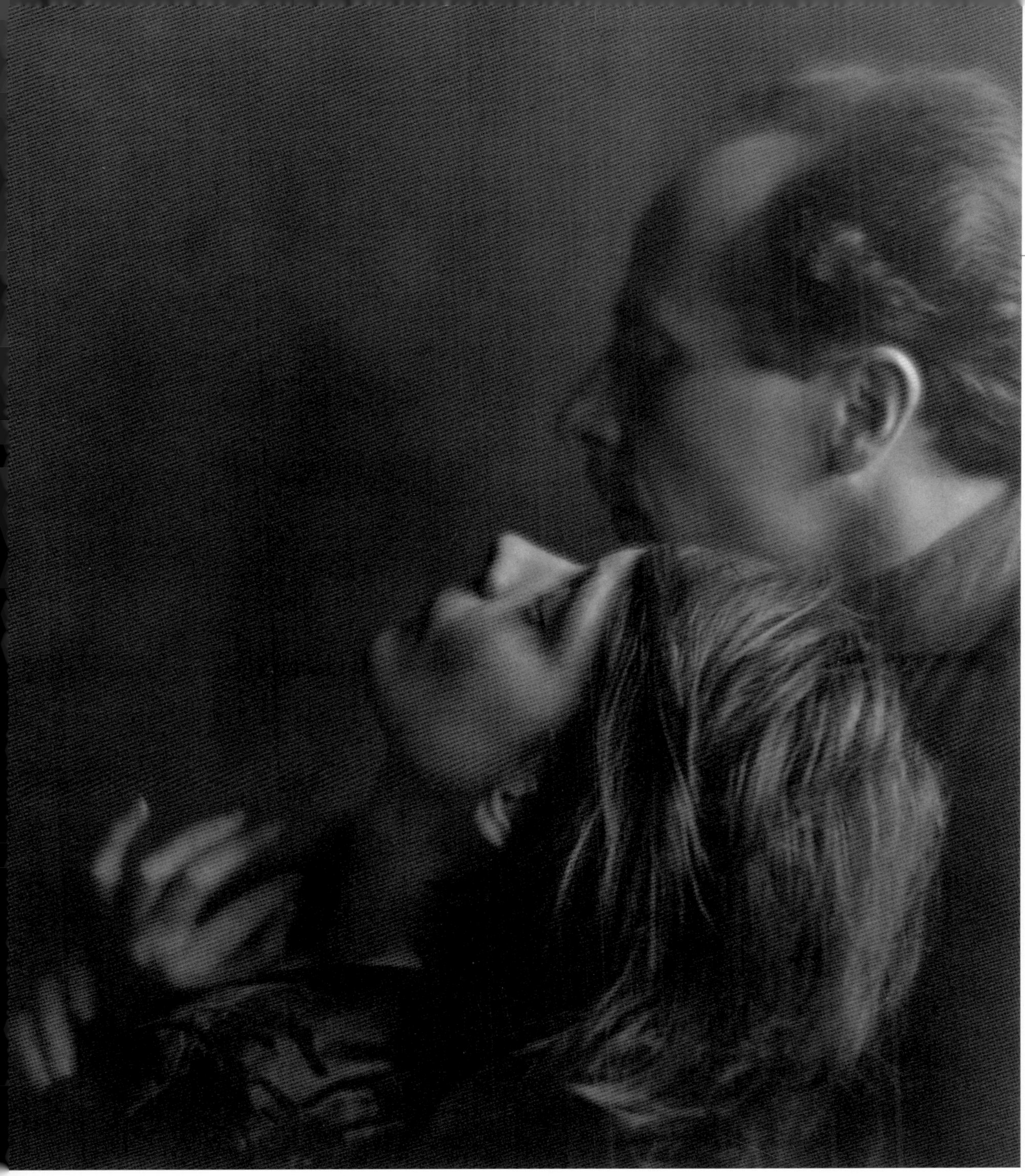

IMOGEN CUNNINGHAM
Edward Weston and Margrethe Mather, 1922
Platinum print
9¼ x 7⅜ in.
COLLECTION OF THE OAKLAND MUSEUM OF CALIFORNIA,
GIFT OF THE BELL FUND

WILLIAM ABBENSETH (1898–1972)

Photographer, filmmaker, writer and adviser to the Bay Area artist community, Abbenseth was born in New York City. He was an associate member of Group f.64 and participated in a 1934 exhibition organized by Willard Van Dyke in Oakland. He produced photographs of local architecture and urban infrastructure for the Federal Works Progress Administration (WPA), c. 1935–39, and during World War II was engaged as a photographer and filmmaker for the Office of War Information. In his later years he photographed the Avery Brundage Art Collection for the M. H. de Young Memorial Art Museum in San Francisco. The San Francisco Museum of Art presented a retrospective exhibition of his work in 1974. Abbenseth was known as an avid reader and connoisseur of theater and film. Photographer John Gutmann said of him, ". . . his greatest and most permanent love affair was with San Francisco. He loved to walk its streets, especially North Beach where he lived so many years and knew everybody."

ANSEL EASTON ADAMS (1902–1984)

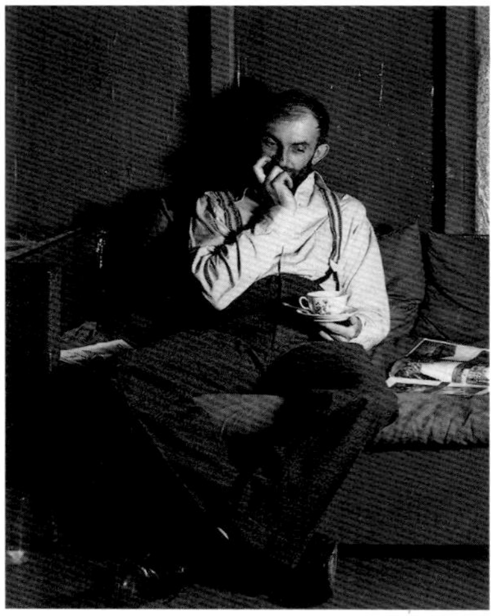

A brilliant recorder of the natural world, Adams achieved international fame as a photographer and master printmaker, a devoted environmentalist and champion of the wilderness ideal. He served for many years as a member of the board of directors of the Sierra Club, and was an educator, author, musician and poet. A native of San Francisco, Adams began wilderness photography in 1916 on a family trip to Yosemite. By 1930 he had set aside a promising career as a concert pianist to devote his energies to photography, publishing the photo-essay *Taos Pueblo* with text by Mary Austin. In the thirties he was a founding member of Group f.64 and wrote a photography column for *Fortnightly*, as well as a number of technical articles, including "Making a Photograph" (1934) and "Personal Credo" (1935), both published in *Camera Craft*. His best-known contribution to photographic technique, the Zone System, systematized the task of making fine negatives and prints, and is widely employed to this day. He mounted a solo exhibition at Alfred Stieglitz's gallery An American Place in 1936, and helped found the photography department at New York's Museum of Modern Art in 1940. In 1946 Adams was awarded a fellowship from the John Simon Guggenheim Memorial Foundation to photograph America's national parks; it was renewed in 1948. By 1962 he had moved to Carmel, California, where he continued his publishing career with both technical and fine art publications. In 1979 his exhibition *Yosemite and the Range of Light* was mounted at the Museum of Modern Art, New York and the Oakland Museum. The following year he received the Presidential Medal of Freedom, the nation's highest civilian honor, from President Jimmy Carter. Adams's achievements and awards are countless, and his appeal to the world remains profound.

PHOTO: Willard Van Dyke, *Ansel Adams at 683 Brockhurst,* c. 1933. Gelatin silver print, collection of the Oakland Museum of California, Prints and Photo Fund.

HUGH ANDERSON (c.1820s– ?)

Born in Scotland, Anderson was one of Northern California's earliest photographers. He is known to have been active in Eureka (1858–65), Petaluma (c. 1875) and San Francisco (c. 1866–95), offering "ambrotypes, pearl ambrotypes, melainotypes, crayon pictures and photographs on patent leather," before embracing the ubiquitous carte de visite. The Civil War greatly depressed California's economy, causing him to look for work in various San Francisco galleries. At one point he operated the Sunbeam Gallery on Clay Street. By 1890 he had become a photographic supplier and camera manufacturer. He also photographed part-time until at least 1895 and is known to have lived in San Francisco until about 1900.

P. DOUGLAS ANDERSON (?–?)

An amateur photographer, Anderson was active in Northern California from around 1910 to about 1935. He was a member of the Pictorial Photographic Society of San Francisco, and in May 1923 was appointed Associate Editor of *Camera Craft*. He briefly served as the magazine's Editor-in-Chief (1924). He continued to participate in pictorial exhibitions between 1918 and 1935, exhibiting three photographs in the Fifth International Exhibition of Pictorial Photography at the California Palace of the Legion of Honor in 1928.

LAURA MAY ADAMS ARMER (1874–1963)

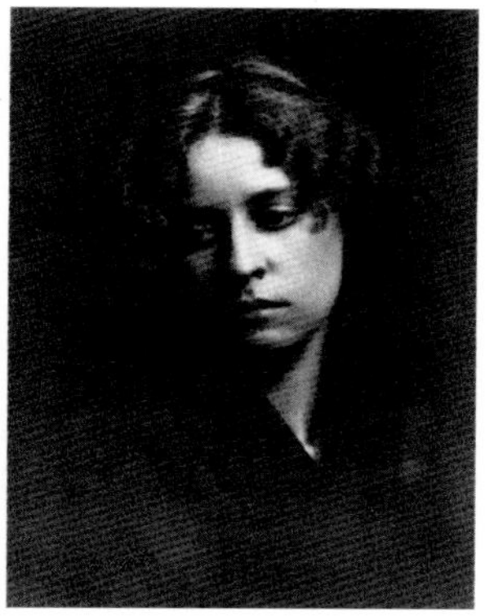

An artist, photographer, filmmaker and author, Armer was born in Sacramento and grew up in San Francisco, where she attended the Mark Hopkins Institute of Art (now the San Francisco Art Institute). In September 1900 her influential article, "The Picture Possibilities of Photography" was published in *Camera Craft* magazine, and in 1902 she opened a photography studio in the Flood Building at Powell and Market Streets in San Francisco. That year she traveled to Tucson, Arizona where she was "first inoculated with the desert delirium" that came to dominate her life, photography and writings. Upon her return, she married classmate Sidney Armer and, following the birth of their first child, moved her photography operation to their home in Berkeley. In addition to photographic art portraits, she made numerous pictorial studies of the Bay Area, regularly exhibiting at photographic salons well into the 1920s. In 1923 she returned to the Southwest, beginning a prolonged cycle of annual pilgrimages to the region, where she recorded many Navajo sand paintings with camera and brush. In 1928, with no previous experience, Armer wrote and directed a film, *The Mountain Chant*. Some of the public showings were narrated in Navajo, making the film the first "all Indian" motion picture "in an aboriginal language." In 1931 she published her first children's book, *Waterless Mountain*, which received the Newberry Medal for Juvenile Literature. Other books followed, including the largely autobiographical *The Trader's Children* (1937). Armer's late years were spent writing and reminiscing about the Southwest and art generally.

PHOTO: Arnold Genthe, *Untitled (Portrait of Laura Adams Armer)*, 1901. Gelatin silver print, collection of the Oakland Museum of California, gift of Mr. and Mrs. Austin Armer.

MORLEY BAER (1916–1995)

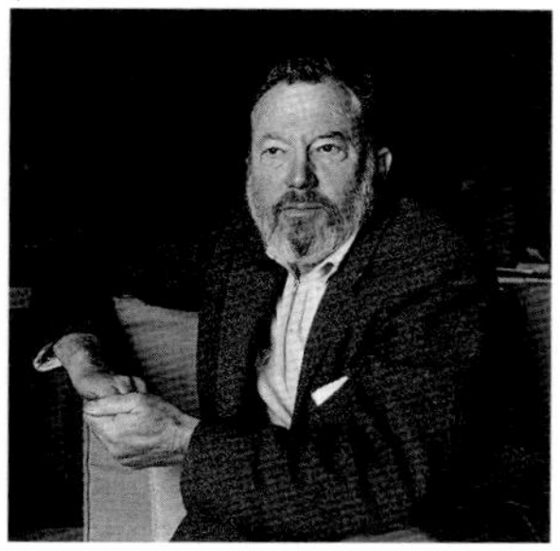

A native of Toledo, Ohio, Baer photographed the California landscape for nearly five decades, focusing on the Pacific Ocean near his home in the Carmel Highlands, as well as the Sierra and Central Valley regions. Following an M.A. degree in English at the University of Michigan, in 1939 he apprenticed himself to a commercial photographer in Chicago before becoming a photographic officer for the U.S. Navy during World War II. He moved to California in 1946, where he met Edward Weston and other photographers of the San Francisco/Carmel area. Like Weston, most of his work was done with an eight-by-ten-inch view camera. Though best known for his California landscapes, Baer photographed for extended periods in Italy, Spain and the American Southwest. He was a frequent exhibitor and an instructor for the Friends of Photography. His work has appeared in several books, including: *Adobes in the Sun* (1973), *Room and Time Enough* (1980), and *The Wilder Shore* (1984). Baer was also known for his architectural photography (including the book *Painted Ladies*, 1978), and in 1966 he received the Architectural Photography Medal from the American Institute of Architects.

PHOTO: Joan Murray, *Morley Baer, Carmel*, 1971. Gelatin silver print, collection of the Oakland Museum of California, gift of Joan Murray.

ISAAC WALLACE BAKER (1818–c.1862)

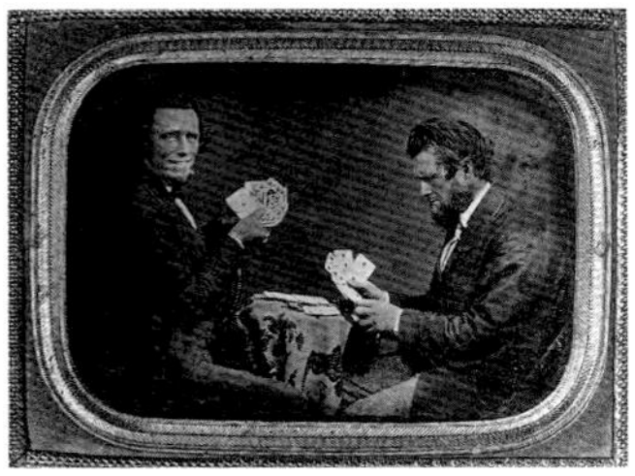

A daguerreotypist, painter, sailor and lecturer, Baker was born in Beverly, Massachusetts. He spent his young adulthood as a sailor. In 1849 he joined the Beverly Joint Stock Company and traveled to California in search of gold. Unsuccessful, he went home to the East after a short stay, but returned to the gold fields in 1852, apprenticing himself the following year to daguerreotypist Perez Mann Batchelder in Sonora. Working as an operator for Batchelder, Baker traveled the mining districts in a portable daguerreian wagon. By the end of 1853, he had returned to the East to tour and lecture on his California experiences, illustrating his talks with large paintings based on his eyewitness sketches. The Oakland Museum of California holds the majority of daguerreotypes attributable to Baker.

PHOTO: Isaac Wallace Baker, *Isaac Wallace Baker (left) and a Friend Playing Poker,* c. 1855. Quarter plate ambrotype, collection of the Oakland Museum of California, gift of anonymous donor.

JOHN ANTHONY BALDESSARI (1931–)

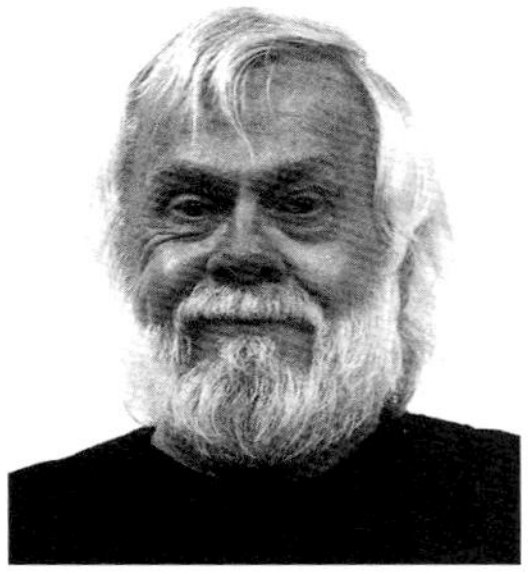

Baldessari once stated: "I have no particular interest in photography, other than it's quick." Born in National City, California, to a Danish mother and Austrian father, Baldessari briefly studied art history at the University of California, Berkeley (1954) before switching to studio art. He earned his B.A. (1953) and M.A. (1957) degrees in art from San Diego State College, where he has also taught. Known as a conceptual artist, Baldessari was among the first to legitimize the use of imagery from popular media, including television, movies and advertising, in fine art. He did not begin working with photography until 1965 when he experimented with photographic emulsions on canvas combined with texts. Most of his work is narrative in nature and often humorous. "I try to make things deceptively simple," he has said. Though a native Californian, Baldessari made his reputation first in Europe and then New York before actively exhibiting on the West Coast. His exhibitions include scores of group and individual shows, and his work has been collected by major institutions throughout the United States and abroad Baldessari has twice been awarded National Endowment for the Arts grants (1973 and 1974–75).

PHOTO: *John Baldessari,* n.d. Courtesy of International Center of Photography, New York.

LEWIS BALTZ (1945–)

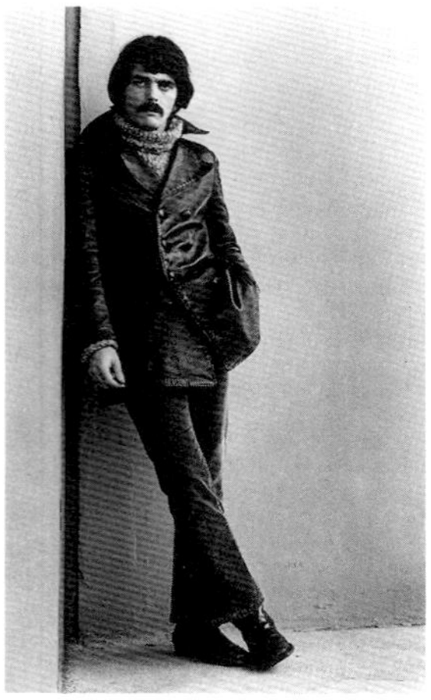

A masterful observer of the contemporary landscape, Baltz was born in Newport Beach, California. He came to prominence as a member of the "New Topographic" movement of the 1970s, which proposed a photographic counter-aesthetic and pursued images of despoiled landscapes. Baltz holds a B.F.A. from the San Francisco Art Institute (1969) and an M.F.A. from Claremont Graduate School in California (1971). He has taught at Pomona College in Claremont, California, the California Institute of the Arts in Valencia and at the University of California campuses in Davis, Santa Cruz and Riverside. In 1973 he was awarded a National Endowment for the Arts Fellowship, and in 1976 received both a John Simon Guggenheim Memorial Fellowship and a second NEA grant. Baltz has exhibited widely since 1971, and his photographs are held in numerous museum collections. Significant publications include: *The New Industrial Parks Near Irvine, California* (1975), *Maryland* (1976), *Nevada* (1977) and *Park City* (1980). Recently his work has appeared at the Musée d'Art Moderne de la Ville de Paris, the Stedelijk Museum, Amsterdam, the Centre Pompidou, Paris and the New York Institute for Contemporary Art. Baltz currently resides and works in France.

PHOTO: Joan Murray, *Lewis Baltz,* 1972. Gelatin silver print, collection of the Oakland Museum of California, gift of Joan Murray.

RUTH-MARION BARUCH (1922–1997)

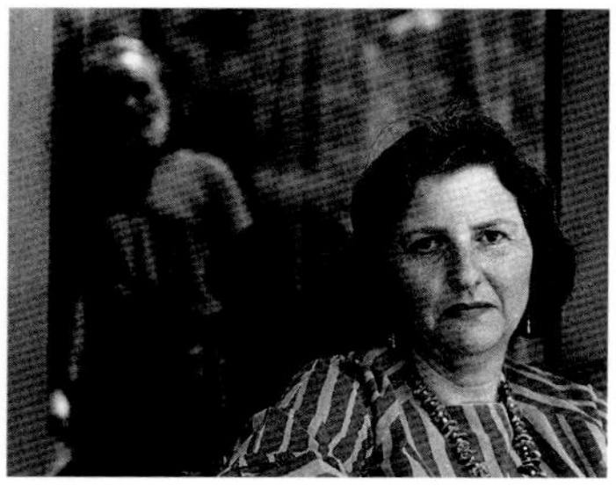

A documentary photographer born in Berlin, Germany, Baruch became interested in photography at the age of twelve when she was given a Brownie box camera. By 1944 she had earned two degrees from the University of Missouri in Columbia: a B.A. in Creative Writing and Literary Criticism and a B.A. in Journalism. She went on to receive her M.F.A. in Photography from the School of Fine Arts, Ohio University, Athens, in 1946. After moving to California, she studied at the California School of Fine Arts under Ansel Adams, Minor White and Homer Page (1946–47). Baruch married photographer Pirkle Jones, who shared her interest in social issues, in 1949. The two began documenting the Black Panther Party in 1968, which culminated in an exhibition at the M. H. de Young Memorial Museum, entitled *The Black Panthers: A Photographic Essay,* later published as *The Vanguard: A Photographic Essay on the Black Panthers* (1970). During the 1970s she was a frequent guest artist at the San Francisco Art Institute.

PHOTO: Joan Murray, *Ruth-Marion Baruch (Pirkle Jones in Reflection),* 1971. Gelatin silver print, collection of the Oakland Museum of California, gift of Joan Murray.

RUTH BERNHARD (1905–)

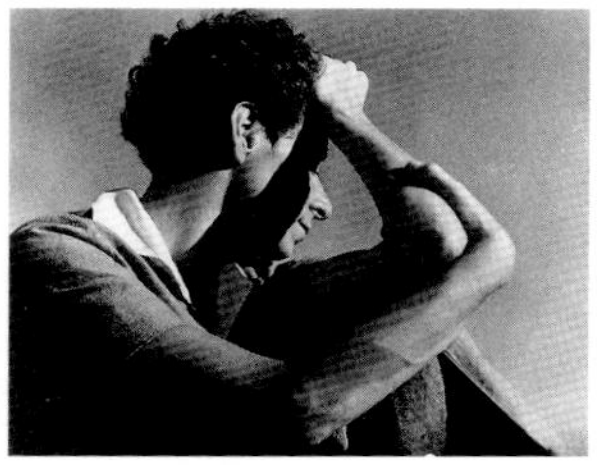

Born in Berlin, Germany, Bernhard studied at the Academy of Art in Berlin (1925–27) before immigrating to New York in 1927. She purchased her first camera with severance pay from a brief job at *Delineator* magazine and entered the world of freelance advertising and fashion photography. She was profoundly influenced by Edward Weston, who she met in 1935 and with whom she studied after moving to Los Angeles. She became a naturalized American citizen in 1937. In 1953 Bernhard settled in San Francisco, and in the 1960s taught for the extension programs of the University of California, Berkeley and San Francisco. She has also been an instructor at Utah State University, Logan, and Columbia University, New York. Bernhard has exhibited widely and her work has been collected by major museums throughout the United States and Europe. She received the National Urban League Award (1961), the Dorothea Lange Award (1976), the City and County of San Francisco Award (1978) and the Award of Honor for Outstanding Achievement in Photography, San Francisco Art Commission (1984). Publications include: *The Big Heart* (1957) and *Collected Light: The Photographs of Ruth Bernhard* (1979). She was also featured in Margaretta K. Mitchell's *Recollections: Ten Women of Photography* (1979).

PHOTO: Edward Weston, *Portrait of Ruth Bernhard,* 1935. Gelatin silver print, collection of the Oakland Museum of California, gift of the Estate of Helen Johnston.

SIGISMUND BLUMANN (1872–1956)

Born Simon Blumann in New York City, Blumann used the name "Sigismund" as an adult. His mother hoped he would become a concert pianist, and music played a prominent role throughout his life. At about age ten he moved to San Francisco, and by age eighteen was working as a teacher, musician and music publisher. During the 1890s he took up amateur photography, eventually becoming deeply involved in the California Camera Club. Between 1924 and 1932 he served as editor of *Camera Craft,* the club's official journal. In 1933 he received the Austrian Gold Medal for outstanding service to photography, and a Fellowship in the Royal Photographic Society of Great Britain. By 1936 he was a member of more than sixty camera clubs around the world. Seeking to promote the pictorialist school of photography, Blumann launched *Photo-Art Monthly,* a magazine devoted to photography as art. He also wrote poetry, as well as a number of articles and several books about photography.

HARRY BOWDEN (1907–1965)

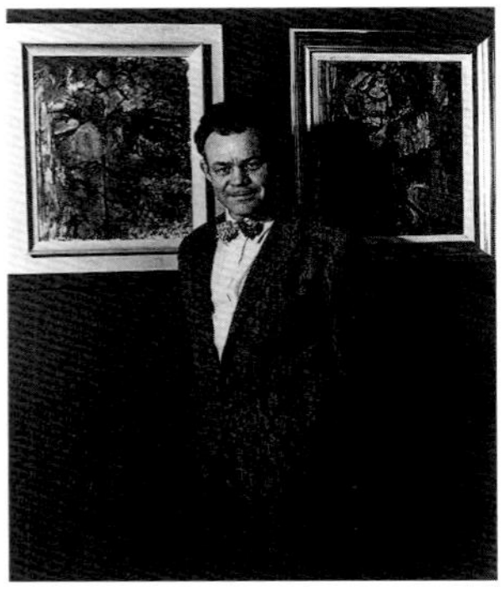

An abstract painter and photographer, Bowden was raised in Los Angeles. He became interested in the arts in high school, going on to attend the Los Angeles Art Institute (1927). He also studied at the National Academy of Design and the Art Students League, both in New York City, at the Chouinard School of Art, Los Angeles and the University of California, Berkeley. By the age of twenty he had already produced a commercial motion picture. From 1929 to 1931 he worked as an art director and designer with several California advertising agencies, receiving a number of awards. His first solo painting exhibition was at the Paul Elder Gallery in San Francisco (1932). By 1935 he was working as Hans Hoffmann's assistant in New York. It was not until the start of World War II, when he returned to California and settled in Sausalito, that he rekindled his interest in photography. Much of the remainder of his life was devoted to both painting and photography. Often his photographs served as references for his paintings. Bowden's art has been widely exhibited, including a Memorial Exhibition in New York in December 1965, following his death from a heart attack in January of that year.

PHOTO: Unknown, *Harry Bowden at the Louvre, Inc., S.F., Exhibition,* 1951. Paul Mills Archives of California Art, Oakland Museum of California.

JULIUS THEODORE BOYSEN (1868–1939)

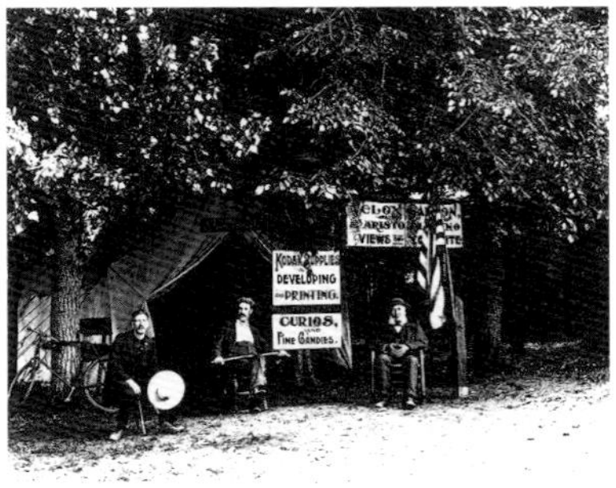

Born in San Francisco, Julius Theodore Boysen may be the J. Boysen known to have operated a portrait studio in Sacramento in the years 1892–93. By 1898 Julius Theodore had opened a studio and curio shop in Yosemite, where he also did photofinishing for the tourist trade until his death. The business was continued by his wife, Mabel, until her death in 1943 when the building was sold to the Yosemite Park and Curry Company. In 1901 Boysen exhibited three photographs of Yosemite at the San Francisco Photographic Salon. He was perhaps best known for his stereographs and lantern slides of Yosemite's Native Americans. A collection of his lantern slides, stereographs and prints is presently held by the Yosemite Museum, Yosemite National Park.

PHOTO: Unknown, *Julius T. Boysen (left) at Yosemite,* n.d. Courtesy of Peter E. Palmquist.

BRADLEY & RULOFSON — Henry William Bradley (1813–1891) and William Herman Rulofson (1826–1878)

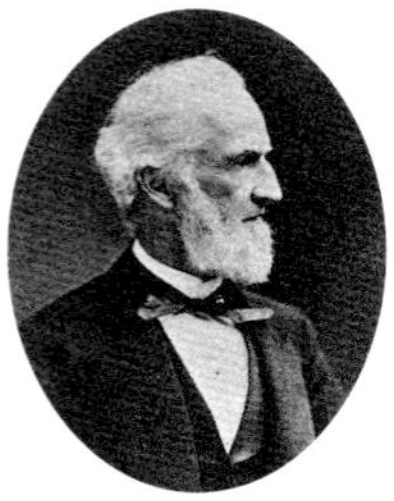

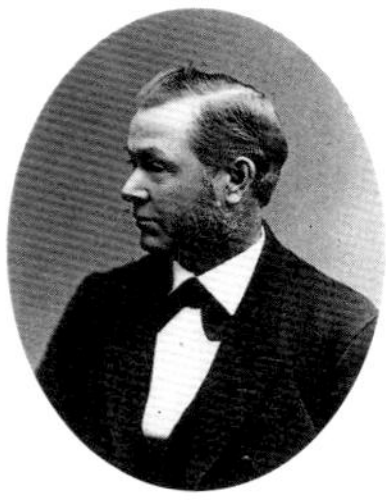

Bradley and Rulofson operated San Francisco's most prominent portrait studio from 1863 to 1878. Bradley, a native of North Carolina, had previously been a daguerreotypist and photographic supply dealer, while Rulofson, a Canadian by birth, excelled at showmanship, self-promotion and business acumen. By 1873 Bradley & Rulofson had branched out into photographic publishing, notably stereographs and mammoth plate views by Eadweard J. Muybridge. The firm also specialized in celebrity portraits, publishing the *Men of Mark* series of prominent individuals. In 1878 Rulofson plunged to his death from the firm's gallery roof, a mysterious incident which may have been either an accident or a suicide. Although the gallery continued under the name Bradley & Rulofson, Bradley's portion of the business was defaulted to William H. Dall, who operated the business with diminished success until 1889. Upon closing, the firm's tens of thousands of glass plate negatives were destroyed. Twenty-thousand of them were used to build a greenhouse.

PHOTOS: Unknown, *Henry W. Bradley* (top), n.d., and *William H. Rulofson* (bottom), n.d. Courtesy of Peter E. Palmquist.

ANNE WARDROPE (NOTT) BRIGMAN (1869–1950)

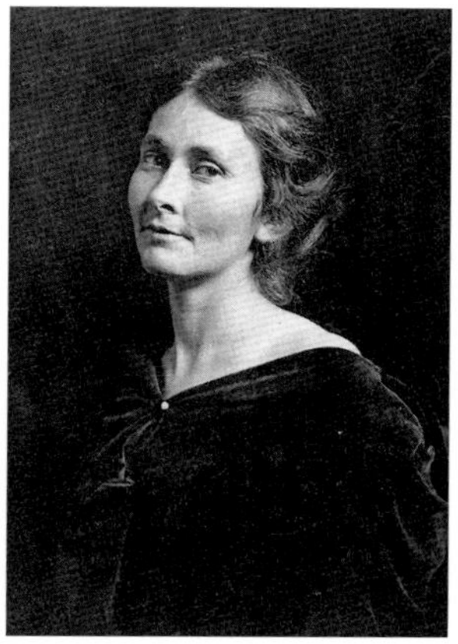

Best known for allegorical studies of nudes and draped figures in Sierran landscapes, Brigman was born and educated in Hawaii, moving to California with her family around 1886. In 1894 she married Martin Brigman, a sea captain, with whom she traveled in the Pacific; their home was in Oakland. Self-taught as a photographer, she embraced the tenets of Alfred Stieglitz's Photo-Secession. Brigman exhibited in the second and third San Francisco Salons of 1902 and 1903, where she established a link with Photo-Secessionist members Stieglitz, Gertrude Käsebier and Edward Steichen. Nearly every year from 1904 to 1927 she took camping and photographic trips to the Sierra Nevadas, where she produced her best-known work. In 1904 she exhibited with the Photo-Secessionists in Hamburg, Germany, at the Corcoran Gallery of Art in Washington, D.C. and at the Carnegie Institute in Pittsburgh. She developed a strong friendship with Stieglitz (their correspondence continued until 1930), who actively promoted her. He exhibited her work at his Little Galleries of the Photo-Secession (known by its address, 291) in New York (1905–6), and he published gravures of her photographs in his magazine *Camera Work* (1909). Brigman was elected a Fellow of the Photo-Secession in 1906, became a member of the Linked Ring in 1909 and, that same year, was awarded a gold medal at the Alaska-Yukon Pacific Exhibition in Seattle. Upon separating from her husband in 1910, she traveled to New York to visit Stieglitz and other members of the Photo-Secession, participating in a class with Clarence White at Fire Island, Maine. She received first prize from the John Wanamaker exhibition of 1913 and joined Francis Bruguière in organizing a Photo-Secession display at San Francisco's Panama-Pacific International Exposition in 1915. In 1930 she moved to Long Beach, California, and by the end of the decade, due to failing eyesight, had turned from photography to poetry. Her book *Songs of a Pagan,* with poetry and photographs, was published in 1949.

PHOTO: Mary L. Bisbee, *Portrait of Anne Brigman,* 1909. Gelatin silver print, collection of the Oakland Museum of California, gift of Mr. and Mrs. W. M. Nott.

ELLEN BROOKS (1946–)

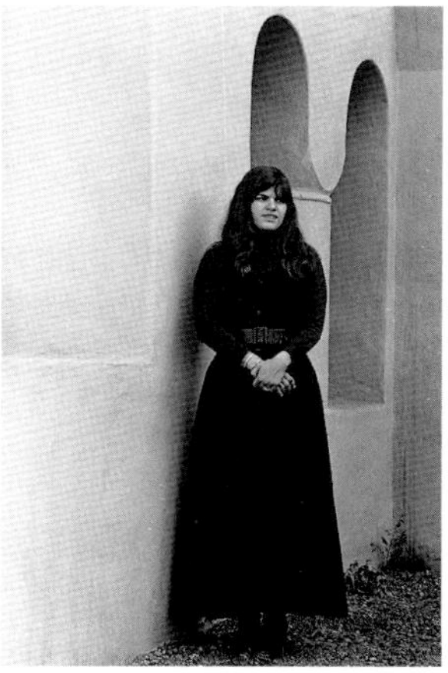

Born in Los Angeles, Brooks attended the University of Wisconsin (1963–65) and the University of California, Los Angeles (1965–71), where she studied under Robert Heinecken, Robert Fichter and Lynn Foulkes. From 1973 until 1982 she taught at the San Francisco Art Institute. She has also taught at the Chicago Art Institute (1976), the extension programs of the University of California, Los Angeles and Berkeley (1971–75) and Franconia College in New Hampshire (1974). Brooks has received a Phelan award (1971), two National Endowment for the Arts grants (1976 and 1979) and a UCLA Alumni Award (1971). Her work has been widely exhibited, including solo exhibitions in New York, Rotterdam, Chicago and San Francisco. In 1988 a retrospective titled *Ellen Brooks: Photographs and Configurations* was mounted at the Freedman Gallery, Albright College. Since 1984 she has taught at the Tisch School of the Arts, New York University.

PHOTO: Joan Murray, *Ellen Brooks, Los Angeles,* 1972. Gelatin silver print, collection of the Oakland Museum of California, gift of Joan Murray.

FRANCIS JOSEPH BRUGUIÈRE (1879–1945)

Bruguière was a painter, musician and innovative abstract photographer. One of four sons of a San Francisco banking family, he spent his early years in a private boarding school in the East. In 1905 he visited New York, where he studied with Frank Eugene and became a member of Alfred Stieglitz's Photo-Secession (1905). A year later, following the great earthquake and fire, he opened a studio in San Francisco. Although a member of the Photo-Secession, he was not considered one of the inner circle and exhibited with the group only once, in 1910 at the Albright-Knox Art Gallery in Buffalo. Instead, he navigated his own aesthetic course. As early as 1910, Bruguière was experimenting with surreal light abstractions and multiple exposures, and by 1915 he had begun experimenting with type-setting and printing. In 1917 he contracted tuberculosis; he suffered from bronchial weakness for the remainder of his life. His book *San Francisco* was published in 1918. From 1919 to 1927 he worked in New York, becoming an official photographer for the Theatre Guild. In 1929 he was invited to show his work in the landmark Modernist exhibition *Film und Foto* in Stuttgart, Germany. He moved to England in 1928 and made several motion pictures there, including *Light Rhythms* (1931), England's first abstract film, made in collaboration with writer and film critic Oswell Blakeson. In 1937 he served as official designer for the gateway to the British Pavilion at the Paris Exposition. By 1940, his health increasingly fragile, he began an autobiography, which he was unable to finish. He died in London on May 8, 1945 on the day peace was declared in Europe.

WYNN BULLOCK (1902–1975)

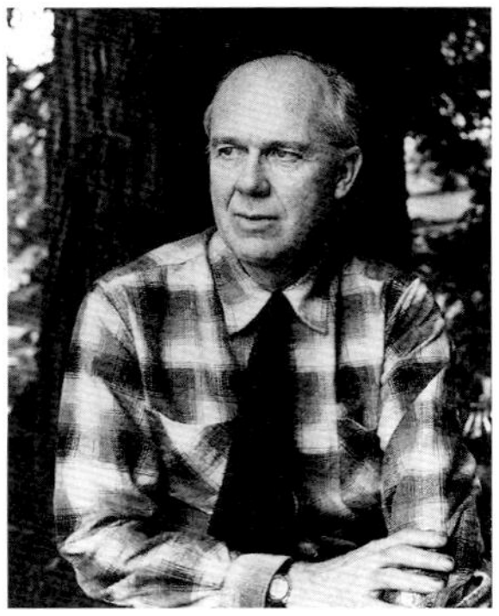

Born Percy Wingfield Bullock in Chicago, Wynn Bullock began his professional life as a singer, performing as a leading tenor in Irving Berlin's *Music Box Review* (1921–24). He studied voice, music and language, performing professionally in Europe (1928–30) before entering a pre-law program at West Virginia University, Morgantown. In 1938 he began law school at the University of Southern California, but quit to study photography at the Art Center School, Los Angeles (1938–40). In 1941 he had his first one-man exhibition at the Los Angeles County Museum of Art. During World War II he obtained the photographic concession at the Fort Ord Army base near Monterey (1943–44). Though strongly influenced by Edward Weston, Bullock did not strictly adhere to "straight" photography, employing various techniques to evoke symbolic meaning. From 1946 to 1948 he obtained several patents for a process to control line effects in solarization. Later experiments using prolonged time exposures and superimposed images expressed his interest in spatial and temporal principals. Bullock's photograph *Let There Be Light* was voted the favorite in the influential *The Family of Man* exhibition at the Museum of Modern Art, New York (1958). In 1960 he received the highest annual award of the Professional Photographers of Northern California for his contributions to Professional Photography as a Fine Art. He taught at San Francisco State College (1945–58), Monterey Peninsula College (1959–60) and at the Institute of Design in Chicago (1967). Bullock served as trustee and chairman of the exhibition committee at the inception of the Friends of Photography in Carmel, and continued to write and lecture about photography until his death in 1975.

PHOTO: Larry Colwell, *Wynn Bullock, n.d.* Gelatin silver print, collection of the Oakland Museum of California, gift of Van Deren Coke.

JERRY BURCHARD (1931–)

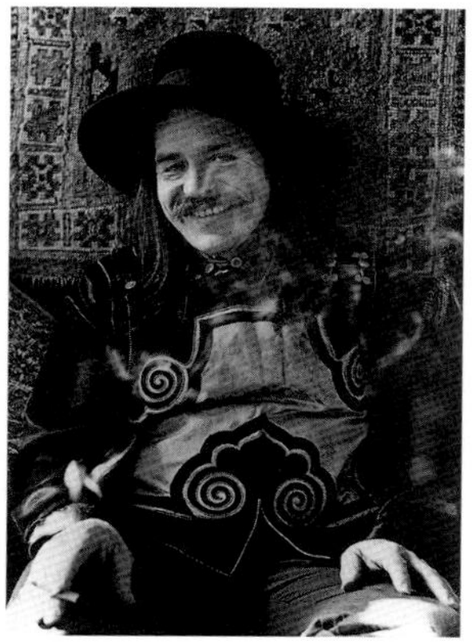

A native of Rochester, New York (home of Eastman Kodak Company), Burchard was a third-generation Kodak employee (1950–1952). Following a stint as a photographer in the United States Navy (1952–56), Burchard studied at the California School of Fine Arts (later renamed the San Francisco Art Institute), earning a B.F.A. in 1960. He began teaching at the Art Institute in 1966, twice serving as chair of the Photography Department (1968–71 and 1978–79). Burchard's work has appeared in numerous exhibitions and publications. He has received two National Endowment for the Arts fellowships (1976 and 1978) and an NEA Photo Survey Grant (1979). Burchard has stated: "My camera is my friend. We go for walks together, sometimes late at night. Sometimes we meet people or landscapes and we make love to them. Sometimes the camera gets more than I do. Sometimes the other way. In any case, the camera, a wizened 1957 SP Nikon, sees what I don't, what I can't, what I'd like to. That's why we're friends."

PHOTO: Joan Murray, *Gerald Burchard*, 1972. Gelatin silver print, collection of the Oakland Museum of California, gift of Dr. and Mrs. Dudley P. Bell.

SHIRLEY C. BURDEN (1908–1989)

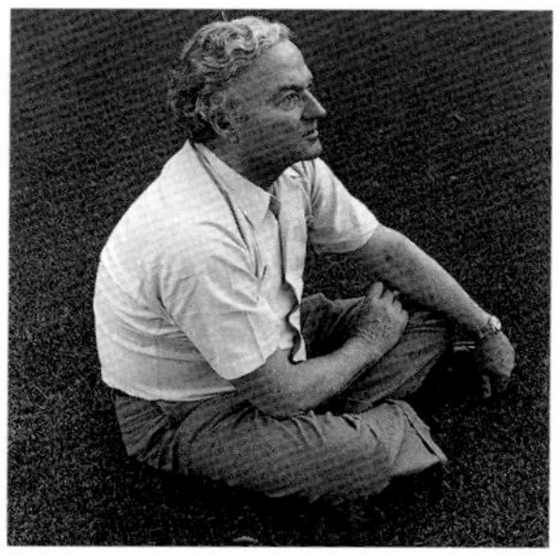

A photographer and filmmaker, Burden was raised in New York and educated through high school. At seventeen he joined his cousin, W. Douglas Burden, in the production of a motion picture on the life of the American Indian, *The Silent Enemy*. He learned the motion picture sound business at Paramount's Long Island Studio under Walter Wanger. In 1929 he came to Hollywood to work at R.K.O. Studios, where he directed and co-produced several films, among them *She* starring Helen Gahagan. He formed Tradefilms, Inc. to produce motion pictures, including training films for the U.S. military and the U.S. Office of Education. By 1946 he had opened a commercial still photography studio in Beverly Hills, his work appearing in periodicals such as *House and Garden* and *McCall's*. Beginning in the 1950s, Burden became increasingly interested in photography as art, his work appearing in numerous exhibitions over the next thirty-five years, including *The Family of Man* at the Museum of Modern Art, New York. He became a photography teacher at the Art Center College of Design, Pasadena, in 1978. Burden's photographs have been widely published and he is the author of at least five books, among them *God is My Life* (1960) and *The Vanderbilts is My Life* (1981).

PHOTO: Joan Murray, *Shirley Burden, Los Angeles*, 1972. Gelatin silver print, collection of the Oakland Museum of California, gift of Joan Murray.

ALICE BURR (1883–1968)

One of three daughters of a prominent San Francisco family with strong New England associations, Burr was active as a pictorialist photographer from about 1910 through at least 1925. She studied at the California School of Design in San Francisco, exhibiting as a student at both the M. H. de Young Museum, San Francisco, and the San Diego Museum of Fine Arts. At that time her media were listed as oil, watercolor, chalk, pencil, and linoleum block printing. During the 1915–16 season, she studied at the Clarence White School of Photography, New York, where she participated in at least two alumni exhibitions (1917 and 1921). She exhibited at various salons including the Fifth Pittsburgh Salon (1918) and the Fourth International Exhibition of Pictorial Photography in San Francisco (1926). In 1927 she was elected president of the California League of Women Voters, later gaining recognition as a devoted worker for the American Red Cross in both World Wars. A retrospective exhibition of her paintings was held in San Francisco in 1953 when Burr was 70 years old.

JO ANN CALLIS (1940–)

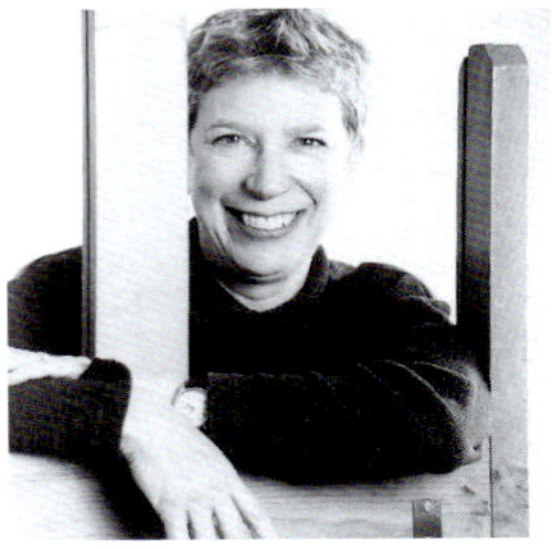

Best known for staged and fabricated tableaux that combine sculpture with photography, Callis creates narrative images in color. She holds a B.A. in Art (1974) and an M.F.A. in Photography (1977) from the University of California, Los Angeles, where she studied with Robert Heinecken, a major influence. She has taught at the California Institute of the Arts, Valencia (1976–82), the UCLA extension program, and California State University, Fullerton. She received the Ferguson Grant from the Friends of Photography, Carmel (1978) and was twice awarded National Endowment for the Arts grants (1980 and 1985). Other awards include a Mellon Leave Grant (1982) and a Guggenheim Fellowship (1990). Callis has had a number of solo exhibitions and her work is widely published.

PHOTO: John Ellis, *Jo Ann Callis*, n.d. Courtesy of Jo Ann Callis.

LINDA CONNOR (1944–)

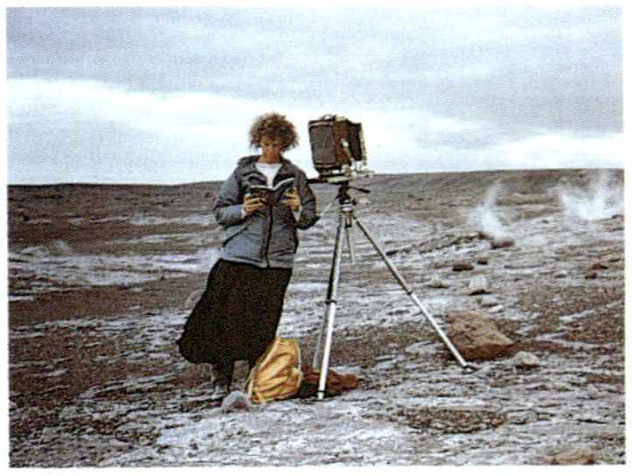

Known for landscape, architectural documentation and portrait photography, Connor is particularly interested in manifestations of religious belief and myth in diverse cultures. She holds a B.F.A. from the Rhode Island School of Design (1967), where she studied with Harry Callahan and used a large-format camera, and an M.S. from the Illinois Institute of Technology, Chicago (1969), where she studied with Aaron Siskind. Since her graduation in 1969 she has been an instructor at the San Francisco Art Institute. She has also taught at the California College of Arts and Crafts in Oakland, the University of California, Berkeley Extension program and the School of the Museum of Fine Arts in Boston. Awarded a National Endowment for the Arts Grant in 1976, she photographed in the Caribbean, Mexico and Guatemala, and a Guggenheim Fellowship enabled her to work in Asia for seven months in 1979. She received the Photographer of the Year award from the Friends of Photography in 1986, the Charles Pratt Memorial Award, New York, and another NEA grant (both 1988). In 1994 she received an NEA travel grant. Connor's photographs appear in many collections and have been featured in numerous exhibitions and publications. Selected recent solo exhibitions include *Spiral Journey*, Museum of Contemporary Art, Chicago, and two traveling exhibitions, *Earthly Constellations* (San Francisco Museum of Modern Art, 1992), and *Sacred Places from Around the World* (Cuesta College Art Gallery, San Luis Obispo, 1993). Her exhibit *Tibet: A Land of Light and Shadow* was mounted at the Haines Gallery, San Francisco in 1993. In 1997 Connor received the Falkirk Cultural Center's Annual Life Work Award. Monographs include *Solos: Photographs by Linda Connor* (1979) and *Spiral Journey* (1990).

PHOTO: Linda Connor, *Linda Connor in Hawaii,* c.1990. Copyright Linda Connor.

IMOGEN CUNNINGHAM (1883–1976)

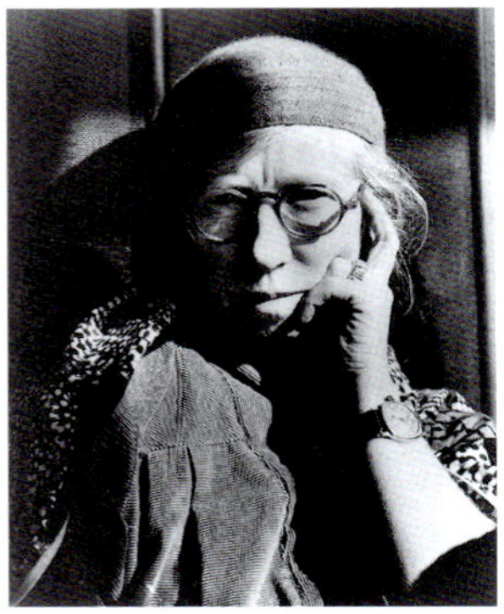

Considered the grande dame of California photography, Cunningham produced a wide range of portraits, still lifes, plant studies, nudes, industrial landscapes and allegorical studies for over seventy years. Inspired to become a photographer by the work of Gertrude Käsebier in 1901, Cunningham studied chemistry at the University of Washington, Seattle, graduating in 1907. She assisted Edward S. Curtis before moving to Dresden, Germany, where she studied photographic chemistry at Technische Hochschule. In 1910 she visited New York, where she met Käsebier and Alfred Stieglitz. Later that year she opened a portrait studio in Seattle, specializing in soft-focus work in the pictorialist style. In 1915 she married etcher Roi Partridge with whom she had three sons. The family moved to San Francisco in 1917, then to Oakland in 1920 where, restricted by domestic concerns, she began to make plant studies in her garden. In 1923 she met Edward Weston, who placed ten of her plant studies in the landmark *Film und Foto* exhibition in Stuttgart, Germany (1929). Cunningham was a founding member of Group f.64, appearing in its first exhibition at the M. H. de Young Memorial Museum in 1932. She photographed political figures and Hollywood stars for *Vanity Fair* (1932–34). She divorced Partridge in 1934. During the 1950s and '60s she lived in San Francisco, photographing poets and members of the Beat generation, as well as the flower children of San Francisco's Haight-Ashbury district. Late in life she was awarded a Guggenheim Fellowship to print from her early negatives. A beloved Bay Area figure, at ninety-two she began a project to photograph people over ninety, culminating in her book *After Ninety*, published posthumously in 1977.

PHOTO: Imogen Cunningham, *Self-Portrait 2*, 1932 (printed later). Gelatin silver print, collection of the Oakland Museum of California, gift of the Estate of Helen Johnston.

EDWARD SHERIFF CURTIS (1868–1952)

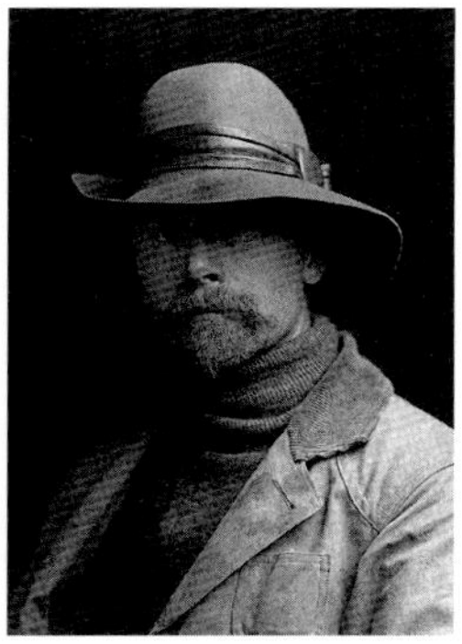

A photographer, author, ethnologist and filmmaker, Curtis is best known for his seminal twenty-volume work on aboriginal life, *The North American Indian*. Born in White Water, Wisconsin, Curtis began photography in the late 1880s and by 1891 had moved to Seattle where he joined the photographic firm of Rothi & Curtis. By 1893 he had entered the partnership of Curtis & Guptil, assuming sole proprietorship in 1897. At about this time he became interested in photographing Indians, accompanying the Edward H. Harriman Expedition to Alaska in 1899, a trip that stimulated his obsession with ethnographic images. In 1903 he traveled to the Southwest to photograph the Mojave, Zuni and Apache, exhibiting fifty portraits in his Seattle gallery. Other field work followed on a regular basis, often taking Curtis away from his studio for months at a time. *The North American Indian* was published in series from 1907 to 1930, eventually totaling 1,500 images in photogravure and copperplate engravings. The project received vital support around 1905 when President Theodore Roosevelt, impressed with Curtis's work, introduced him to capitalist J. P. Morgan, who advanced Curtis $75,000 to complete the enterprise. Other writings include two books, *Indian Days of Long Ago* (1914) and *In the Land of the Head-Hunters* (1915). By 1919 Curtis had moved to Los Angeles where he opened a portrait studio associated with the Hollywood film industry. In 1927 he made his last expedition, this time to Arctic Alaska in a fifty-foot boat which nearly cost him his life in the rigors of the Bering Sea (the resulting images were included in the final volume of *The North American Indian*). His full-length film *In the Land of the Headhunters* (1914) was briefly popular, then languished until the late 1940s, when a surviving copy was salvaged by the Field Museum of Chicago, who restored and reissued it with sound under the title *In the Land of the War Canoes* (1974). By way of epitaph, his daughter Florence said: "My father was a man with great singleness of purpose."

PHOTO: Edward Sheriff Curtis, *Self-Portrait,* 1899, printed circa 1930. Photogravure, Los Angeles County Museum of Art, The Audrey and Sydney Irmas Collection (AC1992.197.37).

WILLIAM EDWARD DASSONVILLE (1879–1957)

An artist, photographer, self-taught chemist and entrepreneur, Dassonville also invented, manufactured and distributed Dassonville Charcoal Black photographic printing paper. He received his first camera as a youth, and during the late 1890s became active in the California Camera Club. In December 1900 he joined forces with Oscar Mauer, opening a portrait studio on Stockton Street in San Francisco, and in 1901 he took his only trip to Europe, visiting Paris, Belgium and the Netherlands. He exhibited at the First San Francisco Photographic Salon and participated in the California Camera Club Exhibition of Industrial Arts, both in 1901. By 1904 Dassonville was already a veteran of the salon circuit and had established friendships with Alvin Langdon Coburn and others active in the "new school" of art photography. The 1906 earthquake and fire destroyed his studio; in its aftermath he established a close relationship with painter William Keith. By 1908 Dassonville had become interested in printing photographs on Japanese tissue, leading him to undertake a wide range of experimentation with new printing materials, and culminating in his manufacture of Charcoal Black paper beginning in 1924. He continued portrait and landscape photography, exhibiting well into the 1930s. Dassonville sold his Charcoal Black manufacturing business in the early 1940s, finding employment at Stanford University Hospital in San Francisco, where he photographed people with physical abnormalities.

JUDY DATER (1941–)

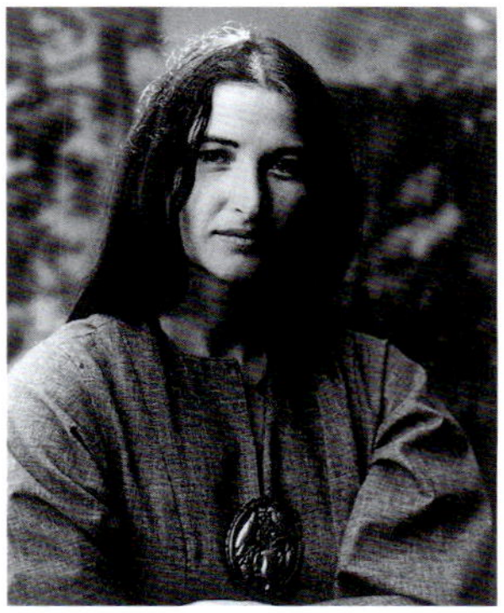

"My creative process is a composite event and encompasses whatever is going on," Dater has written, "dreams, revelations, psychiatry, talk, something I saw in a movie, a passage from a book." Born Judy Rose Lichtenfeld in Hollywood, Dater studied drawing and painting at the University of California, Los Angeles (1959). Briefly married (1962–64) to Dennis Dater, she began taking photographs in 1962 while studying art at San Francisco State, earning an M.A. degree in 1966. Her early mentor was Imogen Cunningham (then in her eighties), with whom she developed a close friendship. She also studied with Jack Welpott at the San Francisco Art Institute; the two were married from 1971 to 1977. Dater's early work was primarily black and white nudes and portraits. After 1979 she began working in color, beginning a series of self-portraits in 1980, many of them satirical comments on gender roles. Recent work includes installations and performance art. Dater has participated in innumerable group and solo exhibitions across the country and internationally. She has taught at the extension program of the University of California, San Francisco (1966–77) and the San Francisco Art Institute (1974–78). She has received numerous grants and awards, among them a Dorothea Lange Award (1974), National Endowment for the Arts grants (1976 and 1988), a Guggenheim Fellowship (1978), and a Marin Arts Council Individual Artist Grant (1987). Her work has been widely published, including the monographs *Judy Dater: Twenty Years* (1986) and *Judy Dater: Cycles* (1994).

PHOTO: Imogen Cunningham, *Judy Dater,* 1976. Gelatin silver print, collection of the Oakland Museum of California, gift of Judy Dater.

ROBERT DAWSON (1950–)

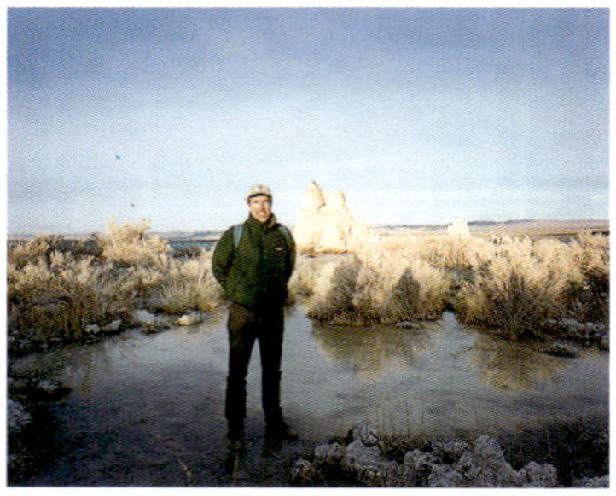

Born in Sacramento, Dawson holds a B.A. in psychology from the University of California, Santa Cruz (1972) and an M.A. in Interdisciplinary Creative Arts (with an emphasis in photography) from California State University, San Francisco (1979). Active as an educator, he has taught at a number of colleges and universities and conducted numerous photography workshops. Since the late 1970s Dawson has involved himself in environmental photographic projects, including *Mono Lake Series* (1979), the *Great Central Valley Project* (1982 and 1986), the *Water in the West Project* (1983), and his *Pyramid Lake Project with Peter Goin* (1989). From 1991 through 1993 he served as the chair of photography at the City College of San Francisco. Dawson continues to be involved in many Bay Area photographic organizations including San Francisco Camerawork, where he served as Vice President of the Board of Directors from 1986 to 1991. In 1988 he received a National Endowment for the Arts fellowship. Dawson's photographs have been published in the monograph *Robert Dawson: Photographs* and *Farewell, Promised Land,* and have been collected by various museums including the National Museum of American Art.

PHOTO: Ellen Manchester, *Robert Dawson*, 1999. Courtesy of Robert Dawson, copyright Ellen Manchester.

THEOPHILUS HOPE D'ESTRELLA (1851–1929)

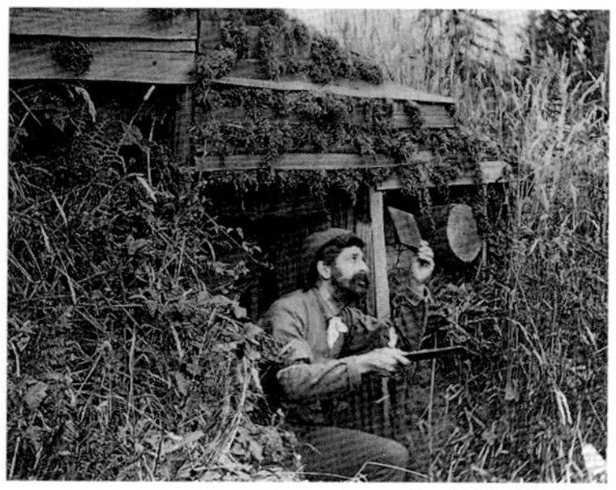

A painter, photographer and educator, d'Estrella was born Theophilus de Rutte but changed his name (d'Estrella is Spanish for "of the stars") to disassociate himself from his father, who had abandoned him as a baby. Born deaf, he was orphaned at the age of five when his mother died. As a child he roamed the streets of Gold Rush San Francisco, in 1860 becoming the first pupil of the newly formed California Institution for the Education and Care of the Indigent Deaf, Dumb, and Blind. Upon graduation in 1873 he became the first deaf student accepted at the University of California, Berkeley. He spent three years there, followed by five years at the San Francisco Art Association's California School of Design. He served as the drawing and painting instructor for the California School for the Deaf, Berkeley, holding that position until his death in 1929. He took up photography in 1886 and a few years later became a charter member of the California Camera Club. In 1901 he won a first prize medal at the first San Francisco Photographic Salon. A regular participant on Sierra Club jaunts, d'Estrella was a prolific writer and journalist, but his primary interest was always his students. He regularly used photography (in the form of lantern slides) in his classroom, to illustrate stories and lectures given in sign language and pantomime. In 1910 a fire destroyed his studio and all of his equipment, effectively ending his photographic career, although he continued to be an influential teacher.

PHOTO: Unknown, *Theophilus Hope D'Estrella Examining a Negative,* n.d. Courtesy of Peter E. Palmquist.

JOHN M. DIVOLA, JR. (1949–)

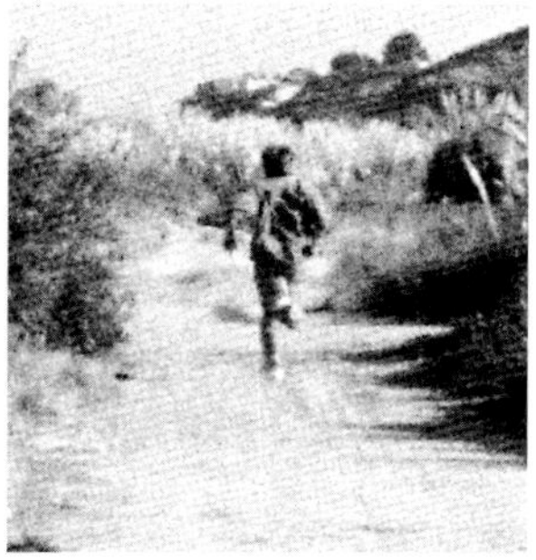

Divola's photographs explore the dialectical discourse between a known experience and visual sensation. For example, a series called *Vandalism* consists of black and white photographs of spray-painted markings which Divola made on the interior surfaces of abandoned houses. Divola's education includes a B.A. from California State University, Northridge (1971) and an M.A. (1973) and an M.F.A. (1974), both from the University of California, Los Angeles. He has received three National Endowment for the Arts Photography Fellowships (1973, 1976 and 1979). In 1986 he was awarded a Guggenheim Fellowship. Since 1973 his photographs have appeared in over one hundred exhibitions in the United States, Europe, Australia and Japan.

PHOTO: John Divola, *As Far As I Can Get,* 1996. Gelatin silver print, courtesy of John Divola.

WILLIAM DOHERTY (1940–1972)

Doherty earned a B.A. degree in History from Stanford University in 1962 before attending Harvard Law School for two years. From 1965 to 1967 he studied art with Robert Heinecken at the University of California, Los Angeles, and in 1967 received an M.A. degree in film history and esthetics through the Theater Arts Department. At that time he was employed as a filmmaker and worked as a photographer for the UCLA Museum of Cultural History. He also taught at the UCLA Extension program from 1971 until his death. A posthumous retrospective exhibition of his work was held at the Ohio Silver Gallery, Los Angeles, in October 1973.

JOHN PAUL EDWARDS (1884–1968)

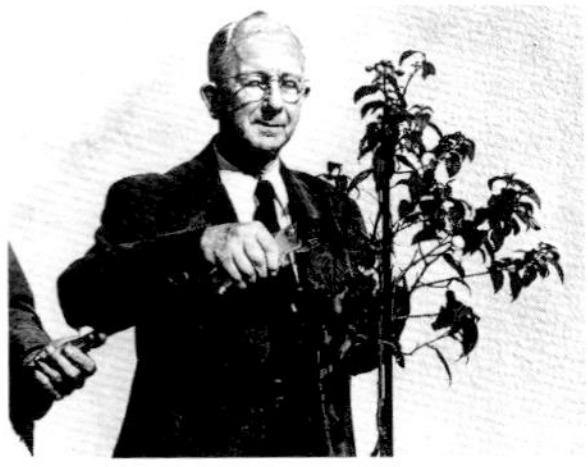

A well-known pictorialist photographer, Edwards rejected Pictorialism to become a founding member of Group f.64. Born in Minnesota, Edwards moved to California in 1902, becoming a member of the Oakland Camera Club and the Pictorial Photographers of America. He exhibited widely, participating in pictorialist salons in San Francisco, Los Angeles, Pittsburgh, New York, Toronto and London. A prominent member of the Pictorial Photographic Society of San Francisco, Edwards exhibited three prints in the group's Fifth International Exhibition in 1928. His daughter, photographer Mary Jeanette Edwards, opened the f.64 Gallery with Willard Van Dyke in Oakland and was instrumental in turning Edwards away from Pictorialism to embrace "straight" photography. As a charter member of the group, he participated in their landmark exhibition at the M. H. de Young Memorial Museum in 1932, and contributed an article on the group to *Camera Craft* in 1935.

PHOTO: Unknown, *John Paul Edwards Pruning Roses,* 1930s. Gelatin silver print, courtesy of Norman Donant.

GUSTAVUS A. F. FAGERSTEEN (c.1830–c.1890)

A portrait painter and photographer, Fagersteen was born in Prussia. He was active in San Antonio, Texas, in the firm of Vivier & Fagersteen in 1858–59 (he was listed as a "portrait artist" and Vivier as a "chemist.") Located in New Orleans at the end of the Civil War, he moved to California in the 1870s, where he joined in partnership with Benjamin Howland in a San Francisco gallery from about 1871 to 1873. In 1874 he moved to San Jose. By the summer of 1875 he had briefly relocated to Merced before beginning a tenure of many years in Yosemite as a photographer, painter and dealer in images of Yosemite Valley.

GEORGE ROBINSON FARDON (1807–1886)

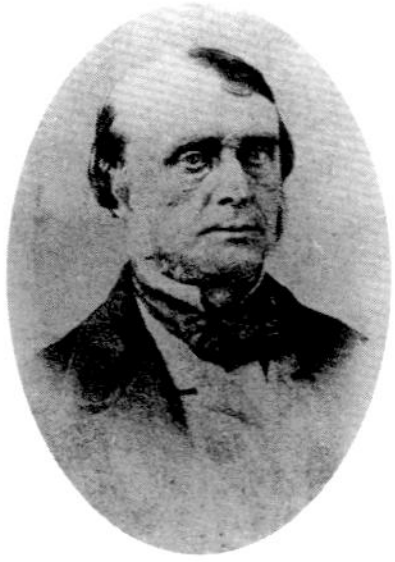

Fardon's reputation is based almost entirely on his seminal, photographically illustrated book, *San Francisco Album: Photographs of the Most Beautiful Views and Public Buildings of San Francisco* (1856). Illustrated with salt prints from wet collodion negatives, this volume is the earliest published photographic book of any American city, perhaps of any city in the world. An Englishman by birth, Fardon came to California by way of New York, arriving by 1854. He is known to have produced photographs on leather in San Francisco, several examples of which are extant. In 1858 he was attracted to British Columbia on the heels of the Fraser River gold discovery, and by 1861 was operating a studio in Victoria. In 1862 his panorama, *View of Victoria, Vancouver Island, from Hospital Point,* was exhibited at the World's Fair in London; it appeared as an engraving in the *London Illustrated News* on January 14, 1863. Fardon continued working in Victoria through 1871 before returning to California in 1876 as a partner in the portrait establishment of Bluett & Fardon, at 1157 Broadway, Oakland. He died in Victoria in 1886.

PHOTO: Unknown, *George Robinson Fardon,* 1860s. British Columbia Archives.

GEORGE FISKE (1835–1918)

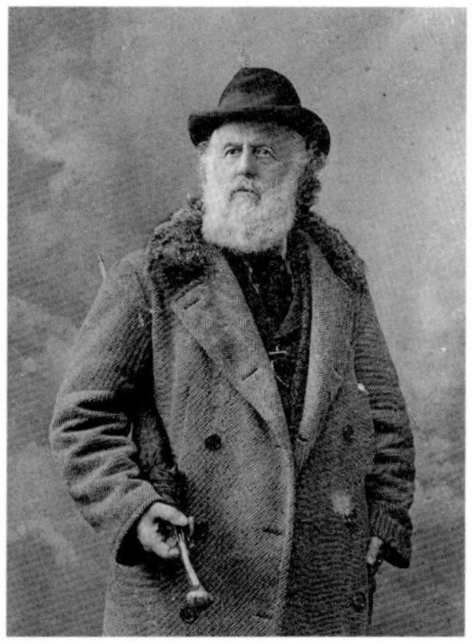

Raised on a farm in Amherst, New Hampshire, Fiske traveled to California in 1858, where he found work in a Sacramento banking house next door to photographer Robert H. Vance's branch gallery. By October 1864 he had relocated to San Francisco and was employed as a photographer. He worked for Carleton E. Watkins in 1868, then for Thomas Houseworth & Company from 1869 to 1874. In 1875 he accompanied Watkins to Yosemite, but after Watkins's gallery went bankrupt, Fiske went into business as a co-owner of a boarding house. He returned to landscape photography in 1878, and from the Fall of 1879 through the Fall of 1881 he lived with his wife in Yosemite, becoming the first photographer to reside in the valley year-round. In 1883 he received a silver medal at the Eighteenth Industrial Exhibition held at the Mechanic's Institute of San Francisco. Around this time the Fiskes received permission to build a house and darkroom across from the Yosemite Chapel; this would be their home until a fire destroyed it in 1904. By 1917 Fiske was suffering from a brain tumor, and on October 20, 1918 he committed suicide. He is buried in Yosemite's Pioneer Cemetery.

PHOTO: Elite Gallery, San Francisco, *Untitled (Portrait of George Fiske),* c. 1890. Mat collodion print, collection of the Oakland Museum of California, gift of Leonard Bardsley, Jr.

ROBBERT FLICK (1939–)

Born in the Netherlands, Flick traveled to Canada where he received a B.A. from the University of British Columbia, Vancouver, in 1967. He received Canada Council bursaries in 1967 and 1969, and was awarded M.A. and M.F.A. degrees (1970 and 1971) from the University of California, Los Angeles, where he studied with Robert Heinecken. He taught at the University of Illinois, Urbana-Champaign, from 1971 to 1976, and at the University of Southern California (USC) in Los Angeles (1976–78). In 1973 he was named a Fellow at the Center for Advanced Studies at the University of Illinois. Working primarily in black and white, he has concentrated on landscape and urban photography, including such series as *L.A. Diary, Midwest Diary, Wall Series* and *Inglewood Diary.* His book *Sequential Views, 1980–1986* was published in 1987. In 1998 he participated with Allan Sekula in *Port and Corridor: Working Sites in Los Angeles* in connection with the J. Paul Getty Research Institute Exhibition Gallery. He currently teaches at USC.

ROBERT FRANK (1924–)

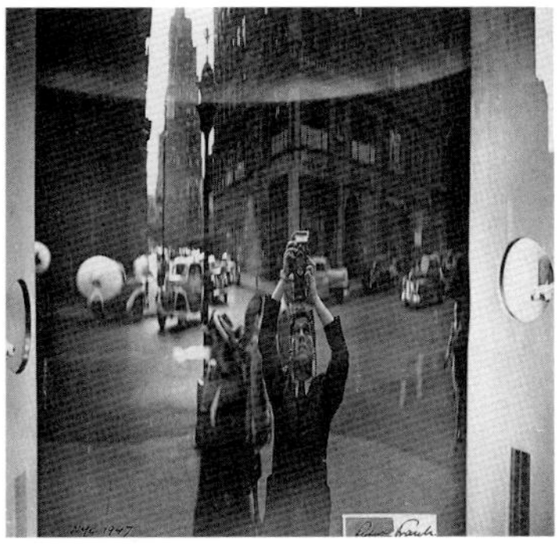

A photographer and filmmaker, Frank is best known for his book *The Americans* (1959), a record of his road travels in 1955 and 1956. Born in Zurich, Switzerland, Frank served as an apprentice in the film industry in 1942. The following year he worked as a photographer for Gloria Films in Zurich and freelanced for *Harper's Bazaar,* Paris, through the 1940s. He came to the United States in 1947, freelancing for *Fortune, LIFE, The New York Times* and other publications. In 1955 he became the first European to receive a Guggenheim Fellowship, the award that funded the two year cross-country trip which became *The Americans.* He began making motion pictures in 1958. His films include: *Pull My Daisy* (1959), *Kaddish* (c. 1965–66), *Me and My Brother* (c. 1965–68), *Conversations in Vermont* (c. 1969), *About Me—A Musical* (1971), *Life Dances On* (1980), *Home Improvements* (1985), and *Candy Mountain* (c. 1987). Publications include: *Pull My Daisy* (1961), *Zero Mostel Reads a Book* (1963), *The Lines of My Hand* (1971), and revised editions of *The Americans* in 1969 and 1978.

PHOTO: Robert Frank, *NYC, 1947 (Self-Portrait),* 1947 (printed later). Gelatin silver print, Los Angeles County Museum of Art, The Audrey and Sydney Irmas Collection (AC1992.55). Copyright Robert Frank, courtesy of Pace/MacGill Gallery, New York.

GEOFFREY FRICKER (1947–)

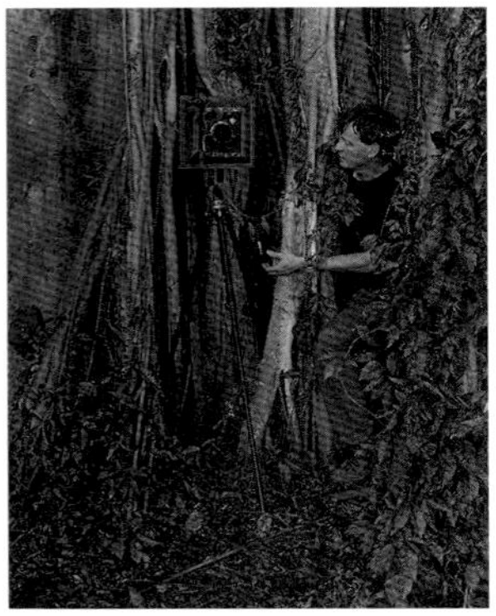

A photographer and educator concerned with water in the West, Fricker uses an 8-by-10-inch view camera perched atop a hydraulic lift to create sweeping black and white landscapes. He earned a B.A. degree in art at Raymond College, University of the Pacific in Stockton (1968) and an M.F.A. in photography from the San Francisco Art Institute (1972). He was employed as a medical photographer at the University of California, Davis (1971–73) and as a staff photographer for the Public Information Office of the United States Air Force (1971–75). He has taught photography at various locations from 1973 to the present, and is currently Chair of the Photography Department, Butte College, Oroville, California. Since 1980 Fricker has had a number of international exhibitions. He received a Phelan Award from the Oakland Museum (1971), a National Science Foundation Grant for Exploratory Research (1993) and Department of Water Resources contracts (1995 and 1996). From 1995 to 1997 he served as photographer and director of photography for the Watershed Restoration Project. In 1999 Fricker received a National Endowment for the Arts photography grant to continue his *Watershed* project and to shape it into a traveling exhibition.

PHOTO: Geoffrey Fricker, *From the Sugar Mill—Hamakuapoho (Self-Portrait),* 1999. Gelatin silver print, courtesy of Geoffrey Fricker.

ARNOLD GENTHE (1869–1942)

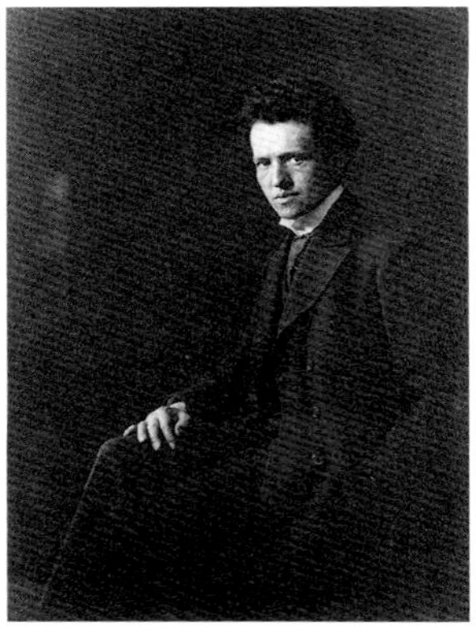

Although his name will always be linked with candid street photographs of San Francisco's Chinatown, Genthe was a man of wide-ranging interests and tastes. In 1938, writer Robert W. Marks referred to Genthe as "a Don Juan, a Hermit Monk, a Chinese Sage, a University Professor—all rolled into one." A German immigrant, Genthe held a doctorate in Philology from the University of Jena in Germany (1894). He also studied at the Sorbonne in Paris (1894–95). He arrived in San Francisco in 1895 to tutor the eldest son of Baron and Baroness von Schroeder, one of the city's wealthiest couples. Genthe quickly became an intimate of San Francisco's artistic and literary elite, joining both the Bohemian Club and the California Camera Club. He was a regular participant in photographic salons. In 1898 he opened a portrait gallery on Sutter Street which catered to the rich and famous. His two books, *Pictures of Old Chinatown* (1908) and *Old Chinatown: A Book of Pictures* (1913), with essays by Will Irwin, were popular and precedent-setting, documenting the intricate blending of modern and traditional cultures to which he remained drawn throughout his life. In 1910 he moved to New York City to become a highly respected professional photographer with a long list of celebrities, financiers and politicians as clients. His autobiography, *As I Remember,* was published in 1936.

PHOTO: Laura Adams Armer, *Untitled (Portrait of Arnold Genthe),* c. 1900. Gelatin silver print, collection of the Oakland Museum of California, gift of Mr. and Mrs. Austin Armer.

JOHN GUTMANN (1905–1998)

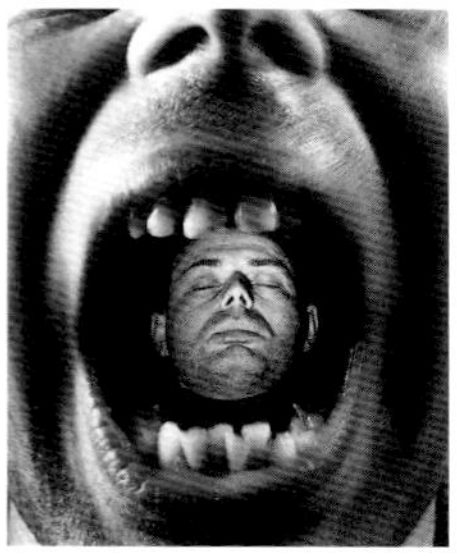

"I believe a good picture is open to many individual (subjective) associations." A leading artist and photojournalist during the Great Depression, Gutmann was born in Breslau, Germany. With degrees from German art schools, he spent his early adulthood in the raucous and revolutionary Berlin of the 1920s. Following Hitler's takeover, he emigrated to San Francisco in 1934, where he worked for the German agency Presse-Photo (1933–34). Work for a variety of popular American photo and weekly news magazines followed, including *PIX, Inc.,* through 1962. Gutmann began teaching at California State University, San Francisco in 1936, founding the photography department there in 1946. He received a Guggenheim Fellowship in 1978, and in 1984 his collection of images from the Great Depression, *The Restless Decade,*

was published with an introduction by the critic Max Kozloff. A selection of his paintings and drawings was shown at the M. H. de Young Memorial Museum in 1995. Considered a modernist, Gutmann maintained a high profile in the wider literary and artistic circles of San Francisco. A retrospective exhibition, *The Photography of John Gutmann: Culture Shock,* was mounted at the Cantor Arts Center, Stanford University, in 2000.

PHOTO: John Gutmann, *Death Trap. Self-Portrait,* 1936. © The Estate of John Gutmann.

OTTO HAGEL (1909–1973)

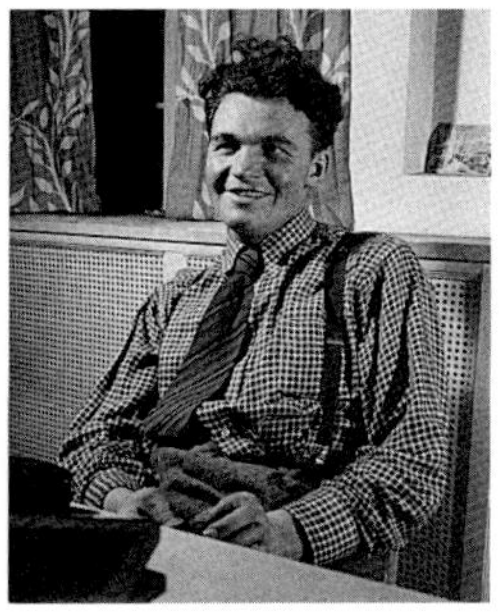

Like his wife Hansel Mieth, photojournalist Otto Hagel spent his life as a social documentarian. Both were born in Germany, running away together at age fifteen in order to find "truth in life." Their travels took them to Vienna, Yugoslavia, Romania, Bulgaria and Turkey. By the 1920s they were supporting themselves by selling snapshots to local newspapers. Hagel left for the United States in 1928, followed by Mieth in 1930 (they were married in 1941). Both became involved in freelance photojournalism, Hagel with *Time* and Mieth with *LIFE.* Their primary focus was the human condition, particularly issues of labor and poverty. In 1933 they made a documentary film on the California cotton strike, followed by another called *Century of Progress* (1934). During the 1940s they lived near Glen Ellen in the Sonoma Valley, while Mieth continued with *LIFE* and Hagel worked for *Fortune* and other publications. After World War II they visited their childhood home in Fellbach, Germany, publishing the photo-essay *We Return to Fellbach,* in *LIFE.* Stateside, the onset of the McCarthy era subjected them to political suspicion, causing them to lose work. Despite this, Hagel participated in the landmark exhibition *The Family of Man* at the Museum of Modern Art in New York in 1955. In 1994 a retrospective solo exhibit of Hagel's work was held at the International Center of Photography, Midtown, New York. Hagel died in Santa Rosa, California.

PHOTO: Hansel Mieth, *Portrait of Otto Hagel,* c. 1938. Courtesy of Debra Heimerdinger/Fine Art Photographs.

JOHAN HAGEMEYER (1884–1962)

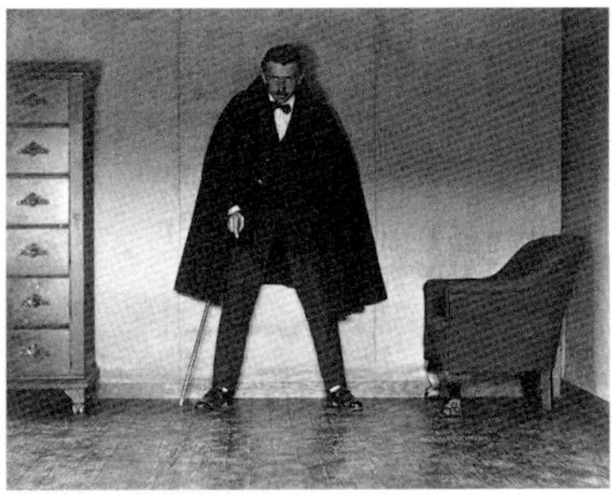

Called the "man who paints with a camera," Hagemeyer was born in Amsterdam, Holland, immigrating to California in 1911 to work as a horticulturist. During a trip to Washington, D.C. he contracted pneumonia and, while recuperating, saw an issue of Alfred Stieglitz's *Camera Work* at the Library of Congress. Intrigued, Hagemeyer found his way to New York in 1916 where he met Stieglitz and decided to become a photographer. Returning to California, he completed a short apprenticeship in Berkeley before becoming Edward Weston's assistant in Los Angeles in 1917. By 1919 he had returned to the Bay Area, where he operated a succession of portrait galleries and in 1927 served as a photographer for *The San Franciscan.* In 1938 he held a one-man retrospective at the M. H. de Young Memorial Museum in San Francisco, and in 1939 he exhibited at the Golden Gate International Exposition. In 1952 Hagemeyer moved to Berkeley, where he remained until his death in 1962.

PHOTO: Edward Weston, *Portrait of Johan Hagemeyer,* c. 1920. Platinum print, collection of the Oakland Museum of California, The Oakland Museum Founders Fund.

ADELAIDE HANSCOM (1876–1932)

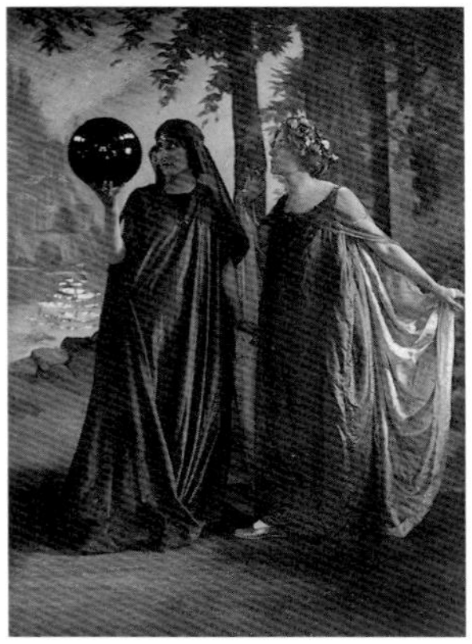

Known for portraits and narrative tableaux, Hanscom was born in Empire City, Oregon. By 1892 she had entered the Mark Hopkins Institute of Art (now the San Francisco Art Institute). In 1901, she exhibited at the Channing Club Exhibition, Berkeley, winning two second prizes. A year later she took over the San Francisco studio of Laura Adams Armer, whose clients included many prominent Bay Area families. With her partner Blanche Cumming, she produced a photographically illustrated version of *The Rubáiyát of Omar Khayyám* (1905), a popular success which was eventually issued in a number of editions, including a color version in 1912. She exhibited regularly until the San Francisco earthquake and fire of 1906 destroyed her studio, the *Rubáiyát* negatives and most of her exhibition prints. She established a gallery in Seattle, and in 1908 married Gerald Leeson, a British mining engineer and former Canadian Mountie. The marriage was not a happy one. Following a stormy argument, Leeson enlisted in the Canadian army during World War I and was killed in his first battle (1915). Widowed and with two children, Hanscom's mental health began to deteriorate and she retreated to an artist's colony in Berkeley, where she did illustrations for Elizabeth Browning's *Sonnets from the Portuguese* (1916). From 1922 to 1924 she lived in a mental-health facility in Napa. In 1924 she took her inheritance and moved to England, but soon returned to California to be near her daughter. Hanscom was killed in a hit-and-run accident in Los Angeles in 1932.

PHOTO: Adelaide L. Hanscom, *Anne Brigman (left) and Adelaide L. Hanscom,* c. 1906. Gelatin silver print, collection of the Oakland Museum of California, Willard Nott Exchange.

ALFRED A. HART (1816–1908)

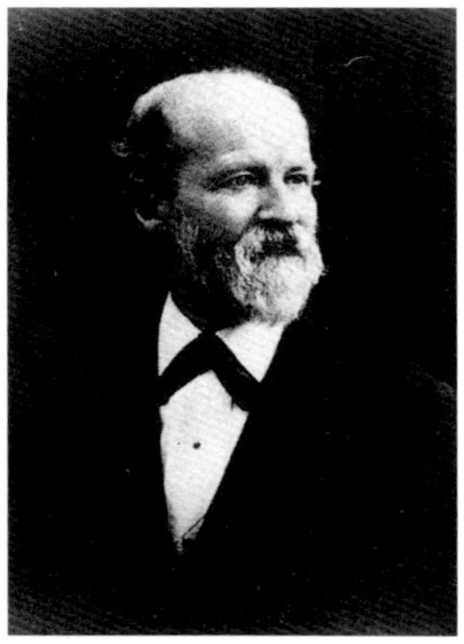

Best known as the photographer who recorded construction of the Transcontinental Railroad over the Sierra Nevadas, Hart was born in Connecticut and trained as a portrait painter. In 1852 he painted a panorama depicting biblical scenes in the Holy Land, which he supplemented with lectures and commentary. Five years later he opened a daguerreotype studio in Hanford, Connecticut, before moving to Cleveland, Ohio, to open an art store. He came to California in 1863, opening a gallery in La Porte before teaming with the Central Pacific Railroad (C.P.R.R.), which hired him to record the arduous task of building a railroad over the Sierras. After producing hundreds of stereo negatives, Hart's connection with the company was severed and Carleton E. Watkins—thanks, no doubt, to Watkins's connection with C.P.R.R. official Collis P. Huntington—replaced Hart as official photographer. Watkins proceeded to publish Hart's negatives as his own. Hart moved to Denver, Colorado, and worked as a portrait painter, but in 1872 he was back in California, winning first prize for the Most Meritorious Exhibition of Paintings at the State Agricultural Exhibition in Sacramento. In 1874, living in San Francisco, he was listed as a landscape and portrait painter. During the 1880s Hart moved to New York, where he was awarded patents for a folding magic lantern device and a new "Method for Making Photographic Pictures." Returning to California, he died in the Alameda County Infirmary in 1908, a few days before his ninety-second birthday.

PHOTO: Unknown, *Alfred A. Hart,* n.d. Courtesy of Peter E. Palmquist.

ROBERT F. HEINECKEN (1931–)

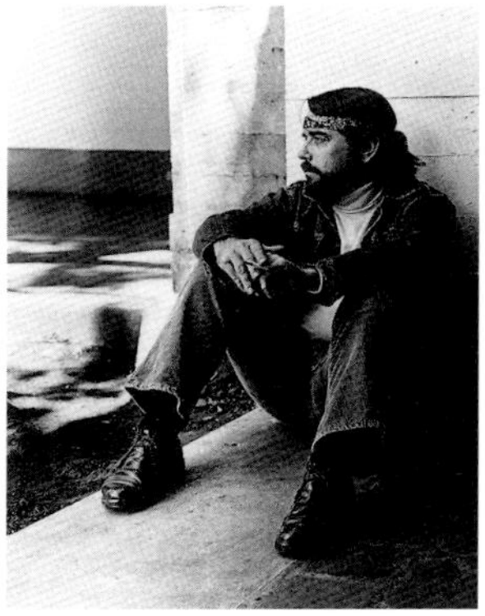

Born in Denver, Colorado, Heinecken served as a Marine fighter pilot in the 1950s and earned his M.A. degree in printmaking from the University of California, Los Angeles in 1960. He worked briefly in graphic design before becoming interested in photography around 1962. Describing himself as a "photographist," Heinecken's work consists of photographic material appropriated from print media and television that has been reworked to reveal new meanings and context. Although he claims to be unconcerned with technical mastery, Heinecken founded the photography program at UCLA in the early 1960s and continued to teach there until 1991. Known as a teacher and mentor to a generation of UCLA-trained photographers, Heinecken has also been an instructor at the State University of New York, Buffalo (1969), the School of the Art Institute of Chicago (1970), San Francisco Art Institute (1971) and Harvard University (1972). He has received a John Simon Guggenheim Fellowship (1976), two National Endowment for the Arts grants (1977 and 1981), a Peer Award from the Friends of Photography, Carmel (1985), and the First Annual Members Award of the California Museum of Photography, Riverside (1985). He held his first solo photography exhibition in 1964 and his work has continued to be exhibited and published on a regular basis. A retrospective, *Robert Heinecken: Photographist,* was exhibited at the Museum of Contemporary Art in Chicago in 1999 and traveled to Los Angeles in 2000.

PHOTO: Joan Murray, *Robert Heinecken,* 1971. Gelatin silver print, collection of the Oakland Museum of California, gift of Joan Murray.

ANTHONY LOUIS HERNANDEZ (1947–)

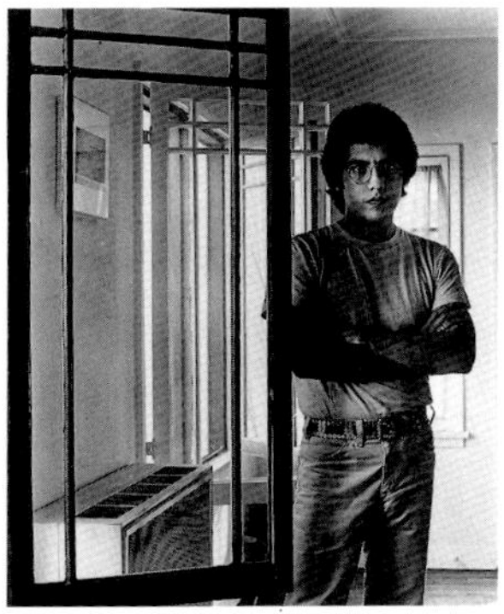

Born in Los Angeles, Hernandez is known for California cityscapes such as those in his 1995 exhibition *Landscapes for the Homeless.* His education includes East Los Angeles College (1966–67) and the Center of the Eye in Aspen, Colorado (1969), where he studied with Lee Friedlander. In 1971 he was one of three Los Angeles photographers in the exhibition *Crowded Vacancy* at the Memorial Union Art Gallery, University of California, Davis. Hernandez has garnered a number of grants and awards, including the Friends of Photography Ferguson Grant (1972) and three National Endowment for the Arts Photographer's Fellowships (1975, 1978 and 1980). In 1987 he participated with photographer Lewis Baltz in an exhibition and publication titled *Nevada.* His work has been collected by museums across the United States and in Europe.

PHOTO: Joan Murray, *Anthony Hernandez,* 1972. Gelatin silver print, collection of the Oakland Museum of California, gift of Joan Murray.

LYNN LESTER HERSHMAN-LEESON (1941–)

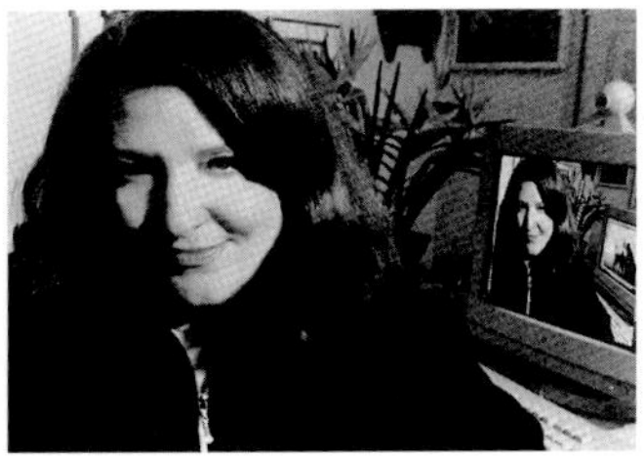

Hershman-Leeson is widely recognized for her exploration of contemporary social, gender and political issues through interactive art. In addition to photography, her work has included video, installation and Internet-based art. She is also credited with developing the first interactive video disc, *Lorna,* as early as 1979. She has received numerous awards, including the 1995 Media Arts Award, shared with Peter Greenaway and Jean Baudrillard. She was the first woman to receive a tribute and retrospective at the San Francisco International Film Festival (1994). Her first feature film, *Conceiving Ada,* was shown at the 1998 Sundance Film Festival and as many as thirty-five other festivals worldwide. The film, which used pioneering digital processes to create virtual sets, has been recognized for technical achievement. Her work is held by numerous collections in the United States and abroad. She is currently a Professor of Digital Art at the University of California, Davis, and is the author of *Clicking In: Hotlinks to a Digital Culture* (1996). A new monograph on her work, published by the University of California Press, will be available in 2001.

PHOTO: *Lynn Hershman,* n.d. Courtesy of Lynn Hershman.

TODD HIDO (1968–)

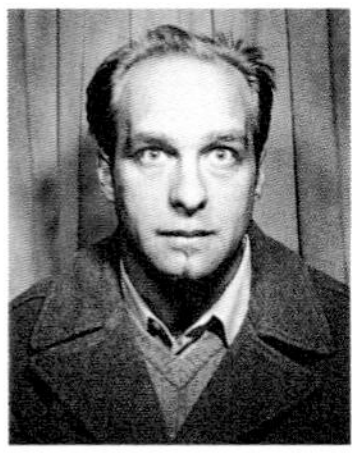

Born in Kent, Ohio, Hido earned a B.F.A. from Tufts University in 1991 before attending the Rhode Island School of Design for two years. He received his M.F.A., from the California College of Arts and Crafts in Oakland, in 1996. He has exhibited widely since 1988, including two recent exhibitions: *Immodest Gazes* in Barcelona, Spain, and a solo exhibition, *Homing In* at the Stephen Wirtz Gallery, San Francisco. In 1996 Hido was awarded the Barclay Simpson Award and in 1998 received the Wallace Alexander Gerbode Foundation Visual Arts Award. He also garnered the Eureka Fellowship from the Fleishhacker Foundation, and the Recent Graduate of Distinction Award from his alma mater, California College of Arts and Crafts.

PHOTO: *Todd Hido, 2000.* Courtesy of Stephen Wirtz Gallery.

THOMAS HOUSEWORTH (1828–1915)

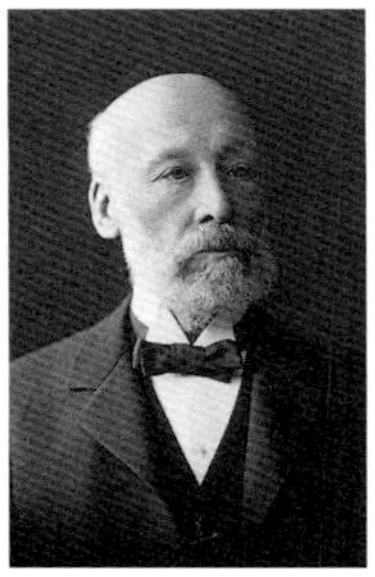

An optician, photographer and publisher, Houseworth came to California from New York by way of Cape Horn in 1849. After a period of mining in Calaveras and Trinity counties, he joined George S. Lawrence in opening an optical store in San Francisco in 1851, the first on the Pacific Coast. By 1860 the firm was offering stereoscopes for sale, and by 1863 it had begun stereo production in earnest, publishing the work of photographers such as Charles L. Weed. In 1867 Lawrence retired and the business was renamed Thomas Houseworth & Company. It continued until 1886, when it fell on hard times. Houseworth worked as an independent photographer with indifferent success until 1894, when he briefly found work as an accountant. A few years later he returned to optometry, becoming president of the San Francisco Association of Optometrists. In 1908 he received recognition as the "longest practicing member of that profession in San Francisco."

PHOTO: Unknown, *Thomas Houseworth,* n.d. Courtesy of Peter E. Palmquist.

GEORGE HURRELL (1904–1992)

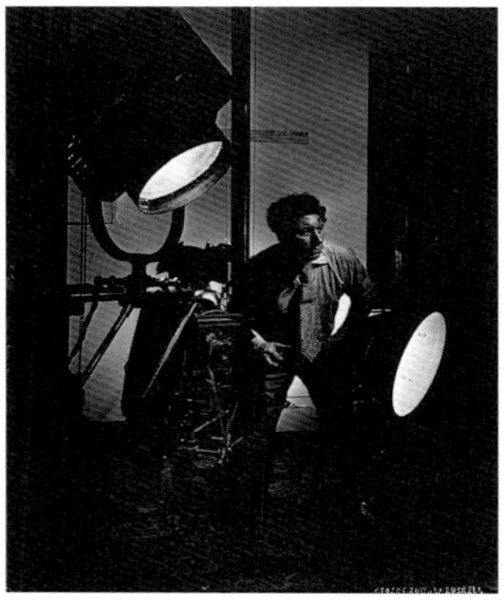

Hurrell's name is synonymous with Hollywood glamour photography. Born in Cincinnati, Ohio, He attended the Chicago Art Institute in 1920 and apprenticed to portrait photographer Eugene Hutchinson in 1922. He moved to California in 1925 and opened a studio in Los Angeles two years later, producing portraits of motion picture stars for Metro-Goldwyn-Mayer (1930–32), 20th Century-Fox (1932–34) and Warner Brothers (1935–38). During World War II he served as a staff photographer for the Pentagon. Following the war he worked for Columbia Pictures before joining the Walt Disney Studios in 1956. From 1960 to 1975 Hurrell worked as a freelance production and publicity still photographer for the motion picture and television industry. In 1977 he published a book, *The Hurrell Style.*

PHOTO: George Hurrell, *Self-Portrait,* 1947. Gelatin silver print, Los Angeles County Museum of Art, The Audrey and Sydney Irmas Collection (AC1992.197.71). Reproduced courtesy of George Hurrell, Hurrell's Hollywood.

HENRY ALBERT HUSSEY (1887–1959)

Born in Sacramento, Hussey was a graduate of the University of California, Berkeley (1909). He purchased his first camera while stationed in Germany during World War I, and in 1920 became a founding member of the Pictorial Photographic Society of San Francisco. He was a regular participant in international photographic salons between 1917 and 1930. Hussey also frequently published photographs, criticism and essays in photographic periodicals such as *Camera Craft.* By 1939 he had begun to photograph exclusively with Kodachrome, a color transparency film.

GEORGE HOWARD JOHNSON (c. 1923– ?)

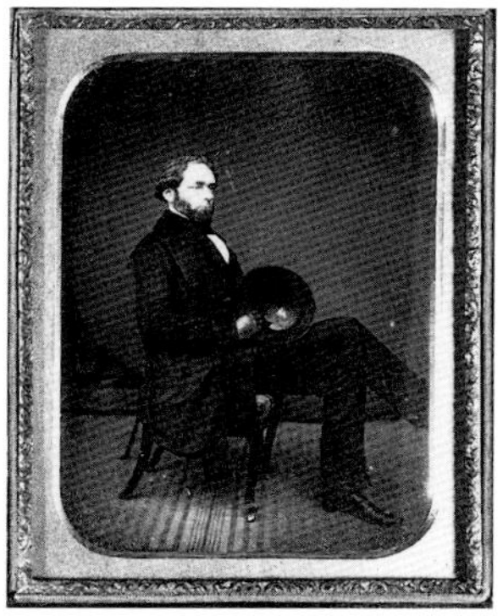

A pioneer photographer of the Gold Rush, Johnson arrived in California in January of 1849. Establishing a studio in Sacramento (referred to in advertising as a "Facial and Landscape Gallery"), he photographed miners on their way to the gold fields, sometimes taking his camera into the "diggins" as well. In 1850 he made daguerreotypes of the Sacramento Squatter's Riot which were published, as wood engravings, in the *Illustrated California News.* That same year he lost his Sacramento gallery to fire and moved to San Francisco, joining Seth Louis Shaw in a brief partnership known as the Eureka Daguerrean Rooms, on Montgomery Street. He continued in San Francisco, working in various partnerships, until 1873, when he moved to New York City. He was known to be active as a photographer in the late 1880s, apparently living in Denver, Colorado, but details of the closing years of his life and death are unknown.

PHOTO: George H. Johnson studio, *Portrait of George H. Johnson,* c.1852. Quarter plate daguerreotype, courtesy of Peter E. Palmquist.

STEPHEN JOHNSON (1955–)

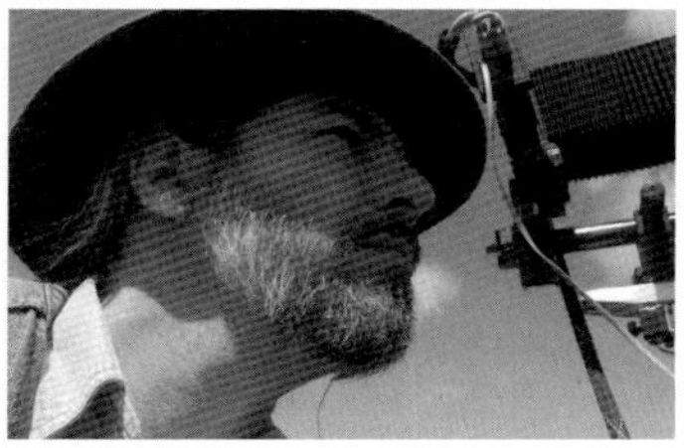

Johnson is a photographer, designer and teacher who explores the dilemmas that confront a landscape artist in an increasingly industrialized world. He is particularly interested in refining the new tools of digital photography, and since 1989 has worked on a groundbreaking national parks project, *With a New Eye,* which records images on digital sensors instead of film. Johnson received his B.A. (1978) and M.A. (1982) degrees from California State University, San Francisco. He served as curator, editor and designer for *At Mono Lake,* a book and National Endowment for the Arts-funded exhibition that toured the United States from 1980 to 1983. In 1988 he was awarded a congressional Special Recognition Award for his work on behalf of Mono Lake. He was co-creator of *The Great Central Valley Project,* a photographic exhibit focusing on the human-altered heartland of California. Using a Macintosh computer, he edited, designed, and created the graphics for the award-winning *The Great Central Valley: California's Heartland,* a companion book published by the University of California Press in 1993. Johnson has taught digital imaging courses in numerous venues, including the Center for Creative Imaging in Camden, Maine, and regularly lectures at leading digital and photographic industry forums. Examples of his work have appeared in many publications, including *LIFE, American Photographer,* and *Sierra.*

PHOTO: Stephen Johnson, *Stephen Johnson at Badlands National Park,* 1997. Kodak DCS 460M digital camera image, courtesy of Stephen Johnson.

PIRKLE JONES (1914–)

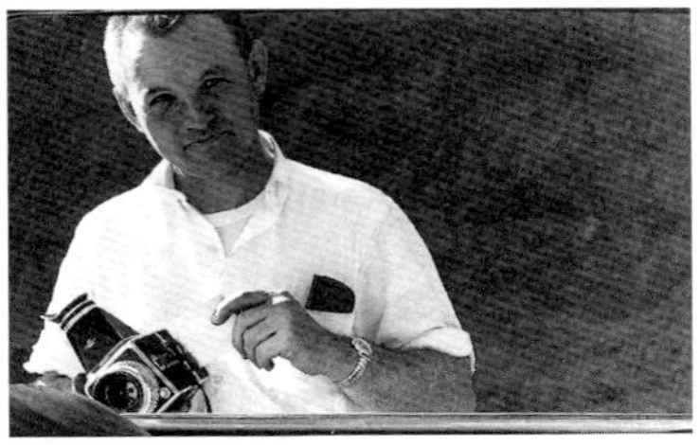

A native of Shreveport, Louisiana, Jones graduated from the California School of Fine Arts (now the San Francisco Art Institute). He studied with Ansel Adams and Minor White, crediting them, along with Dorothea Lange, Edward Weston and Alfred Stieglitz, with shaping his vision. Jones served in the U.S. Army Signal Corps (1941–46) before working as an assistant to Ansel Adams (1949–52). In 1960 he created *Death of a Valley* with Dorothea Lange, a photo-essay and book focusing on the last days of the Berryessa Valley in Napa County before it was flooded to create a reservoir. In 1970 he joined the staff of the San Francisco Art Institute, where he taught until the late 1980s. In 1961 he received a certificate of recognition from the National Urban League for photographic excellence and participation in *America's Many Faces,* and in 1977 he won a National Endowment for the Arts grant. His work has been widely published and is held in collections throughout the United States.

PHOTO: Dorothea Lange, *Untitled (Pirkle Jones with Hasselblad),* n.d. © Oakland Museum of California, the City of Oakland. Gift of Paul S. Taylor.

ARTHUR F. KALES (1882–1936)

Born in Phoenix, Arizona, Kales grew up in Oakland and completed a law degree at the University of California, Berkeley, in 1903. While living in the Bay Area he became interested in pictorial photography, participating in a number of photographic salons. He worked briefly in Los Angeles in 1916, where he was active with the Camera Pictorialists of Los Angeles. Between 1922 and his death in 1936, Kales wrote a number of essays on developments in pictorial photography in western America for the prestigious *Photograms of the Year.* He was a fellow of the Royal Photographic Society and exhibited in the John Wanamaker Salon of 1918 and the London Salons of 1920 and 1931. In 1928 he mounted a fifty-print retrospective at the Smithsonian Institution. He died in Los Angeles.

MARK KLETT (1952–)

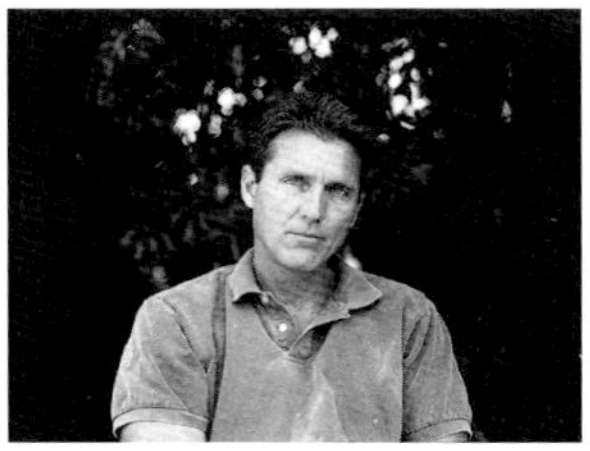

A native of Albany, New York, Klett earned a B.S. degree in geology from St. Lawrence University, Canton, New York (1974), followed by an M.F.A. in photography from the Visual Studies Workshop in Rochester (1977). After undergraduate studies, Klett worked for the U.S. Geological Survey (1974–76) and took an early interest in photographing the land. Klett has written or co-authored several books, including *Second View: The Rephotographic Survey Project* (1984); *Traces of Eden: Travels in the Desert Southwest* (1986); *One City / Two Visions: San Francisco Panoramas, 1878 and 1990* (1990); *Revealing Territory: Photographs of the Southwest* (1992); *Capital View: A New Panorama of Washington, D.C.* (1994); and *Desert Legends: Re-storying the Sonoran Borderlands* (1994). Klett is the recipient of four National Endowment for the Arts Fellowships (1979, 1982, 1984 and 1993) and two awards from The Friends of Photography (1980 and 1992). His interactive exhibition, *Participant Observer: Photography by Mark Klett* was featured at the Virginia Steele Scott Gallery, Huntington Library, in 1999. Klett's photographs have appeared in numerous individual and group exhibitions across the country and abroad. Venues include the National Museum of American Art, the Center for Creative Photography, the Amon Carter Museum, the Los Angeles County Museum of Art, and the Art Institute of Chicago.

PHOTO: Emily Matyas, *Mark Klett, March 31, 2000, Tempe Arizona,* 2000. Gelatin silver print, collection of the Oakland Museum of California, gift of Mark Klett and Emily Matyas, courtesy of Fraenkel Gallery, San Francisco.

VILEM KRIZ (1921–1994)

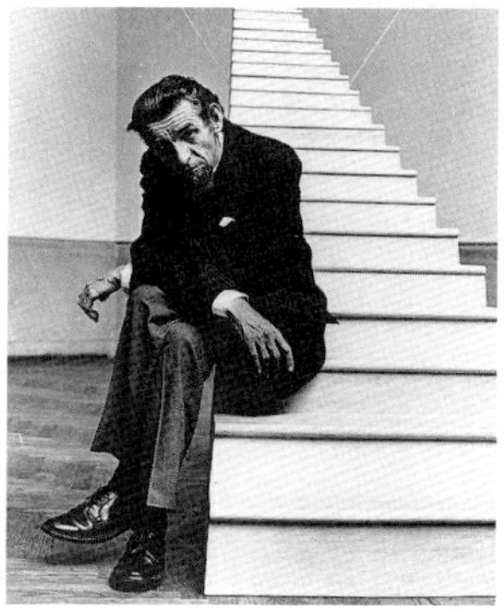

Born in Prague, Czechoslovakia, Kriz attended the School of Graphic Arts in Prague, where he studied with Jaromír Funke, Josef Ehm and František Drtikol. From 1946 to 1952 he lived in Paris, working as a press photographer. He attended the Ecole Cinématographique et Photographique and worked with Jean Cocteau and other artists. Throughout these years he was active in the surrealist movement. In 1952 he moved to the United States, becoming a naturalized citizen in 1958. He settled in Berkeley, where he worked as a freelance photographer. He also taught at various Bay Area institutions including Mills College, Oakland, Holy Names College, Oakland, and at the University of California, Berkeley. From 1975 until his retirement in 1991, he taught surrealism and photography at the California College of Arts and Crafts, Oakland. *San Francisco Chronicle* art critic Thomas Albright called Kriz among "the last of the true Surrealists." Kriz was also a poet. His photographs have been published in several books and shown internationally.

PHOTO: Joan Murray, *Vilem Kriz,* 1969. Gelatin silver print, collection of the Oakland Museum of California, gift of Joan Murray.

VICTOR LANDWEBER (1943–)

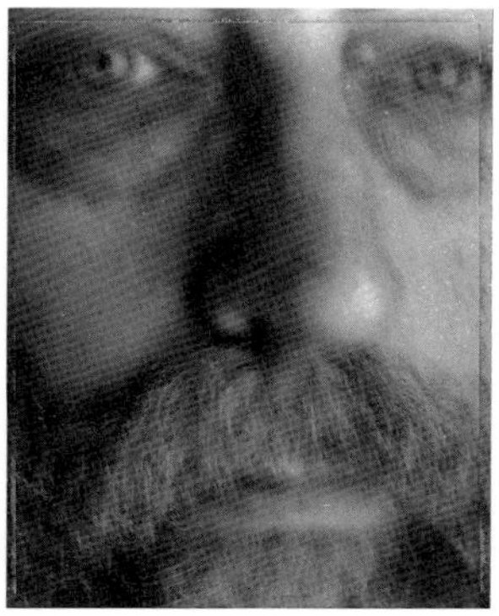

Born in Washington, D.C., Landweber received a B.A. from the University of Iowa in 1966 and an M.F.A. from the University of California, Los Angeles, in 1976. His mentor at UCLA was Robert Heinecken. A self-employed photographer and art publisher, Landweber has taught photography at various California institutions, including the University of California, Berkeley (1988 and 1994–97), UCLA's Extension Program (1971–73 and 1977–87), Otis Art Institute, Los Angeles, (1982–84), and Orange Coast College, Costa Mesa (1973–76). He currently teaches at Academy of Art College, San Francisco (since 1988). His work has been widely published and is represented in a number of public collections. A retrospective book, *Victor Landweber Photographs, 1967–1984* was published in 1985. His work recently appeared in the exhibition *L.A. Current: the Photographers' Perspective* at the Armand Hammer Museum of Art, Los Angeles.

PHOTO: Marion Brenner, *Victor,* 2000. Courtesy of Marion Brenner and Victor Landweber.

DOROTHEA MARGARETTA LANGE (1895–1965)

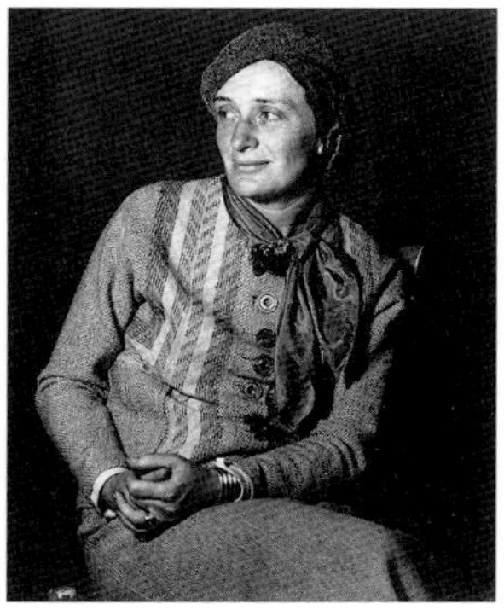

Born Dorothea Margaretta Nutzhorn in Hoboken, New Jersey, Lange is best remembered for her documentary photographs of migrant farm workers, including *Migrant Mother,* one of the great icons of photography. Lange contracted polio at age seven, which left her with a malformed right leg. She studied at the New York Training School for Teachers (1914–15), and worked as an assistant to Arnold Genthe in his New York studio (c. 1915). She took a class in fine art photography from Clarence White at the extension division of Teacher's College, Columbia University (1917). In 1918 she and a friend began an around-the-world tour during which she hoped to make a living with her camera. Stranded in San Francisco, she found work as a photofinisher. Shortly thereafter she opened her own portrait studio (1919) and married painter Maynard Dixon (1920). In 1933, after years of studio work, Lange took her camera to the streets to photograph victims of the Depression. This first outing resulted in *White Angel Breadline,* a pivotal work that brought her to the attention of Paul S. Taylor, an economist at the University of California, Berkeley. He hired Lange to document migratory workers for the State Resettlement Administration. Their joint report, seen by Roy Stryker in Washington, led to Lange's employment as a photographer for the Farm Security Administration (FSA), an agency of the Department of Agriculture, in 1935. Lange divorced Dixon and married Taylor the same year. For the next five years, she traveled extensively for the FSA, photographing in every part of the United States except New England. In 1941 she became the first woman to receive a Guggenheim Fellowship for photography. During World War II she documented the internment of Japanese-Americans for the War Relocation Authority, and defense industry workers in the Bay Area. Despite failing health, Lange continued to photograph until the end of her life, working in Southeast Asia, Egypt and Ireland, as well as near her home in Berkeley. Her final days were spent working on a retrospective exhibition at the Museum of Modern Art in New York, which opened posthumously. The Oakland Museum of California holds her creative estate, including 25,000 negatives, 6,000 prints and hundreds of personal papers. In 1971 the Museum established the Dorothea Lange Award for women photographers; the first recipient was Lange's friend Imogen Cunningham.

PHOTO: Unknown, *Dorothea Lange,* 1930s. Gelatin silver print, collection of the Oakland Museum of California, gift of John Eaglefeather Dixon.

ALMA RUTH LAVENSON (1897–1989)

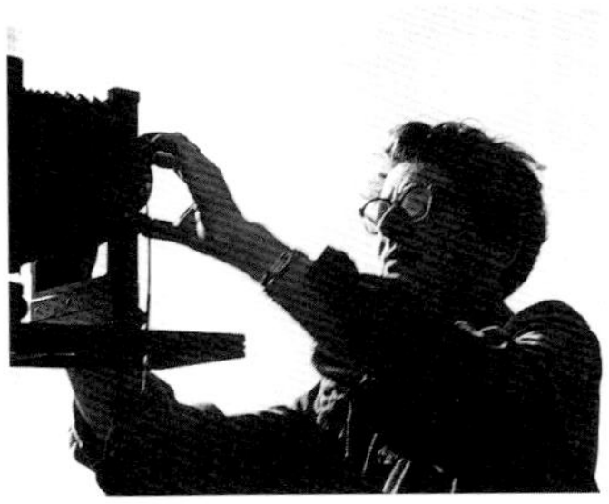

Born in San Francisco, Lavenson moved to Oakland with her family following the 1906 earthquake. She earned a B.A. in Psychology from the University of California, Berkeley (1919) and embarked on a seven-month tour of Europe during which she began to use a camera. She is known to have participated in photographic salons as early as the 1920s. Although she was not formally trained as a photographer, Lavenson was influenced by Imogen Cunningham, Consuelo Kanaga and Edward Weston. In 1932, she showed with them in the landmark Group f.64 exhibition at the M. H. de Young Memorial Museum, San Francisco. A year later, her work appeared in solo shows at the de Young and the Brooklyn Art Museum. In 1941, she received an award at the First Annual West of the Rockies Photographic Salon, San Francisco Museum of Art. Following the death of her husband in 1957, Lavenson traveled widely. A retrospective exhibition was held at the California Museum of Photography, University of California, Riverside, in 1979, and in 1991 *Alma Lavenson: Photographs,* was shown at the Ansel Adams Center in San Francisco.

PHOTO: Imogen Cunningham, *Alma Lavenson with Camera,* 1942. ©The Imogen Cunningham Trust, courtesy Alma Lavenson Associates and Susan Ehrens.

LAWRENCE & HOUSEWORTH

San Francisco-based stereopublishing and optical firm operating from about 1860 to 1867. Very little is known about George Lawrence; see entry for Thomas Houseworth.

JOANNE LEONARD (1940–)

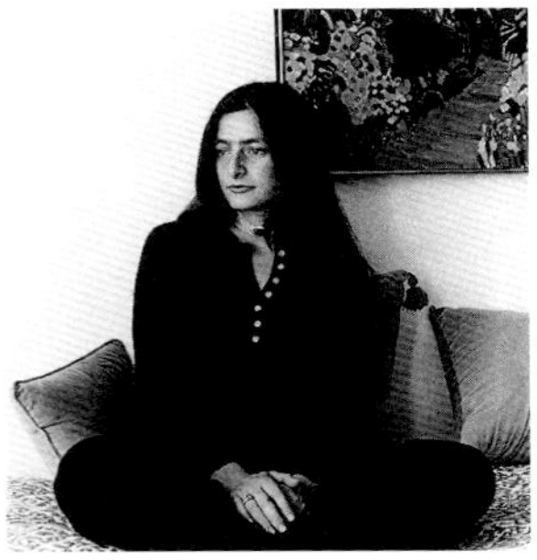

A photographer and educator, Leonard earned a B.A. from the University of California, Berkeley (1962) and studied photography at San Francisco State College (1963–64). She cites John Collier, Jr., one of her instructors, as a major influence. She has taught at various California colleges including the San Francisco Art Institute (1973–75), California State University, Hayward (1974–75), the extension programs of the University of California, Berkeley and Davis (1974–77), Mills College, Oakland (1975–78), and Cornell University, Ithaca, New York (1977). Since 1978 she has been an Assistant Professor of Art at the University of Michigan, Ann Arbor. In 1971 she won the Phelan Award in Art and Literature, followed in 1977 by a National Endowment for the Arts Photo Survey Grant. She served as the official photographer for the 1972 American Olympic Team in Sapporo, Japan. Her photographs have been widely exhibited and published. In 1992 her exhibit *Not Losing Her Memory: Stories in Photographs, Words and Collage* was shown at the University of Michigan Museum of Art.

PHOTO: Joan Murray, *Joanne Leonard,* 1971. Gelatin silver print, collection of the Oakland Museum of California, gift of Dr. and Mrs. Dudley P. Bell.

REAGAN LOUIE (1951–)

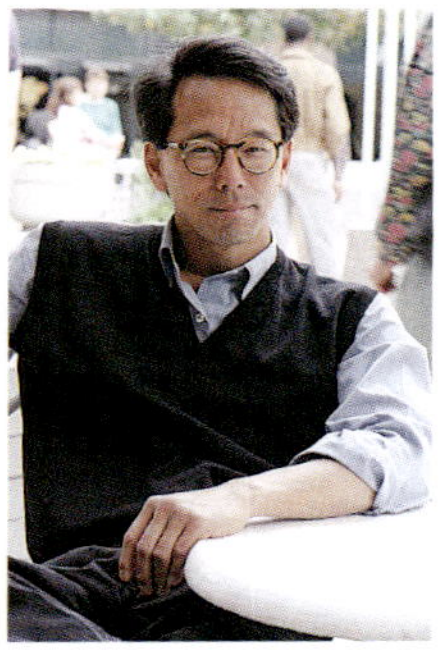

Louie holds a B.A. from the University of California, Los Angeles (1973), and an M.F.A. from Yale University (1975). A native Californian of Chinese ancestry, Louie did not make his first visit to China until 1980. A year later he and his father visited his father's former village in China, beginning a photographic journey of self-discovery that resulted in the publication *Toward a Truer Life: Photographs of China 1980–1990* (co-published by Aperture and the Friends of Photography as *Untitled 52*). He is the recipient of two National Endowment for the Arts grants (1979 and 1980), a James Phelan Art Award (1988), a John Simon Guggenheim Fellowship (1989), and the Oakland Museum of California's Dorothea Lange/Paul Taylor Prize (1994). In 1997 he was awarded a Fulbright Fellowship and served as a Distinguished Visiting Professor at National Central University, Taipei, Taiwan. In 1999 he received an "Indivisible" Commission from Duke University and the Center for Creative Photography. Louie is presently a professor of photography at the San Francisco Art Institute.

PHOTO: Joe Samberg, *Reagan Louie,* 1994. Courtesy of Joe Samberg.

GREGORY ALLEN MACGREGOR (1941–)

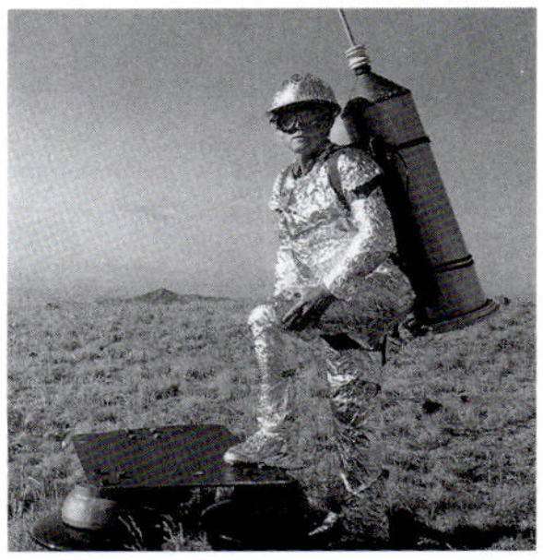

A native of Wisconsin, MacGregor holds an M.S. degree in physics from the South Dakota School of Mines and Technology, Rapid City (1964) and worked as an astrophysicist at the Lawrence Radiation Laboratory in Berkeley from 1966 to 1970. MacGregor earned his M.A. in photography from California State University, San Francisco in 1970, and has taught both photography and physics at the university level. He is currently a professor of art at California State University, Hayward. For the past twenty-five years, MacGregor has been actively photographing the Great Basin Desert between Colorado and California. A number of series have resulted, including: *Oddities in the Western Landscape* (1969–74), *Explosions* (1978–present) and the *Overland Historic Emigrants* project. The latter was the basis for MacGregor's publication *Overland: The California Emigrant Trail of 1841–1870* (1996). MacGregor has mounted more than twenty-five solo exhibitions of his work and participated in numerous group shows in the United States and abroad. He lives in Oakland with his wife, photographer Jo Whaley.

PHOTO: Greg MacGregor, *Greg MacGregor as Human Lightning Rod,* 1994. Courtesy of Greg MacGregor.

MAN RAY (1890–1976)

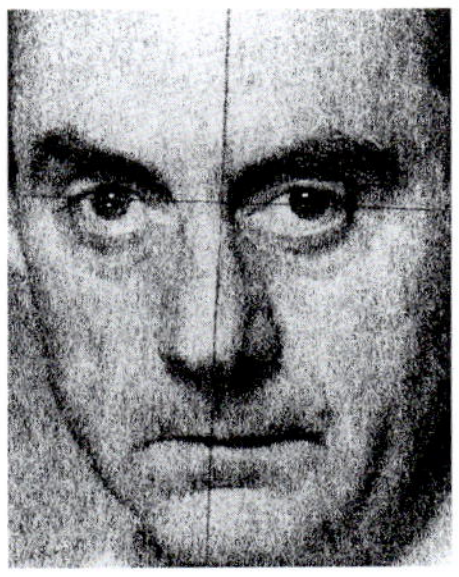

Born Emmanuel Rudnitzky in Philadelphia, Man Ray has been described as the single most influential artist of the twenties, thirties and forties. As an expatriate painter, sculptor and photographer living most of his adult life in Europe, he bridged European abstract and Surrealist art movements with West Coast photography. Jean Cocteau called him "the poet of the darkroom." He studied at the National Academy of Design, New York (1908–12), becoming interested in photography after meeting Alfred Stieglitz. He co-founded the Society of Independent Artists, New York (1915), the New York Dadaist Movement (1917) and Société Anonyme, New York (1920). In 1921 he traveled to Paris, where he maintained close ties with surrealist groups and worked as a freelance photographer, filmmaker and painter. From 1940 to 1950 he resided in Hollywood, where he taught at the Art Center School in Los Angeles and worked as a fashion photographer and painter. He returned to Europe in 1951, where he remained for the rest of his life. As a photographer, Man Ray was an innovator. He reinvented the photogram, calling these cameraless photographs Rayograms or Rayographs, and explored the aesthetic possibilities of solarization. He was also among the first to fuse photography with painting to create assemblages. First a Dadaist, then a Surrealist, in his later years he said: "If I contradict myself, if I move from style to style, so does nature." Man Ray has been the subject of numerous books, writings and documentary films.

PHOTO: Man Ray, *Self-Portrait,* 1947. Gelatin silver print, collection of the Oakland Museum of California, Museum Income Purchase.

MARGRETHE MATHER (c. 1885–1952)

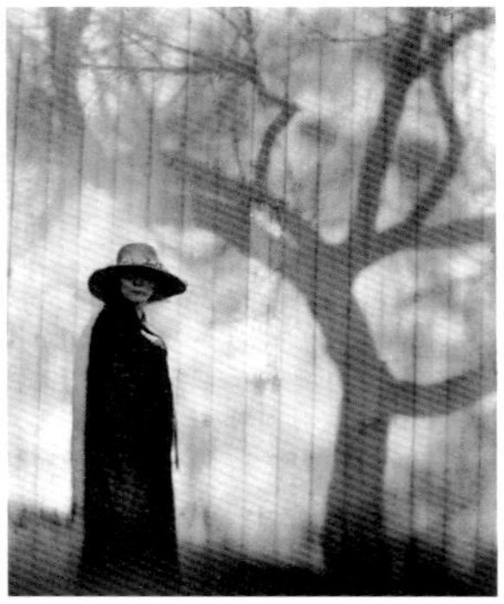

Born in Salt Lake City, Utah, Mather was adopted from an orphanage by a professor of mathematics and his common-law wife. Her home life was unhappy, and as a young teenager she left for San Francisco where she supported herself as a prostitute (c. 1910–11). Shortly thereafter, she moved to Los Angeles and lived with her wealthy protector and mentor, a woman named "Beau." Already an accomplished photographer, Mather met Edward Weston in 1912, probably in connection with the Los Angeles Camera Club. The two became partners in his small but elite studio in Glendale (1914). Mather exhibited in a number of photographic salons, among them the Sixth and Eighth Pittsburgh Salons (1919 and 1921), the *Frederick and Nelson Exhibition,* Seattle (1919) and the Oakland Photographic Salon (1921). Published work by Mather appeared in *American Photography and Camera Craft* from 1919 to 1921. Though her partnership with Weston ended in 1922, Mather continued to photograph on her own, doing portraiture and work for interior designers, through 1930. In 1931 she collaborated with her friend, designer William Justema, on an exhibition at the M. H. de Young Memorial Museum, San Francisco, entitled *Patterns by Photography.* From 1934 until her death from multiple sclerosis in 1952, Mather made few photographs except occasional portraits of friends.

PHOTO: Edward Weston, *Margrethe,* 1921 (printed later). Gelatin silver print, collection of the Oakland Museum of California, gift of the Estate of Helen Johnston.

OSCAR MAURER (1871–1965)

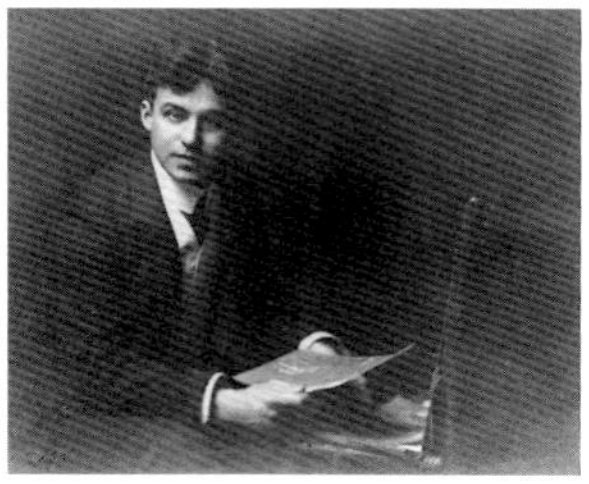

Born the son of a German chemist in New York, Maurer studied chemistry and physics at the University of California, Berkeley. By 1897 he had become a member of the California Camera Club and was elected a director in 1900. In 1898 he traveled to Mexico where he made a photograph called *The Storm,* which was widely praised and exhibited at the Chicago Salon of 1900. In 1899, he traveled with William E. Dassonville to France and Holland, a trip which resulted in a portfolio titled *Life Under Foreign Skies* that was published in *Camera Craft.* Working in the pictorialist tradition, Maurer entered ten prints in the First San Francisco Photographic Salon (1901) and fifteen prints, including several images he had taken while in Holland, in the Second San Francisco Salon (1902). In 1907, Following the destruction of his San Francisco studio (which he briefly shared with Arnold Genthe) in the 1906 earthquake and fire, Maurer set up shop in Berkeley and exhibited at the Photo-Secession Gallery in New York. He continued to exhibit his photographs, many of which were published in the *American Annual of Photography,* over the next two decades. He also actively wrote technical articles and essays on his photographic excursions, sometimes publishing in *Sunset* magazine. In 1965, the Oakland Art Museum (now the Oakland Museum of California) presented a retrospective exhibition of Maurer's images taken in the aftermath of the 1906 earthquake. He was 94 at the time.

PHOTO: Arnold Genthe, *Portrait of Oscar Maurer*, n.d. Gelatin silver print, collection of the Oakland Museum of California, gift of E. Wilhelm.

KENNETH McGOWAN (1940–)

Born the son of painter John Thomas McGowan in Ogden, Utah, Kenneth McGowan began working in photography in 1959. He earned his M.A. at the University of California, Los Angeles in 1966, and served as an assistant to Robert Heinecken and Edmund Teske. McGowan credits motion pictures as a major influence in his work and has done special effects for the film industry as well as portraits of film, recording and television personalities. McGowan's photographs have appeared in a number of publications and museum collections.

ANDREW BARNABY McKINNE (1881–1966)

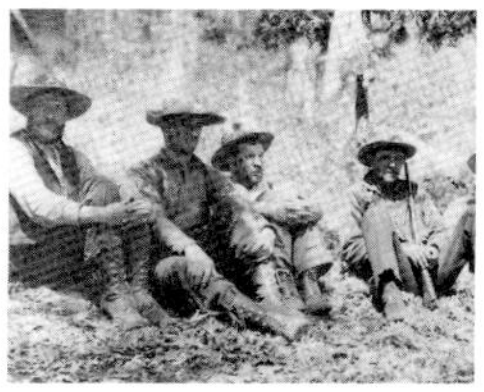

McKinne is known primarily from a group of albums donated to the Oakland Museum of California by his widow in 1969. An amateur photographer, he was apparently an active member of the Sierra Club.

PHOTO: Unknown, *Andrew Barnaby McKinne (Second from Left) on a Sierra Club Jaunt,* c. 1908. Gelatin silver print, collection of the Oakland Museum of California, Gift of Mrs. Andrew Barnaby McKinne.

ROGER MINICK (1944–)

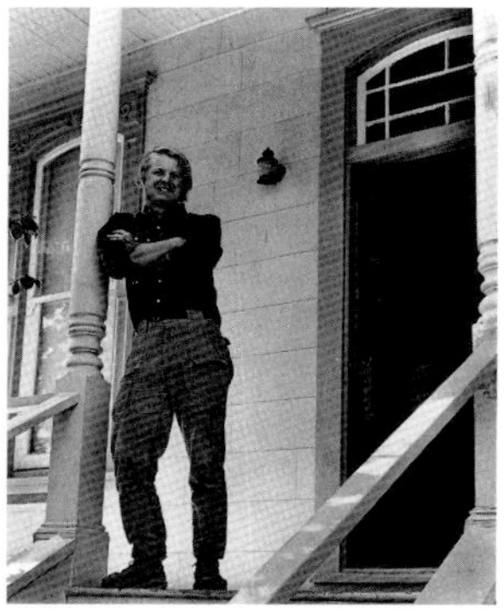

Born in Oklahoma, Minick earned a B.A. in History from the University of California, Berkeley, in 1969. While at Berkeley, he apprenticed at the Associated Students of the University of California (ASUC) photography studio (1964–69), directing the studio upon graduation (1970–75). Before entering graduate school at the University of California, Davis (where he received his M.F.A. in 1986), Minick worked as a photographer for the Mexican American Legal Defense and Educational Fund's (MALDEF) Photo Survey (1977–79). His work has appeared in numerous individual and group exhibitions and he has published three monographs, *Hills of Home: The Rural Ozarks of Arkansas* (1976), *The Oakland Paramount* (1981) and *Delta West* (1969). Minick has been recognized by the National Endowment for the Arts twice (1977–78 and 1980) and has received a John Simon Guggenheim fellowship (1972) and a Gyorgy Kepes Photography Grant (1988). Over the past twenty-five years, Minick has taught at California State University, Sonoma (beginning in 1988), and at many other California institutions. He currently teaches at the Academy of Art College in San Francisco. He is presently involved in four projects: *Perambulations,* ironic and often surreal scenes drawn from everyday American life; *Dialogues,* a series of mixed media works combining photographs and painting; *American Biographics,* black and white photographs forming a visual time capsule of American landscapes; and a series of dreamlike images taken with a fifteen dollar, medium-format Holga camera.

PHOTO: Joan Murray, *Roger Minick,* 1971. Gelatin silver print, collection of the Oakland Museum of California, gift of Dr. and Mrs. Dudley P. Bell.

RICHARD MISRACH (1949–)

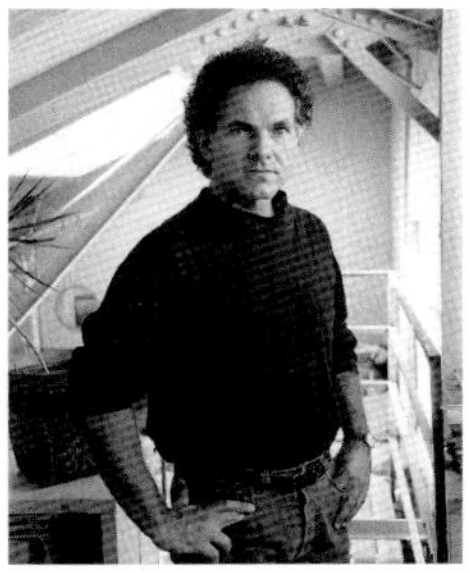

Best known for his images of western deserts, Misrach has had a distinguished thirty-year career in photography. A native Californian, Misrach earned a B.A. degree in psychology at the University of California, Berkeley in 1971. His self-published book *Telegraph 3 A.M.: The Street People of Telegraph Avenue, Berkeley* (1974), which documents street life along the notorious Berkeley thoroughfare, received the Western Books Award in 1975. He has received four National Endowment for the Arts grants (1973, 1977, 1984 and 1992), a John Simon Guggenheim Memorial Fellowship (1979) and a Ferguson Grant from the Friends of Photography (1976). Misrach has participated in more than twenty solo traveling exhibitions, and his work is found in more than fifty museum and corporate collections around the world. Monographs include: *(a photographic book)* (1979); *Desert Cantos* (1987); *Richard Misrach: Photographs, 1975–1987* (1988), *Bravo 20: The Bombing of the American West* (1990); *Violent Legacies: Three Cantos* (1992); and *Crimes and Splendors: The Desert Cantos of Richard Misrach* (by Anne Tucker, 1996). In 1994 Misrach was awarded the Distinguished Career in Photography Award from the Los Angeles Center for Photographic Studies, and in 1996 *Crimes and Splendors* garnered him a coveted Golden Lights Award for Best Retrospective Book. In 1998 he received a commission from the Center for Creative Photography, Tucson, Arizona, and another from the High Museum of Art, Atlanta, Georgia.

PHOTO: Joan Murray, *Richard Misrach,* 1992. Gelatin silver print, collection of the Oakland Museum of California, gift of Joan Murray.

WILLIAM MORTENSEN (1897–1965)

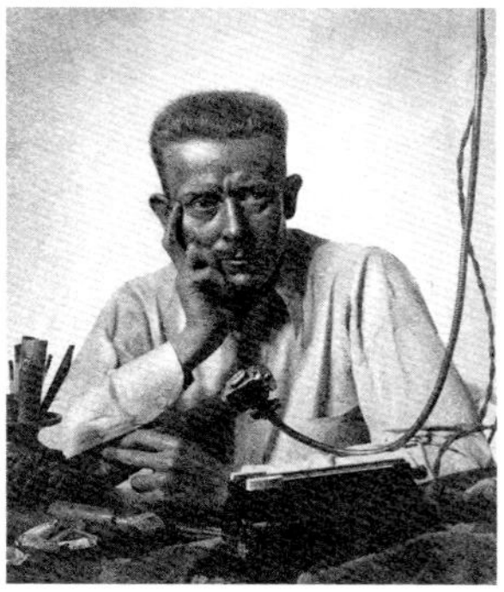

In the words of critic A. D. Coleman: "Along with his romanticism and his classicism, Mortensen had a Gothic mood; an obsession with the grotesque and . . . a belief in evil as an actual presence in the world." Mortensen came to photography with a background in art, and his first photographic work was as a high school student in Salt Lake City. He later studied at the Art Students League in New York City where he was instructed by Arthur Kales. In 1920, he moved to Los Angeles, opening a studio a few years later on Hollywood Boulevard. He took still photographs for Hollywood films such as Cecil B. De Mille's *King of Kings* (1926). Mortensen moved to Laguna Beach in the early 1930s and founded the Mortensen School of Photography, which prospered for some thirty years. He was a prolific and opinionated author, writing nine books, countless magazine articles and technical guides on photography, including his magnum opus *Monsters and Madonnas* (1936). In 1935 he began experiments with the Metalchrome process, which enabled him to transform black and white images into color. Working against the predominant ethic of "straight" photography, he employed pigment printing to create ink renderings from his photographs, claiming that any alteration of an image through chemical, optical, or manufactured means was legitimate.

PHOTO: William Mortensen, *Self-Portrait,* 1932. Gelatin silver print with texture screen, Los Angeles County Museum of Art, The Audrey and Sydney Irmas Collection (AC1992.197.94). Reproduced courtesy of Deborah Irmas.

DOUGLAS MUIR (1940–)

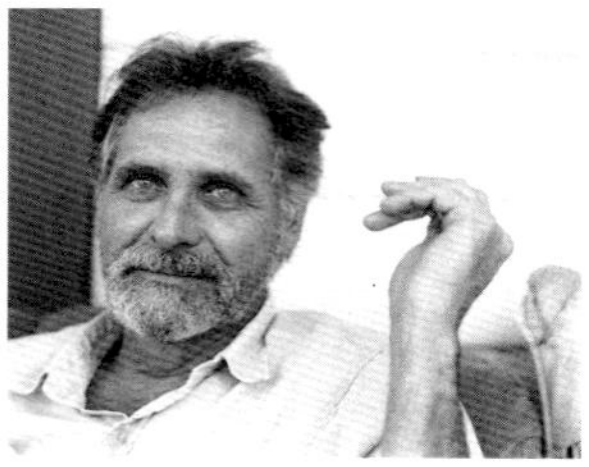

The first of six children, Muir grew up in Syracuse, New York. He claims he was a poor student, his mind often wandering to the view outside the school windows. At thirteen he received his first camera, a Christmas gift from his parents. After a number of jobs, including short order cook, caddie and pinsetter in a bowling alley, Muir followed his father into the Syracuse Steam Fitters' Union. In 1962, inspired by the novels of Jack Kerouac, he and two friends drove from Syracuse to San Francisco in an Austin Healy sportscar, and in 1967 he, his wife and daughter settled in Berkeley. While working as a steam fitter, Muir took photography classes from Jack Welpott, Michael Harris and Margo Davis at the University of California Extension program. He photographed Magic Theater productions from 1968 to 1971 and covered protests against the Vietnam War. Inspired by his grandfather's flower gardens, he has photographed gardens over the years. Muir has presented solo exhibitions at the Focus Gallery, San Francisco (1984), the Menschel Photography Gallery, Syracuse, New York (1993), the California Museum of Photography, Riverside (1996) and *Family Album: An Installation* at the Falkirk Cultural Center, San Rafael, California (2000). Group shows include: *Picturing California* at the Oakland Museum (1989), *California Cityscapes* at the San Diego Museum of Art (1991) and *Facing Eden: One Hundred Years of Landscape Art in the Bay*

Area, at the M. H. de Young Museum in San Francisco (1995). He has been awarded the Society for the Encouragement of Contemporary Art Award, San Francisco Museum of Modern Art (1982), the Eugene Atget International Photography Award (1984) and the Marin Arts Council Award, Marin County, California (1987). Muir lives in Mill Valley, California, where he continues to photograph his favorite subjects: his family, his community and the garden in its many forms.

PHOTO: Susan Page, *Doug Muir,* n.d. Courtesy of Douglas Muir.

EADWEARD JAMES MUYBRIDGE (1830–1904)

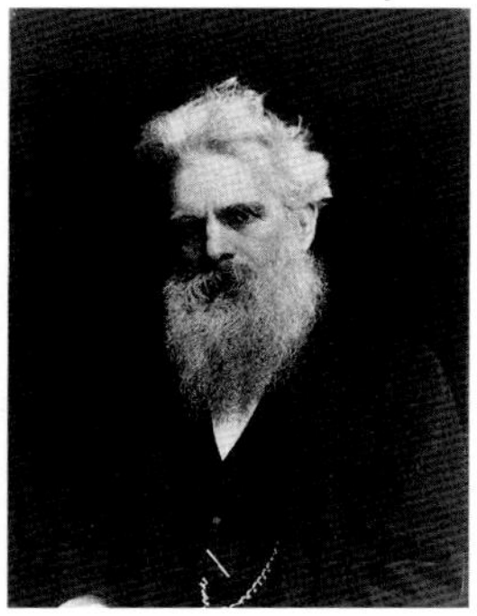

Famous as the man who used Leland Stanford's race horses for some of the first photographic studies of motion, he is also remembered for magnificent landscapes, an enormous ego and for killing his wife's lover. Born Edward James Muggeridge in Kingston on Thames, England, Muybridge joined his family's stationery and paper-making business. In 1852 he emigrated to the United States, opening a bookstore in San Francisco. The circumstances of his entry into photography are obscure; in 1867, using the name "Helios," he photographed Yosemite Valley with his "Flying Studio" (a darkroom on wheels). Some of the resulting photographs were used in John S. Hittell's book, *Yosemite: Its Wonders and Its Beauties* (1868). By 1873, Muybridge had linked up with the San Francisco firm of Bradley & Rulofson, who served as his publisher. Much of his output consisted of stereographic images, including a series on California lighthouses in 1871 and the Modoc Indian War of 1873–74, as well as extensive coverage of Central and Northern California. He also traveled to Mexico and Central America, and was the first photographer to document the newly acquired territory of Alaska in 1868. During the mid-1870s he made several spectacular photographic panoramas of San Francisco, including one in mammoth plate (20 x 24 inches) format. In 1875 Muybridge was tried in Napa County for the murder of his wife's lover. After a sensational trial which included an early use of the insanity defense, he was acquitted. His interest in motion studies began in 1872 when Stanford, a former California governor, commissioned him to prove that all four of a horse's legs are off the ground simultaneously at some point in its trot. In 1878 he succeeded in devising a series of drop shutters that captured Stanford's horse, Occident, at each stage of his gallop, proving Stanford's theory. Muybridge later created a device called the Zoopraxiscope, which projected sequential images on a screen in rapid succession, paving the way for the motion picture. He followed his initial success with studies of many other animals, and in 1879 began his first efforts to show human locomotion. In 1884 Muybridge began work at the University of Pennsylvania, culminating in the eleven-volume *Animal Locomotion* in 1887, containing 781 plates. Most of the remainder of his life was spent on the lecture circuit. He returned to England in 1894.

PHOTO: Unknown, *Eadweard Muybridge,* 1881. Courtesy of Peter E. Palmquist.

PATRICK AUGUST NAGATANI (1945–)

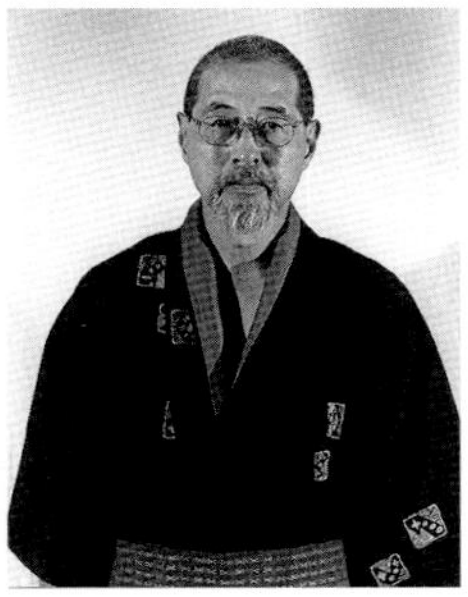

Born in Chicago to Japanese-American parents who had been relocated to an internment camp during World War II, Nagatani's work takes an ironic look at cultural identity and history. He earned a B.A. from California State University, Los Angeles in 1968 and an M.F.A. from the University of California, Los Angeles in 1980. He has taught at various institutions, including West Los Angeles Community College (1980–83), The School of the Art Institute of Chicago (1983) and Otis Art Institute of Parsons School of Design, Los Angeles (1987). He has been the recipient of two National Endowment for the Arts Visual Arts Fellowships (1984–85 and 1992–93), the Kraszna-Krausz Photographic Book Innovation Award (1992) and an Aaron Siskind Foundation Individual Photographer's Fellowship (1998). Nagatani's work, typically fabricated and then photographed, is characterized by a dark sense of humor, a fascination with the apocalyptic and an interest in the intersection of science and popular culture. This is evident in his published works, *Patrick Nagatani/Andrée Tracey: Polaroid 20 x 24 Photographs 1983–1986* (1987) and *Nuclear Enchantment* (1991). Nagatani's photographs have appeared in numerous individual and group exhibitions in the United States, Europe and Japan. Most recently, his series *Ryoichi/Nagatani Excavations,* a narrative of a staged, fourteen-year archaeological journey told through photographs, journal entries and artifacts, was shown at the University Art Museum, University of New Mexico, Albuquerque (1999). Currently, Nagatani is a Professor of Art at the University of New Mexico, Albuquerque.

PHOTO: Patrick Nagatani, *Portrait of Ryoichi/Nagatani,* 1999.

HELEN NESTOR (1924–)

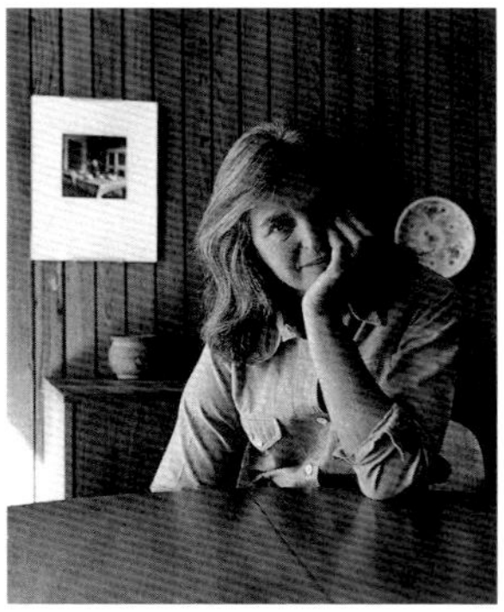

Documentarian Helen Nestor earned her B.S. in public health at the University of California, Berkeley, in 1945. In 1951, when her first child was two, Nestor contracted polio, which left her permanently disabled. Fiercely independent, Nestor has pursued photography, first with the aid of crutches, and later with a motorized scooter and wheelchair. In the early 1960s, she studied with Ansel Adams, Morley Baer, Minor White and fellow polio victim Dorothea Lange—her spiritual mentor. Nestor took an interest in the political and social changes of the 1960s and 70s, documenting the Free Speech Movement at Berkeley, the flower children of San Francisco's Haight-Ashbury district and the early days of busing in the Berkeley Unified School District. Her work appeared in publications such as *Ramparts* magazine as well as in several monographs, including: *Equal Start* (1968), *On the Go* (1968), *The Trouble in Berkeley* (1965), and *Field Trips* (1966). In the 1970s, she became increasingly interested in changing family constellations, creating a series entitled *Non-Traditional American Families,* which exhibited in several galleries, including the Focus Gallery, San Francisco. In 1988 she rephotographed these families for a book titled *Family Portraits in Changing Times* (1992). Nestor has also photographed the disabled, focusing on disabled working women and artists. She has mounted ten solo exhibitions and participated in numerous group showings. Her archive of negatives, prints and papers is held by the Oakland Museum of California.

PHOTO: Joan Murray, *Helen Nestor, Berkeley, California,* 1971. Gelatin silver print, collection of the Oakland Museum of California, gift of Joan Murray.

SAMUEL NEWSOM, SR. (1848–1908)

A renowned Bay Area architect and amateur photographer, Samuel Newsom emigrated from Canada in 1855. With his brother Joseph, he founded the San Francisco architectural firm of Newsom & Newsom. Known for fanciful Victorian designs, the Newsoms were responsible for nearly six hundred buildings throughout California, among them the Alameda County Courthouse (c. 1875), the Berkeley Town Hall (1884), and the William Carson residence in Eureka, recognized as the quintessential West Coast Victorian mansion (1884–85). In 1894 they designed the gardens and Horticultural Building for the California Midwinter Fair in Golden Gate Park, San Francisco. Samuel Newsom was also involved in restoring and rebuilding some of California's Missions, possibly under the employ of the Franciscans. He often made watercolor sketches and photographs of the Missions as a hobby. His interest in Mission architecture is reflected in his articles "The Santa Barbara Mission" and "The Romantic House of the Castros," both published in *Overland Monthly* (October 1907 and August 1908) with Newsom's photographs. The Newsom brothers' designs were published in a series of pattern books, one of which was republished by the Oakland Museum in the 1970s.

SONYA NOSKOWIAK (1900–1975)

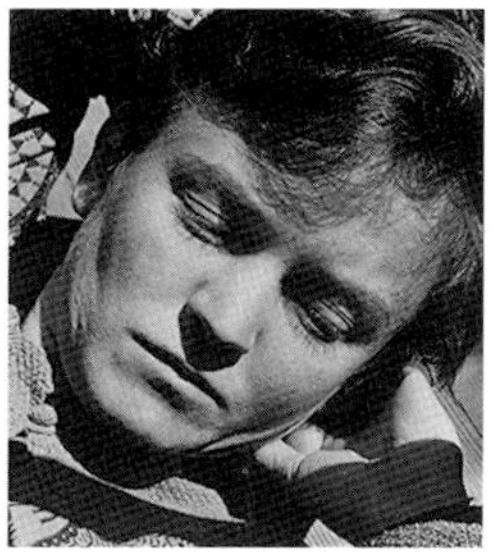

Born in Leipzig, Germany, Noskowiak spent her childhood in Valparaiso, Chile before her family moved to Sacramento in 1915. In the late 1920s, she worked as a receptionist in Johan Hagemeyer's Los Angeles studio. Through Hagemeyer she met Edward Weston (1929) and began a personal and professional relationship with him that lasted until 1934. She was a founding member of Group f.64, contributing ten prints to the group's first exhibition in 1932 at the M. H. de Young Memorial Museum, San Francisco. In 1935, Noskowiak opened her own commercial studio in San Francisco, specializing in portrait and fashion photography. Around the same time she was hired by the Federal Arts Project and was awarded a prize in decorative arts by the San Francisco Society of Women Artists (1936). In 1939 she was represented in the exhibition *Scenes from San Francisco* at the San Francisco Museum of Art. In 1940 she photographed for the Oakland Army Base, and was featured in the Oakland Museum's exhibition of photographs from the WPA in 1965.

PHOTO: Imogen Cunningham, *Sonya Noskowiak,* 1928. Gelatin silver print, The J. Paul Getty Museum, Los Angeles

TED ORLAND (1941–)

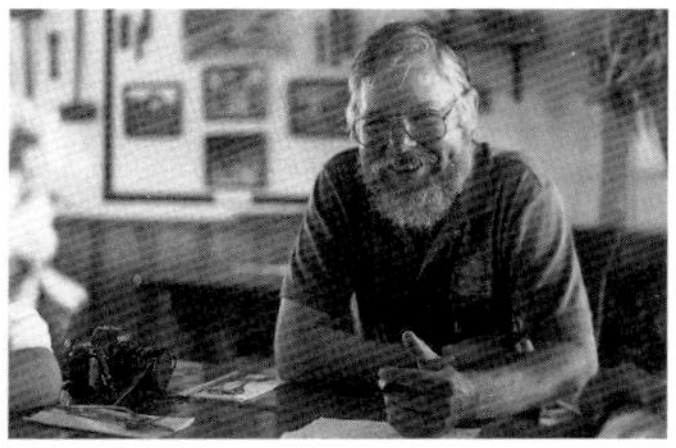

A third generation Californian, Orland earned a B.S. in Industrial Design from the University of Southern California and an M.A. in Interdisciplinary Creative Arts from California State University, San Francisco (1974), where he studied with Wynn Bullock, Dave Bohn and Paul Caponigro. From 1967 to 1990 he was a teacher at, then director of, the Ansel Adams Yosemite Workshops. During that time, he worked as Adams's personal assistant, printing his Special Edition Yosemite negatives (1972–75). In 1973 he founded *The Image Continuum Journal,* serving as publisher and contributing editor. Orland has taught at the University of California, Berkeley Extension program as well as at Stanford University. He has been recognized twice by the National Endowment for the Arts, with grants to work at Volcanos National Park, Hawaii (1976) and to photograph the Diablo Valley (1978). He has also been the recipient of a National Park Service artist-in-residence award to photograph Yosemite National Park. Since 1985 he has been an instructor at Cabrillo College, Aptos, California. Orland founded and owns The Image Continuum Press and has been president of the Center for Photographic Art in Carmel. He continues to live and work in Santa Cruz, California. His book *Scenes of Wonder & Curiosity: The Photographs & Writings of Ted Orland* was published in 1988.

PHOTO: Allison Smith, *Ted Orland,* n.d. Courtesy of Ted Orland.

TIMOTHY H. O'SULLIVAN (c. 1840–1882)

Best known for landscape photographs of the Great West, O'sullivan previously photographed battlefields of the civil war as an employee of both Mathew Brady and Alexander Gardner. Following the war, he served as the official photographer for Clarence King's Fortieth Parallel Expedition in Nevada, California and Utah (1867–69), a government survey excursion. He also accompanied Thomas O. Selfridge's expedition to Panama's Isthmus of Darien (1870) and the George M. Wheeler survey along the hundredth meridian (1870 and 1873–74). He was appointed chief photographer for the United States Department of the Treasury in 1880.

PAUL OUTERBRIDGE, JR. (1896–1959)

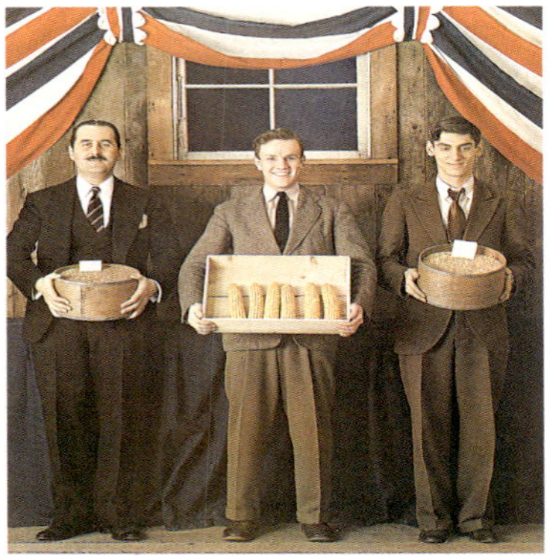

Born to a wealthy New York family and educated in private schools, Outerbridge studied sculpture at the Art Students League in New York in 1915. He took up photography in 1917 while serving in the armed forces, and by 1921 had enrolled in the Clarence H. White School of Photography, New York. He later taught aesthetics and composition at the same institution. His photographs appeared in *Vanity Fair, Vogue,* and *Harper's Bazaar.* He moved to Paris in 1925, where he became art director of *Paris Vogue* and established an advertising studio. Outerbridge also worked briefly as an assistant film director in Berlin and London (1928–29). He returned to New York in 1929 and began experimenting with the three-color carbro process. His forays into color work culminated in the 1940 publication *Photographing in Color.* By 1943 he had moved to Hollywood and then Laguna Beach, California, where he established a small commercial studio. Variously considered a dandy, playboy and aesthete, he became one of photography's great technicians. Outerbridge was a contributor to *U.S. Camera* (1954–58), the recipient of the Photography Medal at the *11th Annual Exhibition of Advertising Photography* (1932) and an honorary member of the Royal Photographic Society, London (1925).

PHOTO: Paul Outerbridge, *Untitled (Test Shot for 4 Roses Advertisement),* c. 1938. Carbro print (original in color), Los Angeles County Museum of Art, The Audrey and Sydney Irmas Collection. © Courtesy G. Ray Hawkins Gallery.

WILLIAM ("BILL") ELMO OWENS (1938–)

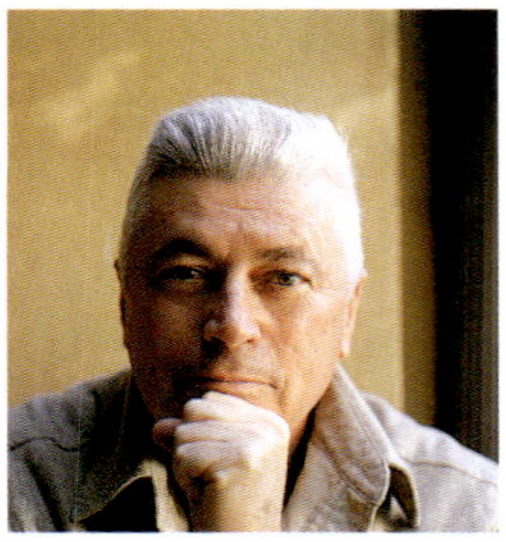

A documentary photographer and photojournalist, Owens was born in San Jose, California, and earned a B.A. from California State University, Chico in 1963. Following service in the Peace Corps (1964–66), Owens worked as a photographer for the Livermore *Independent* newspaper (1968–78). During that time he created his landmark series and book *Suburbia,* which documented the social life and customs of residential communities surrounding Livermore. He was awarded a Guggenheim Fellowship in 1964 and National Endowment for the Arts grants in 1976, 1977, 1978 and 1979. Until the mid 1980s, Owens continued to work as a freelance photographer in Livermore. His book, *Suburbia,* has recently been republished.

PHOTO: Marion Brenner, *Bill Owens,* 2000. Courtesy of Marion Brenner.

RONDAL PARTRIDGE (1917–)

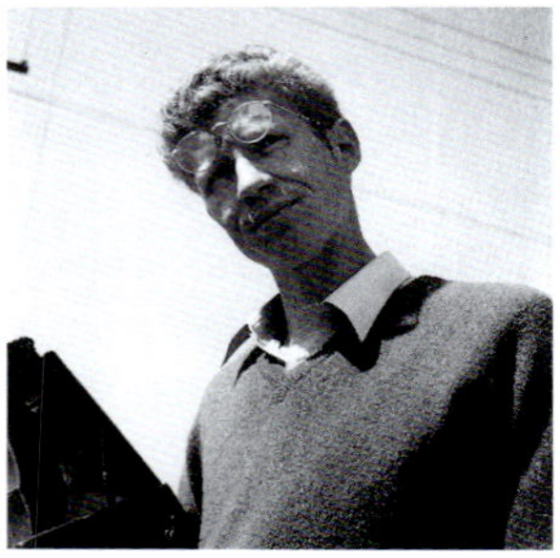

The son of etcher Roi Partridge and photographer Imogen Cunningham, Ron Partridge was apprenticed to Dorothea Lange from 1934 to 1937, and to Ansel Adams for two years beginning in 1937. He studied at California State University, San Francisco in 1938. He served as a photographer for the National Youth Administration (1939) and, during World War II, was a photographer for United States Navy Intelligence and Edward Steichen's naval aviation photographic unit. In 1947 he attended the Cornish School of Music, Seattle, and in 1951 studied with Minor White at the San Francisco Art Institute. Partridge has taught at California State University, Hayward, the University of California, Santa Barbara, the Academy of Art, San Francisco, and the San Francisco Art Institute, among other institutions. Since 1965 he has been involved in the Art Institute's film-making department. His film credits include *Pave It and Paint It Green, They're Your Kids, Wayne Thiebaud,* and *The Water Movie.* Lately he has worked extensively in the platinum process and continues to print his mother's negatives for the Imogen Cunningham Trust.

PHOTO: Dorothea Lange, *Untitled (Ron Partridge),* 1940. © Oakland Museum of California, the City of Oakland. Gift of Paul S. Taylor.

EMILY PITCHFORD (1878–1956)

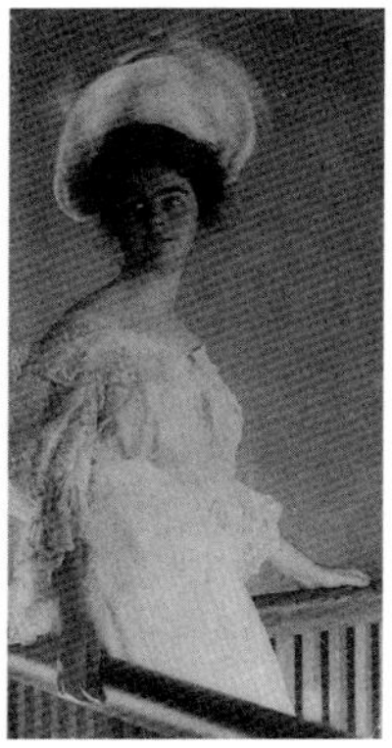

Born in Gold Hill, Nevada, Pitchford attended the Mark Hopkins Institute of Art (later called the San Francisco Art Institute) in San Francisco, where she became interested in photography. By 1902 she began sharing a studio with Laura Adams Armer in Berkeley. Specializing in portraiture and genre images, Pitchford exhibited at the Fourth Annual Exhibition of Photographs, Worcester Art Museum, Massachusetts in 1907. In 1908 she participated in the Second Annual Exhibition of the Berkeley Art Association, and won a bronze medal at the Alaska-Yukon-Pacific Exposition held in Seattle. She exhibited with Anne Brigman at the California Camera Club, and her photographs appeared in *Camera Craft* (1907–8) and *Photograms of the Year* (1908). In 1911 she married William Leo Hussey, a mining engineer from Johannesburg, South Africa. The couple lived in South Africa until 1921, when they returned to Berkeley, but by then Pitchford had apparently given up photography.

PHOTO: Emily Pitchford, *Emily Pitchford,* n.d. Gelatin silver print, collection of the Oakland Museum of California, gift of Mr. Henley Miller.

CHARLES L. POND (c.1832–1891)

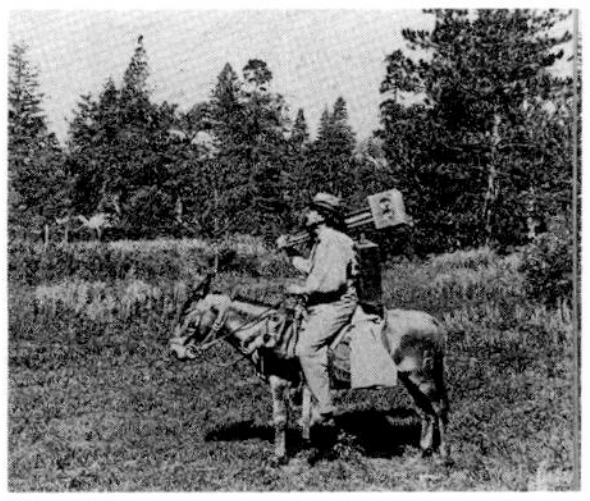

A photographer, manufacturer and publisher of stereographs, Pond worked in Buffalo, New York, for twenty years (1862–82). He had previously been a bookbinder. Among his stereoscopic series are views of Buffalo's harbor taken in the late 1860s and the *Governor Cushman Disaster* in which the boiler of a grain ship exploded on May 1, 1868. In 1871 Pond visited California, travelling to Yosemite where he joined with Martin Mason Hazeltine to produce a series of Yosemite and Big Trees stereographs, the work for which he is best remembered. In 1882, at the age of fifty, Pond abandoned photography and took up the manufacture of railroad shipping accessories.

PHOTO: C. L. Pond, *Photographer's first Glimpse of the Yo Semite Valley, California (self-portrait),* c. 1871. Albumen stereograph (detail), courtesy of Peter E. Palmquist.

JOHN JAMES REILLY (1838–1894)

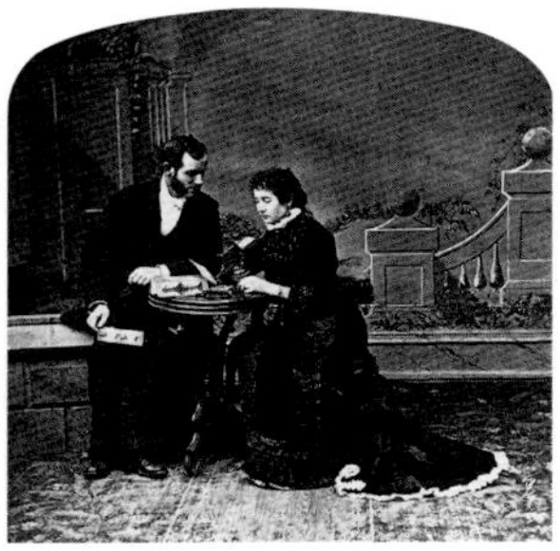

A native of Scotland, Reilly settled in Niagara County, New York, in the early 1860s, where he worked as a photographer. He enlisted in the Union Cavalry in December 1863, received a disability discharge in October 1864, and returned to photography, taking stereographs of Niagara Falls and vicinity. In 1870 he traveled to California by train, eventually settling in Yosemite, where he established the valley's first photographic gallery, housed in a tent. In the ensuing years Reilly spent his summers in Yosemite and wintered in nearby towns, producing views of the valley, railroads and the Marysville and San Francisco areas. He relocated to San Francisco in 1878 and thence to Marysville, where he was active until 1886, when he abandoned his wife and business. For a few years he worked for others, but in 1894 took his own life during a fit of depression.

PHOTO: J. J. Reilly, *Mr. and Mrs. J. J. Reilly,* c. 1875. Albumen stereograph (detail), collection of James P. Crain, courtesy of Peter E. Palmquist.

LELAND DAVID RICE (1940–)

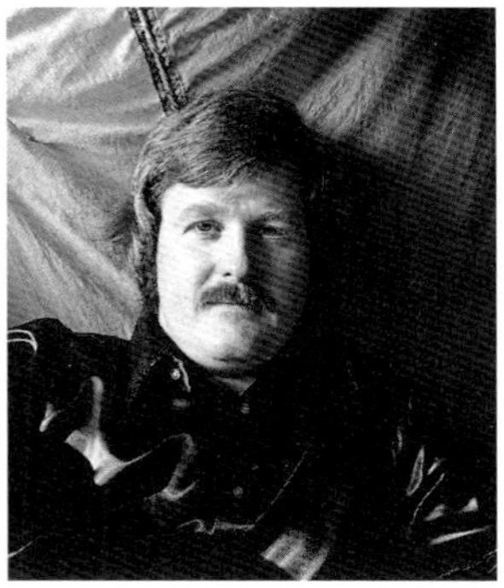

A photographer, teacher and curator, Rice earned a B.S. from Arizona State University, Tempe (1964), where he studied with Van Deren Coke, and an M.A. from California State University, San Francisco (1969). He also studied at the Chouinard Art Institute in Los Angeles (1964–65). Rice became assistant professor at the California College of Arts and Crafts in Oakland (1969–72) and a visiting artist-in-residence at the University of California, Los Angeles (1972). He has served as curator of photography and lecturer in art at Pomona College (1973–79) and taught at the extension program of the University of California, Los Angeles. He has conducted numerous workshops, including the Ansel Adams Workshop in Yosemite (1978) and courses at the University of New Mexico, Albuquerque (1977). Rice joined the Council of the Center for Southern California Studies in the Visual Arts at California State University, Long Beach (1979), and he has been on the board of trustees of The Friends of Photography since 1978. He received a National Endowment for the Arts Photographic Fellowship in 1978, and a Survey Grant in 1980. He was awarded a Guggenheim Fellowship in 1979 and earned a commission from the Graphic Arts Council of the Los Angeles County Museum of Art in 1978. A retrospective exhibition, *Leland Rice, Photographs 1968–1980* was mounted at New Mexico State University in 1980.

PHOTO: Joan Murray, *Leland Rice (California College of Arts and Crafts),* 1972. Gelatin silver print, collection of the Oakland Museum of California, gift of Joan Murray.

ARTHUR ROTHSTEIN (1915–1985)

A documentary photographer, Rothstein is best known for his work with the Farm Security Administration (FSA) during the Great Depression. Rothstein earned a B.A. from Columbia University, New York (1935), where he studied with Roy Stryker (later the head of the FSA photographic division), and is credited with founding the University Camera Club. From 1935 to 1940 he served as a photographer for the FSA. During World War II he worked as a picture editor for the U.S. Office of War Information (1941–44) before becoming a U.S. Army Signal Corps photographer (1943–46). After the war he was director of photography for *Look* magazine (1946–71) and *Parade* magazine (beginning in 1972). Rothstein was a member of the New York Press Photographers Association (NPPA), the American Association of Magazine Photographers (ASMP), and the Royal Photographic Society (RPS). He won the NPPA Sprague Award in 1967 and the International Award from the Photographic Society of America in 1968. He wrote numerous magazine articles and six books, including *The Depression Years* (1978).

EDWARD JOSEPH RUSCHA (1937–)

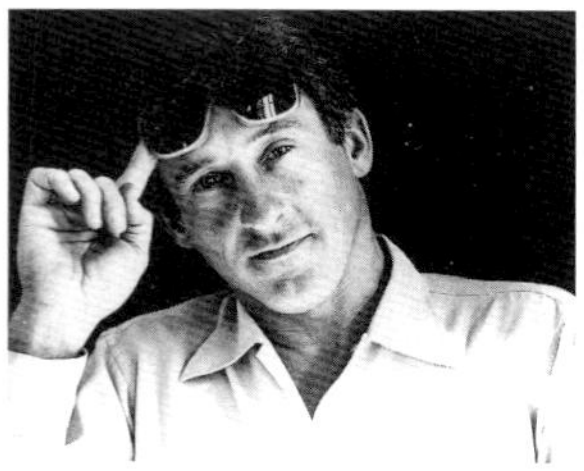

Pop and conceptual artist Ruscha is well known for his paintings and prints, but he has also contributed to photography and film. He does not consider himself a photographer and sees the camera only as a means to an end. Ruscha was born in Omaha, Nebraska and educated at the Chouinard Art Institute, Los Angeles (1956–60). Though he questions the artistic potential of photography, he has produced several important photographic books, including: *26 Gasoline Stations* (1962), *Nine Swimming Pools* (1967), *Some Los Angeles Apartments* (1965), *34 Parking Lots* (1967), *Sunset Strip* (1966), *Real Estate Opportunities* (1969) and *A Few Palm Trees* (1970). Ruscha's work has been internationally recognized in countless solo and group exhibitions and he has garnered numerous awards, including two National Endowment for the Arts grants (1969 and 1978) and a Guggenheim Foundation Fellowship (1971). In 1997, he completed a commission for the J. Paul Getty Museum in Los Angeles consisting of a twenty-three-foot-tall mural entitled *Picture Without Words* for the lobby of the Harold Williams Auditorium. In 1998 he was awarded the Coutts Contemporary Art Foundation Award.

PHOTO: Mimi Jacobs, *Ed Ruscha, Artist,* n.d. Gelatin silver print, collection of the Oakland Museum of California, gift of Mimi Jacobs.

ANDREW J. RUSSELL (1830–1902)

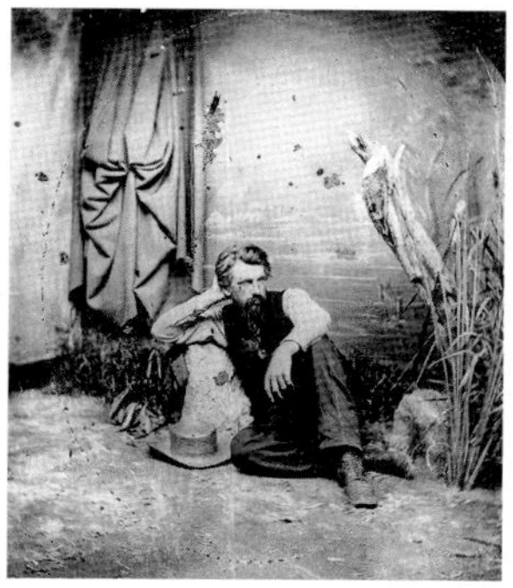

A photographer and painter, Russell is best known for documenting construction of the Union Pacific Railroad. His famous photograph of the last spike driven at Promontory, Utah, on May 10, 1869 marked the meeting of the Union Pacific with the Central Pacific and completion of the transcontinental railway. Russell worked for photographer Mathew Brady during the Civil War before becoming a captain in the Union Army, photographing construction on the U.S. Military Railroad (1861–65). Following his epic work for the Union Pacific, Russell joined the Clarence King Geological Survey of the Bear River area, venturing as far as Sacramento (1869). He later opened a photographic studio in New York, where he did work for Leslie's *Illustrated Weekly*. Russell's collodion glass plate negatives of the Union Pacific are held by the Oakland Museum of California.

PHOTO: Unknown, *Portrait of Andrew J. Russell,* n.d. Tintype, location of original unknown.

JOE SAMBERG (1946–)

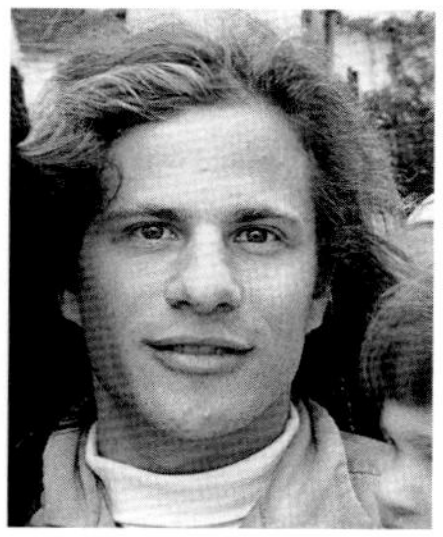

Attracted to the fine arts as a youth, Samberg began a career in photography in 1969, photographing Manhattan neighborhoods around Washington Square Park. In February of 1970 he left New York for Berkeley. His first major work in California was a documentary series, *Telegraph Avenue* (1970–73), in which he photographed the Berkeley youth scene with an eye for "the decisive moment." His immersion in the Telegraph Avenue milieu gave him an open window into the culture of "sex, drugs and broken couches." In 1975, struggling to support a young family, Samberg almost gave up photography, but was hired by the Oakland Museum as a staff photographer for the graphic design department. It was at the museum that he learned studio lighting technique, which served him well when he returned to freelance photography in 1981. In 1984 he launched a series of still-life photographs using organic materials such as iridescent scarab beetles, dried flowers, pieces of textured paper, newsprint, glass and stone. Since 1998, while continuing still-life and freelance work, he has adopted the computer as a creative tool, adjusting and altering his photographs to create digital prints on watercolor paper. He maintains an Oakland studio.

PHOTO: Margie Marrow Samberg, *Joe Samberg,* c. 1971. Courtesy of Joe Samberg.

WILLIAM SHEW (1820–1903)

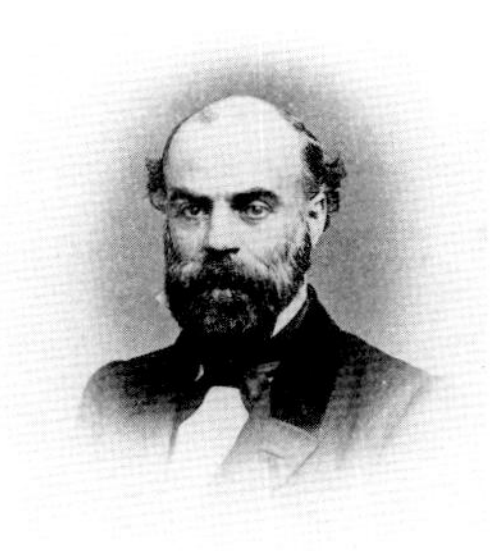

One of California's most prolific and successful early photographers, Shew was born in Providence, Fulton County, New York. He learned to make daguerreotypes from Samuel F.B. Morse in 1841, becoming supervisor of John Plumbe's Boston gallery. By 1844 he had opened a miniature case manufactory, which he operated until 1848. He joined with daguerreotypist Marsena Cannon in a portrait venture in Boston until 1850, when he traveled to California via the Isthmus of Panama. Beginning in a portable daguerreian studio, Shew operated a successful portrait business at various San Francisco locations for more than fifty years. He is known to have supplied daguerreotypes for John Wesley Jones's *Great Pantoscope of California* in 1851, an enormous panoramic painting based on 1,500 daguerreotypes. Upon his death his widow continued the business until the studio was destroyed in the 1906 earthquake and fire. Shew's photographs are found today in countless family albums and museum collections.

PHOTO: William Shew Studio, *Portrait of William Shew,* c. 1867. Albumen carte de visite, collection of the Oakland Museum of California, gift of Mrs. Carolyn K. Louderback.

STEPHEN SHORE (1947–)

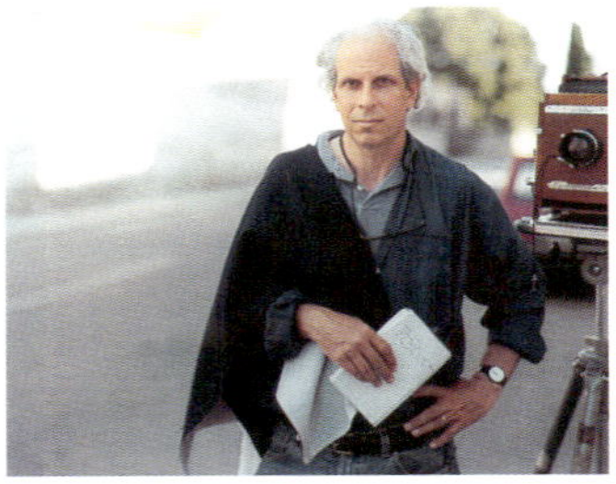

A native of New York City, Shore taught himself photography at an early age, later studying under Minor White at the Hotchkiss Workshop (1970). In the early 1970s, Shore began working in large-format color, concentrating on landscapes and cityscapes. He is known as one of the leading photographers of the so-called color movement of the mid-1970s. Shore has been the recipient of two National Endowment for the Arts photography grants (1974 and 1979) and a Guggenheim Fellowship (1975). His work is held in numerous American collections and he has published several books, including: *Uncommon Places* (1982), *The Gardens at Giverny* (1983), *Stephen Shore: Photographs 1973–1993* (1993), *Stephen Shore: Luzzara* (1993), *The Nature of Photographs* (1998) and *American Surfaces* (1999). Presently, he is Chair of the Arts Division and Professor of Art at Bard College in New York. Recently his work has appeared in several solo and group exhibitions in Europe as well as in shows at the Photographic Resource Center, Boston (1997), 303 Gallery, New York City (2000) and the Whitney Museum's retrospective *The American Century, 1950–2000* (1999).

PHOTO: Guido Guido, *Photograph of Stephen Shore,* n.d. Courtesy of Stephen Shore.

WILLIAM SIMPSON (?–?)

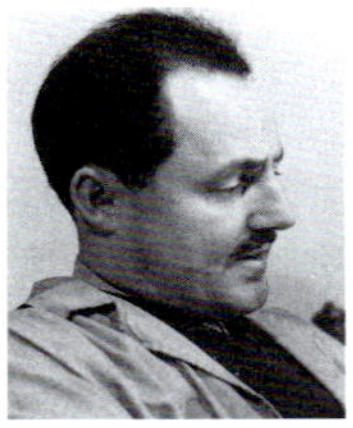

An artist for the *Oakland Tribune* in the 1930s, Simpson was recommended by Willard Van Dyke for membership in Group f.64. He is known to have contributed photographs to *Camera Craft*. His work is known today primarily from this published work and a large group of photographs given to the Oakland Museum of California by his widow, Anita Simpson, in 1992.

PHOTO: Unknown, *Untitled (Portrait of William Simpson),* n.d. Gelatin silver print, collection of the Oakland Museum of California, gift of Anita Simpson.

PETER STACKPOLE (1913–1997)

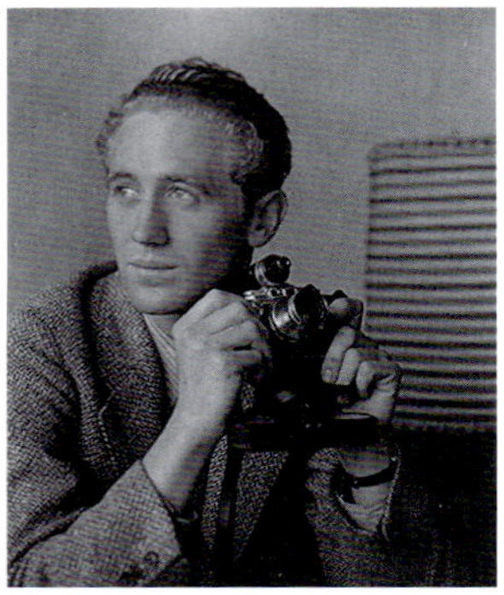

A renowned photojournalist, Stackpole had a strong interest in photographing people in their environment. The son of sculptor Ralph Stackpole and a native of San Francisco, his early mentor was Willard Van Dyke of Group f.64. Along with Alfred Eisenstaedt, Stackpole became one of the first staff photographers for *LIFE* magazine, a position which lasted from 1936 to 1960. For fifteen years he also wrote a column entitled "35mm Techniques" for *U.S. Camera*. As a war correspondent he covered the invasion of Saipan in 1945. He was a member of the Circle of Confusion, a New York group specializing in underwater photography, for many years. Among his early accomplishments were series on the building of the Golden Gate and San Francisco–Oakland Bay bridges (1934–36). Stackpole's photographs and articles have appeared in many journals, including *The Saturday Evening Post, Smithsonian, Time,* and *Scientific American,* as well as *LIFE*. Exhibitions include a retrospective show at the Stanford Art Gallery in 1986 and *Peacetime, Wartime & Hollywood: Photographs of Peter Stackpole,* at the Oakland Museum of California in 1992. It was during preparation for this show that Stackpole lost his home and much of his photographic archive in the devastating Oakland firestorm of 1991.

PHOTO: Sonya Noskowiak, *Portrait of Peter Stackpole,* c. 1932. Gelatin silver print, courtesy of Peter Stackpole.

FRANK M. STIFFLER

A commercial photographer active in Los Angeles in the 1890s, Stiffler is best known for his (or possibly his brother George L.'s) photographs of the Fresno Jack Rabbit Drive which took place on March 10, 1892. In this bizarre event, sponsored by an Encampment of the Grand Army of the Republic, some eight thousand people rounded up more than twenty thousand jack rabbits, enclosed them in a corral, and clubbed them to death. Stiffler published six different photographs of the event. He was a partner in Stiffler & Gill, along with his brother George, (1896) and in Stiffler & Potter (1897).

KARL STRUSS (1886–1981)

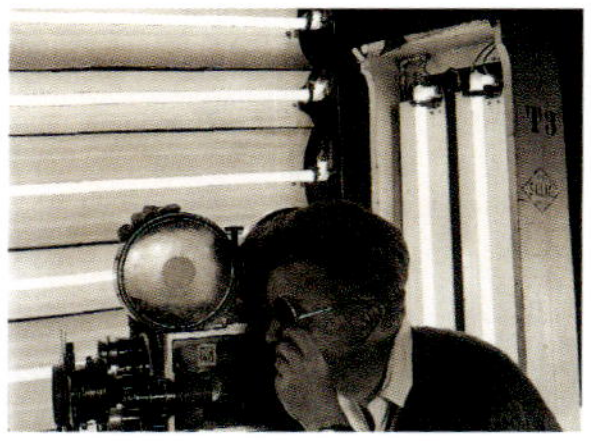

A distinguished cinematographer and photographer, Struss was born in New York City. He took up photography in 1896, later studying under Clarence White at Columbia University, New York from 1908 to 1912. He served in the armed forces during World War I, after which he established a studio in New York, serving clients such as *Vogue, Harper's Bazaar,* and *Vanity Fair.* Three years later he moved to Hollywood, where he worked as a cameraman for Cecil B. DeMille (1919–22). He then freelanced as a cinematographer for various studios until his retirement in 1970. Struss was a co-founder of the Pictorial Photographers of America, and was involved in Alfred Stieglitz's Photo-Secession from 1912 to 1917. He was also a founding member of the Academy of Motion Picture Arts and Sciences, and in 1928 won the first Academy Award for cinematography, for the film *Sunrise.* His credits as cinematographer are impressive: *Ben Hur* (1925), *Dr. Jekyll and Mr. Hyde* (1931), *Island of Lost Souls* (1932), *The Great Dictator* (1940), *Limelight* (1952), and *The Fly* (1958). He was a pioneer in early 3-D films, and in 1959 won the Cannes Grand Prix First Award for a Chevrolet commercial. A retrospective exhibition and catalogue, *Karl Struss: Man With a Camera,* traveled in 1976–77.

PHOTO: Edward Weston, *Karl Struss,* 1922. Collection Center for Creative Photography, The University of Arizona, Tucson.

ROGER STURTEVANT (1903–1982)

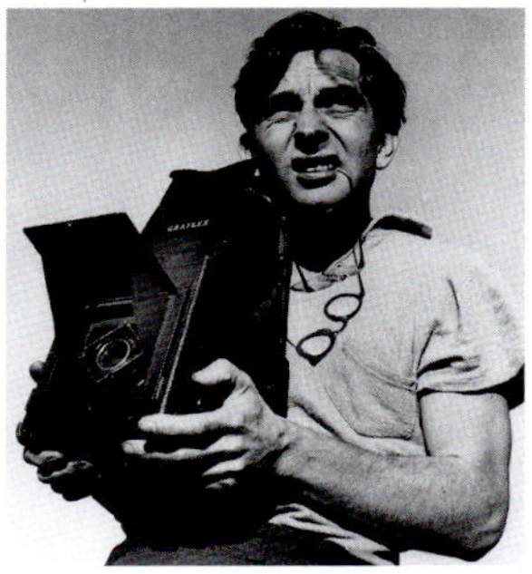

One of the premier architectural photographers of the twentieth century, Sturtevant also produced pictorial, surrealist, modernist and advertising photography. Born in Alameda, California, Sturtevant opened a portrait studio in his home in 1921. He was informally apprenticed to both Dorothea Lange and Imogen Cunningham, but soon developed an eccentric style all his own. During the 1920s and '30s he did commercial photography for the Southern Pacific Railroad, M. J. B. Coffee, Caterpillar Tractor, and other industrial and manufacturing companies. The photographer of choice for West Coast architects such as William Wurster, Sturtevant was awarded the first American Institute of Architecture Medal for Architectural Photography in 1960. His creative estate, including more than twenty-thousand negatives, is held by the Oakland Museum of California.

PHOTO: Roger Sturtevant, *He Flunked in Sandpile (Self-Portrait),* n.d. Gelatin silver print, collection of the Oakland Museum of California, gift of Roger Sturtevant.

LARRY SULTAN (1946–)

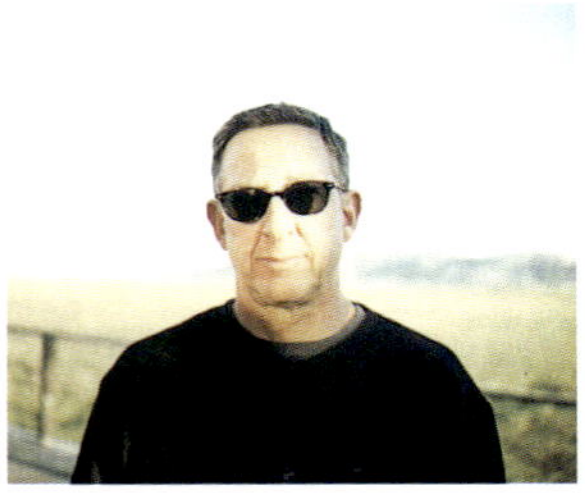

A photographer and educator, Sultan earned a B.A. in Political Science from the University of California, Santa Barbara (1968) and an M.F.A. in Photography from the San Francisco Art Institute (1973). He won a California Arts Council Special Projects Grant in 1978 and a National Endowment for the Arts, Art in Public Places Grant, in 1976–77 and again in 1986. He received a Guggenheim Fellowship in 1983–84, a Marin Arts Council Fellowship in 1986 and an Englehard Award in 1988. Sultan has taught photography at the San Francisco Art Institute beginning in 1978, and has co-directed the photography programs at Lone Mountain College, San Francisco, from 1974 to 1978. He has written various publications including *How to Read Music in One Evening* (1974), and *Evidence* (1977), both in collaboration with Mike Mandel, and *Pictures from Home* (1995), a solo effort. Sultan has exhibited regularly, and his photographs are in numerous collections.

PHOTO: Larry Sultan, *Self-Portrait,* 2000. Courtesy of Larry Sultan.

ISAIAH WEST TABER (1830–1912)

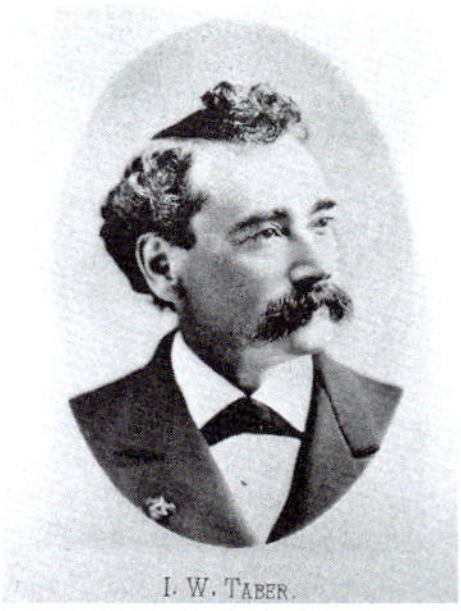

For thirty years Taber was one of the most prominent and ambitious studio operators in California. He sailed from his Home in New Bedford, Massachusetts to California in 1850. He tried his hand at gold mining before returning to the East, where he learned dentistry, then photography, establishing a studio in New Bedford in 1857. A few years later he returned to California to work for Bradley & Rulofson (1864–73), and in 1871 he purchased the gallery of the Nahl Brothers. He then became a portrait photographer for Carleton Watkins's Yosemite Art Gallery in San Francisco. By 1876 Watkins was bankrupt, enabling Taber to acquire a large number of Watkins's landscape negatives. With a financial backer, Taber established a major new gallery in which he could boast, thanks to Watkins, an "immense collection of views of Pacific Coast Scenery, from Alaska to Mexico." He proceeded to publish the views under his own name, also offering high-quality portraits. In 1894 he served as official photographer for the California Midwinter Fair, and in 1897 traveled to London to photograph Queen Victoria's Jubilee, where he took a portrait of the future King Edward VII. So prestigious had Taber become that in 1900 his gallery employed more than fifty people, and he presented a major exhibit at the Paris Exposition that year. His studio was destroyed by the San Francisco earthquake and fire of 1906, with estimated losses of twenty tons of view negatives and eighty tons of portrait negatives!

Photo: Unknown, *Isaiah West Taber,* n.d. Courtesy of Peter E. Palmquist.

DR. HENRY MORIYA TAKAHASHI (1904–1978)

A San Francisco optometrist and amateur pictorial photographer, Takahashi was a member of the Japanese Camera Club of San Francisco (c. 1930). He was included in the book *Japanese Photography in America 1920–1940* (1986) by Dennis Reed. Takahashi lived in Berkeley.

EDMUND TESKE (1911–)

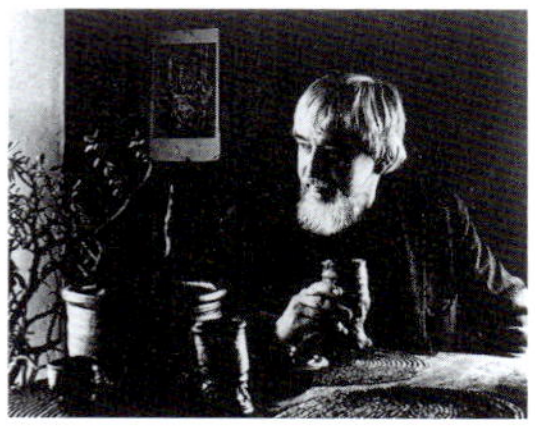

A photographer and educator, Teske credits an elementary school teacher with encouraging an early interest in photography. He went on to study painting and drawing at the Huttle Art Studio in Chicago. He also became interested in set design, acting and theatrical makeup after taking a residency in the theater department of the Jane Addams Hull House. Obtaining a Frank Lloyd Wright Taliesin Fellowship in 1936, he began to photograph some of Wright's architectural works. In 1945, attracted to Vedantic thought through the teachings of the

Hindu Swami Prabhavananda, he immersed himself in Hindu mythology and symbolism. By 1962 he had become a member of Moholy-Nagy's New Bauhaus School of Design in Chicago. Teske later taught at various California schools (1965–70) before becoming a visiting professor at California State University, Los Angeles in 1979. He received a Certificate of Recognition from the Photographic Society of America in 1969, and a National Endowment for the Arts Photography Fellowship in 1975. Teske is best known for multiple-image montages in which he invokes the Hindu mythology of the Shiva (male) and Shakhti (female) principles at work.

PHOTO: Joan Murray, *Edmund Teske,* 1972. Gelatin silver print, collection of the Oakland Museum of California, gift of Dr. and Mrs. Dudley P. Bell.

ANDRÉE TRACEY (1948–)

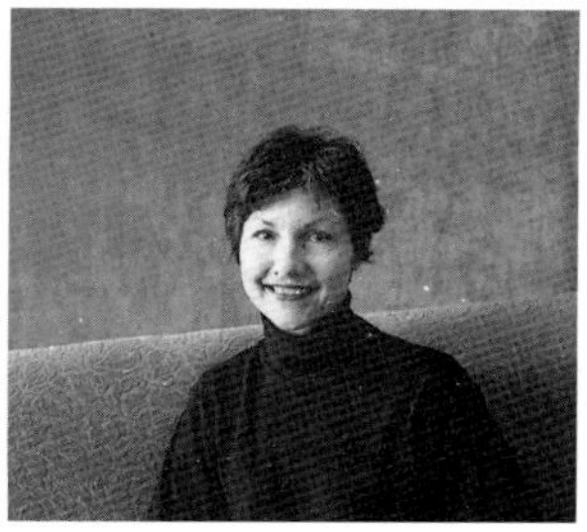

A painter and photographer with an interest in popular culture, Tracey holds a B.F.A. from the University of Iowa (1970) with additional work at the Otis Art Institute, Los Angeles, in 1972. She was awarded Polaroid Corporation Artist Support Grants between 1983 and 1989, and again in 1992. She has received the Leopold Godowsky, Jr., Color Photography Award, a Grody Arts Fellowship and the McKnight Photography Fellowship (1994). Tracey sometimes collaborates with photographer Patrick Nagatani, including a 1989 exhibition at the Northlight Gallery, School of Art, Arizona State University. She has participated in more than eighty group exhibitions and nearly sixty individual exhibitions since 1977. Tracey has worked as a freelance artist since 1976.

PHOTO: David Dick, *Andrée Tracey,* n.d. Courtesy of Andrée Tracey.

WILLARD VAN DYKE (1906–1986)

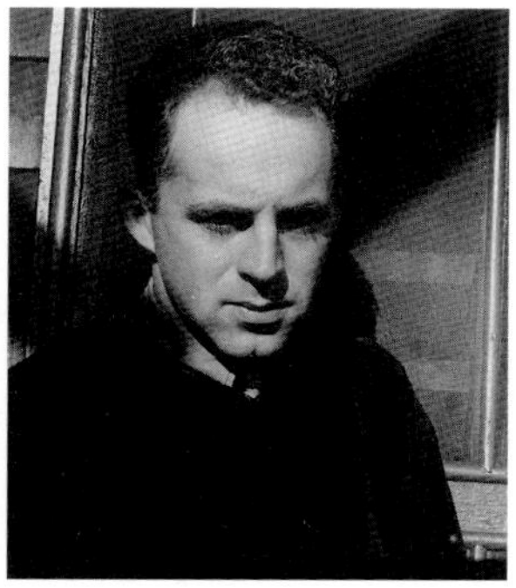

Born in Denver, Colorado, Van Dyke moved to Oakland in 1918, the same year he was given his first camera. After studying at the University of California, Berkeley, Van Dyke became acquainted with Edward Weston and Ansel Adams, his major artistic influences. In 1930 he took over Anne Brigman's studio at 683 Brockhurst street in Oakland. He operated the studio with then-girlfriend Mary Jeanette Edwards (daughter of photographer John Paul Edwards), which became a gathering place for the photographers who would become known as Group f.64. In 1932 his work appeared in a solo show and Group f.64's famous first exhibition, both at the M. H. de Young Memorial Museum in San Francisco. His growing interest in social documentation, however, earned him the displeasure of fellow members Adams and Weston. In 1934 he photographed for the Public Works Art Project. In 1937 he photographed the groundbreaking documentary film *The River* for director Pare Lorentz, and in 1939 he photographed and directed *The City* with Ralph Steiner (with music by Aaron Copland). Having given up still photography altogether, he served as a film director for the U.S. government during World War II. From 1965 to 1973 Van Dyke was director of the Department of Film at the Museum of Modern Art, New York. He was also employed as adjunct professor at the State University of New York, Purchase (beginning in 1974). He operated his own company, Van Dyke Productions, Inc., from 1958 to 1981.

PHOTO: Imogen Cunningham, *Willard Van Dyke,* 1933. Gelatin silver print, collection of the Oakland Museum of California, gift of Imogen Cunningham.

ROBERT H. VANCE (1825–1876)

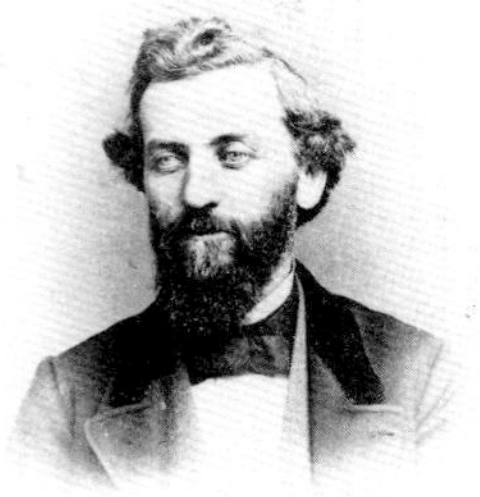

Known as "the Mathew Brady of California," Vance is arguably the most influential photographer of the American West during the daguerreian era. Born and raised in Maine, Vance had established his first portrait gallery in Boston by the time he was twenty-one. Traveling to South America, he opened galleries there sometime between 1848 and 1850. He left South America for California in the winter of 1850, and upon arrival almost immediately began to make his famous *Views In California,* a series of three hundred whole-plate-size daguerreotypes of San Francisco and the California gold fields. This remarkable collection, now lost, was exhibited in New York City in the fall of 1851. The exhibition was not financially successful, and Vance returned to California, where he established galleries in Sacramento, Marysville and San Francisco; by 1860 he had added branch establishments in Nevada and Hong Kong. His "First Premium Gallery" in San Francisco was the largest and most luxurious portrait gallery west of the Mississippi; many of his former employees went on to success as photographers and gallery owners in their own right. In 1858 Vance devised a way to make photographic reproductions of forged Spanish land grant records, enabling the courts to disavow the fraudulent claims of a man named Limantour who claimed to own all of San Francisco. During the Comstock silver mining rush of 1860 he overinvested in mining stock and was forced to sell his San Francisco gallery to competitors Bradley & Rulofson. Returning to New York City, he worked as a mining broker until his sudden and unexplained death at the age of 51.

PHOTO: Unknown, *Untitled (Robert H. Vance),* c. 1865. Albumen carte de visite, collection of the Oakland Museum of California, gift of Mrs. Carolyn K. Louderback.

MICHELLE MARIE VIGNES (1928–)

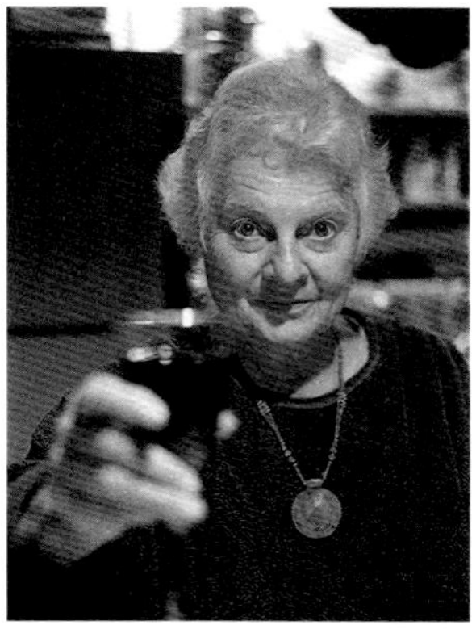

Vignes was born in France, where she studied philosophy. From 1953 to 1957 she worked for Henri Cartier-Bresson as an editor in the Paris office of the photo agency Magnum. She began taking photographs on her own in 1958. By 1966 she was working as a freelance photojournalist in San Francisco, with clients such as *Vogue, Time, LIFE, Ramparts, Der Spiegel, McCall's* and others. Vignes specializes in sympathetic portrayals of outsiders, ranging from the Native American protesters who occupied Alcatraz in 1969–71, to blues musicians, the Black Panthers and Angela Davis. She has recently produced a series on members of gospel churches in Oakland. From 1989 to 1993 she taught ethnology & photography at the College of Academy of Arts in San Francisco. Vignes is a co-founder, with the magazine *Mother Jones,* of the International Fund for Documentary Photography. She has several books to her credit, including *Eli's Mile High Club* (1982), *The Blues* (1986), *Oakland Blues* (1990), and *Bay Area Blues* (1993).

PHOTO: Alex Subrizi, *Portrait of Michelle Vignes,* 1999. Gelatin silver print, courtesy of Michelle Vignes, copyright Alex Subrizi.

LAURA VOLKERDING (1939–1996)

Born in Kentucky, Volkerding studied photography at the University of Louisville, receiving a bachelor's degree in fine arts in 1961. In 1964 she earned an M.A. degree in graphic design from the Chicago Institute of Design. She taught for nearly thirty years, first as an instructor at Rosary College in Illinois, and later as a lecturer in photography at Stanford University. She was awarded a Guggenheim Fellowship in photography in 1989. Working primarily with large-format cameras, she created panoramic photographs of California's changing architecture and environment, as well as a series documenting the lives of the Compagnons de Devoir, a centuries-old organization of crafts-people devoted to the upkeep and restoration of historical monuments.

CATHERINE WAGNER (1953–)

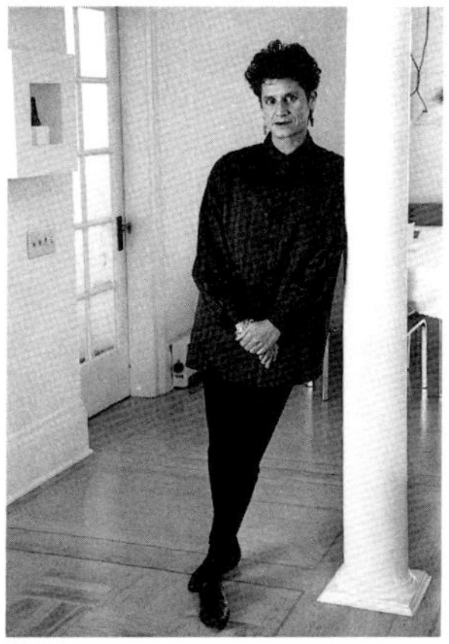

Wagner photographs social archetypes, creating images that explore the construction of American culture. Born in San Francisco, Wagner earned her B.A. (1975) and M.A. (1977) degrees from California State University, San Francisco. She also studied at Instituto del Arte in San Miguel de Allende, Mexico (1970–71), the San Francisco Art Institute (1971) and the College of Marin in Kentfield, California (1972–73). Since 1978 she has taught art and photography at Mills College, Oakland, and at California State University, San Francisco. Wagner has garnered two National Endowment for the Arts photography grants (1981 and 1991), a Ferguson Grant from The Friends of Photography (1984), and a Guggenheim Fellowship in 1987. Her exhibition *The American Classroom* was shown at the Oakland Museum in 1985, and *Home and Other Stories* was shown at the Fraenkel Galley in 1993 and at The Center for Creative Photography in Tucson, Arizona, in 1994. Her work also appeared in *Investigating Matter, Photographs by Catherine Wagner* (1996) and other publications.

PHOTO: Joan Murray, *Catherine Wagner,* 1992. Gelatin silver print, collection of the Oakland Museum of California, gift of Joan Murray.

HERALD TODD WALKER (1917–1998)

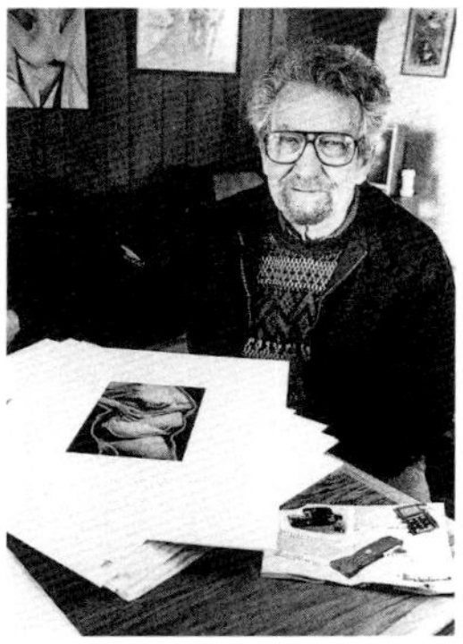

A native of Utah, Walker was educated at Glendale Junior College in California (1939–40) and at the Art Center School, Los Angeles (1939–41). He worked in Hollywood as a photographer for the Scenic Department of R.K.O. Studios (1934–42) and for Tradefilms, Inc. (1941–43), and he operated his own studio in Los Angeles and Beverly Hills from 1946 to 1970. Walker was a recipient of a photography fellowship from the Florida Council for the Arts in 1976 and a grant from the National Endowment for the Arts in 1971. He employed a wide range of photographic processes, including gum-bichromate, lithography, collotype and silkscreen. He taught at the University of Florida, Gainesville (1970–77), the University of Arizona, Tucson (beginning in 1978), California State University, Northridge and other California institutions. Walker's photographs have been widely published and collected.

PHOTO: Anthony Friedkin, *Portrait of Todd Walker in his Arizona Home,* mid-1990s. Courtesy of Steven K. Josefsberg.

CARLETON EUGENE WATKINS (1829–1916)

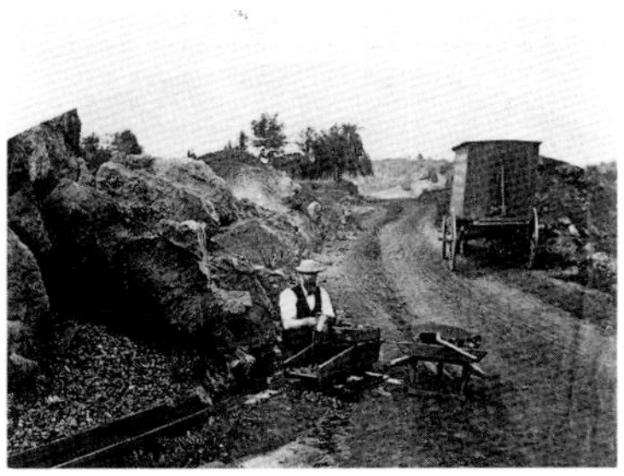

Relatively obscure until recent decades, Watkins has emerged as perhaps the single most important American photographer of the nineteenth century. He is best remembered for visionary and technically polished mammoth plate (18 by 22 inches) landscape views of the West. Born in Oneonta, New York, Watkins came to California during the Gold Rush. He first worked in a bookstore and then for daguerreotypist Robert Vance (c. 1851). By 1857 he had opened his own studio which he operated for nearly fifty years. During his long career, Watkins traveled from British Columbia in the north to Mexico in the south, westward to the Farallon Islands and eastward as far as Yellowstone. His work took him to the top of Mount Shasta in 1870, and to the bottom of a Montana copper mine in 1890, where he suffered horribly from dampness and vertigo. He is best known, however, for his photographs of Yosemite. His breathtakingly detailed images of the valley brought worldwide attention to Yosemite and helped pave the way for its preservation as a national park. Watkins won international recognition and dozens of awards for his photographs, yet could barely support himself. In 1875 he went bankrupt, losing many of his precious negatives to a competitor, Isaiah Taber. In 1906 he lost his studio and all of its contents in the San Francisco earthquake and fire. He died 10 years later in the Napa State Mental Hospital in Imola, California.

PHOTO: Carleton E. Watkins, *Primitive Mining: The Rocker, Calaveras, Co., Cal. (Self-Portrait),* c. 1880. Albumen print, collection of the Society of California Pioneers.

LEWIS WATTS

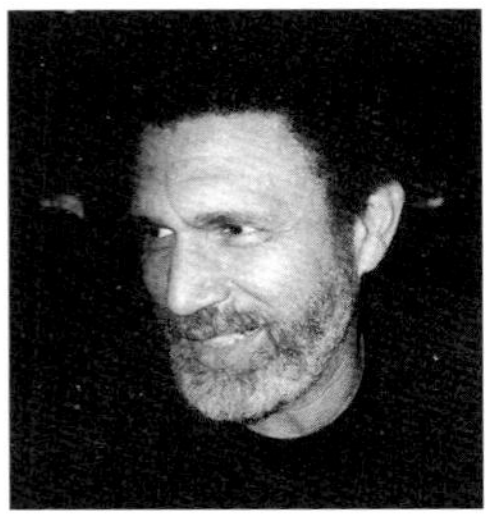

Born in Little Rock, Arkansas, Watts grew up in Seattle and spent his high school years in the Northeast while his father completed a Ph.D. at Brandeis University. His father's dissertation, *The Middle-Income Negro Family Faces Urban Renewal,* contained themes which would later inspire the younger Watts in his photography. Watts earned his B.A. in Political Science (1969) and his M.A. in Photography and Design (1973) from the University of California, Berkeley. After graduation he studied architecture, which led to much work as an architectural photographer. Since 1978 he has taught photography in the Department of Architecture at U.C. Berkeley. His personal work has focused on black neighborhoods in Los Angeles, San Francisco, Harlem, Atlanta, New Orleans and Chicago, as well as the Caribbean. "The thing that opened the door to photographing in the community," he says, "was those photographs where people were not in the pictures." Since 1993, he has conducted a concentrated study of West Oakland, producing work which was exhibited as *Urban Footprints: The Photography of Lewis Watts* at the Oakland Museum of California (1998). Other exhibitions of his photographs include *Black Photographer's Annual* at the San Francisco Museum of Modern Art (1979), *Lewis Watts, South to West Oakland* (1999) at the Robert B. Menschel Photography Gallery, Syracuse University and *Reflections in Black: A History of Black Photographers, 1840 to the Present* (2000) at the Anacostia Museum Center for African American History and Culture, Smithsonian Institution. Watts has also curated several shows, including *Picturing San Francisco* at the San Francisco Public Library (1988) and *Harlem of the West: The Filmore Jazz Archives* at the San Francisco Art Commission Gallery.

PHOTO: *Lewis Watts,* n.d. Courtesy of Lewis Watts.

CHARLES LEANDER WEED (1824–1903)

The first photographer of Yosemite, Weed came to California from Wisconsin, working as a daguerreotypist in Sacramento in 1854. By February 1858 he had become a junior partner in the Sacramento studio of Robert H. Vance, who sponsored Weed's first trip to Yosemite in 1859. Many of the resulting photographs were published as wood engravings in Hutchings's *California* magazine. Weed then traveled to Asia to become manager of Vance's Hong Kong gallery. When Vance became financially overextended in a Comstock mining venture, Weed returned to operate the San Francisco gallery, which was sold to Bradley & Rulofson in 1863. He made photographs of Nevada towns and mining camps in 1862 and made a second trip to Yosemite in 1863, which resulted in a set of mammoth plate (eighteen-by-twenty-two-inch) views. Many of his images were published, without credit, as stereoviews and cartes de visite by Lawrence & Houseworth. By 1865 Weed had left California, establishing himself in Hawaii, where he was the first to document Haleakala Crater, an active volcano, with a camera. He moved back to Hong Kong (1865–71) and then returned to California in 1871. The following year Weed assisted Eadweard Muybridge in producing a set of photographs of Yosemite and Big Trees, for which Muybridge took sole credit. Weed continued to work as a photographer until 1877, becoming a photoengraver until his retirement in about 1887. He died in Oakland.

CARRIE MAE WEEMS (1953–)

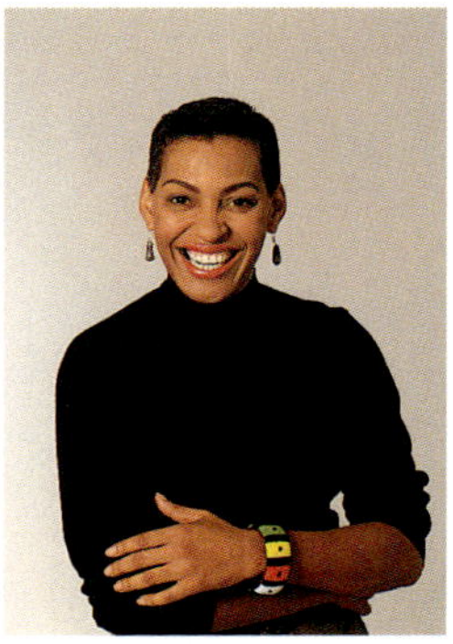

Weems's narrative photographs, often combined with text, confront issues of race, identity, gender and class. Born in Portland, Oregon, she had an early background in modern dance and a deep involvement in grassroots socialist and feminist organizations. She earned a B.F.A. from the California Institute of the Arts (CalArts), Valencia (1981), and an M.F.A. in Photography from the University of California, San Diego (1984). Her early series *Family Pictures and Stories* (1978–84), a kind of family album with text, explored African American social life from an insider's perspective. Weems's interest in storytelling led her to study African American Folklore at the University of California, Berkeley (1984–1987). Her studies informed her provocative 1987 series *Ain't Jokin,* which explored the implications of stereotypes and racist humor by pairing images of African Americans with ethnic jokes. In 1990, at the invitation of the Polaroid Corporation, Weems made her first color work, using a twenty-by-twenty-four-inch Polaroid camera to create an installation titled *And 22 Million Very Tired and Very Angry People.* Weems has taught at various institutions including Hampshire College, Amherst, Massachusetts (1987–91), Hunter College, New York City (1988–89) and the California College of Arts and Crafts in Oakland (1991). She has exhibited in numerous solo and group exhibitions, including the touring show *Carrie Mae Weems,* organized by the National Museum of Women in the Arts, Washington, D.C. in 1993. Weems has also been the recipient of several awards, including a California Arts Council Grant (1983), a Smithsonian Fellowship (1987) and a Louis Comfort Tiffany Award (1992).

PHOTO: Ray Manikowski, *Carrie Mae Weems,* n.d. Courtesy of P.P.O.W., New York.

THOMAS ALGERNON WEIR (1935–)

A self-taught photographer, Weir is also a printer and designer of photographic equipment. He attended Iowa State University, Drake University and the Free University of Berlin. Weir photographed in California from 1961 through 1968, exhibiting at the Sun Gallery in San Francisco in 1967 and the Van der Voort Gallery in 1968. He was also involved in *Light Sound Dimension* in June 1968, in conjunction with the Rolling Renaissance Festival of the Arts. In October 1968 Weir was the subject of a one-man exhibition at the University of California, Santa Cruz. He currently lives in Marin County, California.

JACK WARREN WELPOTT (1923–)

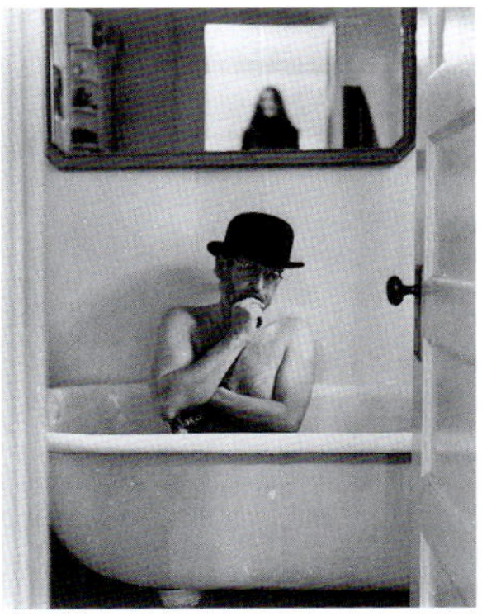

Originally from Kansas, Welpott earned his B.S. (1949), M.S. (1955) and M.F.A. (1959) degrees at Indiana University. He began teaching at California State University, San Francisco in 1959, and has conducted many international workshops in photography. He was married to photographer Judy Dater from 1971 to 1977. He received a National Endowment for the Arts photography grant in 1979. Welpott has participated in numerous solo and group exhibitions and his photographs appear in many publications, including *Women & Other Visions* (with Judy Dater; 1975) and *Photography in America* (1974). A catalogue, *Jack Welpott: The Artist as Teacher, the Teacher as Artist* was published in 1975.

PHOTO: Joan Murray, *Jack Welpott (Judy Dater in Mirror),* 1971. Gelatin silver print, collection of the Oakland Museum of California, gift of Dr. and Mrs. Dudley P. Bell.

HENRY WESSEL, JR. (1942–)

Wessel's photographs have been described as ordinary scenes of the human environment. Born in Teaneck, New Jersey, Wessel earned his B.A. from Pennsylvania State University, University Park (1965) and his M.F.A. from the Visual Studies Workshop at State University of New York, Buffalo (1972). He has received two National Endowment for the Arts Photographer's Fellowships (1974 and 1976) and two Guggenheim grants (1971 and 1978). In 1968 he taught in Project Upward Bound, a program funded by the U.S. Government Office of Economic Opportunity, offering photography workshops for underprivileged rural youths. Wessel has taught at the San Francisco Art Institute (1973), the University of California, Berkeley (1973), the Center of the Eye in Aspen, Colorado (1973), and California State University, San Francisco (1974) before serving as a visiting artist at the California College of Arts and Crafts in Oakland (1977) and the University of California, Davis (1977). Solo exhibitions include *Henry Wessel, Jr.* shown at the Grossmont College Art Gallery in 1976, *Henry Wessel: Still Photographs* (1989) and *Henry Wessel: House Pictures* (1992) both at the Fraenkel Gallery, San Francisco. Wessel currently teaches at the Academy of Art College in San Francisco.

BRETT WESTON (1911–1993)

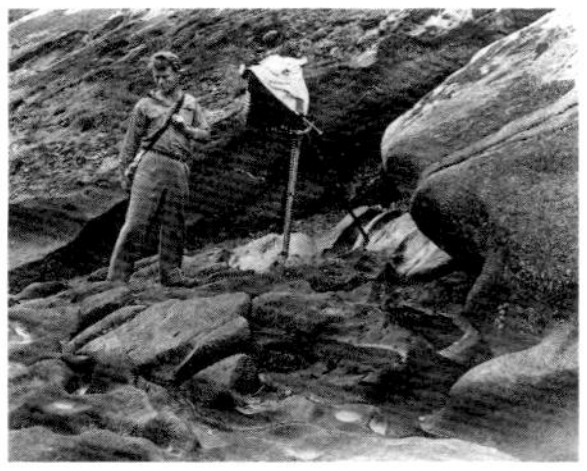

A master of sharply delineated landscapes, plant forms, sand dunes and other natural objects along the California coast, Weston learned photography at age thirteen from his father, Edward. After serving an apprenticeship in his father's Glendale studio (1925–27), he moved with him to San Francisco (1928) and Carmel (1929). In 1930 he set up his own studio in Glendale, later moving to Santa Monica. His first major solo exhibition was at the M. H. de Young Memorial Museum in San Francisco in 1932. Later that year, he was invited to become a member of Group f.64, and was included in their famous first exhibition at the de Young. After serving in the U.S. Army, (1943–45), he received a Guggenheim Fellowship to photograph the Atlantic coast from Maine to Florida (1947). Beginning in 1960, he made a series of trips to Europe, Baja California, Japan and Hawaii. In 1973 he received a National Endowment for the Arts grant to photograph in Alaska. Weston was particularly renowned as a photographic craftsman who could make large prints with exceptional detail and subtle tonalities. In December 1991 he created an international stir when, on his eightieth birthday, he destroyed all but twelve of his negatives, stating he alone was capable of making the kind of print needed to fully express his vision.

PHOTO: Edward Weston, *Brett Weston and Camera at Point Lobos,* 1942. Gelatin silver print, collection of the Oakland Museum of California, gift of Tom Curran.

EDWARD WESTON (1886–1958)

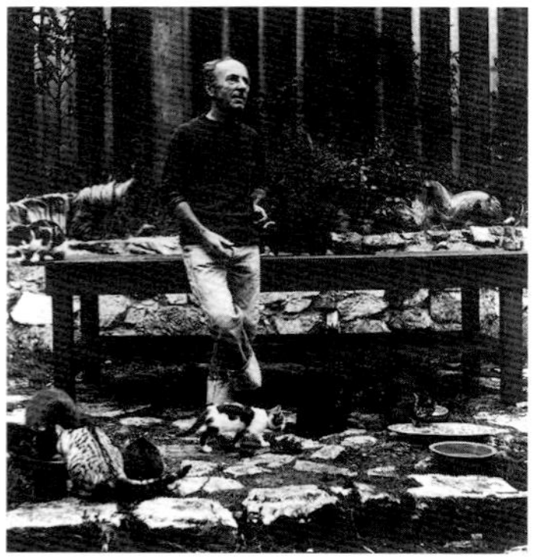

A mythic figure of twentieth-century photography, Weston is considered a pioneering Modernist. Born in Highland Park, Illinois, he began taking pictures at age sixteen and attended the Illinois College of Photography in Chicago (1908). By 1911 he had established a portrait studio in Tropico (now Glendale), California. Adhering to the then-fashionable mode of Pictorialism, Weston prospered artistically. Between 1914 and 1917, he received many awards for his highly-stylized, atmospheric images and was selected to show in prestigious pictorial salons around the world. In 1922 he had a solo exhibition at the Academia Bellas Artes in Mexico City, and upon the show's enthusiastic reception, he decided to move there with his companion, Tina Modotti. Weston had already renounced Pictorialism, and in Mexico he and Modotti embraced the European-influenced Modernism favored by revolutionary artists of the Mexican Renaissance. Returning to Los Angeles in 1926, he continued his new interest in abstract form through extreme close-up views of shells, vegetables and nudes. In

1929 he established a studio in Carmel, and in 1932 was a founding member of Group f.64. In 1937 he became the first photographer to win a Guggenheim Fellowship. Weston's life and work have been the subject of numerous publications. His own published diaries, or *Daybooks,* describe the development of his aesthetic thought and his many relationships, which included Margrethe Mather, Tina Modotti, Sonya Noskowiak and Charis Wilson.

PHOTO: Imogen Cunningham, *Edward Weston, Photographer, with His Cats,* 1945. Gelatin silver print, collection of the Oakland Museum of California, gift of the Estate of Helen Johnston.

JO WHALEY (1953–)

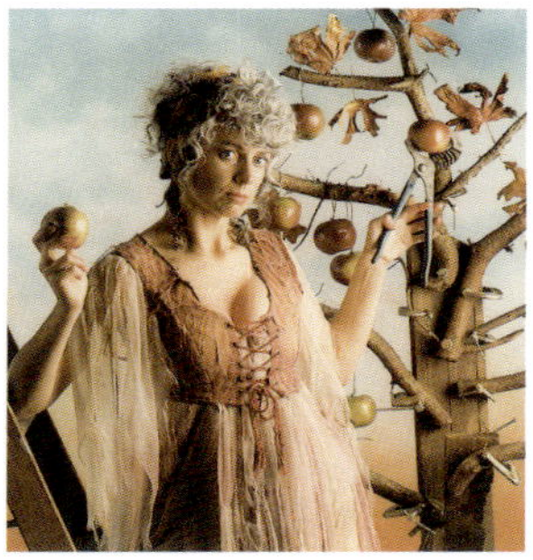

A native Californian, Whaley earned her B.A. (1975), M.A. (1978), M.F.A. (1979) and M.A. in Photography (1980) at the University of California, Berkeley. She has exhibited regularly since 1981 and received numerous awards, including a National Endowment for the Arts, Visual Artist fellowship (1994), an Eisner Award in art (1979), an Eisner Award in photography (1980), a California Arts Council Grant, Artist in Residence (1981) and a Phelan Award in photography (1985). Whaley has taught at the California College of Arts and Crafts in Oakland (1984–86), California State University, Hayward (1985–86), and the San Francisco Art Institute (1987). Her most recent teaching position was at The Pont-Aven School of Art in Brittany, France. Other teaching assignments include the University of California, Berkeley (1984), San Francisco Art Institute (1987 and 1990), the University of New Mexico (1994 & 1996), and California State University, San Jose (1986–99). Whaley is on the board of San Francisco Camerawork. She has had many solo exhibitions including *Natura Morta (Still Life/Dead Nature)* which was shown at the Robert Koch Gallery, San Francisco in 1992. In 1991 and again in 1993 she received a Polaroid Corporation 20 by 24 Studio Grant, as well as a National Endowment for the Arts, Visual Artist Fellowship in 1994. A solo exhibition of her latest work is planned at the San Jose Museum of Art in 2001. She lives in Oakland with her husband, photographer Greg MacGregor.

PHOTO: Jo Whaley, *Self Portrait with Still-Life for "Harvest, the Fall,"* n.d. Chromogenic color print, copyright and courtesy of Jo Whaley.

MINOR MARTIN WHITE (1908–1976)

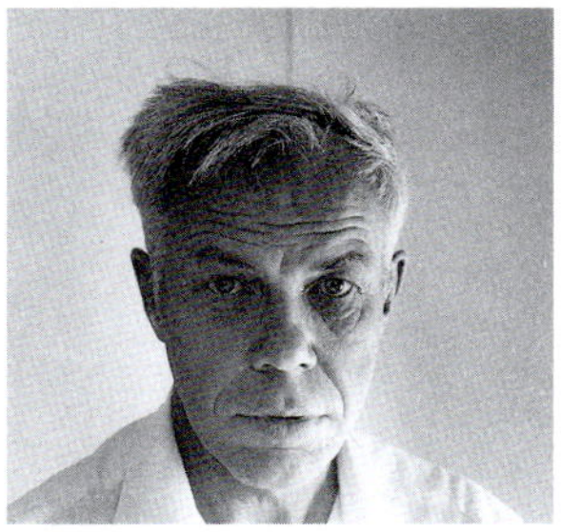

An influential photographer, editor, writer and teacher, White was born in Minneapolis, Minnesota. His work had diverse influences, including Catholicism, Meyer Schapiro's psychological approach to creativity and art, Zen, Gestalt, and perhaps most significant, the teachings of the mystic G. I. Gurdjieff. He enjoyed close relationships with Alfred Stieglitz, Edward Weston and Ansel Adams. White received a B.S. in Botany from the University of Minnesota in 1933 and studied Art history and Aesthetics at Columbia University, New York (1945–46). Self-taught in photography, he was hired as a photographer by the Works Progress Administration (WPA) in Portland, Oregon, in 1938. He became director of the La Grande Art Center, La Grande, Oregon (1940–41) before serving a tour in the U.S. Army (1942–45), and began teaching at the California School of Fine Arts (now the San Francisco Art Institute), where he stayed until 1953. White was one of the founders of the influential *Aperture* magazine in 1952, serving as its editor until 1975. During these years he was assistant curator to Beaumont Newhall at the George Eastman House (1953–57), taught at the Rochester Institute of Technology (1956–74) and was a senior lecturer at MIT. White was a founding member of the Society for Photographic Education in 1962. His photographs are notable for a sharply focused beauty and realism, which serve as metaphors for personal inner experience. In 1976 he was awarded an Honorary Doctorate of Fine Arts from the San Francisco Art Institute.

PHOTO: Dorothea Lange, *Untitled (Minor White),* c. 1959. © Oakland Museum of California, the City of Oakland. Gift of Paul S. Taylor.

MARION POST WOLCOTT (1910–1990)

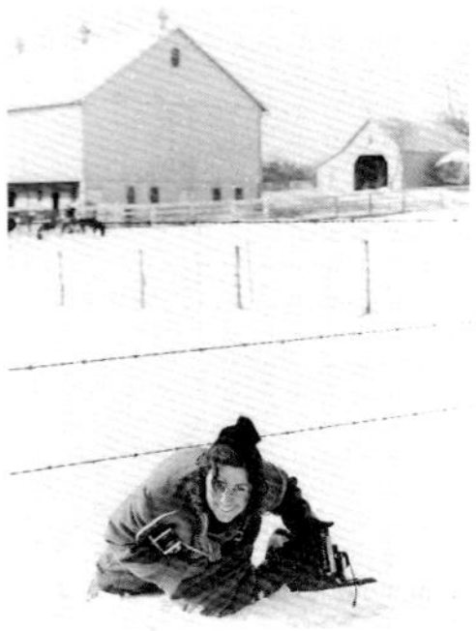

A social documentarian, Wolcott studied at the New School for Social Research, New York (1928) and New York University (1929). On a visit to Europe, she heard Adolf Hitler speak in Berlin, an experience which turned her personal politics sharply to the left. Wolcott earned her B.A. from the University of Vienna, Austria in 1935. Returning to New York, she began to take photographs and undertook freelance work, also attending the Photo League. In 1937 Paul Strand and Ralph Steiner invited her to act as still photographer for their film on labor organizations in the South, *People of the Cumberlands*. She took a photojournalist position at the *Philadelphia Evening Bulletin* (1937) and then joined the Farm Security Administration (FSA) from 1938 to 1941. Her work for the FSA took her to the South, New England, and the West. Wolcott continued to photograph intermittently until the late 1960s.

PHOTO: Unknown photographer, *Marion Post Wolcott on Assignment in Vermont,* 1940. Courtesy of Linda Wolcott-Moore.

AMOS WOODS (c. 1826–1887)

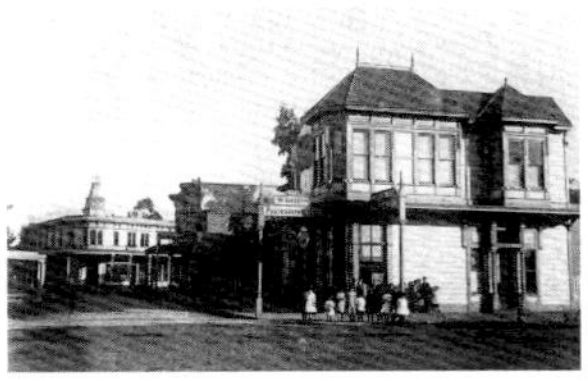

Born in Massachusetts, Woods operated a commercial portrait gallery in the Odd Fellows Building in Marysville, California, from 1874 to about 1879. The following year he relocated to 541 Sixteenth Street, Oakland, California, where he worked until his death.

PHOTO: Amos Woods, *Woods's Photographic Gallery,* Oakland, c. 1880. Albumen carte de visite, private collection.

WILLARD ELMER WORDEN (1868–1946)

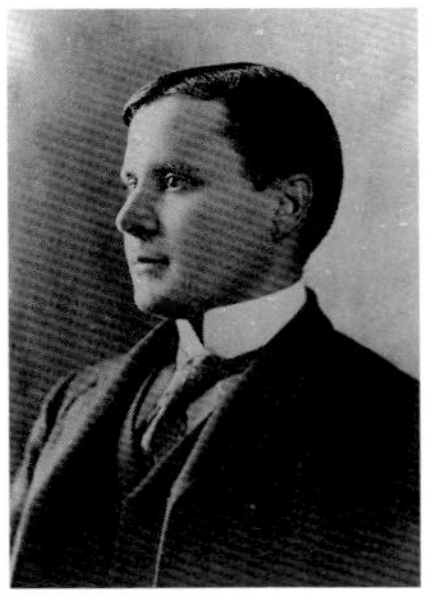

A painter and photographer, Worden grew up in Philadelphia, where he studied painting. In 1898 he enlisted as an officer in the Spanish-American War stationed in the Philippines, the period in which he became interested in photography. He established a studio in San Francisco in 1902, producing photographs of the Sierra Nevadas, the Pacific Coast and the San Francisco Bay Area. Worden was noted for his images of Chinatown (taken about 1903) and for his photographs of the devastation and aftermath of the 1906 San Francisco earthquake and fire. He served as official photographer for the Panama-Pacific International Exposition in 1915 and operated a studio at 316 Stockton Street, San Francisco for many years. A retrospective exhibition, *Photographs of San Francisco by Willard E. Worden,* was shown at the Focus Gallery, San Francisco, in 1977.

PHOTO: Willard Worden, *Untitled (Self-Portrait),* c. 1905. Courtesy of Wells Fargo Bank Historical Services.

CEDRIC WRIGHT (1889–1959)

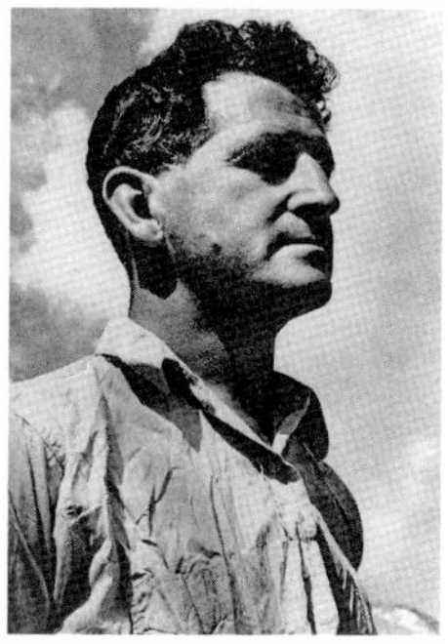

A photographer, writer and musician, Wright was trained as a violinist, studying for six years in Prague and Vienna. He gravitated to photography in his middle years, in part because of increasingly arthritic fingers. He taught music at Mills College, Oakland and the University of California, Berkeley Extension program. During World War II he worked as a photographer for Livermore Radiation Laboratories in Berkeley. Wright also made more than thirty-five trips to the High Sierras as the official trip photographer for the Sierra Club. "Cedric believed that any man's spiritual horizon would be expanded through contact with nature," Ansel Adams said of him, "and his life was dedicated to this idea." His work has been featured in solo exhibitions at Mills College, Stanford Art Museum, and the University of California, Santa Barbara.

PHOTO: *Cedric Wright,* n.d.

MAX YAVNO (1911–1985)

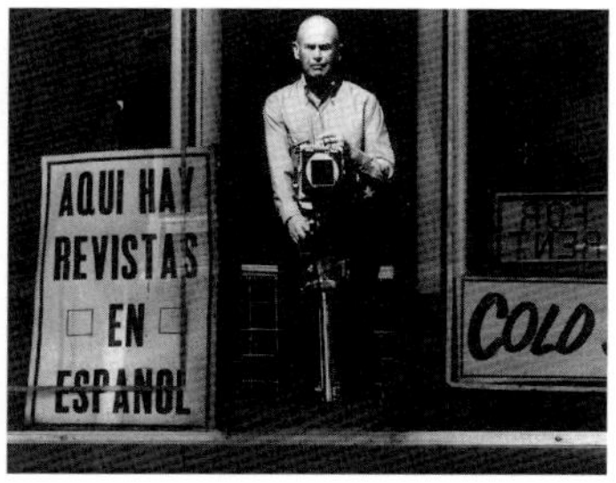

Born in New York, Yavno earned a B.S. degree in 1932 from City College of New York. He also attended the Graduate School of Business Administration (1932–33) and the Graduate Faculty of Political Science (1933–34) at Columbia University, New York. In 1938 and 1939 he served as president of the Photo League, and from 1939 to 1942 roomed with photographer Aaron Siskind. He was awarded a Guggenheim fellowship in 1953. Yavno operated a commercial photography studio in San Francisco (1954–75) and studied cinematography at the University of California, Los Angeles (1972–75). His books include *The San Francisco Book* with Herb Caen (1948), and *The Los Angeles Book* with Lee Shippey (1950). Edward Steichen acquired twenty of Yavno's photographs for the permanent collection of the Museum of Modern Art in 1952.

PHOTO: Max Yavno, *Untitled, Self-Portrait, Los Angeles,* 1977. Gelatin silver print, courtesy of Jan Kesner Gallery, Los Angeles.

INDEX

Illustrations are indicated in bold face.

A

Abbenseth, William, **160, 180,** 316
Adams, Ansel, viii, x, 67, **105,** 127, 130, 133, **146, 186,** 193, 195, 198, 199, 202, 206, **211, 212,** 303, 307, 308, **316**
Adams, Robert, 206, **207**
American Exodus, An, **136,** 137–38
Americans, The, 198
Anderson, Hugh, **42,** 298, 316
Anderson, P. Douglas, **94,** 317
Anger, Kenneth, 198
Anthony, Edward, 14
Aperture, 195, **196**
Arbus, Diane, xi
Archer, Fred, 71
Armer, Laura Adams, 68, **88, 108,** 303, **317, 320**
Atkinson, Dorothy, **55,** 300
Atkinson, Nell, **55,** 300

B

Baer, Morley, 195, 199, **234, 317**
Bailey, Clayton, 312
Baker, Isaac Wallace, 9, **10, 22, 24, 26,** 295, **318**
Baldessari, John, 197, 204, 206, 208, **285,** 313, **318**
Ball, George, **100,** 302
Baltz, Lewis, 141, 200, 206, **272–73,** 312, **318**
Barton, Nancy, 208
Baruch, Ruth Marion, 198, **217, 319**
Batchelder, Benjamin P., 8
Batchelder, Perez M., 8, 9, **10**
Becher, Bernd and Hilla, 206
Bell, Mr. and Mrs. Dudley, viii
Berman, Wallace, 198
Bernhard, Ruth, **155,** 194, 195, 197, **232, 233,** 304–5, 309, **319**
Bisbee, Mary L., **321**
Bishop, Michael, 200, **201**
Bixby-Smith, Llewellyn, 302
Blumann, Sigismund, 64, **112–13,** 303, 319
Boardman, William F., **30,** 296
Bowden, Harry, **226,** 309, **320**
Boysen, Julius T., **83, 320**
Bradley, Henry William (*see also* Bradley & Rulofson), 7, 295, 320
Bradley & Rulofson (Henry William Bradley and William Herman Rulofson), 15, **39, 40, 49, 50,** 299, **320**
Brady, Matthew, 130
Brenner, Marion, **337, 346**
Brigman, Anne, viii, x, 67, 70, **90, 91,** 121, **122,** 123, 126, 127, **140,** 141, **154,** 301, 304, **321**
Briggs, Henry, 4
Bristol, Horace, **136**
Britt, Peter, 8–9
Brooks, Ellen, 202, 208, **267, 321**
Bruguière, Francis, viii, **96,** 302, 322
Brumfield, John, 208
Bullock, Wynn, 195, 197, 198, 200, **222, 223,** 308, **322**
Burchard, Jerry, 200, **281,** 313, **323**
Burden, Shirley, viii, 198, **220, 323**
Burr, Alice, **109,** 323

C

Cabot, Dr. Samuel, Jr., 5
Caffin, Charles, 63
Cagney, James, **150,** 304
Callis, Jo Ann, 202, 208, **269,** 312, **324**
Camera Craft, 64, **65,** 66, 70, 130, 131
Camera Work, 64, 123, 124
Cameron, Julia Margaret, 61
Carr, Richard H., 6, 7
Carvalho, Solomon Nuñes, 5
Catherwood, Frederick, 5
Chau, Ka, 8
Coburn, Alvin Langdon, xi, 70, **71**
Coffin, Isaac T., 16
Collier, John, 198, 199
Colwell, Larry, **322**
Connell, Will, 72
Conner, Bruce, 194, 198
Connor, Linda, 200, **265,** 312, **324**
Coombs, Frederick, 3, **4,** 7, 19 (note 2)
Corso, Gregory, 198
Cowin, Eileen, 208
Coyote, Peter, 310
Cumming, Blanche, 68
Cumming, Robert, **205,** 206
Cunningham, Imogen, viii, 69, 70, **95, 99,** 121, **122,** 123, 125–26, 127, **132,** 133, **152, 153, 168,** 200, **227, 229, 240,** 302, 304, 306, 307, 309, 310, 311, **315, 324, 326, 338, 345, 353, 358,** 359
Curran, Darryl, **201,** 202
Curtis, Edward S., viii, 67, **86, 87,** 301, **325**

D

Daguerre, Louis J. M., ix, 61
Dassonville, William, 66, 70, **106,** 325
Dater, Judy, ix, 200, **248, 249,** 311, **326**
Dawson, Robert, viii, 206, **293,** 314, **326**
Day, F. Holland, 64, 67
Deal, Joe, 206, **207**
Del Monte Corporation, **84,** 300
Derrida, Jacques, 208
Deshon, Florence, **98,** 302
D'Estrella, Theophilus Hope, **77, 327**
Dick, David, **353**
Dietrich, Marlene, **185,** 307
Divola, John, 202, 206, **268, 327**
Dixon, Harry St. John, **104,** 303
Dixon, Maynard, 127, **212,** 303, 308
Doherty, William, **238,** 327
Dow, Arthur Wesley, 70

E

Edwards, John Paul, 69, 72, **107,** 127, **148, 149,** 303, 304, **328**
Elite Gallery, **329**
Ellis, John, **324**
Emerson, Peter Henry, **62,** 63
English, Patricia, 307
Eugene, Frank, **65**
Evans, Vernon, **175,** 306
Evans, Walker, 133, 206

F

Fagersteen, Gustavus, **41,** 298, 328
Family of Man, The, 198
Fardon, George Robinson, 13, **31,** 296, **328**
Farm Sercurity Administration (FSA), 131, 138, 197, 306–7, 308
Farquhar, Francis, 303
Ferlinghetti, Lawrence, 198
Ferus Gallery, 198
Fichter, Robert, 202
Film un Foto, 194, 305
Fiske, George, viii, 17, **54, 55,** 300, **329**
Fitzgerald, Edward, 68
Fleckenstein, Louis, 71
Flick, Robbert, 202, **264,** 312, 329
Focus Gallery, 202, 311
Fraenkel Gallery, 204
Frank, Robert, 198, **228,** 309, **329**
Freedlander, Lee, 200
Freeman, Emma Belle, 67, **68**
Frémont, Jesse Benton, **43,** 298
Frémont, John Charles, 5, 298
French, Nora May, **80,** 300
Fricker, Geoffrey, **292,** 314, 330
Friedkin, Anthony, **355**
Friends of Photography, 206
Fulton, Jack, 200, **201**

G

Gazan & Mazzuchelli, 13
Genthe, Arnold, viii, 66, 67, **78, 79, 80,** 299, 300, **317, 330, 340**
Gilfillian, A. W., 15
Ginsberg, Allen, 198
Gold, Norman Leon, 131
Gradwohl, Raoul, 197
Grapestake Gallery, 204
Graves, Morris, **240,** 310
Griffith, Millen, 298
Grogan, Emmett, 310
Group f.64, 124, 127, 128, 194, 200, 304
Guido, Guido, **350**
Gundlach, Jacob, 296
Gutmann, John, **135,** 136, 137, **182,** 200, 307, **330**

H

Hagel, Otto, 135, **136,** 137–38, **172, 173,** 198, 306, **331**
Hagemeyer, Johan, 72, **100, 101,** 121, **122,** 123, 302, **331**
Hallidie, Andrew S., 299
Hanscom, Adelaide, **54,** 68, 301, **332**
Hanscom, Moses, 8
Hare, Chauncey, 208
Harlow, Jean, **184,** 307
Hart, Alfred A., vii, 14, **36,** 297, **332**
Hawkins, G. Ray, 204
Hazeltine, Martin M., 14
Heinecken, Robert, 197, 198, 200–02, 203, 206, **250,** 311, **333**
Herms, George, 198, **199**
Hernandez, Anthony, viii, **275, 333**
Herschel, Sir John, 301
Hershman, Lynn, **276,** 312, **333**
Hido, Todd, **289,** 314, 334
Holder, Preston, 127, 129
Homer, Winslow, 70
Hoover, Herbert, 127, **132,** 133
Hopps, Walter, 198
Houseworth, Thomas (*see also* Lawrence & Houseworth), 15, **35, 45, 48, 51,** 298, 299, **334**
Huebler, Douglas, 208
Hurrell, George, **184,** 197, 307, **334**
Hussey, Henry, 72, **102, 103,** 302, 335
Hutchings, James M., 12, 297

J

Jacobs, Mimi, **348,** 349
James, George Wharton, 67
Jeffers, Robinson, **151,** 304
Johnson, George H., 6–7, **27,** 296, **335**
Johnson, Larry, 208
Johnson, Stephen, **294,** 134, **335**
Johnston, Helen, 202, 311
Jones, Pirkle, 195, **221, 319, 336**
Jordan, Lois, 306

K

Kales, Arthur F., 72, **110,** 303, 336
Kaminsky, Ed, 200
Kanaga, Consuelo, 127, 129
Käsebier, Gertrude, 67
Kerouac, Jack, 309
Kidd, G. W., 298
Kienholz, Ed, 198
King, Clarence, 13
Kipling, Rudyard, **100,** 302
Kismaric, Susan, 209
Klain, Nathan, 13
Klett, Mark, **286–87,** 313, 336
Kramer, Hilton, 204
Kriz, Vilem, **215,** 308, **337**

L

LaFarge, John, 70
Landweber, Victor, 202, 206, **251, 261,** 311, **337**
Lange, Dorothea, **vi,** viii, x, 68, **104,** 121, **122,** 127–28, 129–33, **131,** 134–35, **136, 137,** 138, **139, 140,** 141, **169, 170, 171, 188, 189,** 197, 198, 199, 206, 230, 231, 303, 306, 307, 309, 311, **336, 337, 346, 359**
Lavenson, Alma, **147, 165,** 304, 305, 308, **338**
Lawrence & Houseworth (George Lawrence and Thomas Houseworth), 14, **36, 37,** 42, 297, 298, 338
Leibovitz, Annie, 200
Leonard, Joanne, 200, **236, 338**
Liebert, Alphonse, 15
London, Jack, 137
Louie, Reagan, **288,** 314, **339**

M

MacGregor, Greg, 206, **266,** 312, **339**
Man Ray, viii, 193, 197, **214,** 308, 311, **339**
Manchester, Ellen, **326**
Mandel, Mike, 200, 208
Manikowski, Ray, **357**
Martinez, Xavier Tizoc, **62,** 301
Mather, Margrethe, viii, 68, **98,** 126–27, 302, **315, 340**
Matyas, Emily, **336**
Maurer, Oscar, viii, 66, **92, 340**
McGowan, Kenneth, **277**
McKinne, Andrew Barnaby, **82, 341**
Meltzer, Milton, 128
Mieth, Hansel, 137, **331**
Miller, Joaquin, 301
Minick, Roger, **263,** 312, 341
Misrach, Richard, viii, ix, 206, **245, 262,** 310, 312, **341**
Modotti, Tina, 126, 305
Morse, George D., **46, 47**
Morse, Samuel F. B., vii,
Mortensen, William, 72, **116, 117,** 303–4, **342**
Muir, Douglas, **280, 342**
Murphy, John and Daniel, 295
Murray, Joan, **317, 318, 319, 321, 323, 333, 337, 338, 341, 344, 348, 352,** 353, **355, 357**
Muybridge, Eadweard J., viii, ix, 3, 4, 13, 14–15, **39, 40, 46, 47,** 297, 298, 299, 312, **343**

N

Nagatani, Patrick, 208, **283,** 313, **343**
Nauman, Bruce, 204, 206
Nestor, Helen, **237,** 310, **344**
Newhall, Beaumont and Nancy, 193, 206, 305
Newsom, Samuel, **85,** 301, 344
Norcross, Oliver H. P., 9
Noskowiak, Sonya, viii, 126, 127, **151, 159,** 304, 305, **345, 350**

O

Orland, Ted, 206, **255,** 311, **345**
Osburn & Searles, 8
O'Sullivan, Timothy, **38,** 297, 345
Outerbridge, Paul Jr., **166,** 197, **346**
Owens, Bill, 141, 208, **242, 243,** 310, **346**

P

Page, Homer, 198
Page, Susan, 341, **342**
Partridge, Roi, **122,** 307
Partridge, Rondal, **176, 177,** 198, 307, **346**
Pichel, Irving, **108,** 303
Pierpont, James, 7
Pitchford, Emily, 68, **89, 347**
Pond, Charles L., 14, **37, 347**
Pulich, Martin, 309

R

Rauschenberg, Robert, 198, 203
Reilly, John James, 15, **16, 37, 347**
Rice, Leland, 200, **252,** 311, **348**
Robinson, Henry Peach, 61, **62**
Rolling Stone, 200
Roosevelt, Franklin, 127, 128, **132,** 133
Rothstein, Arthur, 138, **175,** 306, 348
Rulofson, William Herman (*see also* Bradley & Rulofson), 7, **12,** 295, **320**
Ruscha, Ed, 141, 203–4, 205, 206, **284,** 313, **348**
Russell, Andrew J., vii, **34,** 297, **349**
Russell, Sol. Smith, **49,** 299
Ryan, Marah Ellis, 301

S

Sabattier, Armand, 309
Saergent, Jill, 303
Samberg, Joe, **244, 339, 349**
Samberg, Margie Marrow, **349**
Scripture, John Calvin, 16–17
Shannon, Julia, 7
Sheeler, Charles, 69
Shepard, Claire, 302
Shew, William, **21, 29,** 295, 296, **349**
Shore, Stephen, 206, **256, 350**
Silveira, Joseph N., 8
Simpson, Marion, **153,** 304,
Simpson, William, **132,** 133–34, **161, 174, 183, 350**
Sinclair, Upton, 129
Smith, Allison, 345
Smith, G. S., 12
Smith, Henry Holmes, 200
Sontag, Susan, 204
Speer, Jennie, **48,** 299
Spiritus, Susan, 204
Spooner, John Pitcher, 16
Stackpole, Peter, viii, **164, 178, 179, 185,** 198, 307, **350**

Stanford, Leland, 299
Starr, Kevin, 136
Steichen, Edward, 198
Stephens, John Lloyd, 5
Sterling, George, 301
Stieglitz, Alfred, viii, x, 64, **65,** 67, 69, 123, 124, 126, 195
Stiffler, Frank M., **56,** 300, 351
Stiffler, George L., **56,** 300, 351
Strand, Paul, 69, **70**
Struss, Karl, 71, **75,** 300, **351**
Sturtevant, Roger, **115,** 121, **122,** 123, 127, 128, **156, 187,** 303, 305, **351**
Subrizi, Alex, **354**
Suck, Kai, **8**
Sultan, Larry, 200, 208, **291,** 314, **352**
Sunby, Dorothy, **164**
Survey Graphic, 131, 133
Sutter, John, 9
Sutton, E., 7
Swift, Henry, 127

T

Taber, Isaiah West, **52, 53,** 299, **352**
Takahashi, Henry, **114,** 303, 352
Talbot, William Henry Fox, 61
Taylor, Paul S., viii, 127, 131, 133, **136,** 137–38, 306
Teske, Edmund, 193, 202, **253,** 311, **352**
Thiebaud, Twinka, 311
Thiebaud, Wayne, 311
Thomas, Lew, 206
Thompson, Florence, viii
Tracey, Andrée, **283,** 313, **353**
Truman, Stanley, viii

V

Vallejo, Epifania de Guadalupe, xiv (note 1), 6
Vallejo, Mariano Guadalupe, 6
Van Dyke, Willard, viii, 123, 127, 128, 129–30, 131, 133, **145, 158, 181,** 304, **316, 353**
Vance, Robert H., 4, 7, 9–11, 13, **28, 30,** 296, 297, 299, **354**
Vignes, Michelle, **239, 354**
Visual Dialogue Foundation, 200
Volkerding, Laura, 206, **270–71,** 312, 354

W

Wagner, Catherine, **274,** 312, **355**
Wales, R. E., 299
Walker, Todd, 200, 202, **235,** 309, **355**
Wanamaker, John, 303
Warhol, Andy, 198, 203
Watkins, Carleton, vii, 3, 4, 13, **14, 32, 33, 44,** 296, 307, 311, **355**
Watts, Lewis, **290,** 314, **356**
Weed, Charles Leander, **11,** 13, **35, 36, 37,** 297, 299, 356
Weems, Carrie Mae, **279,** 313, **357**
Wegman, William, 205–6
Weir, Thomas, **241,** 310, 357
Welling, James, 208
Welpott, Jack, 200, **246, 247,** 311, **357**
Welsh, John Oliver, 15
Wessel, Henry, 206, **278,** 313, 358
Weston, Brett, 127, **167,** 195, **224, 225, 254,** 305, 311, **358**
Weston, Chandler, 302
Weston, Charis Wilson, 126, **162,** 305
Weston, Edward, viii, ix, 66, 67, 68, 69, 71, 72, **97, 111,** 121, **122,** 123, **125,** 126–27, 133, **150, 162, 163,** 194, 195, 198, **213,** 302, 304, 305, 308, **315, 319, 331, 340, 351, 358**
Weston Gallery, 204
Whaley, Jo, **282,** 313, **359**
Wheeler, George M., 297
White, Clarence, 67, 69
White, Minor, 141, 195–97, **218, 219, 359**
White, Stephen, 204
Whitehurst, Jesse, 11
Williams, Otis, 71
Withington, Eliza, 17
Witkin, Joel Peter, 72
Wolcott, Marion Post, **190,** 308, **360**
Woods, Amos, **43, 360**
Worden, Willard, **76, 81,** 300, **360**
Wright, Cedric, **157,** 305, **361**

Y

Yavno, Max, 197–98, **216, 361**
Yong, Lai, 8